D1376223

Performance Measurement for Health System Improvement

In a world where there is increasing demand for the performance
of health providers to be measured, there is a need for a more
strategic vision of the role that performance measurement can play
in securing health system improvement. This volume meets this
need by presenting the opportunities and challenges associated
with performance measurement in a framework that is clear and
easy to understand. It examines the various levels at which health
system performance is undertaken, the technical instruments and
tools available, and the implications using these may have for those
charged with the governance of the health system.

Leading authorities in the field present technical material in an
accessible way and illustrate with examples from all over the world.
Performance Measurement for Health System Improvement is an
authoritative and practical guide for policy makers, regulators,
patient groups and researchers.

Edited by
Peter C. Smith is Professor of Health Policy in the Business School
and Institute for Global Health at Imperial College, London.

Elias Mossialos is Professor of Health Policy at the London School
of Economics and Political Science, Co-Director of the European
Observatory on Health Systems and Policies and Director of LSE
Health, United Kingdom.

Irene Papanicolas is Research Associate and Brian Abel-Smith
Scholar at LSE Health, the London School of Economics and
Political Science.

Sheila Leatherman is Research Professor at the Gillings School of
Global Public Health, University of North Carolina and Visiting
Professor at the London School of Economics and Political Science,
United Kingdom.

The Cambridge Health Economics, Policy and Management series

Series Editor: Professor Elias Mossialos, the London School of Economics and Political Science

This series is for scholars in health policy, economics and management. The series publishes texts that provide innovative discourses, comprehensive accounts and authoritative approaches to scholarship. The Cambridge Health Economics, Policy and Management series creates a forum for researchers to participate in interdisciplinary conversations on contemporary issues in healthcare. Concerns in health policy, economics and management will be featured in the context of international healthcare practices and on-going discussions on the latest developments in scholarly research and theoretical issues from a variety of perspectives.

Presenting clear, concise and balanced accounts of topics, particularly those that have developed in the field in the last decade, the series will appeal to healthcare scholars, policy makers, practitioners and students.

Performance Measurement for Health System Improvement:
Experiences, Challenges and Prospects

Edited by Peter C. Smith, Elias Mossialos, Irene Papanicolas, Sheila Leatherman

Health Systems Governance in Europe:
The Role of European Union Law and Policy

Edited by Elias Mossialos, Govin Permanand, Rita Baeten, Tamara Hervey

Private Health Insurance and Medical Savings Accounts:
History, Politics, Performance

Edited by Sarah Thomson, Elias Mossialos, Robert G. Evans

Performance measurement for health system improvement

Experiences, challenges and prospects

EDITED BY

PETER C. SMITH
(Imperial College Business School)

ELIAS MOSSIALOS
(LSE Health and European Observatory on Health Systems and
Policies, the London School of Economics and Political Science)

IRENE PAPANICOLAS
(LSE Health and European Observatory on Health Systems and
Policies, the London School of Economics and Political Science)

SHEILA LEATHERMAN
(School of Public Health, University of North Carolina)

CAMBRIDGE UNIVERSITY PRESS
Cambridge, New York, Melbourne, Madrid, Cape Town, Singapore,
São Paulo, Delhi, Dubai, Tokyo

Cambridge University Press
The Edinburgh Building, Cambridge CB2 8RU, UK

Published in the United States of America by Cambridge University Press,
New York

www.cambridge.org
Information on this title: www.cambridge.org/9780521133487

© Cambridge University Press 2009

First published 2009
Reprinted 2010

Printed in the United Kingdom at the University Press, Cambridge

A catalogue record for this publication is available from the British Library

ISBN   978-0-521-11676-3 Hardback
ISBN   978-0-521-13348-7 Paperback

Contents

Foreword

NATA MENABDE
Deputy Regional Director, WHO Regional Office for Europe

The provision of relevant, accurate and timely performance information is essential for assuring and improving the performance of health
systems. Citizens, patients, governments, politicians, policy-makers,
managers and clinicians all need such information in order to assess
whether health systems are operating as well as they should and to
identify where there is scope for improvement. Without performance
information, there is no evidence with which to design health system
reforms; no means of identifying good and bad practice; no protection for patients or payers; and, ultimately, no case for investing in the
health system.

Performance information offers the transparency that is essential
for securing accountability for health system performance, thereby
improving the health of citizens and the efficiency of the health system. However, most health systems are in the early stages of performance measurement and still face many challenges in the design and
implementation of these schemes. This book brings together some of
the world's leading experts on the topic and offers a comprehensive
survey of the current state of the art. It highlights the major progress
that has been made in many domains but also points to some unresolved debates that require urgent attention from policy-makers and
researchers.

This book arises from the WHO European Ministerial Conference on
Health Systems: 'Health Systems, Health and Wealth', Tallinn, Estonia,
25–27 June 2008. During the conference, the WHO, Member States
and a range of international partners signed the Tallinn Charter that
provides a strategic framework, guidance for strengthening health systems and a commitment to promoting transparency and accountability.

Following on from Tallinn, the WHO Regional Office for Europe is
committed to support Member States in their efforts to develop health
system performance assessment. Measurable results and better performance data will help countries to support service delivery institutions

in their efforts to learn from experience; strengthen their health intelligence and governance functions; and contribute to the creation of a common ground for cross-country learning. By enabling a wide range of comparisons (for example, voluntary twinning or benchmarking) improved performance measurement should facilitate better performing health systems and thus the ultimate goal of a healthier Europe.

Acknowledgements

The editors would like to thank all those who contributed their expertise to this volume. The authors responded with great insight, patience and forbearance. Furthermore, the project benefited enormously from the contributions of participants at the WHO Ministerial Conference in Tallinn, Estonia and the associated preparatory meetings. The editors thank WHO and the Estonian Government for organizing and hosting the WHO Ministerial Conference and the pre-conference workshop at which some of the book's material was presented.

Particular thanks go to Isy Vromans, Claudia Bettina Maier and Susan Ahrenst in the WHO Secretariat for planning and organizing the workshop, as well as to Govin Permanand for his guidance and help in writing the WHO policy brief based on the book.

The pre-conference workshop could not have happened without the contributions of Nata Menabde, Niek Klazinga, Enis Bariş, Arnold Epstein, Douglas Conrad, Antonio Duran, David McDaid, Paul Shekelle, Gert Westert, Fabrizio Carinci and Nick Fahy. Sara Allin, Cristina Hernández-Quevedo and Cristina Masseiria would like to thank Julian Le Grand for his comments on an earlier version of Chapter 2.6. In addition, the editors would like to thank Jonathan North for managing the production process along with Caroline White, Jo Woodhead for the copy editing and Peter Powell for the typesetting. Thanks are also due to Chris Harrison and Karen Matthews at Cambridge University Press for their invaluable guidance throughout the project. Finally, we would like to thank Josep Figueras and Suszy Lessof at the European Observatory on Health Systems and Policies for their guidance and useful comments.

Nigel Rice and Silvana Robone acknowledge funding from the United Kingdom Economic and Social Research Council under their Public Services Programme.

List of contributors

Sara Allin is Post-Doctoral Fellow in the Department of Health Policy, Management and Evaluation at the University of Toronto, Canada.

David C. Aron is Co-Director of the VA Health Services Research and Development Quality Enhancement Initiative (QUERI) Center for Implementation Practice and Research Support (CIPRS) at the Louis Stokes Cleveland Department of Veterans Affairs Medical Center and Professor of Medicine, Epidemiology and Biostatistics at Case Western Reserve University School of Medicine, Cleveland, Ohio, USA.

Chris Bain is Reader in Epidemiology in the School of Population Health, University of Queensland, Australia.

David W. Bates is Chief at the Division of General Internal Medicine and Primary Care, Brigham and Women's Hospital and Professor of Medicine, Harvard Medical School, Boston, MA, USA.

Reinhard Busse is Professor of Health Management at Technische Universität, Berlin.

Somnath Chatterji is Team Leader of Multi-Country Studies, Health Statistics and Informatics (HSI), World Health Organization, Geneva.

Douglas A. Conrad is Professor of Health Services and Department of Health Services Director at the Center for Health Management Research, University of Washington.

Jean-Noël DuPasquier is Chief Economist at Me-Ti SA health and private consultant, Carouge, Switzerland.

Arnold M. Epstein is John H. Foster Professor and Chair of the Department of Health Policy and Management at the Harvard School of Public Health and Professor of Medicine and Health Care Policy at Harvard Medical School, Boston, MA, USA.

Harriet Finne-Soveri is Senior Medical Officer and RAI project manager at the National Institute for Health and Welfare STAKES, Finland.

Ray Fitzpatrick is Professor at the Division of Public Health and Primary Health Care, University of Oxford and Fellow of Nuffield College, Oxford.

Sandra Garcia-Armesto is Health Economist/Policy Analyst for the Health Care Quality Indicators project at the OECD Directorate for Employment, Labour and Social Affairs

Ruedi Gilgen is Attending Physician and Geriatrician at Waid City Hospital, Zürich, Switzerland and a principle in Q-Sys, a health information company providing quality data to participating providers.

Maria Goddard is Professor of Health Economics at the Centre for Health Economics, University of York.

Olivia Grigg is a scientist at the MRC Biostatistics Unit, Institute of Public Health, University of Cambridge.

Unto Häkkinen is Research Professor at the Centre for Health Economics (CHESS) in the National Institute for Health and Welfare (STAKES), Helsinki, Finland.

Cristina Hernández-Quevedo is Research Fellow at the European Observatory on Health Systems and Policies based at the London School of Economics and Political Science, London.

John P. Hirdes is Professor in the Department of Health Studies and Gerontology at the University of Waterloo, Ontario, Canada.

Lisa I. Iezzoni is Professor of Medicine at Harvard Medical School and Director of the Institute for Health Policy, Massachusetts General Hospital.

Rowena Jacobs is Senior Research Fellow at the Centre for Health Economics, University of York.

Sowmya Kadandale is Technical Officer at the Department for Health System Governance and Service Delivery, World Health Organization, Geneva.

Niek Klazinga is Coordinator, Health Care Quality Indicator Project, OECD, Paris and Professor of Social Medicine, Academic Medical Centre, University of Amsterdam.

Helen Lester is Professor of Primary Care at the University of Manchester.

Cristina Masseria is Research Fellow in Health Economics at the London School of Economics and Political Science, London.

David McDaid is Senior Research Fellow at the London School of Economics and Political Science and European Observatory on Health Systems and Policies.

Elizabeth A. McGlynn is Associate Director of RAND Health.

Martin McKee is Professor of European Public Health at the London School of Hygiene & Tropical Medicine and Head of Research Policy at the European Observatory on Health Systems and Policies.

Vincent Mor is Professor and Chair of the Department of Community Health at the Brown University School of Medicine.

Ellen Nolte is Director, Health and Healthcare, RAND Europe, Cambridge.

Amit Prasad is Technical Officer at WHO Kobe Centre, Kobe, Japan.

Nigel Rice is Professor of Health Economics at the Centre for Health Economics, University of York.

Silvana Robone is Research Fellow at the Centre for Health Economics, University of York.

Martin Roland is Professor of Health Services Research in the University of Cambridge.

Thomas D. Sequist is Assistant Professor of Medicine and Health Care Policy at Harvard Medical School and Brigham and Women's Hospital, Boston, MA, USA.

Paul G. Shekelle is Staff Physician, West Los Angeles Veterans Affairs Medical Center, Los Angeles and Director, Southern California Evidence-Based Practice Center, RAND Corporation, Santa Monica, California.

David Speigelhalter is Senior Scientist at the MRC Biostatistics Unit, Institute of Public Health, University of Cambridge.

Andrew Street is Professor of Health Economics at the Centre for Health Economics, University of York.

Darcey D. Terris is Senior Scientist at the Mannheim Institute of Public Health, Social and Preventive Medicine, Universitätsmedizin Mannheim, Medical Faculty Mannheim, Heidelberg University, Mannheim, Germany.

Nicole Valentine is Technical Officer in the Department of Ethics, Equity, Trade and Human Rights at the World Health Organization, Geneva.

Jeremy Veillard is Regional Adviser, *ad interim*, Health Policy and Equity Programme at the World Health Organization Regional Office for Europe, Copenhagen.

Adam Wagstaff is Lead Economist (Health) in the Development Research Group (Human Development and Public Services Team) at The World Bank, Washington DC, USA.

Editors

Sheila Leatherman is Research Professor at the Gillings School of Global Public Health, University of North Carolina and Visiting Professor at the London School of Economics and Political Science.

Elias Mossialos is Professor of Health Policy at the London School of Economics and Political Science, Co-Director of the European Observatory on Health Systems and Policies and Director of LSE Health.

Irene Papanicolas is Research Associate and Brian Abel-Smith Scholar at LSE Health, the London School of Economics and Political Science.

Peter C. Smith is Professor of Health Policy in the Business School and Institute for Global Health at the Imperial College, London.

List of boxes, figures and tables

Boxes

Figures

Tables

PART I

Principles of performance measurement

1.1 | *Introduction*

PETER C. SMITH, ELIAS MOSSIALOS,
IRENE PAPANICOLAS, SHEILA LEATHERMAN

Introduction

Information plays a central role in a health system's ability to secure improved health for its population. Its many and diverse uses include tracking public health; determining and implementing appropriate treatment paths for patients; supporting clinical improvement; monitoring the safety of the health-care system; assuring managerial control; and promoting health system accountability to citizens. However, underlying all of these efforts is the role that information plays in enhancing decision-making by various stakeholders (patients, clinicians, managers, governments, citizens) seeking to steer a health system towards the achievement of better outcomes.

Records of performance measurement efforts in health systems can be traced back at least 250 years (Loeb 2004; McIntyre et al. 2001). More formal arguments for the collection and publication of performance information were developed over 100 years ago. Pioneers in the field campaigned for its widespread use in health care but were impeded by professional, practical and political barriers (Spiegelhalter 1999). For example, Florence Nightingale and Ernest Codman's efforts were frustrated by professional resistance and until recently information systems have failed to deliver their promised benefits in the form of timely, accurate and useful information.

Nevertheless, over the past twenty-five years there has been a dramatic growth in health system performance measurement and reporting. Many factors have contributed to this growth. On the demand side health systems have come under intense cost-containment pressures; patients expect to make more informed decisions about their treatment choices; and there has been growing demand for increased oversight and accountability in health professions and health service institutions (Power 1999; Smith 2005). On the supply side great advances in information technology (IT) have made it much cheaper and easier to collect, process and disseminate data.

The IT revolution has transformed our ability to capture vast quantities of data on the inputs and activities of the health system and (in principle) offers a major resource for performance measurement and improvement. Often, the immediate stimulus for providing information has been the desire to improve the delivery of health care by securing appropriate treatment and good outcomes for patients. When a clinician lacks access to reliable and timely information on a patient's medical history, health status and personal circumstances this may often lead to an inability to provide optimal care; wasteful duplication and delay; and problems in the continuity and coordination of health care. Similarly, patients often lack useful information to make choices about treatment and provider in line with their individual preferences and values.

Information is more generally a key resource for securing managerial, political and democratic control of the health system, in short – improving governance. Over the last twenty-five years there have been astonishing developments in the scope, nature and timeliness of performance data made publicly available in most developed health systems. The publication of those data has had a number of objectives, some of which are poorly articulated. However, the overarching theme has been a desire to enhance the accountability of the health system to patients, taxpayers and their representatives, thereby stimulating efforts to improve performance.

Notwithstanding the vastly increased potential for deploying performance measurement tools in modern health systems, and the large number of experiments under way, there remain many unresolved debates about how best to deploy performance data. Health systems are still in the early days of performance measurement and there remains an enormous agenda for improving its effectiveness. The policy questions of whether, and what, to collect are rapidly being augmented by questions concerning how best to summarize and report such data and how to integrate them into an effective system of governance.

This book summarizes some of the principal themes emerging in the performance measurement debate. The aim is to examine experience to date and to offer guidance on future policy priorities, with the following main objectives:

- to present a coherent framework within which to discuss the opportunities and challenges associated with performance measurement.

- to examine the various dimensions and levels of health system performance;
- to identify the measurement instruments and analytical tools needed to implement successful performance measurement;
- to explore the implications for the design and implementation of performance measurement systems;
- to examine the implications of performance measurement for policy-makers, politicians, regulators and others charged with the governance of the health system.

In this first chapter we set the scene by offering a general discussion on what is meant by health system performance and why we should seek to measure it. We also discuss the various potential users of such information and how they might respond to its availability. The remainder of the chapter summarizes the contents of the book that fall into four main sections: (i) measurement of the various dimensions of performance; (ii) statistical tools for analysing and summarizing performance measures; (iii) examples of performance measurement in some especially challenging domains; and (iv) how policy instruments can be attached to performance measurement.

What is performance measurement for?

Health systems are complex entities with many different stakeholders including patients, various types of health-care providers, payers, purchaser organizations, regulators, government and the broader citizenry. These stakeholders are linked by a series of accountability relationships. Accountability has two broad elements: the rendering of an account (provision of information) and the consequent holding to account (sanctions or rewards for the accountable party). Whatever the precise design of the health system, the fundamental role of performance measurement is to help hold the various agents to account by enabling stakeholders to make informed decisions. It is therefore noteworthy that, if accountability relationships are to function properly, no system of performance information should be viewed in isolation from the broader system design within which the measurement is embedded.

Each of the accountability relationships has different information needs in terms of the nature of information, its detail and timeliness; validity of the data; and the level of aggregation required. For example, a patient choosing which provider to use may need detailed comparative data on health outcomes. In contrast, a citizen may need highly aggregate summaries and trends when holding a government to account and deciding for whom to vote. Many intermediate needs arise. A purchaser (for example, social insurer) may require both broad, more aggregate information (for example, readmission rates) and detailed assurance on safety aspects when deciding whether providers are performing adequately. Performance measurement faces the fundamental challenge of designing information systems that are able to serve these diverse needs. Table 1.1.1 summarizes some of the information needs of different stakeholders.

Table 1.1.1 *Information requirements for stakeholders in health-care systems*

Stakeholder	Examples of needs	Data requirements
Government	• Monitoring population health • Setting health policy goals and priorities • Assurance that regulatory procedures are working properly • Assurance that government finances are used as intended • Ensuring appropriate information and research functions are undertaken • Monitoring regulatory effectiveness and efficiency	• Information on performance at national and international levels • Information on access to and equity of care • Information on utilization of services and waiting times • Population health data
Regulators	• To protect patients' safety and welfare • To assure broader consumer protection • To ensure the market is functioning efficiently	• Timely, reliable and continuous information on health system performance at aggregate and provider levels • Information on probity and efficiency of financial flows

Table 1.1.1 *cont'd*

Stakeholder	Examples of needs	Data requirements
Payers (taxpayers and members of insurance funds)	• To ensure money is being spent effectively and in line with expectations	• Aggregate, comparative performance measures • Information on productivity and cost-effectiveness • Information on access and equity of care
Purchaser organiz-ations	• To ensure that the contracted providers deliver appropriate and cost-effective health services	• Information on health needs and unmet needs • Information on patient experiences and patient satisfaction • Information on provider performance • Information on the cost-effectiveness of treatments • Information on health outcomes
Provider organiz-ations	• To monitor and improve existing services • To assess local needs	• Aggregate clinical performance data • Information on patient experiences and patient satisfaction • Information on access and equity of care • Information on utilization of services and waiting times
Physicians	• To provide high-quality patient care • To maintain and improve knowledge and skills	• Information on individual clinical performance • State-of-the-art medical knowledge • Benchmarking performance information
Patients	• Ability to make a choice of provider when in need • Information on alternative treatments	• Information on health-care services available • Information on treatment options • Information on health outcomes
Citizens	• Assurance that appropriate services will be available when needed • Holding government and other elected officials to account	• Broad trends in, and comparisons of, system performance at national and local levels across multiple domains of performance: access, effectiveness, safety and responsiveness

In practice the development of performance measurement has rarely been pursued with a clear picture of what specific information is needed by the multiple users. Instead, performance measurement systems typically present a wide range of data, often chosen because of relative convenience and accessibility, in the hope that some of the information will be useful to a variety of users. Yet, given the diverse information needs of the different stakeholders in health systems, it is unlikely that a single method of performance reporting will be useful for everybody. Moreover, some sort of prioritization is needed as an unfeasibly large set of data may result from seeking to satisfy all information needs. One of the key issues addressed in the following chapters is how data sources can be designed and exploited to satisfy the demands of different users (often using data from the same sources in different forms) within health systems' limited capacity to provide and analyse data.

Defining and measuring performance

Performance measurement seeks to monitor, evaluate and communicate the extent to which various aspects of the health system meet key objectives. There is a fair degree of consensus that those objectives can be summarized under a limited number of headings, such as:

- health conferred on citizens by the health system
- responsiveness to individual needs and preferences of patients
- financial protection offered by the health system
- productivity of utilization of health resources.

'Health' relates to both the health outcomes secured after treatment and the broader health status of the population. 'Responsiveness' captures dimensions of health system behaviour not directly related to health outcomes, such as dignity, communications, autonomy, prompt services, access to social support during care, quality of basic services and choice of provider. Financial protection from catastrophic expenditure associated with illness is a fundamental goal of most health systems, addressed with very different levels of success across the world. 'Productivity' refers to the extent to which the resources used by the health system are used efficiently in the pursuit of its goals. Furthermore, as well as a concern with the overall attainment in each of these domains, *The world health report 2000* (WHO 2000) highlighted the importance of distributional (or equity) issues, expressed in terms of inequity in health outcomes, in responsiveness and in payment. Part 2 of the book summarizes progress in these dimensions of health performance measurement.

The fundamental goal of health systems is to improve the health of patients and the general public. Many measurement instruments have therefore focused mainly on the health of the populations under scrutiny. Nolte and colleagues (2009) (Chapter 2.1) summarize progress to date. Population health has traditionally been captured in broad measures such as standardized mortality rates, life expectancy and years of life lost, sometimes adjusted for rates of disability in the form of disability-adjusted life years (DALYs). Such measures are frequently used as a basis for international and regional comparison. However, whilst undoubtedly informative and assembled relatively easily in many health systems, they have a number of drawbacks. Most notably, it is often difficult to assess the extent to which variations in health outcome can be attributed to the health system. This has led to the development of the concept of avoidable mortality and disability. Nolte, Bain and McKee assess the current state of the art of population health measurement and its role in securing a better understanding of the reasons for variations.

Health care is a field in which the contribution of the health system can be captured most reliably, using measures of the clinical outcomes for patients. Traditionally, this has been examined using post-treatment mortality but this is a blunt instrument and interest is focusing increasingly on more general measures of improvements in patient health status, often in the form of patient-reported outcome measures (PROMs). These can take the form of detailed condition-specific questionnaires or broad-brush generic measures and numerous instruments have been developed, often in the context of clinical trials. Fitzpatrick (2009) (Chapter 2.2) assesses progress to date and seeks to understand why implementation for routine performance assessment has been piecemeal and slow.

Clinical outcome measures are the gold standard for measuring effectiveness in health care. However, there are numerous reasons why an outcome-oriented approach to managing performance may not always be appropriate. It may be extremely difficult or costly to collect the agreed outcome measure and outcomes may become evident only after a long period of time has elapsed (when it is too late to act on the data). Measures of clinical process then become important signals of future success (Donabedian 1966). Process measures are based on actions or structures known from research evidence to be associated with health system outcomes. Examples of useful process measures include appropriate prescribing, regular blood pressure monitoring for hypertension or glucose monitoring for diabetics (Naylor et al. 2002). McGlynn (2009) (Chapter 2.3) assesses the state of the art in clinical process measurement, describes a number of schemes now in operation and assesses the circumstances in which it is most appropriate.

Most health systems have a fundamental goal to protect citizens from impoverishment arising from health-care expenditure. To that end, many countries have implemented extensive systems of health insurance. However, much of the world's population remains vulnerable to catastrophic health-care costs, particularly in low-income countries. Even where insurance arrangements are in place, often they offer only partial financial protection. Furthermore, there is considerable variation in the arrangements for making financial contributions to insurance pools, ranging from experience rating (dependent on previous health-care utilization) to premiums or taxation based on, say, personal income, unrelated to any history of health-care utilization. Wagstaff (2009) (Chapter 2.4) shows that the measurement of financial protection is challenging as in principle it seeks to capture the extent to which payments for health care affect people's savings and their ability to purchase other important things in life. He examines the concepts underlying financial protection related to health care and current efforts at measuring health system performance in this domain.

The world health report 2000 highlights the major role of the concept of responsiveness in determining levels of satisfaction with the health system amongst patients, carers and the general public (WHO 2000). Responsiveness can embrace concepts as diverse as timeliness and convenience of access to health care; treatment with consideration for respect and dignity; and attention to individual preferences and values. Generally, although certainly not always, it is assumed that responsiveness reflects health system characteristics that are independent of the health outcomes achieved. Valentine and colleagues (2009) (Chapter 2.5) explain the concept of responsiveness as developed by the World Health Organization (WHO) and discuss it in relation to closely related concepts such as patient satisfaction. They explain the various concepts of health system responsiveness, examine current approaches to their measurement (most notably in the form of the World Health Survey (WHS)) and assess measurement challenges in this domain.

The pursuit of some concept of equity or fairness is a central objective of many health systems and indicates a concern with the distribution of the burden of ill health across the population. The prime focus is often on equity of access to health care or equity of financing of health care but there may also be concern with equity in eventual health outcomes. The formulation and measurement of concepts of equity are far from straightforward. They require quite advanced analytical techniques to be applied to population surveys that measure individuals' health status, use of health care, expenditure on health care and personal characteristics. Furthermore, it is often necessary to replicate measurement within and across countries in order to secure meaningful benchmarks. Allin and colleagues (2009) (Chapter 2.6) explain the various concepts of equity applied to health systems and the methods used to measure them. They examine the strengths and limitations of these methods, illustrate with some examples and discuss how policy-makers should interpret and use measures of equity.

Productivity is perhaps the most challenging measurement area of all as it seeks to offer a comprehensive framework that links the resources used to the measures of effectiveness described above. The need to develop reliable productivity measures is obvious, given the policy problem of ensuring that the funders of the health system (taxpayers, insurees, employers, patients) get good value for the money they spend. Measurement of productivity is a fundamental requirement for securing providers' accountability to their payers and for ensuring that health system resources are spent wisely. However, the criticisms directed at *The world health report 2000* illustrate the difficulty of making an operational measurement of productivity, even at the broad health system level (WHO 2000). Also, the accounting challenges of identifying the resources consumed become progressively more acute as the levels of detail become finer, for example, for the meso-level (provider organizations), clinical department, practitioner or – most challenging of all – individual patient or citizen. Street and Häkkinen (2009) (Chapter 2.7) examine the principles of productivity and efficiency measurement in health and describe some existing efforts to measure the productivity of organizations and systems. They discuss the major challenges to implementation and assess the most promising avenues for future progress.

Statistical tools for analysing and summarizing performance measures

Understanding performance measures for health care and public health is a complex undertaking. In health care, it is frequently the case that physicians and provider organizations treat patients with very significant differences in their severity of disease, socio-economic status, behaviours related to health and patterns of compliance with treatment recommendations. These differences make it difficult to draw direct performance comparisons and pose considerable challenges for developing accurate and fair comparisons. The problems are magnified when examining broader measures of population health improvement. Furthermore, health outcomes are often subject to quite large random variation that makes it difficult to detect genuine variation in performance. Performance measures that fail to take account of such concerns will therefore lack credibility and be ineffective. Statistical methods move to centre stage as the prime mechanism for addressing such concerns.

Hauck and colleagues (2003) show that there are very large variations in the extent to which local health-care organizations can influence performance measures in different domains. Broadly speaking, measures of the processes of care can be influenced more directly by the organ-izations whilst measures of health outcome exhibit a great deal of variation beyond health system control. One vitally important element in performance measurement therefore is how to attribute causality to observed outcomes or attribute responsibility for departures from approved standards of care. There are potentially very serious costs if good or poor performance is wrongly attributed to the actions of a practitioner, team or organization. For example, physicians working in socio-economically disadvantaged localities may be wrongly blamed for securing poor outcomes beyond the control of the health system. Conversely, mediocre practitioners in wealthier areas may enjoy undeservedly high rankings. In the extreme, such mis-attributions may lead to difficulties in recruiting practitioners for disadvantaged localities. Terris and Aron (2009) (Chapter 3.3) discuss the attribution problem – assessing progress in ensuring that the causality behind observed measures is attributed to the correct sources in order to inform policy, improve service delivery and assure accountability.

Risk adjustment is used widely to address the attribution problem. This statistical approach seeks to enhance comparability by adjusting outcome data according to differences in resources, case-mix and environmental factors. For example, variations in patient outcomes in health care will have much to do with variations in individual attributes such as age, socio-economic class and any co-morbidities. Iezzoni (2009) (Chapter 3.1) reviews the principles of risk-adjustment in reporting clinical performance, describes some well-established risk adjustment schemes, explains the situations in which they have been deployed and draws out the future challenges.

Random fluctuation is a specific issue in the interpretation of many performance data, by definition emerging with no systematic pattern and always present in quantitative data. Statistical methods become central to determining whether an observed variation in performance may have arisen by chance rather than from variations in the performance of agents within the health system. There is a strong case for routine presentation of the confidence intervals associated with all performance measures. In the health-care domain such methods face the challenge of identifying genuine outliers in a consistent and timely fashion, without signalling an excessive number of false positives. This is crucial when undertaking surveillance of individual practitioners or teams. When does a deviation from expected outcomes become a cause for concern and when should a regulator intervene? Grigg and Spiegelhalter (2009) (Chapter 3.2) show how statistical surveillance methods such as statistical control charts can squeeze maximum information from time series of data and offer considerable scope for timely and focused intervention.

Health systems are complex entities with multiple dimensions that make it very difficult to summarize performance, especially through a single measure. Yet, when separate performance measures are provided for the many different aspects of the health system under observation (for example, efficiency, equity, responsiveness, quality, outcomes, access) the amount of information provided can become overwhelming. Such information overload makes it difficult for users of performance information to make any sense of the data. In response to these problems it has become increasingly popular to use composite indicators. These combine separate performance indicators into a single index or measure, often used to rank or compare the performance of different practitioners, organizations or systems by providing a bigger picture and offering a more rounded view of performance.

However, composite indicators that are not carefully designed may be misleading and lead to serious failings if used for health system policy-making or planning. For example, one fundamental challenge is to decide which measures to include in the indicator and with what weights. Composite indicators aim to offer a comprehensive performance assessment and therefore should include all important aspects of performance, even those that are difficult to measure. In practice, it is often the case that there is little choice of data and questionable sources may be used for some components of the indicator, requiring considerable ingenuity to develop adequate proxy indicators. Goddard and Jacobs (2009) (Chapter 3.4) discuss the many methodological and policy issues that arise when seeking to develop satisfactory composite indicators of performance.

Performance measurement in challenging domains

Health problems and health care are enormously heterogeneous and performance measurement in specific health domains often gives rise to special considerations. It is therefore important to tailor general principles of good performance measurement to specific disease areas or types of health care. This book examines the performance measurement issues that arise for particularly challenging domains that involve large volumes of health system expenditure.

Primary care is an important element of most health-care systems and usually accounts for by far the highest number of encounters with patients. However, the importance and meaning of primary care varies between countries and there is often a lack of clarity about its composition. Lester and Roland (2009) (Chapter 4.1) therefore first provide an underlying conceptual framework for performance measurement in primary care based on concepts such as access, effectiveness, efficiency, equity and organization. From a generic perspective they discuss how existing measures have been developed and selected and explain why it may be especially important to measure the processes of care (rather than outcomes) in a primary care setting. The chapter discusses a variety of case studies (including the Quality and Outcomes Framework in the United Kingdom; changes in the Veterans Health Administration in the United States; European Practice Assessment indicators for practice management); assesses their effectiveness and any unintended consequences; and sets out the prerequisites for successful implementation.

Chronic illnesses are the primary cause of premature mortality and the overall disease burden within Europe, and a growing number of patients are facing multiple chronic conditions (WHO 2002). WHO estimates that chronic illnesses globally will grow from 57% to around 65% of all deaths annually by 2030 (WHO 2005). Some initiatives are in place but the measurement of performance in the chronic disease sector has traditionally been a low priority and there is an urgent need to develop and test a broader range of more sensitive measurement instruments.

There are several challenges in assessing health system performance in relation to chronic disease. Studies of the process of care identify the critical importance of coordinating the elements of care but the models proposed to ensure this coordination have proved extremely difficult to evaluate, partly because often they are implemented in different ways in different settings. The problems that need to be addressed may also differ in these different settings, making comparisons problematic. McKee and Nolte (2009) (Chapter 4.2) examine progress to date. They analyse the particular issues that arise in seeking to measure performance in chronic care, such as the heightened tension between reporting the processes and the outcomes of care; the difficulty of measuring performance across a range of settings (such as prescribing, outpatient clinic, hospital); the challenges of accounting for co-morbidities and other patient circumstances; and the need for process measures that keep pace with the rapidly expanding body of medical evidence.

Mental health problems account for a very large proportion of the total disability burden of ill health in many countries but are often afforded much lower policy priority than other areas of health services. Every year up to 30% of the population worldwide has some form of mental disorder and at least two thirds of those people receive no treatment, even in countries with the most resources. In the United States, 31% of people are affected by mental disorders every year but 67% of them are not treated. In Europe, mental disorder affects 27% of people every year, 74% of whom receive no treatment. The treatment gap approaches 90% in many developing countries (Lancet Global Mental Health Group 2007).

Mental health is still a hugely neglected policy area – stigma, prejudice and discrimination are deeply rooted and make it complex to discuss the challenges for policy-makers. The Organisation for Economic Co-operation and Development (OECD) and the European Union (EU) have recognized the importance of mental health performance indicators and have developed plans to monitor mental health in their member countries, but the policy drive and state-of-the-art measurement are still young. Jacobs and McDaid (2009) (Chapter 4.3) examine performance measurement in mental health and map out the progress in performance measurement instruments in terms of outcome, process, quality and patient experience. They pay particular attention to the important issue of equity in mental health services.

Long-term care for elderly people has become a central policy concern in many industrialized countries. This is likely to assume increasing importance in many transitional and developing countries as longevity increases and traditional sources of long-term care come under pressure. Long-term care systems in most countries have evolved idiosyncratically, facing different demographic imperatives and responding to different regulatory and medical care systems. One prime requirement is therefore to assess the needs of the population of long-term care users and the types and quality of services they receive. A particular challenge for this sector is the need to address both quality-of-life and quality-of-care issues as the long-term care setting provides the individual's home. Mor and colleagues (2009) (Chapter 4.4) describe the American-designed long-term care facility Resident Assessment Instrument (interRAI) and its adoption for use in several European countries' long-term care systems. They describe how these types of data are being used to monitor and compare the quality of care provided and enumerate some challenges for the future.

Health policy and performance measurement

In many respects, performance information is what economists refer to as a public good – unlikely to develop optimally within a health system without the guidance and encouragement of governments. Performance measurement is therefore a key stewardship issue that requires conscious policy attention in a number of important domains. Part 5 of the book discusses some of the ways in which policy can translate performance measurement into real health system improvement.

Much of the modern performance measurement movement is predicated on implementing rapid improvements in the IT systems required to capture electronically the actions and outcomes of health systems and advances in the science of health informatics. Electronic guidelines provide the latest available evidence on chronic diseases, enabling physicians to tailor them for specific patients; electronic health cards that track information such as prescriptions can reduce contraindications and inappropriate prescribing. Although designed primarily for improving the quality and continuity of patient care, the electronic health record offers extraordinary potential for transforming the range, accuracy and speed of data capture for performance measurement purposes. However, progress has not been as rapid or as smooth as many commentators had hoped and it is clear that many of the benefits of IT have yet to be realized. Sequist and Bates (2009) (Chapter 5.3) examine progress to date, describe examples of good practice and offer an assessment of the most important priorities for future IT and health informatics developments.

Setting targets for the attainment of health-care improvement goals expresses a commitment to achieve specified outputs in a defined time period and helps to monitor progress towards the realization of broader goals and objectives. Targets may be based on outcomes (reducing infant mortality rates) or processes (regular checks of a patient's blood pressure by a physician). They are viewed as a means of defining and setting priorities; creating high-level political and administrative commitment to particular outputs; and providing a basis for follow-up and evaluation. In short, they can become central to the governance of the health system. However, targets are selective and focus on specific areas, thereby running the risk of neglecting untargeted areas (Smith 1995). As Goodhart (1984) emphasized, "any observed statistical regularity will tend to collapse once pressure is placed upon it for control purposes", therefore existing targets should be scrutinized routinely for continued relevance and effectiveness. McKee and Fulop (2000) also emphasize that targets monitoring progress in population health require knowledge of the natural history of diseases. For some, changes in risk factors now will affect disease only many years hence, for example, smoking and lung cancer. Therefore, process measures (such as changes in attitudes or behaviour) are more appropriate than outcome measures (such as fewer deaths). The relation is more immediate for other risk factors (such as drunk driving and injuries)

(McKee & Fulop 2000). Many individual countries have implemented national, regional or local health target schemes that are yielding some successes but also some that have had little measurable impact on system performance. Smith and Busse (2009) (Chapter 5.1) summarize experiences with health targets to date and seek to draw out some general lessons for their design and implementation in guiding and regulating the health system.

Governments and the public increasingly are demanding that providers should be more accountable for the quality of the clinical care that they provide. Publicly available report cards that document the comparative performance of organizations or individual practitioners are a fundamental tool for such accountability. Public reporting can improve quality through two pathways: (i) selection pathway whereby patients select providers of better quality; and (ii) change pathway in which performance data help providers to identify areas of underperformance and public release of the information acts as a stimulus to improve (Berwick et al. 2003). Information about the performance of health-care providers and health plans has been published in the United States for over fifteen years. Many other health systems are now experimenting with public disclosure and public reporting of performance information is likely to play an increasingly significant part in the governance, accountability and regulation of health systems. Shekelle (2009) (Chapter 5.2) summarizes experience to date with public disclosure of performance data. He describes some of the major public reporting schemes that have been implemented; the extent to which they have affected the behaviour of managers, practitioners and patients; and the impact of the reports on quality of care.

Performance measurement has a central purpose to promote better performance in individual practitioners by offering timely information that is relevant to their specific clinical practice. In some countries there is growing pressure to demonstrate that practising physicians continue to meet acceptable standards. This is driven in part by concerns that the knowledge obtained during basic training may rapidly become out of date and is also used increasingly as a way of holding physicians to account. Professional improvement schemes are often implemented in conjunction with guidelines on best practice and seek to offer benchmarks against which professionals can gauge their own performance. They seek to harness and promote natural professional interest in 'doing a good job' and those advocating measurement for professional improvement argue that they should offer rapid, anonymous feedback that practitioners are able to act upon quickly. Such schemes should be led by the professionals themselves and not threaten professional autonomy or livelihood, except in egregious cases. These principles can challenge the philosophy of public disclosure inherent in report card initiatives. Epstein (2009) (Chapter 5.5) describes experience with performance measurement for professional improvement; discusses the successes and failures; and explains how such schemes can be reconciled with increasing demands for public reporting and professional accountability.

Most performance measurement of any power offers some implicit incentives, for example in the form of provider market share or reputation. Furthermore, there is no doubt that physicians and other actors in the health system respond to financial incentives. This raises the question of whether performance measurement can be harnessed to offer *explicit* incentives for performance improvement, based on reported performance. The design of such purposive incentive schemes needs to consider many issues, including which aspects of performance to target; how to measure attainment; how to set targets; whether to offer incentives at individual or group level; the strength of the link between achievement and reward; and how much money to attach to the incentive. Furthermore, constant monitoring is needed to ensure that there are no unintended responses to incentives; the incentive scheme does not jeopardize the reliability of the performance data on which it relies; and unrewarded aspects of performance are not compromised. Pay for performance can also challenge the traditions of professional clinical practice (that is, principles of autonomous decision-making) and the need to do the best for patients even in the absence of direct incentives. Conrad (2009) (Chapter 5.4) sets out the issues and assesses the limited evidence that has emerged to date.

International comparison has become one of the most powerful tools for securing national policy-makers' attention to deficiencies in their health systems and prompting remedial action. The response to *The world health report 2000* (WHO 2000) is an indication of the power of international comparison. A number of information systems aimed at facilitating such comparison are now in place, including those provided by WHO and the OECD. Notwithstanding the power of international comparison, its use gives rise to many philosophical and practical difficulties. For example – are data definitions transportable between countries? How valid are comparisons made using different classification systems? How should one adjust for economic, climatic and physical differences between countries? To what extent should comparison take account of differences in national epidemiological variations? Is it possible to make meaningful cost comparisons in the absence of satisfactory currency conversion methodologies? Veillard and colleagues (2009) (Chapter 5.6) examine the major issues involved in undertaking meaningful comparison of countries' health systems.

Conclusions

The broad scope of the chapters outlined above is an indication of the size of the task of conceptualizing performance; designing measurement schemes; understanding and communicating performance information; and formulating policies to seize the opportunities offered by performance measurement. The chapters raise numerous challenges of concept, design, implementation and evaluation. Many also highlight government's crucial role in guiding performance measurement policy and the numerous political considerations that must be examined alongside technical measurement issues. In the final chapter the editors seek to draw together the main themes emerging from the book and set out key research, policy and evaluation priorities for the future.

References

Allin, S. Hernández-Quevedo, C. Masseria, C (2009). Measuring equity of access to health care. In: Smith, PC. Mossialos, E. Papanicolas, I. Leatherman, S (eds.). *Performance measurement for health system improvement: experiences, challenges and prospects.* Cambridge: Cambridge University Press.

Berwick, DM. James, B. Coye, MJ (2003). 'Connections between quality measurement and improvement.' *Medical Care*, 41(Suppl. 1): 30–38.

Conrad, D (2009). Incentives for health-care performance improvement. In: Smith, PC. Mossialos, E. Papanicolas, I. Leatherman, S (eds.). *Performance measurement for health system improvement: experiences, challenges and prospects.* Cambridge: Cambridge University Press.

Donabedian, A (1966). 'Evaluating the quality of medical care.' *Milbank Memorial Fund Quarterly*, 44(3): 166–206.

Epstein, AM (2009). Performance information and professional improvement. In: Smith, PC. Mossialos, E. Papanicolas, I. Leatherman, S (eds.). *Performance measurement for health system improvement: experiences, challenges and prospects*. Cambridge: Cambridge University Press.

Fitzpatrick, R (2009). Patient-reported outcome measures and performance measurement. In: Smith, PC. Mossialos, E. Papanicolas, I. Leatherman, S (eds.). *Performance measurement for health system improvement: experiences, challenges and prospects*. Cambridge: Cambridge University Press.

Goddard, M. Jacobs, R (2009). Using composite indicators to measure performance in health care. In: Smith, PC. Mossialos, E. Papanicolas, I. Leatherman, S (eds.). *Performance measurement for health system improvement: experiences, challenges and prospects*. Cambridge: Cambridge University Press.

Goodhart, CAE (1984). *Monetary theory and practice: the UK experience*. London: Macmillan.

Grigg, O. Spiegelhalter, D. (2009). Clinical surveillance and patient safety. In: Smith, PC. Mossialos, E. Papanicolas, I. Leatherman, S (eds.). *Performance measurement for health system improvement: experiences, challenges and prospects*. Cambridge: Cambridge University Press.

Hauck, K. Rice, N. Smith, P (2003). 'The influence of health care organisations on health system performance.' *Journal of Health Services Research and Policy*, 8(2): 68–74.

Iezzoni, LI (2009). Risk adjustment for performance measurement. In: Smith, PC. Mossialos, E. Papanicolas, I. Leatherman, S (eds.). *Performance measurement for health system improvement: experiences, challenges and prospects*. Cambridge: Cambridge University Press.

Jacobs, R. McDaid, D (2009). Performance measurement in mental health services. In: Smith, PC. Mossialos, E. Papanicolas, I. Leatherman, S (eds.). *Performance measurement for health system improvement: experiences, challenges and prospects*. Cambridge: Cambridge University Press.

Lancet Global Mental Health Group (2007). 'Scale up services for mental disorders: a call for action.' *Lancet*, 370(9594): 1241–1252.

Lester, H. Roland M (2009). Performance measurement in primary care. In: Smith, PC. Mossialos, E. Papanicolas, I. Leatherman, S (eds.). *Performance measurement for health system improvement: experiences, challenges and prospects*. Cambridge: Cambridge University Press.

Loeb, JM (2004). 'The current state of performance measurement in health care.' *International Journal for Quality in Health Care*, 16(Suppl. 1): 5–9.

McGlynn, EA (2009). Measuring clinical quality and appropriateness. In: Smith, PC. Mossialos, E. Papanicolas, I. Leatherman, S (eds.). *Performance measurement for health system improvement: experiences, challenges and prospects.* Cambridge: Cambridge University Press.

McIntyre, D. Rogers, L. Heier, EJ (2001). 'Overview, history, and objectives of performance measurement.' *Health Care Financing Review*, 22(3): 7–43.

McKee, M. Fulop, N (2000). 'On target for health? Health targets may be valuable, but context is all important.' *British Medical Journal*, 320(7231): 327–328.

McKee, M. Nolte, E (2009). Chronic care. In: Smith, PC. Mossialos, E. Papanicolas, I. Leatherman, S (eds.). *Performance measurement for health system improvement: experiences, challenges and prospects.* Cambridge: Cambridge University Press.

Mor, V. Finne-Soveri, H. Hirdes, JP. Gilgen, R. DuPasquier, J (2009). Long-term care quality monitoring using the interRAI common clinical assessment language. In: Smith, PC. Mossialos, E. Papanicolas, I. Leatherman, S (eds.). *Performance measurement for health system improvement: experiences, challenges and prospects.* Cambridge: Cambridge University Press.

Naylor, C. Iron, K. Handa, K (2002). Measuring health system performance: problems and opportunities in the era of assessment and accountability. In: Smith, P (ed.). *Measuring up: improving health systems performance in OECD countries.* Paris: Organisation for Economic Co-operation and Development.

Nolte, E. Bain, C. McKee, M (2009). Population health. In: Smith, PC. Mossialos, E. Papanicolas, I. Leatherman, S (eds.). *Performance measurement for health system improvement: experiences, challenges and prospects.* Cambridge: Cambridge University Press.

Power, M (1999). *The audit society: rituals of verification.* Oxford: Oxford University Press.

Shekelle, PG (2009). Public performance reporting on quality information. In: Smith, PC. Mossialos, E. Papanicolas, I. Leatherman, S (eds.). *Performance measurement for health system improvement: experiences, challenges and prospects.* Cambridge: Cambridge University Press.

Sequist, TD. Bates, DW (2009). Developing information technology capacity for performance measurement. In: Smith, PC. Mossialos, E. Papanicolas, I. Leatherman, S (eds.). *Performance measurement for health system improvement: experiences, challenges and prospects.* Cambridge: Cambridge University Press.

Smith PC (1995). 'On the unintended consequences of publishing performance data in the public sector.' *International Journal of Public Administration*, 18(2&3): 277–310.

Smith, PC (2005). 'Performance measurement in health care: history, challenges and prospects.' *Public Money & Management*, 25(4): 213–220.

Smith, PC. Busse, R (2009). Targets and performance measurement. In: Smith, PC. Mossialos, E. Papanicolas, I. Leatherman, S (eds.). *Performance measurement for health system improvement: experiences, challenges and prospects*. Cambridge: Cambridge University Press.

Spiegelhalter, DJ (1999). 'Surgical audit: statistical lessons from Nightingale and Codman.' *Journal of the Royal Statistical Society*, 162(1): 45–58.

Street, A. Häkkinen, U (2009). Health system productivity and efficiency. In: Smith, PC. Mossialos, E. Papanicolas, I. Leatherman, S (eds.). *Performance measurement for health system improvement: experiences, challenges and prospects*. Cambridge: Cambridge University Press.

Terris, DD. Aron, DC (2009). Attribution and causality in health-care performance measurement. In: Smith, PC. Mossialos, E. Papanicolas, I. Leatherman, S (eds.). *Performance measurement for health system improvement: experiences, challenges and prospects*. Cambridge: Cambridge University Press.

Valentine, N. Prasad, A. Rice, N. Robone, S. Chatterji, S (2009). Health systems responsiveness: a measure of the acceptability of health-care processes and systems from the user's perspective. In: Smith, PC. Mossialos, E. Papanicolas, I. Leatherman, S (eds.). *Performance measurement for health system improvement: experiences, challenges and prospects*. Cambridge: Cambridge University Press.

Veillard, J. Garcia-Armesto, S. Kadandale, S. Klazinga, N (2009). International health system comparisons: from measurement challenge to management tool. In: Smith, PC. Mossialos, E. Papanicolas, I. Leatherman, S (eds.). *Performance measurement for health system improvement: experiences, challenges and prospects*. Cambridge: Cambridge University Press.

Wagstaff, A (2009). Measuring financial protection in health. In: Smith, PC. Mossialos, E. Papanicolas, I. Leatherman, S (eds.). *Performance measurement for health system improvement: experiences, challenges and prospects*. Cambridge: Cambridge University Press.

WHO (2000). *The world health report 2000. Health systems: improving performance*. Geneva: World Health Organization.

WHO (2002). *The world health report 2002: reducing the risks, promoting healthy life*. Geneva: World Health Organization.

WHO (2005). *Preventing chronic disease: a vital investment.* Geneva: World
    Health Organization.

PART II

Dimensions of performance

2.1 *Population health*

ELLEN NOLTE, CHRIS BAIN,
MARTIN MCKEE

Introduction

Health systems have three goals: (i) to improve the health of the populations they serve; (ii) to respond to the reasonable expectations of those populations; and (iii) to collect the funds to do so in a way that is fair (WHO 2000). The first of these has traditionally been captured using broad measures of mortality such as total mortality, life expectancy, premature mortality or years of life lost. More recently these have been supplemented by measures of the time lived in poor health, exemplified by the use of disability-adjusted life years (DALYs).

These measures are being employed increasingly as a means of assessing health system performance in comparisons between and within countries. Their main advantage is that the data are generally available. The most important drawback is the inability to distinguish between the component of the overall burden of disease that is attributable to health systems and that which is attributable to actions initiated elsewhere. *The world health report 2000* sought to overcome this problem by adopting a very broad definition of a health system as "all the activities whose primary purpose is to promote, restore or maintain health" (WHO 2000) (Box 2.1.1). A somewhat circular logic makes it possible to use this to justify the use of DALYs as a measure of performance. However, in many cases policy-makers will wish to examine a rather more narrow question – how is a particular health system performing in the delivery of health care?

This chapter examines some of these issues in more detail. It does not review population health measurement per se, as this has been addressed in detail elsewhere (see, for example, Etches et al. 2006; McDowell et al. 2004; Murray et al. 2000; Murray et al. 2002; Reidpath 2005). However, we give a brief overview of some measures that have commonly been used to assess population health in relation

---

Box 2.1.1 Defining health systems

Many activities that contribute directly or indirectly to the provision of health care may or may not be within what is considered to be the health system in different countries (Nolte et al. 2005). Arah and colleagues (2006) distinguish between the *health* system and the *health-care* system. The latter refers to the "combined functioning of public health and personal health-care services" that are under the "direct control of identifiable agents, especially ministries of health." In contrast, the health system extends beyond these boundaries "to include all activities and structures that impact or determine health in its broadest sense within a given society". This closely resembles the World Health Organization (WHO) definition of a health system set out in *The world health report 2000* (WHO 2000). Consequently, health-care performance refers to the "maintenance of an efficient and equitable system of health care", evaluating the system of health-care delivery against the "established public goals for the level and distribution of the benefits and costs of personal and public health care" (Arah et al. 2006). Health system performance is based on a broader concept that also takes account of determinants of population health not related to health care, principally building on the health field concept advanced by Lalonde and thus subsuming health-care performance (Lalonde 1974).

---

to health-care performance (Annex 1 & 2). We begin with a short historical reflection of the impact of health care on population health. We discuss the challenges of attributing population health outcomes to activities in the health system, and thus of identifying indicators of health system performance, before considering indicators and approaches that have been developed to relate measures of health at the population level more closely to health-care performance.

Does health care contribute to population health?

There has been long-standing debate about whether health services make a meaningful contribution to population health (McKee 1999). Writing from a historical perspective in the late 1970s, several authors argued that health care had contributed little to the observed decline in mortality that had occurred in industrialized countries from the mid-nineteenth to the mid-twentieth century. It was claimed that mortality improvements were most likely to be attributable to the influence of factors outside the health-care sector, particularly nutrition, but also to general improvements in the environment (Cochrane et al. 1978; McKeown 1979; McKinlay & McKinlay 1977).

Much of this discussion has been linked to the work of Thomas McKeown (Alvarez-Dardet & Ruiz 1993). His analysis of the mortality decline in England and Wales between 1848/1854 and 1971 illustrated how the largest part of an observed fall in death rates from tuberculosis (TB) predated the introduction of interventions such as immunization or effective chemotherapy (McKeown 1979). He concluded that "specific measures of preventing or treating disease in the individual made no significant contribution to the reduction of the death rate in the nineteenth century" (McKeown 1971), or indeed into the mid-twentieth century. His conclusions were supported by contemporaneous work which analysed long-term trends in mortality from respiratory TB until the early and mid-twentieth century in Glasgow, Scotland (Pennington 1979); and in England and Wales, Italy and New Zealand (Collins 1982); and from infectious diseases in the United States of America in the early and mid-twentieth century (McKinley & McKinley 1977).

Recent reviews of McKeown's work have challenged his sweeping conclusions. They point to other evidence, such as that which demonstrated that the decline in TB mortality in England and Wales in the late nineteenth and early twentieth centuries could be linked in part to the emerging practice of isolating poor patients with TB in workhouse infirmaries (Fairchild & Oppenheimer 1998; Wilson 2005). Nolte and McKee (2004) showed how the pace at which mortality from TB declined increased markedly following the introduction of chemotherapy in the late 1940s, with striking year-on-year reductions in death rates among young people. Others contended that McKeown's focus on TB may have overstated the effect of changing living standards and nutrition (Szreter 1988) and simultaneously underestimated the role of medicine. For example, the application of inoculation converted smallpox from a major to a minor cause of death between the late eighteenth and early nineteenth centuries (Johansson 2005).

Similarly, Schneyder and colleagues (1981) criticized McKinley and McKinley's (1977) analysis for adopting a narrow interpreta-

tion of medical measures, so disregarding the impact of basic public health measures such as water chlorination. Evidence provided
by Mackenbach (1996), who examined a broader range of causes
of death in the Netherlands between 1875/1879 and 1970, also suggests that health care had a greater impact than McKeown and others
had acknowledged. Mackenbach (1996) correlated infectious disease
mortality with the availability of antibiotics from 1946 and deaths
from common surgical and perinatal conditions with improvements in
surgery and anaesthesia and in antenatal and perinatal care since the
1930s. He estimated that up to 18.5% of the total decline in mortality in the Netherlands between the late nineteenth and mid-twentieth
centuries could be attributed to health care.

However, this debate does not address the most important issue.
McKeown was describing trends in mortality at a time when health
care could, at best, contribute relatively little to overall population
health as measured by death rates. Colgrove (2002) noted that there
is now consensus that McKeown was correct to the extent that "curative medical measures played little role in mortality decline prior to the
mid-20th century." However, the scope of health care was beginning
to change remarkably by 1965, the end of the period that McKeown
analysed. A series of entirely new classes of drugs (for example, thiazide
diuretics, beta blockers, beta-sympathomimetics, calcium antagonists)
made it possible to control common disorders such as hypertension
and chronic airways diseases. These developments, along with the
implementation of new and more effective ways of organizing care
and the development of evidence-based care, made it more likely that
health care would play a more important role in determining population health.

How much does health care contribute to population health?

Given that health care can indeed contribute to population health – how
much of a difference does it actually make? Bunker and colleagues (1994)
developed one approach to this question, using published evidence
on the effectiveness of specific health service interventions to estimate
the potential gain in life expectancy attributable to their introduction.
For example, they examined the impact of thirteen clinical preventive
services (such as cervical cancer screening) and thirteen curative services
(such as treatment of cervical cancer) in the United States and estimated

a gain of eighteen months from preventive services. A potential further gain of seven to eight months could be achieved if known efficacious measures were made more widely available. The gain from curative services was estimated at forty-two to forty-eight months (potential further gain: twelve to eighteen months). Taken together, these calculations suggest that about half of the total gain in life expectancy (seven to seven and a half years) in the United States since 1950 may be attributed to clinical preventive and curative services (Bunker 1995).

Wright and Weinstein (1998) used a similar approach to look at a range of preventive and curative health services but focused on interventions targeted at populations at different levels of risk (average and elevated risk; established disease). For example, they estimated that a reduction in cholesterol (to 200 mg/dL) would result in life expectancy gains of fifty to seventy-six months in thirty-five year-old people with highly elevated blood cholesterol levels (> 300 mg/dL). In comparison, it was estimated that life expectancy would increase by eight to ten months if average-risk smokers aged thirty-five were helped to stop smoking.

Such analyses provide important insights into the potential contribution of health care to population health. However, they rest on the assumption that the health gains reported in clinical trials translate directly to the population level. This is not necessarily the case (Britton et al. 1999) as trial participants are often highly selected subsets of the population, typically excluding elderly people and those with co-morbidities. Also, evaluations of individual interventions fail to capture the combined effects of integrated and individualized packages of care (Buck et al. 1999). The findings thus provide little insight into what health systems actually achieve in terms of health gain or how different systems compare.

An alternative approach uses regression analysis to identify any link between inputs to health care and health outcomes although such studies have produced mixed findings. Much of the earlier work failed to identify strong and consistent relationships between health-care indicators (such as health-care expenditure, number of doctors) and health outcomes (such as (infant) mortality, life expectancy) but found socio-economic factors to be powerful determinants of health outcomes (Babazono & Hillman 1994; Cochrane et al. 1978; Kim & Moody 1992). More recent work has provided more consistent evidence. For example, significant inverse relationships have been established between health-care expenditure and infant and premature mortality (Cremieux et al. 1999; Nixon & Ulmann 2006; Or 2000); and between the number of doctors per capita and premature and infant mortality, as well as life expectancy at age sixty-five (Or 2001).

Other studies have asked whether the organization of health-care systems is important. For example, Elola and colleagues (1995), and van der Zee and Kroneman (2007) studied seventeen health-care systems in western Europe. They distinguished national health service (NHS) systems (such as those in Denmark, Ireland, Italy, Spain, United Kingdom) from social security systems (such as those in Germany, Austria, the Netherlands). Controlling for socio-economic indicators and using a cross-sectional analysis, Elola and colleagues (1995) found that countries with NHS systems achieve lower infant mortality rates than those with social security systems at similar levels of gross domestic product (GDP) and health-care expenditure. In contrast, van der Zee and Kroneman (2007) analysed long-term time trends from 1970 onwards. They suggest that the relative performance of the two types of systems changed over time and social security systems have achieved slightly better outcomes (in terms of total mortality and life expectancy) since 1980, when inter-country differences in infant mortality became negligible.

These types of study have obvious limitations arising from data availability and reliability as well as other less-obvious limitations. One major weakness is the cross-sectional nature that many of them display. Gravelle and Blackhouse (1987) have shown how such analyses fail to take account of lagged relationships. An obvious example is cancer mortality, in which death rates often reflect treatments undertaken up to five years previously. Furthermore, a cross-sectional design is ill-equipped to address adequately causality and such models often lack any theoretical basis that might indicate what causal pathways may exist (Buck et al. 1999). However, the greatest problem is that the majority of studies of this type employ indicators of population health (for example, life expectancy and total mortality) that are influenced by many factors outside the health-care sector. These include policies in sectors such as education, housing and employment, where the production of health is a secondary goal.

This is also true of more restricted measures of mortality. Thus, infant mortality rates are often used in international comparisons to capture health-care performance. Yet, deaths in the first four weeks of life (neonatal) and those in the remainder of the first year (postneonatal) have quite different causes. Postneonatal mortality is strongly related to socio-economic factors while neonatal mortality more closely reflects the quality of medical care (Leon et al. 1992). Consequently, assessment of the performance of health care per se requires identification of the indicators of population health that most directly reflect that care.

Attributing indicators of population health to activities in the health system

As noted in the previous section, the work by Bunker and colleagues (1994) points to a potentially substantial contribution of health care to gains in population health, although that contribution has not been quantified. In some cases the impact of health care is almost self-evident, as is the case with vaccine-preventable disease. This is illustrated by the eradication of smallpox in 1980 that followed systematic immunization of entire populations in endemic countries, and also by antibiotic treatment of many common infections. The discovery of insulin transformed type I diabetes from a rapidly fatal childhood illness to one for which optimal care can now provide an almost normal lifespan. In these cases, observed reductions in mortality can be attributed quite clearly to the introduction of new treatments. For example, there was a marked reduction in deaths from testicular cancer in the former East Germany when modern chemotherapeutic agents became available after unification (Becker & Boyle 1997). In other situations the influence is less clear, particularly when the final outcome is only partly attributable to health care. In this chapter we use the examples of ischaemic heart disease, perinatal mortality and cancer survival to illustrate some of the challenges involved in using single indicators of population health to measure health system performance.

Ischaemic heart disease

Ischaemic heart disease is one of the most important causes of premature death in industrialized countries. Countries in western Europe have had great success in controlling this disease and death rates have fallen, on average, by about 50% over the past three decades (Kesteloot et al. 2006) (Fig. 2.1.1). Many new treatments have been introduced including new drugs for heart failure and cardiac arrhythmias; new

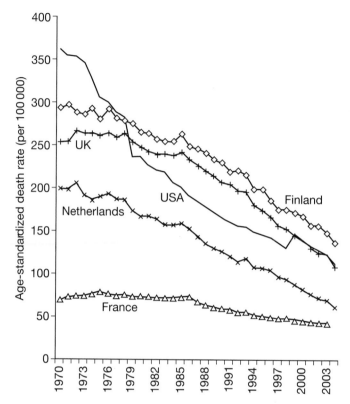

Fig. 2.1.1 Mortality from ischaemic heart disease in five countries, 1970–2004
Source: OECD 2007

technology, such as more advanced pacemakers; and new surgical techniques, such as angioplasty. Although still somewhat controversial, accumulating evidence suggests that these developments have made a considerable contribution to the observed decline in ischaemic heart disease mortality in many countries.

Beaglehole (1986) calculated that 40% of the decline in deaths from ischaemic heart disease in Auckland, New Zealand between 1974 and 1981 could be attributed to advances in medical care. Similarly, a study in the Netherlands estimated that specific medical interventions (treatment in coronary care units, post-infarction treatment, coronary artery bypass grafting (CABG)) had potentially contributed to 46% of the observed decline in mortality from ischaemic heart disease between 1978 and 1985. Another 44% was attributed to primary prevention efforts such as smoking cessation, strategies to reduce cholesterol levels and treatment of hypertension (Bots & Grobee 1996).

Hunink and colleagues (1997) estimated that about 25% of the decline in ischaemic heart disease mortality in the United States between 1980 and 1990 could be explained by primary prevention and another 72% was due to secondary reduction in risk factors or improvements in treatment. Capewell and colleagues (1999, 2000) assessed the contribution of primary (such as treatment of hypertension) and secondary (e.g. treatment following myocardial infarction) prevention measures to observed declines in ischaemic heart disease mortality in a range of countries during the 1980s and 1990s. Using the IMPACT model, they attributed between 23% (Finland) and almost 50% (United States) of the decline to improved treatment. The remainder was largely attributed to risk factor reductions (Table 2.1.1) (Ford et al. 2007). These estimates gain further support from the WHO Multinational Monitoring of Trends and Determinants in Cardiovascular Disease (MONICA) project which linked changes in coronary care and secondary prevention practices to the decline in adverse coronary outcomes between the mid-1980s and the mid-1990s (Tunstall-Pedoe et al. 2000).

In summary, these findings indicate that between 40% and 50% of the decline in ischaemic heart disease in industrialized countries can be attributed to improvements in health care. Yet, it is equally clear that large international differences in mortality predated the advent of effective health care, reflecting factors such as diet, rates of smoking and physical activity. Therefore, cross-national comparisons of ischaemic heart disease mortality have to be interpreted in the light of wider policies that determine the levels of the main cardiovascular risk factors in a given population (Box 2.1.2).

The nature of observed trends may have very different explanations. This is illustrated by the former East Germany and Poland, which both experienced substantial declines in ischaemic heart disease mortality during the 1990s – reductions of approximately one fifth between 1991/1992 and 1996/1997 among those aged under seventy-five years (Nolte et al. 2002).

In Poland, this improvement has been largely attributed to changes in dietary patterns, with increasing intake of fresh fruit and vegetables and reduced consumption of animal fat (Zatonski et al. 1998). The contribution of medical care was considered to be negligible,

Table 2.1.1 *Decline in ischaemic heart disease mortality attributable to treatment and to risk factor reductions in selected study populations (%)*

Country	Period	Risk factors	Treatment
Auckland, New Zealand (Beaglehole 1986)	1974–1981	–	40%
Netherlands (Bots & Grobee 1996)	1978–1985	44%	46%
United States (Hunink et al. 1997)	1980–1990	50%	43%
Scotland (Capewell et al. 1999)	1975–1994	55%	35%
Finland (Laatikainen et al. 2005)	1982–1997	53%	23%
Auckland, New Zealand (Capewell et al. 2000)	1982–1993	54%	46%
United States (Ford et al. 2007)	1980–2000	44%	47%
Ireland (Bennett et al. 2006)	1985–2000	48%	44%
England & Wales (Unal et al. 2007)	1981–2000	58%	42%

although data from the WHO MONICA project in Poland suggest that there was a considerable increase in intensity of the treatment of acute coron-ary events between 1986/1989 and the early 1990s (Tunstall-Pedoe et al. 2000). However, Poland has a much higher proportion of sudden deaths from ischaemic heart disease in comparison with the west. This phenomenon has also been noted in the neighbouring Baltic republics and in the Russian Federation (Tunstall-Pedoe et al. 1999; Uuskula et al. 1998) and has been related to binge drinking (McKee et al. 2001). From this it would appear that health care has been of minor importance in the overall decline in ischaemic heart disease mortality in Poland in the 1990s.

The eastern part of Germany experienced substantial increases in a variety of indicators of intensified treatment of cardiovascular disease during the 1990s (for example, cardiac surgery increased by 530%

Box 2.1.2 Comparing mortality across countries

International variations in ischaemic heart disease mortality and, by extension, other cause-specific mortality may be attributable (at least in part) to differences in diagnostic patterns, death certification or cause of death coding in each country. This problem is common to all analyses that employ geographical and/or tem-poral analyses of mortality data. However, it must be set against the advantages of mortality statistics – they are routinely available in many countries and, as death is a unique event (in terms of its finality), it is clearly defined (Ruzicka & Lopez 1990). Of course there are some cave-ats. Mortality data inevitably underestimate the burden of disease attributable to low-fatality conditions (such as mental illness) or many chronic disorders that may rarely be the immediate cause of death but which contribute to deaths from other causes. For example, diabetes contributes to many deaths from ischaemic heart disease or renal failure (Jougla et al. 1992). Other problems arise from the different steps involved in the complex sequence of events that leads to allocation of a code for cause of death (Kelson & Farebrother 1987; Mackenbach et al. 1987). For example, the diag-nostic habits and preferences of certifying doctors are likely to vary with the diagnostic techniques available, cultural norms or even professional training. The validity of cause of death statistics may also be affected by the process of assigning the formal International Classification of Diseases (ICD) code to the statements on the death certificate. However, a recent evaluation of cause of death statis-tics in the European Union (EU) found the quality and compara-bility of cardiovascular and respiratory death reporting across the region to be sufficiently valid for epidemiological purposes (Jougla et al. 2001). Where there were perceived problems in comparability across countries, the observed differences were not large enough to explain fully the variations in mortality from selected causes of cardiovascular or respiratory death.

Overall, mortality data in the European region are generally considered to be of good quality, although some countries have been experiencing problems in ensuring complete registration of all deaths. Despite some improvements since the 1990s, problems remain with recent figures estimating completeness of mortality

---

Box 2.1.2   cont'd

data covered by the vital registration systems range from 60% in
Albania; 66% to 75% in the Caucasus; and 84% to 89% in
Kazakhstan and Kyrgyzstan (Mathers et al. 2005). Also, the vital
registration system does not cover the total resident population
in several countries, excluding certain geographical areas such as
Chechnya in the Russian Federation; the Transnistria region in
Moldova; or Kosovo, until recently part of Serbia (WHO Regional
Office for Europe 2007).

---

between 1993 and 1997) (Brenner et al. 2000). However, intensified
treatment does not necessarily translate into improved survival rates
(Marques-Vidal et al. 1997). There was a (non-significant) increase in
the prevalence of myocardial infarction among people from the east
of Germany aged twenty-five to sixty-nine years, between 1990/1992
and 1997/1998, which accompanied an observed decline in ischaemic
heart disease mortality, suggesting that the latter is likely to be attributable to improved survival (Wiesner et al. 1999).

In summary, a fall in ischaemic heart disease mortality can generally
be seen as a good marker of effective health care and usually contributes to around 40% to 50% of observed declines. However, multiple
factors influence the prevalence of ischaemic heart disease. As some lie
within the control of the health-care sector and others require intersectoral policies, it may not be sufficient to use ischaemic heart disease
mortality as a sole indicator of health-care performance. At the same
time, ischaemic heart disease may be considered to be an indicator
of the performance of national systems as a whole. Continuing high
levels point to a failure to implement comprehensive approaches that
cover the entire spectrum – from health promotion through primary
and secondary prevention to treatment of established disease.

Perinatal mortality

Perinatal mortality (see Annex 2) has frequently been used as an indicator of the quality of health care (Rutstein et al. 1976). However,
comparisons between countries and over time are complicated because
rates are now based on very small numbers which are "very dependent on precise definitions of terms and variations in local practices

and circumstances of health care and registration systems" (Richardus et al. 1998). For example, advances in obstetric practice and neonatal care have led to improved survival of very preterm infants. These outcomes affect attitudes to the viability of such infants (Fenton et al. 1992) and foster debate about the merits of striving to save very ill newborn babies (who may suffer long-term brain damage) or making the decision to withdraw therapy (De Leeuw et al. 2000). Legislation and guidelines concerning end-of-life decisions vary among countries – some protect human life at all costs; some undertake active interventions to end life, such as in the Netherlands (McHaffie et al. 1999).

A related problem is that registration procedures and practices may vary considerably between countries, reflecting different legal definitions of the vital events. For example, the delay permitted for registration of births and deaths ranges from three to forty-two days within western Europe (Richardus et al. 1998). This is especially problematic for small and preterm births, as deaths that occur during the first day of life are most likely to be under-registered in countries with the longest permitted delays.

Congenital anomalies are an important cause of perinatal mortality. However, improved ability of prenatal ultrasound screening to recognize congenital anomalies has been shown to reduce perinatal mortality as fetuses with such anomalies are aborted rather than surviving to become fetal or infant deaths (Garne 2001; Richardus et al. 1998). This phenomenon may distort international comparisons (van der Pal-de Bruin et al. 2002). Garne and colleagues (2001) demonstrated how a high frequency of congenital mortality (44%) among infant deaths in Ireland reflected limited prenatal screening and legal prohibition of induced abortion. Conversely, routine prenatal screening in France is linked to ready access to induced abortion throughout gestation. Congenital mortality was cited in 23% of infant deaths although the total number of deaths from congenital malformations (aborted plus delivered) was higher in France (Garne et al. 2001). However, recent work in Italy has demonstrated that the relative proportion of congenital anomalies as a cause of infant deaths tends to remain stable within countries (Scioscia et al. 2007). This suggests that perinatal mortality does provide important insights into the performance of (neonatal) care over time.

In summary, international comparisons of perinatal mortality should be interpreted with caution. However, notwithstanding improvements in antenatal and obstetric care in recent decades, perinatal audit studies that take account of these factors show that improved quality of care could reduce current levels of perinatal mortality by up to 25% (Richardus et al. 1998). Thus, perinatal mortality can serve as a meaningful outcome indicator in international comparisons as long as care is taken to ensure that comparisons are valid. The EuroNatal audit in regions of ten European countries showed that differences in perinatal mortality rates may be explained in part by differences in the quality of antenatal and perinatal care (Richardus et al. 2003).

Cancer survival

Cancer survival statistics have intrinsic appeal as a measure of health system performance – cancer is common; causes a large proportion of total deaths; and is one of the few diseases for which individual survival data are often captured routinely in a readily accessible format. This has led to their widespread use for cross-sectional assessments of differences within population subgroups (Coleman et al. 1999) and over time (Berrino et al. 2007; Berrino et al. 2001). Comparisons within health systems have clear potential for informing policy by providing insight into differences in service quality, for example: timely access, technical competence and the use of standard treatment and follow-up protocols (Jack et al. 2003).

International comparisons of cancer registry data have revealed wide variations in survival among a number of cancers of adults within Europe. The Nordic countries generally show the highest survival rates for most common cancers (Berrino et al. 2007; Berrino et al. 2001) (Fig. 2.1.2) and there are marked differences between Europe and the United States (Gatta et al. 2000).

Prima facie, these differences might suggest differing quality of care, so cancer survival has been proposed as an indicator of international differences in health-care performance (Hussey et al. 2004; Kelley & Hurst 2006). However, recent commentaries highlight the many elements that influence cancer outcomes (Coleman et al. 1999; Gatta et al. 2000). These include the case-mix, that is, the distribution of tumour stages. These will depend on the existence of screening programmes, as with prostate and breast cancer; the socio-demographic composition of the population covered by a registry (not all registries cover the entire population); and time lags (personal and system induced)

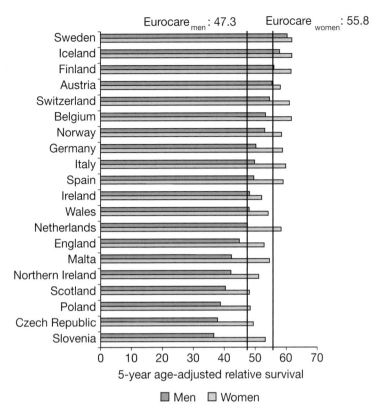

Fig. 2.1.2 Age-adjusted five-year relative survival of all malignancies of men and women diagnosed 2000–2002

Source: Verdecchia et al. 2007

between symptom occurrence and treatment (Sant et al. 2004). Data from the United States suggest that the rather selected nature of the populations covered by the registries of the Surveillance Epidemiology and End Results (SEER) Program, widely used in international comparisons, account for much of the apparently better survival rates in the United States for a number of major cancers (Mariotto et al. 2002). Death rates increased by 15% for prostate cancer; 12% for breast cancer; and 6% for colorectal cancer in men when SEER rates were adjusted to reflect the characteristics of the American population. This brings them quite close to European survival figures.

Presently, routine survival data incorporate adjustments only for age and the underlying general mortality rate of a population.

Use of stage-specific rates would improve comparability (Ciccolallo et al. 2005) but these are not widely available, nor are they effective for comparisons of health systems at different evolutionary stages. A more sophisticated staging system based on intensive diagnostic workup can improve stage-specific survival for all stages – those transferred from the lower stage will usually have lower survival than those remaining in the former group, but better survival than those initially in the higher stage.

Sometimes there is uncertainty about the diagnosis of malignancy (Butler et al. 2005). For example, there is some suggestion that apparently dramatic improvements in survival among American women with ovarian cancer in the late 1980s may be largely attributable to changes in the classification of borderline ovarian tumours (Kricker 2002). The ongoing CONCORD study of cancer survival is examining these issues in detail across four continents, supporting future calibration and interpretation of cancer survival rates (Ciccolallo et al. 2005; Gatta et al. 2000). There is little doubt that survival rates should be considered as no more than a means to flag possible concerns about health system performance at present.

Yet, it is important to note that while cross-national comparisons – whether of cancer survival (illustrated here) or other disease-specific population health outcomes (such as ischaemic heart disease mortality, described earlier) can provide important insights into the relative performance of health-care systems. It will be equally important for systems to benchmark their progress against themselves over time. For example, cross-national comparisons of breast cancer survival in Europe have demonstrated that constituent parts of the United Kingdom have relatively poor performance in comparison with other European countries (Berrino et al. 2007) (Fig. 2.1.3).

However, this has to be set against the very rapid decline in mortality from breast cancer in the United Kingdom since 1990 (Fig. 2.1.4), pointing to the impact of improvements in diagnostics and treatment (Kobayashi 2004). Thus, a detailed assessment of progress of a particular system optimally includes a parallel approach that involves both cross-sectional and longitudinal analyses. In the case of cancer survival these should ideally be stage-specific so as to account for inherent potential biases that occur when short-term survival is used to assess screening effects.

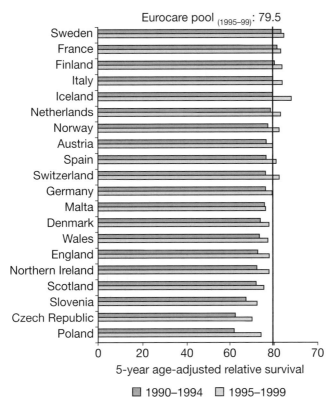

Fig. 2.1.3 Age-adjusted five-year relative survival for breast cancer for women diagnosed 1990–1994 and 1995–1999

Source: Berrino et al. 2007

In summary, these examples of ischaemic heart disease mortality, perinatal mortality and cancer survival indicate the possibilities and the challenges associated with particular conditions. Each provides a lens to examine certain elements of the health-care system. In the next section these are combined with other conditions amenable to timely and effective care to create a composite measure – avoidable mortality.

Concept of avoidable mortality

The concept of avoidable mortality originated with the Working Group on Preventable and Manageable Diseases led by David Rutstein of Harvard Medical School in the United States in the 1970s

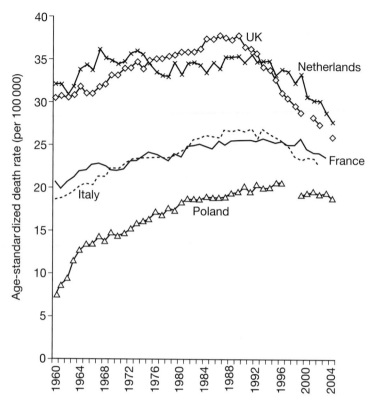

Fig. 2.1.4 Age-standardized death rates from breast cancer in five countries, 1960–2004

Source: OECD 2007

(Rutstein et al. 1976). They introduced the notion of 'unnecessary untimely deaths' by proposing a list of conditions from which death should not occur in the presence of timely and effective medical care. This work has given rise to the development of a variety of terms including 'avoidable mortality' and 'mortality amenable to medical/ health care' (Charlton et al. 1983; Holland 1986; Mackenbach et al. 1988). It attracted considerable interest in the 1980s as a way of assessing the quality of health care, with numerous researchers, particularly in Europe, applying it to routinely collected mortality data. It gained momentum with the European Commission Concerted Action Project on Health Services and 'Avoidable Deaths', established in the early 1980s. This led to the publication of the *European Community*

Atlas of Avoidable Death in 1988 (Holland 1988), a major work that
has been updated twice.

Nolte and McKee (2004) reviewed the work on avoidable mortality
undertaken until 2003 and applied an amended version of the original
lists of causes of death considered amenable to health care to countries
in the EU (EU15)[1]. They provide clear evidence that improvements in
access to effective health care had a measurable impact in many countries during the 1980s and 1990s. Interpreting health care as primary
care, hospital care, and primary and secondary preventive services
such as screening and immunization, they examined trends in mortality from conditions for which identifiable health-care interventions can
be expected to avert mortality below a defined age (usually seventy-
five years). Assuming that, although not all deaths from these causes
are entirely avoidable, health services could contribute substantially
by minimizing mortality but demonstrated how such deaths were still
relatively common in many countries in 1980. However, reductions in
these deaths contributed substantially to the overall improvement in
life expectancy between birth and age seventy-five during the 1980s.
In contrast, declines in avoidable mortality made a somewhat smaller
contribution to the observed gains in life expectancy during the 1990s,
especially in the northern European countries that had experienced the
largest gains in the preceding decade.

Importantly, although the rate of decline in these deaths began to
slow in many countries in the 1990s, rates continued to fall even in
countries that had already achieved low levels. For example, this was
demonstrated for 19 industrialized countries between 1997/1998 and
2002/2003, although the scale and pace of change varied (Nolte &
McKee 2008) (Fig. 2.1.5). The largest reductions were seen in countries with the highest initial levels (including Portugal, Finland, Ireland,
United Kingdom) and also in some countries that had been performing
better initially (such as Australia, Italy, France). In contrast, the United
States started from a relatively high level of avoidable mortality but
experienced much smaller reductions.

The concept of avoidable mortality provides a valuable indicator
of general health-care system performance but has several limitations.
These have been discussed in detail (Nolte & McKee 2004). We here
focus on three aspects that need to be considered when interpreting observed trends: the level of aggregation; the coverage of health

[1]   EU15: Member States belonging to the European Union before 1 May 2004.

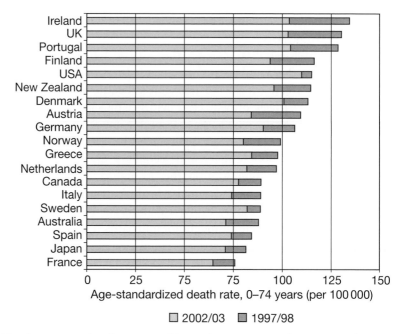

Fig. 2.1.5 Mortality from amenable conditions (men and women combined), age 0–74 years, in 19 OECD countries, 1997/98 and 2002/03 (Denmark: 2000/01; Sweden: 2001/02; Italy, United States: 2002)

Source: Adapted from Nolte & McKee 2008

outcomes; and the attribution of outcomes to activities in the health system.

Nolte and McKee (2008) noted that there are likely to be many underlying reasons for an observed lack of progress on the indicator of amenable mortality in the United States. Any aggregate national figure will inevitably conceal large variations due to geography, race and insurance coverage, among many other factors. Interpretation of the data must go beyond the aggregate figure to look within populations and at specific causes of death if these findings are to inform policy.

The focus on mortality is one obvious limitation of the concept of avoidable mortality. At best mortality is an incomplete measure of health-care performance and is irrelevant for those services that are focused primarily on relieving pain and improving quality of life. However, reliable data on morbidity are still scarce. There has been progress in setting up disease registries other than the more widely established cancer registries (for example, for conditions such as diabetes, myocardial infarction or stroke) but information may be misleading where registration is not population-based. Population surveys provide another potential source of data on morbidity, although survey data are often not comparable across regions. Initiatives such as the European Health Survey System currently being developed by Eurostat and the European Commission's Directorate-General for Health and Consumers (DG SANCO) will go some way towards developing and collecting consistent indicators (European Commission 2007). Routinely collected health service utilization data such as inpatient data or consultations of general practitioners and/or specialists usually cover an entire region or country. However, while potentially useful, these data (especially consultation rates) do not include those who need care but fail to seek it.

Finally, an important issue relates to the list of causes of death considered amenable to health care. Nolte and McKee (2004) define amenable conditions "[as] those from which it is reasonable to expect death to be averted even after the condition develops". This interpretation would include conditions such as TB, in which the acquisition of disease is largely driven by socio-economic conditions but timely treatment is effective in preventing death. This highlights how the attribution of an outcome to a particular aspect of health care is intrinsically problematic because of the multi-factorial nature of most outcomes. As a consequence, when interpreting findings a degree of judgement, based on an understanding of the natural history and scope for prevention and treatment of the condition in question, is needed. Thus it will be possible to distinguish more clearly between conditions in which death can be averted by health-care intervention (amenable conditions) as opposed to interventions reflecting the relative success of policies outside the direct control of the health-care sector (preventable conditions). Preventable conditions thus include those for which the aetiology is mostly related to lifestyle factors, most importantly the use of tobacco and alcohol (lung cancer and liver cirrhosis). This group also includes deaths amenable to legal measures such as traffic safety (speed limits, use of seat belts and motorcycle helmets). This refined concept of avoidable mortality makes it possible to distinguish between improvements in health care and the impact of policies outside the health sector that also impact on the public's health, such as tobacco and alcohol policies (Albert et al. 1996; Nolte et al. 2002).

In summary, the concept of avoidable mortality has limitations but provides a potentially useful indicator of health-care system performance. However, it is important to stress that high levels should not be taken as definitive evidence of ineffective health care but rather as an indicator of potential weaknesses that require further investigation. The next section explores the tracer concept – a promising approach that allows more detailed analysis of a health system's apparent suboptimal performance.

Tracer concept

The Institute of Medicine (IoM) in the United States proposed the concept of tracer conditions in the late 1960s as a means to evaluate health policies (Kessner et al. 1973). The premise is that tracking a few carefully selected health problems can provide a means to identify the strengths and weaknesses of a health-care system and thereby assess its quality.

Kessner et al. (1973) defined six criteria to define health problems appropriate for application as tracers. They should have: (i) a definitive functional impact, i.e. require treatment, with inappropriate or absent treatment resulting in functional impairment; (ii) a prevalence high enough to permit collection of adequate data; (iii) a natural history which varies with the utilization and effectiveness of health care; (iv) techniques of medical management which are well-defined for at least one of the following: prevention, diagnosis, treatment, rehabilitation; and (v) be relatively well-defined and easy to diagnose, with (vi) a known epidemiology.

The original concept envisaged the use of tracers as a means to evaluate discrete health service organizations or individual health care. Developed further, it might also be used at the system level by identifying conditions that capture the performance of certain elements of the health system. This approach would not seek to assess the quality of care per se but rather to profile the system's response to the tracer condition and aid understanding of the strengths and weaknesses of that system. By allowing a higher level of analysis such an approach has the potential to overcome some of the limitations of the cruder comparative studies outlined earlier.

The selection of health problems suitable for the tracer concept will depend on the specific health system features targeted. Thus, vaccine-preventable diseases such as measles might be chosen as an indicator for public health policies in a given system. Measles remains an important preventable health problem in several European countries, as illustrated by continuing outbreaks and epidemics (WHO Regional Office for Europe 2003). This is largely because of inadequate routine coverage in many parts of Europe, despite the easy availability of vaccination. These problems persist despite successes in reducing measles incidence to below one case per 100 000 in most EU Member States except Greece (1.1/100 000), Malta (1.5/100 000), Ireland (2.3/100 000) and Romania (23.2/100 000) (WHO Regional Office for Europe 2007).

Neonatal mortality has been suggested as a possible measure for assessing access to health care. For example, there were substantial declines in birthweight-specific neonatal mortality in the Czech Republic and the former East Germany following the political transition in the 1990s (Koupilová et al. 1998; Nolte et al. 2000). Thus, in east Germany neonatal mortality fell markedly (by over 30%) between 1991 and 1996 due to improvements in survival, particularly among infants with low and very low birth weight (<1500 g) (Nolte et al. 2000). This has been attributed, in part, to reform of the system of health care after unification which increased the availability of modern equipment and drugs for high-quality neonatal care. As with perinatal mortality, international comparisons of neonatal mortality can be problematic. However, temporal comparisons within a given country can provide important insights into potential weaknesses or advances in the quality of neonatal care, as demonstrated in east Germany.

Other work has examined the use of diabetes as a measure of health system performance in relation to chronic illness (Nolte et al. 2006). Deaths from diabetes among young people have been interpreted as 'sentinel health events' that should raise questions about the quality of health-care delivery (McColl & Gulliford 1993). The optimal management of diabetes requires coordinated inputs from a wide range of health professionals; access to essential medicines and monitoring; and, ideally, a system that promotes patient empowerment. Measures of diabetes outcome may therefore provide important insights into primary and specialist care and their systems of communication.

Nolte and colleagues (2006) generated a measure of 'case-fatality' among young people with diabetes, using published data on diabetes incidence among young people for the period 1990–1994 and mortality under the age of 40 years for the period 1994–1998 in twenty-nine countries. This mortality-to-incidence ratio varied more than ten-fold across countries, consistent with findings of cohort studies of mortality among young people with type I diabetes. The mortality-to-incidence ratio for diabetes thus appears to provide a means of differentiating countries' quality of care for people with diabetes. While solely an indicator of potential problems, this can stimulate more detailed assessments of the problems raised and what can be done to address them. Chapter 4.2 (Chronic care) explores this in more detail.

The way ahead

A large body of work aims to define how best to analyse health system performance at the level of population health and the multiplicity of strategies and approaches employed. This demonstrates that there is no definitive solution for this central challenge of managing a health (care) system effectively. The main goals of a health system can be defined easily but it is more difficult to identify a way of assessing whether these goals are being achieved and the extent to which apparent progress can be attributed to the health system or to other factors.

The overview presented here illustrates the conceptual underpinning of different measures in use, the information they provide and their major problems. General indicators of population health (for example, total and infant mortality, life expectancy, DALYs) remain important and provide tools that allow quick and simple assessments of total societal health system performance. Careful age- and sex-specific demographic measures of mortality over time can be strongly suggestive but generally such indicators provide only limited insights into specific components of the health-care system that impact on health. In contrast, more specific indictors of population health, such as cancer survival, give more detailed insights into discrete aspects of the health-care system but when used in isolation do not reveal information on other areas of the system that may be equally important. Also, single indicators often identify only the need for more in-depth investigation of process.

In conclusion, assessments of health system performance require a set of probes in order to examine different levels. Given the variation of settings within and between countries it is equally clear that there will be no single best combination. The range and balance across levels will differ according to the context within which each system sits; the expectations and norms of those who assess performance; and whether longitudinal (within system) or cross-sectional (across populations) comparisons are employed. Of necessity, the combination will also vary according to the availability of appropriate data and the resultant limitations of those data.

Despite its many limitations, the concept of avoidable mortality remains a valuable indicator of health-care system performance. However, it is important to reiterate that the underlying concept should not be mistaken as definitive evidence of differences in the effectiveness of health care. Avoidable mortality should be interpreted as an indicator of potential weaknesses in health care that may require further investigation.

References

Albert, X. Bayo, A. Alfonso, J. Cortina, P. Corella, D (1996). 'The effectiveness of health systems in influencing avoidable mortality: a study in Valencia, Spain, 1975–90.' *Journal of Epidemiology and Community Health*, 50(3): 320-325.

Alvarez-Dardet, C. Ruiz, M (1993). 'Thomas McKeown and Archibald Cochrane: a journey through the diffusion of their ideas.' *British Medical Journal*, 306(6887): 1252–1255.

Arah, O. Westert, G. Hurst, J. Klazinga, N (2006). 'A conceptual framework for the OECD Health Care Quality Indicators Project.' *International Journal for Quality in Health Care*, 18 (Suppl. 1): 5–13.

Babazono, A. Hillman, A (1994). 'A comparison of international health outcomes and health care spending.' *International Journal of Technology Assessment in Health Care*, 10(3): 376–381.

Beaglehole, R (1986). 'Medical management and the decline in mortality from coronary heart disease.' *British Medical Journal*, 292(6512): 33–35.

Becker, N. Boyle, P (1997). 'Decline in mortality from testicular cancer in West Germany after reunification.' *Lancet*, 350(9079): 744.

Bennett, K. Kabir, Z. Unal, B. Shelley, E. Critchley, J. Perry, I. Feely, J. Capewell, S (2006). 'Explaining the recent decrease in coronary heart disease mortality rates in Ireland, 1985–2000.' *Journal of Epidemiology and Community Health*, 60(4): 322–327.

Berrino, F. De Angelis, R. Sant, M. Rosso, S. Bielska-Lasota, M. Coebergh, J. Santaquilani, M. & EUROCARE Working Group (2007). 'Survival for eight major cancers and all cancers combined for European adults diagnosed in 1995–99: results of the EUROCARE-4 study.' *Lancet Oncology,* 8(9): 773–783.

Berrino, F. Gatta, G. Sant, M. Capocaccia, R (2001). 'The EUROCARE study of survival of cancer patients in Europe: aims, current status, strengths and weaknesses.' *European Journal of Cancer,* 37(6): 673–677.

Bots, M. Grobee, D (1996). 'Decline of coronary heart disease mortality in the Netherlands from 1978 to 1985: contribution of medical care and changes over time in presence of major cardiovascular risk factors.' *Journal of Cardiovascular Risk,* 3(3): 271–276.

Brenner, G. Altenhofen, L. Bogumil, W. Heuer, J. Kerek-Bodden, H. Koch, H (2000). *Gesundheitszustand und ambulante medizinische Versorgung der Bevölkerung in Deutschland im Ost-West-Vergleich.* Cologne: Zentralinstitut für die kassenärztliche Versorgung.

Britton, A. McKee M. Black, N. McPherson, K. Sanderson, C. Bain, C (1999). 'Threats to applicability of randomised trials: exclusions and selective participation.' *Journal of Health Services Research and Policy,* 4(2): 112–121.

Buck, D. Eastwood, A. Smith, P (1999). 'Can we measure the social import-ance of health care?' *International Journal of Technology Assessment in Health Care,* 15(1): 89–107.

Bunker, J (1995). 'Medicine matters after all.' *Journal of the Royal College of Physicians,* 29(2): 105–112.

Bunker, J. Frazier, H. Mosteller, F (1994). 'Improving health: measuring effects of medical care.' *Milbank Memorial Fund Quarterly,* 72(2): 225–258.

Butler, C. Currie, G. Anderson, W (2005). 'Do differences in data report-ing contribute to variation in lung cancer survival?' *Journal of the National Cancer Institute,* 97(18): 1385.

Capewell, S. Beaglehole, R. Seddon, M. McMurray, J (2000). 'Explanation for the decline in coronary heart disease mortality rates in Auckland, New Zealand, between 1982 and 1993.' *Circulation,* 102(13): 1511–1516.

Capewell, S. Morrison, C. McMurray, J (1999). 'Contribution of modern cardiovascular treatment and risk factor changes to the decline in coronary heart disease mortality in Scotland between 1975 and 1994.' *Heart,* 81(4): 380–386.

Charlton J. Hartley, R. Silver, R. Holland, W (1983). 'Geographical varia-tion in mortality from conditions amenable to medical intervention in England and Wales.' *Lancet,* 1(8326 Pt 1): 691–696.

Ciccolallo, L. Capocaccia, R. Coleman, M. Berrino, F. Coebergh, J. Damhuis, R. Faivre, J. Martinez-Garcia, C. Moller, H. Ponz de Leon,

M. Launoy, G. Raverdy, N. Williams, E. Gatta, G (2005). 'Survival differences between European and US patients with colorectal cancer: role of stage at diagnosis and surgery.' *Gut,* 54(2): 268–273.

Cochrane, A. Leger, A. Moore, F (1978). 'Health service 'input' and mortality 'output' in developed countries.' *Journal of Epidemiology and Community Health,* 32(3): 200–205.

Coleman, M. Babb, P. Damiecki, P. Grosclaude, P. Honjo, S. Jones, J. Knerer, G. Pitard, A. Quinn, M. Sloggett, A. De Stavola, B (1999). *Cancer survival trends in England and Wales 1971–1995: deprivation and NHS region.* London: The Stationary Office.

Colgrove, J (2002). 'The McKeown thesis: a historical controversy and its enduring influence.' *American Journal of Public Health,* 92(5): 725–729.

Collins, J (1982). 'The contribution of medical measures to the decline of mortality from respiratory tuberculosis: an age-period-cohort model.' *Demography,* 19(3): 409–427.

Cremieux, PY. Ouellette, P. Pilon, C (1999). 'Health care spending as determinants of health outcomes.' *Health Economics,* 8(7): 627–639.

De Leeuw, R. Cuttini, N. Nadai, M. Berbik, I. Hansen, G. Kucinskas, A. Lenoir, S. Levin, A. Persson, J. Rebagliato, M. Reid, M. Schroell, M. De Vonderweid, U. EURONIC Study Group (2000). 'Treatment choices for extremely preterm infants: an international perspective.' *Journal of Pediatrics,* 137(5): 608–616.

Elola, J. Daponte, A. Navarro, V (1995). 'Health indicators and the organization of health care systems in western Europe.' *American Journal of Public Health,* 85(10): 1397–1401.

Etches, V. Frank, J. Di Ruggiero, E. Manuel, D (2006). 'Measuring population health: a review of indicators.' *Annual Review of Public Health,* 27: 29–55.

European Commission (2007). *The European Health Survey System.* Brussels: European Commission (http://ec.europa.eu/health/ph_information/dissemination/reporting/ehss_en.htm).

Fairchild, A. Oppenheimer, G (1998). 'Public health nihilism vs pragmatism: history, politics, and the control of tuberculosis.' *American Journal of Public Health,* 88(7): 1105–1117.

Fenton, A. Field, D. Mason, E. Clarke, M (1992). 'Attitudes to viability of preterm infants and their effect on figures for perinatal mortality.' *British Medical Journal,* 300(6722): 434–436.

Ford, E. Ajani, U. Croft, J. Critchley, J. Labarthe, D. Kottke, T. Giles, W. Capewell, S (2007). 'Explaining the decrease in US deaths from coronary disease, 1980–2000.' *New England Journal of Medicine,* 356(23): 2388–2398.

Garne, E (2001). 'Perinatal mortality rates can no longer be used for compar-
    ing quality of perinatal health services between countries.' *Paediatric
    and Perinatal Epidemiology,* 15(3): 315–316.

Garne, E., Berghold, A. Johnson, Z. Stoll, C (2001). 'Different policies
    on prenatal screening programmes and induced abortions explain
    regional variations in infant mortality with congenital malforma-
    tions.' *Fetal Diagnosis and Therapy,* 16(3): 153–157.

Gatta, G. Capoccacia, R. Coleman, M. Ries, L. Hakulinen, T. Micheli, A.
    Sant, M. Verdecchia, A. Berrino, F (2000). 'Toward a comparison of
    survival in American and European cancer patients.' *Cancer,* 89(4):
    893–900.

Gravelle, H. Blackhouse, M (1987). 'International cross-section analysis of the
    determination of mortality.' *Social Science and Medicine,* 25(5): 427–441.

Holland, W (1986). 'The 'avoidable death' guide to Europe.' *Health Policy,*
    6(2): 115–117.

Holland, W (1988). *European Community atlas of 'avoidable death'.*
    Oxford: Oxford University Press.

Hunink, M. Goldman, L. Tosteson, A. Mittelman, M. Goldman, P. Williams,
    L. Tsevat, J. Weinstein, M (1997). 'The recent decline in mortality
    from coronary heart disease, 1980–1990.' *Journal of the American
    Medical Association,* 277(7): 535–542.

Hussey, PS. Anderson, GF. Osborn, R. Feek, C. McLaughlin, V. Millar,
    J. Epstein, A (2004). 'How does the quality of care compare in five
    countries?' *Health Affairs (Millwood),* 23(3): 89–99.

Jack, R. Gulliford, M. Ferguson, J. Moller, H (2003). 'Geographical inequal-
    ities in lung cancer management and survival in south east England:
    evidence of variation in access to oncology services?' *British Journal
    of Cancer,* 88(7): 1025–1031.

Johansson, S (2005). 'Commentary: the pitfalls of policy history. Writing the
    past to change the present.' *International Journal of Epidemiology,*
    34(3): 526–529.

Jougla, E. Papoz, L. Balkau, B. Maguin, P. Hatton, F (1992). 'Death
    certificate coding practices related to diabetes in European coun-
    tries – the 'EURODIAB Subarea C' study.' *International Journal of
    Epidemiology,* 21(2): 343–351.

Jougla, E. Rossolin, F. Niyonsenga, A. Chappert, J-L. Johansson, L. Pavillon,
    G (2001). *Comparability and quality improvement of the European
    causes of death statistics.* Paris: INSERM.

Kelley, E. Hurst, J (2006). *Health care quality indicators project. Conceptual
    framework paper.* Paris: Organisation for Economic Co-operation
    and Development (OECD Health Working Papers No. 23).

Kelson, M. Farebrother, M (1987). 'The effect of inaccuracies in death certification and coding practices in the European Economic Community (EEC) on international cancer mortality statistics.' *International Journal of Epidemiology*, 16(3): 411–414.

Kessner, D. Kalk, C. Singer, J (1973). 'Assessing health quality – the case for tracers.' *New England Journal of Medicine*, 288(4): 189–194.

Kesteloot, H. Sans, S. Kromhaut, D (2006). 'Dynamics of cardiovascular and all-cause mortality in western and eastern Europe between 1970 and 2000.' *European Heart Journal*, 27(1): 107–113.

Kim, K. Moody, P (1992). 'More resources better health? A cross-national perspective.' *Social Science and Medicine*, 34(8): 837–842.

Kobayashi, S (2004). 'What caused the decline in breast cancer mortality in the United Kingdom?' *Breast Cancer*, 11(2): 156–159.

Koupilová, I. McKee, M. Holcik, J (1998). 'Neonatal mortality in the Czech Republic during the transition.' *Health Policy*, 46(1): 43–52.

Kricker, A (2002). *Ovarian cancer in Australian women*. Camperdown, NSW: National Breast Cancer Center.

Laatikainen, T. Critchley, J. Vartiainen, E. Salomaa, V. Ketonen, M. Capewell, S (2005). 'Explaining the decline in coronary heart disease mortality in Finland between 1982 and 1997.' *American Journal of Epidemiology*, 162(8): 764–773.

Lalonde, M (1974). *A new perspective on the health of Canadians*. Ottawa: Government of Canada.

Leon, D. Vagerö, D. Olausson, P (1992). 'Social class differences in infant mortality in Sweden: comparison with England and Wales.' *British Medical Journal*, 305(6855): 687–691.

Lopez, AD. Mathers, CD. Ezzati, M. Jamison, DT. Murray, CJL (2006). *Global burden of disease and risk factors*. New York: Oxford University Press and World Bank.

Mackenbach, J (1996). 'The contribution of medical care to mortality decline: McKeown revisited.' *Journal of Clinical Epidemiology*, 49(11): 1207–1213.

Mackenbach, J. Looman, C. Kunst, A. Habbema, J. van der Maas, P (1988). 'Post-1950 mortality trends and medical care: gains in life expectancy due to declines in mortality from conditions amenable to medical intervention in the Netherlands.' *Social Science and Medicine*, 27(9): 889–594.

Mackenbach, J. Van Duyne, W. Kelson, M (1987). 'Certification and coding of two underlying causes of death in the Netherlands and other countries of the European Community.' *Journal of Epidemiology and Community Health*, 41(2): 156–160.

Mariotto, A. Capocaccia, R. Verdecchia, A. Micheli, A. Feuer, E. Pickle, L. Clegg, L (2002). 'Projecting SEER cancer survival rates to the US: an ecological regression approach.' *Cancer Causes Control,* 13(2): 101–111.

Marques-Vidal, P. Ferrieres, J. Metzger, M. Cambou, J. Filipiak, B. Löwel, H. Keil, U (1997). 'Trends in coronary heart disease morbidity and mortality and acute coronary care and case fatality from 1985–1989 in southern Germany and south-western France.' *European Heart Journal,* 18(5): 816–821.

Mathers, C. Ma Fat, D. Inoue, M. Rao, C. Lopez, A (2005). 'Counting the dead and what they died from: an assessment of the global status of cause of death data.' *Bulletin of the World Health Organization,* 83(3): 171–77.

McColl, AJ. Gulliford, MC (1993). *Population health outcome indicators for the NHS. A feasibility study.* London: Faculty of Public Health Medicine and the Department of Public Health Medicine, United Medical and Dental Schools of Guy's and St Thomas' Hospitals.

McDowell, I. Spasoff, R. Kristjansson, B (2004). 'On the classification of population health measurements.' *American Journal of Public Health,* 94(3): 388–393.

McHaffie, H. Cuttini, M. Brolz-Voit, G. Randag, L. Mousty, R. Duguet, A. Wennergren, B. Benciolini, P (1999). 'Withholding/withdrawing treatment from neonates: legislation and official guidelines across Europe.' *Journal of Medical Ethics,* 25(6): 440–446.

McKee, M (1999). 'For debate – Does health care save lives?' *Croatian Medical Journal,* 40(2): 123–128.

McKee, M. Shkolnikov, V. & Leon, D (2001). 'Alcohol is implicated in the fluctuations in cardiovascular disease in Russia since the 1980s.' *Annals of Epidemiology,* 11(1): 1–6.

McKeown, T (1971). Medical issues in historical demography. In: Clarke, E (ed.). *Modern methods in the history of medicine.* London: Athlone Press.

McKeown, T (1979). *The role of medicine: dream, mirage or nemesis?* Oxford: Blackwell.

McKinlay, J. McKinlay, S (1977). 'The questionable contribution of medical measures to the decline of mortality in the United States in the twentieth century.' *Milbank Memorial Fund Quarterly,* 55(3): 405–428.

Murray, C. Salomon, J. Mathers, C (2000). 'A critical examination of summary measures of population health.' *Bulletin of the World Health Organization,* 78(8): 981–994.

Murray, C. Salomon, J. Mathers, C. Lopez, A (eds.) (2002). *Summary measures of population health. Concepts, ethics, measurement and applications.* Geneva: World Health Organization.

Nixon, J. Ulmann, P (2006). 'The relationship between health care expenditure and health outcomes. Evidence and caveats for a causal link. *European Journal of Health Economics,* 7(1): 7–18.

Nolte, E. Bain, C. McKee, M (2006). 'Chronic diseases as tracer conditions in international benchmarking of health systems: the example of diabetes.' *Diabetes Care,* 29: 1007–1011.

Nolte, E. Brand, A. Koupilova, I. McKee, M (2000). 'Neonatal and postneonatal mortality in Germany since unification.' *Journal of Epidemiology and Community Health,* 54(2): 84–90.

Nolte, E. McKee, M (2004). *Does healthcare save lives? Avoidable mortality revisited.* London: The Nuffield Trust.

Nolte, E. McKee, M (2008). 'Measuring the health of nations: updating an earlier analysis.' *Health Affairs,* 27(1): 58–71.

Nolte, E. McKee, M. Wait, S (2005). Describing and evaluating health systems. In: Bowling, A. Ebrahim, S (eds.) *Handbook of health research methods: investigation, measurement and analysis.* Maidenhead: Open University Press.

Nolte, E. Scholz, R. Shkolnikov, V. McKee, M (2002). 'The contribution of medical care to changing life expectancy in Germany and Poland.' *Social Science and Medicine,* 55(11): 1907–1923.

OECD (2007). *OECD health data 2007.* Paris: Organisation for Economic Co-operation and Development.

Or, Z (2000). 'Determinants of health outcomes in industrialised countries: a pooled, cross-country, time-series analysis.' *OECD Economic Studies,* 30: 53–77.

Or, Z (2001). *Exploring the effects of health care on mortality across OECD countries.* Paris: Organisation for Economic Co-operation and Development (Labour Market and Social Policy Occasional Paper No. 46).

Pennington, C (1979). 'Mortality and medical care in nineteenth-century Glasgow.' *Medical History,* 23(4): 442–450.

Reidpath, D (2005). 'Population health. More than the sum of the parts?' *Journal of Epidemiology and Community Health,* 59(10): 877–880.

Richardus, J. Graafmans, W. Verloove-Vanhorick, S. Mackenbach, J (1998). 'The perinatal mortality rate as an indicator of quality of care in international comparisons.' *Medical Care,* 36(1): 54–66.

Richardus, J. Graafmans, W. Verloove-Vanhorick, S. Mackenbach, J. EuroNatal International Audit Panel, EuroNatal Working Group (2003). 'Differences in perinatal mortality and suboptimal care between 10 European regions: results of an international audit.' *British Journal of Obstetrics and Gynaecology,* 110(2): 97–105.

Rutstein, D. Berenberg, W. Chalmers, T. Child, C. Fishman, A. Perrin, E (1976). 'Measuring the quality of medical care. A clinical method.' *New England Journal of Medicine*, 294(11): 582–588.

Ruzicka, L. Lopez, A (1990). 'The use of cause-of-death statistics for health situation assessment: national and international experiences.' *World Health Statistics Quarterly*, 43(4): 249–258.

Sant, M. Allemani, C. Berrino, F. Coleman, M. Aareleid, T. Chaplain, G. Coebergh, J. Colonna, M. Crosignani, P. Danzon, A. Federico, M. Gafà, L. Grosclaude, P. Hédelin, G. Macè-Lesech, J. Garcia, C. Møller, H. Paci, E. Raverdy, N. Tretarre, B. Williams, E. European Concerted Action on Survival and Care of Cancer Patients (EUROCARE) Working Group (2004). 'Breast carcinoma survival in Europe and the United States.' *Cancer*, 100(4): 715–722.

Schneyder, S. Landefeld, J. Sandiffer, F (1981). 'Biomedical research and illness: 1900–1979.' *Milbank Memorial Fund Quarterly*, 59(1): 44–58.

Scioscia, M. Vimercati, A. Maiorano, A. Depalo, R. Selvaggi, L (2007). 'A critical analysis on Italian perinatal mortality in a 50-year span.' *European Journal of Obstetrics, Gynecology, and Reproductive Biology*, 130(1): 60–65.

Szreter, S (1988). 'The importance of social interventions in Britain's mortality decline.' *Social History of Medicine*, 1(1): 1–37.

Tunstall-Pedoe, H. Kuulasmaa, K. Mahonen, M. Tolonen, H. Ruokokoski, E. Amouyel, P (1999). 'Contribution of trends in survival and coronary-event rates to changes in coronary heart disease mortality: 10-year results from 37 WHO MONICA project populations.' *Lancet*, 353(9164): 1547–1557.

Tunstall-Pedoe, H. Vanuzzo, D. Hobbs, M. Mähönen, M. Cepatis, Z. Kuulasmaa, K. Keil, U (2000). 'Estimation of contribution of changes in coronary care to improving survival, event rates, and coronary heart disease mortality across the WHO MONICA project populations.' *Lancet*, 355(9205): 688–700.

Unal, B. Critchley, J. Capewell, S (2007). 'Explaining the decline in coronary heart disease mortality in England and Wales between 1981 and 2000.' *Circulation*, 109(9): 1101–1107.

Uuskula, M. Lamp, K. Vali, M (1998). 'An age-related difference in the ratio of sudden coronary death over acute myocardial infarction in Estonian males.' *Journal of Clinical Epidemiology*, 51(7): 577–580.

Van der Pal-de Bruin, K. Graafmans, W. Biermans, M. Richardus, J. Zijlstra, A. Reefhuis, J. Mackenbach, J. Verloove-Vanhorick, S (2002). 'The influence of prenatal screening and termination of pregnancy on perinatal mortality rates.' *Prenatal Diagnosis*, 22(11): 966–972.

Van der Zee, J. Kroneman, M (2007). 'Bismarck or Beveridge: a beauty contest between dinosaurs.' *BMC Health Services Research*, 7(1): 94.

Verdecchia, A. Francisci, S. Brenner, H. Gatta, G. Micheli, A. Mangone, L. Kunkler, I. EUROCARE-4 Working Group (2007). 'Recent cancer survival in Europe: a 2000–02 period analysis of EUROCARE-4 data.' *Lancet Oncology*, 8(9): 784–796.

WHO (2000). *The world health report 2000. Health systems: improving performance*. Geneva: World Health Organization.

WHO Regional Office for Europe (2003). *Strategic plan for measles and congenital rubella infection in the European region of WHO*. Copenhagen: WHO Regional Office for Europe.

WHO Regional Office for Europe (2007). European Health for All database [offline database]. Copenhagen: WHO Regional Office for Europe (January update).

Wiesner, G. Grimm, J. Bittner, E (1999). 'Zum Herzinfarktgeschehen in der Bundesrepublik Deutschland: Prävalenz, Inzidenz, Trend, Ost-West-Vergleich.' *Gesundheitswesen*, 61(Suppl. 2): 72–78.

Wilson, L (2005). 'Commentary: medicine, population, and tuberculosis.' *International Journal of Epidemiology*, 34(3): 521–524.

Wright, J. Weinstein, M (1998). 'Gains in life expectancy from medical interventions – standardizing data on outcomes.' *New England Journal of Medicine*, 339(6): 380–386.

Zatonski, W. McMichael, A. Powles, J (1998). 'Ecological study of reasons for the sharp decline in mortality from ischaemic heart disease in Poland since 1991.' *British Medical Journal*, 316(7137): 1047–1051.

Annex 1 Summary measures of population health

Recent decades have seen a growing interest in, and work on, indicators that combine information on mortality and non-fatal health outcomes to summarize population health. Etches et al. (2006) distinguish two general categories of summary measures of population health: (i) health expectancies; and (ii) health gaps. Health expectancies determine how long people can expect to live free of certain diseases or limitations on their normal activities. In contrast, health gaps measure the difference between a specified health norm for the population (e.g. seventy-five as the average age at death) and the actual health of the population. The latter is most commonly assessed using DALYs.

Key issues include how to define and measure disability and select the weights to apply to particular health states. Disability weighting means that conditions which are disabling but rarely cause death (particularly mental illness) are ranked as more important than they would be if ranked by mortality alone. This is related to the highly controversial debate on the value placed on a year of life at different stages. For example, The Global Burden of Disease project (Lopez et al. 2006) placed more weight on a year of life of a young adult than on that of a child. This has the effect of reducing the burden of disease arising from deaths in childhood. One further issue concerns how to obtain estimates for countries from which data are unavailable. At present, these are often modelled on the relationships between mortality and other variables in countries which have data available. Given all of these issues, it is important to note that continuing debate surrounds the use of measures such as DALYs in policy-making.

Annex 2 Overview of selected measures of population health in health system performance assessment

Indicator	Definition	Advantages	Limitations
Life expectancy	Summary measure of the probability of dying at different ages in a population in a given year	Easy to understand and calculate as underlying mortality data are available for high- and most middle-income countries	Summarizes total mortality experience in a given population and therefore cannot be linked directly to activities within the health system
Age-standardized mortality rates by cause	Number of deaths per 100 000 population from a given cause adjusted for differences in the age-distribution between populations or over time	Easy to understand and calculate as underlying mortality data are available for high- and most middle-income countries	Cross-national comparisons might be limited by differences in cause of death certification in different settings and completeness of data registration
Infant mortality rate* (IMR)	Number of deaths in children within the first year of life, per 1000 live births in a given year	Easy to understand and calculate as underlying mortality data are available for high- and most middle-income countries	Combines neonatal and postneonatal deaths which are differentially sensitive to health-care quality (see text)

*Under-five mortality rate is also widely used, although mainly in low-income settings. This has the same structure but extends capture of deaths to five years so it is weighted more heavily than IMR towards influences of nutrition and primary care.

Perinatal mortality rate	Number of foetal deaths and deaths in the first week of life (early neonatal death) per 1000 live and stillbirths in a given year	Commonly used measure of quality of high-level care	Many challenges to interpretation, especially in international comparisons (see text)
Healthy life expectancy at birth (HALE)	Average number of years that a person can expect to live in 'full health' by taking into account years lived in less than full health because of disease and/or injury	Similar to life expectancy; takes account of the disease burden estimates available from the Global Burden of Disease study	Particular challenges in assigning acceptable disability weights
Disease-specific survival	Summary measure of the average length of time that individuals survive following diagnosis. It is most commonly used in respect to cancer.	Reasonably good comparative measure (but see text for limitations); data for cancer survival widely available	For cancers stage-specific data usually unavailable; inappropriate for evaluating screening programmes

2.2 Patient-reported outcome measures and performance measurement

RAY FITZPATRICK

Introduction

One of the most important developments in the assessment of health-care performance in recent years has been the demonstration that patients' and users' experiences of health and illness can be reliably and accurately captured by very simple means. It is now possible to capture aspects of health that are of most concern to individuals and populations – usually with self-completed and fairly short questionnaires. Typically these ask respondents to report, describe or assess aspects of their current health (e.g. symptoms); and the physical, psychological and social impact of health problems. The technical and scientific developments that have resulted in this capacity to capture patients' experiences have occurred over the last thirty years and these methods can now be considered mature, established and well-understood.

This chapter reviews the range of measures available and describes key considerations for selecting these for particular applications. It also considers the scope for widespread use of these measures to monitor health-care performance and the barriers that may limit such uses. Instruments in this field have been variously termed measures of quality of life, health status, health-related quality of life, subjective health status and functional status. The most important use of these questionnaires is for assessing outcomes of health care and increasingly they are referred to as patient-reported outcome measures (PROMs), the term used here.

Uses of PROMs

One of the simplest applications of PROMs is their use in surveys to assess the health of populations or segments of populations, e.g. users of particular facilities such as a hospital or clinic. For example, the Health Survey for England (Joint Health Surveys Unit, 2008) is a household survey (usually of over 10 000 randomly selected adults) that gathers physiological and blood-sample based data and invites respondents to complete several questionnaire items about their health. The survey is conducted regularly and the information is an important resource to identify trends over time and geographical and social variations in health. Other more specialist national surveys are carried out from time to time to assess the prevalence and impact of disability in England and to assess the health of older people.

Increasingly, survey research to assess population levels of health is conducted on an international basis. For example, the Survey of Health, Ageing and Retirement in Europe (SHARE) is a multidisciplinary and cross-national database of micro data on health, socio-economic status and social and family networks of individuals aged fifty or more, carried out across eleven European countries (Siegrist et al. 2007). Self-reported health is a major feature of this survey.

Health professionals also use PROMs in the context of individual patient care. Clinicians have argued that standard care in rheumatology is improved if, in addition to other clinical measures, PROMs are used regularly to assess a patient's current status with regard to pain and function (Pincus & Wolfe 2005). There are similar arguments that PROMs are essential to assess patients' needs and communication between patient and provider in routine care in other contexts such as oncology, dermatology and neurology (Lipscomb et al. 2007; Salek et al. 2007; Wagner et al. 1997).

In clinical trials PROMs can provide evidence that cannot be obtained by other means. This includes all the intended and unintended consequences of health-care interventions, whether drugs, new surgical techniques or innovations in the organization and delivery of services. In this sense they provide a necessary form of evidence of patient impact that complements the traditional clinical and laboratory measures employed. It is not yet standard practice to use PROMs in clinical trials (Sanders et al. 1998) but such uses have provided invaluable evidence of one key feature – they can provide evidence of change over time in an individual's health-related quality of life that can, in principle, be used as a means of assessing the performance or effectiveness of an intervention. Cross-sectional application of PROMs can be extended to longitudinal studies to offer a potential source of evidence of outcomes for determining health care's contribution to changes in health status.

PROMs are also being used more generally as evidence of outcomes to assess the contribution of health services to health in contexts such as professional quality assurance and audit and funders' assessments of the performance and value for money of services that they provide. Twenty years ago Ellwood (1988) proclaimed that PROMs offered a breakthrough for health services by providing funders and providers with evidence (for the first time) of benefits experienced by patients. It was argued that PROMs are uniquely important not only because they measure what matters to patients but also because they do so in ways that are feasible for large scale and regular use, such as through simple questionnaires. Claims are beginning to emerge, for example, in the Veterans Health Administration in the United States, that performance measurement (including PROMs) can be shown to improve the quality of care (Kerr & Fleming 2007).

Types of instruments

A bewildering number of PROMs exist. In 2002 my colleagues and I reported that our systematic review had identified at least 1275 such instruments in the English language alone (Garratt et al. 2002). We estimate that at least 3215 different instruments were reported in the English language literature in 2007.

PROMs can be classified into two basic types. *Generic* instruments have been developed to be relevant to the widest possible range of health problems. By contrast, *disease- or condition-specific* instruments are intended to be relevant to a limited disease or specific aspect or dimension of illness.

Generic instruments

Short-form 36 (SF-36) is by far the most commonly used generic measure (Ware & Sherbourne 1992). Thirty-six standard questions about the respondent's health in the last month are grouped into eight different dimensions of health: (i) physical functioning; (ii) role limitations due to physical problems; (iii) role limitations due to emotional problems; (iv) social functioning; (v) mental health; (vi) energy; (vii) pain; and (viii) health perceptions. As with most such instruments, responses are scored and all items in a given dimension (or scale) are combined to provide a single scale score, for example, for physical functioning. Responses can also be used to produce just two, more general scale scores: a physical component summary and a mental component summary. Short-form 12 (SF-12) was developed as a shorter version that is normally scored to produce physical component summary and mental component summary scores. SF-36 has been translated into at least fifty languages and has been the object of more studies than any other instrument (Garratt et al. 2002). Its measurement properties (discussed in the following section) have been examined exhaustively, largely with very positive results.

Several other generic instruments have been widely used, notably the Sickness Impact Profile (Bergner et al. 1981), the Nottingham Health Profile (Hunt et al. 1985) and Dartmouth Primary Care Cooperative Information Project (Coop) Charts (Nelson et al. 1990). However, currently there is less supporting evidence for their use than for SF-36.

Utility instruments

In many ways utility instruments can be classed as generic instruments because they are all intended to have the widest applicability. However, unlike instruments such as SF-36, they were developed for one distinctive purpose – to assign overall values (or utilities) to respondents' health states. This overall value is particularly useful for analyses of the cost-effectiveness of health-care interventions. It allows researchers to estimate the overall aggregated value of the health states of the samples receiving an intervention, to allow comparisons of the costs. Traditional PROMs do not allow this overall calculation of the value of health states for individuals or aggregations of individuals.

EuroQol (EQ-5D) is the most commonly used utility instrument in Europe (Brooks 1996). This generic measure of health has five dimensions: (i) mobility; (ii) self-care; (iii) usual activities; (iv) pain/discomfort; and (v) anxiety/depression. Respondents choose between three levels of severity for each of the five dimensions and identify their position on a visual analogue scale ranging from zero (worst imaginable health state) to one hundred (best imaginable health state). A single weighted score (value) of the individual's health can be calculated from the five selected responses, using weights of values provided by a general population survey.

The Health Utilities Index (HUI) is the next most commonly used approach for deriving the values, preferences or utilities of respondents. To date, less evidence is available to support the questionnaire-based versions of the HUI. Potential users have to decide between different interview formats and weigh the benefits of interview-based methods against the extra costs.

Disease-specific instruments

Disease-specific instruments have increased most rapidly in the last ten years (Garratt et al. 2002). They are developed to provide questionnaire content that is tailored to the specific disease for which they are intended. Thus, an instrument to assess health-related quality of life in rheumatoid arthritis might include specific items that would not feature in a generic instrument, e.g. on stiffness, fatigue or the difficulties of performing household tasks with hands. An instrument for Parkinson's disease might contain items concerning the consequences of tremor (e.g. holding objects, embarrassment in public) that would not be salient in a generic instrument. Typically disease-specific instruments are developed and explicitly identified as having relevance for an identified illness. The Arthritis Impact Measurement Scales and Parkinson's Disease Questionnaire (PDQ-39) have the specialist function conveyed by their titles.

The main reason for the growing interest in disease-specific PROMs is the belief that they are necessary to identify the small but important benefits and harms associated with novel interventions in clinical trials. This has some supporting evidence. Also, the broadly-based questionnaire content of generic instruments may miss both types of consequence.

Other instruments have been developed for more specific purposes, for example to assess outcomes in relation to specific health-care interventions. The Oxford knee score was developed specifically to assess outcomes of knee replacement surgery; a parallel PROM (Oxford hip score) is used to assess outcomes of hip replacement surgery. There is substantial evidence that these instruments are more sensitive to the specific problems of severe pain and the function of the patients receiving these procedures (Murray et al. 2007).

Individualized instruments

Recent years have seen the emergence of a number of instruments based on a single important principle – individuals have their own personal goals and concerns in relation to health. Hence, traditional questionnaires with fixed items that are uniform for all respondents run contrary to the personal nature of health-related quality of life. Several new instruments attempt to elicit individuals' personal goals and concerns in a more flexible form. For example, the Patient Generated Index (Ruta et al. 1994) asks respondents to list the five most important areas of their lives that are affected by a disease or health problem; to rate how badly affected they are in each area; and to allocate points to the areas in which they would most value an improvement. Individual area ratings are weighted by the points given and summed to produce a single index. This is designed to measure the extent to which a patient's actual situation falls short of their hopes and expectations in those areas of life in which they would most value improvement. Such approaches are quite different to PROMs but the most obvious disadvantage of all the individualized instruments developed to date is the limited evidence for large-scale use. Generally, they require quite time-consuming and complex interviews.

Evaluating PROMs

A disciplined approach is needed to select an instrument for a particular application and formal criteria can inform the selection of sound choices from among the enormous number of instruments. Seven criteria are commonly used to assess PROMs: (i) reliability; (ii) validity; (iii) responsiveness; (iv) precision; (v) interpretability; (vi) acceptability; and (vii) feasibility (Fitzpatrick et al. 1998). It is possible to inspect the published evidence and weigh the amount of positive evidence for an instrument under each of these criteria. However, appropriateness is the eighth and arguably the most important criterion as it asks whether an instrument is relevant to the specific purpose of a given user. This requires judgements on (for example) the match between the content of the instrument and the purpose of the user. Such judgements are context specific and less easily informed by the general literature on an instrument.

Reliability is a fundamental requirement of any system of measurement. The more reliable an instrument, the more it is free of error. The literature is written as if reliability is a fixed feature of a PROM but it is dependent on the specific population in which it is used.

The reliability of PROMs is usually estimated in terms of internal consistency and reproducibility. It has already been pointed out that PROMs commonly take the form of scales (e.g. SF-36) – questionnaire items that combine to measure a construct such as pain or social isolation. The greater the agreement between the items of the scale the higher its internal consistency. This is one aspect of reliability and a variety of statistical tests have been developed to assess the extent to which scales reach perfect consistency. However, there is a complication to this approach. Perfect internal consistency is achieved most easily when questionnaire items are virtually identical to each other (i.e. asking the same question). Such an instrument is not desirable in practice. Instruments require scales that capture the different facets or aspects of, say, pain or social isolation. This is more likely to be achieved with items that do not correlate perfectly. As a result of these contrasting requirements, internal consistency statistics of instruments are expected to be high, but not too high (no higher than 0.90 on a range from 0.00 to 1.00).

Reproducibility is the other aspect of reliability. This the extent to which a measuring instrument produces the same result on repeated use, as long as the construct it is measuring does not change. A variety of test statistics have been developed to express the extent to which instruments are consistent over time. Typically instruments are retested on respondents between two and fourteen days after the first administration. An additional check to confirm that respondents have not experienced any change in their health (for example, using a simple global question) can be used to focus reproducibility estimates on stable respondents when assessing the reproducibility of a PROM.

Validity concerns the extent to which an instrument measures what it purports to measure. As with reliability, an instrument is only validated in the contexts in which its validity has been tested. Again, the literature generally overlooks this point but it is misleading to call an instrument validated without some qualification. Thus, an instrument validated to assess disability in multiple sclerosis may not be valid to assess disability in epilepsy as the measurement properties need to be re-established in the new context. The literature on validation of PROMs is dense and complex and only three key points are emphasized here.

Firstly, criterion validity assesses the extent to which scores from a new instrument agree with those of a gold standard. This has little relevance as it is rare for a new instrument to be necessary or justified if a gold standard exists. Second, content validity is always crucial in judging a PROM, although it is a matter of judgement rather than statistical testing. Evidence of content validity is provided by clear explanation of what the instrument is intended to measure; how the items were developed and chosen; and whether these items appear to cover the intended construct. Third, the construct validity of an instrument is statistical. This assesses the available evidence in relation to the extent to which scores from the instrument agree with other measures in ways that are expected. Increasingly, authors of new PROMs are required to specify hypotheses of how they expect the test instrument to relate to other variables in order to avoid the biases of retrospective logic.

Responsiveness addresses the extent to which an instrument is able to detect changes over time in respondents' health. Since the overarching goal of health care is to bring about beneficial change, it may be argued that the most important requirement is that an instrument should accurately capture changes in health when they occur. Sometimes an instrument needs to detect clinically important changes (that is, not minor or 'noise'). However, it is argued increasingly that the term 'clinically' is unhelpful – changes have to be important and significant for the patient, not the health professional. A wide array of different statistical techniques is used to assess responsiveness, but no single approach dominates. The common thread is to assess the amount of variability in the change scores of an instrument that is due to change relative to other sources of variability (measurement error, patient characteristics, and so on).

Precision presents a problem for PROMs. This stems from the basic requirement to transform answers to questionnaires into quantitative scores that reflect accurately the full spectrum of the underlying phenomenon – pain, disability, social function, and so on. The following simplified example demonstrates how measurement assumptions may be problematic. An instrument with a physical mobility scale of, say, ten questionnaire items may be summed simply to produce a disability score. By accident of development, the majority of these items assess quite mild disability, for example, being unable to walk very long distances. An intervention that enabled a patient to improve at the mild end of the spectrum could produce improvements in the majority of items when assessed on the hypothetical scale. A patient with more disability could improve at the severe end of the spectrum but show improvement on a smaller number of items. The latter result would be purely an artefact of questionnaire selection. An elegant study by Stucki and colleagues (1996), in which patients completed the physical mobility scale of SF-36 before and after hip-replacement surgery, shows that this is not just a hypothetical problem. Recently applied statistical techniques such as Rasch analysis are intended to address this problem by ensuring that scales for newly developed instruments provide unidimensional and interval-level measurement of domains (Norquist et al. 2004).

Interpretability is concerned with the meaning and inferences that may be drawn from an instrument. Typically, a PROM expresses changes that arise from a health-care intervention in terms of quantitative change scores on a scale that has little inherent meaning. It is possible to address the statistical significance of a given change score but less easy to give the result intuitive meaning. One approach is to equate a PROM's change scores to some other life event (if such evidence is available), for example to show that a change score is equivalent to the deterioration in health associated with a major life event such as bereavement. Another approach is to relate change scores to different levels of severity of illness, for example by comparing inpatients with less-severely ill patients in the community. Such approaches have not found much favour and it is likely that the field will increasingly resort to a different approach to identify minimal important differences for PROMs. This is outlined below.

Acceptability is an essential requirement. If respondents do not like a PROM they will either leave items incomplete or fail to answer the questionnaire at all, with major risk of bias in the interpretation of results. Instruments vary substantially in simple factors such as length and completion time. There are also less obvious variations, such as the amount of distressing or complex judgements required from the respondent.

Few studies directly address the issue of acceptability. One exception is a study of patients who were followed up after attendance at eighteen Swedish hospitals (Nilsson et al. 2007). Respondents were asked to complete both SF-36 and EQ-5D and to comment on their satisfaction with the two instruments. The majority appeared equally happy with both but a minority expressed a clear preference. Of these, more preferred SF-36 and commonly stated that it allowed them to

report their health more comprehensively or that the response categories allowed more nuanced answers. In another study (Moore
et al. 2004), patients with multiple sclerosis received SF-36, EQ-5D
and a fifty-four item disease-specific instrument. The majority were
happy with all three instruments but the longer disease-specific instrument was preferred among the minority who expressed a preference.
By way of contrast, patients in a follow-up to a major trial of treatment
for stroke were randomized to report their health using either EQ-5D
or SF-36 (Dorman et al. 1997). Respondents who received EQ-5D
showed a higher response rate and fewer responses with incomplete
data. However, acceptability may depend as much on specific features
of the respondent group such as age, co-morbidity and the reason for
involvement in a survey.

Feasibility needs to be considered separately as more resources are
necessary for instruments that require trained staff or that involve significant transformation or processing of data to derive results. Costs
become a major consideration if PROMs are to be delivered to large
samples and/or over long periods of time.

Evidence to aid choice of instrument

It is clear that there is a burgeoning number of instruments from which
to choose for any given problem and that evidence of their measurement properties and performance is potentially complex. It is not surprising that increasing attention is given to comparing instruments
to identify those PROMs that have overall superior performance. It
is rare to randomize respondents between instruments to compare
performance as in the study cited above (Dorman et al. 1997). It is
far more common for patients to be asked to complete two or more
PROMs in the context of a trial and to compare their performance.
This can be very informative if the trial provides other information
about health as a benchmark. Such studies have tended to focus on the
comparative evidence of the responsiveness of instruments since this is
the most critical requirement for evaluations of interventions.

Several studies have shown that shorter instruments are as sensitive to change as longer instruments (Fitzpatrick et al. 1993; Katz et al.
1992). This is significant because it suggests that instruments may be
shortened and reduce respondents' burden without loss of important
information. Studies have reported statistically driven reductions of

longer instruments such as the Sickness Impact Profile in which the short-form versions appear to produce similar results (de Bruin et al. 1994). Moran et al. (2001) used simulation techniques and results of a dataset of three trials of respiratory rehabilitation to analyse the consequences of reducing items in the scales of the widely used Chronic Respiratory Questionnaire. They found modest losses of reliability, validity and responsiveness that became serious losses only when the number of items was reduced to one per scale. It is likely that content validity, the degree of coverage of the underlying construct, is adversely affected when a scale comprises only one item.

Coste et al. (1997) reviewed a series of forty-two studies that used shorter but equivalent instruments and identified a number of problems. For example, analysis of the shorter version from the dataset in which respondents had completed a longer version produced artificially elevated correlations between the shorter and longer versions. Studies seldom re-examined the content validity of the new, shorter instrument. Coste et al. concluded that a shortened PROM needs to be re-assessed as if it is a brand new instrument, distinct from the longer original.

Disease-specific versus generic instruments

Comparative studies have also investigated the widely debated issue of the relative merits of disease-specific and generic PROMs. The argument for disease-specific instruments is based on the belief that such measures will be more sensitive to changes in the health-related quality of life produced by an intervention, mainly because they contain a higher proportion of supposedly relevant items for the illness and intervention being studied. However, some studies have failed to identify such advantages empirically. Walsh et al. (2003) invited patients with various conditions that produce back pain to participate in a longitudinal survey of health-related quality of life involving the completion of both disease-specific and generic PROMs. They found no evidence that the disease-specific instrument was more sensitive to change over time.

Wiebe et al. (2003) carried out a structured review and identified forty-three randomized controlled trials which included direct comparison of disease-specific and generic PROMs completed by the same patients. The Sickness Impact Profile, Nottingham Health

Profile and SF-36 generic instruments were most commonly used in the sample of trials. No significant difference between the two types of instrument was found when the trials with modest and small overall effects were sub-divided according to the size of the underlying treatment effect. The difference between the two types of measure became greater and more significant as the true underlying therapeutic effect became greater in trials, with disease-specific instruments consistently more responsive. This evidence of the superior responsiveness of disease-specific PROMs is consistent with a review by Murawski and Miederhoff (1998) who used a wider array of observational, as well as randomized, studies. Wiebe et al. (2003) caution that such evidence does not prove that all disease-specific measures are more responsive than all generic measures.

Increasingly, it is becoming necessary to carry out reviews that assess all of the available evidence in order to inform choices between instruments. For practical, largely clinical, reasons such reviews tend to focus on the evidence on PROMs that relate to specific illnesses. Some of these reviews are relatively informal in terms of how evidence is sought, assessed and described (Carr et al. 1996). However, they are becoming more formal with increasing use of explicit search and inclusion criteria for relevant studies and scoring of the strength and quality of evidence for instruments included in the review (Garratt et al. 2004; Haywood et al. 2005). This enables readers to draw independent assessments of the evidence to determine whether or not they agree with reviewers' recommendations.

It is has been argued that such reviews are helpful in facilitating evidence-based recommendations but frequently are still limited by their reliance on informal and implicit criteria for what constitutes good measurement properties (Terwee et al. 2007). For example, a review may report and rate all the available evidence on the validity, responsiveness and interpretability of instruments. Typically, this will not spell out explicitly what counts as evidence of good validity or responsiveness. As an example, Terwee et al. (2007) suggest that reviewers might require at least 75% of the specific hypotheses spelt out in advance of a study to be supported as positive evidence for an instrument's construct validity. Evidence falling short of this standard would be rated either indeterminate or negative. Terwee et al. argue that wide application of such standards would make reviews even more transparent and offer easy choices. These standards would drive up the quality of reporting in original studies that assess the measurement properties of PROMs as these tend to be vague about most details of procedure.

Broad problems remain with reviews of the comparative value and performance of PROMs. Firstly, these are heavily influenced as much by the volume of evidence as by its quality – instruments tend to be rated as relatively poor largely because of a lack of evidence. Secondly, even the most explicit reviews require difficult judgments of the relative importance of different criteria. For example, many would argue that content validity is fundamentally important and cannot be substituted by good evidence on other criteria. Those who use PROMs in evaluative research often tend to prioritize responsiveness as their most important criterion for evaluating and selecting the instrument. The third and related problem is the difficulty of reviewing the evidence for instruments against all possible uses in all contexts. Unavoidable elements of judgment remain regardless of the methodological thoroughness of reviews.

Barriers to implementation

Clearly, a substantial number of well-validated PROMs are available to provide important evidence of health from users' and the community's perspectives. Nevertheless, health-care providers do not use PROMs widely on a regular basis. A number of studies have examined potential barriers to more widespread implementation. These may be grouped into two broad categories: (i) cognitive; and (ii) logistic and resource factors. Evidence for each of these is examined in turn.

Cognitive barriers

Health professionals' attitudes to PROMs have had a major influence on implementation. This is particularly true among doctors who have been found to be generally sceptical about their value. An early and influential review (Deyo & Patrick 1989) argued that doctors' training leads them to be distrustful of data that they consider subjective and soft. Information from questionnaires is viewed as inherently less reliable than biologically derived data. A study of oncologists found that they considered quality of life to be a very important issue for their patients but preferred to collect data informally. They were not convinced of the validity of PROMS outside clinical trials (Taylor et al. 1996). A study of UK psychiatrists found that few clinicians regularly used PROMs in their daily practice (Gilbody et al. 2002). Many respondents explained this infrequent use by expressing scepticism about the reliability, validity and responsiveness of the available instruments. McHorney and Bricker (2002) asked doctors in a primary-care setting about the value of PROMs when assessing patients' function. Doctors were sceptical that questionnaire-based information could add to what was established by traditional history taking. A related problem was found in a study of Dutch paediatricians (Baars et al. 2004). They acknowledged that PROMs could provide valuable information in principle but were concerned that they lacked the skills and professional background to interpret and use the information provided by such instruments.

These reservations relate to a broader set of concerns. PROMs are seen to be of doubtful value as they do not improve a doctor's ability to diagnose and treat problems more effectively; they identify problems that a doctor can do nothing about and are therefore not an effective resource or intervention. Certainly randomized controlled trials that evaluated PROMs as an addition to clinical services have tended to be disappointing. For example, Kazis et al. (1990) randomized doctors to receive or not receive information from disease-specific health status instruments completed by their patients with rheumatoid arthritis every three months for a year. Doctors who received this form of feedback found it useful. However, comparison with controls showed no differences in processes of care such as medication, referral or satisfaction and no differences in health status at one year follow-up.

An early structured review of studies that experimentally evaluated the benefits of PROMs for patient care and outcomes was unable to find clear evidence to support their use (Greenhalgh & Meadows 1999). A variety of reasons have been suggested for these predominantly negative results. It may be that it is not inherent problems of data from PROMs per se but rather that the details of the timing, presentation and feed-back of data to health professionals limit their impact in trials. PROMs have been of particular and long-standing interest in cancer services and some more encouraging and more focused studies have started to emerge in that field. Detmar et al. (2002) randomized doctors in a outpatient palliative care clinic to provide standard care alone or, with the addition of three consecutive outpatient visits, in combination with graphic summaries of patients' quality of life recorded by a cancer-specific questionnaire. Audiotapes of consultations were analysed. Health-related quality of life was discussed significantly more frequently in the consultations for which doctors received patients' quality of life scores. Also, the experimental consultations identified a higher proportion of health problems than the controls.

A similarly positive result was obtained in a trial by Velikova et al. (2004). They randomly assigned patients to be either controls receiving usual care or in an experimental arm that involved regular completion of a cancer-specific PROM with results fed back to their doctors. At the end of the study the experimental group's consultations had more discussion of health-related quality of life and also experienced more favourable quality of life than the controls. The investigators noted greater improvement in health-related quality of life in those patients who had explicitly discussed the subject during consultations. In discussing the differences with other, negative, studies the investigators also note that their patients saw different clinicians sequentially. PROMs may be more valuable in these situations than where there is strong continuity of care. More encouraging evidence from more recent trials probably reflects more appropriate instruments and better ways of feeding information into clinicians' routines (Marshall et al. 2006).

The uptake of PROMs may also have been hindered by the belief that such questionnaires are intrusive or burdensome to patients and therefore jeopardize the professional-client relationship. Studies that have included a separate assessment of patients have invariably found that the majority consider that the information conveyed by their responses is important for health professionals to know and are positively satisfied with the task of completing a questionnaire (Detmar et al. 2002; McHorney & Bricker 2002; Nelson et al. 1990). In the study by McHorney et al. (2002), some patients queried the appropriateness of items on anxiety and depression in the context of what they considered to be purely physical presenting problems.

Logistic and resource barriers

Logistic and resource barriers include a set of related practical considerations. Time is one that immediately concerns health professionals.

In the study of oncologists and their views about PROMs described earlier (Taylor et al. 1996), 85% of respondents felt that time constraints made it difficult to integrate PROMs into routine patient care. Time was also the most commonly cited obstacle in the survey of paediatricians (Baars et al. 2004). The doctors in the study by McHorney and Bricker (2000) felt that the economics of managed care meant that there was no time for additional activities such as assessment of patients' answers to PROMs. The psychiatrists in the study by Gilbody et al. (2002) also felt that more time would be required to include PROMs in regular care.

Time is related to the broader challenge described in different ways in the various studies of the use of PROMs in routine practice – the need for significant changes in administrative routines in order to incorporate regular use of PROMs. Gilbody et al. reported that psychiatrists emphasized the need for a 'robust infrastructure, particularly in terms of administration and information technology resources' in order to incorporate the routine use of PROMs (Gilbody et al. 2002, p102). The American doctors would require the whole 'office ecosystem' to be changed (McHorney & Bricker 2002, page 1117). However, administrative changes are not enough. The basic routines of health professionals would require adjustments to enable PROMs to become a core part of a clinical service.

Economic costs are frequently cited as an additional consideration but it is remarkable how few attempts have been made to estimate such costs. Moinpour et al. (2007) were unable to provide any estimate of the costs of including PROMs in cancer trials because they were invariably bundled in with other research costs. They were able to conclude only that the costs of PROMs were likely to prove considerably lower than other clinical and biological endpoints. A recently published study by a group at the London School of Hygiene and Tropical Medicine (2007) provides one of the few explicitly calculated estimates of the total costs of collecting longitudinal data on PROMs. They conclude that the total costs in relation to elective surgical procedures are approximately £ 6.50 per patient included in a longitudinal survey. The majority of costs relate to data entry and they suggest that there may be significant opportunities for cost reduction. This issue will require further investigation if widespread use of PROMs is to be contemplated in health-care systems.

Current and future issues

One trend can confidently be predicted – continued proliferation of PROMs despite the attendant confusion that is risked by the availability of ever larger numbers of instruments. The pharmaceutical industry is likely to be the main driver of this growth as it responds to the growing need to demonstrate impact on ever more specific aspects of health-related quality of life for the burgeoning chronic disease market. Regulatory pressures in particular will drive the industry to use clearly validated instruments to demonstrate ever more precisely pre-specified domains of quality of life in specific diseases.

The proliferation of instruments will be driven by the recognition that disease-specific instruments can be developed to incorporate the preference- or utility-based measurement required for health economic decisions (e.g. Torrance et al. 2004). It is not hard to foresee a plethora of instruments that produce increasingly difficult selection choices and growing problems with the non-comparability of the results of trials and evaluative studies that use increasingly different measures for similar domains of outcome. The capacity to provide reliable reviews and assessments of the quality and performance of the growing array of PROMs will need to be constantly improved.

It is often argued that trials and evaluative studies aiming to address health-related quality of life (particularly health) problems should include both a disease-specific and a generic measure in order optimally to capture the full spectrum of outcomes. It may also be argued that more short generic instruments such as EQ-5D or SF-12 are needed to complement disease-specific PROMs. They will provide some means of maintaining comparability of outcomes across studies given the increasing proliferation of disease-specific measures.

A potentially important development that is intended to solve many of the problems concerning the proliferation of PROMs may simply add to difficulties in the short term. The PROMIS initiative is sponsored by the National Institutes of Health in the United States. As discussed above it is a large-scale collaboration between scientists that will draw on existing instruments and develop new items (Cella et al. 2007a) for investigators to use in trials and evaluative studies. The long-term vision is to ensure that patients and populations will be assessed by items that are maximally relevant to respondents' specific health problems and levels of disability. In some respects this vision resembles that driving the emergence of the individualized PROMs described earlier. However, PROMIS involves two quite new techniques to identify standard questionnaire items that maximally match the health of the respondent (Cella et al. 2007). Firstly, item response theory is a statistical method to select items that match respondents' levels of health or disability. Secondly, computerized adaptive testing uses the many strengths of information technology to facilitate that matching process. To provide a grossly simplified example – a respondent at a computer answers one question on health and is efficiently moved on to the next most appropriate question because the system takes account of the answer to the first question. Overall, the volume and redundancy of items required of the respondent is minimized and the assessment burden is reduced. PROMIS has only been in existence since 2005 so it is difficult to assess achievements. In the short term the very flexibility of such measuring systems may be confusing for potential users who are familiar with conventional, standard, fixed instruments.

Another potentially important recent development has been the publication of a document by the American Food and Drug Administration (FDA) (http://www.fda.gov/CDER/GUIDANCE/5460dft.pdf). This is likely to be widely influential as it describes in some detail how evidence from PROMs for drugs and medical products is assessed and underlines the importance of issues such as analysis of the implications of missing data for PROMs. Its most striking discussion concerns the need for those who use this evidence to have a very clearly developed model of how a product or drug might relate to quite specific aspects of health-related quality of life and to submit detailed evidence of a PROM's validity in measuring those specific domains. At the very least this will require much more careful consideration of the selection and justification of instruments for use in trials. Ritual inclusion of SF-36 or EQ-5D to address quality of life aspects in an unfocused way will no longer be a valid strategy, at least for submissions to the FDA.

These recent trends are emerging from the pharmaceutical industry and its regulators and push PROMs to become ever more specialized and targeted instruments. There will be greater need for health-care funders, providers and regulators to produce broader evidence of outputs and outcomes via PROMs but as yet this is not articulated as forcefully. It might be expected that these needs will push towards more generic solutions that capture the broad impacts of services on patients and the public. It may be that the field increasingly diverges between these increasingly different needs of industry and public services. It will be a challenge for the science to respond to increasingly diverse expectations.

Policy implications

As yet, there is no evidence of PROMs being used extensively and routinely in a health-care system in order to assess performance and improve quality. The National Health Service (NHS) in the United Kingdom requires health-care providers to monitor four major elective surgical procedures (primary hip or knee replacement, groin hernia surgery, varicose vein procedures) by means of specified PROMs from 2009. This decision has enormous significance as it is the first real test of the scale of benefits that may accrue to patients, the public and providers when representative evidence from PROMs is available to assess the outcomes of all public service providers of particular interventions. It is significant that the decision to make monitoring of outcomes by PROMs effectively compulsory for four elective surgical procedures was preceded by structured reviews to identify the best performing PROMs for the four procedures. These were followed by pilot studies to ensure that the most appropriate PROMs could be identified and that it was feasible to use them for longitudinal monitoring. It is also significant that these four surgical procedures have a fairly clear, well-understood and specific role in relation to patients' health status. It will be interesting to see how readily the NHS moves from applying PROMs in the relatively simple environment of elective surgery to assessing the outcomes of long-term conditions for which the benefits of interventions may be less clear cut.

To date, PROMs' real world impact on routine services is largely theoretical and assumed. The NHS is field-testing the potential for PROMs to improve decisions about health care. The real challenge will be to examine their contribution to patients' and providers' decisions in relation to more complex health problems where multiple services over time make modest and often hard to define contributions to the quality of life. These contributions will need careful piloting and evaluation before services will feel confident to embrace PROMs on a widespread and regular basis.

References

Baars, R. van der Pal, S. Koopman, H. Wit, J (2004). 'Clinicians' perspective on quality of life assessment in paediatric clinical practice.' *Acta Paediatrica*, 93(10): 1356–1362.

Bergner, M. Bobbitt, R. Carter, W. Gilson, B (1981). 'The sickness impact profile: development and final revision of a health status measure.' *Medical Care*, 19(8): 787–805.

Brooks, R (1996). 'EuroQol: the current state of play.' *Health Policy*, 37(1): 53–72.

Carr, AJ. Thompson, PW. Kirwan, JR (1996). 'Quality of life measures.' *British Journal of Rheumatology*, 35(3): 275–281.

Cella, D. Gershon, R. Lai, J. Choi, S (2007). 'The future of outcomes measurement: item banking, tailored short-forms, and computerized adaptive assessment.' *Quality of Life Research*, 16(Suppl. 1): 133–141.

Cella, D. Yount, S. Rothrock, N. Gershon, R. Cook, K. Reeve, B. Ader, D. Fries, JF. Bruce, B. Rose, M (2007a). 'The patient-reported outcomes measurement information system (PROMIS): progress of an NIH roadmap cooperative group during its first two years.' *Medical Care*, 45(Suppl. 1): 3–11.

Coste, J. Guillemin, F. Fermanian, J (1997). 'Methodological approaches to shortening composite assessment scales.' *Journal of Clinical Epidemiology*, 50(3): 247–252.

de Bruin, A. Diederiks, J. de Witte, L. Stevens, F. Phillipsen, H (1994). 'The development of a short generic version of the sickness impact profile.' *Journal of Clinical Epidemiology*, 47(4): 407–418.

Detmar, S. Muller, M. Schornagel, J. Wever, L. Aaronson, N (2002). 'Health-related quality of life assessments and patient physician communication: a randomized controlled trial.' *Journal of the American Medical Association*, 288(23): 3027–3034.

Deyo, R. Patrick, D (1989). 'Barriers to the use of health status measures in clinical investigation, patient care and policy research.' *Medical Care*, 27(Suppl. 3): 254–268.

Dorman, P. Slattery, J. Farrell, B. Dennis, M. Sandercock, P (1997). 'A randomised comparison of the EuroQol and short form-36 after stroke.' *British Medical Journal*, 315(7106): 461–462.

Ellwood, P (1988). 'Shattuck lecture – outcomes management. A technology of patient experience.' *New England Journal of Medicine*, 318(23): 1549–1556.

Fitzpatrick, R. Ziebland, S. Jenkinson, C. Mowat, A (1993). 'A comparison of the sensitivity to change of several health status instruments in rheumatoid arthritis.' *Journal of Rheumatology*, 20(3): 429–436.

Fitzpatrick, R. Davey, C. Buxton, M. Jones, D (1998). 'Evaluating patient-based outcome measures for use in clinical trials.' *Health Technology Assessment*, 2(14): 1–74.

Garratt, AM. Brealey, S. Gillespie, WJ. DAMASK Trial Team (2004). 'Patient-assessed health instruments for the knee: a structured review.' *Rheumatology*, 43(11): 1414–1423.

Garratt, A. Schmidt, L. Mackintosh, A. Fitzpatrick, R (2002). 'Quality of life measurement: bibliographic study of patient assessed health outcome measures.' *British Medical Journal*, 324(7351): 1417–1422.

Gilbody, S. House, A. Sheldon, T (2002). 'Psychiatrists in the UK do not use outcomes measures.' *British Journal of Psychiatry*, 180: 101–103.

Greenhalgh, J. Meadows, K (1999). 'The effectiveness of the use of patient-based measures of health in routine practice in improving the process and outcomes of patient care: a literature review.' *Journal of Evaluation and Clinical Practice*, 5(4): 401–416.

Haywood, K. Garratt, AM. Fitzpatrick, R (2005). 'Quality of life in older people: a structured review of generic self-assessed health instruments.' *Quality of Life Research*, 14(7): 1651–1668.

Hunt, S. McEwan, J. McKenna, S (1985). 'Measuring health status: a new tool for clinicians and epidemiologists.' *Journal of Royal College of General Practitioners*, 35(273): 185–188.

Joint Health Surveys Unit (2008). *Health survey for England 2007: latest trends*. Leeds: NHS Information Centre (http://www.ic.nhs.uk).

Katz, J. Larson, M. Phillips, C. Fossel, A. Liang, M (1992). 'Comparative measurement sensitivity of short and longer health status instruments.' *Medical Care*, 30(10): 917–925.

Kazis, L. Callahan, L. Meenan, R. Pincus, T (1990). 'Health status reports in the care of patients with rheumatoid arthritis.' *Journal of Clinical Epidemiology*, 43(11): 1243–1253.

Kerr, E. Fleming, B (2007). 'Making performance indicators work: experiences of US Veterans Health Administration.' *British Medical Journal*, 335(7627): 971–973.

Lipscomb, J. Gotay, C. Snyder, C (2007). 'Patient-reported outcomes in cancer: a review of recent research and policy initiatives.' *CA: A Cancer Journal for Clinicians*, 57(5): 278–300.

London School of Hygiene and Tropical Medicine (2007). *Patient reported outcome measures (PROMs) in elective surgery*. Report to the

Department of Health. London: London School of Hygiene and Tropical Medicine (http://www.lshtm.ac.uk/hsru/research/PROMs-Report-12-Dec-07.pdf).

Marshall, S. Haywood, K. Fitzpatrick, R (2006). 'Impact of patient-reported outcome measures on routine practice: a structured review.' *Journal of Evaluation and Clinical Practice*, 12(5): 559–568.

McHorney, C. Bricker, D (2002). 'A qualitative study of patients' and physicians' views about practice-based functional health assessment.' *Medical Care*, 40(11): 1113–1125.

Moinpour, C. Denicoff, A. Bruner, D. Kornblith, A. Land, S. O Mara, A. Trimble, E (2007). 'Funding patient-reported outcomes in cancer clinical trials.' *Journal of Clinical Oncology*, 25(32): 5100–5115.

Moore, F. Wolfson, C. Alexandrov, L. Lapierre, Y (2004). 'Do general and multiple sclerosis specific quality of life instruments differ?' *Canadian Journal of Neurological Sciences*, 31(1): 64–71.

Moran, L. Guyatt, G. Norman, G (2001). 'Establishing the minimal number of items for a responsive, valid, health-related quality of life instrument.' *Journal of Clinical Epidemiology*, 54(6): 571–579.

Murawski, M. Miederhoff, P (1998). 'On the generalizability of statistical expressions of health-related quality of life instrument responsiveness: a data synthesis.' *Quality of Life Research*, 7(1): 11–22.

Murray, DW. Fitzpatrick, R. Rogers, K. Pandit, H. Beard, DJ. Carr, AJ. Dawson, J (2007). 'The use of the Oxford hip and knee scores.' *Journal of Bone & Joint Surgery*, 89(8): 1010–1014.

Nelson, E. Landgraf, J. Hays, R. Wasson, J. Kirk, J (1990). 'The functional status of patients. How can it be measured in physicians' offices?' *Medical Care*, 28(12): 1111–1126.

Nilsson, E. Wenemark, M. Bendtsen, P. Kristenson, M (2007). 'Respondent satisfaction regarding SF-36 and EQ-5D, and patients' perspectives concerning health outcome assessment within routine health care.' *Quality of Life Research*, 16(10): 1647–1654.

Norquist, J. Fitzpatrick, R. Dawson, J. Jenkinson, C (2004). 'Comparing alternative Rasch-based methods vs raw scores in measuring change in health.' *Medical Care*, 42(Suppl. 1): 125–136.

Pincus, T. Wolfe, F (2005). 'Patient questionnaires for clinical research and improved standard patient care: is it better to have 80% of the information in 100% of patients or 100% of the information in 5% of patients?' *Journal of Rheumatology*, 32(4): 575–577.

Ruta, D. Garratt, A. Leng, M. Russell, I. Macdonald, L (1994). 'A new approach to the measurement of quality of life: the patient-generated index.' *Medical Care*, 32(11): 1109–1126.

Salek, S. Roberts, A. Finlay, A (2007). 'The practical reality of using a patient-reported outcome measure in a routine dermatology clinic.' *Dermatology,* 215(4): 315–319.

Sanders, C. Egger, M. Donovan, J. Tallon, D. Frankel, S (1998). 'Reporting on quality of life in randomised controlled trials: bibliographic study.' *British Medical Journal,* 317(7167): 1191–1194.

Siegrist, J. Wahrendorf, M. von dem Knesebeck, O. Jürges, H. Börsch-Supan, A (2007). 'Quality of work, well-being, and intended early retirement of older employees: baseline results from the SHARE study.' *European Journal of Public Health,* 17(1): 62–68.

Stucki, G. Daltroy, L. Katz, J. Johannesson. M. Liang, M (1996). 'Interpretation of change scores in ordinal clinical scales and health status measures: the whole may not equal the sum of the parts.' *Journal of Clinical Epidemiology,* 49(7): 711–717.

Taylor, K. Macdonald, K. Bezjak, A. Ng, P. DePetrillo, A (1996). 'Physicians' perspectives on quality of life: an exploratory study of oncologists.' *Quality of Life Research,* 5(1): 5–14.

Terwee, C. Bot, S. de Boer, M. van der Windt, D. Knol, D. Dekker, J. Bouter, L. de Vet, H (2007). 'Quality criteria were proposed for measurement properties of health status questionnaires.' *Journal of Clinical Epidemiology,* 60(1): 34–42.

Torrance, GW. Keresteci, MA. Casey, RW. Rosner, AJ. Ryan, N. Breton, MC (2004). 'Development and initial validation of a new preference-based disease-specific health-related quality of life instrument for erectile function.' *Quality of Life Research,* 13(2): 349–359.

Velikova, G. Booth, L. Smith, A. Brown, P. Lynch, P. Brown, J. Selby, P (2004). 'Measuring quality of life in routine oncology practice improves communication and patient well-being: a randomized controlled trial.' *Journal of Clinical Oncology,* 22(4): 714–724.

Wagner, AK. Ehrenberg, BL. Tran, TA. Bungay, KM. Cynn, DJ. Rogers, WH (1997). 'Patient-based health status measurement in clinical practice: a study of its impact on epilepsy patients' care.' *Quality of Life Research,* 6(4): 329–341.

Walsh, TL. Hanscom, B. Lurie, JD. Weinstein, JN (2003). 'Is a condition-specific instrument for patients with low back pain/leg symptoms really necessary? The responsiveness of the Oswestry Disability Index, MODEMS, and the SF-36.' *Spine,* 28(19): 607–615.

Ware, J. Sherbourne, C (1992). 'The MOS 36-item short-form health survey (SF-36).1. Conceptual framework and item selection.' *Medical Care,* 30(6): 473–483.

Wiebe, S. Guyatt, G. Weaver, B. Matijevic, S. Sidwell, C (2003). 'Comparative responsiveness of generic and specific quality of life instruments.' *Journal of Clinical Epidemiology*, 56(1): 52–60.

2.3 Measuring clinical quality and appropriateness

ELIZABETH A. MCGLYNN

Introduction

The purpose of this chapter is to review the state of the art in developing clinical process measures and to describe some of the schemes that are using these measures for health system improvement. A high-level summary of the major steps involved in constructing good clinical process measures is provided to enable policy-makers to appreciate some of the complexities involved. There is not enough detail for novices to be able to develop measures from this source alone, but interested readers will be pointed towards examples of best practice.

The section on current schemes that employ clinical process measures includes a greater number of examples from the United States. This reflects the fact that clinical process measurement has been undertaken systematically in the United States for a longer period. Much activity is currently underway in several countries but the measures being used are not readily accessible. Some of these schemes may therefore be under-represented in this chapter.

The chapter concludes with some thoughts on the best uses of process measures, particularly in comparison to outcomes measures. In general, both play an important role in stimulating quality improvement at different levels in the health system and neither type of measure alone is sufficient for all applications. Some directions for future research in this area are also proposed.

State-of-the-art development of clinical process measures

Developers generally pass through five steps to create state-of-the-art measures: (i) selecting topics; (ii) reviewing clinical evidence; (iii) identifying clinical process indicators; (iv) constructing process measures; and (v) creating scoring methods. The importance of each step is discussed below, together with what constitutes best practice.

Selecting topics

Process measurement occurs within a context and the selection of the topics for measurement is a critical step in defining this. The availability and use of performance measures will result in other resources being directed at the measured areas ('what gets measured, gets done') and therefore topic selection should be undertaken systematically. This is particularly important if measures are being developed across multiple clinical areas or for a specific population.

Topics for clinical process measures are generally defined by conditions (e.g. hypertension, upper respiratory infection) although these may be identified for different age groups (children, older people), settings (ambulatory, hospital, nursing home), or events (discharge from hospital, end of life). Ideally, topics are selected because they represent critical dimensions of a strategic plan for improving the health outcomes for a particular group.

The first consideration is to select the outcomes that are of greatest interest – mortality, morbidity, functioning and well-being are the most common outcomes used to identify clinical areas. The availability of systematic data on these outcomes across the group of interest will facilitate topic selection. Mortality data are the most likely to be available (through national data systems) followed by morbidity. Systematic, national (or system-level) information on functioning and well-being are much less likely to be available. Data collection may be best informed by a review of published studies or through a group process that obtains input from experts or community leaders.

A second consideration is the condition's relative impact on the population of interest. In general, priority is given to conditions that are highly prevalent (e.g. the top ten causes of death) or have a substantial impact on health (e.g. those with the condition have a very high probability of dying). For example, heart disease and cancer are the leading causes of death in the United States and so would be high priorities to support plans for reducing premature mortality. Severe depression is one of the leading causes of functional limitations worldwide and would likely be included in a strategy to improve functioning.

A third consideration is whether outcomes are likely to be affected by actions taken in the health-care system. A number of potential actions to improve population health do not operate through the health-care system (e.g. ensuring adequate sanitation, safe food, clean environments) and some areas do not have health services that are effective in changing an outcome. Neither of these areas is fruitful for developing clinical process measures.

There are a number of examples of systematic selection of topics for quality improvement or measurement. For example, the Institute of Medicine (2003) identified twenty priority areas for quality measurement representing clinical areas across the age spectrum. The Danish National Indicator Project selected clinical areas representing the greatest use of resources in hospitals (Mainz et al. 2004). The Assessing Care of Vulnerable Elders (ACOVE) project selected twenty-six conditions representing clinical problems of the elderly population using a group judgment process (Wenger et al. 2007).

Reviewing clinical evidence

Once a topic (or topics) has been selected, the next step is to review what is known about effective interventions. The starting point is to construct the questions that will be answered by the literature search. For example, if heart disease was selected as a topic the questions might include the following.

- What interventions have been shown to be effective in preventing heart disease (primary and secondary prevention)? What interventions have been shown to be ineffective in preventing heart disease?
- Is there evidence that early identification of heart disease through general population screening reduces premature mortality or morbidity, or leads to higher functioning?
- What methods are effective in accurately diagnosing the presence (or absence) of heart disease? What methods are not effective or are unnecessary aspects of the diagnostic process?
- What interventions have been shown to be effective in treating established heart disease? What interventions have been shown to be ineffective in treating heart disease?
- What interventions have been shown to be effective in helping people return to higher levels of functioning following a heart attack? What interventions have been shown to be ineffective?

- What interventions have been shown to be effective for the ongoing management of persons with established heart disease? What interventions have been shown to be ineffective?

In this example, separate questions are posed for primary and secondary prevention, screening, diagnosis, treatment, rehabilitation and ongoing maintenance. This is appropriate for developing measures across the continuum of care but measures focused on a single aspect of the continuum would require only questions related to that area. Positive (what is effective) and negative (what is not effective) questions are asked to illustrate how evidence for measures of underuse (failure to use effective interventions) or overuse (use of interventions known to be ineffective) might be developed.

A formal strategy for identifying relevant articles is developed once the questions have been agreed upon. Several components are involved and the choices within each will depend on the time and resources available; degree to which an exhaustive search is necessary to meet the goals; and the likelihood of reaching a different conclusion by broadening the search strategy. This must include consideration of the type of studies that will be included (e.g. only randomized trials or a broad range of study designs); whether particular outcomes have been measured (e.g. include only studies that examine the impact on premature mortality or on functioning); the characteristics of participants (e.g. development of measures for the elderly might require only studies on this population); and what specific interventions are included (e.g. only those that can be provided in ambulatory settings vs. any setting). In addition, the reviewer must consider what databases to search; how far back to look; whether to supplement electronic searches with other information (e.g. literature cited in articles, hand search of specific journals); or whether to include information that has not been published in peer reviewed journals (e.g. private reports, data from unpublished studies).

Generally, the articles that will be included in a review are determined via three steps. First, a list of article titles is obtained by the application of search terms and other strategies. This list is screened to identify those that are relevant for the particular question and to exclude those that are not. Second, these selected titles undergo a more formal screen of abstracts to further determine which of these should be included. This step can be used to apply some of the selection criteria (e.g. type of study, population, outcomes). Third, a full review is conducted on the articles selected during the abstract review and relevant information is collated. Some articles may be excluded at this step if greater detail available in the full article indicates that they do not meet the inclusion criteria (or do meet the exclusion criteria). These review results are generally summarized in an evidence table.

Clinical practice guidelines are another source of evidence for constructing process measures. Evidence-based guidelines will incorporate conclusions from the scientific research literature about preferred approaches to prevention, screening, diagnosis, treatment, rehabilitation and monitoring. Even evidence-based guidelines will include some guidance that reflects professional consensus rather than scientific studies. Well-documented guidelines should enable the reviewer (or user) to identify easily the foundation for each recommendation (Shiffman et al. 2003). The Agency for Healthcare Research and Quality (AHRQ) maintains the National Guideline Clearinghouse (www.guideline.gov). This holds guidelines from a variety of sources and currently has 2083 individual summaries from eight countries; European medical societies and WHO. A search for myocardial infarction identified 252 related guidelines, ranging from those providing guidance on the use of a single technology (e.g. electrocardiographic monitoring in the hospital setting) to the management of a diagnosis (e.g. ischaemic heart disease). It is not unusual to find some disagreement between guidelines developed by different groups and these may be worth noting because of their potential impact on the development of process measures.

Two important principles should be kept in mind when developing the evidence base for process measures. First, it is important to document the strategy used to retrieve articles because it allows others to replicate the approach. Second, it is important to consider how the review of evidence might be biased. For example, the search for unpublished literature is designed to deal with publication bias – studies that report positive findings will be published more often than those that report negative or no findings.

The approach described here is consistent with the practices for identifying articles used by the Cochrane Collaboration (http://www.cochrane.org/reviews/revstruc.htm), the AHRQ Evidence-based Practice Centers (http://effectivehealthcare.ahrq.gov/) and the National Institute for Health and Clinical Excellence (NICE) (http://www.nice.

org.uk/guidance/index.jsp). The process is similar to that used in creating evidence-based guidelines.

Identifying clinical process indicators

Process indicators are descriptive statements about the aspect of care that is being evaluated and the type of patient that should receive the indicated care. Most clinical process indicators are written in a general style, such as:

- Persons with diabetes mellitus should have their blood sugar measured at least once each year.

The style introduced by the ACOVE project makes the eligibility and expected process statements more explicit by using if/then statements in which the 'if' describes the eligible population and the 'then' describes the expected care process (Wenger et al. 2007). For example:

- *If* a vulnerable elder has diabetes mellitus, *then* glycated haemoglobin (HbA1c) should be measured annually.

Clinical practice guidelines are 'systematically developed statements to assist practitioner and patient decisions about appropriate health care for specific clinical circumstances' (Institute of Medicine 1990). Clinical process indicators have a different purpose as they are designed to guide the evaluation of health service delivery. As a result, they have some key distinguishing features:

- selective rather than comprehensive;
- usually focus on areas for which a link to outcomes has been established in the scientific literature;
- inclusion and exclusion criteria are explicit rather than left to clinical judgment;
- intended to apply to the average patient seeing the average physician;
- applied retrospectively to a population of patients (guidelines are used prospectively in the management of a single patient).

Process indicators should be selected in a way that maintains a link to the evidence that supports the underlying scientific rationale. The RAND/UCLA Appropriateness Method established an approach to selecting indicators that combines a review of published evidence with a formal expert panel process (Brook 1994). This method is reliable (Shekelle et al. 1998) and has been shown to have content, construct and predictive validity in other applications (Hemingway et al. 2001; Kravitz et al. 1998; Selby et al. 1998; Shekelle et al. 1998a).

In this approach, the development staff produces a set of draft quality indicators based on a review of the literature and guidelines (as described above) and measurement expertise. An expert panel is recruited based on nominations from appropriate specialty societies. The panels generally have nine doctors and include multiple specialties (e.g. primary care and specialty care doctors, proceduralists and non-proceduralists) and are diverse with respect to geography, gender, practice setting and other factors relevant to the purpose of the quality indicator set.

The draft process indicators and the literature review described above are referred to an expert panel (usually of nine members) that votes on which indicators should be included. Each panel member rates each indicator privately on a scale from one (i.e. indicator is not a valid measure of quality) to nine (i.e. indicator is a very valid measure of quality). The development staff summarizes results from the initial round of ratings for each indicator to produce the median score on validity (central tendency) and the mean absolute deviation from the median (spread) and to show whether the indicator ratings demonstrate substantial agreement or disagreement. Panellists assemble to discuss the indicators in a face-to-face meeting that allows them all to benefit from the perspectives of those with different views. Discussion usually focuses on the indicators for which there was substantial disagreement in the first round of ratings (for a nine-member panel defined as three or more ratings ≤ 3 and three or more ratings ≥ 7).

There are two common reasons for disagreement. First, if the indicator language is unclear the panellists may interpret the intent differently. In this case staff can rewrite the indicator or clarify definitions for key terms so that all panellists consider the same group of patients in their ratings. Second, the indicator may address a clinical process for which no strong evidence or consensus exists. In this case the indicator is likely to be rejected because reasonable people could disagree and there is no strong case for choosing one process over another. Panellists vote again after the group discussion and these results determine which indicators will be included. The standard for the RAND/UCLA method is to include indicators with a median validity score of seven or more that are rated without disagreement.

This method can be used to create appropriateness of care indicators as well as process quality indicators. The panel process is described in detail in the volumes on the RAND Quality Assessment (QA) Tools measures (Asch et al. 2000; Kerr et al. 2000; Kerr et al. 2000a; McGlynn et al. 2000; McGlynn et al. 2000a). Although it is common for countries to conduct their own indicator selection processes, they frequently refer to indicators that have been developed elsewhere. Many indicators transfer well from one country to another because the scientific basis is often common internationally (Steel et al. 2004). However, transferability may be limited by the organization of the delivery system in a country, as was noted in the development of the German indicators for the quality of acute stroke care (Heuschmann et al. 2006).

Constructing process measures

Ideally, the data source is decided prior to the development of process indicators as the type of data available will determine the types of indicators that can be constructed. When this does not happen some indicators will likely be dropped during measure development because it will not be feasible to collect the necessary data from the intended source.

Data sources
There are three major sources of data for measuring process quality: (i) medical records (electronic or paper); (ii) billing data; and (iii) surveys (patient or doctor). Each of these has strengths and weaknesses which limit the types of indicators that can be evaluated and the validity of results. Some of the main considerations are highlighted in the following paragraphs but there is not sufficient space for full descriptions of all.

Medical records contain the greatest amount of clinical information and allow the construction of measures that are clinically detailed with respect to defining eligibility, exclusions and scoring criteria. Collecting data from paper-based medical records is labour intensive and this may limit their utility for routine assessments. Paper-based medical records also lack standardized nomenclature which means that data collectors need to be carefully trained and supervised to ensure that results are reliable and valid across providers. Electronic medical records may offer greater ease of access but many such systems face the same limitations as paper-based records (lack of standard nomenclature, need to abstract key pieces of information manually). Developers (and purchasers) of electronic medical records systems face difficult tradeoffs between ease of implementation for users and the utility of the information produced for secondary uses. To date ease of use by clinicians (which may be necessary to stimulate adoption of the technology) has been prioritized.

Billing data have the advantages of being available electronically and constructed using standardized coding schemes but they lack clinical detail. In most cases a bill indicates that an encounter took place but contains no information on its content, apart from separately billed interventions (e.g. laboratory tests, immunizations, other procedures). Also, there is usually no information about the clinical profile of the patient (e.g. severity and extent of disease, co-morbid conditions, behavioural risk factors). Thus, billing data are most useful for quality indicators that require little clinical detail to identify the eligible population (e.g. presence of disease is sufficient and exclusions are rare) and to determine whether the process occurred (e.g. whether a laboratory test was ordered rather than whether counselling about a health-related behaviour occurred). Most billing data do not include the results of tests ordered (e.g. HbA1c level; LDL cholesterol level; imaging) although such information is increasingly becoming available electronically and integrated into data warehouses.

Patient survey data are useful when the patient is a reliable reporter about the eligibility conditions (e.g. presence of disease, age, health risk behaviour, symptoms) and whether or not a process occurred (e.g. various screening tests, advice from a doctor). Patients have more difficulty reporting specific test values although they may be aware of whether intermediate outcome measures for chronic diseases (e.g. blood pressure, blood sugar, cholesterol) are high, low or normal. Patient surveys can be difficult to collect on a representative sample because people are unwilling to participate or may be hard to reach.

Surveys of doctors are useful when evaluating knowledge about particular care processes or using scenarios to test what the doctor might do. Doctors are less likely than patients to respond to surveys. Studies have shown that knowledge does not necessarily translate into action so knowledge-based surveys may not be indicative of actual performance. Scenario-based studies are more reliable but there is a limit to the number of scenarios that can be tested in a single survey.

Development of measures

Detailed specifications must be developed to enable reliable assessment of the frequency with which a clinical process is delivered. The specifications should define unambiguously the criteria for identifying patients who are eligible for a clinical process indicator and for determining whether eligible patients received the indicated care. The specifications will take different forms depending on the data source. To illustrate the approach to developing specifications, consider the following indicator:

* Persons with diabetes mellitus should have their blood sugar measured at least once per year.

The first step is to develop specifications to identify those who have diabetes mellitus. It is common to consider first whether the eligible population needs to be restricted in any way. This is illustrated in Table 2.3.1 below.

These questions illustrate a major point in constructing process quality measures. In general, such measures are designed with a tendency to specificity rather than sensitivity: appropriate for the population identified as eligible for a measure (with only rare exceptions) to receive the care process. The difference between these considerations and a clinical guideline is that guidelines can allow for clinical judgment – the doctor is responsible for determining the tradeoffs based on knowledge of the patient's full spectrum of health concerns.

To ensure that data are collected reliably for a process measure, the data collector's judgment must be largely removed. It is rarely possible to include all possible clinical exceptions to eligibility. It may not be necessary to include an exception that is 'rare or random' but those that are 'common or biased' should likely be included. This requires consideration of the application of the measure by asking whether a particular clinical exception occurs less than, for example, 1% of the time in the population of interest and whether the exceptions would be expected to be distributed randomly (without any discernable pattern) across the entities likely to be evaluated. If that test is met, it may not be worthwhile to include exceptions for those considerations.

Table 2.3.1 *Assessing the eligible population for clinical process indicators*

Consideration	Issue for measurement
Does the measure apply to patients at all ages or should lower and/or upper age limits be established?	There may be ages (e.g. children, older adults) where the clinical judgment is more critical than the standard reflected in the indicator.
Does the measure apply to both type 1 and type 2 diabetes?	Subgroups within a diagnosis may be excluded. In this case, it is often difficult to distinguish between type 1 and type 2 in various data sources and routine measurement of blood sugar is the standard of care for both.
Does the measure apply to women with gestational diabetes?	The nature of the diagnosis and the routine management indicators are different for this subgroup.
Does the measure apply only to patients with a confirmed or established diagnosis of diabetes or can other factors (e.g. high HbA1c value) be used to identify the eligible population?	When assessing potential underuse it is sometimes appropriate to include persons who have signs of disease but diagnosis has not been recognized in the medical record. The conservative approach requires a confirmed diagnosis.
Should persons with a new diagnosis be included or does the patient have to have had the diagnosis for some period of time?	Process measures often distinguish between new diagnoses (where measures related to the quality of the diagnostic process are appropriate) and prevalent or existing diagnoses (where routine management measures are appropriate). This indicator is intended to apply to those with an established diagnosis.
Should there be exclusions for co-morbid conditions?	In some cases management of a co-morbid condition (cancer, AIDS) will take priority over routine care for the condition under consideration for process measures.

Table 2.3.1 *(cont)*

Consideration	Issue for measurement
Should there be exclusions for health status (e.g. end of life)?	Similar to the above consideration, some routine management of chronic conditions will be inappropriate at the end of life or in the face of other health status concerns.

The inclusion criteria are the next consideration and some of the questions that typically determine these are shown in Table 2.3.2.

Together, the exclusion and inclusion criteria form the basis for identifying the eligible population but the way in which these considerations are operationalized varies with the data source. Medical records require instructions related to notation; billing data require instructions that include the common codes used (e.g. ICD-9 or 10, CPT-4); and patient surveys need a set of questions that will elicit information about the inclusion and exclusion criteria. Most process measures are constructed by putting together a sequence of events and determining whether these occurred within an acceptable time frame. For this reason, it is generally better to collect the date associated with an event (e.g. visit for diabetes) rather than a dichotomous answer (yes/no) to a question about whether criteria are met. This allows maximum flexibility in assessing whether an indicated process has been met.

Finally, the criteria for determining whether or not the indicated care has been delivered are specified. The questions in Table 2.3.3 illustrate how this might be done.

The specifications must include instructions about the type of documentation or the names of laboratory tests that meet the conditions. Specific codes must be listed if billing data are being used.

Creating scoring methods

The last major development step is to create the scoring instructions. For process measures, the basic approach for an individual indicator is to count the number of times that a patient in the population of interest is eligible for an indicator and then the number of times the

Table 2.3.2 *Determining the inclusion criteria for clinical process indicators*

Consideration	Issue for measurement
What evidence is sufficient to determine that the patient has diabetes?	Options for a chronic disease include: (i) visit where the reason for visit is the diagnosis; (ii) medication orders consistent with the diagnosis (insulin, oral hypoglycaemics); (iii) mention of diabetes as a co-morbid factor in a visit for another reason.
Will the measure be limited to those with evidence of the disease in the year in which the measure is constructed?	When looking for evidence of underuse, and when the diagnosis is not likely to resolve, evidence of disease in a time period prior to the one in which the care process is being evaluated is acceptable. The look-back period may be limited in order to improve data collection efficiency.

indicated process was delivered to those who are eligible. Table 2.3.4 illustrates this process for a simple indicator with five patients in the population of interest.

In this example, four of the five patients are eligible for the indicator and two passed for a score of two out of four, or 50%.

Some process indicators require multiple events. For example, if the example indicator requires two blood sugar tests per year it needs to be decided whether the scoring method is 'all or nothing'. This means that the indicator is not passed if a patient receives fewer than two tests in a year. Alternatively, partial credit can be granted by counting the proportion of required tests received. This can be seen as giving each patient two eligibilities (one for each test that should be received) and counting the number of times the process was received. The scores for an individual patient would be 0%, 50% or 100%.

Increasingly, process indicators are being combined to create composite scores. For example, a diabetes composite score could be compiled from multiple process indicators related to routine management of diabetes. Similarly, composites can be created across conditions (for example, all chronic disease care in a population). Composites are constructed in three common ways.

Table 2.3.3 *Specifying the criteria for determining whether indicated care has been delivered*

Consideration	Issue for measurement
What type of blood sugar test is sufficient to meet the conditions for the indicator?	This has generally been limited to an HbA1c test, but multiple tests might be allowed to meet a criterion for other indicators. Possible question for this indicator is whether home monitoring tests are an acceptable alternative – they would not be accepted as they do not meet the intent of this indicator.
Is there evidence that an HbA1c test was ordered or that laboratory results are available?	Tests (and medications) have two signals – whether the test was ordered and whether it was completed. Accounting for orders gives the doctor the benefit of the doubt, particularly in systems where the patient goes elsewhere for the test. Alternatively, orders may not be recorded in some records but laboratory reports show that a test was done. Standard practice at RAND is to take account of both orders and test results.
Is there evidence that the patient refused the test?	Look for documentation that the patient refused a recommended procedure (only possible in medical record-based data collection or surveys) and allow refusals to count toward passing an indicator. Refusals could also be used to exclude a patient from an indicator.
Does the sequence of events matter?	Some instances may require evidence that a diagnosis occurred on or before the date of the indicated process (blood sugar test). Here, the sequence is not important because prevalent cases of diabetes are sought. Those with a new diagnosis have been excluded. However, this type of consideration illustrates why it is useful to have the dates on which events occur.

Table 2.3.4 *Sample scoring table for a simple performance indicator*

Patient	Eligible?	Received process?
1234	Yes	Yes
5678	No	NA
9101	Yes	No
1112	Yes	No
1314	Yes	Yes

1. Opportunity score counts all instances in which a patient is eligible for an indicator in the denominator and all instances in which the indicated care was delivered in the numerator. The implicit weight in this case is the prevalence of eligibility for different indicators – more common care processes account for a greater portion of the total score and patients who are eligible for more indicators contribute more to the total score.
2. Average of averages approach creates a score for each patient and then averages the patients' scores. In this case, each patient counts equally toward the total score.
3. All or nothing approach counts the proportion of patients who receive all the care for which they are eligible. Each patient counts equally although patients eligible for a larger number of indicators may be less likely to get all indicated care.

Weights can be added within each of these general approaches in order to reflect the different levels of clinical importance attached to certain indicators.

Risk adjustment is used less commonly for process measures. The rationale is that most of the risk adjustment occurs in constructing the conditions of eligibility. If the process measures are being used to compare the performance of different entities, this might include consideration of whether one entity has a greater number of patients or eligibility events associated with indicators that have low empirical scores (i.e. appear to be harder to pass). At RAND, adjustments to scores have been constructed to account for this.

Process measurement schemes in operation

Process measures can be used in a variety of ways to improve quality, for example as part of accreditation of facilities or providers; in public reporting; as part of the structure of benefit designs; and in payment incentive programmes. In this section, some of the current uses of process measures outside of the research setting are described. This is not exhaustive but is intended to illustrate some of the ways in which clinical process and appropriateness measures can be used to promote quality.

Accreditation

Accreditation is the recognition by an independent body that an organization meets an acceptable standard. Traditionally, accrediting organizations have set standards related to the way in which an organization functions (e.g. whether specific procedures are in place, certain committees exist and meet regularly, safety codes are met) and assessed compliance with these standards through on-site visits. It is less common for accrediting bodies to use process measures to assess actual performance.

In the United States, the National Committee for Quality Assurance (NCQA) uses about twenty measures of process quality as part of its accreditation programme for managed care and preferred provider organizations. A description of NCQA's accreditation programme is available on its web site (http://www.ncqa.org/). The process measures selected for accreditation are drawn from the Healthcare Effectiveness Data and Information Set – HEDIS (Lacourciere 2007). They meet the best practice for measure development described above. The process quality and patient experience measures account for about 40% of the total accreditation score. Managed care organizations participate in accreditation voluntarily but about 90% of such organizations in the United States seek NCQA accreditation.

At the time of writing, no European countries were identified that had incorporated clinical process measures into any voluntary accreditation schemes. To the extent that accreditation is used in Europe, the performance measures included are more likely to relate to the volume of procedures performed or the waiting times to access a procedure. Sometimes volume is used as a proxy for quality but it is not considered a clinical process measure. In this context waiting times also do not constitute a clinical process measure.

Public reporting

The results of clinical process and appropriateness assessments have been reported at various levels in the health-care system. National reporting is perhaps the most common and in recent years there has been an interest in common measures that allow for cross-national comparisons. Results can also be reported anonymously or by the name of the provider (health plan, hospital, nursing home, medical group physician).

The AHRQ has produced an annual report on health-care quality since 2003. The 2008 report is available from the web site (http://www.ahrq.gov/qual/qrdr08.htm#toc). A variety of data sources are used to construct the measures which report on the following clinical areas: cancer; diabetes; end stage renal disease; heart disease; HIV and AIDs; maternal and child health; mental health and substance abuse; and respiratory diseases. Process indicators constitute the largest portion of the indicators.

The Organisation for Economic Co-operation and Development (OECD) is conducting a project to collect national-level information on process quality suitable for cross-national comparisons. The project started in 2001 and involves twenty-three countries. The initial report contained seventeen indicators, primarily outcomes measures but including some process quality indicators for cancer screening (breast, cervical) and vaccinations (childhood, adult influenza) (Mattke et al. 2006). An indicator for retinal screening among persons with diabetes has been added subsequently (OECD 2007).

There are a number of examples of public reporting for managed care organizations, hospitals and nursing homes in the United States. Some organizations are also working to develop public reports of performance at the medical group practice and individual doctor level. Since 1999, NCQA has released public reports using clinical process measures. A subset of the information collected by NCQA is available on the web site (http://hprc.ncqa.org/tabid/836/Default.aspx) and more detailed information can be purchased. The web site provides a high level summary (one to four stars) of performance in a category (e.g. chronic disease category = living with illness) and scores for a sub-set of eleven individual measures for asthma, diabetes, heart disease and mental health are available. These results are shown for each health plan along with a comparison to the score for each measure for the top 10% of plans nationally and the top 25% and 50% of plans regionally.

Public reports on hospital performance in the United States are available from the Centers for Medicare and Medicaid Services (http://www.hospitalcompare.hhs.gov/). Bar graphs show the results for three clinical areas (heart attack, heart failure, pneumonia) and for surgi-cal care (prevention of infections). Results are displayed for hospitals selected by the user and are compared to the United States' average, the average for the state in which the hospital is located and the top 10% of hospitals nationwide. The information is also available as a table that includes the number of patients who were eligible for the measure. The Joint Commission provides reports on the same mea-sures in a different format – symbols provide a high-level summary of performance in the category and detailed information is provided on each process measure within the category available. There are compar-isons with the top 10% and average scores both nationally and for the state in which the hospital is located (http://www.qualitycheck.org/).

The Netherlands Health Care Inspectorate (IGZ) has developed a set of hospital performance indicators that include a combination of structure, process and outcomes measures (Dutch Institute for Healthcare Improvement 2004). The process measures are based on national guidelines. The Danish National Indicator Project focuses on hospital-delivered care in eight clinical areas: stroke, hip fracture, upper gastrointestinal bleeding, lung cancer, schizophrenia, heart fail-ure, diabetes and chronic obstructive lung disease (Bartels et al. 2007). Participation in reporting is mandatory for hospitals and the results are reported using both opportunity and all-or-nothing scoring methods.

Process measures are not used as commonly in public reports on nursing homes in the United States. These include only two process measures – on influenza and pneumococcal vaccinations (http://www.medicare.gov/NHCompare). Public reports of performance on clinical process measures have been available at the medical group and clinic level in Minnesota for the past four years through a private nonprofit group. MN Community Measurement was founded by the Minnesota Medical Association and seven of the nonprofit health plans operat-ing in the state (http://www.mnhealthscores.org/Report/). The reports include measures of care processes and outcomes in nine clinical areas: asthma, cancer screening, childhood immunizations, chlamydia screening, diabetes, pharyngitis (sore throat), upper respiratory infection, vascular care and coronary artery disease care. Reports for the optimal care measurement areas (diabetes, cancer screening, vascular and coronary artery disease) use the all-or-nothing scoring method and are dominated by outcomes measures.

In the United Kingdom, the Quality and Outcomes Framework (QOF) uses process measures to assess the performance of general practices. The clinical domain currently includes eighty indicators across nineteen clinical areas. The results are available on multiple web sites providing overall statistics for the nation (proportion of practices achieving 100% performance, average performance levels) and an online database that allows users access to detailed information about specific practices. The online database (http://www.qof.ic.nhs.uk/) has a number of display options including comparisons between a selected practice and the averages for the local primary care trust (PCT) and England, respectively.

Benefit design

The use of process measures for benefit design is a relatively new phenomenon in the United States. Essentially, process measures are used to assess the relative performance of hospitals, medical groups or physicians. Patients pay copayments based on relative rankings – lower copayments are due if patients see providers with relatively better performance. The purpose is to provide patients with a financial incentive to seek care from better quality providers. These schemes are used by both private insurance companies (e.g. UnitedHealthcare, Aetna) and in government run programmes (e.g. the General Insurance Commission for the state of Massachusetts). In these schemes, process quality measures are generally combined with measures related to the cost of care and the most favourable copayments are assigned to providers who deliver high quality care at low relative cost.

Payment incentives

Process measures have also been used as the basis for payment incentives for providers. These schemes are commonly referred to as pay-for-performance programmes and have been implemented at hospital and medical group level in the United States and at practice level in the United Kingdom.

About twenty-three hospital pay-for-performance programmes currently operate in the United States. Most draw on the process measures that the Centers for Medicare and Medicaid Services require for reporting (heart attack, heart failure, pneumonia, surgical infection prevention). Typically, composite scores are constructed at the condition level and hospitals are eligible for bonuses (lump sum or percentage) based on the level of achievement. For example, the Premier Hospital Quality Incentive Demonstration paid a 2% bonus to hospitals in the top decile and a 1% bonus to hospitals in the second decile (Lindenauer 2007).

The Integrated Healthcare Association in California has one of the longest running pay-for-performance schemes in the United States. The programme is designed to incentivize medical groups to improve quality. About half of the payment incentive is based on quality measures and eight of the ten measures used in 2005/2006 were clinical process measures (Integrated Healthcare Association 2006).

The pay-for-performance scheme for general practices in the United Kingdom has the most extensive use of process quality measures to date. At the outset of the programme, the government increased the amount of funding for general practices by more than £ 1 billion, an approximately 20% increase in general practice budgets (Roland 2004). Incentives are based on a complex formula that includes minimum and maximum thresholds of performance and a number of points allocated for each indicator. Practice size and the prevalence of different chronic disease are also included in the calculations. At the beginning of the scheme each point was worth £120.

Best uses of process measurement

Most schemes to monitor quality include a combination of different types of measures – structure, process and outcomes. This is reasonable because no single approach to quality measurement addresses all issues. Measures should be selected after consideration of the intended use of the results as this may inform the type of measure preferred.

Process measures have four main advantages. First, care processes occur more frequently thereby enabling deficits in care to be identified more rapidly. Many quality measurement schemes encounter too few cases to be able to draw robust conclusions; a problem that tends to be more pronounced with outcome measures. Second, process measures describe the care delivery expectations and thus define what needs to be done to achieve optimal care delivery. When monitoring outcomes, the reasons for poor results are not always clear and it may be necessary to collect process measures to identify the steps that must be taken to improve these outcomes. Third, process measures generally do not require risk adjustment beyond the specifications associated with identifying eligible patients. This increases the potential for greater acceptability of the measures as risk adjustment of outcome measures is challenging (and rarely satisfies those being measured). Fourth, processes reflect the way in which the scientific literature is organized. Most studies involve investigations of the effect of a particular intervention and allow direct links to an evidence base.

So when are these attributes most important? As a general rule, process measures are preferred when quality is being measured for the purpose of holding organizations or individuals accountable for meeting standards. This is particularly true when organizations or individuals are being compared.

Recommendations for developing countries

Increasing research has been conducted to investigate the clinical quality improvement efforts being undertaken in developing countries. Successful efforts that have been documented show that these use similar meta-analyses to those undertaken in developed countries (Leatherman et al., forthcoming). Some conclusions on successful monitoring of quality in settings with limited resources can be drawn from projects that have shown favourable outcomes (Berwick 2004; Ovretveit 2004).

Developing countries face the major barrier of a lack of available resources for quality measurement and monitoring. This makes it more difficult to introduce not only the infrastructure necessary for measurement and monitoring, but also staff training and supervision programmes. Yet, investment in these areas has long-term potential as it will enable gaps in quality to be identified and addressed to produce more efficient allocation of financial resources.

Given the limited information technology available in developing countries it is important to measure only what is necessary to inform policy and not to waste resources by attempting to measure too much. Furthermore, quality measurement and monitoring should be directed at areas in which quality improvements will have the most impact. These may differ from the clinical areas targeted by developed countries. For example, much of the current literature on quality improvement in developing countries describes efforts in the areas of acute illnesses, child care and maternity care. Such efforts may result in increases in immunization rates or reductions in childhood and maternal mortality which have a larger impact on the mortality and morbidity of developing countries.

Where there is a distinct lack of infrastructure, managers should be encouraged to think innovatively about alternative ways of measuring quality. Berwick (2004) gives the example of a maternal and child health clinic in northern Pakistan that wanted to measure the effect of a project on early intervention in pregnancy. The lead doctor on the project suggested counting the small graves as an outcome measure. This shows a creative way of overcoming the lack of IT infrastructure to address the problem at hand.

Physical infrastructures need to be developed in tandem with training programmes that provide all levels of staff with the skills to carry out a systematic measurement of indicators. Moreover, teamwork should be encouraged amongst those employing interventions at the provider, patient and system levels to ensure that measurement and monitoring is integrated throughout.

Finally, it may be useful to develop different systems to reward the practitioners or facilities that undertake quality monitoring. These can take the form of self-assessment, peer review, certification, accreditation or licensing. Such mechanisms allow recognition of more successful endeavours as well as the identification of areas where quality monitoring efforts are less effective and can be improved.

Directions for future research

Clinical process measures offer an important tool for assessing the current quality of care being delivered by a system or in a country. They are also useful for evaluating whether interventions have improved quality performance. This chapter has described the challenges associated with developing robust process measures and with implementing assessments on a large scale. One promising direction for future research is the development of streamlined approaches to measure the development and translation of measures across systems and countries. This activity may be performed most effectively by a limited number of centres with special expertise in combination with government or nongovernmental organizations that translate measures into routine use. Methods to assess the appropriateness of a measure or set of measures for use in a new country or system could increase the potential to use or adapt measures in new settings.

There is considerable interest in cross-national comparison of quality performance. Much of what is known today is derived from surveys but a number of clinical process measures cannot be assessed adequately in this way. The development of a core set of process measures that could be used across countries with different health systems would increase the ability of countries to learn from one another. This would likely require investment from a group that takes the lead on this activity as well as cooperation from participating countries. Such efforts are underway but have encountered considerable difficulties.

Another critical area for research is to find ways to integrate measurement and clinical practice. Too often, quality measurement activities are separate from the delivery of health services. Quality will not reach its full potential until methods for measuring and delivering care can be integrated.

It would be useful to identify a set of strategies that are effective in improving quality in different settings and countries. Research in this area is fairly rudimentary and requires considerable work to identify the best ways of converting information generated from process assessments into action plans for improvement. With few effective ways of sharing lessons learned across different entities and countries, much time is spent on unnecessary duplication.

Quality measurement in developing countries offers an opportunity for innovative thinking and approaches that could well translate to developed countries. Developing countries may offer fresh perspectives on common quality problems and be less tied to a history of how such problems have been solved. It should be a high priority to find ways to draw upon the lessons learned from these experiences and to make this learning widely available.

Conclusions

The methods for developing clinical process and appropriateness measures are well established and the use of state-of-the-art methods has been demonstrated in multiple countries. There has been a substantial increase in the number of measures available but their use for quality improvement and other applications remains limited. The United States appears to lead the world in the use of clinical process measures in different applications, although the United Kingdom's pay-for-performance scheme is far more comprehensive. It is beyond the purview of this chapter to comment on how effective these measures have been in stimulating quality improvement but examples from several countries show positive trends.

One of the greatest limitations to the rapid uptake of clinical process measures is the inadequate data infrastructure in place to support measurement. Health care lags behind most modern industries in its use of electronic systems for the management of essential processes. Without this type of infrastructure, quality measurement is likely to be relegated to a minor role and is unlikely to realize its full potential. Significant investments will be required to develop the necessary information infrastructure to manage patients effectively in the face of accelerating advances in knowledge as the cognitive processes necessary to process the match between patients' problems and the available solutions exceed human abilities. A by-product of this investment will be the development (if done well) of systems that will also allow quality measurement to accelerate. It will be necessary to take account of the information requirements for clinical process measurement as the functional requirements for future health-care information systems are developed.

References

Asch, S. Kerr, EA. Hamilton, EG. Reifel, JL. McGlynn, EA (eds.) (2000). *Quality of care for oncologic conditions and HIV: a review of the literature and quality indicators*. Santa Monica, CA: RAND Corporation (Publication No. MR-1281-AHRQ).

Bartels, PD. Mainz, J. Hansen, A-M. Ingeman, A. Bunk, A. Nakano, A. Kaersvang L (2007). *Nationwide performance measurement can improve the quality of care.* Presentation at International Society for Quality in Health Care, 1 October 2007 (http://www.isqua.org/isqua-Pages/Conferences/Boston/slides/BOSTONMonday.html).

Berwick, DM (2004). 'Lessons from developing nations on improving health care.' *British Medical Journal*, 328(7448): 1124–1129.

Brook, RH (1994). The RAND/UCLA Appropriateness Method. In: McCormick, KA. Moore, SR. Siegel, RA (eds.). *Clinical practice guideline development: methodology perspectives.* Rockville, MD: Agency for Health Care Policy and Research, Public Health Service, US Department of Health and Human Services (Publication No. 95–0009).

Dutch Institute for Healthcare Improvement (2004). *Vision of quality 2004.* Utrecht: Dutch Institute for Healthcare Improvement (http://www.cbo.nl/algemeen/visionofquality.pdf/view).

Field, MJ. Lohr, KN (eds.) (1990). *Clinical practice guidelines: directions for a new program.* Washington, DC: Institute of Medicine National Academies Press.

Hemingway, H. Crook, AM. Feder, G. Banerjee, S. Dawson, JR. Magee, P. Philpott, S. Sanders, J. Wood, A. Timmis, AD (2001). 'Underuse of coronary revascularization procedures in patients considered appropriate candidates for revascularization'. *New England Journal of Medicine*, 344(9): 645–654.

Heuschmann, PU. Biegler, MK. Busse, O. Elsner, S. Grau, A. Hasenbein, U. Hermanek, P. Janzen, RW. Kolominsky-Rabas, PL. Kraywinkel, K. Lowitzsch, K. Misselwitz, B. Nabavi, DG. Otten, K. Pientka, L. von Reutern, GM. Ringelstein, EB. Sander, D. Wagner, M. Berger, K (2006). 'Development and implementation of evidence-based indicators for measuring quality of acute stroke care: the Quality Indicator Board of the German Stroke Registers Study Group (ADSR).' *Stroke*, 37(10): 2573–2578.

Institute of Medicine (2003). *Priority areas for national action: transforming health care quality.* Washington, DC: National Academy Press.

Integrated Healthcare Association (2006). *Advancing quality through collaboration: the California pay for performance program.* Oakland, CA: Integrated Healthcare Association.

Kerr, EA. Asch, S. Hamilton, EG. McGlynn, EA (eds.) (2000). *Quality of care for cardiopulmonary conditions: a review of the literature and quality indicators.* Santa Monica, CA: RAND Corporation (Publication No. MR-1282-AHRQ).

Kerr, EA. Asch, S. Hamilton, EG. McGlynn, EA. (eds.) (2000a). *Quality of care for general medical conditions: a review of the literature and quality indicators.* Santa Monica, CA: RAND Corporation (Publication No. MR-1280-AHRQ).

Kravitz, RL. Park, RE. Kahan, JP (1997). 'Measuring the clinical consistency of panelists' appropriateness ratings: the case of coronary artery bypass surgery.' *Health Policy*, 42(2):135–143.

Lacourciere, J (ed.) (2007). *HEDIS 2007 technical specifications.* Washington, DC: National Committee for Quality Assurance (No. 2).

Leatherman, S. Ferris, TG. Berwick, D. Omaswa, FM, Crisp, N (forthcoming). *The role of quality improvement in strengthening health systems in developing countries.*

Lindenauer, PK. Remus, D. Roman, S. Rothburg, MB. Benjamin, EM. Ma, A. Bratzler, DW (2007). 'Public reporting and pay for performance in hospital quality improvement.' *New England Journal of Medicine*, 356(5): 486–496.

Mainz, J. Krog, BR. Bjornshave, B. Bartels, P (2004). 'Nationwide continuous quality improvement using clinical indicators: the Danish National Indicator Project.' *International Journal for Quality in Health Care*, 16(Suppl.1): 45–50.

Mattke, S. Kelley, E. Scherer, P. Hurst, J. Lapetra, MLG. HCQI Expert Group Members (2006). *Health care quality indicators project: initial indicators report.* Paris: OECD Publications Service (OECD Health Working Papers No. 22).

McGlynn, EA. Damberg, C. Kerr, E. Schuster, M (eds.) (2000). *Quality of care for children and adolescents: a review of selected clinical conditions and quality indicators.* Santa Monica, CA: RAND Corporation (Publication No. MR-1283-HCFA).

McGlynn, EA. Kerr, EA. Damberg, C. Asch, S (eds.) (2000a). *Quality of care for women: a review of selected clinical conditions and quality indicators.* Santa Monica, CA: RAND Corporation (Publication No. MR-1284-HCFA).

OECD (2007). *Health at a glance 2007: OECD indicators.* Paris: Organisation for Economic Co-operation and Development.

Ovretveit, J (2004). 'Formulating a health quality improvement strategy for a developing country.' *International Journal of Health Care Quality Assurance*, 17(7): 368–376.

Roland, M (2004). 'Linking physicians' pay to the quality of care – a major experiment in the United Kingdom.' *New England Journal of Medicine*, 351(14): 1448–1454.

Selby, JV. Fireman, BH. Lundstrom, RJ. Swain, BE. Truman, AF. Wong, CC. Froelicher, ES. Barron, HV. Hlatky MA (1996). 'Variation among hospitals in coronary-angiography practices and outcomes after myocardial infarction in a large health maintenance organization.' *New England Journal of Medicine*, 335(25): 1888–1896.

Shekelle, PG. Chassin, MR. Park, RE (1998). 'Assessing the predictive validity of the RAND/UCLA appropriateness method criteria for performing carotid endarterectomy.' *International Journal of Technology Assessment in Health Care*, 14(4): 707–727.

Shekelle, PG. Kahan, JP. Bernstein, SJ. Leape, LL. Kamberg, CJ. Park, RE (1998a). 'The reproducibility of a method to identify the overuse and underuse of medical procedures.' *New England Journal of Medicine*, 338(26): 1888–1895.

Shiffman, RN. Shekelle, P. Overhage, JM. Slutsky, J. Grimshaw, J. Deshpande, AM (2003). 'Standardized reporting of clinical practice guidelines: a proposal from the Conference on Guideline Standardization.' *Annals of Internal Medicine*, 139(6): 493–498.

Steel, N. Melzer, D. Shekelle, PG. Wenger, NS. Forsyth, D. McWilliams, BC (2004). 'Developing quality indicators for older adults: transfer from the USA to the UK is feasible.' *Quality and Safety in Health Care*, 13(4): 260–264.

Wenger, N. Roth, CP. Shekelle, P. & ACOVE Investigators (2007). 'Introduction to the assessing care of vulnerable elders-3 quality indicator measurement set.' *Journal of the American Geriatrics Society*, 55(Suppl. 2): 247–52.

2.4 | *Measuring financial protection in health*

ADAM WAGSTAFF

Introduction

Health systems are not just about improving health. Good ones also ensure that people are protected from the financial consequences of illness and death, or at least from the financial consequences associated with the use of medical care. Anecdotal evidence suggests that health systems often perform badly in this respect, with devastating consequences especially for poor and near-poor households. The World Bank participatory poverty study in fifty countries – *Voices of the Poor* (Narayan et al. 2000a) – found that poor health and illness are universally dreaded as a source of destitution, not only because of the costs of health care but also because of the income lost. The study documents the case of a twenty-six year-old Vietnamese man who was the richest man in his community but became one of the poorest as a result of the health-care costs incurred for his daughter's severe illness (Narayan 2000). Another case concerned a thirty year-old Indian mother of four who was forced to sell the family's home and land and must walk 10 km a day transporting wood on her head in order to finance the cost of her diabetic husband's medical care (Narayan 2000).

How can a health system's success in protecting people against the financial consequences of ill health be measured? What do successful systems have in common? How far do health system reforms improve people's financial protection against health expenses? This chapter provides an overview of the methods and issues arising in each case and presents empirical work on financial protection in health, including the impacts of government policy. The chapter also reviews a recent critique of the methods used to measure financial protection.

Some preliminaries

The measures of financial protection developed to date are based on out-of-pocket spending on medical care and relate these payments to

114

a threshold (Wagstaff & van Doorslaer 2003). The idea is that out-of-pocket spending is largely involuntary and does not contribute to household well-being in the way that spending on (say) a new car might. A household unfortunate enough to have to pay for medical care is deprived of resources that could be used to purchase other goods and services, including necessities such as food and shelter. One approach is to classify spending as catastrophic if it exceeds a certain fraction of household income. Another is to classify it as impoverishing if it is sufficiently large to make the difference to a household being above or below the poverty line, i.e. in the absence of the medical outlays the household's resources would have been sufficient to keep living standards above the poverty line; with the outlays living standards are pushed below the poverty line.

Three general issues arise with these approaches. First, the focus is the cost of medical care; income losses associated with illness, injury and death are not captured, even though they may have greater impacts on household welfare. The justification is that these measures aim to assess financial protection related to health-care expenses and that the social protection system should be responsible for protecting households against income losses. Second, the assumptions that out-of-pocket spending on health is involuntary and automatically deprives households of resources should be considered. They are discussed further below. Third, some argue that the focus on what households spend misses an important point – high out-of-pocket costs may deter some people from using health services. A country in which people pay little out of pocket (and which therefore looks good from a financial protection perspective) may be one in which people do not use health services. Some argue that this should be captured by a financial protection measure.

On the face of it, it seems reasonable that financial protection measures should capture forgone utilization caused by high out-of-pocket costs. However, this confuses policy objectives with policy instruments. Policy-makers seek to influence multiple (focal) variables including health outcomes and people's expenditure on health (and by implication their available resources for other goods and services). They have a number of instruments at their disposal, including the share of the cost of health care that people pay out of pocket. A change in a given instrument will likely affect several focal variables. For example, exempting poor people from user fees at public facilities will likely affect their use of services (non-use and under-utilization should fall) and the amount that they pay out of pocket.

The natural approach to a health system assessment is to examine how the system functions in terms of the focal variables and works backwards to see how far this is attributable to specific set policies that have been adopted. For example, a country might show good financial protection but poor health outcomes and health inequalities if out-of-pocket payment policies discourage most people from using health services but those that are used are high quality and appropriate. Another country might have poor financial protection and poor health outcomes and inequalities because people use services (despite high cost at the point of use) that are poor quality or inappropriate for their needs. This example highlights that performance on financial protection depends not just on policies for narrowly defined health financing but also (amongst other things) on the way that providers are paid and regulated.

Catastrophic expenditures

The basics

Many studies simply examine the distribution of catastrophic health expenditures. These are defined as health spending that exceeds a threshold usually defined in relation to the household's pre-payment income. This is illustrated in Fig. 2.4.1 which plots out-of-pocket spending on medical care (M) against non-medical spending (NM) on other items such as food, housing, transport, etc. In Fig. 2.4.1 a household has income equal to x (intercept on x and y axes) and outgoings on medical care (M_0) and other items (NM_0). The 45° budget line indicates that each dollar spent on medical care means one dollar less to spend on other things. It is this fact that underpins the concern over financial protection – that medical care outlays are different from spending on other goods and services. They are viewed as involuntary responses to unwanted health shocks and are considered to have entirely negative effects on households by diverting resources that could have been spent on goods and services that contribute to welfare. Waters et al. (2004) define out-of-pocket medical spending as catastrophic if it exceeds a certain amount.

Wagstaff and van Doorslaer (2003), by contrast, consider spending is catastrophic if it exceeds some specified fraction of pre-payment income (x) defined as the sum of observed medical outlays (M_0) and observed

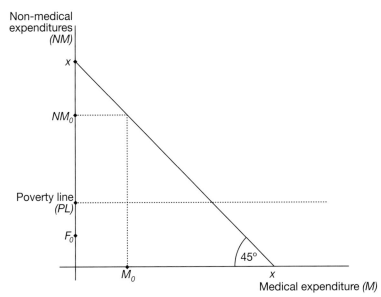

Fig. 2.4.1 Defining catastrophic health spending

Source: Author's own compilation

non-medical spending (NM_0). The threshold could also be defined in terms of pre-payment income less a deduction for food and (possibly) other necessities (Wagstaff & van Doorslaer 2003; Xu et al. 2003). The idea is that these deductions for basic necessities offer a better idea of an individual's ability to pay. These deductions could be an individual's (or household's) actual food expenditure (F_0) or what is considered to be the minimum acceptable level of expenditure on food (and perhaps other necessities) as reflected in a poverty line (PL). The latter approach is problematic when a household's pre-payment income falls short of the poverty line. In such cases, households have a negative estimated ability to pay that automatically falls below the catastrophe threshold whatever the medical care outlay (Wagstaff & van Doorslaer 2003).[1]

---

[1] Xu et al. (2003) use this approach. Their poverty line is just for food expenditures, which is subtracted from non-medical consumption (NM_0) rather than pre-payment income (x). Ability to pay is defined as NM_0-PL except for households for whom this is negative. In such cases, ability to pay is defined as NM_0 less *actual* food expenditure. This leads to the rather unsatisfactory outcome that a household just below their poverty line could be judged to have the same ability to pay as one just above it.

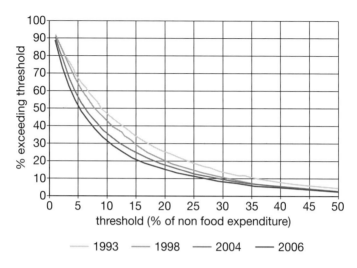

Fig. 2.4.2 Catastrophic spending curves, Viet Nam

Source: Author

Of course, the precise fraction of pre-payment income (with or without some deduction for basic necessities) is arbitrary; therefore it is sensible to examine the sensitivity of results to the threshold chosen. Fig. 2.4.2 shows catastrophic spending curves for a variety of years for Viet Nam – plotting the fraction of households experiencing catastrophic out-of-pocket spending (y-axis) for a given threshold (x-axis). In this instance, the incidence of catastrophic spending has fallen continuously over the period, whatever the threshold, and therefore the choice of threshold is irrelevant.

It may be desirable to move beyond counting the number of households who overshoot the threshold to capturing the amount by which they overshoot it. This is common in the poverty literature which assesses not only the number of people in poverty but also the poverty gap – the extent to which they fall below the poverty line. The catastrophic payment gap is simply the aggregate or average amount by which out-of-pocket spending exceeds the threshold (Wagstaff & van Doorslaer 2003). Fig. 2.4.3 plots out-of-pocket payments as a share of income (y-axis) against the cumulative share of the population (x-axis), ranked in decreasing order of out-of-pocket payments as a share of income. The catastrophic payment headcount (those whose payments exceed the threshold) is obtained by reading off the curve

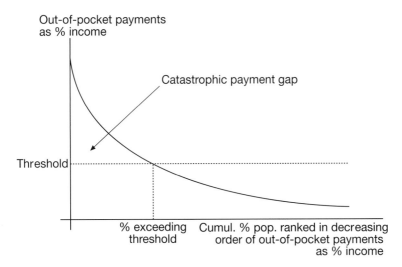

Fig. 2.4.3 Catastrophic spending gap

Source: Wagstaff & van Doorslaer 2003.

at the threshold. The (aggregate) catastrophic payment gap shows the overall amount by which payments exceed the threshold in the sample.

A final modification is to make some allowance for whether well-off or worse-off households exceed the threshold. It is likely that policy-makers would be more concerned about the latter. The incidence of catastrophic payments and the catastrophic payment gap could be tabulated by pre-payment income quintile or by computing a concentration index for each (Wagstaff & van Doorslaer 2003). For example, the concentration index for the catastrophic health expenditure head-count would be negative if catastrophic expenditures were, on aver-age, more common among the worse off. Of course, it may be that the fraction of the population experiencing catastrophic spending has increased over time but become less concentrated among the poor. Multiplying the catastrophic payment headcount by the complement of the concentration index provides a natural summary measure that takes both into account (Wagstaff & van Doorslaer 2003). This is equivalent to constructing a rank-weighted average of the binary vari-able indicating whether or not the person in question had expenses exceeding the catastrophic payment threshold, where the weight is decreasing in the person's rank in the income distribution.

Empirical studies

Xu et al. (2003) found large differences when they reported the incidence of catastrophic health spending (using a 40% threshold) in fifty-nine countries (Fig. 2.4.4). Xu et al. (2007) recently produced estimates for eighty-nine countries covering 89% of the world's population, again using the 40% threshold. Their estimates range from 0% in the Czech Republic, Slovakia and the United Kingdom to more than 10% in Brazil and Viet Nam. Several OECD countries (Portugal, Spain, Switzerland, United States) record rates in excess of 0.5%.

Van Doorslaer et al. (2007) looked at catastrophic spending in ten Asian territories. They found relatively low rates in Malaysia, Sri Lanka and Thailand and relatively high rates in China, Viet Nam and Bangladesh. This study also looked at the pre-payment income distribution of those experiencing catastrophic payments. For the most part, catastrophic spending was concentrated among the better off although this was dependent to some degree on the threshold chosen. Taiwan is the exception – catastrophic spending was concentrated among the poor whatever the threshold. A different picture emerges in Waters et al's (2004) study in the United States. They found a higher incidence of catastrophic spending among poor families and those with multiple chronic conditions. In Belgium, too, the incidence was found to be higher among poorer families (De Graeve & Van Ourti 2003).

A number of studies explore how policies and institutions impact on the incidence of catastrophic health spending. Xu et al. (2003 & 2007) found that rates of catastrophic spending are higher in poorer countries and in those with limited prepayment systems. Xu et al's (2007) most recent study (controlling for whether prepayment as a share of health spending exceeds 50%) found that the incidence of catastrophic spending does not vary between tax-financed or social health insurance systems. Looking at cross-country differences, van Doorslaer et al. (2007) speculate that the low incidence of catastrophic spending in Sri Lanka, Malaysia and Thailand reflects the low reliance on out-of-pocket spending to finance health care and the limited use of user fees in the public sector. By contrast, the high rate of incidence in the Republic of Korea is argued to reflect the high copayments in that country's social insurance system and the partial coverage of inpatient care. De Graeve and Van Ourti (2003) found that the incidence of catastrophic spending in

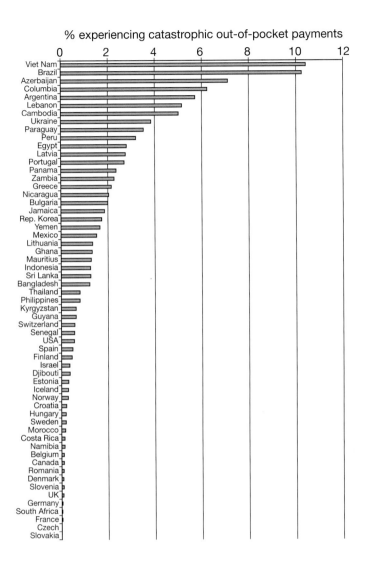

Fig. 2.4.4 Incidence of catastrophic out-of-pocket payments in fifty-nine countries

Source: Xu et al. 2003

Belgium would have been higher without a policy that imposes a ceiling on official out-of-pocket payments linked to a family's income. This ceiling has greatest effect in the middle of the income distribution.

Several country-level studies conclude that insurance reduces the risk of catastrophic health spending. Gakidou et al. (2006) and Knaul et al. (2006) found that the introduction of the Popular Health Insurance scheme in Mexico from 2001 led to a reduction in the incidence of catastrophic health expenditures. Limwattananon et al. (2007) found that rates of catastrophic spending in Thailand were lower after the universal health-care scheme was introduced in 2001. Habicht et al. (2006) found that the risk of catastrophic spending in Estonia increased during the late 1990s and early 2000s. They attribute this partly to rising copayments (hence a decrease in the depth of coverage) linked to a decline (in real terms) in government health spending and partly to the ageing of the population – elderly people have shallower coverage, especially for medicines.

Other studies point to the limitations of using insurance to reduce and eliminate catastrophic spending. Wagstaff and Pradhan (2005) found that the introduction of a social health insurance scheme in Viet Nam in 1993 reduced the incidence of catastrophic expenses. Wagstaff (2007) found that the scheme's subsequent extension to the poor (financed through general revenues) produced similar results. However, the percentage reductions were estimated to be small and high rates of catastrophic spending were observed even among those with insurance. These results may be explained partly by the fact that insurance appears to have increased the utilization of services in Viet Nam. Xu et al. (2006) found lower rates of catastrophic out-of-pocket spending among the Ugandan population following the removal of user fees in 2001 although the rate increased among the poor. They speculate that this was due to the frequent unavailability of drugs at government facilities following the removal of user fees – patients were forced to buy drugs from private pharmacies and informal payments to health workers increased to offset lost revenues from fees. Devadasan et al. (2007) examined how two community health insurance schemes in India affected the risk of catastrophic out-of-pocket payments and concluded that they halved the risk. This limited impact on benefit packages is attributed to low maximum limits; the exclusion of some conditions from the package; and the use of the private sector for some inpatient admissions.

Ekman (2007) found that insurance increases the risk of catastrophic spending in Zambia and suggests that the amount of care per illness episodes may have increased. He contends that quality assurance and the oversight of service providers is important in determining how far insurance reduces the risk of catastrophic spending. Three recent studies from China reinforce these points. Wagstaff and Lindelow (2008) found that China's urban insurance scheme increases the risk of catastrophic out-of-pocket spending. These results are attributed in part to weak regulation of providers; a fee-for-service payments system; and a fee schedule that allows providers to profit from drugs and the high-tech care results for insured patients receiving more complex care and from higher-level (hence more costly) providers. Wagstaff et al. (2007) found that China's new rural insurance scheme does not appear to have reduced the incidence of catastrophic health spending. They attribute this to exclusions, high deductibles, low reimbursement ceilings and similar supply responses to those seen in the urban setting. By contrast, Wagstaff and Yu (2007) found that supply-side interventions in rural China (including the introduction of treatment protocols and essential drug lists) reduced the incidence of catastrophic health spending.

Impoverishing expenditures

The basics

The catastrophic payment approach is limited by its failure to show the extent of the hardship caused by catastrophic payments. One household might spend more than 25% of its pre-payment income on health and yet be nowhere near the poverty line. Another might spend only 1% of its pre-payment income before crossing the poverty line. Impoverishment offers an alternative perspective – the core idea being that health-care expenses should push no one into (or further into) poverty.

A household may be classified as impoverished by out-of-pocket payments on medical care if pre-payment income (x in Fig. 2.4.1) lies above the poverty line (PL) and non-medical spending (NM_0) lies below (Wagstaff & van Doorslaer 2003). Comparison of the pre-payment poverty headcount (fraction of households where $x > PL$) and the post-payment poverty headcount (fraction of households where

$NM_0 < PL$) can indicate how far out-of-pocket payments cause impoverishment by identifying the fraction of the population that crosses the poverty line as a result of health expenditures. This approach does not capture how far people are pushed below the poverty line as a result of health spending or the possibility that health spending may push already poor households (in terms of their pre-payment discretionary income) into greater poverty. This can be established by comparing the pre-payment poverty gap (aggregate shortfall from poverty line using x as the living standards measure) with the post-payment poverty gap (aggregate shortfall from poverty line using NM_0 as the living standards measure).

Empirical studies

Wagstaff and van Doorslaer (2003) looked at health-care payments and poverty in Viet Nam in 1993 and 1998. Fig. 2.4.5 shows their pre-payment income Pen's parade for Viet Nam in 1998. This paint drip chart also shows households' out-of-pocket payments and a food-based poverty line. The difference between the pre-payment and post-payment poverty headcount is around 3.5% and the difference between the pre-payment and post-payment (normalized) poverty gaps is around 1%. In 1993, the difference between the pre-payment and post-payment poverty headcounts was 4.4%. This greater fall in the headcount for post-payment income reflects the fall in the share of income absorbed by health spending over this period in Viet Nam (Wagstaff 2002).

Results for rural China over the same period show a reduction in the difference between pre-payment and post-payment headcounts (Liu et al. 2003). However, Gustafsson and Li (2004) found the opposite in their analysis of changes between 1988 and 1995. The poverty headcount fell by 2.2% at the dollar-a-day poverty line when health expenditures were not deducted from disposable income; and by only 0.7% percentage points when they were. This reflects the fact that the share of income spent on health care increased in rural China during the period 1988–1995.

Two studies have looked at trends before and after the introduction of a reform. Limwattananon et al. (2007) found that impoverishment rates in Thailand were lower (but not zero) following the introduction of the universal health-care scheme in 2001. The failure to eliminate

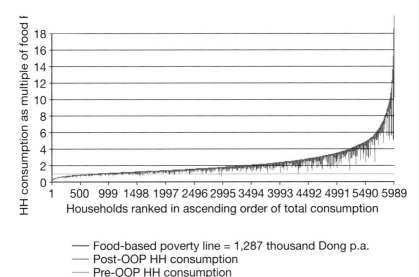

Fig. 2.4.5 Out-of-pocket payments and poverty in Viet Nam, 1998

Source: Wagstaff & van Doorslaer 2003.

impoverishment caused by out-of-pocket expenses is attributed to people who bypass their designated provider and thus make themselves unnecessarily liable for out-of-pocket payments and non-coverage of certain interventions, e.g. renal dialysis and chemotherapy. Knaul et al. (2006) report that the difference between the pre-payment and post-payment poverty gap narrowed following the introduction of the Popular Health Insurance scheme in Mexico.

Van Doorslaer et al. (2006) used data from eleven Asian countries to compare pre- and post-payment poverty headcounts and poverty gaps using the World Bank's dollar-a-day poverty line (as well as its US$ 2-a-day poverty line). On average, they found that the dollar-a-day poverty headcount is almost three percentage points higher when out-of-pocket spending is deducted from household consumption. The difference is almost four percentage points in Bangladesh and India but just 0.1 and 0.3 percentage points in Malaysia and Sri Lanka, respectively.

Alam et al. (2005) compared pre-payment and post-payment poverty headcounts in ten countries in eastern Europe and the former Soviet Union using a US$ 2.15-a-day poverty line at 2000 prices and purchasing power parities. On average, out-of-pocket payments raise the poverty headcount by 2% percentage points – Armenia (3.4), Georgia (3.6) and Tajikistan (3.3) recorded the highest increases. Interestingly, the average share of income spent on out-of-pocket health care payments is quite different in Armenia (around 12%) and Georgia (around 7%). However, the shares among the poorest and second poorest quintiles are quite similar at around 14% and 8%, respectively. The high incidence of impoverishment due to health-care spending in these countries likely reflects the collapse of publicly-financed health systems and increasing reliance on out-of-pocket payments, including informal ones. The rate in Armenia would probably have been even higher if the government's 2001 reform had not provided the services in the health insurance scheme's benefit package free of charge to households receiving social assistance.

Is health spending involuntary?

The catastrophe and impoverishment approaches outlined above make two key assumptions. The first is that health-care payments should be seen as involuntary and non-discretionary – the result of an unforeseen and unwanted shock and rarely the result of a deliberate choice by the individual concerned. In this view, health-care payments stand apart from other items of household consumption that contribute to household welfare or utility.

This view can be challenged as in some cases individuals may well have some discretion (at least at the margin) over health expenditures. However, generally it seems more reasonable to treat health spending as non-discretionary and to consider that it does not contribute to household welfare. This would exclude it from household spending in consumption aggregates used in studies of household living standards. Deaton and Zaidi (1999) reached a similar conclusion based partly on the low income elasticities of health spending they found in six of the seven developing countries they studied. Burtless and Siegel (2001) also argue for this approach in their discussion of proposals to take explicit account of health-care spending when computing poverty rates in the United States.

It seems reasonable to treat health expenditures as involuntary but the implied practice of excluding out-of-pocket spending from consumption aggregates for measuring poverty is often not followed. For example, the World Bank's official dollar-a-day poverty figures are based on measures of household consumption that include out-of-pocket spending on medical care. This produces poverty rates that are lower than they would be if out-of-pocket spending on medical care was treated as involuntary and excluded from the consumption aggregate (van Doorslaer et al. 2006).

Asset sales, dissaving and borrowing

The second assumption that underpins the catastrophe and impoverishment approaches is that a household's non-medical expenditure in the period under consideration would have increased by an amount equal to its out-of-pocket expenditures on medical care had it not incurred the out-of-pocket spending. In other words, it is assumed that the household was forced to finance the health spending entirely from its current non-medical consumption.

This assumption fails if the household is able to finance some (or all) of the expenditure by running down its stock of financial and physical assets (dissaving) or by borrowing. In both cases, current income (gross of proceeds of asset disposals and loans taken) is higher when medical costs are incurred than when they are not. Fig. 2.4.6 illustrates a household that spends M_0 on medical care and NM_0 on other things. If the household member needing medical care had not fallen ill, the household's income would have been x' not x. The difference between the two reflects the proceeds of asset sales or funds from a gift or loan. The drop in non-medical consumption caused by the use of medical care (ultimately the quantity of interest) is equal to the difference between x' and NM_0. This is less than out-of-pocket spending (M_0) in cases such as that illustrated in Fig. 2.4.6 when people are able to borrow or sell assets to reduce the impact of health spending on non-medical consumption. Indeed, it may well be that the household is completely able to smooth its non-medical consumption in the face of health shocks that necessitate health expenditure. In the case illustrated, x' and NM_0 coincide and the medical expenses cause no reduction in non-medical consumption. The household is only partially able to smooth non-medical consumption in the face of health shocks and non-medical consumption is cut back in the period when the health shock occurs. However, this reduction is less than the amount of the medical expenditure. The reduction in non-medical consumption equals the amount of health expenditures only in extreme cases when

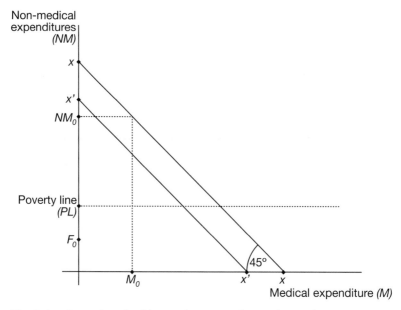

Fig. 2.4.6 Case where health spending is not financed out of current income
Source: Author

the household is unable to use savings or borrow, as illustrated in Fig.
2.4.1.

Empirical evidence suggests that people do prevent drops in non-
medical consumption by selling assets or borrowing. The World Health
Survey (WHS) asked how people finance their health expenditures
(http://www.who.int/healthinfo/survey/instruments/en/index.html).
Respondents were able to choose from the following sources: savings;
selling items; borrowing from relatives; borrowing from others; health
insurance; current income; and other. Fig. 2.4.7 shows the cumulative
percentages for a selection of countries; the y-axis would have been
700% if people had used all seven sources. It seems likely that people
in countries with pre-payment schemes financed from general revenues and no out-of-pocket payments would select none of the seven
options. These people are unlikely to consider that the pre-payment
scheme is insurance. This explains why South Africa and Sri Lanka
average less than 100%. The clear message from Fig. 2.4.7 and from
other surveys is that people borrow, sell assets and dissave to protect
their living standards in the face of health shocks that necessitate out-

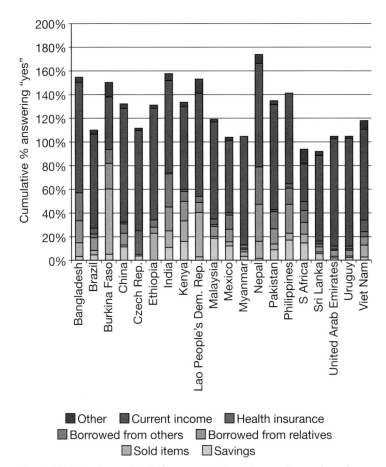

Fig. 2.4.7 How households finance their health spending, selected countries

Source: World Health Surveys (http://www.who.int/healthinfo/survey/whsresults/en/index.html)

of-pocket spending on care. The mix of strategies varies from country to country. Countries where asset disposals feature prominently are likely be those in which households find it difficult to get credit.

Whatever the sources used to protect living standards in the face of health shocks, it is important to allow for such strategies when estimating people's financial protection against health expenditures. Failure to do so will result in an overestimate of the extent to which health expenditures are catastrophic and impoverishing and an underestimate of the related degree of financial protection (provided by one method or another). As far as catastrophic spending is concerned, the numerator in Fig. 2.4.6 (originally M_0) should be replaced by the drop in non-medical consumption caused by the medical expenditure $(x'-NM_0)$ and the denominator (x) should be replaced by the amount of non-medical consumption that would have been enjoyed in the absence of the health shock (x'). For impoverishment, the pre-payment headcount should be assessed on the basis of x', rather than x, and the post-payment poverty headcount computed using observed non-medical consumption (NM_0). Further doubt is raised about including out-of-pocket payments in the consumption aggregate for measuring poverty when dissaving, asset sales and borrowing are factored in (van Doorslaer et al. 2006). Medical outlays financed largely by dissaving and borrowing may push a household above the poverty line when non-medical and medical expenditure is combined. A health financing reform that cuts out-of-pocket payments and reduces the need for households to dissave and borrow would actually increase measured poverty.

Modification of estimates of catastrophe and impoverishment to take account of dissaving, asset sales and borrowing requires an estimate of the counterfactual income (x') – a household's income in the absence of the health expenditures. The WHS is one of the few household surveys to ask how households financed their health expenditures. Questions about what was raised by selling assets or borrowing are asked sometimes in specialized vulnerability surveys but rarely in health surveys. The 1995 Indian National Sample Survey is an exception. In their analysis of the data, Flores et al. (2008) found heavy use of coping strategies including drawing down of savings, asset sales, borrowing and transfers. They found that such strategies finance three quarters of the cost of inpatient care in rural areas and two thirds in urban areas. They also find that these sources fully finance hospital costs in 52% of rural and 44% of urban households. Ignoring the use of coping strategies to protect current income suggests that 2.2% of rural Indian households incur catastrophic payments for inpatient care using a 5% threshold. This estimate is reduced to just 0.2% following the adjustments outlined above.

Flores et al. (2008) found similar dramatic differences for impoverishment in urban households. In rural areas, the poverty headcount for actual non-medical consumption (NM_0 in Fig. 2.4.6) is 39.45% and the headcount corresponding to the naive estimate of what non-medical consumption would have been in the absence of medical outlays

(x) is 8.94%. The naive approach would indicate that out-of-pocket payments have raised poverty dramatically. However, the headcount for what non-medical consumption would have been in the absence of medical outlays and factoring in people's coping strategies (x') is just 39.39%, barely different from the actual poverty rate.

These results indicate that households are generally able to smooth non-medical consumption in the face of large outlays on medical care. This appears at odds with the econometric literature that looks at the effects of health shocks on household non-medical consumption. Typically, that literature finds that households are unable to smooth consumption in the face of health shocks, at least large ones (Gertler & Gruber 2002; Wagstaff 2007). However, outlays on medical care are just one channel through which health shocks affect non-medical consumption. Losses in earned income (possibly offset at least in part by increases in unearned income) are another, possibly more important, channel and evidence suggests that households are unable to smooth consumption in the face of income shocks (Jalan & Ravallion 1999). Therefore, the two literatures are, in fact, not at odds with one another.

Intertemporal considerations

Flores et al. (2008) acknowledge that the argument in the previous section misses the fact that households incur costs to finance out-of-pocket payments. These costs should not be disregarded when measuring catastrophic and impoverishing payments. Households with insurance cover for out-of-pocket payments likely have reduced uncertainty about future expenditures and are able to hold their wealth in less liquid forms that offer higher returns. In addition, loans have to be repaid (possibly at very high interest rates) in subsequent periods and returns on assets and savings are lost when these have been sold or used.

Flores et al. (2008) provide an example of an Indian high-spending household in which per capita consumption is INR 6866 and inpatient out-of-pocket payments are INR 2760. The household finances these payments by borrowing INR 1020; drawing INR 823 from savings; and raising INR 298 from asset sales, INR 439 from other sources and INR 180 from current income. Flores et al. (2008) focus on the INR 180 financed from current income and ignore the other expenses.

They compute the coping-adjusted expense ratio by dividing 180 (sum financed by current income) by 4286 (6866 consumption less 2580 out-of-pocket payments financed through coping strategies). This is just 4%, one tenth of the conventional ratio of out-of-pocket spending divided by consumption (2760/6866=40%). Even for the current period, 4% is likely to underestimate the hardship caused by medical care costs – forgone returns accrue from the moment that assets and savings are cashed in and loan repayments are likely to start well within twelve months of the expenses being incurred. In any case, costs incurred beyond the current period should not simply be ignored.

What might the time path of expenses look like for this Indian household? Banerjee and Duflo (2007) report monthly interest rates of 3%–4% among India's poor. If the INR 1020 loan was repaid over three years at a 3.5% monthly interest rate then the household's annual repayments would be INR 607. Suppose that in the absence of medical-care expenses the household would have held the savings and assets for three years. If the INR 823 of savings and the INR 298 of assets earned 10% per annum then, on average, they would have produced combined annual returns of INR 129. Loan interest and lost returns give a total cost of INR 736 for each of the three years following the inpatient expenditure. This can be compared with the household's per capita consumption in the absence of the interest payments and forgone returns – INR 4842 (6866-2760+736). The ratio of 736 to 4842 is 15%, considerably less than the 40% produced by the naive calculation but a good deal higher than the 4% from the calculation above. For some thresholds this might be considered catastrophic. Obviously these calculations hinge on assumptions about the duration of the loan; loan interest rates; the number of years the assets and savings would have been held in the absence of the shock; and the interest that the household would have earned on them.

The example above provides a somewhat truer picture but still misses something. It overlooks the fact that households are likely to incur at least some medical outlays every year – possibly even quite high costs for several years in a row. So, while it is true that a health shock in year t may not cause a major drop in consumption in that year (if any) because the household borrows to finance the cost of medical care, it is also possible that the household may already be paying off a loan for a previous health shock in year t-2. This is more likely to be the case if health expenditures are highly correlated across years at the household level, i.e. if households that incur expenditures in one year are more likely to incur expenditures in subsequent years.

The rank correlation for health expenditures over the five years between the two waves of the Viet Nam 1993-98 Living Standards Measurement Study panel is 0.36. This is lower than the rank correlation for non-medical consumption (0.66) but still quite high.[2] Over the two years between the two waves of the China panel used by Wagstaff et al. (2007) the rank correlation for medical outlays at household level is 0.31, compared to 0.66 for household income. With correlations of this size, episodes of coping with expenses incurred following health shocks will likely overlap. In the example of the Indian household given above this might require the estimated interest payments and forgone returns for the INR 2760 medical bill to be added to similar charges incurred earlier. Thus, Flores et al's (2008) 15% figure is likely to be an underestimate of the hardship caused by medical bills, possibly a considerable underestimate.

Conclusions

There has been a good deal of progress in designing and implementing measures of financial protection in health but, perhaps inevitably, the work is incomplete. One major challenge concerns how to take account of how people finance their medical outlays and when they incur the costs. The recent literature (Flores et al. 2008) is right to reiterate that, contrary to what is assumed by the naive approach used to date, households may not experience much of a drop in living standards during the period in which the outlays are made. However, households do have to make sacrifices at some stage. Borrowing allows the sacrifice to be deferred and spread over multiple periods, although interest rates will add to the bill. Furthermore, households are unlikely to incur out-of-pocket payments on a one-off basis and more likely to incur at least some expenses every year. A household may have to borrow to finance a medical care bill precisely because it has not yet repaid the loan that financed earlier charges. The challenge is to move from the snapshot approach that assumes that outlays entail

---

[2] Author's calculation from the Viet Nam 1993 and 1998 Living Standards Measurement Study data.

consumption sacrifices in the period in which they are incurred to an intertemporal approach that takes account of the (possibly quite different) time paths of outlays and forgone consumption.

The naive approach assumes that consumption drops pari passu with medical outlays and is therefore likely to underestimate the hardship caused by out-of-pocket spending. However, it remains useful as it has the merit of capturing the amount of money that households must find (one way or another) and relating this to their standard of living. Furthermore, it can be implemented with a standard household expenditure or multipurpose survey. By contrast, the alternative approach focuses (purportedly) on costs incurred in the current period and ignores those incurred in other periods. For this reason, and because it overlooks the fact that some costs (e.g. forgone returns on assets and loan repayments) are likely to be incurred in the period in which the medical bills are incurred, it is likely to provide a lower, possibly highly conservative, bound.

Subject to the caveats associated with the naive methods of measuring financial protection, some general points emerge from the empirical literature. Financial protection in health appears to vary across countries, partly reflecting the role of per capita income. On average, higher rates of catastrophic payments are found in poorer countries and therefore those who can least afford large out-of-pocket payments for health care are at greatest risk. However, differences exist across countries at a given per capita income. These appear to reflect income inequality and also the extent to which health-care payments are pre-paid through some form of insurance.

The roles of insurance, pre-payment and other forms of financial protection emerge from country studies. Expansion of insurance coverage tends to reduce the incidence of catastrophic spending and impoverishment, while a reduction in the depth of coverage has tended to be associated with higher rates. As expected, ceilings on out-of-pocket payments reduce the incidence of catastrophic spending. But there are caveats. Studies point to a variety of factors that together influence the degree to which insurance influences financial protection.

- Insurance tends to increase the quantity of care received and puts upward pressure on out-of-pocket payments.
- Some benefit packages are not especially generous, with high deductibles, high coinsurance rates, low reimbursement ceilings

and multiple exclusions (for example, drugs which often use a large share of household health spending).

- Providers may not be properly compensated by third-party payers. They may look to informal payments to make up lost income and may be unable to procure drugs on the terms offered by the third-party payer.

In China, recent research suggests that supply-side interventions (treatment protocols, drug lists, and so on) have had more success in improving financial protection than expansion of insurance coverage. This reinforces the point made earlier in this chapter – policy-makers have a variety of instruments available to increase financial protection in health. Insurance coverage is just one important instrument and it may not be the most effective for all applications.

References

Alam, A. Murthi, M. Yemtsov, R. Murrugarra, E. Dudwick, N. Hamilton, E. Tiongson, E (2005). *Growth, poverty, and inequality: eastern Europe and the former Soviet Union.* Washington, DC: World Bank.

Banerjee, AV. Duflo, E (2007). 'The economic lives of the poor.' *Journal of Economic Perspectives*, 21(1): 141–167.

Burtless, G. Siegel, S (2001). *Medical spending, health insurance, and measurement of American poverty.* Washington, DC: Brookings Institution (CSED Working Paper No. 22).

Deaton, A. Zaidi, S (1999). *Guidelines for constructing consumption aggregates for welfare analysis.* Princeton, NJ: Princeton University Woodrow Wilson School of Public and International Affairs (Research Program in Development Studies Working Paper No. 192).

De Graeve, D. van Ourti, T (2003). 'The distributional impact of health financing in Europe: a review.' *World Economy*, 26(10): 1459–1479.

Devadasan, N. Criel, B. Van Damme, W. Ranson, K. Van der Stuyft, P (2007). 'Indian community health insurance schemes provide partial protection against catastrophic health expenditure.' *BMC Health Services Research*, 7: 43.

Ekman, B (2007). 'Catastrophic health payments and health insurance: some counterintuitive evidence from one low-income country.' *Health Policy*, 83(2–3): 304–313.

Flores, G. Krishnakumar, J. O Donnell, O. van Doorslaer, E (2008). 'Coping with health-care costs: implications for the measurement of catastrophic expenditures and poverty.' *Health Economics*, 17(12): 1393–1412.

Gakidou, E. Lozano, R. Gonzalez-Pier, E. Abbott-Klafter, J. Barofsky, JT. Bryson-Cahn, C. Feehan, DM. Lee, DK. Hernandez-Llamas, H. Murray, CJL (2006). 'Health system reform in Mexico 5 – assessing the effect of the 2001–06 Mexican health reform: an interim report card.' *Lancet*, 368(9550): 1920–1935.

Gertler, P. Gruber, J (2002). 'Insuring consumption against illness.' *American Economic Review*, 92(1): 51–76.

Gustafsson, B. Li, S (2004). 'Expenditures on education and health care and poverty in rural China'. *China Economic Review*, 15(3): 292–301.

Habicht, J. Xu, K. Couffinhal, A. Kutzin, J (2006). 'Detecting changes in financial protection: creating evidence for policy in Estonia.' *Health Policy and Planning*, 21(6): 421–431.

Jalan, J. Ravallion, M (1999). 'Are the poor less well insured? Evidence on vulnerability to income risk in rural China.' *Journal of Development Economics*, 58(1): 61–81.

Knaul, FM. Arreola-Ornelas, H. Mendez-Carniado, O. Bryson-Cahn, C. Barofsky, J. Maguire, R. Miranda, M. Sesma, S (2006). 'Health system reform in Mexico 4. Evidence is good for your health system: policy reform to remedy catastrophic and impoverishing health spending in Mexico.' *Lancet*, 368(9549): 1828–1841.

Limwattananon, S. Tangcharoensathien, V. Prakongsai, P (2007). 'Catastrophic and poverty impacts of health payments: results from national household surveys in Thailand.' *Bulletin of the World Health Organization*, 85(8): 600–606.

Liu, Y. Rao, K. Hsiao, WC (2003). 'Medical expenditure and rural impoverishment in China.' *Journal of Health Population and Nutrition*, 21(3): 216–222.

Narayan, D. Chambers, R. Shah, MK. Petesch, P (2000). *Voices of the poor: crying out for change*. New York, NY: Oxford University Press.

Narayan, D. Patel, R. Schafft, K. Rademacher, A. Koch-Schulte, S (2000a). *Voices of the poor: can anyone hear us?* New York, NY: Oxford University Press.

Van Doorslaer, E. O Donnell, O. Rannan-Eliya, RP. Somanathan, A. Adhikari, SR. Garg, CC. Harbianto, D. Herrin, AN. Huq, MN. Ibragimova, S. Karan, A. Ng, CW. Pande, BR. Racelis, R. Tao, S. Tin, K. Tisayaticom, K. Trisnantoro, L. Vasavid, C. Zhao, Y (2006). 'Effect of payments for health care on poverty estimates in 11 countries in Asia: an analysis of household survey data.' *Lancet*, 368(9544): 1357–1364.

Van Doorslaer, E. O Donnell, O. Rannan-Eliya, RP. Somanathan, A. Adhikari, SR. Garg, CC. Harbianto, D. Herrin, AN. Huq, MN. Ibragimova, S.

Karan, A. Lee, TJ. Leung, GM. Lu, JF. Ng, CW. Pande, BR. Racelis, R. Tao, S. Tin, K. Tisayaticom, K. Trisnantoro, L. Visasvid, C. Zhao, Y (2007). 'Catastrophic payments for health care in Asia'. *Health Economics*, 16(11): 1159–1184.

Wagstaff, A (2002). 'Reflections on and alternatives to WHO's fairness of financial contribution index.' *Health Economics*, 11(2): 103–115.

Wagstaff, A (2007). *Health insurance for the poor: initial impacts of Vietnam's health care fund for the poor*. Washington, DC: World Bank (Impact Evaluation Series no. 11. Policy Research Working Paper No. WPS 4134).

Wagstaff, A (2007a). 'The economic consequences of health shocks: evidence from Vietnam.' *Journal of Health Economics*, 26(1): 82–100.

Wagstaff, A. Lindelow, M (2008). 'Can insurance increase financial risk? The curious case of health insurance in China.' *Journal of Health Economics*, 27(4): 990–1005.

Wagstaff, A. Pradhan, M (2005). *Health insurance impacts on health and nonmedical consumption in a developing country*. Washington, DC: World Bank (Policy Research Working Paper No. 3563).

Wagstaff, A. van Doorslaer, E (2003). 'Catastrophe and impoverishment in paying for health care: with applications to Vietnam 1993–1998.' *Health Economics*, 12(11): 921–934.

Wagstaff, A. Yu, S (2007). 'Do health sector reforms have their intended impacts? The World Bank's Health VIII project in Gansu province, China.' *Journal of Health Economics*, 26(3): 505–535.

Wagstaff, A. Lindelow, M. Gao, J. Xu, L. Qian, J (2007). *Extending health insurance to the rural population: an impact evaluation of China's new cooperative medical scheme*. Washington, DC: World Bank (Impact Evaluation Series no. 12. Policy Research Working Paper No. WPS 4150).

Waters, HR. Anderson, GF. Mays, J (2004). 'Measuring financial protection in health in the United States.' *Health Policy*, 69(3): 339–349.

Xu, K. Evans, DB. Kawabata, K. Zeramdini, R. Klavus, J. Murray, CJ (2003). 'Household catastrophic health expenditure: a multicountry analysis.' *Lancet*, 362(9378): 111–117.

Xu, K. Evans, DB. Kadama, P. Nabyonga, J. Ogwal, PO. Nabukhonzo, P. Aguilar, AM (2006). 'Understanding the impact of eliminating user fees: utilization and catastrophic health expenditures in Uganda.' *Social Science & Medicine*, 62(4): 866–876.

Xu, K. Evans, DB. Carrin, G. Aguilar-Rivera, AM. Musgrove, P. Evans, T (2007). 'Protecting households from catastrophic health spending.' *Health Affairs (Project Hope)*, 26(4): 972–983.

2.5 Health systems responsiveness: a measure of the acceptability of health-care processes and systems from the user's perspective

NICOLE VALENTINE, AMIT PRASAD,
NIGEL RICE, SILVANA ROBONE,
SOMNATH CHATTERJI

Introduction

The World Health Organization (WHO) developed and proposed the concept of responsiveness, defining it as aspects of the way individuals are treated and the environment in which they are treated during health system interactions (Valentine et al. 2003). The concept covers a set of non-clinical and non-financial dimensions of quality of care that reflect respect for human dignity and interpersonal aspects of the care process, which Donabedian (1980) describes as "the vehicle by which technical care is implemented and on which its success depends". Eight dimensions (or domains) are collectively described as goals for health-care processes and systems (along with the goals of higher average health and lower health inequalities; and non-impoverishment – as measured through other indicators): (i) dignity, (ii) autonomy, (iii) confidentiality, (iv) communication, (v) prompt attention, (vi) quality (of) basic amenities, (vii) access to social support networks during treatment (social support), and (viii) choice (of health-care providers).

Building on extensive previous work, this chapter directs the conceptual and methodological aspects of the responsiveness work in three new directions. First, the given and defined domains (Valentine et al. 2007) are used to link responsiveness (conceptually and empirically) to the increasingly important health system concepts of access to care and equity in access. The concept of equity used in this chapter was defined by a WHO working group with experts on human rights, ethics and equity. It is defined as the absence of avoidable or remediable differences among populations or groups defined socially, economically, demographically or geographically (WHO 2005). Health inequities involve more than inequality – whether in health determinants or outcomes, or in access to the resources needed to improve and maintain health. They also represent a failure to avoid or overcome such inequality which infringes human rights norms or is otherwise unfair. Second, it expands on the issue of measurement strategies. Third, the psychometric results of the responsiveness module from the WHS are compared with its survey instrument predecessor in the Multi-country Survey (MCS) Study.

The chapter concludes with analysis of the most recent results for responsiveness from the WHS for ambulatory and inpatient health-care services for sixty-five countries (with special reference to subsets of European countries) to see how European countries' health-care systems perform with respect to responsiveness.

Responsiveness operationalized as a population health concept

Responsiveness is measured using criteria related to the importance of users' views. Individuals who use (or decide not to use) the health-care system are viewed as the appropriate source of information on non-technical aspects of care. This approach implies measuring responsiveness through household or other types of user surveys rather than, for example, expert opinion or facility audits.

Concepts such as quality of life and general satisfaction are also measured in surveys. However, self-reports have the additional criterion that they should be linked to one or several actual experiences with health services in the respondent's recent past (previous year) and upon which they base their views. These experiences are usually based on some type of interaction with the health-care system including interaction with a specific person in that system; a communication campaign; or another type of health system event or action that did not entail direct personal interactions. This criterion places the focus on what actually happened during contact with the health-care system, rather than the respondent's satisfaction or expectations of the health-care system in general.

WHO (2000) broadly defines the health-care system as: 'all actions whose primary intent is to produce health'. The responsiveness measure proposed by WHO conceptually aims to measure the responsiveness of the *whole health-care system* to the *whole population* (Murray

& Frenk 2000). When the self-report measurement approach based on the criterion of an actual (recent) experience is combined with the concept of measuring the *whole* population's experience of the *whole* health-care system then the measurement challenges are multiplied. We outline aspects of these challenges below.

Spheres of health events

Seven different types of health events that require interactions with health-care systems or services are listed below. The list is intended to be relevant generically, regardless of the configuration of providers, financing, technology, medicines and human resources:

1. ambulatory care in response to acute needs;
2. ambulatory care for chronic conditions;
3. inpatient care for short-term stays (>24 hours; <3 months);
4. long-term institutionalized care e.g. for populations with mental illnesses, disabilities related to physical health conditions or elderly populations;
5. non-excludable public health interventions e.g. public health promotion for communities or population groups such as access to improved water and sanitation, smoking bans;
6. opportunities for participation in health system governance e.g. shaping the health system and issues affecting health;
7. administrative and financial transactions: e.g. ease of making payments for services and medicines or of obtaining medicines with prescriptions, receiving reimbursement from insurance if needed.

This list illustrates that the design of questions in household or user surveys and the actual survey coverage would require significant work to cover the entire typology of interactions and abide by the criterion of obtaining user reports. For example, individuals receiving long-term institutionalized care cannot respond to household surveys and require more targeted designs. Also, questions may need to be tailored to the specific institutional arrangements of services (including insurance coverage) for a particular country, region or sector.

Roles of the users

Given that the health-care system is a socially constructed system, individuals' interactions with that system will differ according to circumstances. These can be categorized into four non-mutually exclusive groupings. For any given time period, a single survey respondent may have experiences of interactions that relate to all, none or some of these roles:

a. a patient or user (with or without personal contact);
b. a patient or user *by proxy* e.g. chiefly for children, but also for people with mental illness or elderly persons;
c. a relative or close friend of a patient;
d. a member of society who uses health services but has not done so in the defined period of the previous year, and who has some ability to shape the structure of health institutions. This citizen role is facilitated by the mechanisms for social participation in decision-making on health.

Combining health events and user roles – interactions

The full range of interactions combines user roles and different types of health events. When these are stated explicitly they help policy-makers to understand which aspects of responsiveness they are most interested in capturing. A strategy to measure all these combinations of interactions and user roles would need to identify the most important in order to avoid overburdening respondents. This breadth of responsiveness is operationally challenging and to date has not been undertaken systematically in any country. Nevertheless, from a heuristic point of view, it is important to observe the potential implications of a concept if operationalized fully. It is also vital to decide whether measurement is necessary for all domains of responsiveness or a more limited set. WHO designed the WHS responsiveness instrument to cover interactions represented by the combination of events and user roles matching the alphanumeric labels listed above - 1ab, 2ab, 3ab, and 6d (involvement in decision-making only).

Responsiveness and equity in access

The link between responsiveness and equity in access is important. It derives from the impact of service qualities described by the responsiveness domains on utilization patterns. An explicit framework that describes how responsiveness is linked to access to care via the care context and process can inform empirical work aimed at describing responsiveness across countries. Fig. 2.5.1 presents such a framework that builds on other frameworks in the literature covering the medical-care process (Donabedian 1973); access to care (Aday & Andersen 1974; Tanahashi 1978); utilization (Andersen 1995; Bradley et al. 2002); and the conceptual framework proposed to the Commission on Social Determinants of Health (Solar & Irwin 2007).

The framework has three broad components: (i) environment; (ii) agents defining need for care; and (iii) process of care and outcomes (Fig 2.5.1). The first two components delineate context and together define the need for care at the population level. Their development was informed by the Aday and Andersen framework (1974) of 'health policy'; 'population characteristics'; 'health service characteristics'; and 'utilization', with some adaptations. For example, the decision-making agents component in the Fig. 2.5.1 framework draws attention to the role of both providers and users in defining need and setting the context for utilization. It evokes three agency groupings: (i) providers and their accepted protocols (which may differ across countries); lay persons (with their socially accepted protocols/norms); and the specific epidemiological or biological agents which produce different responses from the other two groups of decision-makers.

Recognition of the separate groupings of providers and lay persons is an important innovation that was raised in the Solar and Irwin (2007) framework and the work of the Health Systems Knowledge Network of the Commission on Social Determinants of Health (Gilson et al. 2007). This distinction is important for understanding the context in which responsiveness is measured and the implications for policy discussions. Responsiveness reports on convenience of access or confidentiality will reflect different profiles of services which have been negotiated by decision-making groups in society. For example, midwives in one country may make home visits that are not part of population health needs in another. Differences are to be expected and

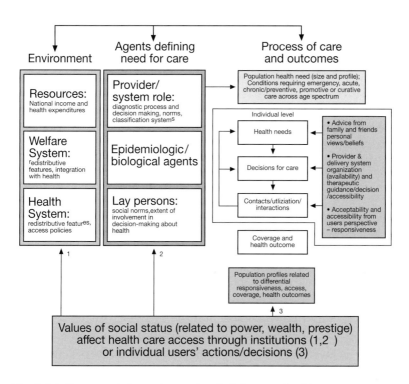

Fig. 2.5.1 Framework for understanding link between health system responsiveness and equity in access

may provide explanations for varying responsiveness across countries. However, it is important that these factors are explicit in analytical frameworks in order to understand how to improve responsiveness across different countries.

The third component of the framework is most relevant to the measurement of responsiveness – the process of care and outcomes. An individual who has a specific need for care moves from (a) recognition of health needs, to (b) decisions for care, to (c) contact with the system/utilization, and to (d) coverage. The latter is defined as the single, multiple or perpetual contacts to ensure adherence that may be required to guarantee adequate care for a particular condition (adapted from Tanahashi 1978). Care-seekers' decisions related to utilization and the possible achievement of full coverage (explained below) for a particular condition are influenced by three broad factors shown in Fig. 2.5.1: (i) the *personal* context (advice from family and friends, personal beliefs); (ii) *providers* (administering therapeutic guidelines/decisions, organization of delivery e.g. being able to see a general doctor or specialist directly); and (iii) the health system's capacity to be responsive. The responsiveness domains mostly relate to Tanahashi's (1978) definitions of accessible (users able to reach and use health services) and acceptable care or coverage (users willing to use accessible services).

The concept of full coverage is introduced into the framework as coverage, although this term is used infrequently in the traditional access literature (except Tanahashi 1978 and, more recently, Shengelia et al. 2005). It usefully communicates the concept of a norm related to interventions for particular conditions. This differs from utilization rates for which high or low values indicate only the use of health-care resources without explicit reference to norms or need related to particular conditions. Health outcomes are affected by the extent of coverage reached and may not be affected by utilization rates. Of course, there is room for both concepts in the same framework as utilization rates for which the vulnerability of the population group is proxied (e.g. by income) do give some indication of the resources consumed relative to need.

The literature does make reference to definitions of coverage at population and individual levels. Shengalia et al. (2005) define *effective* coverage at the individual level as 'the fraction of maximum possible health gain an individual with a health care need can expect to receive from the health system.' Tanahashi (1978) refers to a population level measure of coverage as 'the number of people for whom the service has satisfied certain criteria relating to its intended health intervention, compared with the total target population.'

The third component of the framework also shows the links between responsiveness and equity in access. Responsiveness affects access at the individual level first. Responsiveness that is systematically worse for certain social groups with the same or greater need than other social groups could lead to inequities in access. These are defined as arising when anticipated, perceived or actual responsiveness attributes of the service dissuade certain social groups from seeking and receiving adequate care.[1] By adapting Tanahashi's (1978) population-level definition of coverage to the individual level, 'adequate care' would refer

[1] Definition suggested by Elias Mossialos, who commented on the draft chapter.

to services striving to meet a predefined technical norm in response to a variety of health conditions (completion of treatment; or continued, on-going treatment for chronic or palliative cases). Given this relationship between responsiveness, equity in responsiveness and equity in access, it is possible to use measures of responsiveness inequalities by different social groups (stratified according to need, e.g. proxied by income) to anticipate inequities in access.

Equity considerations for responsiveness survey design

A service that is perceived to have poor responsiveness may not be used optimally (or even at all) or as required by the health condition. Yet responsiveness measurement needs to be based on actual interactions. Thus, one weakness of the measurement approach is that measures will be biased upwards. This is not only because self-reports of this nature are usually biased upwards (see Ware & Hays 1988) but also because they do not fully capture the experiences of respondents who are in need but have not used services recently. Responsiveness measurement will not record the experience of care of someone who is excluded from care by failing to initiate (Aday & Andersen 1974) or obtain contact with the system (Tanahashi 1978).

Fig. 2.5.2 illustrates how populations may be excluded, with reference to two types of problems. In some cases, populations may not have sought care in the defined time period due to responsiveness or other factors e.g. financial barriers. These denied users would be excluded by screening questions on when they last came into contact with a health service. In other cases, the very nature of their vulnerability (e.g. homelessness) may put certain populations beyond the reach of traditional survey techniques. In both instances, surveys will be biased upwards and potentially underestimate inequalities in responsiveness. For the first problem, denied users can be asked about the barriers to care in order to gain qualitative information on the responsiveness measures. The second problem will require special survey efforts (e.g. surveys of institutionalized, homeless or migratory populations).

Special consideration should be given to the inclusion of service contacts with children as exposures at early stages of the life course have not only equity impacts that transmit into adulthood, but also intergenerational consequences. Minors cannot report for themselves but reporting by parents has been shown to be effective. This was used

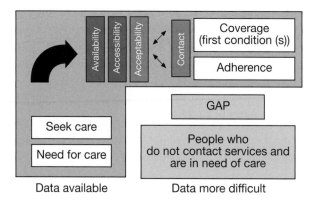

Fig. 2.5.2 Traditional survey methods omit data from certain population groups, overestimating responsiveness

Source: WHO & EQUINET (forthcoming)

for children up to the age of twelve in the WHS, as recommended by experts (WHO 2001).

Some critics have argued for special attention for sicker populations (Blendon et al. 2003) to ensure equity and because they know the services better. A strategy focusing on the sick may use health-facility exit-based surveys rather than household surveys, although this approach may omit those who have not used health services.

Responsiveness questionnaires

The responsiveness domains were derived from existing patient questionnaires and studies as reported in the extensive literature review conducted by De Silva (2000). This review profiled the questionnaire work undertaken by the AHRQ, Harvard Medical School, the Research Triangle Institute and the RAND Corporation. None of the existing questionnaires and studies captured all the dimensions that they covered collectively. WHO developed an instrument (questionnaire) that covered the collection of dimensions (described in the literature review) related to non-technical aspects of the process of care: dignity, autonomy, communication, confidentiality, prompt attention (related to convenience and peace of mind rather than urgent medical attention), quality of basic amenities, access to social support networks during treatment (labelled 'social support' in the MCS Study

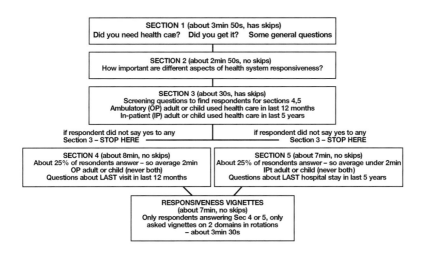

Fig. 2.5.3 Responsiveness questionnaire as a module in the WHS questionnaire: interview structure and timing

and 'access to family and community support' in the WHS) and choice (of health-care providers).

WHO's responsiveness questionnaire has been developed and refined. Questions (items) were initially fielded in a key informants' survey of thirty-five countries and the results described in *The world health report 2000* (WHO 2000). A household survey instrument which included pre-testing was then developed as part of the MCS Study covering sixty countries (Ustun et al. 2001; Valentine et al. 2007). Following the launch of the MCS Study, the concept of responsiveness and the questionnaire were refined and a revised instrument was included in the WHS implemented across seventy countries in 2002–2003.

The WHS basic survey mode used an in-person interview conducted in one of three possible forms: ninety-minute in-household interview (fifty-three countries) (long-form); thirty-minute face-to-face interview (short-form) (thirteen countries); or computer-assisted telephone interview. Samples were randomly selected (those above eighteen years) resulting in sizes of between 600 and 10 000 for each country surveyed. Descriptive statistics about individuals sampled in each country are reported in Annex 2. Data collection was performed on a modular basis, addressing different aspects of health and the health system and including information on health insurance, health expenditures, socio-demographics and income, health state valuations, health system responsiveness and health system goals (Üstün et al. 2003). Fig. 2.5.3 provides an overview of the responsiveness module in the WHS. The measurement of responsiveness was obtained by asking respondents to rate their most recent experience of contact with the health system within each of the eight domains by responding to the set of questions listed in Fig. 2.5.4. The response categories available were very good, good, moderate, bad and very bad.

Like health, responsiveness is viewed as a multidimensional concept. Each domain is measured as a categorical variable for which there is an assumed underlying latent scale. Certain domains are more suited to patient evaluation, e.g. quality of basic amenities and prompt attention. In contrast, it is more difficult to evaluate whether full details of the nature of an illness and all relevant treatments and available options have been disclosed as this requires specialist knowledge. Accordingly, it is more problematic to maintain objectivity in the evaluation of some domains. Samples have undergone extensive quality assurance pro-cedures at data collection stage at country and inter-country levels.

The MCS Study and WHS modules on responsiveness have strong similarities. However, they have a number of different ways of expanding coverage and alleviating the burden on survey respondents. More notable changes in the WHS include: more face-to-face interviews or computer-assisted telephone interviews (MCS Study included twenty-eight postal surveys); eliciting the experiences of children up to twelve (reported through a parent); and reducing the number of items that individuals are required to respond to on each domain. The WHS module also tried to identify barriers to access by asking people if they needed care and, if so, whether they sought care or why they did not (Fig. 2.5.3 section 1). The analyses that follow focus on the questions asked in sections four and five of the responsiveness module and cover the ambulatory and hospital (inpatient) experiences of adult and child populations.

Fig. 2.5.4 Operationalization of responsiveness domains in the WHS

Responsiveness domain label (short description)	Item questions
Prompt attention (convenient travel and short waiting times)	How would you rate: 1- travelling time to the hospital 2- time you waited before being attended to[b]
Dignity (respectful treatment and communication)	How would you rate: 1- being greeted and talked to respectfully[a] 2- respect for privacy during physical examinations and treatments[a,b]
Communication (clarity of communication)	How would you rate: 1- how clearly health-care providers explained things to you[a] 2- the time you get to ask questions about your health problems or treatment[a,b]
Autonomy (involvement in decisions)	How would you rate: 1- being involved in making decisions about your health care or treatment[a] 2- the information you get about other types of treatments or tests[b]
Confidentiality (confidentiality of personal information)	How would you rate the way: 1- health services ensured you could talk privately to health-care providers[a] 2- your personal information was kept confidential[a,b]
Choice (choice of health-care provider)	How would you rate: 1- your freedom to choose the health-care providers that attended to you
Quality of basic amenities (surroundings)	How would you rate: 1- cleanliness of the rooms inside the facility, including toilets[a] 2- amount of space you had[a,b]
Access to family and community support (contact with outside world and maintenance of regular activities)	How would you rate: 1- ease of having family and friends visit you 2- experience of staying in contact with the outside world when you were in hospital[a,b]

[a] Similar items appear in the MCS Study
[b] Item omitted from short version of WHS

Psychometric properties of the responsiveness domain questions

Psychometrics examines the quality of survey instruments and has been used extensively to assess the quality of the responsiveness instrument in both the MCS Study and the WHS. This section briefly considers three key desirable properties of a survey instrument (feasibility, reliability, validity) and compares them in the MCS Study and the WHS. The results on these properties are presented in combination for ambulatory and home care (as ambulatory care) and separately for inpatients. A more detailed description of the psychometric properties of the MCS Study is provided by Valentine et al. (2003a & 2007).

Feasibility

Feasibility refers to the ease of administering an instrument in the field and can be assessed by considering factors such as survey response rates, the proportion of missing items in a respondent interview (inappropriate missing responses) and item missing rates (percentage of respondents who omitted a particular item). The literature provides little indication of an acceptable survey response or inappropriate response missing rates but, in general, guidance indicates that item missing rates below 20% can be considered acceptable (Valentine et al. 2007; WHO 2005a).

Survey response rates measured as a percentage of attempted and effective contacts were available only for the MCS. The comparison of reliability between the two surveys rests mainly on interview completion (a form of survey response rates) and item missing rates. It is important to note that interview completion rates may be as high as 100% as they give the number of persons who started and completed interviews as a percentage of the number of persons who started interviews.

The MCS Study shows high measures of feasibility with a response completion rate greater than 95% for each of the countries considered, except Colombia (73%). Furthermore, no country exceeded a 20% item missing rate and only three countries had item missing rates in excess of 10% (Switzerland, Turkey, Tobago). Valentine et al. (2007) provide full results of the psychometric properties of the MCS

Table 2.5.1 *Item missing rates, ambulatory care (%)*

	MCS Study	WHS
Prompt attention	0.86	1.72
Dignity	1.13	1.75
Communication	0.55	0.38
Autonomy	2.70	2.03
Confidentiality	6.40	2.43
Choice	7.50	3.25
Quality of basic amenities	2.30	3.25
Average	3.06	2.12

Study. A similar analysis of the responsiveness instrument in the WHS showed that response completion rates per country were greater than 80% for all countries except Israel (63%). No country exceeded the accepted item missing rate threshold of 20% for ambulatory care and only Swaziland exceeded this threshold for inpatient care.

Additional information on the feasibility of the WHS responsiveness instrument is provided by the percentage of respondents that report missing values for zero; one; two; or three or more items. In countries where the long-form questionnaire was implemented, in responses on ambulatory care 88% of respondents reported no missing items; 6% reported one; 2% reported two and 4% reported three or more. Corresponding values for inpatient care were 87%, 5%, 1% and 7%. In countries where the short-form questionnaire was implemented, in responses for ambulatory care 87% returned no missing items, 11% reported one, 3% reported two and 2% reported three or more. The corresponding figures for inpatient care are 81%, 11%, 4% and 4%.

Table 2.5.1 offers a more direct comparison of the item missing rates. The values for the MCS Study are taken from Valentine et al. (2007) and consider only the forty-one countries in which interviewer administered interviews were held, corresponding to the method used in the WHS. Item missing rates are provided for ambulatory care by domain (calculated as the arithmetic mean of missing rates of individual items present in a domain) by averaging across countries. As can be seen, the WHS reported lower item missing rates for four of the seven domains and failed to exceed 3.25% in any domain. Averaged across countries and domains, the overall missing item rate in the WHS is nearly 1% lower than that in the MCS Study.

Reliability

The reliability of an instrument refers to the test-retest property of measurement, usually over time, all other things being equal. Temporal reliability can be measured using the kappa statistic. Landis and Koch (1977) suggest that statistics in the range 0.41–0.60 indicate moderate reproducibility; 0.61–0.80 substantial reproducibility and 0.81–1.00 almost perfect reproducibility.

Instrument reliability in the MCS Study was assessed by re-administering the entire responsiveness questionnaire to respondents in ten country sites one month after the initial interview. There is high reliability of all items by domain when averaged across the countries (see Valentine et al. 2007). The lowest kappa value reported for any domain was 0.64 (for dignity in home care). However, there is variability in reliability when results are averaged across domains within countries. Reproducibility is substantial in five countries, moderate in three and low in two.

The reliability of the WHS instrument was assessed by re-interviewing 10% of the original sample in each country. The re-interviewed respondents were selected randomly and asked to complete the follow-up questionnaire one to seven days after the first interview (Üstün et al. 2005). We consider reliability in fifty-three countries for ambulatory care and fifty-five countries for inpatient care where sufficient data points (>20) were available in the follow-up survey. When the kappa statistics are averaged across items within countries, at least moderate reliability was reported for ambulatory care in twenty-four countries and for inpatient care in twenty-seven countries. When results are averaged across countries for each item separately all items satisfy at least the condition for moderate reproducibility.

Table 2.5.2 compares kappa statistics for the MCS Study and the WHS. The kappa statistic is provided for each domain, averaged across countries and overall for countries and domains. The first and second columns in Table 2.5.2 show kappa statistics averaged across the ten countries in the MCS Study and the fifty-three countries of the WHS in which the responsiveness instrument was re-administered to respon-

Table 2.5.2 *Reliability in MCS Study and WHS*

	MCS+ (10 countries)	WHS (53 countries)	MCS+ (India, China)	WHS (India, China)
Prompt attention	0.60	0.49	0.66	0.73
Dignity	0.61	0.45	0.69	0.71
Communication	0.57	0.45	0.67	0.73
Autonomy	0.65	0.46	0.71	0.70
Confidentiality	0.59	0.45	0.74	0.71
Choice	0.63	0.40	0.75	0.72
Quality of basic amenities	0.65	0.44	0.71	0.72

+*Source*: Valentine et al. 2007

dents. When considering all available countries, the kappa statistics are considerably lower for the WHS. However, this does not provide a like-for-like comparison. Consideration of the two countries common to both surveys (India and China) provided in columns three and four indicates very similar comparisons of reliability in each survey.

Psychometric measures can also be investigated where data are stratified by population groups of interest. This allows an assessment of whether any revealed systematic variations suggest caution in interpreting results or indicate a need for greater testing before a survey is implemented.

We investigated the reliability of the WHS responsiveness instrument across European countries for two population groups defined by educational tenure. Table 2.5.3 presents average kappa statistics for each domain separately for western European countries and those of Central and Eastern Europe and the former Soviet Union (CEE/FSU) (listed in Annex 1). Results are further presented by level of educational tenure (defined as people having studied for either more or less than twelve years). Table 2.5.3a and Table 2.5.3b report results for ambulatory care and inpatient care, respectively. Overall, the reliability of the responsiveness instrument appears to be greater in CEE/FSU countries than in western European countries, irrespective of levels of education.

Table 2.5.3a *Reliability across European countries: ambulatory care*

	Western Europe		CEE/FSU		Europe overall	
	Education		Education		Education	
	Low	High	Low	High	Low	High
Prompt attention	0.49	0.44	0.59	0.56	0.54	0.50
Dignity	0.40	0.40	0.57	0.60	0.49	0.50
Communication	0.42	0.42	0.52	0.49	0.47	0.45
Autonomy	0.43	0.41	0.55	0.46	0.49	0.43
Confidentiality	0.25	0.52	0.58	0.52	0.41	0.52
Choice	0.37	0.26	0.61	0.52	0.49	0.39
Quality of basic amenities	0.24	0.37	0.54	0.53	0.39	0.45
Average	0.37	0.40	0.56	0.52	0.47	0.46

Table 2.5.3b *Reliability across European countries: inpatient care*

	Western Europe		CEE/FSU		Europe overall	
	Education		Education		Education	
	Low	High	Low	High	Low	High
Prompt attention	0.30	0.38	0.68	0.53	0.49	0.45
Dignity	0.34	0.40	0.65	0.53	0.50	0.47
Communication	0.25	0.34	0.56	0.52	0.41	0.43
Autonomy	0.19	0.24	0.61	0.48	0.40	0.36
Confidentiality	0.21	0.37	0.60	0.49	0.41	0.43
Choice	0.23	0.34	0.64	0.49	0.43	0.42
Quality of basic amenities	0.29	0.43	0.62	0.52	0.46	0.47
Social support	0.26	0.38	0.60	0.49	0.43	0.43
Average	0.26	0.36	0.62	0.51	0.44	0.43

CEE: Central and eastern Europe; FSU: Former Soviet Union

Interestingly, country groupings indicate that the reliability of the instrument is greater for less educated individuals in CEE/FSU countries but generally the opposite appears to hold for western Europe. Taken in their totality across both groups of countries, the results suggest that (with the exception of the domain for confidentiality and choice) educational achievement has little influence on the reliability of the responsiveness instrument. Further, the reliability of the instrument for ambulatory care appears marginally better than for inpatient care (except for quality of basic amenities domain).

Validity

The psychometric property of validity focuses on exploring the internal structure of the responsiveness concept, particularly the homogeneity or uni-dimensionality of responsiveness domains. The property is often measured through factor analysis and Cronbach's alpha. Stronger evidence of uni-dimensionality (factor loadings close to +1 or -1) supports greater validity of the instrument; a minimum value in the range of 0.6 to 0.7 has been suggested for Cronbach's alpha (e.g. Labarere 2001; Steine et al. 2001).

Validity was assessed by pooling data from different countries and analysing each domain independently. For the MCS Study, values of Cronbach's alpha suggested that all domains lay within the desired range and were greater than 0.7 for all except one (prompt attention = 0.61) (Valentine et al. 2007). For the WHS all countries satisfied the requirement that Cronbach's alpha is greater than 0.6 – the minimum value across countries was 0.66 for inpatient care and 0.65 for ambulatory care. This requirement was also satisfied for all domains except prompt attention for ambulatory care (alpha = 0.56).

We further evaluated the construct validity of the WHS questionnaire using maximum likelihood exploratory factor analysis, as performed by Valentine et al. (2007) when analysing the MCS Study ambulatory responsiveness questions (inpatient sector of MCS Study contained only one item per domain, except for prompt attention and social support). The method makes reference to Kaiser's eigenvalue rule which stipulates that item loadings on factors should be 0.40 or greater (Nunnally & Bernstein 1994). The results of the MCS Study analysis are presented by Valentine et al. (2007).

Table 2.5.4 *Promax rotated factor solution for ambulatory responsiveness questions in the WHS*

Domain	Item	Latent underlying factor							Uniqueness
		1	2	3	4	5	6	7	
Prompt attention	1	-0.018	0.115	0.135	-0.006	0.056	-0.013	0.288	0.774
	2	0.010	-0.019	-0.038	0.013	-0.019	0.019	**1.023**	0.000
Dignity	1	0.048	**0.728**	0.045	-0.046	0.044	-0.027	0.061	0.352
	2	0.025	**0.719**	-0.079	0.225	-0.009	-0.003	-0.041	0.311
Communication	1	0.523	0.321	-0.063	0.076	0.048	0.014	-0.014	0.327
	2	**0.855**	-0.017	0.038	0.000	0.048	0.011	0.019	0.157
Autonomy	1	**0.476**	-0.027	0.042	0.020	0.371	0.034	0.021	0.294
	2	-0.011	0.029	0.010	-0.005	**0.924**	0.028	-0.017	0.116
Confidentiality	1	0.072	0.039	-0.030	**0.614**	0.194	0.013	0.032	0.327
	2	-0.005	0.028	0.033	**0.849**	-0.050	-0.005	0.010	0.257
Choice	1	0.072	-0.055	**0.629**	0.037	0.145	-0.042	-0.038	0.462
Facilities	1	-0.021	0.169	0.185	0.134	-0.058	**0.444**	-0.043	0.462
	2	0.016	-0.050	-0.063	-0.028	0.034	**1.052**	0.026	0.000

Valentine et al's (2007) results confirmed the hypothesized domain taxonomy for the majority of the domains. The high human development countries have a few exceptions within the domains of prompt attention and dignity, where items tend to load on multiple factors. For the WHS questionnaire, Table 2.5.4 reports the promax rotated factor solutions for ambulatory care computed across all countries (pooled) in which the long-form questionnaire was implemented.[2] In general, results confirmed the hypothesized domain taxonomy, as the items belonging to particular domains (except autonomy) loaded on a single factor. For autonomy, the largest loading for the first item was on the factor for communication but the second largest loading (0.371) corresponded to the largest loading on the second item (factor 5). For prompt attention, the two largest loadings fell on a single factor (7) but did not reach the threshold suggested by Nunnally and Bernstein (1994).

As seen in Table 2.5.5, the hypothesized domain taxonomy was also confirmed for inpatient care and, again, the items failed to load on a single factor in only two domains (prompt attention, communication). The communication item related to information exchange loaded more strongly on the autonomy domain. In general, the strong association between autonomy, communication and dignity domain items supports the assertions made in previous MCS Study work and elsewhere that communication is an important precondition or accompaniment to being treated with dignity and involvement in decision-making about care or treatment.

Measuring responsiveness

Calculating the measures

Two measures are used to capture health system responsiveness in the analyses that follow. The first is the level of responsiveness; the second is the extent of inequalities in responsiveness across socio-economic groups in a country. This second measure can be used as a proxy for equity in responsiveness as explained below. Both measures are applied to user reports from ambulatory and inpatient health-care settings, resulting in four indicators per country.

---

[2] This type of analysis is not suitable for countries in which the short-version questionnaire was implemented as only one item was present in each domain.

Table 2.5.5 Promax rotated factor solution for inpatient responsiveness questions in the WHS

| Domain | Item | Latent underlying factor | | | | | | | | | | Uniqueness |
		1	2	3	4	5	6	7	8	9	10	
Prompt attention	1	0.009	0.002	-0.073	-0.011	0.005	-0.004	-0.011	-0.011	**1.041**	0.007	0.000
	2	-0.007	-0.004	**0.446**	0.063	-0.021	0.031	0.051	0.044	0.233	-0.037	0.543
Dignity	1	0.036	-0.051	**1.007**	-0.023	-0.018	-0.007	0.014	-0.012	-0.081	0.005	0.134
	2	0.052	0.263	**0.437**	0.008	0.172	0.024	-0.099	-0.002	0.010	0.029	0.371
Communication	1	0.150	-0.016	0.038	0.004	**0.786**	0.005	0.019	0.022	0.009	-0.005	0.131
	2	**0.526**	-0.002	0.032	0.003	0.144	0.015	0.025	0.292	-0.012	-0.001	0.239
Autonomy	1	**0.757**	0.040	-0.009	0.028	-0.021	0.009	-0.030	0.167	-0.002	0.002	0.253
	2	**0.951**	-0.011	0.046	-0.004	0.009	0.010	0.017	-0.219	0.028	-0.004	0.184
Confidentiality	1	0.178	**0.632**	0.011	0.098	0.032	0.010	0.028	-0.022	-0.034	-0.134	0.307
	2	0.026	**0.874**	-0.016	-0.055	-0.033	0.017	0.009	0.014	0.021	0.013	0.269
Choice	1	0.254	0.053	0.006	0.007	0.021	0.024	**0.475**	0.007	-0.017	0.012	0.455
Facilities	1	0.026	0.091	0.060	**0.501**	0.004	0.034	0.067	-0.013	0.019	0.141	0.417
	2	0.017	-0.045	-0.037	**0.959**	-0.002	0.035	-0.032	0.007	-0.014	0.007	0.147
Social support	1	-0.014	0.031	0.029	0.121	0.016	**0.747**	-0.027	-0.019	-0.011	-0.003	0.294
	2	0.039	-0.011	-0.021	-0.034	-0.010	**0.871**	0.024	0.016	0.006	0.003	0.244

The level of responsiveness (also called the responsiveness score) is calculated by averaging the percentage of respondents reporting that their last interaction with the health-care system was good or very good across the relevant domains (seven domains for ambulatory care; eight for inpatient). This average is referred to as overall ambulatory or inpatient responsiveness. A higher value indicates better responsiveness. Scores or rates per country are age-standardized using the WHO World Standard Population table, given that increasing age is associated with increasingly positive reports of experiences with health services (Hall et al. 1990).

The inequality measure is based on the difference across socio-economic groups, in this case identified by income quintiles and a reference group.[3] From a theoretical perspective, the reference group could be chosen on the basis of the best rate in the population; the rate in the highest socio-economic group; a target external rate; or the mean rate of the population. The highest income quintile reference group was selected here. Each difference between the highest and other quintiles is weighted by the size of the group with respect to the reference group. The measure is calculated for each domain and an average is taken across all domains to derive a country inequality indicator (again, for ambulatory or inpatient services separately).[4] Higher value for the inequality measure indicates higher inequalities and, by proxy, higher inequities (see below).

The assumption behind the link between the inequality measure of responsiveness calculated here and an inequity measure is based on the equity criterion that there should be an equal level of responsiveness for people with equal levels of health need. To the extent to which income may proxy as health needs (assuming a negative relationship between income and ill-health), then a positive gradient between income quintiles and responsiveness levels provides evidence of inequity. In other

---

[3] Harper, S. Lynch, J (2006). Measuring health inequalities. In: Oakes, JM. Kaufman, JS (eds.). *Methods in social epidemiology*. San Francisco: John Wiley & Sons. The indicator was further modified by Dr. Ahmad Hosseinpoor (WHO/IER). The title of the paper is "Global inequalities in life expectancy among men and women" (tentative).

[4] The formula: $\sum_{j=1}^{J} N_j |y_j - \mu| \Big/ N$; y_j : *the rate in group j,μ : the rate in*

reference group, N_j : population size of each group,N: Total population

words, a positive gradient from low to high income groups would imply inequities in responsiveness. Lower income groups would presumably have greater health service needs and be entitled to at least the same, or better, responsiveness from the health system.

All domain results were sample weighted and average responsiveness scores were age-standardized because of the widespread evidence of a systematic upward bias in rating in the literature and reports on responsiveness and quality of care in older populations (Valentine et al. 2007).

Interpreting the measures

In interpreting the indicators of responsiveness, there is no clear cut-off between acceptable and unacceptable. Clearly, higher responsiveness levels and lower inequality measures are better. The literature shows that self-reported measures (e.g. responsiveness, quality of life, satisfaction) are right-skewed. This was illustrated in the WHO's raw survey results in which 81% of respondents reported in the highest two categories (range 52%-96%) in the MCS Study and an average of 72% (range 38%-92%) in the WHS. Therefore, the framework for interpreting the results on the WHS presented here adopts a benchmarking approach, comparing countries with similar resource levels based on the World Bank income classification of countries (see Annex 1, Fig. A). The WHS classification of countries was incorporated for the European results – western European, and eastern European and former Soviet Union countries (Annex 1, Fig.B).

Using this benchmarking approach and the analytical framework shown in Fig. 2.5.1, we had some expectations of how the WHS results would look. We expected responsiveness to be greater in high resource settings because of the increased availability of human resources and better infrastructure. Human resources are the main conduit for the respect of person domains and, to some degree, prompt attention and choice. The higher the quality of the basic infrastructure in a country (e.g. better transport networks) the greater the impact on the domains of prompt attention and quality of basic amenities in health services.

We anticipate that there will be differences between responsiveness measures and general satisfaction measures for the same country although no direct comparison is drawn in this chapter. Measures of general satisfaction may respond to the contextual components described in Fig. 2.5.1 but measures of responsiveness are based on actual experiences and will reflect the care process from the perspective of users.

WHS 2002 results

Sample statistics

The WHS 2002 was conducted in seventy countries, sixty-nine of which reported back to WHO on their responsiveness data. Turkey did not complete the responsiveness section. The average interview completion response rate was 91% for all countries, ranging from 44% for Slovenia and up to 100% for as many as twenty-two countries. Note that the measure of survey response rates was interview completion rates – as mentioned, these may be as high as 100% as they express the number of persons who started and completed interviews as a percentage of the number of persons starting interviews. Sample sizes for ambulatory and inpatient care services averaged 1530 and 609 respectively, across all countries. A wide range across countries (130–19 547 for ambulatory use in the last twelve months; 72–1735 for inpatient use in the last three years) depended on both overall survey samples and different utilization rates across the different countries. Female participation in the overall survey sample averaged 56%, ranging from 41% (Spain) to 67% (Netherlands). The average age across all surveys was forty-three, ranging from thirty-six in Burkina Faso to fifty-three in Finland. Details on country-specific samples are provided in Annex 2.

Ambulatory care responsiveness

All countries

Overall results followed expected trends,[5] with higher overall levels of responsiveness in higher-income countries as shown in Fig. 2.5.5. Inequalities between lower- and middle-income countries changed slightly but, in general, large reductions in inequalities were only observed when moving from middle- to high-income countries.

---

[5] Australia, France, Norway and Swaziland were not included as they did not record an ambulatory section. Italy, Luxembourg, Mali and Senegal were dropped as their datasets lacked (minimum) sufficient observations for each quintile (thirty or more).

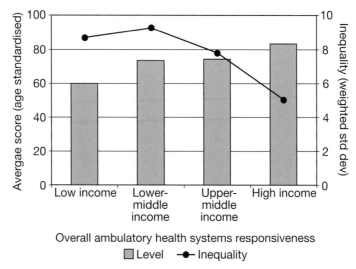

Fig. 2.5.5 Level of inequalities in responsiveness by countries grouped according to World Bank income categories

Respondents from different country groupings consistently reported low responsiveness levels and high inequalities for the prompt attention domain. The dignity domain was consistently reported as high and with low inequalities. The overall gradient between country groupings as described in Fig. 2.5.5 held for all domains. In other words, no domain was performing significantly better in a lower income grouping of countries than in the higher income grouping.

European countries
Within Europe, western European countries showed notably higher mean levels of responsiveness and lower inequalities than the CEE/FSU countries (Fig. 2.5.6). Responsiveness levels across all twenty-five European countries ranged from 56% in Russia to 92% in Austria (Fig. 2.5.7). Inequalities ranged from 2.2 in Spain to 14.3 in Bosnia and Herzegovina. Strikingly, nine of the twelve CEE/FSU countries had inequalities higher than the European average and only four of the twelve CEE/FSU countries had responsiveness levels greater than the average levels for Europe as a whole. By contrast, twelve of the thirteen western European countries had responsiveness levels higher than the European average.

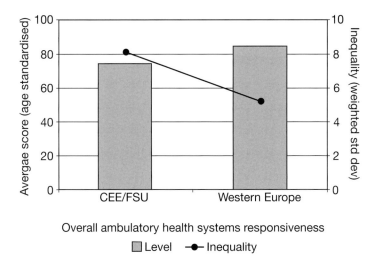

Fig. 2.5.6 Level of inequalities in responsiveness by two groups of twenty-five European countries

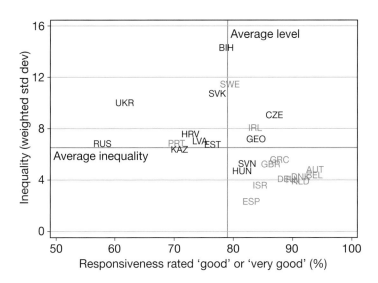

Fig. 2.5.7 Inequalities in ambulatory responsiveness against levels for twenty-five European countries

On average, responsiveness for all domains in western European countries was higher than in CEE/FSU countries. Differences were largest for the choice and autonomy domains. Prompt attention was the worst performing domain in western Europe, while autonomy and prompt attention were the worst performing domains in CEE/FSU countries. Dignity was the best performing domain in both groups of countries, as found for the global average.

Inequalities were higher for all domains in CEE/FSU countries. Both groups of countries had the highest inequalities in the prompt attention domain. Inequalities were lowest in the communication domain in CEE/FSU countries and in the basic amenities and dignity domains in western Europe.

Inpatient health services

All countries

The level of responsiveness for inpatient services increased across the four income groupings of countries (Fig. 2.5.8).[6] However, the pattern for inequalities was surprising. Unlike the trend in ambulatory care, inpatient inequalities reached a peak in upper middle-income countries (greatest values in South Africa and Slovakia).

Responsiveness domain levels (except for autonomy and choice) increased across country groupings. Upper middle-income countries had lower levels of both domains than lower middle-income countries. In general, these domains were also the worst performing (compared with prompt attention for ambulatory services). The dignity domain performed best in all groupings of countries, followed closely by social support. The spike in inequalities observed for upper middle-income countries seems to have arisen from sharply higher inequalities for the autonomy, basic amenities and social support domains.

European countries

For ambulatory services, responsiveness levels and inequalities in inpatient services differed between western Europe and CEE/FSU countries

---

[6] Australia, France and Norway were not included because they lacked data on assets necessary for construction of wealth index; Swaziland had too few observations in the ambulatory section. Ethiopia, Italy, Mali, Senegal and Slovenia were dropped from the analysis as their datasets did not have (minimum) sufficient observations for each quintile.

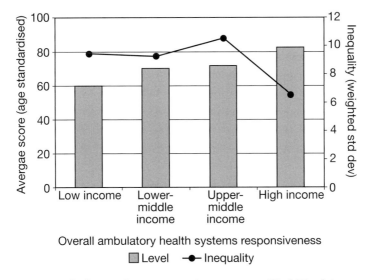

Fig. 2.5.8 Level of inequality in responsiveness across World Bank income categories of countries

(Fig. 2.5.9). The average level of responsiveness levels across eleven CEE/FSU countries is 70% compared to 80% for fourteen countries in western Europe.[7] Inequalities were also higher in CEE/FSU countries.

Across all twenty-five European countries, responsiveness levels range from 51% in Ukraine to 90% in Luxembourg. Inequities range from a low of 3.4 in Austria to 18.9 in Slovakia. Ten of the eleven CEE/FSU countries (shown in grey in Fig. 2.5.10) have responsiveness inequalities higher than the European average (for inequalities). Only five of the eleven CEE/ FSU countries have responsiveness levels higher than the average level for Europe, whereas all fourteen western European countries have a responsiveness level higher than the European average.

As for ambulatory services, western European countries show higher levels for each of the eight domains of inpatient services. Dignity was the best performing domain in CEE/FSU countries; in western Europe both dignity and social support had the highest (similar) levels. Choice was the worst performing domain for both groups of countries.

[7]   Italy and Slovenia were omitted from the inpatient services analysis as their datasets did not have the minimum number of observations required for reliable results.

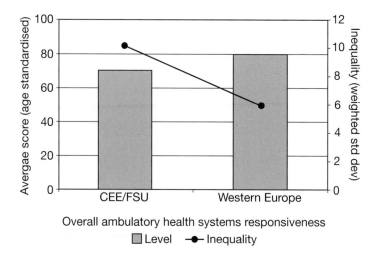

Fig. 2.5.9 Level of inequalities in responsiveness by two groups of twenty-five European countries

Inequalities in all domains were higher for CEE/FSU countries; the highest inequality was seen in the prompt attention domain. In western Europe, inequalities were highest in the domains of autonomy and confidentiality. In CEE/FSU countries the lowest inequalities were seen in the dignity domain while in western Europe the lowest inequalities were seen in social support.

Responsiveness gradients within countries

Ambulatory health services

The values for the inequality indicator ranged between five and ten for the different groups of countries. Fig. 2.5.11 shows how these values translate into a gradient in responsiveness for different wealth or income quintiles within countries. Low- and middle-income countries showed a gradient but no gradient was seen in the high-income countries when averaged together.

In Europe, the CEE/FSU countries showed a gradient in the level of responsiveness across wealth quintiles with richer populations reporting better responsiveness (Fig. 2.5.12). The gradient was nearly flat for western European countries.

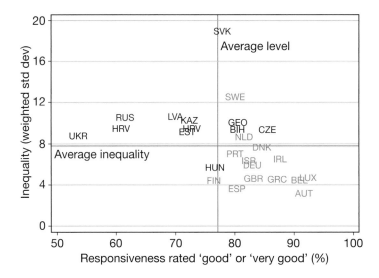

Fig. 2.5.10 Responsiveness inequalities against levels for twenty-five European countries

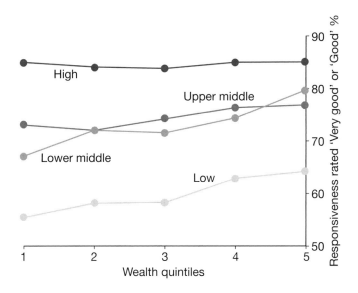

Fig. 2.5.11 Gradient in responsiveness for population groups within countries by wealth quintiles

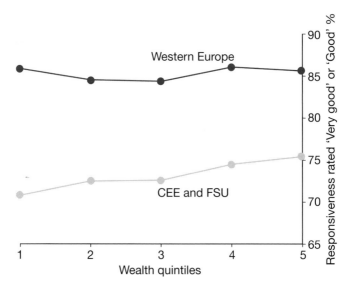

Fig. 2.5.12 Gradient in responsiveness for population groups within countries in Europe by wealth quintiles

Inpatient health services

The gradient in responsiveness for inpatient services is flatter than that observed for ambulatory services and most marked in low-income countries (Fig. 2.5.13). Similarly, no gradient can be observed across wealth quintiles in the two groups of European countries. However, people in all quintiles in CEE/FSU countries clearly face worse levels of responsiveness than people in any quintile of western Europe (Fig. 2.5.14).

Health system characteristics and responsiveness

Fig. 2.5.1 shows the rather obvious observation that factors such as resources in the health system provide a context to the process of care. It also shows the less obvious result that responsiveness affects the process of care, especially with respect to completion of treatment. We refer to this as coverage. With this understanding, we first explored the relationship between health expenditure and responsiveness in order to assess which domains might be more affected. Second, we explored the relationship between responsiveness and indicators of

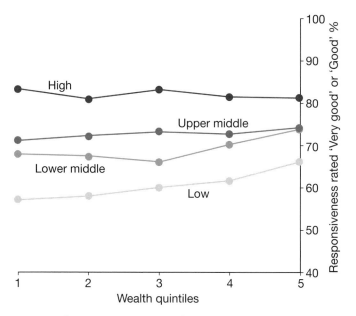

Fig. 2.5.13 Gradient in responsiveness for population groups within countries by wealth quintiles

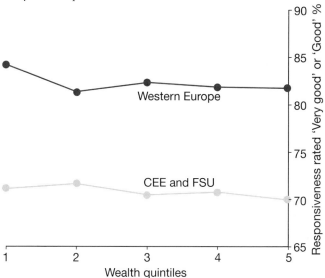

Fig. 2.5.14 Gradient in responsiveness for population groups within countries in Europe by wealth quintiles

completion of valid antenatal care as a means of understanding the relationship between responsiveness and coverage in general.

Keeping all other factors constant, well-resourced health system environments should be able to afford better quality care and receive better responsiveness ratings from users. Using a simple correlation for each responsiveness domain and keeping development contexts constant (by looking at correlations within World Bank country income groups), we observed whether higher health expenditures are associated with higher responsiveness and for which domains. Fig. 2.5.15 lists the domains for which the correlations between total and government health expenditures and responsiveness are significant (p=0.05). In general, there is a positive association across many of the domains for most country income groupings, with the exception of lower middle-income countries. This indicates that increases in health expenditures in this grouping of countries are not being translated into improvements in patients' experiences of care, perhaps because absolute levels of expenditure are too low to create even a basic health system.

Where particular health needs require multiple contacts with the health system (e.g. chronic conditions or treatment protocols for TB or maternal care), the interaction between provider and user behaviours can influence utilization patterns. Under- or incorrect utilization can influence technical care and health outcomes (Donabedian 1973).[8]

A few simple analyses of responsiveness and adherence-related data give a sense of the extent of validity in the WHS responsiveness results and how the acceptability and accessibility of services, as measured by responsiveness, can lead to adherence. Fig. 2.5.16 shows a scatterplot of responsiveness and antenatal coverage rates. The latter rates were obtained from the WHS question which asked whether the respondent had completed four antenatal visits. Overall, a significant linear correlation was observed between the level of responsiveness and the percentage of respondents reporting that they had completed all four antenatal visits (r=0.51, p=0.000). The highest correlations were observed for the level of dignity (r=0.55), communication (0.54) and confidentiality (0.50). The responsiveness measure of inequality was less strongly correlated (r=0.35).

---

[8]   This assumes that, when applied technically correctly, health interventions have a positive impact on health.

Fig. 2.5.15 Correlations of average total health expenditure per capita and overall responsiveness for countries in different World Bank income categories

	AMBULATORY		INPATIENT	
	Total health expenditure per capita	Government health expenditure per capita	Total health expenditure per capita	Government health expenditure per capita
Low income (n, 19)	• Higher levels for basic amenities, confidentiality • Lower inequalities for dignity and autonomy	• Higher levels for basic amenities, dignity, confidentiality • Lower inequalities for dignity and basic amenities	• Higher levels for basic amenities • Lower inequalities for all domains except prompt attention.	• Higher levels for basic amenities • Lower inequalities for dignity
Lower-middle income (n, 15)	• None	• None	• None.	• Higher levels for dignity
Higher-middle income (n,12)	• Higher levels for communication, choice	• Higher levels for dignity, communication, choice	• Higher levels for choice, social support	• Higher levels for prompt attention, choice, social support
High income (n,15)	• Higher levels for communication, autonomy, choice, basic amenities. • Lower inequalities for basic amenities	• Higher levels for all domains except confidentiality. • Lower inequalities for basic amenities.	• Higher levels for all domains except communication and confidentiality.	• Higher levels for all domains except confidentiality • Lower inequalities for prompt attention, dignity, social support

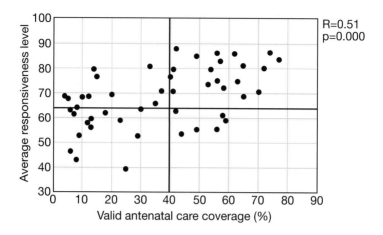

Fig. 2.5.16 Responsiveness and antenatal coverage

Conclusions

Empowering patients and equity in access are founding values that underpin the outlook for the new European health strategy. These values are expressed in the *White Paper: Together for Health: A Strategic Approach for the EU 2008-2013* (Commission of the European Communities 2007). Ensuring high responsiveness performance from health systems, with respect to both level and equity, is one key strategy to support these values. Measuring responsiveness is one approach to keeping the issue high on the health systems performance agenda.

The analyses for this chapter used inequalities in responsiveness across income groups as a proxy for inequities in responsiveness. The discussion below refers to these two aspects of responsiveness.

Common concerns

A wide array of results on health system responsiveness has been presented in this chapter. Health systems across the world show some common strengths and failings. Nurses' and doctors' respectful treatment of users is encapsulated in the responsiveness domain – dignity. This is a relative strength in comparison to systemic issues such as prompt attention, involvement in decision-making (autonomy) or choice (/continuity of provider).

Our analysis has generally confirmed the hypothesis of a positive relationship between a country's level of development (represented by national income) and the responsiveness of its health system (as is observed for health outcomes). However, while there is a linear relationship between the income level in a country and the average level of responsiveness, dramatic reductions in responsiveness inequalities are only observed in the high-income country category. This observation was true for both inpatient and ambulatory care.

Elevated levels of health expenditures are no guarantee that a system's responsiveness has improved. For lower middle-income countries no gains in responsiveness are observed for increases in health expenditures, probably due to inadequate general funding. Increased health expenditure (particularly in the public sector) for the other country groupings does yield gains in the overall responsiveness level and equality, but usually in some specific domains. On the other hand, lower responsiveness is associated with lower coverage and inequalities in responsiveness are associated with greater inequity in access, regardless of development setting. Hence, explicit steps are needed to build good levels of responsiveness performance into all systems.

The European analysis showed substantial differences in mean levels and within-country inequalities between western European and CEE/FSU countries. Average responsiveness levels are higher in western European (85%) than in CEE/FSU (73%) countries. In both groups of countries, ambulatory services had the highest levels for dignity and the highest inequalities for prompt attention. In inpatient services, levels of dignity were highest in both country groupings but prompt attention inequities were highest in CEE/FSU countries and autonomy and confidentiality inequalities were highest in western Europe.

Implementing change

Enhancing communication in the health system provides a potential entry point for improving responsiveness. Clear communication is associated with dignity, better involvement in decision-making and, in addition, supports better coverage or access. It is also an attribute that is highly valued by most societies. In the European context, it is interesting to note that CEE/FSU countries place special importance on communication (Valentine et al. 2008).

As shown here, responsiveness appears to be complementary or contributory to ensuring equity in access (to the technical quality of care). This is in keeping with the Aday and Andersen (1974) framework and with Donabedian (1980) who introduced the concept of the quality of health care and satisfaction with the care received as a valid component for achieving high technical quality of care and high rates of access to care. Inequities in access will result if the process of care systematically dissuades some groups from either initiating or continuing use of services to obtain the maximum benefit from the intervention. It is critical to deliver health interventions effectively and ensure compliance in primary care where a large majority of the population receives preventive and promotive health interventions. This is likely to become an increasing concern with the global epidemiological transition from infectious to chronic diseases. Therefore, primary-care providers need to be aware of their critical role in patient communication and treating individuals with respect.

Responsiveness measurement and future research

The psychometric properties of the responsiveness questions show resilience across different countries and settings and indicate that the responsiveness surveys (when reported as raw data) have face validity. The WHS managed to improve on the MCS Study questions in several ways and provides a useful starting tool for countries embarking on routine assessments of responsiveness.

Some key aspects of responsiveness still need to be researched further. In particular, while theoretically complementary, further investigation could benefit empirical research on the potential trade-offs between health (through investments in improved technical applications) and non-health (through better responsiveness) outcomes.

A second key area relates to gaining a better understanding of how responsiveness and responsiveness inequities may act as indicators of inequities in access or unmet need in the population and what measures can be taken to improve responsiveness in the light of this relationship.

A third key area relates to the self-reported nature of the responsiveness instrument. Self-reported data may be prone to measurement error (e.g. Groot 2000; Murray et al. 2001) where bias results from groups of respondents (for example defined by socio-economic characteristics) varying systematically in their reporting of a fixed level of the measurement construct. The degree of comparability of self-reported survey data across individuals, socio-economic groups or populations has been debated extensively, usually with regard to health status measures (e.g. Bago d'Uva et al. 2007; Lindeboom & van Doorslaer 2004).

Similar concerns apply to self-reported data on health systems responsiveness where the characteristics of the systems and cultural norms regarding the use and experiences of public services are likely to predominate. The method of anchoring vignettes has been promoted as a means for controlling for systematic differences in preferences and norms when responding to survey questions (see Salomon et al. 2004). Vignettes represent hypothetical descriptions of fixed levels of a construct (such as responsiveness) and individuals are asked to evaluate these in the same way that they are asked to evaluate their own experiences of the health system. The vignettes provide a source of external variation from which information on systematic reporting behaviour can be obtained. To date, little use has been made of the vignette data within the WHS (Rice et al. 2008) and these offer a valuable area for future research.

Prospects for measuring responsiveness

Non-health outcomes are gaining increasing attention as valid measures of performance and quality. These require some feedback on what happens when users make contact with health-care systems and that can be easily compared across countries. Routine surveys on responsiveness are by no means a substitute for other forms of participation but, within the theme of patient empowerment, can provide opportunities for users' voices to be heard in health-care systems.

Responsiveness measurement (as opposed to broader patient satisfaction measurement) is increasingly recognized as an appropriate approach for informing health system policy. Work by the Picker Institute (1999) and the AHRQ (1999); the future work envisaged by the OECD (Garratt et al. 2008); and the broader analytical literature have built this case very satisfactorily. The work of the last decade has provided a solid base and an opportunity for individual countries to introduce measures of responsiveness into their health-policy information systems in the short and medium term.

References

Aday, LA. Andersen, R (1974). 'A framework for the study of access to medical care'. *Health Services Research*, 9(3): 208–220.

AHRQ (1999). *CAHPS 2.0 survey and reporting kit.* Rockville, MD: Agency for Healthcare Research and Quality.

Andersen, RM (1995). 'Revisiting the behavioral model and access to medical care: does it matter?' *Journal of Health and Social Behavior*, 36(1): 1–10.

Bago d'Uva, T. van Doorlsaer, E. Lindeboom, M. O Donnell, O (2007). 'Does reporting heterogeneity bias the measurement of health disparities?' *Health Economics*, 17(3): 351–375.

Blendon, RG. Schoen, C. DesRoches. C. Osborn, R. Zapert, K (2003). 'Common concerns amid diverse systems: health care experiences in five countries. The experiences and views of sicker patients are bellwethers for how well health care systems are working.' *Health Affairs*, 22(3): 106–121.

Bradley, EH. McGraw, SA. Curry, L. Buckser, A. King, KL. Kasl, SV. Andersen, R (2002). 'Expanding the Andersen model: the role of psychosocial factors in long-term care use.' *Health Services Research*, 37(5): 1221–1242.

Commission of the European Communities (2007). *White Paper. Together for health: a strategic approach for the EU 2008–2013.* Brussels: European Commission (http://ec.europa.eu/health/ph_overview/Documents/strategy_wp_en.pdf).

De Silva, A (2000). *A framework for measuring responsiveness.* GPE Discussion Paper Series No. 32 (http://www.who.int/responsiveness/papers/en).

Donabedian, A (1973). *Aspects of medical care administration.* Cambridge, MA: Harvard University Press.

Donabedian, A (1980). *Explorations in quality assessment and monitoring: the definition of quality and approaches to assessment.* Ann Arbor, Michigan: Health Administration Press.

Garratt, AM. Solheim, E. Danielsen, K (2008). *National and cross-national surveys of patient experiences: a structured review.* Oslo: Norwegian Knowledge Centre for the Health Services (Report No. 7).

Gilson, L. Doherty, J. Loewenson, R. Francis, V (2007). *Challenging inequity through health systems.* Final Report Knowledge Network on Health Systems (http://www.who.int/social_determinants/knowledge_networks/final_reports/en/index.htm).

Groot, W (2000). 'Adaptation and scale of reference bias in self-assessments of quality of life.' *Journal of Health Economics*, 19: 403–420.

Hall, JA. Feldstein, M. Fretwell, MD. Rowe, JW. Epstein, AM (1990). 'Older patients' health status and satisfaction with medical care in an HMO population.' *Medical Care*, 28: 261–70.

Harper, S. Lynch, J (2006). Measuring health inequalities. In: Oakes, JM. Kaufman, JS (eds.). *Methods in social epidemiology*. San Francisco: John Wiley & Sons.

Labarere, J. Francois, P. Auquier, P. Robert, C. Fourny, M (2001). 'Development of a French inpatient satisfaction questionnaire.' *International Journal for Quality in Health Care*, 13: 99–108.

Landis, JR. Koch, GG (1977). 'The measurement of observer agreement for categorical data.' *Biometrics*, 33: 159–174.

Lindeboom, M. van Doorslaer E (2004). 'Cut-point shift and index shift in self-reported health.' *Journal of Health Economics*, 23(6): 1083–1099.

Murray, CJL. Frenk, J (2000). 'A framework for assessing the performance of health systems.' *Bulletin of the World Health Organization*, 78: 717–731.

Murray, CJL. Tandon, A. Salomon, J. Mathers, CD (2001). *Enhancing cross-population comparability of survey results*. Geneva: WHO/EIP (GPE Discussion Paper No. 35).

Nunnally, JC. Bernstein, IH (1994). *Psychometric theory, 3rd ed*. New York: McGraw-Hill.

Picker Institute (1999). *The Picker Institute Implementation Manual*. Boston, MA: Picker Institute.

Rice, N. Robone, S. Smith, PC (2008). *The measurement and comparison of health system responsiveness*. Presentation to Health Econometrics and Data Group (HEDG), January 2008, University of Norwich (HEDG Working Paper 08/05).

Salomon, J. Tandon, A. Murray, CJ (2004). 'Comparability of self-rated health: cross-sectional multi-country survey using anchoring vignettes.' *British Medical Journal*, 328(7434): 258.

Shengelia, B. Tandon, A. Adams, O. Murray, CJL (2005). 'Access, utilization, quality, and effective coverage: an integrated conceptual framework and measurement strategy.' *Social Science & Medicine*, 61: 97–109.

Solar, O. Irwin, A (2007). *A conceptual framework for action on the social determinants of health*. Draft discussion paper for the Commission on Social Determinants of Health. April 2007 (http://www.who.int/social_determinants/resources/csdh_framework_action_05_07.pdf).

Steine, S. Finset, A. Laerum, E (2001). 'A new, brief questionnaire (PEQ) developed in primary health care for measuring patients' experience of interaction, emotion and consultation outcome.' *Family Practice*, 18(4): 410–419.

Tanahashi, T (1978). 'Health service coverage and its evaluation.' *Bulletin of the World Health Organization*, 56(2): 295–303.

Üstün, TB. Chatterji, S. Mechbal, A. Murray, CJL. WHS Collaborating Groups (2003). The world health surveys. In: Murray, CJL. Evans, DB (eds.). *Health systems performance assessment: debates, methods and empiricism*. Geneva: World Health Organization.

Üstün, TB. Chatterji, S. Mechbal, A. Murray, CJL (2005). Quality assurance in surveys: standards, guidelines and procedures. In: *Household surveys in developing and transition countries: design, implementation and analysis*. New York: United Nations (http://unstats.un.org/unsd/hhsurveys/pdf/Household_surveys.pdf).

Üstün, TB. Chatterji, S. Villanueva, M. Bendib, L. Çelik. C. Sadana, R. Valentine, N. Ortiz, J. Tandon, A. Salomon, J. Cao, Y. Jun, XW. Özaltin, E. Mathers, C. Murray, CJL (2001). *WHO multi-country survey study on health and responsiveness 2000–2001*. Geneva: World Health Organization (GPE Discussion Paper 37) (http://www.who.int/healthinfo/survey/whspaper37.pdf).

Valentine, N. Bonsel, GJ. Murray. CJL (2007). 'Measuring quality of health care from the user's perspective in 41 countries: psychometric properties of WHO's questions on health systems responsiveness.' *Quality of Life Research*, 16(7): 1107–1125.

Valentine, N. Darby, C. Bonel, GJ (2008). 'Which aspects of non-clinical quality of care are most important? Results from WHO's general population surveys of health systems responsiveness in 41 countries.' *Social Science and Medicine*, 66(9): 1939–1950.

Valentine, NB. de Silva, A. Kawabata, K. Darby, C. Murray, CJL. Evans, DB. (2003). Health system responsiveness: concepts, domains and operationalization. In: Murray, CJL. Evans, DB (eds.). *Health systems performance assessment: debates, methods and empiricism*. Geneva: World Health Organization.

Valentine, NB. Lavallee, R. Liu, B. Bonsel, GJ. Murray, CJL (2003a). Classical psychometric assessment of the responsiveness instrument in the WHO multi-country survey study on health responsiveness 2000 –2001. In: Murray, CJL. Evans, DB (eds.). *Health systems performance assessment: debates, methods and empiricism*. Geneva: World Health Organization.

Ware, JE. Hays, RD (1988). 'Methods for measuring patient satisfaction with specific medical encounters.' *Medical Care*, 26(4): 393–402.

WHO (2000). *The world health report 2000. Health systems: improving performance*. Geneva: World Health Organization.

WHO (2001). Report on WHO meeting of experts responsiveness (HFS/FAR/RES/00.1) Meeting on Responsiveness Concepts and Measurement.

Geneva, Switzerland: 13–14 September 2001 (http://www.who.int/ health-systems-performance/technical_consultations/responsiveness_ report.pdf).

WHO (2005). *The health systems responsiveness analytical guidelines for surveys in the multi-country survey study.* Geneva: World Health Organization (http://www.who.int/responsiveness/papers/MCSS_ Analytical_Guidelines.pdf).

WHO (2005a). *WHO glossary on social justice and health.* A report of the WHO Health and Human Rights, Equity, Gender and Poverty Working Group. Available online at WHO, forthcoming.

WHO & EQUINET (forthcoming). *A framework for monitoring equity in access and health systems strengthening in AIDS treatment programmes: options and implementation issues.* Geneva: World Health Organization and EQUINET.

Annex 1

Groupings of World Health Survey countries

Fig. A WHS countries grouped by World Bank income categories

Low income
Bangladesh, Burkina Faso, Chad,
Comoros, Congo, Cote d'Ivoire,
Ethiopia, Ghana, India, Kenya,
Lao People's Democratic Republic,
Malawi, Mali, Mauritania,
Myanmar, Nepal, Pakistan, Senegal,
Viet Nam, Zambia, Zimbabwe

Lower-middle income
Bosnia and Herzegovina, Brazil,
China, Dominican Republic,
Ecuador, Georgia, Guatemala,
Kazakhstan, Morocco, Namibia,
Paraguay, Philippines, Sri Lanka,
Tunisia, Ukraine

Higher-middle income
Croatia, Czech Republic, Estonia,
Hungary, Latvia, Malaysia,
Mauritius, Mexico, Russian
Federation, Slovakia, South Africa,
Uruguay

High income
Austria, Belgium, Denmark, Finland,
Germany, Greece, Ireland, Israel,
Italy, Luxembourg, Netherlands,
Portugal, Slovenia, Spain, Sweden,
United Arab Emirates, United
Kingdom

Fig. B WHS countries in Europe

CEE/FSU
Bosnia and Herzegovina, Croatia,
Czech Republic, Estonia, Georgia,
Hungary, Kazakhstan, Latvia,
Russia, Slovakia, Slovenia, Ukraine

Western Europe
Austria, Belgium, Denmark, Finland,
Germany, Greece, Ireland, Israel,
Italy, Luxembourg, Netherlands,
Portugal, Spain, Sweden, United
Kingdom

Annex 2 *WHS 2002 sample descriptive statistics*

Country	Response rate - interview completion (%)	Users of ambulatory services in last twelve months	Users of inpatient services in last three years	Percentage female	Average age (years)	Percentage high school or more educated	Percentage in good or very good health
Low income							
Bangladesh	85	4020	777	53	39	8	44
Burkina Faso	96	1199	589	53	36	3	70
Chad	92	423	371	53	37	3	58
Comoros	95	526	374	55	42	5	54
Congo	79	381	288	53	36	18	56
Cote d'Ivoire	97	765	305	43	36	13	60
Ethiopia	96	1779	224	52	37	3	75
Ghana	70	1567	677	55	41	4	72
India	93	5003	1735	51	39	21	58

Annex 2 *cont'd*

Country	Response rate - interview completion (%)	Users of ambulatory services in last twelve months	Users of inpatient services in last three years	Percentage female	Average age (years)	Percentage high school or more educated	Percentage in good or very good health
Kenya	82	2228	803	58	38	21	66
Lao People's Democratic Republic	98	735	570	53	38	10	78
Malawi	93	2423	1236	58	36	1	79
Mali	79	130	104	43	42	3	70
Mauritania	98	552	469	61	39	10	69
Myanmar	97	1667	320	57	41	9	79
Nepal	98	3279	1141	57	39	5	62
Pakistan	93	3727	913	44	37	14	75
Senegal	88	222	182	48	38	8	58
Viet Nam	84	1541	548	54	40	24	51
Zambia	88	2188	764	55	36	5	72

Country							
Zimbabwe	94	1660	649	64	37	5	52
Lower-middle income							
Bosnia and Herzegovina	94	394	259	58	47	8	58
Brazil	100	2341	1244	56	42	28	53
China	100	1435	423	51	45	28	62
Dominican Republic	74	1315	1508	54	42	5	56
Ecuador	77	1372	592	56	41	13	57
Georgia	92	763	227	58	49	88	38
Guatemala	98	2063	978	62	40	12	53
Kazakhstan	100	2331	803	66	41	96	48
Morocco	79	2211	800	59	41	14	41
Namibia	91	650	862	59	38	4	72
Paraguay	97	2414	1096	54	40	12	70

Annex 2 *cont'd*

Country	Response rate - interview completion (%)	Users of ambulatory services in last twelve months	Users of inpatient services in last three years	Percentage female	Average age (years)	Percentage high school or more educated	Percentage in good or very good health
Philippines	100	2625	906	52	39	16	60
Sri Lanka	99	2268	1697	53	41	21	72
Tunisia	96	2352	816	53	42	28	62
Ukraine	99	735	580	64	48	87	27
Upper-middle income							
Croatia	100	465	259	59	52	16	51
Czech Republic	49	411	302	55	48	47	55
Estonia	99	395	289	64	50	74	36
Hungary	100	453	489	58	49	63	51
Latvia	92	283	293	67	51	34	33

Malaysia	80	1943	1329	56	41	42	78
Mauritius	88	1702	1180	52	42	13	65
Mexico	97	19457	1440	55	42	23	67
Russian Federation	100	1794	1019	64	51	61	31
Slovakia	99	897	355	62	39	71	66
South Africa	89	384	384	53	38	34	73
Uruguay	100	1029	536	51	46	30	79
High income							
Austria	100	184	351	62	45	26	77
Belgium	100	298	299	56	45	64	74
Denmark	100	316	194	53	51	52	79
Finland	100	464	345	55	53	58	55
Germany	100	428	401	60	50	23	65
Greece	100	433	272	50	51	47	67

Annex 2 *cont'd*

Country	Response rate - interview completion (%)	Users of ambulatory services in last twelve months	Users of inpatient services in last three years	Percentage female	Average age (years)	Percentage high school or more educated	Percentage in good or very good health
Ireland	100	239	214	55	44	19	82
Israel	57	521	412	57	45	85	76
Italy	100	541	232	57	48	51	63
Luxembourg	100	135	237	52	45	43	73
Netherlands	100	624	192	67	44	83	76
Portugal	100	510	212	62	50	20	39
Slovenia	44	284	72	53	47	52	58
Spain	53	2863	1601	41	53	31	64
Sweden	100	300	266	58	51	70	62
United Arab Emirates	100	453	239	48	37	65	86
United Kingdom	100	369	344	63	50	46	68

2.6 | *Measuring equity of access to health care*

SARA ALLIN, CRISTINA HERNÁNDEZ-QUEVEDO, CRISTINA MASSERIA

Introduction

A health system should be evaluated against the fundamental goal of ensuring that individuals in need of health care receive effective treatment. One way to evaluate progress towards this goal is to measure the extent to which access to health care is based on need rather than willingness or ability to pay. This egalitarian principle of equity or fairness is the primary motivation for health systems' efforts to separate the financing from the receipt of health care as expressed in many policy documents and declarations (Judge et al. 2006; van Doorslaer et al. 1993). The extent to which equity is achieved is thus an important indicator of health system performance.

Measuring equity of access to care is a core component of health system performance exercises. The health system performance framework developed in WHO's *The world health report 2000* stated that ensuring access to care based on need and not ability to pay is instrumental in improving health (WHO 2000). It can also be argued that access to care is a goal in and of itself: 'beyond its tangible benefits, health care touches on countless important and in some ways mysterious aspects of personal life and invests it with significant value as a thing in itself' (President's Commission for the Study of Ethical Problems in Medicine and Biomedical and Behavioural Research, 1983 cited in Gulliford et al. 2002). Equitable access to health care has been identified as a key indicator of performance by the OECD (Hurst & Jee-Hughes 2001) and underlies European-level strategies such as those developed at the European Union Lisbon summit in March 2000 and the Open Method of Coordination for social protection and social inclusion (Atkinson et al. 2002).

However, it is far from straightforward to measure equity and translate such measures into policy. This chapter is structured according to three objectives: (i) to review the conceptualization and measurement of equity in the health system, with a focus on access to care; (ii) to present the strengths and weaknesses of the common methodological approaches to measuring equity, drawing on illustrations from the existing literature; and (iii) to discuss the policy implications of equity analyses and outline priorities for future research.

Defining equity, access and need

Libertarianism and egalitarianism are two ideological perspectives that dominate current debates about individuals' rights to health care (Donabedian 1971; Williams 1993; Williams 2005). Libertarians are concerned with preserving personal liberty and ensuring that minimum health-care standards are achieved. Moreover, access to health care can be seen as a privilege and not a right: people who can afford to should be able to pay for better or more health care than their fellow citizens (Williams 1993). Egalitarians seek to ensure that health care is financed according to ability to pay and delivery is organized so that everyone has the same access to care. Care is allocated on the basis of need rather than ability to pay, with a view to promote equality in health (Wagstaff & van Doorslaer 2000). Egalitarians view access to health care as a fundamental human right that can be seen as a prerequisite for personal achievement, therefore it should not be influenced by income or wealth (Williams 1993).

These debates are also informed by the comprehensive theory of justice developed by Rawls (1971) that outlines a set of rules which would be accepted by impartial individuals in the 'original position'. This original position places individuals behind a 'veil of ignorance' – having no knowledge of either their place in society (social standing) or their level of natural assets and abilities. The Rawlsian perspective has been interpreted to suggest that equity is satisfied if the most disadvantaged in society have a decent minimum level of health care (Williams 1993). This would be supported by libertarians provided that government involvement was kept to a minimum. However, if health care is considered one of Rawls' social primary goods[1] then an equitable society depends on the equal distribution of health care, in line with egalitarian goals. Furthermore, to the extent that health care can be considered essential for individuals' capability to function, then the egalitarian perspective is also consistent with Sen's theory of equality of capabilities (Sen 1992).

No perfectly libertarian or egalitarian health system exists but the egalitarian viewpoints are largely supported by both the policy community and the public. This support is evidenced by the predominantly publicly funded health systems with strong government oversight that separate payment of health care from its receipt and offer programmes to support the most vulnerable groups. At international level the view that access to health care is a right is illustrated by the 2000 Charter of Fundamental Rights of the European Union and the 1948 Universal Declaration of Human Rights.

The debate between libertarian and egalitarian perspectives is not resolved in practice. Policies that preserve individual autonomy and freedom of choice exist alongside policies of redistribution, as evidenced by the existence of a private sector in health care that allows those able or willing to pay to purchase additional health services. Thus the design of the health system impacts equity of access to health care. For instance, patient cost sharing may introduce financial barriers to access for poorer populations and voluntary health insurance may allow faster access or access to better quality services for the privately insured (Mossialos & Thomson 2003). Policy-makers appear to be concerned about the effects of health-care financing arrangements on the distribution of income and the receipt of health care (OECD 1992; van Doorslaer et al. 1993). Chapter 2.4 on financial protection provides an in-depth review of the extent to which health systems ensure that the population is protected from the financial consequences of accessing care.

---

[1] Social primary goods are those that are important to people but created, shaped and affected by social structures and political institutions. These contrast with the natural primary goods (intelligence, strength, imagination, talent, good health) that inevitably are distributed unequally in society (Rawls 1971).

What objective of equity do we want to evaluate?

The idea that health systems should pursue equity goals is widely supported. However, it is not straightforward to operationalize equity in the context of health care. Many definitions of equity in health-care delivery have been debated and Mooney identifies seven in the economics literature (Mooney 1983 & 1986). The first two (equality of expenditure per capita, equality of inputs across regions) are unlikely to be equitable since they do not allow for variations in levels of need for care. The third (equality of input for equal need) accounts for need but does not consider factors that may give rise to inequity beyond the size of the health-care budget. The fourth and fifth are the most commonly cited definitions – equality of access for equal need (individuals should face equal costs of accessing care) and equality of utilization for equal need (individuals in equal need should not only face equal costs but also demand the same amount of services). The sixth suggests that if needs are prioritized/ranked in the same way across regions, then equity is achieved when each region is just able to meet the same 'last' or 'marginal' need. The seventh argues that equity is achieved if the level of *health* is equal across regions and social groups, requiring positive discrimination in favour of poorer people/regions and an unequal distribution of resources.

All the above goals are concerned with health-care delivery. Equity in health care is often defined in terms of health-care financing whereby individuals' payments for health care should be based on their ability to pay and therefore proportional to their income. Individuals with higher incomes should pay more and those with lower incomes should pay less, regardless of their risk of illness or receipt of care. This concept is based on the vertical equity principle of unequal payment for unequals in which unequals are defined in terms of their level of income (Wagstaff & van Doorslaer 2000; Wagstaff et al. 1999). It has direct implications for access to care since financial barriers to access may arise from inequitable (or regressive) systems of health-care finance. The financial arrangements of the health system not only impact on equity of access to health care but also have the potential to exacerbate health inequalities: "unfair financing both enhances any existing unfairness in the distribution of health and compounds it by making the poor multiply deprived" (Culyer 2007, p.15).

The policy perspective requires a working definition of equity that is feasible (i.e. within the scope of health policy) and makes intuitive sense. In an attempt to clarify equity principles for policy-makers, Whitehead (1991) builds on Mooney's proposed equity principles to develop an operational definition encompassing the three dimensions of accessibility, acceptability and quality.

1. Equal access to available care for equal need – implies equal entitlements (i.e. universal coverage); fair distribution of resources throughout the country (i.e. allocations on basis of need); and removal of geographical and other barriers to access.
2. Equal utilization for equal need – to ensure use of services is not restricted by social or economic disadvantage (and ensure appropriate use of essential services). This accepts differences in utilization that arise from individuals exercising their right to use or not use services according to their preferences. This is consistent with the definition of equity that is linked to personal choice, such that an outcome is equitable if it arises in a state in which all people have equal choice sets (Le Grand 1991).
3. Equal quality of care for all – implies an absence of preferential treatments that are not based on need; same professional standards for everyone (for example, consultation time, referral patterns); and care that is considered to be acceptable by everyone.

In a similar exercise to identify an operational definition of equity that is relevant to policy-makers and aligned with policy objectives, equal access for equal need is argued to be the most appropriate definition because it is specific to health care and respects the potentially acceptable reasons for differentials in health-care utilization (Oliver & Mossialos 2004). Moreover, unequal access across groups defined by income or socio-economic status is the most appropriate starting point for directing policy and consistent with many governments' aims to provide services on the basis of need rather than ability to pay (Oliver & Mossialos 2004).

The goal of equal (or less unequal) health outcomes appears to be shared by most governments, as expressed in policy statements and international declarations (such as European Union's Health and Consumer Protection Strategy and Programme 2007-2013; WHO's Health 21 targets) (Judge et al. 2006). However, two factors complicate the adoption of equality in health to evaluate health-care performance.

First, social and economic determinants of health fall outside the health system and beyond the scope of health policy and health care. Second, such an action might require restrictions on the ways in which people choose to live their lives (Mooney 1983). In the 1990s the policy support for improving equity of access or receipt of care was more evident than the commitment to improve equality in health (Gulliford 2002). However, more recently the reduction of avoidable health inequalities has become a priority government objective in the United Kingdom (Department of Health 2002 & 2003). The formula used to allocate resources to the regions seeks to improve equity in access to services and to reduce health inequalities (Bevan 2008).

These two principles are clearly linked. Much support for the equity objective based on access derives from its potential for achieving equality in health. Some argue that an equitable distribution of health leads to a more equal distribution of health (Culyer & Wagstaff 1993). Health care is instrumental in improving health or minimizing ill-health. In fact, no one wants to consume health care in a normal situation but it becomes essential at the moment of illness. Demand for health care is thus derived from the demand for health itself (Grossman 1972). Ensuring an equitable distribution of health-care resources serves a broader aim of health improvement and reduction of health inequalities. From the egalitarian viewpoint it is often argued that allocating health-care resources according to need will promote, if not directly result in, equality in health (Wagstaff & van Doorslaer, 2000). Culyer and Wagstaff (1993) demonstrate that this is not necessarily the case but Hurley argues that equality of access is based on the ethical notion of equal opportunity or a fair chance and not necessarily on the consequences of such access, such as utilization or health outcomes (Hurley 2000).

How to define access?

The equity objective of equal access for equal need commands general policy support but the questions of how to define and measure access need to be clarified. Narrowly defined, access is the money and time costs people incur obtaining care (Le Grand 1982; Mooney 1983). One definition of access incorporates additional dimensions: 'the ability to secure a specified set of health care services, at a specified level of quality, subject to a specified maximum level of personal inconvenience and cost, whilst in possession of a specified amount of information' (Goddard & Smith 2001, p.1151).

Accessing health care depends on an array of supply- and demand-side factors (Healy & McKee, 2004). Supply-side factors that affect access to and receipt of care include the volume and distribution of human resources and capital; waiting times; referral patterns; booking systems; how individuals are treated within the system (continuity of care); and quality of care (Gulliford et al. 2002b; Starfield, 1993; Whitehead, 1991). The demand-side has predisposing, enabling and needs factors (Aday & Andersen, 1974), including socio-demographics; past experiences with health care; perceived quality of care; perceived barriers; health literacy; beliefs and expectations regarding health and illness; income levels (ability to pay); scope and depth of insurance coverage; and educational attainment.

The complexity of the concept of access is apparent in the multitude of factors that affect access and potential indicators of access. As a result, many researchers use access synonymous with utilization, implying that an individual's use of health services is proof that he/she can access these services. However, the two are not equivalent (Le Grand 1982; Mooney 1983). As noted, access can be viewed as opportunities available but receipt of treatment depends on both the existence of these opportunities and whether an individual actually makes use of them (Wagstaff & van Doorslaer 2000). Aday and Andersen suggest that a distinction must be made between 'having access' and 'gaining access' – the *possibility* of using a service if required and the actual *use* of a service, respectively (Aday & Andersen 1974; Aday & Andersen 1981). Similarly, Donabedian (1972, p. 111) asserts that: 'proof of access is use of service, not simply the presence of a facility' and thus it is argued that utilization represents *realized* access. In order to evaluate whether an individual has gained access, this view requires measurement of the actual utilization of health care and possibly also the level of satisfaction with that contact and health improvement.

A consensus about the most appropriate metric of access remains to be found. Many different elements or indicators of access can be measured (e.g. waiting time, availability of resources, access costs) and utilization can be directly observed. Therefore, while 'equal access for equal need' is arguably the principle of equity most appropriate for policy, 'equal utilization for equal need' is what is commonly measured and analysed. In this way, inequity is assumed to arise when individuals in higher socio-economic groups are more likely to use or are using a greater quantity of health services after controlling for their level of need (see section below on defining need). However, it should be remembered that differences in utilization levels by socio-economic status (adjusting for need) do not necessarily imply inequity because they may be driven in part by individuals' informed choices or preferences (Le Grand 1991; Oliver & Mossialos 2004). Also an apparently equal distribution of needs-adjusted utilization by socio-economic status may not imply equity if the services used are low quality or inappropriate (Thiede et al. 2007).

Equity of access to health care could also be assessed directly by measuring the extent to which individuals did not receive the health care needed. Unmet need could be measured with clinical information (e.g. medical records or clinical assessments) or by self-report. Subjective unmet need is easily measurable and has been included in numerous recent health surveys e.g. European Union Statistics on Income and Living Conditions (EU-SILC) and the Survey of Health, Ageing and Retirement in Europe (SHARE). Levels of subjective unmet need and the stated reasons for unmet need could provide some insight into the extent of inequity in the system, particularly if these measures are complemented by information on health-care utilization.

How to define need?

An operational definition of need is required in order to examine the extent to which access or utilization is based upon it. Four possible definitions have been proposed in the economics literature (Culyer & Wagstaff 1993).

1. Need is defined in terms of an individual's current health status.
2. Need is measured by capacity to benefit from health care.
3. Need represents the expenditure a person ought to have i.e. the amount of health care required to attain health.
4. Need is indicated by the minimum amount of resources required to exhaust capacity to benefit.

The authors argue that the first definition is too narrow since it may miss the value of preventive care and certain health conditions may not be treatable (Culyer & Wagstaff, 1993). The second does not take account of the amount of resources spent or establish how much health care a person needs. The third takes this into consideration since need is defined as the amount of health care required to attain equality of health. The fourth definition implies that when capacity to benefit is (at the margin) zero then need is zero; when there is positive capacity to benefit need is assessed by considering the amount of expenditure required to reduce capacity to benefit to zero (Culyer & Wagstaff 1993). However, by combining the level of need with the level of required resources the latter definition implies than an individual requiring more expensive intervention has greater need than someone with a potentially more urgent need but for less expensive treatment (Hurley 2000).

The definition of need as the capacity to benefit commands the widest approval in the economics literature (Folland et al. 2004). However, empirical studies measure need by level (and risk) of ill-health partly because of data availability and relative ease of measurement. The assumption that current health status reflects needs is generally considered to be reasonable – an individual in poor general health with a chronic condition clearly needs more health care than an individual in good health with no chronic condition. Also, individuals with higher socio-economic status have been shown generally to have more favourable prospects for health and thus greater capacity to benefit (Evans 1994) therefore allocation according to capacity to benefit may distort the allocation of resources away from the most vulnerable population groups. These latter groups would have worse ill health and allocating resources according to this principle would exacerbate socio-economic inequalities in health (Culyer 1995). From a utilitarian perspective, and to maximize efficiency, resources should be distributed in favour of those with the greatest capacity to benefit. However, an egalitarian perspective would conflict with the capacity to benefit definition of need because of the potential unintended implications for health inequality.

To measure need for health care, an individual's level of ill health is most commonly captured by a subjective measure of self-assessed health (SAH). This provides an ordinal ranking of perceived health status and is often included in general socio-economic and health surveys at European (e.g. European Community Household Panel; EU-SILC) and national level (e.g. British Household Panel Survey). The usual health question asks the respondent to rate their general health and sometimes includes a time reference (rate your health in the last twelve months) or an age benchmark (compare your current health to individuals of your own age). Five categories are usually available for the respondent, ranging from very good or excellent to poor or very poor. SAH has been used extensively in the literature and has been applied to measure the relationship between health and socio-economic status (Adams et al. 2003); the relationship between health and lifestyles (Kenkel 1995); and the measurement of socio-economic inequalities in health (van Doorslaer et al. 1997).

Numerous methodological problems are associated with relying on SAH as a measure of need. An obvious concern relates to its reliability as a predictor of objective health status, but this may be misplaced. An early study from Canada found SAH to be a stronger predictor of seven-year survival among older people than their medical records or self-reports of medical conditions (Mossey & Shapiro 1982). This finding has been replicated in many subsequent studies and countries, showing that this predictive power does not vary across jurisdictions or socio-economic groups (Idler & Benyamini 1997; Idler & Kasl 1995). In their review of the literature, Idler and Benyamini (1997) argue that self-rated health represents an invaluable source of health status information and suggest several possible interpretations for its strong predictive effect on mortality.

- SAH measures health more accurately because it captures all illnesses a person has and possibly as yet undiagnosed symptoms; reflects judgements of severity of illness; and/or reflects individuals' estimates of longevity based on family history.
- SAH not only assesses current health but is also a dynamic evaluation thus representing a decline or improvement in health. Poor assessments of health may lessen an individual's engagement with preventive or self care or provoke non-adherence to screening recommendations, medications or treatments.
- SAH reflects social or individual resources that can affect health or an individual's ability to cope with illness.

Since this review, mounting evidence shows SAH to be a valid summary measure of health. It relates to other health-related indicators and appears to capture the broader influences of mortality (Bailis et al. 2003; Mackenbach et al. 2002; McGee et al. 1999; Singh-Manoux et al. 2006; Sundquist & Johansson, 1997); health-care use (van Doorslaer et al. 2000); and inequalities in mortality (van Doorslaer & Gerdtham 2003).

Self-assessed measures can be further differentiated into subjective and quasi-objective indicators (Jürges 2007), the latter based on respondents' reporting on more factual items such as specific conditions or symptoms. These quasi-objective indicators include the presence of chronic conditions (where specific chronic conditions are listed); specific types of cancer; limitations in activity of daily living (ADL) such as walking, climbing the stairs, etc; or in instrumental activity of daily living (IADL) such as eating or having a bath.

There is strong evidence that SAH is not only predictive of mortality and other objective measures of health but may be a more comprehensive measure of health status than other measures. However, bias is possible if different population groups systematically under- or over-report their health status relative to other groups. The subjective nature of SAH means that it can be influenced by a variety of factors that impact perceptions of health. Bias may arise if the mapping of true health in SAH categories varies according to respondent characteristics. Indeed, subgroups of the population appear to use systematically different cut-point levels when reporting SAH, despite equal levels of true health (Hernández-Quevedo et al. 2008). Moreover, the rating of health status is influenced by culture and language (Angel & Thoits 1987; Zimmer et al. 2000); social context (Sen 2002); gender and age (Groot 2000; Lindeboom & van Doorslaer 2004); and fears and beliefs about disease (Barsky et al. 1992). It is also affected by the way a question is asked e.g. the ordering of the question with other health-related questions or form-based rather than face-to-face interviews (Crossley & Kennedy 2002). Potential biases of SAH include state-dependence reporting bias (Kerkhofs & Lindeboom 1995); scale of reference bias (Groot 2000); and response category cut-point shift (Sadana et al. 2000).

Various approaches have been developed to correct for reporting bias in the literature. The first is to condition on a set of objective indicators of health and assume that any remaining variation in SAH reflects reporting bias. For example, Lindeboom and van Doorslaer (2004) use Canadian data and the McMaster Health Utilities Index as their quasi-objective measure of health. They find some evidence of reporting bias by age and gender but not for income. However, this approach relies on having a sufficiently comprehensive set of objective indicators to capture the variation in true health. The second approach uses health vignettes such as those in the current WHS (Bago d'Uva et al. 2008). The third approach examines biological markers of disease risk in the countries considered for comparison, for example by combining self-reported data with biological data (Banks et al. 2006). Bias in reporting may affect estimates of inequalities. For example Johnston et al. (2007) report that the income gradient appears significant when using an objective measure of hypertension measured by a nurse as opposed to the self-reported measure of hypertension included in the Health Survey for England (HSE).

The availability of objective measures of health, such as biomarkers, is mostly limited to specific national surveys. At the European level, both the ECHP and EU-SILC include only self-reported measures. Only SHARE and the forthcoming European Health Interview Survey include some objective (e.g. walking speed, grip strength) and quasi-objective (e.g. ADL, symptoms) measures of health. At national level, only a few countries include objective measures, such as Finland (blood tests and anthropometric tests – FINRISK), Germany (anthropometric measures – National Health Interview and Examination Survey; urine and blood samples – German Health Survey for Children and Adolescents) and the United Kingdom – English Longitudinal Study of Ageing (ELSA) and HSE.

Biomarkers thus have limited availability and may still be subject to bias. The main methodological challenge lies with the standardization of data collection, as variations may arise from different methods. For example, a person's blood pressure may vary with the time of day. Often detailed information on data collection methods is not provided. This type of measurement error is particularly problematic if it is correlated with socio-demographic characteristics and hence biases estimates of social inequalities. Moreover, the collection of biological data also tends to reduce survey response rates, limiting sample size and representativeness (Masseria et al. 2007).

Overall, there is widespread support for equity goals in health care. However, no single operational definition of equity can capture the multiple supply- and demand-side factors that affect the allocation of effective, high-quality health care on the basis of need. This complexity necessitates not only a comprehensive set of information on individuals, their contacts with health care and system characteristics, but also on strong methodological techniques to assess these relationships empirically.

Methods for equity analysis

Methods of measuring equity of access to health care originated with comparisons of health-care use and health-care need (Collins & Klein 1980; Le Grand 1978) and have since taken broadly two directions. The first uses regression models to measure the independent effect of some measure of socio-economic status on the likelihood of contact with health services, the volume of health services used or the expenditures incurred (regression method). The second quantifies inequity by comparing the cumulative distribution of utilization with that of needs-adjusted utilization (ECuity method). Alternative metrics of equity are listed in Table 2.6.1.

Regression method

Regression analyses are the most commonly used means of measuring equity in the literature. These studies often draw on the behavioural model of health service use that suggests that health-care service use is a function of an individual's predisposition to use services (social structure, health beliefs); factors which enable or impede use on an individual (income and education) and community level (availability of services); and the level of need for care (Andersen 1995). Inequity thus arises when factors other than needs significantly affect the receipt of health care.

Regression models of utilization address the question – When needs and demographic factors affecting utilization are held constant, are individuals with socio-economic advantage (e.g. through income, education, employment status, availability of private insurance, etc.) more likely to access health care, and are they making more contacts, than individuals with less socio-economic advantage? A comprehensive model of utilization with multiple explanatory variables allows policy-relevant interpretations that can identify the factors that affect utilization and, to the extent that they are mutable, develop policies accordingly.

In the empirical literature, the most comprehensive studies of health service utilization have included explanatory variables that consider factors that capture not only needs but also individual predisposition and ability to use health-care services. Several studies of equity

Table 2.6.1 *Examples of summary measures of socio-economic inequalities in access to health care*

Index	Interpretation
Correlation and regression	
Product-moment correlation	Correlation between health care utilization rate and socio-economic status (SES)
Regression on SES	Increase in utilization rate per one unit increase in SES
Regression on cumulative percentiles (relative index of inequality; Slope index of inequality)	Utilization rate ratio (RI/I) or differences (SII) between the least and most advantaged person
Regression on z-values	Utilization rate difference between group with lower and higher than average morbidity rates (x 0.5)
Gini-type coefficients	
Pseudo-Gini coefficient	0 = no utilization differences between groups; 1 = all utilization in hands of one person
Concentration index	0 = no utilization differences associated with SES; -1/+1 = all utilization in hands of least/most advantaged person
Horizontal inequity index	0 = no utilization differences associated with SES after need standardization; -1/+1 = all need standardized utilization in hands of least/most advantaged person
Generalized concentration index	Based on CI, but includes also mean distribution of health care

Source: adapted from Mackenbach & Kunst 1997

based on regression models have been conducted (Abásolo et al. 2001; Buchmueller et al. 2005; Dunlop et al. 2000; Häkkinen & Luoma 2002; Morris et al. 2005; Van der Heyden et al. 2003).

The study described here illustrates the methodology (Morris et al. 2005). The authors measured inequity in general practitioner consultations, outpatient visits, day cases and inpatient stays in England between 1998 and 2000. A variety of need indicators were used, including not only age and gender but also self-reported indicators such as SAH; detailed self-reported indicators such as type of long-standing illness and GHQ-12 score; and ward-level health indicators including under-75 standardized mortality ratios and under-75 standardized illness ratios. Non-need variables such as income, education, employment status, social class and ethnicity were included. The effect of supply variables such as the Index of Multiple Deprivation access domain score, average number of general practitioners per 1000 inhabitants and average distance to acute providers were also considered, although their classification as needs or non-needs indicators is not straightforward (Gravelle et al. 2006; Morris et al. 2005).

The regression models showed that indicators of need were significantly associated with all health-care services (Table 2.6.2). People in worse health conditions were more likely to consult a general practitioner, to utilize outpatient and day care and to be hospitalized. However, non-need variables also played a significant role in determining access to health care (holding all else constant) which signalled inequity. Table 2.6.2 reports the marginal effects on utilization caused by income, education, ethnicity and supply. For example, people with higher incomes were significantly more likely to have an outpatient visit, those with lower educational attainment had a higher probability of consulting a general practitioner and education significantly affected the use of outpatient services. Distance and waiting time effects on utilization were also found.

This study provides an example of how regression models offer a rigorous and meaningful method of understanding the role of various socio-economic and system factors that affect access to health care within a country. However, this approach does not lend itself easily to cross-country and inter-temporal comparisons.

The ECuity method: concentration index

The ECuity method makes use of a regression model but tests for the existence of inequity by creating a relative index that allows comparisons across jurisdictions, time or sectors (O'Donnell et al. 2008). This method derives from the literature on income inequality based on the Lorenz curve and Gini index of inequality. While the Lorenz curve describes the distribution of income in a population, the

Table 2.6.2 *Effect of specific non-need variables on health-care utilization, marginal effects*

	GP	Outpatient	Day cases	Inpatient
Ln (income)	-0.005	**0.011**	0.002	0.003
Education				
Higher education	0.007	0.023	0.001	**0.014**
A level or equivalent	0.014	0.009	-0.001	0.005
GCSE or equivalent	**0.014**	**0.020**	0.001	0.008
CSE or equivalent	**0.021**	0.021	0.008	0.004
Other qualifications	**0.032**	**0.041**	0.000	0.003
No qualifications	**0.015**	-0.003	-0.006	0.000
Ethnic group				
Black Caribbean	-0.006	-0.011	0.010	-0.009
Black African	0.009	-0.007	0.013	0.013
Black other	0.057	0.019	0.006	-0.016
Indian	**0.030**	-0.009	-0.009	-0.002
Pakistani	0.022	**-0.065**	-0.016	0.004
Bangladeshi	0.029	**-0.085**	0.015	-0.020
Chinese	-0.014	**-0.122**	-0.020	**-0.039**
Other non-white	0.012	**-0.043**	-0.002	0.014
Supply				
Access domain score	**-0.011**			
Proportion of outpatient <26 weeks		**0.351**		
GPs per 1000 patients			0.021	
Average distance to acute providers				**-0.0004**

Numbers in bold are statistically significant with 95% confidence interval

Source: Morris et al. 2005

concentration curve describes the relationship between the cumulative proportion of the population ranked by income (x-axis) and the cumulative proportion of health-care utilization (y-axis). Like the Gini index that provides a measure of income inequality, the concentration index is a measure of income-related inequality in access to health care and is estimated as twice the area between the concentration curve and the line of perfect equality (diagonal).

The concentration curves for actual medical care utilization (*LM*) and for needs-adjusted utilization (*LN*) are shown in Fig. 2.6.1. Individuals are ranked by a socio-economic variable (e.g. income) from the lowest or poorest to the highest or richest individual. If the cumulative proportion of both health-care utilization and needs-adjusted utilization are distributed equally across income then the two curves will coincide with the diagonal (line of perfect equality). If they lie above (below) the diagonal, the receipt of health care and the distribution of health-care need advantage the lower (higher) socio-economic

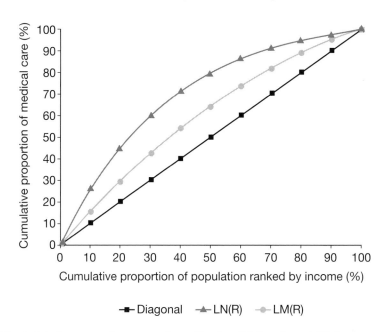

Fig. 2.6.1 Concentration curves for utilization (LM) and need (LN) compared to line of perfect equality (diagonal)

groups, implying pro-poor (pro-rich) inequality. The level of horizontal inequity in the receipt of health care is quantified by comparing the two distributions – when the unadjusted health care utilization and needs-adjusted utilization curves coincide, the horizontal inequity index equals zero (no inequity). Horizontal inequity favours the richer (poorer) if the needs-adjusted concentration curve lies above (below) the unadjusted utilization concentration curve.

Kakwani et al. have shown that it is possible to compute the index using a convenient regression of the concentration index on the relative income rank (Kakwani et al. 1997; O'Donnell et al. 2008). Based on an initial health-care demand model (as in the regression approach described above) it is possible to calculate the concentration index of needs-predicted utilization. This is compared with the concentration index of actual utilization to calculate the index of horizontal inequity.

The concentration index is therefore a relative measure of inequality (Wagstaff et al. 1989) that has the main advantages of capturing the socio-economic dimension of inequities; including information on the whole socio-economic distribution (i.e. income distribution); providing visual representation through the concentration curves; and, finally, allowing checks of stochastic relationships (Wagstaff et al. 1991). Moreover, this approach allows comparisons of inequity across countries and across time in order to understand the specific role that health system characteristics play in inequity.

Horizontal inequity indices were defined primarily to synthesize information from cross-sectional data but they have also been used to measure socio-economic inequalities in health and health-care use with longitudinal data (Bago d'Uva et al. 2007; Hernández-Quevedo et al. 2006). A longitudinal perspective enables the researcher to reveal whether inequalities have reduced or increased with time and to classify them as either short-term (using cross-sectional data) or long-term (aggregated over a series of periods) (Jones & López-Nicolás 2004). A mobility index (MI) can be created to summarize the discrepancy between short- and long-term inequalities. This is equal to one minus the ratio of the long-term inequity index and the weighted sum of all the short-term (cross-sectional) inequity indices. If the long-term index is equal to the weighted sum of the short-term inequity indices then MI equals zero. If it is negative (positive) the long-term inequity is larger (smaller) than the weighted sum of short term inequity:

$$MI= 1- (HI^{LT}/SHI^{ST})$$

This methodology has been used mainly for analyses of inequalities in health (Hernández-Quevedo et al. 2006; Lecluyse 2007).

The concentration index approach has a further advantage of enabling decomposition of the contribution of need (i.e. ill-health) and non-need (i.e. socio-economic) variables to overall inequality in health care (O'Donnell et al. 2008; Wagstaff et al. 2003). The contribution of each determinant to total inequality in health-care utilization can be decomposed into two deterministic components (equal to the weighted sum of the concentration indices of need and non-need regressors) and a residual component that reflects the inequality in health that cannot be explained by systematic variation across income groups. Therefore, the contributors to inequality can be divided into inequalities in each of the need and non-need variables. Each variable's contribution to total inequality would be the sum of three factors: (i) the relative weight of such a variable (measured by its mean); (ii) its income distribution (indicated by the concentration index of the variable of interest); and (iii) its marginal effect on the utilization of health care (regression coefficient). Hence the decomposition method can be a useful instrument for describing the factors that contribute to inequality .

Despite the extensive use of the Concentration Index (CI), the shortcomings associated with this measure have been recently discussed in the literature. Firstly, the CI depends on the mean of the variable and, hence, could confound comparisons of health inequality across time or countries (Wagstaff 2005). Secondly, the ranking differs depending on whether one measures inequalities in health or inequalities in ill-health (Clarke et al. 2000). Finally, the value provided by the CI is arbitrary if one analyses a qualitative measure of health (Erreygers 2006). To overcome these limitations, Erreygers (2009) recently proposed a corrected version of the CI that transforms the standard index by the mean and the bounds of the health variable. This adjusted CI has already been applied in different works (for example, van de Poel et al. 2008).

The concentration index approach has been used mainly for measuring horizontal inequity – equal utilization for people with equal need, independent of income. Few studies have used the vertical equity principle of proportional unequal access for unequals. In contrast, the vertical equity principle has been used mainly for measuring income-related equity in health-care finance (O'Donnell et al. 2008; Wagstaff & van Doorslaer 2000; Wagstaff et al. 1999). The Kakwani index measures the extent to which each source of finance (e.g. taxes, social insurance, private insurance, out-of-pocket payments) or the overall financing system (weighted average of each source of finance index) departs from proportionality.

The empirical research on equity of access to health care has increasingly drawn on the technical methods of the concentration and horizontal inequity indices (Allin et al. 2009; Chen & Escarce 2004; Jiménez-Rubio et al. 2008; Lu et al. 2007; Masseria et al. 2009; van Doorslaer et al. 2004; van Doorslaer et al. 2006). A recent OECD project evaluated income-related inequity across twenty-one countries in physician, hospital and dental sectors (van Doorslaer et al. 2004a; van Doorslaer et al. 2006), standardizing for needs (measured as self-reported health status, health limitations, age and gender). The decomposition approach was also used to disentangle the role of different need and non-need variables. The detailed results of equity in physician visits are discussed here.

Within-country variations in use by income indicate that low-income groups are more likely to visit a doctor than higher income groups in all OECD countries. However, standardizing for population needs, the probability of a doctor visit was higher among richer groups (Fig. 2.6.2). The probability of contacting a general practitioner appeared to be distributed according to need and no statistically significant inequities were found, except in Canada, Finland and Portugal. However, when considering only those who have at least one general practitioner visit, poorer people consulted general practitioners more often. The pattern was very different for specialist visits. In all countries, higher-income individuals had a significantly higher probability of visiting a specialist, and were making more visits, than the poor.

The authors followed the decomposition method to calculate the contributions of need, income, education, activity status, region and insurance to total inequality. Fig. 2.6.3 reports the results for the analysis of specialist visit probability. The contribution of need was negative in all countries (it reduced inequity) but the contribution of income, education and insurance was positive. Table 2.6.3 examines the role of education in inequity in the probability of a specialist visit in Spain.

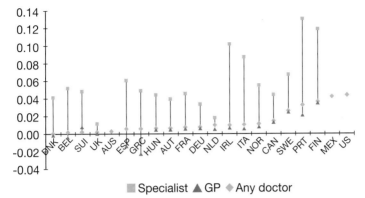

Fig. 2.6.2 Horizontal inequity indices for annual probability of a visit, twenty-one OECD countries

Countries ranked by HI index for doctor visits. HI indices are estimated as concentration indices for need-standardized use. Positive (negative) index indicates a pro-rich (pro-poor) distribution. German general practitioner and specialist indices calculated from ECHP 1996

Source: van Doorslaer, Masseria & Koolman 2006

Low education's contribution to inequity depends on its mean value (63% of the population reported to have low education); relationship with income (measured by the concentration index which indicates that people with low education tend also to have lower incomes); and marginal effect on specialist care (people with low education use specialist care 4.3% less than those with higher education). Thus poor education makes a positive contribution to total inequality, thereby increasing inequity. The total contribution of education is given by the sum of the contributions of low and medium education.

A longitudinal perspective enables the researcher to reveal whether inequalities have reduced or increased with time. Hospital care is a particularly interesting example of the usefulness of this data. Infrequent annual use of hospital care and its skewed distribution may undermine the reliability of estimates of hospital care needs in cross-sectional analysis, particularly when the sample size is relatively small. Masseria et al. (2009) compared the pooled (1994-1998) and wave by wave results of the ECHP. They demonstrated that it was possible to enhance the power of the estimates and to obtain robust estimates of inpatient horizontal inequity by pooling several years of survey data, (see Table 2.6.4). Indeed, inequity in hospital care was found to be

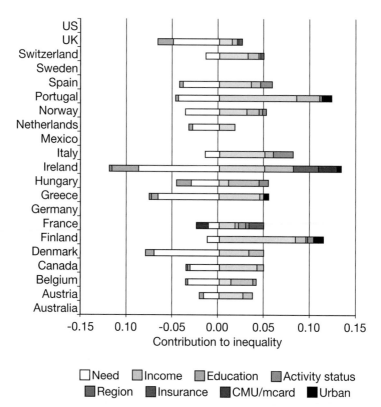

Fig. 2.6.3 Decomposition of inequity in specialist probability

Source: van Doorslaer et al. 2004a

Table 2.6.3 *Contribution of income and education to total specialist inequality in Spain, 2000*

	Mean	Concentration index	Marginal effect	Contribution to inequity	Sum contribution
HI index				0.066	0.066
Logarithm of income	14.121	0.025	0.047	0.036	0.036
Education: medium	0.171	0.139	-0.008	0.000	
Education: low	0.630	-0.159	-0.043	0.010	0.009

Source: van Doorslaer et al. 2004a

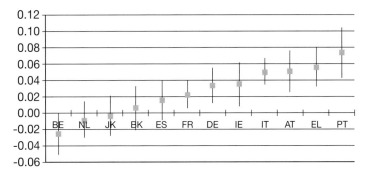

Fig. 2.6.4 Horizontal inequity index for the probability of hospital admission in twelve European countries (1994-1998)

Source: Masseria et al. 2009

significantly pro-rich in seven of the twelve countries analysed and significantly pro-poor in one – Belgium. Conversely, the wave by wave results rarely showed significant inequity, due to their lack of power.

In Table 2.6.4, the MI summarizes the discrepancy between short- and long-term inequalities. The MI was found to be negative in some countries and positive in others. Negative mobility indices mean that the weighted averages of the cross-sectional concentration indices are smaller in absolute value than the longitudinal indices. A negative index suggests that individuals with downwardly mobile incomes have below average levels of health-care use compared to upwardly mobile individuals. This makes long-run income-related inequity greater than would be expected from a cross-sectional measure (contrary applies to a positive index).

Policy implications and directions for future research

Most governments widely accept the goal of equitable access to health care. This goal is motivated by the egalitarian view that access to care is a right and by the potential for equity of access to help reduce health inequalities. Translating this policy goal to a measurable objective is not straightforward. Moreover, considerable debate surrounds the definition of equity, health-care need and access as well as the methods for calculating equity in health care.

Empirical research most commonly measures the goal of treating equals equally; health-care need is measured by levels of ill-health and

Table 2.6.4 *Short-run and long-run horizontal inequity index, MI*

	Wave 1	Wave 2	Wave 3	Wave 4	Wave 5	Pooled	Mobility
Austria		**0.046**	0.070	0.052	0.036	**0.050**	0.029
Belgium	-0.04	-0.029	0.003	-0.019	-0.046	**-0.025**	-0.031
Denmark	0.00	0.049	-0.022	0.022	-0.022	0.006	-0.120
France	0.01	-0.011	0.026	0.030	**0.075**	**0.023**	0.085
Germany	**0.03**	**0.056**	0.015			**0.033**	0.005
Greece	**0.07**	**0.060**	0.037	0.031	**0.074**	**0.055**	-0.015
Ireland	0.04	0.039	0.077	-0.017	0.050	**0.036**	0.025
Italy	0.02	**0.066**	**0.059**	**0.040**	**0.067**	**0.050**	-0.056
Netherlands	0.02	**-0.049**	-0.009	0.029	-0.024	-0.008	0.058
Portugal	0.04	**0.071**	0.087	0.100	0.082	0.074	-0.082
Spain	0.03	0.000	**0.041**	-0.026	0.037	0.016	-0.032
UK	0.00	-0.010	-0.001			-0.003	0.193

Numbers in bold are statistically significant with a 95% confidence interval
Source: authors' calculations based on Masseria et al. 2009

access approximated by utilization. Thus, inequity can be identified where patterns of utilization differ between individuals with the same health-care need (health status and risk of ill-health) across income, social or other socio-economic groups. These analyses require information on socio-economic status, health status and utilization patterns, whether using regression methods or calculating concentration indices of inequity. Analyses of equity can be used to inform policy decisions insofar as the studies are based on accurate and meaningful data.

Empirical analyses may be based on survey, administrative or, ideally, linked datasets. Survey data provide comprehensive information on all these levels but administrative data may provide more accurate information on utilization. This can include the intensity of use measured not just by number of visits but also by total expenditure and the different types of services used (e.g. diagnostic tests received, day surgeries, referrals). Administrative utilization data also address the problems of recall bias and subjectivity, and cover the entire population using health care including those groups typically excluded or underrepresented in surveys (people who are homeless, without tele-phones or living in institutions). However, administrative data provide a less comprehensive source of socio-economic information and health status. Socio-economic data would typically be collected through geo-graphical measures of income or deprivation. Health status could be measured by physician diagnosis but this limits the information avail-able to those who have been in contact with the health system. Linking administrative and survey data is the ideal approach to benefit from the accuracy and detail of utilization information and the comprehen-siveness of self-reported socio-economic and health indicators from surveys.

The majority of studies draw on survey data to undertake equity analyses. Self-reported indicators of health status are the most com-monly used measures of health-care needs as they are available in national and international health surveys. These measures are sub-ject to numerous methodological problems but various studies have shown that they are strong predictors of objective health status and mortality. However, even if ill-health is measured accurately it may not provide an indication of what (and to what extent) services are needed to restore health (Culyer & Wagstaff 1993). A review of equity studies in the United Kingdom noted that the majority pay little attention to the complex concept of need (Goddard & Smith 2001). The majority of studies show widespread acceptance of the assumption that need can be measured using SAH, though many also control for factors that may affect the reporting of health status (e.g. age and sex) and incorporate some indication of an individual's risk of ill-health (e.g. age, obesity, symptoms), while also considering a broad set of SAH indicators.

There has been some growth in the collection of more objective indicators of health. Recent health surveys (e.g. SHARE, Health Interview Survey) include quasi-objective indicators of ill-health, based on respondents' reporting on more factual items such as specific con-ditions or activity limitations (e.g. presence of chronic conditions, spe-cific limitations in ADL or IADL). These indicators have proved useful for building a more general index of ill-health that corrects issues of reporting bias (Jürges 2007). A few surveys (e.g. WHS) have recently introduced vignettes that allow potential biases to be corrected with SAH measures. The availability of objective measures of health, such as biomarkers, is restricted to a few national, cross-sectional surveys and still presents a methodological issue concerning the standardization of data collection.

The methodological difficulties associated with measuring equity are discussed above. In addition, needs-adjusted utilization does not account for potentially acceptable variations in utilization, such as those driven by individuals' choices (Le Grand 1991; Whitehead 1991). Survey data permit further subjective analyses of health-care contacts such as perceived timeliness, quality and overall satisfaction that complement information on utilization. Moreover, subjective unmet need for health care may also be included in surveys. Subjective unmet need has largely been interpreted to represent system-level barriers to access (Elofsson et al. 1998; Mielck et al. 2007; Westin et al. 2004). However, the different reasons for unmet need include personal (e.g. fears and preferences) and system factors (e.g. costs). It is important to differentiate these reasons and to examine the association between reported unmet need and contacts with the health system. Research linking information on levels and reasons for subjective unmet need with actual health-care utilization patterns could therefore complement conventional equity analyses.

Meaningful research on equity in health care relies on the availability of comprehensive and reliable data. Ideally, these would be longitudinal survey and administrative sources linked at the individual level. Population health surveys should include information on health status (including general, specific, subjective and quasi-objective measures, vignettes to test for reporting bias); socio-economic status (including all income sources, assets such as home ownership and financial assets, education, employment); utilization of health care (disaggregated by type of service); experiences with health care (including accessibility, acceptability, waiting times, satisfaction, perceived quality, direct costs, non-use of health care, i.e. unmet need); and other factors that affect access (including details of insurance status and entitlements). Furthermore, information on an individual's residence (post code) makes it possible to calculate the distance to health-care facilities. Finally, clinical appropriateness could be assessed on the basis of available information on diagnoses and health service utilization. This quality aspect of health care remains relatively undeveloped in equity analyses.

Longitudinal data permit more in-depth investigation of the trends and dynamics of inequalities over time. The long-term perspective provides useful information on population-representative disease trajectories; links between outcomes and earlier experiences and behaviours; and the dynamics between individual and family characteristics, take-up of insurance, asset accumulation, health and health care. For the measurement of inequalities in health, it has been shown that the use of longitudinal data captures the mobility of individuals in their ranking according to their socio-economic levels (Hernández-Quevedo et al. 2006; Jones & López-Nicolás 2004). Such mobility is particularly interesting if this variation is systematically associated with changes in levels of health (Hernández-Quevedo et al. 2006). For the study of equity of access to health care, longitudinal data also allow consideration of the possible endogeneity of need variables in the health-care utilization models (Sutton et al. 1999).

A growing evidence base demonstrates inequitable utilization or treatment patterns in many countries, though many questions remain (including whether inequity of access to health care contributes to inequalities in health). There is a need to investigate the link between access to health care, health outcomes and health inequalities. This will not only improve understanding of the processes by which health inequalities arise and can be reduced, but also may increase support for improving efforts to ensure equitable access. It is difficult to address the question of whether inequitable utilization leads to unequal health outcomes on a population level. The research that has been conducted has relied on disease-specific approaches which (although not generalizable to the population level) have the potential to inform policy approaches, e.g. in the treatment of particular conditions such as acute myocardial infarction in Canada (Alter et al. 1999; Alter et al. 2006; Pilote et al. 2003).

It is well-known that the policies needed to reduce inequalities in health call for integrated, multi-sectoral approaches that extend beyond the health system (Mackenbach & Bakker 2002; WHO 2008). These address not only health and social care and poverty alleviation but also health-related behaviours (smoking, alcohol consumption, diet, obesity); psychosocial factors (psychosocial stressors, social support, social integration); material factors (housing conditions, working conditions, financial problems); and access to health care. Many countries have explicit public health policies that address some or all of these (Judge et al. 2006). Equitable access to health care plays a critical role (Dahlgren & Whitehead 2006). Careful monitoring of equity in health care on the basis of robust empirical analyses is vital to measure the impact of health-care policies and broader reform initiatives on health system performance. Continued research is needed to understand not only the causes of inequity but also what policy measures are effective in ensuring that individuals in need receive effective, high-quality health care.

References

Abásolo, I. Manning, R. Jones, A (2001). 'Equity in utilization of and access to public-sector GPs in Spain.' *Applied Economics*, 33(3): 349–364.

Adams, P. Hurd, M. McFadden, D. Merrill, A. Ribeiro, T (2003). 'Healthy, wealthy and wise? Tests for direct causal paths between health and socioeconomic status.' *Journal of Econometrics*, 112: 3–56.

Aday, LA. Andersen, RM (1974). 'A framework for the study of access to medical care.' *Health Services Research*, 9(3): 208–220.

Aday, LA. Andersen, RM (1981). 'Equity of access to medical care: a conceptual and empirical overview.' *Medical Care*, 19(12): 4–27.

Allin, S. Masseria, C. Mossialos, E (2009). 'Measuring socioeconomic differences in use of health care services by wealth versus by income.' *American Journal of Public Health*, 10.2105/AJPH.2008.141499.

Alter, DA. Chong, A. Austin, PC. Mustard, C. Iron, K. Williams, JI. Morgan, CD. Tu, JV. Irvine, J. Naylor, CD. SESAMI Study Group (2006). 'Socioeconomic status and mortality after acute myocardial infarction.' *Annals of Internal Medicine*, 144(2): 82–93.

Alter, DA. Naylor, DC. Austin, P. Tu, JV (1999). 'Effects of socioeconomic status on access to invasive cardiac procedures and on mortality after acute myocardial infarction. *New England Journal of Medicine*, 341(18): 1359–1367.

Andersen, RM (1995). 'Revisiting the behavioral model and access to medical care: does it matter?' *Journal of Health and Social Behaviour*, 36(1): 1–10.

Angel, R. and Thoits, P (1987). 'The impact of culture on the cognitive structure of illness.' *Culture, Medicine and Psychiatry*, 11(4): 465–494.

Atkinson, A. Cantillon, B. Marlier, E. Nolan, B (eds.) (2002). '*Social indicators: the EU and social inclusion*.' Oxford: Oxford University Press.

Bago d'Uva, T. Jones, A. van Doorslaer, E (2007). *Measurement of horizontal inequity in health care utilization using European panel data*. Rotterdam: Erasmus University (Tinbergen Institute Discussion Paper TI 2007 - 059/3).

Bago d'Uva, T. Van Doorslaer, E. Lindeboom, M. O'Donnell, O (2008). 'Does reporting heterogeneity bias the measurement of health disparities?' *Health Economics,* 17(3): 351–375.

Bailis, DS. Segall, A. Chipperfield, JG (2003). 'Two views of self-rated general health status.' *Social Science and Medicine,* 56(2): 203–217.

Banks, J. Marmot, M. Oldfield, Z. Smith, JP (2006). 'Disease and disadvantage in the United States and England.' *Journal of the American Medical Association,* 295(17): 2037–2045.

Barsky, AJ. Cleary, PD. Klerman, GL (1992). 'Determinants of perceived health status of medical outpatients.' *Social Science and Medicine,* 34(10): 1147–1154.

Bevan, G (2008). *Review of the weighted capitation formula.* London: Department of Health.

Buchmueller, T. Grumbach, K. Kronick, R. Kahn, JG (2005). 'The effect of health insurance on medical care utilization and implications for insurance expansion: a review of the literature.' *Medical Research and Review,* 62(1): 3–30.

Chen, AY. Escarce, JJ (2004). 'Quantifying income-related inequality in healthcare delivery in the United States.' *Medical Care,* 42(1): 38–47.

Clarke, PM. Gerdtham, U-G. Johannesson, M. Bingefors, K. Smith, L (2002). On the measurement of relative and absolute income-related health inequality. *Social Science & Medicine,* 55(11):1923–1928.

Collins, E. Klein, R (1980). 'Equity and the NHS: self-reported morbidity, access and primary care.' *British Medical Journal,* 281(6248): 1111–1115.

Crossley, TF. Kennedy, S (2002). 'The reliability of self-assessed health status.' *Journal of Health Economics,* 21(4): 643–658.

Culyer, AJ (1995). 'Need: the idea won't do – but we still need it.' *Social Science and Medicine,* 40(6): 727–730.

Culyer, AJ (2007). 'Equity of what in healthcare? Why the traditional answers don't help policy – and what to do in the future?' *Healthcare Papers,* 8(Spec. No.): 12–26.

Culyer, AJ. Wagstaff, A (1993). 'Equity and equality in health and health care.' *Journal of Health Economics,* 12(4): 431–457.

Dahlgren, G. Whitehead, M (2006). *European strategies for tackling social inequities in health: levelling up. Part 2.* Copenhagen: WHO Regional Office for Europe.

Department of Health (2002). *Tackling inequalities in health: 2002 cross-cutting review.* London: The Stationery Office.

Department of Health (2003). *Tackling inequalities in health: a programme for action.* London: The Stationery Office.

Donabedian, A (1971). 'Social responsibility for personal health services: an examination of basic values.' *Inquiry,* 8(2): 3–19.

Donabedian, A (1972). 'Models for organizing the delivery of personal health services and criteria for evaluating them.' *Milbank Memorial Fund Quarterly*, 50(Pt 2): 103–154.

Dunlop, PC. Coyte, PC. McIsaac, W (2000). 'Socio-economic status and the utilisation of physicians' services: results from the Canadian National Population Health Survey.' *Social Science and Medicine*, 51(1): 123–133.

Elofsson, S. Undén, A-L. Krakau, I (1998). 'Patient charges – a hindrance to financially and psychosocially disadvantaged groups seeking care.' *Social Science and Medicine*, 46(10): 1375–1380.

Erreygers, G (2006). Beyond the health Concentration Index: an Atkinson alternative for the measurement of the socioeconomic inequality of health. In: Paper presented at the Conference Advancing Health Equity, Helsinki, WIDER-UNU.

Erreygers, G (2009). Correcting the Concentration Index. *Journal of Health Economics*, 28(2): 504–515.

Evans, RG (1994). Introduction. In: Evans, RG. Marmor, T. Barer, M (eds.). *Why are some people healthy and others not? The determinants of health of populations*. Berlin: Aldine de Gruyter.

Folland, S. Goodman, AC. Stano, M (2004). *The economics of health and health care*. Upper Saddle River, NJ: Pearson Prentice Hall.

Goddard, M. Smith, P (2001). 'Equity of access to health care services: theory and evidence from the UK.' *Social Science and Medicine*, 53(9): 1149–1162.

Gravelle, H. Morris, S. d Sutton, M (2006). Economic studies of equity in the consumption of health care. In: Jones, AJ (ed.). *The Elgar companion to health economics*. Cheltenham: Edward Elgar.

Groot, W (2000). 'Adaptation and scale of reference bias in self-assessments of quality of life.' *Journal of Health Economics*, 19(3): 403–420.

Grossman, M (1972). 'On the concept of health capital and the demand for health.' *Journal of Political Economy*, 80(2): 223–255.

Gulliford, M (2002). Equity and access to health care. In: Gulliford, M. Morgan, M (eds.). *Access to health care*. London: Routledge.

Gulliford, M. Figueroa-Minoz, J. Morgan, M (2002a). Meaning of 'access' in health care. In: Gulliford, M. Morgan, M (eds.). *Access to health care*. London: Routledge.

Gulliford, M. Figueroa-Munoz, J. Morgan, M. Hughes, D. Gibson, B. Beech, R. Hudson, M (2002b). 'What does 'access to health care' mean?' *Journal of Health Services Research and Policy*, 7(3): 186–188.

Häkkinen, U. Luoma, K (2002). 'Change in determinants of use of physician services in Finland between 1987 and 1996.' *Social Science and Medicine*, 55(9): 1523–1537.

Healy, J. McKee, M (eds.) (2004). *Accessing health care: responding to diversity*. Oxford: Oxford University Press.

Hernández-Quevedo, C. Jones, A. López-Nicolás, A. Rice, N (2006). 'Socioeconomic inequalities in health: a comparative longitudinal analysis using the European Community household panel.' *Social Science and Medicine,* 63(5): 1246–1261.

Hernández-Quevedo, C. Jones, A. Rice, N (2008). 'Reporting bias and heterogeneity in self-assessed health. Evidence from the British Household Panel Survey.' [in Spanish] *Cuadernos Económicos de ICE,* 75: 63–97.

Hurley, J (2000). An overview of the normative economics of the health sector. In: Culyer, AJ. Newhouse, JP (eds.). *Handbook of health economics.* Amsterdam: Elsevier Science BV.

Hurst, J. Jee-Hughes, M (2001). Performance measurement and performance management in OECD health systems. In: *Labour market and social policy occasional papers no. 47.* Paris: OECD.

Idler, E. Benyamini, Y (1997). 'Self-rated health and mortality: a review of twenty-seven community studies.' *Journal of Health and Social Behavior,* 38(1): 21–37

Idler, E. Kasl, SV (1995). 'Self-ratings of health: do they also predict change in functional ability?' *Journal of Gerontology,* 50(6): 344–353.

Jiménez-Rubio, D. Smith, PC. van Doorslaer, E (2008). 'Equity in health and health care in a decentralised context: evidence from Canada.' *Health Economics,* 17(3): 377–392.

Johnston, DW. Propper, C. Shields, MA (2007). *Comparing subjective and objective measures of health: evidence from hypertension for the income/health gradient.* Bonn: Institute for the Study of Labor (IZA Discussion Paper No. 2737).

Jones, AJ. López-Nicolás, A (2004). 'Measurement and explanation of socioeconomic inequality in health with longitudinal data.' *Health Economics,* 13(10): 1015–1030.

Judge, K. Platt, S. Costongs, C. Jurczak, K (2006). Health inequalities: a challenge for Europe. In: *Report prepared for the UK Presidency of the EU.* London: Department of Health.

Jürges, H (2007). 'True health vs response styles: exploring cross-country differences in self-reported health.' *Health Economics,* 16(2): 163–178.

Kakwani, N. Wagstaff, A. van Doorslaer, E (1997). 'Socioeconomic inequality in health: measurement, computation and statistical inference.' *Journal of Econometrics,* 77(1): 87–103.

Kenkel, D (1995). 'Should you eat breakfast? Estimates from health production functions.' *Health Economics,* 4(1): 15–29.

Kerkhofs, M. Lindeboom, M (1995). 'Subjective health measures and state dependent reporting errors.' *Health Economics,* 4(3): 221–235.

Koolman, X. van Doorslaer, E (2004). 'On the interpretation of the concentration index of inequality.' *Health Economics,* 13(7): 649–656.

Lecluyse, A (2007). 'Income-related health inequality in Belgium: a longi-tudinal perspective.' *European Journal of Health Economics*, 8(3): 237–243.

Le Grand, J (1978). 'The distribution of public expenditure: the case of health care.' *Economica*, 45(178): 125–142.

Le Grand, J (1982). *The strategy of equality.* London: George Allen and Unwin.

Le Grand, J (1991). *Equity and choice: an essay in economics and applied philosophy.* London: Harper Collins Academic.

Lindeboom, M. van Doorslaer, E (2004). 'Cut-point shift and index shift in self-reported health.' *Journal of Health Economics*, 23(6): 1083–1099.

Lu, J. F. Leung, GM. Kwon, S. Tin, KY. van Doorslaer, E. O'Donnell, O (2007). 'Horizontal equity in health care utilization evidence from three high-income Asian economies.' *Social Science and Medicine*, 64(1): 199–212.

Mackenbach, JP. Bakker, MJ (2002). *Reducing inequalities in health.* London: Routledge.

Mackenbach, JP. Kunst, AE (1997). 'Measuring the magnitude of socio-eco-nomic inequalities in health: an overview of available measures illus-trated with two examples from Europe.' *Social Science and Medicine*, 44(6): 757–771.

Mackenbach, JP. Simon, JG. Looman, CWN. Joung, IMA (2002). 'Self-assessed health and mortality: could psychosocial factors explain the association?' *International Journal of Epidemiology*, 31(6): 1162–1168.

Masseria, C. Allin, S. Sorenson, C. Papanicolas, I. Mossialos, E (2007). *What are the methodological issues related to measuring health and drawing comparisons across countries? A research note.* Brussels: DG Employment and Social Affairs, European Observatory on the Social Situation and Demography.

Masseria, C. Koolman, X. van Doorslaer, E (2009). 'Income related ine-quality in the probability of a hospital admission in Europe.' *Health Economics Policy and Law*, forthcoming.

McGee, DL. Liao, Y. Cao, G. Cooper, RS (1999). 'Self-reported health sta-tus and mortality in a multiethnic US cohort.' *American Journal of Epidemiology*, 149(1): 41–46.

Mielck, A. Kiess, R. van den Knesebeck, O. Stirbu, I. Kunst, A (2007). Association between access to health care and household income among the elderly in 10 western European countries. In: *Tackling health inequalities in Europe: an integrated approach*. Rotterdam: Erasmus MC Department of Public Health.

Mooney, G (1983). 'Equity in health care: confronting the confusion.' *Effective Health Care*, 1(4): 179–185.

Mooney, G (1986). *Economics, medicine and health care.* Brighton: Wheatsheaf Books Ltd.

Morris, S. Sutton, M. Gravelle, H (2005). 'Inequity and inequality in the use of health care in England: an empirical investigation.' *Social Science and Medicine,* 60(6): 1251–1266.

Mossey, J. Shapiro, E (1982). 'Self-rated health: a predictor of mortality among the elderly.' *American Journal of Public Health,* 72(8): 800–808.

Mossialos, E. Thomson, S (2003). 'Access to health care in the European Union: the impact of user charges and voluntary health insurance. In: Gulliford, M. Morgan, M (eds.) *Access to health care.* London: Routledge.

O'Donnell, O. van Doorslaer, E. Wagstaff, A. Lindelow, M (2008). *Analyzing health equity using household survey data: a guide to techniques and their implementation.* Washington, DC: The World Bank.

OECD (1992). *The reform of health care: a comparative analysis of seven OECD countries.* Paris.

Oliver, A. Mossialos, E (2004). 'Equity of access to health care: outlining the foundation for action.' *Journal of Epidemiology and Community Health,* 58(8): 655–658.

Pilote, L. Joseph, L. Bélisle, P. Penrod, J (2003). 'Universal health insurance coverage does not eliminate inequities in access to cardiac procedures after acute myocardial infarction.' *American Heart Journal,* 146(6): 1030–1037.

President's Commission for the Study of Ethical Problems in Medicine and Biomedical and Behavioural Research (1983). '*Securing access to health care.*' Washington, DC: US Government Printing Office.

Rawls, J (1971). *A theory of justice.* Cambridge, Massachusetts: Harvard University Press.

Sadana, R. Mathers, CD. Lopez, AD. Murray, CJL. Iburg, K (2000). *Comparative analysis of more than 50 household surveys on health status.* Geneva: World Health Organization (GPE Discussion Paper No 15. EIP/GPE/EBD).

Sen, A (1992). *Inequality reexamined.* Cambridge: Harvard University Press.

Sen, A (2002). 'Health: perception versus observation.' *British Medical Journal,* 324(7342): 860–861.

Singh-Manoux, A. Martikainen, P. Ferrie, J. Zins, M. Marmot, M. Goldberg, M (2006). 'What does self rated health measure? Results from the British Whitehall II and French Gazel cohort studies.' *Journal of Epidemiology and Community Health,* 60(4): 364–372.

Starfield, B (1993). *Primary care – concept, evaluation and policy.* Oxford: Oxford University Press.

Sundquist, J. Johansson, SE (1997). 'Self-reported poor health and low educational level predictors for mortality: a population-based follow up study of 39,156 people in Sweden.' *Journal of Epidemiology and Community Health,* 51(1): 35–40.

Sutton, M. Carr-Hill, R. Gravelle, H. Rice, N (1999). 'Do measures of self-reported morbidity bias the estimation of the determinants of health care utilization?' *Social Science and Medicine,* 49(7): 867–878.

Thiede, M. Akweongo, P. McIntyre, D (2007). Exploring the dimensions of access. In: McIntyre, D. Mooney, G (eds.). *The economics of health equity.* Cambridge: Cambridge University Press.

Van de Poel, E. Hosseinpoor, A, Speybroeck, N. Van Ourti, T. Vega, J (2008). Socioeconomic inequality in malnutrition in developing countries. Bulletin of the World Health Organization, 84(4): 282–291.

Van der Heyden, JH. Demarest, S. Tafforeau, J. Van Oyen, H (2003). 'Socio-economic differences in the utilization of health services in Belgium.' *Health Policy,* 65(2): 153–165.

van Doorslaer, E. Gerdtham, UG. (2003). 'Does inequality in self-assessed health predict inequality in survival by income? Evidence from Swedish data.' *Social Science and Medicine,* 57(9): 1621–1629.

van Doorslaer, E. Koolman, X. Jones, A (2004). 'Explaining income-related inequalities in doctor utilisation in Europe.' *Health Economics,* 13(7): 629–647.

van Doorslaer, E. Masseria, C. Koolman, X. OECD Health Equity Research Group (2006). 'Inequalities in access to medical care by income in developed countries.' *Canadian Medical Association Journal,* 174(2): 177–183.

van Doorslaer, E. Masseria, C. OECD Health Equity Research Group Members (2004a). *Income-related inequality in the use of medical care in 21 OECD countries.* Paris: OECD.

van Doorslaer, E. Wagstaff, A. Bleichrodt, H. Calonge, S. Gerdtham, UG. Gerfin, M. Geurts, J. Gross, L. Häkkinen, U. Leu, RE. O'Donnell, O. Propper, C. Puffer, F. Rodríguez, M. Sundberg, G. Winkelhake, O (1997). 'Income-related inequalities in health: some international comparisons.' *Health Economics,* 16(1): 93–112.

van Doorslaer, E. Wagstaff, A. Rutten, F (eds.) (1993). *Equity in the finance and delivery of health care: an international perspective.* Oxford: Oxford University Press.

van Doorslaer, E. Wagstaff, A. van der Burg, H. Christiansen, T. De Graeve, D. Duchesne, I. Gerdtham, UG. Gerfin, M. Geurts, J. Gross, L. Hakkinen, U. John, J. Klavus, J. Leu, RE. Nolan, B. O'Donnell, O. Propper, C. Puffer, F. Schellhorn, M. Sundberg, G. Winkelhake, O (2000). 'Equity in the delivery of health care in Europe and the US.' *Journal of Health Economics,* 19(5): 553–583.

Wagstaff, A (2005). The bounds of the Concentration Index when the variable of interest is binary, with an application to immunization inequality. *Health Economics*, 14(4): 429–432.

Wagstaff, A. Paci, P. van Doorslaer, E (1989). 'Equity in the finance and delivery of health care: some tentative cross-country comparisons.' *Oxford Review of Economic Policy*, 5(1): 89–112.

Wagstaff, A. van Doorslaer, E (2000). Equity in health care finance and delivery. In: Culyer, AJ. Newhouse, JP (eds.). *Handbook of health economics*. Amsterdam: North-Holland, pp. 1803–1862.

Wagstaff, A. van Doorslaer, E. Paci, P (1991). 'On the measurement of horizontal inequity in the delivery of health care.' *Journal of Health Economics*, 10(2): 169–205.

Wagstaff, A. van Doorslaer, E. van Der Burg, H. Calonge, S. Christiansen, T. Citoni, G. Gerdtham, UG. Gerfin, M. Gross, L. Häkinnen, U. Johnson, P. John, J. Klavus, J. Lachaud, C. Lauritsen, J. Leu, R. Nolan, B. Perán, E. Pereira, J. Propper, C. Puffer, F. Rochaix, L. Rodríguez, M. Schellhorn, M. Winkelhake, O. et al (1999). 'Equity in the finance of health care: some further international comparisons.' *Journal of Health Economics*, 18(3): 263–290.

Wagstaff, A. van Doorslaer, E. Watanabe, N (2003). 'On decomposing the causes of health sector inequalities with an application to malnutrition inequalities in Vietnam.' *Journal of Econometrics*, 112(1): 207–223.

Westin, M. Ahs, A. Persson, KB. Westerling, R (2004). 'A large proportion of Swedish citizens refrain from seeking medical care – lack of confidence in the medical services a plausible explanation?' *Health Policy*, 68(3): 333–344.

Whitehead, M (1991). 'The concepts and principles of equity and health.' *Health Promotion International*, 6(3): 217–228.

WHO (2000). *The world health report 2000. Health systems: improving performance*. Geneva: World Health Organization.

WHO (2008). *Closing the gap in a generation. Health equity through action on the social determinants of health*. Geneva: World Health Organization.

Williams, A (1993). Equity in health care: the role of ideology. In: van Doorslaer, E. Wagstaff, A. Rutten, F (eds.). *Equity in the finance and delivery of health care*. Oxford: Oxford University Press.

Williams, A (2005). The pervasive role of ideology in the optimisation of the public-private mix in public healthcare systems. In: Maynard, A (ed.). *The public-private mix for health*. London: The Nuffield Trust.

Zimmer, Z. Natividad, J. Lin, HS. Chayovan, N (2000). 'A cross-national examination of the determinants of self-assessed health.' *Journal of Health and Social Behavior*, 41(4): 465–481.

2.7 Health system productivity and efficiency

ANDREW STREET, UNTO HÄKKINEN

Introduction

In the light of apparently inexorable rises in health-care expenditure, the cost effectiveness of the health system has become a dominant concern for many policy-makers. Do the funders of the health system (taxpayers, insurees, employers or patients) get good value for money? Productivity measurement is a fundamental requirement for securing providers' accountability to their payers and ensuring that health system resources are spent wisely.

Productivity measurement spans a wide range – from the cost effectiveness of individual treatments or practitioners to the productivity of a whole system. Whatever level of analysis is used, a fundamental challenge is the need to attribute both the consumption of resources (costs) and the outcomes achieved (benefits) to the organizations or individuals under scrutiny. The diverse methods used include direct measurement of the costs and benefits of treatment; complex econometric models that yield measures of comparative efficiency; and attempts to introduce health system outcomes into national accounts.

Productivity analysis can be considered via two broad questions: (i) how are resources being used? and (ii) is there scope for better utilization of these resources? These questions can be considered for the whole health system and for organizations within it but most applied research at system level tends to concentrate on the first question. The second question is the primary concern of organizational studies.

This chapter begins with an outline of the fundamental concepts required for productivity analysis, distinguishing productivity from efficiency. This is followed by a discussion of the challenges associated with applying these concepts in the health sector in which it is particularly difficult to define and measure outputs and to determine the relationship between health-care resources (inputs) and outputs.

The chapter continues with an assessment of the use of resources, as posed in the first question. Usually, the concept of productivity is of primary interest in macro-level applications, such as when considering how well an entire health system is using its resources or in analysing labour productivity over time. A growth accounting perspective is often adopted when the objective is to relate a change in outputs to a change of inputs. The productivity change of specific, common and serious health problems has also been analysed by ascribing a monetary value to outputs and relating them to the cost of treating the problem in order to evaluate value for money. In some ways, cost-effectiveness analysis which compares the benefits and cost of two or more health-care services or treatments (health technology assessment) can be seen as a form of productivity analysis. An overview of this type of approach is provided.

A range of methods have been used to consider the second question. The concept of efficiency is usually applied when considering the relative performance of organizations within a health system. These are organizations engaged in production (converting inputs into outputs) and can be hospitals, nursing homes, health centres or individual physicians. Generally speaking, such organizations face few of the competitive pressures that would encourage them to innovate and adopt cost minimizing behaviour. Comparative or benchmarking exercises aim to identify which organizations have more efficient overall operations or specific areas of operation. This information may be used to stimulate better use of resources, either by encouraging organizations to act of their own volition or through tailored incentives imposed by a regulatory authority. The final section of the chapter describes the efficiency analysis techniques that have emerged within the broad evaluative tradition.

Conceptual issues

Four fundamental questions are addressed in this section.

1. What is the relationship between inputs and outputs – i.e. what is the nature of the production process?
2. What does productivity mean and how is this concept distinct from efficiency?

3. What is the output of the health system and of the organizations within the system?
4. What resources (inputs) are employed to produce these outputs?

However, the answers are not straightforward.

Production function – relationship between inputs and outputs

The fundamental building block of productivity or efficiency analysis is the production function. This can be specified for the economy as a whole (macro-level) or for organizations within the economy (meso-level). A more technical description of the macro and meso production functions and their relationships are shown in Box 2.7.1.

Box 2.7.1 Macro-level and meso-level production functions

The production function can be applied at macro-level (for the economy as a whole) or at meso-level (for an organization within the economy). In theory, it is possible to aggregate the production functions for every organization into a function for the economy as a whole, just as total consumer spending is the sum of decisions made by many households.

The standard Cobb-Douglas production function is a useful starting point in which output (Y) is a function of two inputs – labour (L) and capital (K):

1. $$Y = AL^{\alpha} K^{\beta}$$

For calculation purposes this is transformed into logarithmic form, becoming:

2. $$\log Y = \log A + \alpha \log L + \beta \log K$$

In macro-level applications, growth accounting methods are used to assess the contribution of inputs to aggregate output growth and to estimate total productivity change for the economy as a whole or for sectors within it (Jorgenson & Griliches 1967; OECD 2001). These calculations rely on time series data, used to calculate output growth and input growth. The growth in output is defined as:

3. $$\Delta \log Y = \Delta \log A + \alpha \Delta \log L + \beta \Delta \log K$$

Where $\Delta \log Y = \log(Y_t - Y_{t-1})$; $\Delta \log L = \log(L_t - L_{t-1})$; and $\Delta \log K = \log(K_t - K_{t-1})$ with t indexing time. The parameters α and β are usually calculated as the share of income attributable to each input. The fundamental purpose of the growth accounting method is to calculate ΔA which measures the growth in output over and above the growth in inputs. This is termed total factor productivity and, when positive, is interpreted as being due to improvements in methods of production or technical progress. This interpretation rests on three key assumptions: (i) competitive factor markets; (ii) full input utilization; and (iii) constant returns to scale, $\alpha + \beta = 1$ (Inklaar et al. 2005).

Meso-level applications allow analysts to relax assumptions of constant returns to scale and to estimate more flexible functional forms than the Cobb-Douglas. Such applications use organizational data to estimate the production function from observed behaviour, either at a single time point (cross-sectional analysis) or over several time periods (panel data analysis). With cross-sectional data for a set of organizations the Cobb-Douglas production function is estimated as:

4. $$y_i = A + \hat{\alpha} \log L_i + \hat{\beta} \log K_i + \hat{\varepsilon}_i$$

Where y_i is the observed output for organization i, $i = 1...I$; L_i and K_i measure labour and capital input use for organization i; A is an estimated constant; and $\hat{\varepsilon}_i$ is the residual. The purpose is to estimate the relationships between labour and capital and output, given by the estimated parameters $\hat{\alpha}$ and $\hat{\beta}$. Under conditions of perfect competition and profit maximization, marginal productivity will equal the real wage. If these conditions hold, $\hat{\alpha}$ will capture labour's share of total income and $\hat{\beta}$ will capture capital's share, which is consistent with how α and β are calculated in the growth accounting framework (Intriligator 1978). In most econometric applications $\hat{\varepsilon}_i$ is afforded no special attention, other than that it satisfies classical assumptions of being normally distributed with a zero mean. But, analogously to the macro-level interpretation of ΔA, $\hat{\varepsilon}_i$ (or some portion of $\hat{\varepsilon}_i$) has been interpreted as capturing deviations from efficient behaviour among the organizations under scrutiny, with inefficiency defined as the extent to which an organization's output falls short of that predicted by the production function.

At the meso-level, the production function models the maximum output an organization could secure, given its level and mix of inputs. The production process is shown in very simple terms in Fig. 2.7.1. The organization employs inputs (labour, capital, equipment, raw materials) and converts them into some sort of output. The point at which this production process takes place (middle box) is critical for determining whether some organizations are better at converting inputs into outputs.

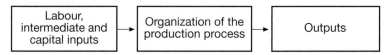

Fig. 2.7.1 Simplified production process

The middle box is something of a black box because it is usually very difficult for outsiders to observe an organization's operation and the organization of the production process. In some industries (e.g. pharmaceutical sector) the production process is a closely guarded secret and the source of competitive advantage.

This inability to observe the production process directly is a fundamental challenge for those seeking to analyse productivity or efficiency. Nevertheless, it is possible to devise a gold standard production process that describes the best possible way of organizing production, given the prevailing technology. The point at which the amount and combination of inputs is optimal is termed the production frontier – any other scale of operation or input mix would secure a lower ratio of output to input. Organizations that have adopted this gold standard are efficient, operating at the frontier of the prevailing technological process. Organizations can operate some way short of this gold standard if equipment is outmoded, the staff underperforms or capital resources stand idle periodically. These, and multiple other reasons, might explain inefficiency.

The analytical problem comprises the following challenges: the gold standard production process is unknown; the particular form of the production process adopted in each organization is difficult to observe; and the various shortcomings associated with each of these particular processes are poorly understood. These challenges can be addressed by comparing organizations involved in similar activities. Such comparative analysis does not attempt to prise open the black box but concentrates on the extremes depicted in Fig. 2.7.1. Information about what goes in (inputs to production process) and what comes out (outputs of production process) tends to be available in some form or another and allows comparison of input-output combinations between organizations that produce similar things. An organization is more *productive* if it uses less input to produce one unit of output than another organization. If we want to assess organizations that produce different amounts of output, we need to make judgements about whether there are economies of scale which, in turn, relies on understanding the gold standard production process. If this is known, organizations can be judged in terms of their *efficiency*.

Distinguishing productivity and efficiency

Productivity and efficiency are often used interchangeably but they refer to different concepts. Sometimes they are distinguished according to what is measured – productivity used when output is measured by activities or services and efficiency used when output is measured by health outcomes. The OECD (2005) has separated technical (or cost) effectiveness from technical (or cost) efficiency – efficiency applies when output is measured by activities; effectiveness when output is measured by outcomes such as health gains or equity.

In country surveys the OECD distinguishes between the concepts of macro- and micro-efficiency (OECD 2003). Macro-efficiency relates to the question of whether total health expenditure is at a socially desirable level. Micro-efficiency involves either minimizing the cost needed to produce a given output or maximizing output for given costs. Within the concept of micro-efficiency, the OECD defines productivity as the volume of services per dollar of expenditure on inputs and effectiveness as quality of care, including health improvement and responsiveness (e.g. timely provision of care).

The definitions used in this chapter are given below.

- Productivity is the ratio of a measure of output to a measure of input.
- Technical efficiency is the maximum level of output that can be produced for a given amount of input under the prevailing technological process – the gold standard.

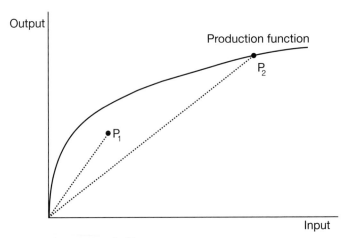

Fig. 2.7.2 Productivity and efficiency

- Allocative efficiency is the maximum level of output that can be produced assuming the cheapest mix of inputs given their relative prices.

The difference between the first two measures is shown in Fig. 2.7.2. Two organizations (P_1, P_2) use a single input to produce a single type of output but P_1 has a higher level of productivity i.e. a higher ratio of output to input. However, technical efficiency is measured in relation to the production function – the maximum amount of output that can be produced at different levels of input. This function suggests diminishing marginal productivity – each additional unit of input produces progressively less output. Diminishing marginal productivity implies decreasing returns to scale – the more inputs used, the lower the return in the form of outputs.

In this illustration, P_2 is operating on the production function, producing the maximum level of output that is technically feasible given its input levels. In contrast, P_1 is operating inefficiently given its size – P_1 has a higher output/input ratio than P_2 but at its scale of operation it would be technically feasible to produce more output. The technical inefficiency of P_1 is measured by its vertical distance from the production function.

Organizations can be allocatively inefficient if they do not use the correct mix of inputs according to their prices. This can be illustrated

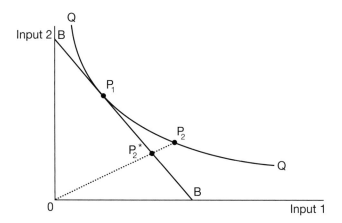

Fig. 2.7.3 Allocative efficiency with two inputs

in a simple two input model. For some known production process, the isoquant QQ in Fig. 2.7.3 shows the use of minimum combinations of the two inputs required to produce a unit of output. In this figure, the organizations P_1 and P_2 lie on the isoquant and therefore (given the chosen mix of inputs) cannot produce more outputs. They are both technically efficient. Organizations might not adopt the best combination of inputs given their prices. Suppose the market prices of the two inputs are V_1 and V_2 – the cost minimizing point on the isoquant occurs where the slope is $-V_1/V_2$ (shown by the straight line BB). In Fig. 2.7.3 this is at the point where P_1 lies, which is allocatively efficient. However, although P_2 lies on the isoquant the organization is not efficient with respect to prices, as a reduction in costs is possible. The allocative inefficiency of P_2 is given by the ratio OP_2^*/OP_2.

Organizations may exhibit both allocative and technical inefficiency. This is illustrated in Fig. 2.7.4 by comparing organizations P_3 and P_4. Organization P_3 purchases the correct mix of inputs but lies inside the isoquant QQ. It therefore exhibits a degree of technical inefficiency, as indicated by the ratio OP_1/OP_3. Organization P_4 purchases an incorrect mix of inputs (given their prices) and lies inside the isoquant QQ. Its overall level of inefficiency is measured as OP_2^*/OP_4, which comprises two components: (i) the organization's allocative inefficiency indicated by the ratio OP_2^*/OP_2; and (ii) its technical inefficiency indicated by the ratio OP_2/OP_4.

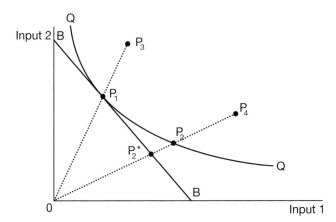

Fig. 2.7.4 Technical and allocative efficiency

Defining, measuring and valuing output

Specification of the inputs consumed and the valued outputs produced is central to the examination of any production process. Analysts usually refer to the outputs of the production process but regulators and other decision-makers are usually more interested in the outcomes produced, in terms of their impact on individual and social welfare.

Physical output is usually a traded product in competitive industries. Even in a reasonably homogeneous market, the products (e.g. cars) can vary considerably in various dimensions of quality such as reliability or safety features (Triplett 2001). The quality of the product is intrinsic to its social value but that value can be readily inferred by observing the price that people are prepared to pay. For this reason there is usually no need explicitly to consider the ultimate outcome of the product, in terms of the value it bestows on the consumer.

Prices do not exist and outputs are difficult to define in many parts of the economy. This is particularly true for many of the goods and services funded by governments (Atkinson 2006). Some of these are classic public goods (non-rival and non-excludable) that would be underprovided if left to the market, e.g. national defence. Government financing of other services (e.g. education, health care) might be justified to ensure universal access. Two fundamental issues need to be considered in the context of productivity and efficiency analysis. How should the outputs of the non-market sector be defined? What value should be attached to these outputs when market prices are not available?

Defining health outcomes

When defining health outcomes the starting point is to consider the objectives of the health system or organization(s) under consideration. The primary purpose of the health-care system is generally considered to be to enhance the health of the population. Individuals do not demand health care for its own sake but for its contribution to health. Presuming that the health system and its constituent organizations aim to satisfy individual demands (however imperfectly) it follows that health should enter the social welfare function and organizational objective functions. Ideally, the measure of health should indicate the value added to health as a result of an individual's contact with the health system. This requires a means of defining and measuring individual health profiles and of attributing changes in these to the actions of the health system or its constituent organizations.

Health is multidimensional and – like utility – there is no objective means of measuring and ordering health across individuals or populations. A diversity of definitions have been used including life expectancy; capacity to work; personal and social functioning; and need for health care (Fuchs 1987). One option is to use avoidable deaths or amenable mortality as an output measure. This is based on a list of causes of deaths that should not occur in the presence of effective and timely health care (Nolte & McKee 2003; Nolte et al. 2009). The aim is to ascertain health services' effect on mortality by disentangling other influences that are unrelated to the health system.

Data on the impact of health services on morbidity or health-related quality of life (HRQoL) are seldom collected outside of clinical trial settings and therefore have rarely been used in productivity analyses. This may change as more countries start to collect such data, even from patients who are not enrolled in clinical trials (Department of Health 2007; Räsänen 2007; Vallance-Owen et al. 2004).

Defining the quantity of output

Given the current absence of data on the amount of health produced, most productivity analyses define output in terms of the numbers and types of patients treated. Sometimes they adjust for the quality of treatment. This is in line with a common approach in theoretical expositions wherein the particular interest is often the analysis of situations in which quality substitutes for quantity (Chalkey & Malcomson 2000, Hodgkin & McGuire 1994). Consistent with such theoretical models, Eurostat's guidance for the compilation of national accounts for European Union countries defines health-care output as: 'the quantity of health care received by patients, adjusted to allow for the qualities of services provided, for each type of health care' (Eurostat 2001).

It is difficult to define even the quantity of health care. This involves consideration of many diverse activities as the production of health care is complex and individually tailored. Contributions to the care process often come from multiple agents or organizations; a package of care may be delivered over multiple time periods and in different settings; and the responsibilities for delivery may vary from place to place and over time. This means that the production of the majority of health-care outputs rarely conforms to a production-line type technology in which clearly identifiable inputs are used to produce a standard type of output (Harris 1977).

Patient classification systems have been developed to address this problem. Patients are described reasonably well in the hospital sector as many countries use some form of diagnosis related groups (DRGs) to quantify hospital activity and to describe the different types (casemix) of patient receiving inpatient care (Fetter et al. 1980). DRGs are best suited to describe patients in hospital settings, where patients tend to be admitted with specific problems that can be managed as discrete events. Casemix adjustment methods for patients treated in outpatient, primary or community care settings are still at the development stage, although a number of classification systems are being explored (Bjorkgren et al. 1999; Carpenter et al. 1995; Duckett & Jackson 1993; Eagar et al. 2003; Street et al. 2007). A major challenge is that many patients treated in these settings have complex health-care requirements and may suffer from multiple problems that require ongoing contact with multiple agencies over a long period. Patients can be tracked across settings in countries that use unique personal identification numbers (Linna & Häkkinen 2008). Elsewhere, activity is described in fairly crude terms, such as number of attendances; or visits or consultations by setting or professional group.

Defining the quality of output

Quantity is difficult to define but it is even more challenging to assess the quality of health care. The majority of empirical studies of the efficiency of health-care organizations fail to consider quality and include only measures of casemix-adjusted quantity (Hollingsworth et al. 1999). In effect, this assumes that there are no differences or variations over time in the quality of treatment among the organizations under consideration.

However, quality improvements are likely to be of value to patients and therefore an important aspect of health-care productivity. As mentioned, health care's impact on health status is of primary interest. Various productivity analyses have attempted to quantify improvements over time in both the amount and quality of treatment, often by considering specific conditions. For example, Shapiro and Shapiro (2001) argue that the value of cataract extraction has risen steadily because of lower rates of complication and better post-operative visual outcomes; Cutler et al. (2001) consider improvements in survival rates following treatment for heart attack; and Castelli et al. (2007) show how improvements in post-operative survival can be incorporated into measures of productivity for the whole health system.

Patients are concerned not only with the outcomes associated with care but also about the process of health-care delivery, such as the reassurance and guidance they receive; waiting times for treatment; and whether they are treated with dignity and respect. It is likely that the process of care delivery also has improved in most countries over time. These improvements ought to be included in measures of health service productivity, insofar as they represent valued improvements in the characteristics of health-care activity. This requires each dimension of quality to be measured consistently over time and a means of valuing unit changes in quality and in quantity on the same valuation scales to enable quality change to be incorporated directly in the output index. It is challenging to value both the quantity and quality of health care.

Valuing outputs

Hospital treatment following cardiac arrest has a different value to a general practitioner consultation about back pain. But how are these values to be derived in the absence of market prices? One source of valuation is based on what these activities contribute to patient welfare. This might be estimated by undertaking discrete choice experiments (Ryan et al. 2004) or by using hedonic methods to assess the value of different characteristics of outputs (Cockburn & Amis 2001). In practice, these approaches are costly and difficult to apply comprehensively across all health-care activities or to update on a routine basis.

Eurostat recommends using cost to reflect the value of non-market outputs in the national accounts (Eurostat 2001). This implies that costs reflect the marginal value that society places on these activities and requires health-care resources to be allocated in line with societal preferences (i.e. health system is allocatively efficient). This strong assumption may not hold but cost-weights have the advantage of being reasonably easy to obtain. As such, costs are likely to remain the dominant source of explicit value weights for the foreseeable future, implying that outputs are valued in terms of their production rather than consumption characteristics.

Defining inputs

The input side of efficiency analysis is usually considered to be less problematic but two issues must be faced. First, how precisely can inputs be attributed to the production of particular outputs? Second, how precisely do specific types of input need to be specified?

Attribution to the unit of analysis (i.e. the organization under consideration) is a serious analytical problem. Rather than taking the organizational form (e.g. hospital) as given, greater insight might be gained from analysing units within it, such as departments or specialties. Comparative analysis at department level makes it more likely that similar production processes are compared and may result in more robust conclusions about relative performance (Olsen & Street 2008).

Disaggregated analysis raises the question of whether it is possible to identify precisely which inputs produce which outputs. This is particularly true in health care as output is often the product of teamwork – sometimes involving collaboration between different organizational entities – and inputs (notably staff) often contribute to the production of different types of output. For instance, one doctor's time may be split between caring for patients in general surgery and in urology; another may work predominantly in dermatology but have a special interest in plastic surgery. Even the managers of the relevant specialties may not know precisely how these doctors divide their time. Ultimately, the analyst has to make a trade-off: specifying the production unit as precisely as possible (disaggregation), may come at the cost of incorrect attribution of inputs to the production process of interest.

As regards the second issue, physical inputs can be measured more accurately than outputs, or are summarized into a single measure in the form of a measure of costs. If costs are used, a cost function can be estimated instead of a production function. The cost function indicates the minimum that an organization can incur in seeking to produce a set of valued outputs. The production function will be equivalent to the cost function (i.e. its dual) if organizations are cost minimizing – which may not be valid if the analytical purpose is to uncover inefficient behaviour. The cost function combines all inputs into a single metric (costs) but does not model the mix of inputs employed or their prices. Therefore, notwithstanding its practical usefulness, a cost function offers little help with detailed understanding of the input side of efficiency.

If there is interest in considering the impact of particular types of input on productivity, these inputs must be specified separately. In particular, separation of labour and capital may be necessary to determine their specific contributions to output (Inklaar et al. 2005).

Labour inputs

Labour inputs usually can be measured with some degree of accuracy. Most health systems collect staffing data, usually by staff type and sometimes by grade, skill level or qualifications. Care must be taken to ensure that such data are strictly comparable as organizations that report different staffing levels may actually have similar inputs. A common reason for this is varying amounts of contracting out of non-clinical (e.g. catering, cleaning, laundry services) and clinical services (laboratory, radiology). Organizations that contract out report lower staffing levels than those that employ staff directly. Differences in employment practices may also affect international comparisons. For instance, in countries such as the United States and Canada doctors are not reimbursed via the hospital and so their input may not be included in the hospital's labour statistics.

More precisely specified data may be useful if there is interest in the relationship between efficiency and the mix of labour inputs employed. This might yield useful policy recommendations about substituting some types of labour for others. But, unless there is a specific interest in the deployment of different labour types, it may be appropriate to construct a single measure of labour input – weighting the various labour inputs by their relative wages. This leads to a more parsimonious model.

Labour inputs may be measured in either physical units (hours of labour) or costs of labour, depending on context. The use of physical inputs fails to capture any variations in organizations' wage rates. This may be desirable (e.g. if there are variations in pay levels beyond the control of organizations) or undesirable (if there is believed to be input price inefficiency in the form of different pay levels for identical workers).

Capital inputs

It is more challenging to incorporate measures of capital into the analysis. This is partly because of the difficulty of measuring capital stock and partly because of problems in attributing its use to any particular period. Measures of capital are often rudimentary and may be misleading. For example, accounting measures for the depreciation of physical stock usually offer little meaningful indication of capital consumed. Many studies of hospital efficiency use beds as a proxy for capital but this is an increasingly poor measure as care moves from inpatient to day case or other settings.

In principle, analysis should use the capital consumed in the current period as an input to the production process but, by definition, capital is deployed across time. Contemporary output may rely on capital investment in previous periods while some current activities are investments that are intended to contribute to future rather than contemporary outputs. Estimates of organizational efficiency will be biased if organizations differ in their (dis)investment strategies and capital use is attributed inaccurately to particular periods.

Macro-level analysis of productivity

Health system level

The key challenge in macro-level applications is to estimate changes in productivity over time. This requires the outputs produced from one period to the next to be measured and valued. In Laspeyres form, where outputs are valued in the base period (*t-1*), the change in output is measured as:

$$\Delta Y = Y_t - Y_{t-1}$$
$$= (outputs_t \times value\_per\_output_{t-1}) - (outputs_{t-1} \times value\_per\_output_{t-1})$$

Changes in inputs can be measured in a similar fashion. If output growth exceeds input growth it is interpreted as an improvement in productivity. However, cross-country comparisons of productivity based on national accounts should be made with caution. Some countries (notably the United States and Canada) continue to apply the output=input convention in which the output of the health system is valued simply by the total expenditure on inputs. This makes it impossible to measure productivity because output is not measured.

Many countries have accepted Eurostat's recommendations to move towards direct measurement of the volume of outputs when constructing their national accounts (Eurostat 2001). However, there are differences in how outputs are defined in those countries that have adopted this recommendation. Many countries define health-care output by counting the number of activities undertaken in different settings – for instance, the number of patients treated in hospital or the number of attendances in outpatient departments. There is no international standard for the way that patients are described and sometimes output definitions are more akin to input measures – such as the use of occupied bed days to count the output of nursing homes or rehabilitation services. Such definitional differences undermine international comparisons (Smith & Street 2007).

A recent study developed a weighted output index to measure changes in the volume of services weighted by health gains (in quality-adjusted life years – QALYs) (Castelli et al. 2007a). No data are currently available to enable a comprehensive index to be calculated for the whole health system but the study indicates where future routine data collection should be focused.

3.2 Disease oriented approach

A number of authors have championed disease-specific assessments of productivity, often undertaken at national level (Cutler et al. 2001). They offer several potential advantages. A more focused assessment has less diversity in the type of activities being considered which simplifies their quantification and aggregation into a single index. A disease-based approach is also more likely to consider health effects and is more clearly a bottom-up approach in which micro-level comparative data on clinical actions, costs and outcomes are essential elements. They may also enable identification of specific aspects of quality change and health gain that can be overlooked when constructing a comprehensive index.

As when considering departments within organizations, there is a particular problem with identifying and attributing the resources devoted to treatment of a particular disease. This disease-based approach also presumes that it is possible to consider each disease in isolation although this may be questionable for conditions associated with multiple co-morbidities (Terris & Aron 2009). Of course, disease-specific productivity assessments should not be extrapolated to draw inferences about the productivity of the health system as a whole.

The disease-oriented approach is based on modelling the natural progress of a disease, with specific interest in the health services' role as a determinant of this progress. The idea is that analyses of time trends and more detailed (particularly individual level) data pertaining to specific health conditions will illuminate the interconnected aspects (i.e. financing, organizational structures, medical technology choices) responsible for health system performance (i.e. health outcomes and expenditure).

Most analyses are undertaken at a national level but there have been three international attempts to apply the disease-based approach during recent years.

1. McKinsey health-care productivity study – breast cancer, lung cancer, gallstone disease, diabetes mellitus: Germany, United Kingdom, United States (McKinsey Global Institute & McKinsey Health Care Practice 1996).
2. OECD Ageing-Related Disease (ARD) Project – ischaemic heart disease, stroke, breast cancer (OECD, 2003a).
3. Technological Change in Healthcare (TECH) Global Research Network (AMI) (McClellan et al. 2001).

The three projects had different perspectives. The McKinsey study analysed productivity, relating outputs (life years saved and estimations of changes in QALYs using information on mortality, complications and treatment patterns) to the resource inputs (physician hours, nursing hours, medication, capital, etc) for treating the four diseases. The study used data available at aggregate national level derived from literature reviews, database analysis and clinical expert interview. The data were limited in key areas such as clinical characteristics and detailed input measurement.

The OECD ARD Project extended the approach by trying to take account of all relevant interrelationships in a broad model. The aim was to provide a holistic innovative framework to understand performance rather than a comparison of the countries' relative productivity. Cost and outcome data were collected on prevention, treatment and rehabilitation; the overall burden of disease; economic incentives; economic conditions; and medical knowledge. The project was implemented by collaborative networks of the participating national experts and represents the first full-scale attempt to use national micro-datasets on national patient records to compute comparable cross-sectional data. In this respect, the project can be seen as a feasibility study to examine what relevant information was available in different countries (Moise 2001). However, patient-level data on well-defined and casemix-adjusted episodes were not available so consideration of outcomes was rudimentary.

The TECH Network's aim was to study the variation in medical technology diffusion; the policy determinants of differing patterns; and the resulting consequences for health outcomes in developed countries. The Network consists of clinicians, health economists and policy-makers from seventeen nations. They have developed a multi-national, standardized summary data set of acute myocardial infarction patients to analyse heart attack procedure utilization; the patient co-morbidity burden; mortality; and demographic characteristics over time and across nations. The data limitations were formidable as most of the participating countries could produce only unlinked event-based administrative or observational data. Longitudinally linked person-based data could be obtained from only seven countries.

Many challenges must still be overcome before reliable comparative studies can be undertaken across countries. Firstly, each disease will require an internationally comparable clinical protocol for measuring an episode to be defined. This should set out inclusion criteria (for example, first-ever cases); definitions of the beginning and end (follow-up) of an episode; and definitions of outcome measures. Secondly, comparable information for measuring inputs and cost must be collected, likely in several stages (Mogyorosy & Smith 2005): identification of resource items used to deliver particular services; selection of the unit of measurement of each resource item; measurement of resource items in natural units; ascribing monetary value to resource items; and expressing results in a single currency.

The disease-based approach is attractive for international productivity analysis but its usefulness is dependent on the following.

- Possibility of linking hospital discharge register to other databases. This requires a unique personal identification number and the legal possibility (confidentiality constrictors) to perform linkages.
- Availability of comprehensive register data. Register-based data are usually available for inpatient care but not primary care and the use of drugs. Hence the data are most useful for well-defined acute conditions (e.g. acute myocardial infarction, stroke) but not chronic conditions (e.g. diabetes).
- Possibility of obtaining good quality comparative input and cost data. In the ARD project, reservations have been expressed about the quality of cost data (Triplett 2002) collected from available administrative data on expenditure, costs and charges (Moise & Jacobzone 2003). The vignette method developed for international comparison of inpatient care is too crude for a disease-based approach since it is based on costing some typical cases. A better option will be to explore the methods developed for gathering comparable cost data for economic evaluations conducted on a multinational basis (Wordsworth et al. 2005) in order to meet the many challenges related to costing (Mogyorosy & Smith 2005).

Meso-level analysis of organizational efficiency

Productivity and efficiency analysis is generally conducted at organizational level. Health-care organizations use costly inputs (labour, capital, etc.) to produce valued outputs. Analysis is concerned with measuring the competence of this production process and relies on comparison of organizations that produce a similar set of outputs. If inefficiency can be revealed, it may be possible to improve the provision of health services without the need for additional resources. A number of challenges are associated with measuring organizational efficiency. The following are discussed in more detail below:

- defining comparable organizations
- identifying the production frontier
- controlling for exogenous production constraints.

Defining comparable organizations

Relative efficiency analysis requires comparison of organizations engaged in similar production processes. This is especially difficult in contexts where the production process is characterized by varying degrees of vertical integration. It is particularly important to ensure that the entire production process is being analysed when several organizations are involved. Variations in the boundaries that define relative contributions to joint production may be a major reason why organizations have differing efficiency. For example, consider an analysis of the efficiency of care delivered to patients with head injury. The organization of care between the trauma and orthopaedics (T&O) department and the intensive care unit (ITU) may differ substantially between hospitals – some T&O departments have more step-down high dependency beds in order to relieve pressure on the ITU. If the unit of analysis is confined to the T&O department and the ITU's contribution is ignored, T&O departments that have made greater investments in high dependency beds will appear relatively inefficient although in reality they will have a better joint production process. This illustrates why sound inferences about relative efficiency cannot be made unless the analyst compares like with like.

Identifying the production frontier

As mentioned earlier, the gold standard or technically feasible production frontier is unknown. Analysis relies on estimation of an empirical frontier based on observed behaviour. Two main analytical techniques are available to assess efficiency – data envelopment analysis (DEA) and stochastic frontier analysis (SFA) (Jacobs et al. 2006).

DEA and SFA use different approaches to establish the location and shape of the production frontier and to determine each organization's location in relation to the frontier. SFA takes an indirect approach by controlling for supposed influences on output and contending that unexplained variations in output are due to inefficiency, at least in part. Standard econometric models are concerned with the explanatory variables but SFA models extract organization-specific estimates of inefficiency from the unexplained part of the model – $\hat{\varepsilon}_i$ (see Box 2.7.1). The implication is that standard econometric tools to test model specification cannot be applied to SFA models because of the interpretation placed on $\hat{\varepsilon}_i$ and because organization-specific rather than average estimates are required. This requires untestable judgments to be made about the adequacy of stochastic frontier models and the inefficiency estimates they yield (Smith & Street 2005).

DEA establishes the location and shape of the frontier empirically. The outermost observations (those with the highest level of output given their scale of operation) are deemed efficient. In Fig. 2.7.2, both P_1 and P_2 would be considered fully efficient under DEA; under SFA both organizations might be considered to exhibit some degree of inefficiency. DEA is highly flexible –by plotting the outermost observations the frontier moulds itself to the data. However, this has the drawback of making the frontier sensitive to organizations that have unusual types, levels or combinations of inputs or outputs. These will have a scarcity of adjacent reference observations and may result in sections of the frontier being positioned inappropriately.

The flexibility of DEA might be thought to increase its value over the SFA method but this is offset by two key differences in how these techniques interpret any distance from the frontier. Firstly, DEA assumes correct model specification and that all data are observed without error; SFA allows for the possibility of modelling and measurement error. Consequently, even if the two techniques yield an identical frontier, the SFA efficiency estimates are likely to be higher than those produced by DEA. Secondly, DEA uses a selective amount of data to estimate each organization's efficiency score. It generates an efficiency score for each organization by comparing it only to peers that produce a comparable mix of outputs. This has two implications.

1. Any output that is unique to an organization will have no peers with which to make a comparison, irrespective of the fact that it may produce other common outputs. An absence of peers results in the automatic assignation of full efficiency to the organization under consideration.
2. When assigning an efficiency score to an organization that does not lie on the frontier, only its peers are considered. Information pertaining to the remainder of the sample is discarded.

In contrast, SFA appeals to the full sample information to estimate relative efficiency and (in addition to making greater use of the available data) makes the sample's efficiency estimates more robust in the presence of outlier observations and atypical input/output combinations. But this advantage over DEA is mainly a matter of degree – the location of (sections of) the DEA frontier may be determined by outliers, but outliers also exert influence on the position of the SFA frontier. Moreover, there are no statistical criteria for sorting these unusual observations into outliers or examples of best practice (Smith & Street 2005).

Controlling for exogenous production constraints

In Chapter 3.3 Terris and Aron (2009) emphasize that many factors might influence the observed performance of an organization and the importance of these situational factors is often under-emphasized. These factors may influence the organization's production frontier and constrain the amount of output it is able to produce for a given level of input. The frontiers for organizations operating in difficult situations will lie inside those of more favourably endowed organizations. For instance, hospital performance may be related to local socio-economic conditions or the organization of community care.

There is considerable debate about which situational factors are considered to be controllable. An analyst's choice will depend on whether the purpose of the analysis is short run and tactical or longer run and strategic. In the short run, many factors are outside the control of an organization; in the longer term a broader set of factors is potentially under an organization's control but the extent and nature of this control will vary with the context. In whatever way the uncontrollable environment is defined, it is usually the case that some organizations operate in more adverse situations than others, that is – external circumstances make it more difficult to achieve a given level of attainment.

Opportunities for meso-level efficiency analysis

The main requirements for meso-level analysis are that the organizations are comparable and outputs are defined in such way that the patient casemix can be standardized. At present, hospitals (or their departments) and nursing homes are most commonly studied as they meet these requirements most closely (Häkkinen & Jourmard 2007). Moreover, information systems are usually most sophisticated in the hospital sector and hospital level discharge data are available in many countries. Unique personal identification numbers allow patients to be followed along their care pathways and enable quality measures (e.g. readmission, complication, mortality) to be included in analyses (Carey & Burgess 1999; McKay & Deily 2005 & 2007).

Conclusion

Productivity and efficiency analyses consider the use of health-care resources and whether there is scope for better utilization. Productivity and efficiency have been defined in this chapter, noting that the former is a measure of the ratio of output to input while the latter incorporates the concept of what level of production might be technically feasible.

There are major challenges in measuring productivity and efficiency in health care, whether measuring the whole health system; organizations within it; or specific types of disease. The most significant challenges relate to the measurement of output although there has been much development, including improved categorization of patients and increased availability of register-based data which enable patients to be tracked over time and across settings. However, there is still a lack of routine data about health-care's impact on health outcomes and the moves to address this deficiency are to be encouraged.

Productivity analysis at health system level is often undertaken to inform national accounts and has been designed for a variety of analytical and policy purposes (macro-economic management; assessing overall economic performance and welfare). One explicit aim has been to develop measures of productivity in the health sector and its sub-sectors that can be compared with other sectors in the economy. The adoption of direct volume measurement has improved what is captured in the national accounts (OECD 2001). Nevertheless, there is some way to go before these accounting measures fully capture changes in health system productivity over time and enable sound international comparisons. Methodological challenges include the measurement of health outcomes, how to quantify and value outputs and how to account for quality change (Smith & Street 2007).

A disease-based approach may provide useful insight, especially if it allows analysis of health gain. Moreover, the development of electronic patient record systems may make it feasible to construct care pathways for patients who receive care from multiple providers over extended time periods. For comparative purposes, standardized definitions of activities and classifications describing the treatments (i.e. diagnosis, procedures) are required. There are analytical challenges concerning attribution, notably how to deal with co-morbidities and how to identify the resources devoted to a specific disease.

Numerous studies have considered the efficiency of health-care organizations, employing empirical techniques to make comparative statements about relative performance. Studies have become more sophisticated over time as better data have allowed improved specification of the production process; greater consideration of the quality of output; and better understanding of the situational factors that may act as constraints on production. Despite these improvements these analyses have limited impact on policy and practice, mainly because of concerns about reliability (Hollingsworth & Street 2006). Greater confidence can be gained by undertaking sensitivity analysis; estimating confidence intervals; and, most importantly, by cautious interpretation of results.

Given the fundamental analytical challenges described in this chapter, rather than claiming that inefficient behaviour can be identified precisely, we should be pursuing the more modest ambition of sorting the inefficient from the efficient. Migration from the first group to the second can then be encouraged by applying regulatory pressure; designing financial incentives; or simply sharing examples of best practice. By systematically detailing the use of resources, productivity and efficiency analyses can contribute to better targeted policy-making.

References

Atkinson, T (2006). 'Measurement of government output and productivity.' *Journal of the Royal Statistical Society, Series A,* 169(4): 659–662.

Bjorkgren, MA. Hakkinen, U. Finne-Soveri, UH. Fries, BE (1999). 'Validity and reliability of Resource Utilization Groups (RUG-III) in Finnish long-term care facilities.' *Scandinavian Journal of Public Health,* 27(3): 228–234.

Carey, K. Burgess, JF Jr. (1999). 'On measuring the hospital cost/quality trade-off.' *Health Economics,* 8(6): 509–520.

Carpenter, GI. Main, A. Turner, GF (1995). 'Casemix for the elderly inpatient: resource utilization groups (RUGs) validation project.' *Age and Ageing,* 24(1): 5–13.

Castelli, A. Dawson, D. Gravelle, H. Jacobs, R. Kind, P. Loveridge, P. Martin, S. O'Mahony, M. Stevens, P. Stokes, L. Street, A. Weale, M (2007). 'A new approach to measuring health system output and productivity.' *National Institute Economic Review,* 200(1): 105–117.

Castelli, A. Dawson, D. Gravelle, H. Street, A (2007a). 'Improving the measurement of health system output growth.' *Health Economics,* 16(10): 1091–1107.

Chalkey, M. Malcomson, J (2000). Government purchasing of health services. In: Culyer, AJ. Newhouse, JP (eds.) *Handbook of health economics*. North Holland: Elsevier.

Cockburn, IM. Amis, AH (2001). Hedonic analysis of arthritis drugs. In: Cutler, DM. Berndt, ER (eds.). *Medical care output and productivity*. Chicago: University of Chicago Press.

Cutler, DM. McClellan, M. Newhouse, JP. Remler, D (2001). Pricing heart attack treatments. In: Cutler, DM. Berndt, ER (eds.). *Medical care output and productivity*. Chicago: University of Chicago Press.

Department of Health (2007). *Guidance on the routine collection of patient reported outcome measures (PROMs)*. London: Department of Health.

Duckett, S. Jackson, T (1993). 'Casemix classification for outpatient services based on episodes of care.' *Medical Journal of Australia*, 159(3): 213–214.

Eagar, K. Gaines, P. Burgess, P. Green, J. Bower, A. Buckingham, B. Mellsop, G (2003). 'Developing a New Zealand casemix classification for mental health services.' *World Psychiatry*, 3(3): 172–177.

Eurostat (2001). *Handbook on price and volume measures in national accounts*. Luxembourg: Office for Official Publications of the European Communities.

Fetter, RB. Shin, YB. Freeman, JL. Averill, RF. Thompson, JD (1980). 'Case mix definition by diagnosis-related groups.' *Medical Care*, 18 (Suppl. 2): 1–53.

Fuchs, VR (1987). Health economics. In: Eatwell, J. Milgate, M. Newman, P (eds.). *The new Palgrave: a dictionary of economics*. London: Macmillan Press Limited.

Harris, JE (1977). 'The internal organisation of hospitals: some economic implications.' *Bell Journal of Economics*, 8(2):467–482.

Hodgkin, D. McGuire, TG (1994). 'Payment levels and hospital response to prospective payment.' *Journal of Health Economics*, 13(1): 1–29.

Hollingsworth, B. Street, A (2006). 'The market for efficiency analysis of health care organisations.' *Health Economics*, 15(10): 1055–1059.

Hollingsworth, B. Dawson, PJ. Maniadakis, N (1999). 'Efficiency measurement of health care: a review of non-parametric methods and applications.' *Health Care Management Science*, 2(3): 161–172.

Inklaar, R. O'Mahony, M. Timmer, M (2005). 'ICT and Europe's productivity performance – industry-level growth account comparisons with the United States.' *Review of Income and Wealth*, 51(4): 505–536.

Intriligator, MD (1978). *Econometric models, techniques and applications*. Englewood Cliffs, New Jersey: Prentice-Hall Inc.

Jacobs, R. Smith, PC. Street, A (2006). *Measuring efficiency in health care: analytical techniques and health policy.* Cambridge: Cambridge University Press.

Jorgenson, DW. Griliches, Z (1967). 'The explanation of productivity change.' *Review of Economic Studies,* 34(3): 249–283.

Linna, M. Häkkinen, U (2008). Benchmarking Finnish hospitals. In: Blank, J. Valdmanis, V (eds.). *Evaluating hospital policy and performance: contributions from hospital policy and productivity research.* Oxford: Elsevier.

McClellan, M. Kessler, D. Saynina, O. Moreland, A. TECH Research Network (2001). 'Technological change around the world: evidence from heart attack care.' *Health Affairs (Millwood),* 20(3): 25–42.

McKay, NL. Deily, ME (2005). 'Comparing high- and low-performing hospitals using risk-adjusted excess mortality and cost inefficiency.' *Health Care Management Review,* 30(4): 347–360.

McKay, NL. Deily, ME (2007). 'Cost inefficiency and hospital health outcomes.' *Health Economics,* 17(7):833–848.

McKinsey Global Institute & the McKinsey Health Care Practice (1996). *Health care productivity.* Los Angeles: McKinsey and Co., Inc.

Mogyorosy, Z. Smith, PC (2005). *The main methodological issues in costing health care services – a literature review,* York, University of York: Centre for Health Economics.

Moise, P (2001). *Using hospital administrative databases for a disease-based approach to studying health care systems.* Paris: OECD.

Moise, P. Jacobzone, S (2003). *OECD study of cross-national differences in the treatment, costs and outcomes of ischaemic heart disease.* Paris: OECD.

Nolte, E. McKee, M (2003). 'Measuring the health of nations: analysis of mortality amenable to medical care.' *British Medical Journal,* 327(7424): 1129–1132.

Nolte, E. Bain, CM. McKee, M (2009). Population health. In: Smith, PC. Mossialos, E. Papanicolas, I. Leatherman, S (eds.). *Performance measurement for health system improvement: experiences, challenges and prospects.* Cambridge: Cambridge University Press.

Olsen, KR. Street, A (2008). 'The analysis of efficiency among a small number of organisations: how inferences can be improved by exploiting patient-level data.' *Health Economics,* 17(6): 671–681.

OECD (2001). *OECD productivity manual: a guide to the measurement of industry-level and aggregate productivity growth.* Paris, Organisation for Economic Co-operation and Development.

OECD (2003) *Ad hoc group on the OECD health project. Assessing the performance of health-care systems: a framework for OECD surveys.* Unpublished report for official OECD use (ECO/CPE/WP1[2003]10).

OECD (2003a). *A disease-based comparison of health systems: what is best and at what cost?* Paris: OECD.

Räsänen, P (2007). *Routine measurement of health-related quality of life in assessing cost-effectiveness in secondary health care.* Helsinki: STAKES (Research Report no. 163).

Ryan, M. Odejar, M. Napper, M (2004). *The value of reducing waiting time in the provision of health care: a review of the evidence.* Aberdeen: Health Economics Research Unit.

Shapiro, I. Shapiro, MD (2001). Measuring the value of cataract surgery. In: Cutler, DM. Berndt, ER (eds.). *Medical care output and productivity.* Chicago: University of Chicago Press.

Smith, PC. Street, A (2005). 'Measuring the efficiency of public services: the limits of analysis'. *Journal of the Royal Statistical Society Series A,* 168(2): 401–417.

Smith, PC. Street, A (2007). 'Measurement of non-market output in education and health.' *Economic and Labour Market Review,* 1(6): 46–52.

Street, A. Vitikainen, K. Bjorvatn, A. Hvenegaard, A (2007). *International literature review and information gathering on financial tariffs.* York: University of York, Centre for Health Economics (Research Paper 30).

Terris, DD. Aron, DC (2009). Attribution and causality in health-care performance measurement. In: Smith, PC. Mossialos, E. Papanicolos, I. Leatherman, S (eds.) *Performance measurement for health system improvement: experiences, challenges and prospects.* Cambridge: Cambridge University Press.

Triplett, JE (2001). What's different about health? Human repair and car repair in national accounts and national health accounts. In: Cutler, DM. Berndt, ER (eds.). *Medical care output and productivity.* Chicago: University of Chicago Press.

Triplett, JE (2002). *Integrating cost-of-disease studies into purchasing power parities (PPP).* Washington: The Brookings Institution.

Vallance-Owen, A. Cubbin, S. Warren, V. Matthews, B (2004). 'Outcome monitoring to facilitate clinical governance: experience from a national programme in the independent sector.' *Journal of Public Health,* 26(2): 187–192.

Wordsworth, S. Ludbrook, A. Caskey, F. Macleod, A (2005). 'Collecting unit cost data in multicentre studies. Creating comparable methods.' *European Journal of Health Economics,* 6(1): 38–44.

PART III

Analytical methodology for performance measurement

3.1 *Risk adjustment for performance measurement*

LISA I. IEZZONI

Introduction

Risk adjustment within health care aims to account for differences in the mix of important patient attributes across health plans, hospitals, individual practitioners or other groupings of interest before comparing how their patients fare (Box 3.1.1).

Box 3.1.1 Definition of risk adjustment

This statistical tool allows data to be modified to control for variations in patient populations. For example, risk adjustment could be used to ensure a fair comparison of the performance of two providers: one whose caseload consists mainly of elderly patients with multiple chronic conditions and another who treats a patient population with a less severe case mix. Risk adjustment makes it possible to take these differences into account when resource use and health outcomes are compared.

Source: Institute of Medicine 2006.

This straightforward purpose belies the complexity of devising clinically credible and widely accepted risk adjustment methods, especially when resulting performance measures might be reported publicly or used to determine payments. Controversies about risk adjustment reach back to the mid-nineteenth century. Florence Nightingale (1863) was criticized for publishing figures that showed higher death rates at London hospitals than at provincial facilities: 'Any comparison which ignores the difference between the apple-cheeked farm-labourers who seek relief at Stoke Pogis [sic] (probably for rheumatism and sore legs), and the wizzened [sic], red-herring-like mechanics of Soho or Southwark, who come into a London Hospital, is fallacious' (Anonymous 1864 pp.187–8). Other critics noted that many provincial hospitals explicitly refused patients with phthisis (consumption), fevers or who were 'dead or dying', whereas urban facilities took everyone (Bristowe & Holmes 1864). Had the figures Nightingale published 'really overlooked the differences in relative severity of cases admitted into ... different classes of Hospitals ...?'[1] (Bristowe 1864 p.492).

Similar complaints echo 150 years later – risk adjustment methods are inadequate and failures of risk adjustment might affect the willingness of health-care institutions and practitioners to accept difficult cases and publicly release performance data. Certainly, there have been advances in what some consider 'the Holy Grail of health services research over the past 30 years' (McMahon et al. 2007 p.234). Statistical techniques for adjusting for risks are increasingly sophisticated. Reasonably well-accepted methods for capturing and modelling patients' clinical risk factors now exist for a variety of conditions, especially those involving surgery and risks of imminent death or post-operative complications. This brief chapter cannot hope to review the full (and growing) range of current risk adjustment methods which span practice settings from intensive inpatient to home-based care. Nevertheless, much remains to be done. In 2006, the Institute of Medicine (2006 p.114) highlighted the need for continuing applied research to support performance measurement, specifically calling for studies of risk adjustment methods. Commenting about inadequate performance measurement methodologies generally, it warned, 'data can be misleading, potentially threatening providers' reputations and falsely portraying the quality of care provided.'

This chapter explores basic issues relating to risk adjustment for quality performance measurement. Another important use of risk adjustment methods involves setting payment levels for health-care services. In 1983, Medicare introduced the earliest widely implemented risk adjustment method by adopting DRGs for prospective hospital payment. These are now utilized worldwide, albeit with nation-specific variations, especially throughout Europe. Langenbrunner et al. (2005) describe the various applications of DRGs for setting hospital payments. Hospital cases are assigned to pre-set reimbursement levels

---

[1] Nightingale (1863) used hospital mortality figures calculated by William Farr. This physician and prominent social reformer shared her passion for motivating hospital improvement through statistical analysis and comparing outcomes across facilities. Farr had conducted analyses for the Registrar-General since 1838.

(or relative weights) based primarily on patients' principal diagnosis, surgery or invasive procedure and whether they have significant co-morbidities or complications. DRGs have evolved over time, mainly to keep abreast of technological advances and newly emerging health conditions but also more recently to account better for severity of illness (US Department of Health and Human Services 2007). Other risk adjustment methods are used to set payment levels for capitated health plans, nursing home stays, home health-care episodes and other types of services. Risk adjustment for payment purposes raises special issues. In particular, critics worry that inadequate risk adjustment exacerbates incentives to avoid or limit care for very sick patients.

Cost-focused and quality performance-targeted risk adjustment methods share important conceptual foundations but are intended to predict different outcomes. Generally they have different specifications and weighting for risk factors but some aspects may overlap. In 2005 the United States Congress mandated that after 1 October 2008 Medicare would no longer pay hospitals for treating preventable complications that shift cases into higher-paying DRGs (Rosenthal 2007). The eight selected complications[2] are generally avoidable so this policy aims to stop financial rewards for substandard care. Pay for performance is another area where cost- and quality-focused risk adjustment may overlap (or collide). As described below, concerns about the validity of these measures (including the adequacy of risk adjustment) have taken centre stage in debates about these efforts worldwide.

Why risk adjust?

Rationale for risk adjustment

Health plans, hospitals, general practitioner practices or other health-care providers are not selected randomly. Many factors affect the way people link with their sources of care, including the nature of their health needs (e.g. acuity and severity of illness); financial resources; geography; previous health-care experiences; and their preferences,

---

[2] Medicare will not pay for any of the following acquired after admission to hospital: air embolism; blood incompatibility; catheter-associated urinary tract infection; pressure ulcer; object left in patient during surgery; vascular catheter-associated infection; mediastinitis after coronary artery bypass grafting; fall from bed (Rosenthal 2007).

values and expectations of health services. Not surprisingly, there may be wide variations in the mix of persons covered by different health plans, hospitals, general practioner practices or other health-care providers. These differences can have consequences. For example, older persons with multiple chronic conditions require more health services than younger healthier people and are thus more costly and complicated to treat. Most importantly from a quality measurement perspective, persons with complex illnesses, multiple coexisting conditions or other significant risk factors are more likely to do poorly than healthier individuals, even with the best possible care.

Most quality performance measures reflect contributions from various patient-related and non-patient factors. For example, hospital mortality rates after open heart surgery reflect not only the technical skills of the surgical team and post-operative nursing care but also the severity of patients' cardiovascular disease, extent of co-morbid illness and level of functional impairment. Screening mammography rates reflect not only recommendations from clinicians and the availability of the test but also women's motivation, ability and willingness to attend. Thus, a complex mix of factors contributes to how patients do and what services they receive. Patient outcomes represent a particularly complicated function of multiple interacting factors:

> Patient outcomes = f (effectiveness of care or therapeutic intervention, quality of care, patient attributes or risk factors affecting response to care, random chance)

Risk adjustment aims to account for the effects of differences when comparing outcomes across groups of patients. It assists in disentangling the variation in patient outcomes attributable to intrinsic patient factors (generally not under the control of clinicians or other health-care providers) from factors under clinicians' or providers' control, such as quality of care. Generally, it is critical to use risk adjustment before using patient outcomes to draw inferences about the relative quality of care across health plans, hospitals, individual practitioners or other units of interest. Risk adjustment aims to give outcome-based performance measures, what Donabedian (1980 p.103) calls 'attributional validity' – the conviction that observed outcome differences causally relate directly to quality of care rather than to other contributing factors.

Despite this straightforward rationale, critics warn that it may be quixotic to believe that quality of care variations can be adequately isolated by adjusting comparisons of patients' risks and other factors (Lilford et al. 2004 p.1147). As Terris and Aron (2009) observe in this volume, proving attribution may require exploration of causality from multiple and varied perspectives. Thus, risk adjustment performed in isolation can produce a false sense that residual differences among providers reflect variations in quality. Different risk adjustment methods can paint divergent pictures of provider performance according to their data sources, variable specifications and weighting schemes. For instance, different risk adjustment methods produced varying impressions of rankings of hospitals based on their relative mortality rates (Iezzoni 1997). Hospitals ranked highly by one risk adjuster may plummet in the rankings of another. Lilford et al. (2004 p.1148) note that, 'case-mix [i.e. risk] adjustment can lead to the erroneous conclusion that an unbiased comparison between providers follows. We term this the case-mix fallacy.' Nonetheless, without any risk adjustment, patient factors can hopelessly confound comparisons of outcomes and of other performance measures.

Consequences of failing to risk adjust

There can be serious consequences from failing to risk adjust before comparing how patients do across health plans or providers. Most importantly, the resulting information could be inaccurate or misleading and consumers, policy-makers and other health-care stakeholders will not have valid information for decision-making (Institute of Medicine 2006).

Intended audiences may grow to distrust, disregard or dismiss poorly-adjusted data. This happened after Medicare first published hospital mortality rates more than twenty years ago (Box 3.1.2). A 2005 national survey of American general internists found that 36% strongly agreed and 52% somewhat agreed that, 'at present, measures of quality are not adequately adjusted for patients' medical conditions.' Interestingly, 38% strongly agreed and 47% somewhat agreed that current quality measures 'are not adequately adjusted for patients' socioeconomic status' (Casalino et al. 2007 p.494). Without clinician buy-in, initiatives that use performance measures to try to

---

Box 3.1.2 Inadequate risk adjustment

In March 1986, the Medicare agency in the United States publicly released for the first time hospital mortality rates for its beneficiaries. According to governmental predictions, 142 hospitals had significantly higher death rates than predicted, while 127 had significantly lower rates. At the facility with the most aberrant death rate 87.6% of Medicare patients had died, compared with a predicted 22.5%. This facility was a hospice caring for terminally ill patients. The government's risk adjustment model had not accounted adequately for patients' risks of death.

Source: Brinkley 1986.

---

influence clinical practices will likely fail or confront controversy and challenges.

Pay-for-performance programmes are a case in point, usually at the forefront of risk adjustment debates. These initiatives aim to align payment incentives with motivations to improve health-care quality but many observers have raised another troubling possibility. If pay-for-performance measures are perceived as unfair or invalid because they do not account adequately for patients' risk factors, then clinicians or health-care facilities may game the system by avoiding high-risk patients who are unlikely to do well (Birkmeyer et al. 2006). To maximize the fairness of pay-for-performance measures, risk adjustment may need to consider not only patients' clinical characteristics but also their socio-demographic complexity and other factors that might affect adherence to treatment regimens, as well as screening and preventive care (Forrest et al. 2006).

Some observers worry that pay-for-performance incentives could potentially precipitate adverse selection – the pressure to avoid severely ill or clinically challenging patients (Petersen et al. 2006; Scott 2007). In addition, vulnerable subpopulations could lose access to care e.g. those with lower socio-economic status and a heavy burden of disease who tend to cluster in specific locales (e.g. distressed inner-city neighbourhoods): '... What happens to providers with a disproportionate number of high-risk patients? They can dump their patients, they can get paid less, or they can move' (McMahon et al. 2007 p.235).

This concern is bolstered by early experiences from the United Kingdom's NHS pay-for-performance initiative targeting general practitioners that began in 2004 (Roland 2004; Velasco-Garrido et al. 2005). Given the nature of some NHS performance measures (see below), general practitioners could perform better by excluding certain high-risk patients from reporting (Doran et al. 2006). Practices could game the incentive system by avoiding such patients or reporting that these patients were exceptions to required clinical actions or outcomes. Evidence of widespread gaming has failed to materialize but a small minority of practices (91 or 1.1%) excluded more than 15% of their patients from performance reporting (Doran et al. 2006). In countries like New Zealand that have not yet widely implemented pay for performance, NHS experiences raise fears of potential gaming incentives and other unintended consequences, leading to caution in specifying initial performance measurement sets. The Effective Practice, Informatics and Quality Improvement (EPIQ) programme at the University of Auckland suggests starting modestly by focusing on childhood immunizations, influenza vaccinations among persons over sixty-five, cervical smears and breast screening (Perkins et al. 2006).

Public reporting of performance measures could also motivate clinicians to turn away or deny care to potentially risky patients although there is scant rigorous evidence of this (Shekelle 2009). The most frequently cited example involves New York State, which has published hospital- and physician-level report cards on coronary artery bypass graft (CABG) surgery deaths since the early 1990s and, more recently, on coronary angioplasty outcomes. Anecdotal rumours among thoracic surgeons and interventional cardiologists, as well as limited objective evidence, suggest that public reporting has made certain New York clinicians reluctant to accept patients with relatively high mortality risks. The concern (not yet proven conclusively) is that high-risk New York residents in need of a CABG or angioplasty must seek physicians elsewhere. Ironically, CABG mortality has one of the most evidence-based, intensively validated and extensively honed risk adjustment methodologies of all performance measures (McMahon et al. 2007). If these reports of avoiding high-risk patients hold true, it would be impossible to forestall gaming behaviour among worried clinicians.

Finally, failure to risk adjust hampers attempts to engage providers in a meaningful dialogue about improving performance. Clinicians may simply argue that unadjusted data are unfair and misrepresent their patient panels, impeding efforts to use these data to direct quality improvement activities. Distinguishing the factors that clinicians can control from those they cannot is a key aim of risk adjustment and essential to identifying productive improvement strategies.

Risk adjustment for different performance measures

The word risk is meaningless without first answering the fundamental question – risk of what? (Iezzoni 2003). In measuring health-care quality this question generates countless answers (from imminent death to satisfaction with care) across diverse health-care settings. For instance, risk adjustment for comparison of CABG death rates differs from that for consumer satisfaction with hospice care. The need for and nature of risk adjustment varies with the topic of interest.

It is necessary to acknowledge limitations in the current science of performance measurement before discussing risk adjusting performance measures. Today, numerous putative performance measures exist for diverse clinical areas and settings of care. Nonetheless, an Institute of Medicine (2006) committee review of more than 800 performance measures identified significant gaps and inadequacies in current quality measures. The scientific evidence base for specifying quality measures remains insufficient in many clinical areas. Numerous existing performance measures focus on actions or activities with limited or unproven clinical value and many concerns relate to risk adjustment and identifying at-risk patients. As Hayward (2007 p.952) observed, the field needs to: "construct performance measures that are much more nuanced and that consider patients' preferences, competing needs, and the complex circumstances of individual patients. Extensive work has shown how simplistic, all-or-nothing performance measurement can mislead providers into prioritizing low-value care and can create undue incentives for getting rid of 'bad' patients."

Growing populations of older persons with multiple co-morbid conditions are especially neglected by current disease-by-disease performance measurement approaches. Boyd et al. (2005) applied established practice guidelines (often the source of performance measures) to a hypothetical 79-year-old woman with hypertension, diabetes mellitus, osteoporosis, osteoarthritis and chronic obstructive pulmonary disease. To meet guideline specifications, the woman would need to pursue fourteen nonpharmaceutical activities and take twelve separate medications in a regimen requiring nineteen daily drug doses. Some recommendations contradicted each other, thus endangering her overall health. There are rapidly ageing populations in many nations worldwide. Accounting for the clinical complexities of persons with multiple chronic conditions and individual preferences for care presents a major challenge for performance measurement and holds important implications for risk adjustment.

Outcome versus process measures

Performance measures often sort into two types: (i) outcomes – how patients do; and (ii) processes of care – what is done to and for patients. Outcomes generally have a clear rationale for risk adjustment. How patients do in the future is closely related to how they are doing now or did in the recent past. Risk adjustment is obviously essential for outcomes heavily influenced by patients' intrinsic clinical characteristics over which clinicians have little control. For example, gravely ill intensive treatment unit (ITU) patients are at greater risk of the outcome 'imminent death' than moderately ill patients. Researchers have developed good methods to risk adjust ITU mortality rates through years of analysing indicators of disease burden and physiological functioning (e.g. vital signs, serum chemistry findings, level of consciousness). Much of the early work on ITU risk adjustment occurred in the United States (Knaus et al. 1981, 1985 & 1991) but these models have been validated and new ones developed in nations worldwide. Methods for risk adjusting paediatric and adult ITU mortality rates are readily available e.g. the United Kingdom's Intensive Care National Audit & Research Centre (www.icnarc.org). It is critically important to validate risk adjustment methods within individual countries for the outcome 'ITU mortality'. Although basic human physiology does not vary, practice patterns (e.g. admission policies, available technologies) and patients' preferences (e.g. use of do-not-resuscitate status) certainly do. These considerations could affect associations of physiological risk factors with mortality outcomes.

Risk adjustment methods pertaining to hospitalization outcomes (primarily mortality and, increasingly, complications of care) have been the most studied over the last thirty years. As noted above, clinically detailed risk adjustment methods for coronary artery bypass graft surgery and coronary interventions are well-developed. In the National Veterans Administration Surgical Risk Study researchers spent more than fifteen years developing risk adjustment methods using clinical variables for other selected surgical specialties (Khuri et al. 1995 & 1997). These methods are now available in the private sector through the American College of Surgeons National Surgical Quality Improvement Program (NSQIP).

This brief chapter cannot itemize the expanding number of publicly available and commercial risk adjustment methods developed to target various outcomes within differing settings of care. Suffice to say that existing risk adjustment methods differ widely in terms of their risk factor specifications, weighting schemes and validation for applications in practice settings beyond those in which they were developed (i.e. other countries with differing practice patterns), depending on the particular outcome, care environment and purpose.

It has been particularly challenging to risk adjust outcomes of routine outpatient care for performance measurement involving common chronic conditions. A number of the 146 indicators chosen for the NHS 2004 pay-for-performance initiative involved outcomes of care. Although patient attributes could certainly affect the selected outcomes, the NHS programme did not conduct formal risk adjustment. Instead, general practitioners received points for their performance between specified minimum and maximum values – an approach that Velasco-Garrido et al. (2005 p.231) describe as 'a kind of simple method for risk adjustment' (Box 3.1.3). However, this characterization is not entirely compatible with the usual goals of risk adjustment. In the example given in Box 3.1.3, if that practice's panel comprised patients with a heavy burden of co-morbid illness and difficult to control diabetes then bringing only 30% to the target blood pressure may represent a significant clinical achievement, perhaps worthy of nearly the full seventeen points. Actual risk adjustment would account for this underlying clinical complexity and pro-rate the point scheme accordingly. The NHS methods' failure to recognize these types of problems might have contributed to concerns about exception report-

---

Box 3.1.3 UK NHS blood pressure indicator

A maximum of seventeen points can be achieved for controlling blood pressure in diabetic patients (i.e. BP 145/85 mmHg or less). The threshold to obtain a score is 25% of patients; the maximum practically achievable has been set at 55%. A practice that achieves this target blood pressure in 55% of its diabetic patients will obtain the full score for this indicator. If the target is achieved for only 30% of the diabetic patients, the practice score for this indicator will be only 5/30, that is 2.8 points.

Source: Velasco-Garrido et al. 2005.

---

ing (i.e. eliminating patients from a particular quality indicator report) (Doran et al. 2006).[3]

Process measures (what is done to and for patients) can also warrant risk adjustment. Beyond patients' clinical attributes, certain process measures may require adjustment for non-clinical factors that may confound performance assessment – factors that can be 'difficult to measure and account for with risk adjustment' (Birkmeyer et al. 2006 p.189). These might include patients' psychosocial characteristics, socio-economic status and preferences for care.

Many process measures build in explicit specifications of patient characteristics that are essentially risk factors for obtaining the service. These factors act as inclusion or exclusion criteria, indicating which subset of patients qualifies to receive the process of care. For example, in the United States it is a widely accepted process mea-

---

[3] Family practitioners can exclude or exception-report patients for reasons including: family practitioner judges indicator inappropriate for the patient because of particular circumstances, such as terminal illness, extreme frailty or the presence of a supervening condition that makes the specified treatment of the patient's condition clinically inappropriate; patient has had an allergic or other adverse reaction to a specified medication or has another contraindication to the medication; patient does not agree to investigation or treatment (Doran et al. 2006).

sure to administer aspirin to patients admitted to hospital with acute myocardial infarction, with the stipulation that patients do not have any of a list of contraindications or exclusion criteria (Kahn et al. 2006).[4] Comparisons of the fraction of acute myocardial infarction patients receiving aspirin across hospitals must recognize that the mix of patients with contraindications may differ across facilities. Here, it is most appropriate to apply contraindication criteria individually, case-by-case (i.e. determining whether aspirin is clinically indicated for each patient). Comparisons across hospitals then focus only on those patients without contraindications and makes it unnecessary to risk adjust for conditions considered as exclusion criteria. This process appears straightforward but even panels of experts can find it challenging to specify inclusion and exclusion criteria in certain clinical contexts (Shahian et al. 2007).

Measures involving patient preferences

Process measures that require a positive action by patients (i.e. obtaining a mammogram, having a child immunized) raise special concerns. These actions are affected by education, motivation, wherewithal (e.g. financial resources, transportation, child care, time off work), preferences for care and outcomes, cultural concerns and various other factors – largely outside clinician control. Different clinicians and providers of care see different mixes of patients along these critical dimensions, raising the need for risk adjustment. For certain purposes, risk stratification might offer a more informative way to present these comparisons (see below).

The underlying goals of process-driven quality measurement initiatives carry implications for risk adjusting the performance measures. For example, health-care administrators may decree that virtually all older women should undergo mammography, regardless of their socio-demographic characteristics. Providers caring for large fractions of

---

[4] The Joint Commission in the United States specifies hospital performance measures widely used in federal reporting initiatives. Exclusions listed for the aspirin on admission measure are: active bleeding on arrival to the hospital or within twenty-four hours of arrival; aspirin allergy; pre-arrival use of warfarin; or other reasons documented by specified clinicians for not administering aspirin before or after admission (Kahn et al. 2006).

women who, for whatever reason (e.g. education, culture, resources), are less apt to obtain a mammogram should nonetheless be held to the same standard as other providers. In this circumstance, risk adjustment becomes moot. This stance might have merit (e.g. equity across patient subgroups) but has practical consequences. Providers that must spend resources boosting their mammography rates may neglect other issues. This also disregards the role of patient preferences, one factor considered in NHS exception reporting (Doran et al. 2006).

Patient preferences are not only an issue for process measures but also might affect some outcomes directly. Mortality rates are a prime example. According to Holloway and Quill (2007 p.802), 'mortality has been criticized as a measure of quality for years and debates about methods of risk adjustment are almost clichéd', but these debates neglect concerns about 'preference-sensitive care.' Hospitals vary widely in the use of early do-not-resuscitate orders and hospital mortality measures erroneously treat all deaths as medical failures. In 2007, Medicare launched Hospital Compare (www.hospitalcompare. hhs.gov), a web site that posts various performance measures including risk adjusted mortality rates for acute myocardial infarction and congestive heart failure for hospitals nationwide. Hospital Compare identified a hospital in Buffalo, New York, as one of the thirty-five worst American hospitals because its mortality rate for congestive heart failure between July 2005 and June 2006 was 4.9% more than the national mean. The hospital reviewed medical records of these deaths and found that eleven decedents (about 40% of the total) were in hospice or receiving only palliative care treatment at patients' requests (Holloway & Quill 2007). More than twenty years after its initial problematic data release (Box 3.1.2), Medicare's risk adjustment method still did not account for patients' preferences for end-of-life care. Some initiatives that report hospital mortality rates exclude all hospice patients from these calculations. This eliminates the need to risk adjust for this patient preference, assuming that all patients with early do-not-resuscitate orders are in hospice (which may not always occur) (Holloway & Quill 2007). In the United Kingdom, whether patients were admitted to palliative care units was recently added to the list of risk factors for computing hospital standardized mortality ratios (Dr Foster Intelligence 2007).

Composite measures

As detailed in Chapter 3.4, there is increasing interest in combining diverse individual performance measures to produce composites or summary assessments of quality-related performance. A conceptual justification for this approach is the complexity of quality, comprised of multifaceted dimensions. A practical impetus for producing composite measures involves common statistical realities – small sample sizes of patients for clinicians, hospitals or other units of interest; and the relative rarity of many targeted single events, such as deaths. The simplicity offered by a single number or score has led some groups to propose the creation of composite performance measures that cut across Donabedian's (1980) classic triad of quality measurement dimensions: outcomes, processes and structures of care (Shahian et al. 2007).

Despite the appeal of simple summary scores the production of composite ratings raises important methodological questions, including whether individual measures within the composite require risk adjustment. The construction of composite measures is complicated and stokes fears about complex statistical arguments masking opportunities for manipulation or misinterpretation. Since September 2001, the NHS in England has published annual star ratings for acute care hospitals, using composite scores to assign hospitals to one of four levels: from zero to three stars. Jacobs et al. (2006) used data from these star ratings to explore the stability of these composite hospital rankings across different methodological choices. They found considerable instability in hospitals' positions in league tables. Beyond those overarching problems, details of individual measures can be lost within the composite. For instance, coronary artery bypass graft mortality is one of the many indicators combined in the star rating composite but these mortality rates are not risk adjusted. Producers of the star ratings aim to ease concerns about these unadjusted mortality figures by comparing institutions within different classes of hospitals – ostensibly a broad attempt to control for patients' risks.

The Society of Thoracic Surgeons (STS) quality measurement task force in the United States has demonstrated the complexities of producing composite measures while paying detailed attention to risk adjustment (O'Brien et al 2007; Shahian et al. 2007). Table 3.1.1 shows

Table 3.1.1 *Individual measures and domains in the STS composite quality score*

Operative care domain
- use of at least one internal mammary artery graft

Perioperative medical care domain
- preoperative beta blockers
- discharge beta blockers
- discharge antiplatelet medication
- discharge antilipid medication

Risk adjusted mortality domain
- operative mortality

Risk adjusted major morbidity domain
- prolonged ventilator (> 24 hours)
- deep sternal wound infection
- permanent stroke
- renal insufficiency
- reoperation

Source: O'Brien et al. 2007

the eleven performance measures selected for producing the composite score. Analysts defined and estimated six different risk adjusted measures to add to their summary model, one for each of the six items requiring risk adjustment. Using clinical data from a large STS data set representing 530 providers, their multivariate random-effects models estimated true provider-specific usage rates for each process measure and true risk-standardized event rates for each outcome. Further analyses suggested that each of the eleven items provided complementary rather than redundant information about performance (O'Brien et al. 2007). Despite their extensive analyses, the STS investigators acknowledge the need to monitor the stability of their composite scores over time; and sensitivity to various threats, such as nonrandomly missing data used for risk adjustment. Future research must explore not only the benefits and drawbacks of composite performance measures but also the role that risk adjustment of individual indicators plays in summary rankings.

Conceptualizing risk factors

The development and validation of credible risk adjustment methods requires substantial time and resources. This chapter does not have the space to describe the steps needed to complete this process but looks briefly at three major issues pertaining to the development of risk adjustment methods: (i) choice of risk factors; (ii) selection and implications of data sources; and (iii) overview of statistical methods.

The essential first step in risk adjusting performance measures involves a thorough understanding of the measure and its validity as a quality indicator. The next step is to develop a conceptual model identifying patient factors that could potentially affect the targeted outcome or process of care. Table 3.1.2 suggests various patient-risk factors grouped along different dimensions although additional attributes could apply to the wide range of potential performance measurement topics and settings of care (Iezzoni 2003).

Initially analysts should develop this conceptual model independently of practical concerns, particularly about the availability of data. Pertinent characteristics and their relative importance as risk factors vary across different performance measures. For example, indicators of acute physiological stability (e.g. vital signs, serum electrolytes, arterial oxygenation) are critical for assessing risk of imminent ITU death but less important for evaluating consumer satisfaction with health plans. It is impossible to risk adjust for all patient dimensions. Nevertheless, it is essential to know what potentially important factors have not been included in risk adjustment. This assists in interpreting comparisons of performance measures across clinicians, hospitals or other providers – attributing residual differences in performance to their root cause (i.e. unmeasured patient characteristics versus other factors).

The selection of potential risk factors can prove controversial, especially items chosen as potential proxies when data about a particular risk factor are unavailable. For example, in England Dr Foster Intelligence produces an annual guide that ranks acute hospital trusts by standardized mortality ratios. Recently, analysts added to their risk adjustment model – each patient's previous emergency admissions within the last twelve months. Presumably, this aims to capture something about the patients' clinical stability and status of chronic illnesses. However, this risk factor could be confounded with the very

Table 3.1.2 *Potential patient risk factors*

Demographic characteristics
- age
- sex/gender
- race and ethnicity

Clinical factors
- acute physiological stability
- principal diagnosis
- severity of principal diagnosis
- extent and severity of co-morbidities
- physical functioning
- vision, hearing, speech functioning
- cognitive functioning
- mental illness, emotional health

Socio-economic/psychosocial factors
- educational attainment, health literacy
- language(s)
- economic resources
- employment and occupation
- familial characteristics and household composition
- housing and neighbourhood characteristics
- health insurance coverage
- cultural beliefs and behaviours
- religious beliefs and behaviours, spirituality

Health-related behaviours and activities
- tobacco use
- alcohol, illicit drug use
- sexual practices ('safe sex')
- diet and nutrition
- physical activity, exercise
- obesity and overweight

Attitudes and perceptions
- overall health status and quality of life
- preferences, values and expectations for health-care services

quantity that standardized mortality ratios aim to highlight – quality of care. Patients may have more emergency readmissions because of poor quality of care (e.g. premature discharges, inadequate care) during prior admissions at that same hospital. In this instance, controlling for frequent readmissions might give hospitals credit for sicker patients rather than highlighting the real problem. Documentation from Dr Foster Intelligence indicates that 'adjustments are made for the factors that are found by statistical analysis to be significantly associated with hospital death rates' (Dr Foster Intelligence 2007). However, as this example suggests, choosing risk factors based only on statistical significance could mask mortality differences related to poor hospital care. Risk factors – and their precise specification (e.g. if using a proxy) – should have clear conceptual justification relating to elucidating provider quality.

Some risk adjustment methods employ processes of care as risk factors, generally as proxies for the presence or severity of disease. Examples include use of certain pharmaceuticals or procedures generally reserved for very ill patients (e.g. tracheostomy, surgical insertion of gastric feeding tube). These processes might have clinical validity as indicators of patients' future risks but in the context of performance measurement for pay for performance or public reporting they are potentially susceptible to manipulation or gaming (see below). These concerns argue against the use of processes of care as risk factors.

Data options and implications

Inadequate information is the biggest practical impediment to risk adjustment. Required information may be simply unavailable or too costly or infeasible to obtain. The conceptual ideal is to have complete information on all potential risk factors (Table 3.1.2) but that goal is not readily unattainable. Therefore, risk adjustment today is inevitably an exercise in compromise, with important implications for interpreting the results. The three primary sources of data for risk adjustment, each with advantages and disadvantages, are now described in more detail.

Administrative data

Administrative data are the first primary source. By definition, they are generated to meet some administrative purpose such as claims submitted for billing or records required for documenting services. The prototypical administrative data record contains a patient's administrative identification and demographic information; one or more diagnoses coded using some version or variant of the WHO

ICD; procedures coded using some local coding classification (unlike ICD, which is used in some form worldwide, there is no universal coding system); dates of various services; provider identifiers; and perhaps some indication of costs or charges, depending on the country and setting of care. To maximize administrative efficiency these records are ideally computerized, submitted electronically and relatively easy to obtain and analyse.

Administrative data offer the significant advantage of ready availability, ease of access and relatively low acquisition costs. Required data elements are typically clearly defined and theoretically recorded using consistent rules, ostensibly making the data content comparable across providers. Administrative records also typically cover large populations, such as all persons covered by a given health plan or living in a specific geographical area. Uniform patient identifiers enable analysts to link records relating to individual patients longitudinally over time (e.g. as when creating the Dr Foster variable relating to prior emergency admissions). Some countries (e.g. United States, United Kingdom, Sweden) have spent considerable resources upgrading their electronic administrative data reporting in anticipation of using this information to manage their health-care systems more effectively (Foundation for Information Policy Research 2005).

However, significant disadvantages can make risk adjustment methods derived from administrative data immediately suspect. Payment-related incentives can skew data content especially when providers produce administrative records to obtain reimbursement. The most prominent example in the United States involved inaccurate reporting of diagnosis codes when Medicare first adopted DRG-based prospective payment. Coding audits found that hospitals engaged in 'DRG creep' (Hsia et al. 1988; Simborg 1981) by assigning diagnoses not supported by medical record evidence but likely intended to move patients into higher-paying DRGs. Inconsistencies and inaccuracies in the assignment of ICD codes across providers can compromise comparisons of their performance using administrative data. Systematic biases across hospitals in under- or over-reporting diagnoses could compromise comparisons. For example, in England, foundation acute hospital trusts have lower rates of uncoded data than other acute trusts. They have prioritized the improvement of coding accuracy and timeliness by investing in training; hiring additional data coders and health information managers; and encouraging coding directly from medical records rather than discharge summaries (Audit Commission 2005). In 2004/2005, the average acute hospital admission in England received only 2.48 coded diagnoses, compared with just over three diagnoses in Australia and six in the United States (Audit Commission 2005 p.47).

Hospital coding of diagnoses raises additional questions about comparing quality performance. Romano et al. (2002) examined results from a reabstraction of 991 discectomy cases admitted to California hospitals. The original hospital codes displayed only 35% sensitivity for identifying any complication of care found during reabstraction (i.e. the gold standard). Under-reporting was markedly worse at hospitals calculated to have lower risk adjusted complication rates. Undercoding extended beyond serious complications to more mild conditions, such as atelectasis, post-haemorrhagic anaemia and hypotension. One study from Canada examined the concordance between medical records and administrative data for conditions included in the Charlson co-morbidity index commonly used in risk adjustment (e.g. Dr Foster uses Charlson co-morbidities in its standardized hospital mortality ratios). Administrative data under-reported ten co-morbidities but slightly over-reported diabetes, mild liver disease and rheumatological conditions (Quan et al. 2002 pp. 675-685).

There are also reservations about the clinical content of ICD codes. Although these aim to classify the full range of diseases and various health conditions that affect humans, they do not capture the critical clinical parameters associated with illness severity (e.g. arterial oxygenation level, haematocrit value, extent and pattern of coronary artery occlusion); nor do they provide insight into functional impairments and disability (see WHO 2001 for that purpose).[5] In the United States[6] these reservations have prompted more than a decade of research controversy as Medicare has tried to produce clinically cred-

---

[5] Representatives from numerous nations participated in specification of WHO's ICF (revision of the International Classification of Impairments, Disabilities and Handicaps). Nonetheless, it is unclear how systematically this is used in administrative data reporting around the world. It does not appear on administrative records required by Medicare or major health insurers in the United States.

[6] United States has switched to ICD-10 for reporting causes of death but still uses a version of ICD-9 specifically designed by American clinicians for morbidity reporting – ICD-9-CM (http://www.eicd.com/EICDMain.htm).

ible risk adjusted mortality figures without the considerable expense of widespread data gathering from medical records. For the Hospital Compare web site, Medicare contracted with researchers at Yale University to develop administrative data-based risk adjustment algorithms for acute myocardial infarction and congestive heart failure mortality within thirty days of hospital admission and to validate the results against methods using detailed clinical information abstracted from medical records (Krumholz et al. 2006). The correlation of standardized hospital mortality rates calculated with administrative versus clinical data was 0.90 for acute myocardial infarction and 0.95 for congestive heart failure. These findings and the results of other statistical testing suggested that the administrative data-based models were sufficiently robust for public reporting.

Cardiac surgeons remain sceptical about whether administrative data can produce meaningful risk adjustment for coronary artery bypass graft hospital mortality rankings. Shahian et al. (2007a) examined this question using detailed clinical data gathered during coronary artery bypass graft admissions in Massachusetts hospitals. The administrative mortality model used risk adjustment methods promulgated by the federal AHRQ and built around all patient refined DRGs (APR-DRGs).[7] The researchers also tested differences between examining in-hospital versus thirty-day post-admission mortality and the implications of using different statistical methodologies (i.e. hierarchical versus standard logistic regression models). At the outset, one major problem was cases misclassified as having had isolated coronary artery bypass graft surgery – about 10% of the administratively identified coronary artery bypass graft cases had some other simultaneous but poorly specified surgery (another subset had concomitant valve surgery). Risk adjusted outcomes varied across the two data sources because of both missing risk factors in the administrative models and case misclassification.

Shahian et al's study (2007a) also highlighted difficulties determining the timing of in-hospital clinical events using coded data. This raises its own set of problems. Administrative hospital discharge data

---

[7] All APR-DRGs were developed by 3M Health Information Systems (Wallingford, CT, USA) to predict two different outcomes: resource use during hospital admissions and in-hospital mortality. The two models use different weighting schemes for the predictor variables (primarily ICD-9-CM discharge diagnoses) and produce different scoring results.

generally have not differentiated diagnoses representing post-admission complications from clinical conditions existing on admission. A tautology could occur if administrative data based risk adjusters use codes indicating virtual death (e.g. cardiac arrest) to predict death, raising the appearance that the model performed well statistically (e.g. producing artifactually high R-squared values or c statistics). Lawthers et al. (2000) looked at the timing of secondary hospital discharge diagnoses by reabstracting over 1200 medical records from hospitalizations in California and Connecticut. Among surgical cases they found many serious secondary diagnosis codes representing conditions that occurred following admission, including 78% of deep vein thrombosis or pulmonary embolism diagnoses and 71% of instances of shock or cardiorespiratory arrest. In our work, discharge abstract-based risk adjusters were generally equal or better statistical predictors of in-hospital mortality than measures derived from admission clinical findings (Iezzoni 1997). Not surprisingly, the administrative risk adjustment models appeared over-specified in the coronary artery bypass graft study (Shahian et al. 2007a).[8] However, even more important than this statistical concern is the possibility that risk adjusters that give credit for potentially lethal in-hospital events might mask the very quantity of ultimate interest – quality of care.

Since 1 October 2008, Medicare has required hospitals in the United States to indicate whether each coded hospital discharge diagnosis was present on admission (POA) or occurred subsequently (e.g. in-hospital complication) for hospitalized beneficiaries. A POA indicator would allow risk adjustment methods to use only those conditions that patients brought with them into the hospital, potentially isolating diagnoses caused by substandard care (Zhan et al. 2007). POA flags could substantially increase the value of hospital discharge diagnosis codes for measuring quality performance. However, California and New York implemented POA flags for discharge diagnoses years ago and subsequent studies have raised questions about the accuracy of these indicators (Coffey et al. 2006).

---

[8] Over-specification could occur when post-operative events virtually synonymous with death (e.g. cardiac arrest) are used in the risk adjustment models. Models containing such rare but highly predictive events may not validate well (e.g. when applied to other data sets or a portion of the model development data set withheld for validation purposes), thus indicating model over-specification.

Medical records or clinical data

The second primary source of risk factor information is medical records or electronic systems containing detailed clinical information in digital formats (e.g. electronic data repositories). The primary benefit of these data is clinical credibility. This clinical face validity is essential for the acceptance of risk adjustment methods in certain contexts, such as predicting coronary artery bypass graft mortality (Shahian et al. 2007a) and deaths following other operations (Khuri et al. 1995 &1997). In certain instances (e.g. when risk adjusting nursing home or home health-care outcomes) coded administrative data provide insufficient clinical content and validity. ICD diagnosis codes do not credibly capture clinical risk factors in these non-acute care settings where patients' functional status typically drives outcomes.

Abstracting information from medical records is expensive and raises other important questions. To ensure good data quality and comparability, explicit definitions of the clinical variables and detailed abstraction guidelines are required when collecting clinical information across providers. Gathering extensive clinical information for performance measurement may demand extensive training and monitoring of skilled staff to maintain data quality. It is hoped that electronic medical records, automated databases and electronic data repositories will eventually ease these feasibility concerns. For instance, Escobar et al. (2008) linked patient-level information from administrative data sources with automated inpatient, outpatient and laboratory databases to produce risk adjusted inpatient and thirty-day post-admission mortality models. In order to avoid confounding risk factors with possible quality shortfalls, they included only those laboratory values obtained within the twenty-four hours preceding hospitalization in their acute physiology measure. It is beyond the scope of this chapter to describe global efforts to develop electronic health information systems but countries worldwide are investing heavily in creating electronic health information infrastructures that are interoperable (i.e. allowing data-sharing readily across borders and settings of care) (Kalra 2006 & 2006a). It may even become possible to download detailed clinical data directly from these electronic systems to support risk adjustment.

Electronic records have obvious advantages (chiefly legibility) but their medical record content may not advance far beyond that of paper records without significant changes in the documentation practices of clinicians. Especially in outpatient settings, medical records have highly variable completeness and accuracy; lengthy medical records in academic medical centres may contain notations from multiple layers of clinicians, sometimes containing contradictory information (Iezzoni et al. 1992). This may partly explain why it is more challenging to capture some variables more reliably than others. For instance, reabstractions of clinical data from the Veterans Affairs National Surgical Quality Improvement Project in the United States found 97.4% exact agreement for abstracting the anaesthetic technique used during surgery; 94.9% for whether the patient had diabetes and 83.4% for whether the patient experienced dyspnea (Davis et al. 2007). Electronic medical records may contain templates with explicit slots for documenting certain data elements; some may even provide completed templates (e.g. clinical information about presumed findings from physical examinations) that allow clinicians to modify automated data entries to reflect individual clinical circumstances. Not surprisingly, concerns arise about the accuracy of such automated records. In the United States, anecdotal reports question whether clinicians actually perform complete physical examinations or just accept template data without validating the information.

Something akin to code creep might also arise when risk adjustment uses detailed clinical information as even these risk adjusters are susceptible to potential manipulation. For example, anecdotal observations suggested that routine blood testing of patients increased after a severity measure (based on extensive medical record reviews and numerous clinical findings) was mandated for publicly reporting mortality and morbidity rates at Pennsylvania hospitals in 1986. Observers have argued about whether reporting of significant clinical risk factors increased in New York following the public release of surgeon-specific coronary artery bypass graft mortality rates. Some manipulation is impossible to detect using routine auditing methods (e.g. re-review of medical records). For example, one risk factor in New York's coronary artery bypass graft mortality model is patients' physical functional limitations caused by their cardiovascular disease. Physicians make this assessment in their offices or at the bedside by questioning and examining patients. Physicians may document functional impairments in the medical record in order to exaggerate their patients' true deficits and make them appear sicker. The only way to detect this problem is by independently re-examining patients – a costly and infeasible undertaking.

Information in administrative and medical records is always susceptible to manipulation but audits to monitor and ensure data integrity and quality are costly and sometimes impossible. The degree of motivation for gaming data reporting relates directly to clinicians' perceptions of whether risk adjusted performance measures are used punitively or unfairly. Once data are systematically and significantly gamed, they generally lose their utility for risk adjustment.

Information directly from patients or consumers

The third, and a popular, source of information is patients themselves, especially when performance measures target patients' perceptions (e.g. satisfaction with care, self-reported functional status). Patients are the only valid source of information about their views of their health-care experiences. Extensive research suggests that persons who say they are in poorer health systematically report lower levels of satisfaction with their health care than healthier individuals. Therefore, surveys asking about satisfaction typically contain questions about respondents' overall health which are then used to risk adjust the satisfaction ratings. Patients do not generally have strong motivations for gaming or manipulating their responses although studies suggest that many patients are reluctant to criticize their clinical caregivers.

Gathering data directly from patients has downsides beyond the considerable expense and feasibility challenges. Patients are not completely reliable sources of information about their specific health conditions or health service use – faulty memories, misunderstanding and misinformation compromise accuracy. Language problems, illiteracy, cultural concerns, cognitive impairments and other psychosocial issues complicate efforts to obtain information directly from patients. Education, income level, family supports, housing arrangements, substance abuse, mental illness and other such factors can affect certain outcomes of care but questions about these generate extreme sensitivities. Concerns about the confidentiality of data and sensitivity of certain issues make it infeasible to gather information on some important risk factors.

Response rates are critical to the validity of results and certain sub-populations are less likely to complete surveys.[9] Unless surveys are administered in accessible formats, persons with certain types of disabilities might be unable to respond. Furthermore, anecdotal reports from some American health insurers suggest that their enrollees are growing impatient with being surveyed about their health-care experiences. Even insurers with affluent enrollees (a population relatively likely to complete surveys) report that many of their subscribers no longer respond. The relatively few completed surveys that are available thus provide information of a highly suspect quality due to possible respondent bias.

Statistical considerations

Researchers developed the earliest generation of severity measures around thirty years ago, before large data sets containing information across numerous providers became available. After identifying risk factors, clinical experts used their judgment and expertise to specify weights (i.e. numbers indicating the relative importance of different risk factors for predicting the outcome of interest) that would be added or manipulated in some other way to produce risk scores. Now that large databases contain information from many providers, researchers can apply increasingly sophisticated statistical modelling techniques to produce weighting schemes and other algorithms to calculate patients' risks. Other chapters provide details about specific statistical methods (e.g. hierarchical modelling, smoothing techniques that attempt to improve predictive performance and recognize various sources of possible variation) but several points are emphasized here.

First, optimal risk adjustment models result from an iterative combination of clinical judgment and statistical modelling. Clinicians specify variables of interest and hypothesized relationships with the dependent variable (e.g. positive or negative correlations) and methodologists confirm whether the associations are statistically significant and satisfy hypotheses. Final models should retain only clinically credible factors that are not confounded with the ultimate goal of perfor-

[9] Surveys of Medicare beneficiaries' perceptions of health-care experiences suggest that certain subpopulations are especially unlikely to respond, e.g. older individuals; people with disabilities; women; racial and ethnic minorities; those living in geographical areas with relatively high rates of poverty and low education.

mance measurement – assessing quality of care. Thus, the creation of a risk adjustment method is a multidisciplinary effort. At a minimum this involves clinicians interacting with statisticians but may require experts in information systems and data production (e.g. medical record and coding personnel); quality improvement; survey design; and management. Analysts should avoid the urge to data dredge. With large databases and fast powerful computers, it is tempting to let the computer specify the risk adjustment algorithm (e.g. select variables) with minimal human input. Users of risk adjustment models should remain sceptical until models are confirmed as clinically credible and statistically validated, preferably on a data set distinct from that used to derive the model.

Second, models developed in one country may not necessarily transfer easily to another. Differences in practice patterns, patient preferences, data specifications and other factors could compromise validity and statistical performance in different settings. Clinicians and methodologists should examine both clinical validity and statistical performance before using models developed elsewhere.

Third, summary statistical performance measures (e.g. R-squared and c statistics) suggest how well risk adjustment models perform at predicting the outcomes of interest or discriminating between patients with and without the outcome. These measures are attractive because they summarize complex statistical relationships in a single number. However, it can be misleading to look only at (for example) relative R-squared values to choose a risk adjustment model. Quirks of the database or selected variables can inflate summary statistical performance measures and experienced analysts know that some data sets are easier to manipulate (e.g. because of the range or distribution of values of variables). Sometimes available predictor (independent) variables may be confounded with the outcome (dependent) variable. An example of this was noted above: when predicting hospital mortality, diagnosis codes that indicate conditions that occurred following admission can elevate c-statistics but obviously confound efforts to find quality problems. Summary statistical performance measures do not indicate how well risk adjustment models predict outcomes for different subgroups of patients. Therefore, decision-makers choosing among risk adjustment methods ideally should not simply search for the highest R-squared or c statistic but should also consider clinical validity and ability to isolate quality deficits.

Finally, other policy considerations may affect decisions about how to risk adjust comparisons of performance measures across practitioners, institutions or other units of interest. Statistical techniques control for the effects of risk factors and allow analysts to ignore these patient characteristics as the explanation for observed outcome differences. However, situations can arise where policy-makers suspect that quality also varies by critical patient characteristics, such as race or social class. Risk stratification can prove useful if the mix of these characteristics differs across the groups being compared (e.g. clinician practices, hospitals) as it examines the performance within strata (i.e. groups) of patients defined by the specific characteristic. Such analyses are especially important when the specific patient attribute has important social policy implications, such as ensuring equitable care across subpopulations.

An example from the United States highlights how risk stratification might work. Research indicates that African-American women are less likely than white women to obtain mammograms. Multiple factors likely contribute to this disparity, including differentials in educational level, awareness of personal breast cancer risks and women's preferences. If two health plans have different proportions of black and white enrollees then risk adjustment controlling for race will not reveal whether the health plans have similar or divergent mammography rates for black and white women. It might also mask a plan's especially poor mammography performance among its black enrollees. In this instance, analysts should perform race-stratified comparisons – looking at mammography rates for black women and for white women respectively across the two plans.

When is risk stratification indicated? The answer underscores the critical importance of understanding the context in which the risk adjusted information will be used and having a conceptual model of the relationships between a given performance measure and various potential risk factors. Risk stratification is desirable when analysts believe that a policy-sensitive patient characteristic (e.g. race, social class) is an important risk factor but could also reflect differences in the treatments patients receive (i.e. quality of care). In this situation, analyses that begin with risk stratification can provide valuable insight. If performance is similar for different comparison groups (e.g. health plans, hospitals) within each patient stratum, then analysts could reasonably combine patients across strata and risk adjust for that characteristic, assuming that the conceptual model provides a valid causal rationale for including that characteristic among the risk factors.[10]

Plea for transparency

As suggested above, risk adjustment is a complicated business – literally so in some health-care marketplaces such as the United States. Many proprietary organizations, health information vendors and others promote or sell their own risk adjustment methodologies for a range of purposes. Policy-makers should be sceptical of marketing claims and would be wise to request details and rigorously evaluate methods to examine whether: they are clinically sound; important risk factors are missing; the data used are sufficiently sound; and the statistical methods are reasonable. However, it is often difficult (if not impossible) to gain access to important details about proprietary methods

When performance measures are either legally mandated or de facto required, policy-makers should consider stipulating that vendors make complete details of the risk adjustment method available for external scrutiny. An ideal strategy would place these methods in the public domain and ensure that they meet minimal explicit standards of clinical credibility and statistical rigour. An external, independent and objective body could operate an accreditation process through a standard battery of evaluations to establish whether the methods meet established explicit criteria of clinical validity and methodological soundness. Analysts should compare competing risk adjustment methods by applying them to the same database as results obtained from different data sets are not truly comparable. Testing would identify not only what the methods adjust for but also what they exclude. Information on critical missing risk characteristics could appear alongside comparisons of risk adjusted performance measures to highlight factors (other than quality) that might explain differences across the units being compared.

---

[10] In the United States, many analysts routinely include race and ethnicity among the predictor variables in modelling a wide range of outcomes (dependent variables). Scientific evidence rarely makes direct causal links between race and ethnicity and outcomes used in performance measurement, other than as perhaps a proxy for social disadvantage (e.g. poor education, low income) or disparate quality of care. Obviously, this raises serious questions about automatic inclusion of race and ethnicity in risk adjustment models for performance measures.

Commercial vendors of risk adjustment methods will argue that putting their products into the public domain will destroy their ability to market their product and fund future developments. This contention has merit and carefully designed policies must balance private sector interests with public needs. However, a method that is mandated for widespread use should be transparent – especially if the results will be publicized. Information produced via opaque methods could compromise the goal of motivating introspection, change and quality improvement.

Conclusions

Risk adjustment is an essential tool in performance measurement. Many risk adjustment methods are now available for users to apply to their own health-care settings, after preliminary testing. However, differences in practice patterns and other factors mean that methods developed in one environment may not transfer directly to other health-care delivery systems. Methods created in resource intensive settings (e.g. the United States) may not readily apply to less technologically driven systems but it may be possible to recalibrate or revise existing risk adjusters to suit local health-care environments. This will be less costly that developing entirely new risk adjustment methods.

Inadequate data sources pose the greatest challenge to risk adjustment. No data source can ever contain information on every personal and clinical attribute that could affect health-care outcomes and unmeasured patient characteristics will always contribute to differences in patient outcomes. Improving clinical data systems – and their linkage with large, population-based administrative records – offers the greatest potential for advancing risk adjustment.

These realities should not deter policy-makers but simply heighten caution about interpreting and using the results, for example when employing risk adjusted performance measures in pay-for-performance programmes or public quality reporting initiatives. Performance measures that are labelled 'risk adjusted' (even with inadequate methods) can engender a false sense of security about the validity of results. Depending on the nature of unmeasured risk factors, it may not be realistic or credible to hold clinicians or other providers fully accountable for performance differences.

Despite these complexities, there are substantial problems associated with *not* risk adjusting. Consumers could receive misleading information; providers might strive to avoid patients perceived as high risk; and any productive dialogue about improving performance could be compromised. Nonetheless, science cannot guarantee perfect risk adjustment and therefore decisions about applying these methods will engender controversy. It is likely that legitimate arguments for and against the use of methods with inevitable shortcomings will continue and policy-makers will need to weigh up the competing arguments when deciding on the appropriate use of risk-adjusted data.

References

Anonymous (1864). 'Untitled. Response to letter by William Farr.' *Medical Times and Gazette:* 13 February 1864, pp. 187–188.

Audit Commission (2005). *Early lessons from payment by results.* London: Audit Commission.

Birkmeyer, JD. Kerr, EA. Dimick, JB (2006). Improving the quality of quality measurement. In: *Performance measurement. Accelerating improvement.* Institute of Medicine Committee on Redesigning Health Insurance Performance Measures, Payment, and Performance Improvement Programs, Washington, DC: The National Academies Press.

Boyd, CM. Darer, J. Boult, C. Fried, LP. Boult, L. Wu, AW (2005). 'Clinical practice guidelines and quality of care for older patients with multiple co-morbid diseases: implications for pay for performance.' *Journal of the American Medical Association,* 294(6): 716–724.

Brinkley, J (1986). 'US releasing lists of hospitals with abnormal mortality.' *New York Times,* 12 March 1986, Sect. A.

Bristowe, JS (1864). 'Hospital mortality.' *Medical Times and Gazette,* 30 April 1864, pp. 491–492.

Bristowe, JS. Holmes, T (1864). *Report on the hospitals of the United Kingdom. Sixth report of the medical officer of the Privy Counci, 1863.* London, UK: George E. Eyre and William Spottiswoode for Her Majesty's Stationery Office.

Casalino, LP. Alexander, GC. Jin, L. Konetzka, RT (2007). 'General internists' views on pay-for-performance and public reporting of quality scores: a national survey.' *Health Affairs,* 26(2): 492–499.

Coffey, R. Milenkovic, M. Andrews, RM (2006). *The case for the present-on-admission (POA) indicator.* Washington, DC (Agency for Healthcare Research and Quality HCUP Methods Series Report).

Davis, CL. Pierce, JR. Henderson, W. Spencer, C. Tyler, DC. Langberg, R. Swafford, J. Felan, GS. Kearns, MA. Booker, B (2007). 'Assessment of the reliability of data collected for the Department of Veterans Affairs National Surgical Quality Improvement Program.' *Journal of the American College of Surgeons,* 204(4): 550–560.

Donabedian, A (1980). *Explorations in quality assessment and monitoring.* Ann Arbor, MI: Health Administration Press.

Doran, T. Fullwood, C. Gravelle, H. Reeves, D. Kontopantelis, E. Hiroeh, U. Roland, M (2006). 'Pay-for-performance programs in family practices in the United Kingdom.' *New England Journal of Medicine,* 355(4): 375–384.

Dr Foster Intelligence (2007) [website]. *Dr Foster hospital guide: methodology for key analyses.* London: Dr Foster Intelligence (http://www.drfoster.co.uk/hospitalGuide/methodology.pdf).

Escobar, GJ. Greene, JD. Scheirer, P. Gardner, MN. Draper, D. Kipnis, P (2008). 'Risk-adjusting hospital inpatient mortality using automated inpatient, outpatient, and laboratory databases.' *Medical Care,* 46(3): 232–239.

Forrest, CB. Villagra, VV. Pope, JE (2006). 'Managing the metric vs managing the patient: the physician's view of pay for performance.' *American Journal of Managed Care,* 12(2): 83–85.

Foundation for Information Policy Research (2005). *Healthcare IT in Europe and North America.* Sandy: National Audit Office.

Hayward, RA (2007). 'Performance measurement in search of a path.' *New England Journal of Medicine,* 356(9): 951–953.

Holloway, RG. Quill TE (2007). 'Mortality as a measure of quality: implications for palliative and end-of-life care.' *Journal of the American Medical Association,* 298(7): 802–804.

Hsia, DC. Krushat, WM. Fagan, AB. Tebbutt, JA. Kusserow, RP (1988). 'Accuracy of diagnostic coding for Medicare patients under the prospective-payment system.' *New England Journal of Medicine,* 318(6): 352–355.

Iezzoni, LI (1997). 'The risks of risk adjustment.' *Journal of the American Medical Association,* 278(19): 1600–1607.

Iezzoni, LI (2003). *Risk adjustment for measuring health care outcomes. Third edition.* Chicago, IL: Health Administration Press.

Iezzoni, LI. Restuccia, JD. Shwartz, M. Schaumburg, D. Coffman, GA. Kreger, BE. Butterly, JR. Selker, HP (1992). 'The utility of severity of illness information in assessing the quality of hospital care. The role of the clinical trajectory.' *Medical Care,* 30(5): 428–444.

Institute of Medicine Committee on Redesigning Health Insurance Performance Measures, Payment, and Performance Improvement Programs (2006).

Performance measurement. Accelerating improvement. Pathways to quality health care. Washington, DC: National Academies Press.

Jacobs, R. Goddard, M. Smith, PC (2006). *Public services: are composite measures a robust reflection of performance in the public sector?* York, UK: Centre for Health Economics (CHE Research Paper 16).

Kahn, CN 3rd. Ault, T. Isenstein, H. Potetz, L. Van Gelder, S (2006). 'Snapshot of hospital quality reporting and pay-for-performance under Medicare.' *Health Affairs*, 25(1): 148–162.

Kalra, D (2006). *eHealth Consortium 2007. Memorandum of understanding.* (http://www.ehealthinitiative.eu/pdf/Memorandum_of_Understanding.pdf).

Kalra, D (2006a). 'Electronic health record standards.' *Methods of Information in Medicine*, 45(Suppl. 1): 136–144.

Khuri, SF. Daley, J. Henderson, W. Barbour, G. Lowry, P. Irvin, G. Gibbs, J. Grover, F. Hammermeister, K. Stremple, JF (1995). 'The National Veterans Administration Surgical Risk Study: risk adjustment for the comparative assessment of the quality of surgical care.' *Journal of the American College of Surgeons*, 180(5): 519–531.

Khuri, SF. Daley, J. Henderson, W. Hur, K. Gibbs, JO. Barbour, G. Demakis, J. Irvin, G 3rd. Stremple, JF. Grover, F. McDonald, G. Passaro, E Jr. Fabria, PJ. Spencer, J. Hammermeister, K. Aust, JB (1997). 'Risk adjustment of the postoperative mortality rate for the comparative assessment of the quality of surgical care: results of the National Veterans Affairs Surgical Risk Study.' *Journal of the American College of Surgeons*, 185(4): 315–327.

Knaus, WA. Draper, EA. Wagner, DP. Zimmerman, JE (1985). 'APACHE II: a severity of disease classification system.' *Critical Care Medicine*, 13(10): 818–829.

Knaus, WA. Wagner, DP. Draper, EA. Zimmerman, JE. Bergner, M. Bastos, PG. Sirio, CA. Murphy, DJ. Lotring, T. Damiano, A (1991). "The APACHE III prognostic system. Risk prediction of hospital mortality for critically ill hospitalized adults.' *Chest*, 100(6): 1619–1636.

Knaus, WA. Zimmerman, JE. Wagner, DP. Draper, EA. Lawrence, DE (1981). 'APACHE – acute physiology and chronic health evaluation: a physiologically based classification system.' *Critical Care Medicine*, 9(8): 591–597.

Krumholz, HM. Normand, SL. Galusha, DH. Mattera, JA. Rich, AS. Wang, Y (2006). *Risk-adjustment models for AMI and HF 30-day mortality – methodology.* Washington, DC: Centers for Medicare & Medicaid Services.

Langenbrunner, JC. Orosz, E. Kutzin, J. Wiley, MM (2005). Purchasing and paying providers. In: Figueras, J. Robinson, R. Jakubowski, E (eds.).

Purchasing to improve health systems performance. New York, NY: Open University Press.

Lawthers, AG. McCarthy, EP. Davis, RB. Peterson, LE. Palmer, RH. Iezzoni, LI (2000). 'Identification of in-hospital complications from claims data. Is it valid?' *Medical Care,* 38(8): 785–795.

Lilford, R. Mohammed, MA. Spiegelhalter, D. Thomson, R (2004). 'Use and misuse of process and outcome data in managing performance of acute medical care: avoiding institutional stigma.' *Lancet,* 363(9415): 1147–1154.

McMahon, LF Jr. Hofer, TP. Hayward RA (2007). 'Physician-level P4P – DOA? Can quality-based payment be resuscitated?' *American Journal of Managed Care,* 13(5): 233–236.

Nightingale, F (1863). *Notes on hospitals. Third edition.* London: Longman, Green, Longman, Roberts and Green.

O'Brien, SM. Shahian, DM. DeLong, ER. Normand, SL. Edwards, FH. Ferraris, VA. Haan, CK. Rich, JB. Shewan, CM. Dokholyan, RS. Anderson, RP. Peterson, ED (2007). 'Quality measurement in adult cardiac surgery: part 2 – Statistical considerations in composite measure scoring and provider rating.' *Annals of Thoracic Surgery,* 83(4) Suppl: 13–26.

Perkins, R. Seddon, M. and Effective Practice Informatics and Quality (EPIQ) (2006). 'Quality improvement in New Zealand healthcare. Part 5: measurement for monitoring and controlling performance – the quest for external accountability.' *New Zealand Medical Journal,* 119(1241): U2149.

Petersen, LA. Woodard, LD. Urech, T. Daw, C. Sookanan, S (2006). 'Does pay-for-performance improve the quality of health care?' *Annals of Internal Medicine,* 145(4): 265–272.

Quan, H. Parsons, GA. Ghali, WA (2002). 'Validity of information on co-morbidity derived from ICD-9-CM administrative data.' *Medical Care,* 40(8): 675–685.

Roland, M (2004). 'Linking physicians' pay to the quality of care – a major experiment in the United Kingdom.' *New England Journal of Medicine,* 351(14): 1448–1454.

Romano, PS. Chan, BK. Schembri, ME. Rainwater, JA (2002). 'Can administrative data be used to compare postoperative complication rates across hospitals?' *Medical Care,* 40(10): 856–867.

Rosenthal, MB (2007). 'Nonpayment for performance? Medicare's new reimbursement rule.' *New England Journal of Medicine,* 357(16): 1573–1575.

Scott, IA (2007). 'Pay for performance in health care: strategic issues for Australian experiments.' *Medical Journal of Australia,* 187(1): 31–35.

Shahian, DM. Edwards, FH. Ferraris, VA. Haan, CK. Rich, JB. Normand, SL. DeLong, ER. O'Brien, SM. Shewan, CM. Dokholyan, RS. Peterson, ED (2007). 'Quality measurement in adult cardiac surgery: Part 1 – conceptual framework and measure selection.' *Annals of Thoracic Surgery*, 83(Suppl. 4): S3–S12.

Shahian, DM. Silverstein, T. Lovett, AF. Wolf, RE. Normand, SL (2007a). 'Comparison of clinical and administrative data sources for hospital coronary artery bypass graft surgery report cards.' *Circulation*, 115(12): 1518–1527.

Shekelle, PG (2009). Public performance reporting on quality information. In: Smith, PC. Mossialos, E. Papanicolas, I. Leatherman, S (eds.). *Performance measurement for health system improvement: experiences, challenges and prospects.* Cambridge: Cambridge University Press.

Simborg, DW (1981). 'DRG creep: a new hospital-acquired disease.' *New England Journal of Medicine*, 304(26): 1602–1604.

Terris, DD. Aron, DC (2009). Attribution and causality in health-care performance measurement.' In: Smith, PC. Mossialos, E. Papanicolas, I. Leatherman, S (eds.). *Performance measurement for health system improvement: experiences, challenges and prospects.* Cambridge: Cambridge University Press.

US Department of Health and Human Services (2007). 'Medicare program: changes to the hospital inpatient prospective payment systems and fiscal year 2008 rates.' *Federal Register*, Vol. 72: Sections 47379–47428.

Velasco-Garrido, M. Borowitz, M. Øvretveit, J. Busse, R (2005). Purchasing for quality of care. In: Figueras, J. Robinson, R. Jakubowski, E (eds.). *Purchasing to improve health systems performance.* Berkshire, UK: Open University Press.

WHO (2001). *International classification of functioning, disability and health: ICF.* Geneva: World Health Organization.

Zhan, C. Elixhauser, A. Friedman, B. Houchens, R. Chiang, YP (2007). 'Modifying DRG-PPS to include only diagnoses present on admission: financial implications and challenges.' *Medical Care*, 45(4): 288–291.

3.2 | *Clinical surveillance and patient safety*

OLIVIA GRIGG, DAVID SPIEGELHALTER

Introduction

Clinical surveillance is the routine collection of clinical data in order to detect and further analyse unusual health outcomes that may arise from a special cause. As in the closely related subject area of statistical surveillance, the aim is typically to isolate and understand special causes so that adverse outcomes may be prevented. Clinical surveillance is a way of providing appropriate and timely information to health decision-makers to guide their choice of resource allocation and hence improve the delivery of health care.

In order to detect unusual data points, first it is important to take account of the measurable factors that are known to affect the distribution and size of the data. Factors typically of key importance in clinical surveillance are discussed in the first section of this chapter. These include important aspects of clinical surveillance data that affect and govern analysis, including patient heterogeneity; the essential size of health-care facilities; and the dimensionality of the data. Given these essential factors, various statistical surveillance tools might be implemented. Statistical control chart options for surveillance are considered, keeping in mind the desirable characteristics of control charts – utility, simplicity, optimality and verity. A variety of such tools are discussed via example data, with an emphasis on graphical display and desirable characteristics. The graphs presented are based on data relating to cardiac surgery performed by a group of surgeons in a single cardiothoracic unit, and on data relating to the practice of Harold Shipman over the period 1987–1998.

Clinical surveillance: important aspects of the data

We consider four aspects of clinical surveillance data in particular: (i) patient demographics; (ii) throughput of health-care facilities or

286

providers; (iii) overdispersion in measured quality indicators; and (iv) dimensionality of the data collected.

Patient demographics

Patients arrive at health-care facilities in varying states of health. Any differences observed in the quality of care that health-care facilities provide might be explained in part by variations in the demography of their catchment populations. Aspects of the demography affecting the burden of the health-care facilities (particularly patient mix and the essential size of the community they serve) might affect measured indicators of quality of care. The relationship between these demographic factors and quality of care indicators might be described through a statistical model of risk (see, for example, Cook et al. 2003; Steiner et al. 2000) that can be used as a guide to express the functional state of health-care facilities and systems. Such a model would predict or describe patients' care experience for a variety of patient categories. Future measurements of quality of care indicators could be compared to the risk model that is updated as and when required.

Alternatively, direct stratified standardization might be applied prospectively to panel or multistream data collected over a group of health-care facilities or providers (Grigg et al. 2009; Rossi et al. 1999). This type of adjustment at each time period for the mix and volume of patients across providers allows for surveillance of change within and between providers, but not overall. The latter requires a well-defined baseline against which to check for change, perhaps in the form of a risk model.

Throughput of providers and health-care facilities

Quality of care measures or indicators that are based on rates or counts require an appropriate denominator that represents, or captures some aspect of, the throughput of the health-care facility. In some circumstances this denominator might be viewed as a surrogate for the absolute size of a health-care facility. In cross-sectional comparisons (across health-care facilities or providers) of measures of quality based on rates or counts, the denominator may vary. If there is a common underlying true rate, measured rates associated with larger denominators should vary less about that rate than those associated with smaller denominators. Hence, in charts that plot the measured rates against an appropriate denominator the points tend to form the shape of a funnel (Spiegelhalter 2005; Vandenbroucke 1988).

Overdispersion amongst outcomes

Unmeasured case-mix or demographic factors may produce overdispersion amongst quality indicators measured across health-care facilities. In such cases the statistical model that relates those factors to quality of care may not apply precisely at all time points to all of the facilities (Aylin et al. 2003; Marshall et al. 2004). Given the risk model, the variability in outcomes may be substantially higher than that expected from chance alone and the excess not explainable by the presence of a few outlying points. This overdispersion (or general lack of fit to the whole population of health-care facilities) might be expressed through hierarchical models that would allow for slack in the fit of the risk model, or in standardized risk measures across facilities (Daniels & Gatsonis 1999; Grigg et al. 2009; Ohlssen et al. 2007). Time-dependent hierarchical models might also allow for flexibility or evolution of the risk model over time (Berliner 1996; West & Harrison 1997).

Dimensionality of the data

The higher the number of health-care facilities or providers that are compared then the greater the potential for false positive results or significant departures from the model describing the normal functional state of the facilities. This is due to the assumed inherent randomness in the system. The potential for false positive results of significance also increases if many quality of care indicators are measured and monitored repeatedly over time. Possible approaches for handling the multivariate nature of the monitoring problem and controlling the multiplicity of false positives include:

- describing the system as a multivariate object and employing multivariate control charts in which signals generally relate only to the system as a whole and require diagnosis to establish any smaller scale causes (Jackson 1985; Lowry & Montgomery 1995);

- employing univariate control charts, mapping the univariate chart statistics to a reference scale and then applying a multiplicity controlling procedure to the multivariate set of mapped values (Benjamini & Kling 1999; Grigg et al. 2009);
- comparing potentially extreme observed chart statistic values to a large population of chart statistic values simulated under null conditions and checking whether those observed values still appear significant (Kulldorf et al. 2007).

Statistical chart options

A wide range of charting tools has been suggested for surveillance of health measures over time, largely adapted from the industrial quality-control context (Woodall 2006). We now describe some of these charting tools, with an emphasis on desirable characteristics.

The charts illustrated include the Shewhart chart; scan statistic, moving average (MA), exponentially weighted moving average (EWMA), sets method, cumulative O – E, cumulative sum (CUSUM) and maximized CUSUM. We illustrate all but the last method using data relating to a group of seven cardiac surgeons in a single cardiac unit. We illustrate the maximized CUSUM using data relating to the practice of the late Harold Shipman, general practitioner and convicted murderer, over the period 1987 to 1998. We consider that the desirable characteristics of a charting tool are:

- *Utility:* ease of interpretation of the graphic; intuitiveness of presentation from a general user's point of view.
- *Simplicity* of the mathematics behind the chart (regarding the chart algorithm calculation of operating characteristics; and calculation of bands, bounds or limits).
- *Responsiveness* (under any circumstances) to important and definable but perhaps subtle changes, where these can be discriminated from false alarms.
- *Verity:* graphical effectiveness and ability to give a close and true description of the process.

It is well known that the CUSUM and EWMA rate highly on responsiveness and the Shewhart chart rates highly on simplicity. Utility and verity are more subjective and therefore it is difficult to say which of the charts, if any, rate highly on these. However, we will attempt to provide some assessment.

Example data: cardiac surgery

Fig. 3.2.1 is a plot (by surgeon) of outcomes adjusted for patient pre-operative risk against operation number. The operation number is the time-ordered operation number and is measured collectively over operations performed by any one of the seven surgeons. The outcomes are coded so that $0 \equiv$ patient survival past thirty days following surgery, $1 \equiv$ death of a patient within thirty days.

The outcomes are adjusted by the use of a model calibrated on the first 2218 operations that relates the patient Parsonnet score to the probability of not surviving beyond thirty days (Parsonnet et al. 1989; Steiner et al. 2000). The adjustment leads to data of the form *observed – expected + baseline*, where the baseline is the mean thirty-day mortality rate in the calibration dataset (= 0.064, given 142 deaths) and the expected outcome is calculated from the risk model. For example, the adjusted outcome for a patient with an expected risk of 0.15 is 1 - 0.15+0.064 = 0.914 if he/she does not survive beyond thirty days following surgery but - 0.15 + 0.064 = -0.086 if she/he does. If the model described predicts patient risk well, the adjustment should increase the comparability of the outcomes of operations performed on differing types of patients.

The adjusted outcomes relating to operations performed by each of the seven surgeons are plotted in grey (Fig. 3.2.1). Points falling at or below zero on the risk-adjusted outcomes scale correspond to patients who survived beyond thirty days; points falling above correspond to those who did not. A smooth mean of the adjusted outcomes is plotted in black (calculated over non-overlapping windows of time, 250 operations in duration) and can be compared to the mean thirty-day mortality rate of 0.064 from the calibration data. These mean adjusted outcomes are plotted on a finer scale in Fig. 3.2.3, with pointwise significance bands or p-value lines (see below).

The extremity of a patient's pre-operative condition is indicated by the extent to which the grey adjusted outcomes in Fig. 3.2.1 fall from the original data values of 0 and 1. For Surgeon 1, a large density of points fall below their original data values of 0 and 1 but Fig.

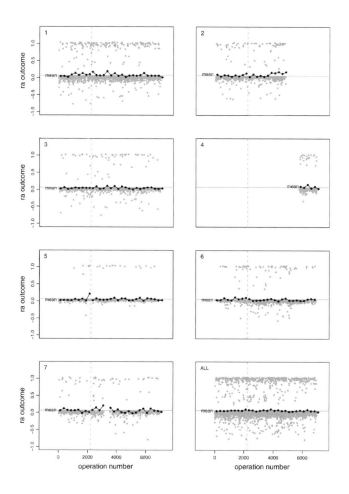

Fig. 3.2.1 Risk-adjusted outcomes (adjusted thirty-day mortality, given patient Parsonnet score) relating to operations performed in a cardiac unit in which there are seven surgeons. First 2218 data are calibration data.

3.2.2 shows that this is because this surgeon consistently receives and treats high-risk patients (with high Parsonnet scores). In contrast, the adjusted outcomes for Surgeon 5 are closer to the original data values as this surgeon consistently receives and treats lower risk patients (see Fig. 3.2.2).

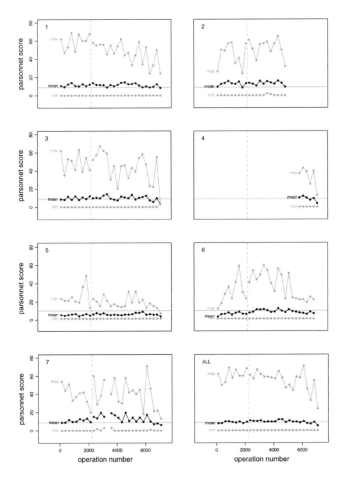

Fig. 3.2.2 Parsonnet score of patients treated in a cardiac unit.

Shewhart charts, scan statistics and MAs

Shewhart charts (Shewhart 1931) plot each individual data point or groups of data points if the data are highly discrete e.g. binary data. Dependent on the size of these groups, the charts can provide quite smooth estimates of the current underlying risk. The charts will only be able to detect departures from baseline risk that affect groups at least as big as those comprising the data-points. A plotted value that falls outside a sufficiently small significance band is evidence of departure from the baseline risk model.

Fig. 3.2.3 is a plot by surgeon of the mean risk-adjusted outcome over disjoint windows of 250 operations performed by all of the surgeons. The plotted binomial significance bands are similar to bands marked on funnel plots (Spiegelhalter 2005) in that they change according to the number of operations performed by an individual surgeon in each window. This number is essentially the denominator used to calculate the bands. If one surgeon performed many of the operations in a window then their chart for that window would have narrow bands. It can be seen that Surgeons 1 and 6 generally perform the most operations out of the group, since the significance bands on charts 1 and 6 are tighter than those on the other charts. The bands on the chart of mean risk-adjusted outcome for all surgeons do not change over time, except for the final incomplete window of 54 observations, as they are based on a constant denominator of 250.

The charts in Fig. 3.2.3 can be viewed as types of Shewhart chart (Shewhart 1931), where the control limits or significance bands are adjusted for the volume of patients treated by a surgeon in each window of time. Equivalent risk-adjusted Shewhart charts could be drawn by plotting the mean of the original data values and adjusting the significance bands for patient case-mix, or Parsonnet score, as well as the denominator (Cook et al. 2003; Grigg & Farewell, 2004).

The charts in Fig. 3.2.3 are also related to the scan statistic method (Ismail et al. 2003). This method retrospectively detects areas or clusters of lack of agreement with the risk model by conditioning on there being such a cluster and then locating it. This method indicates that the most concentrated area of lack of agreement with the model is around operation number 3500 (in an upwards direction) for Surgeon 1 and around operation number 4500 (in a downwards direction) for Surgeon 6. For the group of surgeons as a whole, the method indicates that the most concentrated areas of lack of agreement with the risk model are around operation numbers 4000 (upwards) and 5000 (downwards).

For scan statistic methods it is more typical to scan the data via a moving window (moving one observation at a time) than to scan over neighbouring and non-overlapping windows. The charts in Fig. 3.2.4 can be viewed as performing the former, as they plot each surgeon's MAs for sets of thirty-five adjusted outcomes. The MA is updated for each surgeon for every operation and so is updated more often for those who receive patients regularly (e.g. Surgeon 1) than for those who receive patients less frequently (e.g. Surgeon 5). The MAs can be compared against significance bands calculated in the same way as those in Fig. 3.2.3, but the denominator remains at a constant value of thirty-five. As might be expected, in any particular chart of Fig. 3.2.4, the frequency of evidence indicating lack of agreement with the risk model appears to be related to how frequently the surgeon operates. This can be seen on the chart for all surgeons, which is the most volatile and spiky. In theory the mathematical design of these charts is simple – plotting a summary statistic of groups of data points in which points within groups carry equal weight. The charts should rate quite highly on utility, verity and responsiveness if the aims of the design are met, i.e. the summary statistic summarizes the original data points well and the chosen group size is appropriate. However, the constraint of equal weightings of data points may limit the verity of the charts and their simplicity may be affected if the form of summary statistic and the size of groups of the charts are treated as parameters to be optimized.

EWMAs

Similarly to the charts described immediately above, the EWMA chart (Roberts 1959) provides a smoothed estimate of the current underlying risk but uses all past data since initialization of the chart. Fig. 3.2.5 shows plots of EWMAs (by surgeon) of the risk-adjusted outcomes, with accompanying credible intervals for the mean thirty-day mortality rate at operation number t associated with surgeon j, μ_{tj}, as it evolves from the baseline value μ_0 calculated across all surgeons in the calibration dataset. Any given plotted EWMA value on a particular surgeon's chart is a weighted average of all previous adjusted outcomes for that surgeon. The weights decay geometrically by a factor $\kappa = 0.988$ so that less recent outcomes are given less weight than recent outcomes. The value of κ was chosen so as to minimize the mean squared error of prediction of patient thirty-day mortality in the calibration dataset. The EWMA plotted at operation number t performed by surgeon j can be written as:

$$\omega_{0j} = \mu_0 \qquad\qquad\qquad\qquad\qquad\qquad\qquad (1)$$
$$\omega_{tj} = \kappa\omega_{t-1,j} + (1 - \kappa)Y_{tj}, \quad t = 1, 2, \ldots \qquad j = 1, 2, \ldots, 7.$$

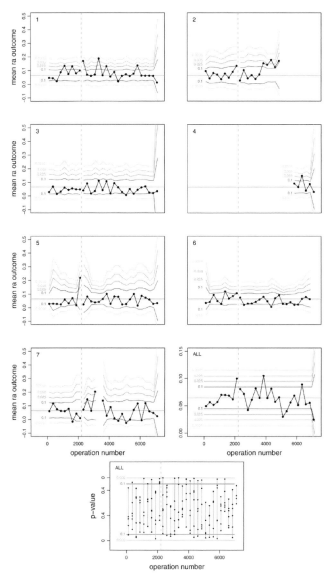

Fig. 3.2.3 Mean risk-adjusted outcome over disjoint windows of 250 operations, where operations are by any of seven surgeons in a cardiac unit. Bands
plotted are binomial percentiles around the mean patient 30-day mortality rate
from the calibration data ($\mu_0 = 0.064$), where the denominator is the number
of operations by a surgeon in a given window. Gaps in the series other than at
the dashed division line correspond to periods of inactivity for a surgeon.

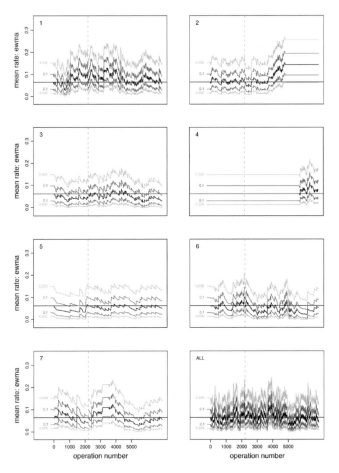

Fig. 3.2.4 Moving average (MA) of risk-adjusted outcomes over overlapping windows of 35 operations by a particular surgeon from a cardiac unit of seven surgeons. Bands plotted are binomial percentiles around the mean patient 30-day mortality rate from the calibration data ($\mu_0 = 0.064$), where the denominator is 35.

where $\mu_0 = 0.064$ is the mean thirty-day mortality rate in the calibration dataset and $Y_{tj} = O_{tj} - E_{tj} + \mu_0$ is the adjusted observation at time t relating to surgeon j.

Equivalently, we can write:

$$\omega_{0j} = \mu_0 \tag{2}$$
$$\omega_{tj} = \omega_{t-1,j} + (1 - \kappa)(O_{tj} - E_{tj}), \, t = 1, 2, \ldots j = 1, 2, \ldots, 7.$$

To calculate the credible intervals it is assumed that a distribution for the mean patient thirty-day mortality rate at operation number t and relating to surgeon j, μ_{tj}, can be described as beta with mean given by the EWMA estimate ω_{tj} and precision given by $(1 - \kappa)^{-1} = 83.3$. Grigg & Spiegelhalter (2007) provide further discussion about these intervals and the risk-adjusted EWMA.

The charts in Figs. 3.2.2–3.2.4 have significance bands or control lines drawn around a calibrated mean but in the EWMA drawn here bounds are placed around the chart statistic. The bounds placed describe uncertainty in the estimate of the current underlying risk. Despite the change of emphasis, lack of agreement with the risk model on any particular chart can still be investigated by checking the extent to which the credible bounds around the EWMA statistic cross the baseline mean patient thirty-day mortality rate, $\mu_0 = 0.064$. A lack of agreement with the risk model is indicated if μ_0 falls far into the tails of the plotted distribution for μ_{tj}.

As seen in Fig. 3.2.5, the outermost credible bounds (at a p-value of ±0.0005) drawn for the distribution of the mean patient thirty-day mortality rate in relation to surgeon j remain mostly below a rate of 0.2 on all the charts. EWMA charts might be considered to have a more complex mathematical design than Shewhart charts as the weighting of data points is not necessarily equal. The chart statistic includes all past data since the start of the chart. This should improve the verity of the estimation of the true current underlying risk but may reduce the responsiveness if the weighting parameter is not well-tuned. The placement of bounds around the chart statistic may affect the utility of the chart, dependent on the user, but again this should improve the verity of estimating the true current underlying risk.

Sets method

The sets method (Chen 1978) measures the number of outcomes occurring between outcomes classified as events. Typically, a signal is given if the set size is less than a value T on n successive occasions, where T and n can be tuned so that the chart is geared towards testing for a specific shift in rate (Gallus et al. 1986). For example, a signal might be given if there were three non-survivors within the space of twenty operations.

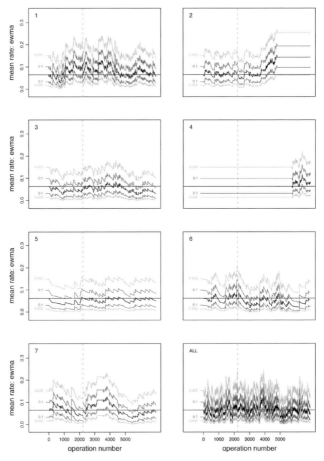

Fig. 3.2.5 Exponentially weighted moving average (EWMA) of risk-adjusted outcomes of surgery by a particular surgeon from a cardiac unit of seven surgeons. Less recent outcomes are given less weight than recent outcomes, by a factor of $k = 0.988$. The EWMA and accompanying bands give a running estimate by surgeon of the mean patient 30-day mortality rate and uncertainty associated with that estimate.

Fig. 3.2.6 shows risk-adjusted sets charts by surgeon, where the adjusted number of operations between surgical outcomes coded 1 (patient survives less than 30 days following surgery) is plotted against operation number. As discussed by Grigg & Farewell (2004b), the adjustment of the accruing set size at each observation is such that higher-than-average risk patients contribute more to the set size than

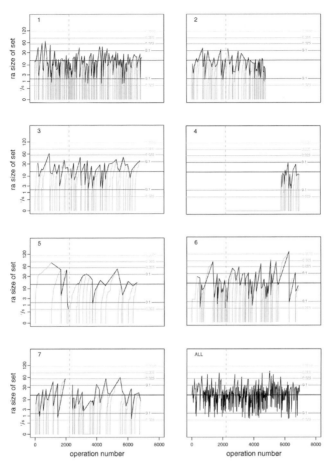

Fig. 3.2.6 Risk-adjusted set size, or adjusted number of operations between outcomes of 1 (where a patient survives less than 30 days following surgery), associated with surgery by a particular surgeon from a cardiac unit of seven surgeons. Bands plotted are geometric percentiles based on the mean patient 30-day mortality rate from the calibration data ($\mu_0 = 0.064$).

those with average risk (risk equal to the baseline risk, $\mu_0 = 0.064$) and lower risk patients contribute less than those with average risk.

The accruing adjusted set size for surgeon j at operation number t, which resets to zero when the observed outcome from the previous operation $O_{t-1,j}$ equals 1, can be written as:

$$S_{0j} = 0 \tag{3}$$

$$S_{tj} = \left(S_{t-1,j} + \frac{E_{tj}}{\mu_0}\right)(1 - 0_{t-1,j}) + \left(\frac{E_{tj}}{\mu_0}\right)0_{t-1,j}, \; t = 1, 2, \ldots j = 1, 2, \ldots, 7.$$

where E_{tj} is the expected outcome at operation number t performed by surgeon j and is calculated from the risk model. This accruing set size is plotted in grey on the charts in Fig. 3.2.6. The absolute set sizes are joined up in black, at the points where the observed outcome O_{tj} equals 1. The significance bands plotted are geometric and calibrated about the baseline expected set size calculated from the first 2218 observations, $1/\mu_0 = 15.63$.

A noteworthy result from these charts is the very large adjusted set size of 132 recorded on the chart for Surgeon 6 at around operation number 6000. This magnitude of set size is interpretable as equivalent to a run of over 132 operations performed on baseline risk patients where those patients all survive beyond 30 days following surgery.

The plots drawn in Fig. 3.2.6 might be viewed as more complex than Shewhart charts of the number of outcomes between events, since the accruing risk-adjusted set size is also plotted. As with runs rules on Shewhart charts (Western Electric Company 1984), a more complex stopping rule may improve the responsiveness, but affect utility. The transformation (Nelson 1994) of the y-axis in Fig. 3.2.6 is intended to ensure that the verity or utility of the charts should not be affected by the fact that they plot time between event data rather than rate data.

Cumulative O – E and CUSUM charts

The cumulative charts described here accumulate measures of departure from the baseline risk model, where the accumulation is either over all outcomes since the start of the chart or is adaptive according to the current value of the chart statistic.

The charts in Fig. 3.2.7 show each surgeon's cumulative sum of *observed-expected* outcomes from surgery (cumulative O – E) where the expected counts are calculated using the risk model relating patient thirty-day mortality to Parsonnet score. This type of chart has also been called a variable life-adjusted display (VLAD) (Lovegrove et al. 1997; Lovegrove et al. 1999) and a cumulative risk-adjusted mortality chart (CRAM) (Poloniecki et al. 1998). The cumulative O – E chart statistic at operation number t relating to surgeon j can be written as:

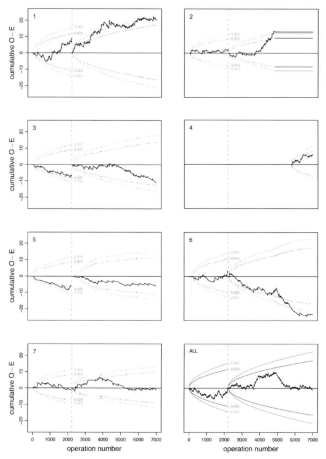

Fig. 3.2.7 Cumulative sum of observed outcome, from an operation by a particular surgeon from a cardiac unit of seven surgeons, minus the value predicted by the risk model given patient Parsonnet score. Bands plotted are centered binomial percentiles based on the mean patient 30-day mortality rate from the calibration data ($\mu_0 = 0.064$).

$$V_{0j} = 0 \qquad\qquad\qquad\qquad (4)$$
$$V_{tj} = V_{t-1,j} + O_{tj} - E_{tj}, \; t = 1, 2, \ldots j = 1, 2, \ldots, 7$$

The charts display each surgeon's accruing excess patient thirty-day mortality above that predicted by the risk model given patient pre-operative risk, where this is assumed to be described by patient Parsonnet score. The measure accrued is simple (except perhaps in its reliance on the accuracy of the risk model) but the charts may be easy to misinterpret. For example, Surgeon 1's chart reaches an excess of 20 patient mortalities above that predicted by the risk model at around operation number 4000. However, the chart retains any past excess and therefore indicates that this excess continues at approximately the same level. Given the accuracy of the risk model, information about a surgeon's current operative performance is mostly contained in the gradient of these charts. This is indicated by the increase in the significance bands on the charts each time a surgeon operates.

The CUSUM chart (Hawkins & Olwell 1997) is closely related to the cumulative O – E chart. However, it accumulates a function of the observed and expected outcomes that reflects the relative likelihood of the baseline risk model compared to that of an alternative model, given the surgical outcomes observed since the start of the chart. This accumulated measure is an optimal measure of departure (Moustakides 1986) and thus these charts are very responsive to important changes, i.e. movement towards alternative models. The chart maintains sensitivity to departure from the baseline model by accumulating only evidence in favour of the alternative model, otherwise it remains at the balance point (zero).

In Fig. 3.2.8, CUSUM charts on the observed outcomes are plotted by surgeon. The upper half of the chart tests for a doubling in the odds of patient thirty-day mortality; the lower half tests for a halving. The significance bands, or p-value lines, are based on the empirical distribution of CUSUM values simulated under baseline conditions. More discussion on associating CUSUM values with p-values can be found in Benjamini and Kling (1999) and Grigg and Spiegelhalter (2008).

The CUSUM chart statistic at operation number t relating to surgeon j can be written as:

$$C_{0j} = 0 \tag{5}$$

$$C_{tj} = max\left\{0, C_{t-1,j} + log\left[\frac{P(0_{tj} \mid alternative)}{P(0_{tj} \mid baseline)}\right]\right\}, \ t = 1, 2, \ldots \ j = 1, 2, \ldots, 7.$$

If, as in the charts plotted in Fig. 3.2.8, the alternative model specifies a uniform change (R) from the baseline model across patient types of the odds of thirty-day mortality, the CUSUM chart statistic can be written as:

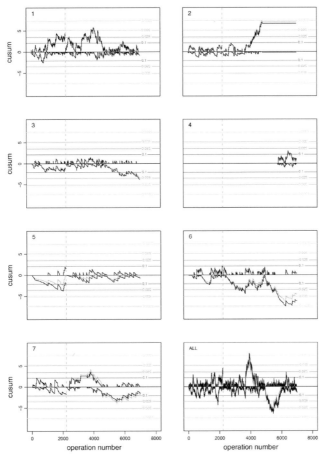

Fig. 3.2.8 Cumulative log-likelihood ratio of outcomes from operations by a particular surgeon from a cardiac unit of seven surgeons, comparing the likelihood of outcomes given the risk model with that given either elevated or decreased risk. Upper chart half is a CUSUM testing for a halving in odds of patient survival past 30 days, lower chart half for a doubling in odds of survival past 30 days.

$$C_{0j} = 0 \tag{6}$$

$$C_{tj} = max\left\{0, C_{t-1,j} + log(R)0_{tj} - \left[\frac{log(1-E_{tj} + RE_{tj})}{E_{tj}}\right]E_{tj}\right\}, \ t = 1, 2, \ldots j = 1, 2, \ldots, 7.$$

As noted by Grigg et al. (2003), the chart statistic increments are then seen to be of the form $aO - b(E)E$, and hence similar to the $O - E$

form in Fig. 3.2.7. In particular, for $R = 2$ the increments are approximately $(\log 2)O_{tj} - E_{tj}$.

Exact risk-adjusted CUSUMs (Steiner et al. 2000) based on the original outcomes and the full likelihood (given the risk model) are plotted in black in Fig. 3.2.8. CUSUMs based on the adjusted outcomes $O_{tj} - E_{tj} + \mu_0$ and the unconditional likelihood are plotted in grey. These closely follow the exact CUSUMs, thereby illustrating that the likelihood contribution from the adjusted outcomes is approximately equivalent to that from the original outcomes. This point is noted in the section on example data for cardiac surgery and described by Grigg and Spiegelhalter (2007).

The Shewhart chart for all surgeons (Fig. 3.2.3) suggests a lack of agreement with the null model around operation numbers 4000 (in an upwards direction) and 5000 (in a downwards direction). This can also be seen in the CUSUM chart for all surgeons (Fig. 3.2.8) but here the evidence of potential lack of agreement is more pronounced. The CUSUM is known to be responsive but this may be at the expense of simplicity and utility. A maximized CUSUM (see section below) may improve the verity of the chart.

Example data: Harold Shipman

Fig. 3.2.9 is a plot of maximized CUSUM charts by age-sex groupings of patients registered with general practitioner Harold Shipman over the period 1987 to 1998 (Baker 2001; Shipman Inquiry 2004). In 2000, Harold Shipman was convicted for murdering fifteen of his patients but he may have killed two hundred (Baker 2001; Shipman Inquiry 2002 & 2004; Spiegelhalter et al. 2003). The chart statistics in Fig. 3.2.9 are as described by equation 5, except that a vector of CUSUM statistics (rather than a single CUSUM statistic) is plotted on each half of the chart. A Poisson likelihood is adopted as the data are grouped mortality counts; the section on cumulative O – E and CUSUM used the Bernoulli likelihood as the data relate to individual patients. The baseline risk for a particular age-sex category is taken to be the England and Wales standard in any given year, as described in Baker (2001).

Each element of the plotted vector corresponds to a CUSUM comparing a particular alternative model to the baseline risk model. On the upper half of the chart, the alternative ranges from no change

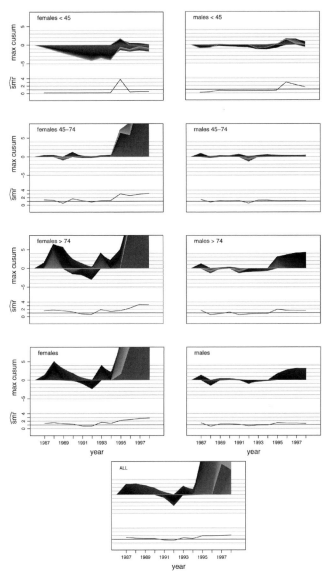

Fig. 3.2.9 Maximised CUSUM of mortality outcomes by age-sex category of patients registered with Harold Shipman over the period 1987–1998, comparing the likelihood of outcomes under the England and Wales standard with that given either elevated or decreased risk. Upper chart half is testing for up to a four-fold increase in patient mortality, lower chart half for up to a four-fold decrease. The estimated standardised mortality rate (SMR) is given.

in risk to a uniform four-fold increase in patient risk across all age-sex categories. Similarly, on the lower half, the alternative ranges from no change in risk to a uniform four-fold decrease in patient risk.

On each half of the chart the external edge of the block of plotted vectors corresponds to the most extreme value in the vector of CUSUM values at any one time. This may relate to different alternative models over time; the alternative model that they relate to represents the best supported alternative to the baseline model (Lai 1995; Lorden 1971). In this way, the maximized CUSUM gives both the maximized evidence in favour of non-baseline risk models and the specific alternative at any one time that corresponds to the maximized evidence.

The pattern of the chart for females over seventy-four can be seen to dominate the chart for all females as well as the overall chart for all patient categories. The estimated standardized mortality ratio (corresponding to the maximized CUSUM value) on the chart for females over seventy-four increases from 1.5 in 1994 to more than 3 in the years 1997 to 1998. From 1995 there is strong evidence of increasing departure from the baseline risk model. A similar increase in estimated SMR is seen on the chart for females aged between forty-five and seventy-four. The increase is mirrored but dampened in the chart for all females and dampened further in the chart for all patients. This dampening is due to information added from the other charts and illustrates why comparisons of outcomes across different aspects of a dataset are hampered by the 'curse of dimensionality' (Bellman 1957).

Conclusions

We have described a selection of statistical control charts that could (individually or in combination) form a basis for clinical surveillance. The charts described include: fixed window methods, e.g. Shewhart, scan statistic and MA charts; continuous window methods, e.g. EWMA and O – E charts; and adaptive window methods e.g. sets method, CUSUM and maximized CUSUM. The charts are graphically illustrated through some example data which include cardiac surgery outcomes, from operations performed in the period 1992-1998 by a group of surgeons in a single cardiothoracic unit, and mortality outcomes of patients registered with Harold Shipman in the period 1987–1998.

We have suggested some desirable characteristics (utility, simplicity, responsiveness, verity) that might be considered when deciding which charts to include in a clinical surveillance system. Our discussion indicates that simpler charts such as the fixed window methods are likely to have better utility but may compromise responsiveness and verity. Verity should be high if a chart gives a running estimate with bounds of the parameter of interest, where these bounds reflect uncertainty surrounding the estimate. The maximized CUSUM can provide such an estimate and is known to be responsive. The EWMA is similarly responsive but may be simpler than the maximized CUSUM, as the chart gives a direct running estimate.

Each of the charts has a variety of characteristics that may be comparable but we recommend the use of a combination of charts, with simpler charts in the foreground. Further, we recommend that any practical application of the charts should be embedded in a structured system for investigating any signals that might be detected.

References

Aylin, P. Best, N. Bottle, A. Marshall, C (2003). 'Following Shipman: a pilot system for monitoring mortality rates in primary care.' *Lancet,* 362(9382): 485–491.

Baker, R (2001). *Harold Shipman's clinical practice 1974–1998: a review commissioned by the Chief Medical Officer.* London: Stationary Office Books.

Bellman, RE (1957). *Dynamic programming.* Princeton, NJ: Princeton University Press.

Benjamini, Y. Kling, Y (1999). *A look at statistical process control through the p-values.* Tel Aviv: Tel Aviv University (Tech. rept. RP-SOR-99-08 http://www.math.tau.ac.il/~ybenja/KlingW.html).

Berliner, L (1996). *Hierarchical Bayesian time series models.* Cite Seer X – Scientific Literature Digital Library and Search Engine. (http://citeseer.ist.psu.edu/121112.html).

Chen, R (1978). 'A surveillance system for congenital malformations.' *Journal of the American Statistical Association*, 73: 323–327.

Cook, DA. Steiner, SH. Farewell, VT. Morton, AP (2003). 'Monitoring the evolutionary process of quality: risk-adjusted charting to track outcomes in intensive care.' *Critical Care Medicine*, 31(6): 1676–1682.

Daniels, MJ. Gatsonis, C (1999). 'Hierarchical generalized linear models in the analysis of variations in health care utilization.' *Journal of the American Statistical Association*, 94(445): 29–42.

Gallus, G. Mandelli, C. Marchi, M. Radaelli, G (1986). 'On surveillance methods for congenital malformations.' *Statistics in Medicine*, 5(6): 565–571.

Grigg, O. Farewell, V (2004). 'An overview of risk-adjusted charts.' *Journal of the Royal Statistical Society: Series A*, 167(3): 523–539.

Grigg, OA. Farewell, VT (2004a). 'A risk-adjusted sets method for monitoring adverse medical outcomes.' *Statistics in Medicine*, 23(10): 1593–1602.

Grigg, OA. Spiegelhalter, DJ (2007). 'A simple risk-adjusted exponentially weighted moving average.' *Journal of the American Statistical Association*, 102(477): 140–152.

Grigg, OA. Spiegelhalter, DJ (2008). 'An empirical approximation to the null unbounded steady-state distribution of the cumulative sum statistic.' *Technometrics*, 50(4): 501–511.

Grigg, OA. Farewell, VT. Spiegelhalter, DJ (2003). 'Use of risk-adjusted CUSUM and RSPRT charts for monitoring in medical contexts.' *Statistical Methods in Medical Research*, 12(2): 147–170.

Grigg, OA. Spiegelhalter, DJ. Jones, HE (2009). 'Local and marginal control charts applied to methicillin resistant Staphylococcus aureus bacteraemia reports in UK acute NHS Trusts.' *Journal of the Royal Statistical Society: Series A*, 172(1): 49–66.

Hawkins, DM. Olwell, DH (1997). *Cumulative sum charts and charting for quality improvement*. New York: Springer.

Ismail, NA. Pettit, AN. Webster, RA (2003). ''Online' monitoring and retrospective analysis of hospital outcomes based on a scan statistic.' *Statistics in Medicine*, 22(18): 2861–2876.

Jackson, JE (1985). 'Multivariate quality control.' *Communication Statistics – Theory and Methods*, 14(11): 2657–2688.

Kulldorff, M. Mostashari, F. Duczmal, L. Yih, WK. Kleinman, K. Platt, R (2007). 'Multivariate scan statistics for disease surveillance.' *Statistics in Medicine*, 26(8): 1824–1833.

Lai, TL (1995). 'Sequential changepoint detection in quality control and dynamical systems.' *Journal of the Royal Statistical Society: Series B*, 57(4): 613–658.

Lorden, G (1971). 'Procedures for reacting to a change in distribution.' *Annals of Mathematical Statistics*, 42(6): 1897–1908.

Lovegrove, J. Sherlaw-Johnson, C. Valencia, O. Treasure, T. Gallivan, S (1999). 'Monitoring the performance of cardiac surgeons.' *Journal of the Operational Research Society*, 50(7): 684–689.

Lovegrove, J. Valencia, O. Treasure, T. Sherlaw-Johnson, C. Gallivan, S (1997). 'Monitoring the results of cardiac surgery by variable life-adjusted display.' *Lancet*, 350(9085): 1128–1130.

Lowry, CA. Montgomery, DC (1995). 'A review of multivariate control charts.' *IIE Transactions*, 27: 800–810.

Marshall, C. Best, N. Bottle, A. Aylin, P (2004). 'Statistical issues in the prospective monitoring of health outcomes across multiple units.' *Journal of the Royal Statistical Society: Series A*, 167(3): 541–559.

Moustakides, GV (1986). 'Optimal stopping times for detecting changes in distributions.' *Annals of Statistics*, 14(4): 1379–1387.

Nelson, LS (1994). 'A control chart for parts-per-million nonconforming items.' *Journal of Quality Technology*, 26(3): 239–240.

Ohlssen, D. Sharples, L. Spiegelhalter, D (2007). 'A hierarchical modelling framework for identifying unusual performance in health care providers.' *Journal of the Royal Statistical Society: Series A*, 170(4): 865–890.

Page, ES (1954). 'Continuous inspection schemes.' *Biometrika*, 41(1–2): 100–115.

Parsonnet, V. Dean, D. Bernstein, AD (1989). 'A method of uniform stratification of risks for evaluating the results of surgery in acquired adult heart disease.' *Circulation*, 779(1): 1–12.

Poloniecki, J. Valencia, O. Littlejohns, P (1998). 'Cumulative risk adjusted mortality chart for detecting changes in death rate: observational study of heart surgery.' *British Medical Journal*, 316(7146): 1697–1700.

Roberts, SW (1959). 'Control chart tests based on geometric moving averages.' *Technometrics*, 42(1): 239–250.

Rossi, G. Lampugnani, L. Marchi, M (1999). 'An approximate CUSUM procedure for surveillance of health events.' *Statistics in Medicine*, 18(16): 2111–2122.

Shewhart, WA (1931). *Economic control of quality of manufactured product*. New York: Van Nostrand.

Shipman Inquiry (2002). *Shipman Inquiry: First Report*. London, UK: HMSO.

Shipman Inquiry (2004). *Shipman Inquiry Fifth Report - Safeguarding patients: lessons from the past, proposals for the future*. London, UK: HMSO (http://www.the-shipman-inquiry.org.uk/fifthreport.asp).

Spiegelhalter, DJ (2005). 'Problems in assessing rates of infection with methicillin resistant *Staphylococcus aureus*.' *British Medical Journal*, 331(7523):1013–1015.

Spiegelhalter, DJ. Grigg, OAJ. Kinsman, R. Treasure, T (2003). 'Risk-adjusted sequential probability ratio tests: applications to Bristol, Shipman and adult cardiac surgery.' *International Journal for Quality in Health Care*, 15(1): 7–13.

Steiner, SH. Cook, RJ. Farewell, VT. Treasure, T (2000). 'Monitoring surgical performance using risk-adjusted cumulative sum charts.' *Biostatistics*, 1(4): 441–452.

Vandenbroucke, JP (1988). 'Passive smoking and lung cancer: a publication bias?' *British Medical Journal*, 296(6619): 319–392.

West, M. Harrison, J (1997). *Bayesian forecasting and dynamic models. Second edition.* New York: Springer-Verlag.

Western Electric Company (1984). *Statistical quality control handbook.* Texas: AT & T Technologies Inc.

Woodall, WH (2006). 'The use of control charts in health-care and public-health surveillance (with discussion).' *Journal of Quality Technology*, 38(22): 89–134.

3.3 | *Attribution and causality in health-care performance measurement*

DARCEY D. TERRIS, DAVID C. ARON

Introduction

The important issue is that a good-quality indicator should define care that is attributable and within the control of the person who is delivering the care.

(Marshall et al. 2002)

A desirable health-care performance measure is one that reliably and accurately reflects the quality of care provided by individuals, teams and organizations (Pringle et al. 2002). The means of attributing causality for observed outcomes, or responsibility for departures from accepted standards of care, is critical for continuous improvement in service delivery. When quality measures do not reflect the quality of care provided then accountability for deficiencies is directed unfairly and improvement interventions are targeted inappropriately. It is both unethical and counterproductive to penalize individuals, teams or organizations for outcomes or processes outside their control.

In addressing attribution in health-care performance measurement, assessors must first face their own imperfections – specifically the likelihood that fundamental attribution error may influence quality assessments. Identified through social psychology research, fundamental attribution error occurs as a result of inherent human bias that arises when viewing another person's actions (Kelley 1967; Ross 1977). Specifically, causality is attributed to their behaviour by overemphasizing an individual's disposition and under-emphasizing situational factors. This bias reflects a widespread cultural norm focusing on individual responsibility and free will that is reinforced by some legal frameworks.

When medical errors occur, it may be easier to recognize the active error that transpires rather than the multiple system-level errors that underlie it (Reason 2000). These latent errors may be more subtle and therefore more difficult to uncover and understand, especially in complex health-care environments. Even when latent errors are exposed, fundamental attribution error can lead us to ignore them and focus blame on the active error. This is problematic as failure to address the latent errors may provide fertile ground for future active errors. Given the tendency for fundamental attribution error, it is critical that health-care performance measurement is designed with scientific rigour. This is especially true when performance measures are linked to consequences (e.g. in reputation or reimbursement) that influence future service delivery. Perceived or experienced fundamental attribution error may lead to unintentional reductions in future health-care quality and equity (Terris & Litaker 2008).

For the purposes of performance measurement, a health outcome is said to be attributable to an intervention if the intervention has been shown in a rigorous scientific way to cause an observed change in health status. The mechanisms and pathways by which the intervention produces the change may not be known but there is some degree of certainty that it does. In this way much understanding of the world derives from experience-based causality, with statistical analysis providing support for the conclusions.

When attributing causality to a given factor or series of factors, typically a change in outcome is observed from manipulating one factor and holding all other factors constant. *Ceteris paribus* thus underlies the process and is a key principle for establishing models of causality. However, a strict *ceteris paribus* approach often cannot be obtained in the real world of health care. For example, when attributing clinical results in chronic disease management many factors outside the physician's actions are potentially involved. The interaction of these many factors (Fig. 3.3.1) further complicates the analysis. Definitive clinical outcomes may take years to manifest or occur so infrequently as to require large sample sizes to ensure detection with any degree of precision. Finally, random variations and systematic influences must be taken into account when differences in measured performance are being interpreted.

This chapter describes the challenges associated with assessing causality and attribution in health-care performance measurement and

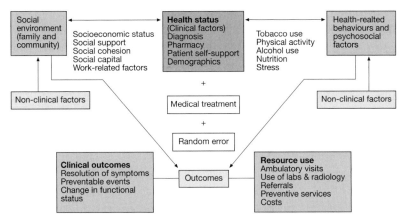

Fig. 3.3.1 Interrelationships of risk factors: relating risks to outcomes*

* Diagnosis-based measures are based on diagnoses, demographics and resource-use outcomes. Patient self-reported approaches are based on patient self-reported information (eg. health-related quality of life) and clinical outcomes.

The model shows that many factors outside a physician's actions can potentially influence the obtainment of a desired outcome of care. The number and interaction of these many factors complicates health-care performance measurement.

Source: Rosen et al. 2003

suggests methods for achieving at least a semblance of holding everything else constant. The concepts within the chapter are offered within the framework of performance measurement of health-care providers but are applicable to quality assessment at other levels including multi-provider practices, health-care facilities, hospitals and health systems. It is important to recognize that the methods presented rest upon a number of key assumptions. Specifically, most of our discussion is based on an underlying assumption of linear causality in which model inputs are assumed to be proportional to outputs. A critique of this approach is provided at the end of the chapter.

Assumptions underlying performance measurement

Donabedian's (1966) classic work on quality assessment identifies three types of performance measures – outcome, process and structure. Of these, outcome and process measures are most commonly used in health-care quality assessment. The reliability and accuracy of performance measurement requires proper definition (operationalization) of the outcome and/or process under evaluation and the availability of good quality data. These are often the first assumptions made and it is dangerous to presume that either or both of these requirements are met.

It is assumed that the outcome or process under evaluation depends upon a number of factors. Iezzoni (2003) uses the phrase 'algebra of effectiveness' to describe health-care outcomes as a function of clinical and other patient attributes, treatment effectiveness, quality of care and random events or chance.

> Patient outcomes = f (effectiveness of care or therapeutic intervention, quality of care, patient attributes or risk factors affecting response to care, random chance)

Each of these domains can be parsed in a variety of ways. For example, patient attributes may include clinical and health status parameters; health behaviours; psychosocial and socioeconomic factors; and individual preferences and attitudes. Effectiveness of care relates to the likelihood that a given intervention will result in the desired outcome e.g. that glycaemic control in a diabetic patient will reduce the occurrence of end-organ complications. Quality of care includes everything attributable to the delivery of health care whether at the physician, nurse, team or organizational level. This includes both the actions of the health-care providers and the context in which they practice. Finally, there are the vagaries of chance – the 'correct' therapy may not work for all patients.

Reliable and accurate assessment of a provider's role in health-care quality is dependent on the ability to divide and assign fairly the responsibility for a patient's receipt of appropriate services and attainment of desired outcomes to the many factors with potential influence. First, it must be known that a provider's given action or inaction *can cause* a process or outcome of care to occur. Then it must be ascertained whether (under the given circumstances and context) an observed process or outcome of care *is attributable* to the provider. The requirement for both causality and attribution implies that a provider's action/inaction may be neither 'necessary' (required to occur) nor 'sufficient' (needs presence of no additional factors in order to occur) for a given process or outcome of care to transpire. Other factors, alone or in combination with the provider's action/inaction, may also cause the observed process or outcome of care to take place.

Similar issues may arise when using process measures even though receipt of a specific guideline recommended therapy (for example) would seem likely to avoid these uncertainties. A patient might not receive a guideline recommended therapy if the provider neglects to prescribe it. Conversely, the observed lack of therapy may occur if a provider prescribes the treatment but the patient refuses treatment because of his/her health beliefs. As illustrated, the provider's failure to prescribe is not 'necessary', i.e. the only possible cause for the observed absence of recommended therapy.

The level of attribution is also important. The provision of guideline-specified screening may occur as a result of a provider's knowledge and attention to standards of care. However, an automatic reminder system in the electronic medical record system utilized by the provider's practice may support the provider's memory and contribute to the observed rate of screening. In this case, the provider's memory alone is not 'sufficient'.

If a provider's actions/inactions are often neither necessary nor sufficient to cause an observed process or outcome of care, how is it possible to assess when the observed process or outcome of care can be ascribed, at least in part, to the provider? Statistical modelling through regression analysis is typically used to evaluate whether a significant relationship exists between providers and a process or outcome variable identified as a quality indicator. Through a process of risk adjustment, control variables are included in the model to account for the potential effects of other factors (confounders) that may influence the incidence of the quality indicator under investigation.

However, even with risk adjustment, more than a single model is necessary to prove that an observed quality indicator is causally linked and attributable to a provider's action/inaction. Measurement and attribution error, complexity in the confounding relationships and provider locus of control must be considered in the analysis of causality and attribution for health-care performance measures (Fig. 3.3.2). The risks associated with causality and attribution bias and the methods to reduce such bias are explored in this chapter.

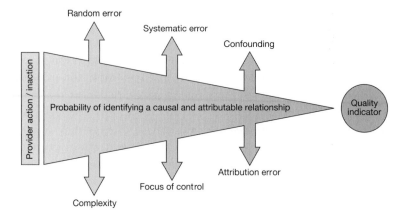

Fig. 3.3.2 Health-care performance measurement: challenges of investigating whether there is a causal and attributable relationship between a provider's action/inaction and a given quality indicator

The vagaries of chance in health-care performance measurement – random error

Variability arising from chance or random error is present in all quantitative data. Two types of random error must be considered in statistical estimates, including those employed in health-care performance measurement. The first is commonly referred to as type I error, or the false positive rate; the second is called type II error, or the false negative rate. Individual variables may be subject to higher or lower rates of random error. For each variable, the errors happen at random without a systematic pattern of incidence within the data elements collected. However, the variance falls evenly above and below the true value of the variable being measured. With increasing random error, the mean value for the variable is unaffected although the variance will increase. In general, variance decreases with increasing sample size.

The acceptable type I error rate of a statistical test (also called the significance level or p value) is typically set at 0.05 or 0.01. This is interpreted to mean that there is a five in one hundred or a one in one hundred chance that the statistical test will indicate that a relationship exists between two variables under consideration (e.g. a provider's action/inaction and a quality indicator) when a relationship *is not present*. Therefore, even when the results of statistical modelling suggest a significant relationship between two variables, it must be recognized that there is a chance that the conclusion is false.

Further, with repetitive testing there is an increasing likelihood that type I error will produce one or more false conclusions unless the analyses adjust for this risk (Seneta & Chen 2005). This problem is especially prevalent in quality measurement due to the proliferation of individual measures and multiple comparisons. Under these circumstances, it may be more common than is acknowledged to see a significant relationship that truly does not exist (Hofer & Hayward 1995 & 1996).

Researchers may also fail to detect differences that are present, i.e. a false negative result may occur. In general, there is more willingness to accept a false negative conclusion (type II error) than a false positive conclusion (type I error). Therefore, the type II error rate (ß) is typically set in the range of 0.20 or 0.10. With ß = 0.20, there is a 20% chance of a conclusion that there is no relationship between two variables when a relationship *does* exist. Statistical testing does not usually refer directly to the type II error rate and the power of the test (1- ß) is more commonly reported. Power analysis is performed before data are collected in order to identify the size of the sample required. This increases the likelihood that the desired type II error rate will not be exceeded. When performed after data collection and statistical testing, power analysis identifies the type II error rate achieved. If the type II error rate is greater than the desired rate, a study may be described as under-powered.

It is not possible to reduce the risk of type I and II error simultaneously without increasing sample size. Sample size may be increased by merging data from smaller units or across time, or through a combination of these approaches. Increasing sample size by these methods may reduce the impact of chance but may also change the focus of the analysis. The results from the aggregated data may be less useful for assessing the health system level and/or time period of interest.

A pervasive statistical phenomenon called regression to the mean may also make natural variation in repeated data look like real change (Barnett et al 2005; Morton & Torgerson 2005). When data regress to the mean, unusually high (or low) measurements tend to be followed by measurements that are closer to the mean. Statistical methods can assess for regression to the mean but have not been used to any great extent (Hayes 1988).

Greater variance from chance (random error) in data makes it more difficult to draw a conclusion as to whether a relationship exists between two variables under analysis. All data are subject to random error which can be minimized through careful adherence to measurement and data recording protocols; with routine checks of data reliability and completeness; and through the use of control groups when possible.

Systematic error in health-care performance measurement

The certainty associated with an estimate of the relationship between two variables is also subject to systematic error. This is also called inaccuracy or bias and results from limitations in measurement and sampling procedures. Systematic error may occur when all measured values for a given variable deviate positively or negatively from the variable's true value, for example – through poor calibration of the measurement instruments employed. This type of bias would equally affect all members of the sample, resulting in the mean for the sample deviating positively or negatively from the true population mean. Bias may also occur when erroneously higher (or lower) values for a given variable are more likely to be measured for a subgroup under analysis. This can occur in resource-limited settings where the measurement instruments used by providers are more likely to be out of calibration than those used in resource-affluent settings.

As with random error, there is no way to avoid all sources of systematic error when assessing the presence of a relationship between two variables. Unlike random error, however, it is not possible to set a maximum rate of permitted systematic error when drawing statistical conclusions. Assessments of systematic error are not included routinely in reports of statistical results (Terris et al. 2007) but recently there has been greater attention to the need for routine, quantitative estimation of bias and its effect on conclusions drawn in statistical analyses (Greenland 1996; Lash & Fink 2003; Schneeweiss & Avorn 2005).

Systematic error obscures assessment of the size and nature of the relationship between two variables. For example, the presence of bias may lead to the conclusion that the relationship between a provider's action/inaction and a given quality indicator is larger (or smaller) than the actual association. Under these circumstances, more (or less) operational significance may be assigned to the identified relationship.

Systematic error can be reduced by proactively considering potential sources of bias in the design and implementation of measurement systems. This enables protocols to be implemented to minimize systematic error in measured values and limit bias among study subgroups.

Confounding in health-care performance measurement

If careful data collection and statistical tests have produced confidence that a relationship exists between two variables under consideration, is it then possible to assume that the relationship is causal? Unfortunately, a significant statistical result only implies that a causal link may be present – it does not prove causality and the relationship can only be said to be correlative. Correlated variables move together, or co-vary, in a pattern that relates to each other. Positive correlation exists when the variables move together in the same direction; negative correlation exists when the variables move in opposition to each other. In both instances, the underlying drivers of the association between the two variables remain unknown.

Correlated variables may be causally linked to each other or both variables under consideration may be affected by a third variable, called a confounder. When the relationship between two variables is confounded by a third variable, the third variable may cause all or a portion of the observed effect between the first two. The confounder's common influence on the first two variables creates the appearance that these two are more strongly connected than they are.

Multivariate statistical modelling controls for confounding by including factors with potential influence on the observed relationship between the primary hypothesized causal agent and the process or outcome variable of interest. This process of controlling is called risk adjustment. The identification of possible confounders and specification of models to control adequately for their effect in health-care performance measurement is discussed in detail in Chapter 3.1.

If an analysis does not adequately account for confounding then the estimated relationship between the two variables of interest will be biased. This type of bias is called missing variable or misspecification bias. As discussed, bias in an assessment of the relationship between two variables can lead to the conclusion that the relationship between the two variables is larger (or smaller) than the actual association. A positive relationship might even be construed as negative, or vice versa.

Complexity in health-care performance measurement

Within a given health-care delivery context, the complexity arising from the number of potential confounders and the complicated relationships between possible confounding factors creates a daunting challenge when seeking to attribute an observed process or outcome of care to a provider's action/inaction. However, variation due to other causes must be accounted for before an observed process or outcome of care can be attributed to a provider's action/inaction (Lilford et al. 2004). Possible confounders arise from patient-level characteristics as well as the health-care resources, systems and policies surrounding the patient and the patient-provider encounter (Rosen et al. 2003; Terris & Litaker 2008). This is further complicated by the need to consider potential confounders that arise outside the health-care environment (see Box 3.3.1 for an example). Adequate risk adjustment for potential confounders is limited by both the knowledge and acknowledgement of potential confounding agents and the ability and available resources to capture confounders for inclusion in quality assessments.

Box 3.3.1 Community characteristics and health outcomes

Empirical studies suggest that community and neighbourhood-level factors have an impact on the health status and outcomes of residents. These factors include the neighbourhood's socioeconomic status; physical environment and availability of resources (recreational space, outlets to purchase fresh foods, etc.); and the social capital within the community. These effects are linked to the context in which people live, not the people themselves (Litaker & Tomolo 2007; Lochner et al. 2003).

For example, Lochner et al. (2003) used a hierarchical modelling approach to demonstrate that neighbourhoods with higher levels of social capital (as assessed by measures of reciprocity, trust and civic participation) were associated with lower all-cause and cardiovascular mortality. This result was found after adjusting for the material deprivation of neighbourhoods. Therefore, individuals living in neighbourhoods with lower social capital may be at greater risk of poor health outcomes, regardless of the quality of care given by their providers.

This discussion can be extended by returning to the previous example in which a patient does not receive a guideline-specified treatment. If the receipt of treatment is used as a quality indicator, this episode reflects negatively on the provider and will be classified as an instance of poor quality care. However, as previously discussed, the patient's health beliefs may have led him/her to refuse the prescribed treatment. Conversely, the patient may have been willing to follow the recommendation but access to the therapy was restricted by policies set by their health-care coverage agency. Limitations in the availability and capacity of facilities dispensing the treatment may also have created insurmountable barriers for the patient. Finally, the patient could have received the treatment but this was not recorded in the health information systems in place (see Box 3.3.2 for a further example). These are just a few of the many factors that may have influenced the observed failure to receive the guideline-recommended treatment, outside of the provider's failure to recommend the therapy.

As the hypothetical example shows, confounding factors that influence an observed process or outcome of care can originate from

---

Box 3.3.2 Missed opportunities with electronic health records

By reducing barriers to longitudinal health and health-care utilization information, electronic health records (EHRs) can be used to improve the quality of care delivered to patients and the reliability and validity of health-care performance measurement. However, in a recent study by Simon et al. (2008) less than 20% of the provider practices surveyed (in Massachusetts, USA) reported having EHRs. Of those practices without, more than half (52%) reported no plans to implement an EHR system in the foreseeable future. Funding was the most frequently reported obstacle to implementation.

Further, less than half of the systems in practices with EHR systems provided laboratory (44%) or radiology (40%) order entry (Simon et al. 2008). This misses the opportunity to, for example, identify whether a provider ordered a guideline-recommended laboratory test. The only information available to assess the quality of care delivered would be the absence of the test result. If the patient did not receive the test for reasons outside the provider's control, this scenario would reflect unfairly upon the provider.

several levels within the health-care delivery environment. In the example given, the confounder was hypothesized to have arisen from patient-level characteristics (patient's health beliefs); provider practice resources (information systems); health system policies (reimbursement policy); or the patient's home community (capability and accessibility of dispensing facilities).

In health-care performance assessment, providers can be sorted into subgroups at different levels, for instance – based on the facilities they practice within; the coverage programmes in which they are included; and/or the communities they serve. The actions/inactions of providers within a given subgroup (e.g. providers practising at a given hospital) tend to have less variation than the actions/inactions of providers in different subgroups (e.g. providers practising at separate hospitals). Hierarchical models can be used to differentiate between the variation arising from differences between providers and between subgroups of providers. If the clustering of data is not accounted for then the estimate of the relationship between the provider's action/inaction and the quality indicator may be biased. Further, the confidence intervals (i.e. estimated range of the effect of the providers' action/inaction on the quality indicator, based on the significance level of the test) may also be narrowed, leading to false conclusions concerning the apparent significance of the relationship (Zyzanski et al. 2004). Therefore, hierarchical modelling approaches have been increasingly recommended (Glance et al. 2003).

Provider locus of control

The example discussed above raises the issue of access hurdles that may prevent a patient from following a provider's recommended therapy. From the provider's perspective, these same hurdles may functionally limit their own control of care-delivery recommendations. For example, health system policies may restrict the number of referrals that a provider can make within a given period. Non-emergency patients who present at the provider's office after the referral limit has been reached may be requested to return for a referral at a later date. However, performance assessment for the time of the postponement would indicate that the recommended process of care had not occurred.

Health system policies may also encourage providers to pursue therapies other than their preferred course of treatment. The new

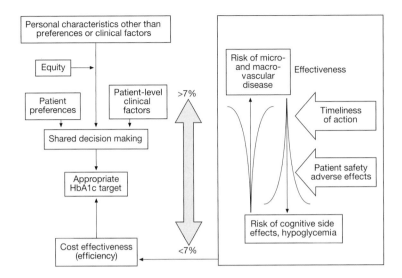

Fig. 3.3.3 Factors in choice of target HbA1c for care of a given patient with diabetes

Source: Based on the model by Aron & Pogach 2007

diabetes care quality measure adopted by the National Committee for Quality Assurance (NCQA) can be used to illustrate this point. The measure is based on the percentage of diabetic patients aged eighteen to seventy-five who have HbA1c levels of less than 7% (Pogach et al. 2007). This target HbA1c level may indicate excellent glycaemic control but a number of factors should be considered before choosing a target HbA1c for a given patient. A conceptual framework illustrating these factors is shown in Fig. 3.3.3.

For example, consider a seventy-four-year-old man with diabetes and heart failure who takes oral medications for glycaemic control. He would require insulin injections to improve his glycaemic control from an HbA1c of 7.2% to less than 7%. However, these injections would increase the patient's risk of hypoglycaemia and its attendant morbidity with little benefit in terms of reduction in cardiovascular risk or microvascular complications. Further, the patient may strongly prefer to continue with the oral agents. Should this patient be counted against his provider because the HbA1c quality target is not met? Of more concern, should the health system's policies lead the provider to strongly recommend (coerce?) the patient to accept insulin injections in order to meet the quality target?

A provider's locus of control can be significantly affected by the policies and infrastructure of their practice environment as directed by local, regional and national health systems and regulatory bodies (Hauk et al. 2003; Landon et al. 2001). Even if a causal relationship is established between a provider's action/inaction and a performance indicator, the responsibility for an observed process or outcome of care may not always be attributable to the provider. Further, providers' locus of control may vary substantially between different practice contexts and for different patient subgroups within a given context. Factors that influence a provider's ability to direct their actions/inactions within their practice environment should be accounted for in health-care performance measurement. These factors are possible confounders to be included in the risk adjustment process.

Attribution theory and fundamental attribution error

Much has been said about the complexity encountered when trying to establish a causal link and attribute a provider's action/inaction to an observed care process or health outcome. It may be that health-care quality researchers have over-emphasized this complexity due to fundamental attribution error. Originating in social psychology research, the term is used to describe bias that arises from differences in perspective when identifying the causal factors for events in which we have been involved and events concerning others (Jones & Harris 1967; Ross 1977). Specifically, there is a known tendency to over-emphasize situational factors (those outside ourselves) when looking for explanations of outcomes related to our own actions. Conversely, when looking at others we are predisposed to under-emphasize these same situational factors and focus more on individual responsibility.

For example, in a recent study by Golomb et al. (2007), physicians were reluctant to attribute patient-reported symptoms to an adverse effect of drugs that they had prescribed. This hesitation occurred even when the reported symptom had strong literature-based support for probable drug causality. Within the framework of fundamental attribution error the physicians could be unconsciously reluctant to attribute reported symptoms to their decision to prescribe the drug. Further, they may be more likely to attribute the reported symptoms to the patient's other health behaviours, downplaying the influence of the external factor of the drug's potential side effects.

Similarly, it might be hypothesized that insiders involved in developing performance measurement systems in a health-care system are more apt to look for external factors as possible confounders. Conversely, when outsiders investigate these performance measurement systems they may be less likely to include external factors as possible confounders. The outsiders may focus instead on the personal responsibility of the agent (e.g. providers, hospitals) under analysis. To limit the effect of fundamental attribution error on the development of health-care performance measures, causality and attribution should be assessed with scientific rigour. Multiple perspectives should be included in the analysis by involving internal and external stakeholders.

Causality and attribution bias in health-care performance measurement

When there is bias in the assessment of causality or attribution for a given quality indicator for a subgroup of providers, the affected providers are ranked more advantageously or disadvantageously (with respect to their true quality) than providers of corresponding quality. If reimbursement is linked to health-care performance assessment then providers subject to this bias are unfairly compensated, receiving a higher or lower rate of payment than providers of equivalent quality. If market-share incentives are offered through published public scorecards, providers who have experienced bias in their assessment will appear relatively more or less attractive to patients than providers of similar quality (Lilford et al. 2004).

Both providers and patients bear the risk of causality and attribution bias in health-care performance measurement. Providers are treated unfairly: well-compensated regardless of the relatively poor quality of care provided or penalized despite the relatively high-quality service delivery. As a consequence, patients may receive lower quality health care. They may leave a relatively high-quality provider because public reporting has misrepresented the provider as delivering low-quality care or because the provider has instituted restrictions in their practice in response to lower reimbursement rates based on this inaccurate assessment.

Who is at risk from causality and attribution bias?

Providers who practise in resource-limited settings are at greater risk of bias in health-care performance measurement than their counterparts in more resource-affluent settings (Casalino & Elster 2007; Terris & Litaker 2008). This bias arises, in part, from differences in the provider's locus of control in acquiring and directing the use of resources in the delivery of care. When resources are generally limited, the choices available to the provider are also limited. The resources to be considered include those that providers apply in service delivery, specifically the facilities, equipment, personnel, management and information systems available (Miller & West 2007).

Limitations in community resources (e.g. neighbourhood's socio-economic status; local public health policy and practice; general infrastructure) may also increase the risk that a provider practising within the community will be subject to bias in health-care performance measurement. These community-level factors influence the health and health-care processes and outcomes obtained by residents. Providers that service resource-limited settings also typically face greater complexity in their practice and this may be difficult to capture and include when risk adjusting in the health-care assessment process (Casalino & Elster 2007). Sources of information outside the practice (such as community-level economic data) are necessary to account adequately for the complexity of the practice context.

Providers that care for more complex patients are also at greater risk of bias in health-care performance measurement (Terris & Litaker 2008). This complexity can arise from the health status of the patient (e.g. severity; comorbidity) or from other patient-level characteristics (e.g. socio-economic status; health beliefs and behaviour). Providers that practise in resource-limited settings generally treat a greater proportion of complex patients (Casalino & Elster 2007). However, complex patients are also more likely to be found within the practices of providers affiliated to teaching hospitals (Antioch et al. 2007) or who specialize in more complex patient subgroups, such as frail older adults (Jette et al. 1996). Risk adjustment for severity and comorbidity is common but again other sources of information are necessary to incorporate the additional patient-level factors that can influence the obtainment of desired processes and outcomes of care.

It should be noted that the bias in health-care performance measurement that arises from limitations in sources and the quality of data and reporting systems is not restricted to providers in resource-limited settings (Terris & Litaker 2008). First, regardless of general resources, few providers have access to or utilize more technologically advanced information systems such as electronic health records (Burt & Sisk 2005). Second, more sophisticated information systems for data recording and reporting are not guaranteed to capture reliably and accurately the patient-level factors that are accessible within the patient-provider encounter (Persell et al. 2006). For example, an electronic health record might not have a clear entry point for specific information on a patient's less common contraindication for a guideline recommended treatment (e.g. patient states he/she is unable to swallow pills). However, a written medical record can afford the provider greater flexibility to note this confounding factor.

What are the potential effects of causality and attribution bias on health-care quality and equity?

Performance measurement is used by health-care managers to both identify targets for improvement and incentivize providers to improve service delivery (Terris & Litaker 2008). If the causality and attribution of a provider's action/inaction to a given quality indicator is not assessed accurately and reliably then the signal that this action/inaction should be repeated (or avoided) will be lost. A high-quality provider may not sustain their current practice policies and procedures as they would not link their current routines with the delivery of high-quality care. As a consequence, new initiatives may be substituted that may/may not result in a similar or better level of care. Conversely, a relatively low-quality provider that is assessed inaccurately as providing higher-quality care does not receive the clear signal that service delivery needs to be improved. The opportunity to maintain and improve quality is clearly affected when providers experience bias in health-care performance measurement.

When health-care performance measurement is linked to reimbursement or other market-based incentives, providers' perception of the risk associated with inaccurate assessment may create disincentives that are contrary to the goal of improving equity in access and health-care quality (Lilford et al. 2004). Providers may seek to avoid including complex patients in their practice or locating their practice in more complex settings. This disincentive may create difficulties in the recruitment and retention of providers for disadvantaged population segments. Further, providers that deliver high-quality care in resource-limited settings may be reimbursed at a lower rate than those that supply a similar level of care in a more resource-affluent environment. This would lead to further restrictions in the resources available for health care in resource-limited settings and likely degradation in the quality of care delivered. In this manner, biased health-care performance measurement could result in increased health disparities (Casalino & Elster 2007).

The probability of fundamental attribution error increases with the increasing risk linked to health-care performance measurement. A provider with a reputation, reimbursement rate or market share at stake may be more likely to point to factors outside their locus of control as responsible for the observed process or outcome of care. Future opportunities for quality improvement are lost as the fear of penalties (fair or unfair) leads providers to avoid self-reflection and instead to identify external causal agents.

Methods to reduce causality and attribution bias in health-care performance measurement

The one certainty in health-care performance measurement is that most often it will not be known with absolute certainty that an observed process or outcome of care is causally linked and attributable to a provider's action/inaction. However, it is possible to address actively the risk of bias in the assessment of causality and attribution in the development and implementation of measurement systems in order to maximize the certainty obtained. A first step is proactive consideration of the possible pathways leading to the desired process and/or outcome of care and where they can diverge (Institute of Medicine 2007).

In industry, failure mode and effects analysis and root cause analysis are advocated during the product or process development stage in order to anticipate risks for adverse events and the need for process control points (McCain 2006). In health care, these methods are increasingly applied to improve patient safety but are most commonly retrospective, in response to an adverse event or near miss (Battles et al. 2006). For example, root cause analysis has been systematically applied for adverse events and near misses that occur in Department of Veterans Affairs' medical facilities. Implementation of this process has shifted the focus from human errors to system vulnerabilities and more actionable root causes (Bagian et al. 2002). Proactive examination of the pathways to episodes of high- and low-quality care enables even more comprehensive understanding of the provider's role and identification of possible confounders, their potential impact and the probability of their influence within a given context. Research can then be designed to investigate whether there is a causal and attributable relationship between a provider's action/inaction and a given process or outcome of care.

The randomized controlled trial (RCT) is considered the gold standard in study design for clinical evidence and has been advocated for building the necessary evidence for quality of care research (Institute of Medicine 2007). Study subjects are assigned randomly to either a treatment (e.g. provider's action) or control (e.g. provider's inaction) group. If the study sample is sufficiently large, random assignment will result in an equal distribution of possible confounders between the treatment and control groups. However, random assignment can account only for confounders represented among the subjects in the study sample. The representativeness of the study sample to more general populations and alternative health-care delivery contexts must be assessed before extending the results of the RCT. Random assignment to a treatment or control group may be neither possible nor ethical in all study scenarios. This may be especially true in quality of care research in which it may be known that a given provider action is preferable (i.e. the action does no harm and may result in benefit) but not whether the action is causal or attributable in a given health-care delivery context. Under such circumstances it may be considered unethical to withhold a potentially beneficial action from study participants (Edwards et al. 1998).

Well-designed observational study designs can be used when an RCT is not possible. Observational studies are potentially affected by hidden bias and therefore sensitivity analyses should be performed routinely in the assessment of results. Propensity score (Johnson et al. 2006) and instrumental variable (Harless & Mark 2006) methods are also recommended increasingly in the analysis of observational study results (see Box 3.3.3 for examples). Propensity score and instrumental variable methods are used to approximate the randomization process of an RCT.

Box 3.3.3 New views on the volume-outcome relationship

Numerous studies have identified a link between the volume of health care delivered and patient outcomes, with higher volume hospitals and providers appearing to provide higher quality of care (Halm et al. 2002). However, prior analysis of the volume-outcome relationship may have been confounded in two important ways. First, the studies may not have risk adjusted adequately for differences in the case mix of patients attending high- and low-volume providers. Second, the relationship may actually be one of reverse causality (Luft 1980). Higher volume may not lead to better outcomes (practice-makes-perfect argument) but providers who are associated with better outcomes may receive more referrals.

New evidence using propensity scores to adjust for selection bias
Zacharias et al. (2005) used a propensity score approach to address systematic differences in patient characteristics before comparing CABG outcomes between a high- and a low-volume hospital. Propensity scores were derived from a logistic regression model, with presentation at the high- or low-volume hospital as the dependent variable. A wide variety of patient-level risk factors were included as covariates. The model was then used to calculate a propensity score for each patient included in the sample. Patients were matched (one from each hospital) based on their propensity score and their CABG outcomes were compared. In the final analysis, hospital volume was not found to be a significant predictor of in-hospital mortality or three-year survival.

Further evidence using an instrumental variable approach
Tsai et al. (2006) used an instrumental variable approach to investigate the volume-outcome relationship among inpatients with congestive heart failure. The instrumental variable used was the linear distance between a patient's residence and the hospital in which care was received. This distance is conceivably related to the exposure of interest (hospital volume, with patients more likely to attend closer hospitals) but not the outcome of interest (thirty-day mortality). The researchers repeated their analysis using limited administrative data and more complete clinical data for risk adjustment and

---

Box 3.3.3 cont'd

including and not including the instrumental variable in the model. A small, potential volume-outcome relationship was only found when the limited administrative data were used and the instrumental variable was not included in the final model. A significant relationship was not found under the other model scenarios.

Propensity scores are derived through multivariate logistic regression models, using receipt of the exposure (e.g. provider's action/inaction) as the outcome variable and factors that influence the receipt of the exposure (e.g. measures of the patients' health status) as covariates. The goal is to include all variables that play a role in receipt of the exposure in order to model propensity for exposure. The model should include interactions among identified covariates although it appears that it is more important to include all the relevant predictors than the correct interaction terms (Dehijia & Wahba 1998; Drake & Fisher 1995).

The exposure model is used to derive a propensity score for each patient, based on the patient's status for each covariate included. Next, patients who did and did not receive the exposure are matched according to their propensity scores. This approximates equal distribution of confounders associated with receipt of treatment between a treatment and control group in an RCT. In a second stage of regression analysis, differences in the outcomes observed between propensity score-matched subjects are then attributed more accurately to the exposure. Propensity score methods work best with large samples and where data are collected expressly for the purpose of deriving propensity scores for subject matching. They can adjust only for measured covariates associated with receipt of exposure and not for unmeasured or omitted variables (Braitman & Rosenbaum 2002). Therefore, the more intensive data collection required for these methods may not be suitable for routine quality assessment.

Instrumental variable models are recommended when there is potential feedback between the outcome (e.g. quality indicator) and exposure (e.g. a provider's action/inaction); unmeasured confounders in the analysis; and/or significant measurement error. A selected instrumental variable should be associated with the exposure variable but not the outcome variable. When the instrumental variable is included in the regression analysis it will appear to be associated with the outcome variable because of its relationship with the exposure variable. The association identified between the instrumental and the outcome variable can then be divided into the association between (i) the instrumental and exposure variable; and, more importantly, (ii) the exposure and outcome variable.

Other techniques have also been developed to address complexity in the assessment of causality and attribution. These methods include multi-level modelling to separate out the hierarchical effects associated with clustered data (Leyland & Goldstein 2001) and selection bias models (Weiner et al. 1997). To date, none of these methods has been widely adopted in health-care performance measurement.

Beyond study design and statistical technique, it is important to recognize that a single RCT or well-designed observational study does not provide sufficient evidence of causality between a provider's action/inaction and a process or outcome of care. A preponderance of evidence is needed from multiple studies among different sample populations and service-delivery contexts. If a plausible pathway is hypothesized and supported through such research results then greater certainty can be assigned to the identified causal link. Further, this derives a richer picture of the health-care delivery contexts in which the process or outcome of care is attributable to the provider's action/inaction, leading to possible multi-factorial interventions to improve future quality.

Critique from the standpoint of complexity theory

The foundation of evidence-based medicine relies upon a particular conceptual model of the world. This model describes a mechanistic world that functions according to deterministic principles in which problems are analysed using a framework of simple linear causality. To illustrate this point, consider an environmental toxin associated with a particular cancer (e.g. aflatoxin and liver cancer). Under the assumption of linear causality, it is presumed that the effect (liver cancer) can be eliminated by eliminating the cause (exposure to aflatoxin). However, health effects are generally not caused by a single agent – there is a web of causal factors, of which the effect itself may be a part. This view is grounded in complexity theory and the behaviour of complex systems.

Complex systems comprise a large number of interacting components that have interconnecting actions. They contain many direct and indirect feedback loops and so the interactions are non-linear with non-proportional effects. Small changes can have large effects on overall system behaviour while large changes can have little effect. The behaviour of the system is determined by the nature and effect of the interactions, not solely by the content or individual actions of component elements (Rouse 2000 & 2003).

If health systems are accepted as complex systems under this definition, there must be a fundamental revision of the understanding of causality and attribution as described within this chapter. Further, the methods used to identify targets and implement health-care quality improvement initiatives will change radically. Until that time, it will be necessary to rely upon the simpler models presented, focusing on individual causal agents but acknowledging the context and systems within which they work.

Conclusions

Health-care managers involved in health-care performance measurement are advised to consider the following recommendations in addressing causality and attribution bias.

1. Access existing reports of research into the possibility of a causal and attributable link between the agents under assessment (e.g. providers, hospitals) and the process or outcome of care proposed as a quality indicator. Evaluate the quality of this research based on study design and control for confounding. Context is important as findings based on a given patient population or setting (health-care venue or system; social, cultural or economic environment; etc.) may not be generalizable to other contexts or countries.
2. Perform a prospective analysis to identify the critical pathways involved in the achievement of desired and undesired processes and outcomes of care. Identify possible confounders to the relationship between the agents under assessment and the process or outcome of care proposed as a quality indicator. Further, identify

how the agents under assessment may be clustered within levels of the health-care context under analysis.

3. Synthesize the results of steps 1 and 2 and identify essential gaps in knowledge. Involve stakeholders internal and external to the health-care level under analysis in order to minimize the risk of fundamental attribution error. Consider root cause analysis as a method to identify system-level sources of variation in the quality of care delivered. These root causes may be more effective targets for sustainable improvement efforts.

4. If a new study is required, prospectively consider sources of random and systematic error in measurement and sampling when developing the study design. This applies to studies utilizing either primary or secondary data sources. Institute policies and procedures for data collection that maximize the reliability and accuracy of the data used for the quality assessment. In resource-constrained settings, it may be more useful to employ a limited number of quality indicators that can be measured in a repeatable and valid manner rather than overburdening reporting mechanisms with many indicators that are less reliable and accurate.

5. Employ risk adjustment when evaluating the relationship between the agents under assessment and the process or outcome of care proposed as a quality indicator. Consider the use of hierarchical models to account for the clustering of data within levels of the health-care context under analysis (see step 2). When confounding cannot be controlled for through randomization, further consider the use of propensity score or instrumental variable methods to approximate randomization.

6. Acknowledge that causality and attribution bias cannot be eliminated completely, even when utilizing best practices as described above. Consider the unintended impacts from experienced or perceived bias in quality assessment on the future improvement of health-care quality and equity, especially when reimbursement or market-share incentives are linked to quality assessment. The risk and potential consequences of causality and attribution bias may be especially severe in resource-constrained and complex settings or for those who care for patients with more complex needs.

References

Antioch, KM. Ellis, RP. Gillett, S. Borovnicar, D. Marshall, RP (2007). 'Risk-adjustment policy options for casemix funding: international lessons in financing reform.' *European Journal of Health Economics,* 8(3): 195–212.

Aron, DC. Pogach, LM (2007). 'One size does not fit all: a continuous measure for glycemic control in diabetes: the need for a new approach to assessing glycemic control.' *Joint Commission Journal on Quality Improvement,* 33: 636–643.

Bagian, JP. Gosbee, J. Lee, CZ. Williams, L. McKnight, SD. Mannos, DM (2002). 'The Veterans Affairs root cause analysis system in action.' *Joint Commission Journal on Quality Improvement,* 28(10): 531–545.

Barnett, AG. van der Pols, JC. Dobson, AJ (2005). 'Regression to the mean: what it is and how to deal with it.' *International Journal of Epidemiology,* 34(1): 215–220.

Battles, JB. Dixon, NM. Borotkanics, RJ. Rabin-Fastmen, B. Kaplan, HS (2006). 'Sensemaking of patient safety risks and hazards.' *Health Services Research,* 41(4 Pt 2): 1555–1575.

Braitman, LE. Rosenbaum, PR (2002). 'Rare outcomes, common treatments: analytic strategies using propensity scores.' *Annals of Internal Medicine,* 137(8): 693–695.

Burt, C. Sisk, J (2005). 'Which physicians and practices are using electronic medical records?' *Health Affairs,* 24(5): 1334–1343.

Casalino, L. Elster, A (2007). 'Will pay-for-performance and quality reporting affect health disparities?' *Health Affairs,* 26(3): 405–414.

Dehejia, R. Wahba, S (1998). *Propensity score-matching methods for non-experimental causal studies.* Cambridge, MA: National Bureau of Economic Research (NBER Working Paper No. 6829).

Donabedian, A (1966). 'Evaluating the quality of medical care.' *Milbank Memorial Fund Quarterly,* 44(3 Pt. 2): 166–203.

Drake, C. Fisher L (1995). 'Prognostic models and the propensity score.' *International Journal of Epidemiology,* 24(1): 183–187.

Edwards, SJL. Lilford, RJ. Hewison, J (1998). 'The ethics of randomised controlled trials from the perspectives of patients, the public and health-care professionals.' *British Medical Journal,* 317(7167): 1209–1212.

Glance, LG. Dick, AW. Osler, TM. Mukamel, D (2003). 'Using hierarchical modeling to measure ICU quality.' *Intensive Care Medicine,* 29(12): 2223–2229.

Golomb, BA. McGraw, JJ. Evans, MA. Dimsdale, JE (2007). 'Physician response to patient reports of adverse drug effects: implications for patient-targeted adverse effect surveillance.' *Drug Safety,* 30(8): 669–675.

Greenland, S (1996). 'Basic methods for sensitivity analysis of biases.' *International Journal of Epidemiology*, 25(6): 1107–1116.

Halm, EA. Lee, C. Chassin, MR (2002). 'Is volume related to outcome in health care? A systematic review and methodologic critique of the literature.' *Annals of Internal Medicine*, 137(6): 511–520.

Harless, DW. Mark, BA (2006). 'Addressing measurement error bias in nurse staffing research. *Health Services Research*, 41(5): 2006–2024.

Hauk, K. Rice, N. Smith, P (2003). 'The influence of health care organisations on health system performance.' *Journal of Health System Research & Policy*, 8(2): 68–74.

Hayes, RJ (1988). 'Methods for assessing whether change depends on initial value.' *Statistics in Medicine*, 7(9): 915–927.

Hofer, TP, Hayward, RA (1995). 'Can early re-admission rates accurately detect poor-quality hospitals?' *Medical Care*, 33(3): 234–245.

Hofer, TP. Hayward, RA (1996). 'Identifying poor-quality hospitals: can hospital mortality rates detect quality problems for medical diagnoses?' *Medical Care*, 34(8): 737–753.

Iezzoni, LI (2003). *Risk adjustment for measuring health care outcomes, Vol. 3*. Chicago: Health Administration Press.

Institute of Medicine (2007). State of the science of quality improvement research. In: *The state of quality improvement and implementation research: expert views. Workshop summary*. Washington DC: The National Academies Press.

Jette, AM. Smith, KW. McDermott, SM (1996). 'Quality of Medicare-reimbursed home health care.' *Gerontologist*, 36(4): 492–501.

Johnson, ML. Bush, RL. Collins, TC. Lin, PH. Liles, DR. Henderson, WG. Khuri, SR. Petersen, LA (2006). 'Propensity score analysis in observational studies: outcomes after abdominal aortic aneurysm repair.' *American Journal of Surgery*, 192(3): 336–343.

Jones, EE. Harris, VA (1967). 'The attribution of attitudes.' *Journal of Experimental Social Psychology*, 3: 1–24.

Kelley, HH (1967). Attribution theory in social psychology. In: Levine, D (ed.). *Nebraska symposium on motivation and emotion, Vol. 15*. Lincoln: University of Nebraska Press.

Landon, BE. Reschovsky, J. Reed, M. Blumenthal, D (2001). 'Personal, organizational, and market level influences on physicians' practice patterns: results of a national survey of primary care physicians.' *Medical Care*, 39(8): 889–905.

Lash, TL. Fink, AK (2003). 'Semi-automated sensitivity analysis to assess systematic errors in observational data.' *Epidemiology*, 14(4): 451–458.

Leyland, AH. Goldstein, H (2001). *Multilevel modeling of health statistics*. Chichester: John Wiley & Sons.

Lilford, R. Mohammed, MA. Spiegelhalter, D. Thomson, R (2004). 'Use and misuse of process and outcome data in managing performance of acute medical care: avoiding institutional stigma.' *Lancet*, 363(9424): 1147–1154.

Litaker, D. Tomolo, A (2007). 'Association of contextual factors and breast cancer screening: finding new targets to promote early detection.' *Journal of Women's Health*, 16(1): 36–45.

Lochner, KA. Kawachi, I. Brennan, RT. Buka, SL (2003). 'Social capital and neighborhood mortality rates in Chicago.' *Social Science & Medicine*, 56(8): 1797–1805.

Luft, HS (1980). 'The relation between surgical volume and mortality: an exploration of causal factors and alternative models.' *Medical Care*, 18(9): 940–959.

Marshall, M. Campbell, C. Hacker, J. Roland, M (2002). *Quality indicators for general practice*. London: Royal Society of Medicine.

McCain, C (2006). 'Using an FMEA in a service setting.' *Quality Progress*, 39(9): 24–29.

Miller, R West, C (2007). 'The value of electronic health records in community health centers: policy implications.' *Health Affairs*, 26(1): 206–214.

Morton, V. Torgerson, DJ (2005). 'Regression to the mean: treatment effect without the intervention.' *Journal of Evaluation in Clinical Practice*, 11(1): 59–65.

Persell, S. Wright, J. Thompson, J. Kmetik, K. Baker, D (2006). 'Assessing the validity of national quality measures for coronary artery disease using an electronic health record.' *Archives of Internal Medicine*, 166(20): 2272–2277.

Pogach, L. Engelgau, M. Aron, D (2007). 'Measuring progress toward achieving hemoglobin A1c goals in diabetes care: pass/fail or partial credit.' *Journal of the American Medical Association*, 297(5): 520–523.

Pringle, M (2002). 'Reflections on quality issues: quality becomes ever more complex.' *British Journal of General Practice*, 52(Suppl.): 47–48.

Reason, J (2000). 'Human error: models and management.' *British Medical Journal*, 320(7237): 768–770.

Rosen, AK. Reid, R. Broemeling, A-M. Rakovski, CC (2003). 'Applying a risk-adjustment framework to primary care: can we improve on existing measures?' *Annals of Family Medicine*, 1(1): 44–51.

Ross, L (1977). The intuitive psychologist and his shortcomings: distortions in the attribution process. In: Berkowitz, L (ed.). *Advances in experimental social psychology, Vol. 10*. New York: Academic Press.

Rouse, WB (2000). 'Managing complexity: disease control as a complex adaptive system.' *Information-Knowledge-Systems Management*, 2(2): 143–165.

Rouse, WB (2003). 'Engineering complex systems: implications for research in systems engineering. *IEEE Transactions on Systems, Man, and Cybernetics – Part C*, 33(2): 154–156.

Schneeweiss, S. Avorn, J (2005). 'A review of uses of health care utilization databases for epidemiologic research on therapeutics.' *Journal of Clinical Epidemiology*, 58(4): 323–337.

Seneta, E. Chen, JT. (2005). 'Simple stepwise tests of hypotheses and multiple comparisons.' *International Statistical Review*, 73(1): 21–34.

Simon, SR. McCarthy, ML. Kaushal, R. Jenter, CA. Volk, LA. Poon, EG. Yee, KC. Orav, EJ. Williams, DH. Bates, DW (2008). 'Electronic health records: which practices have them, and how are clinicians using them?' *Journal of Evaluation in Clinical Practice*, 14(1): 43–47.

Terris, DD. Litaker, DG (2008). 'Data quality bias: an under-recognized source of misclassification in pay for performance reporting?' *Quality Management in Health Care*, 17(1): 19–26.

Terris, DD. Litaker, DG. Koroukian, SM (2007). 'Health state information derived from secondary databases is affected by multiple sources of bias.' *Journal of Clinical Epidemiology*, 60(7): 734–741.

Tsai, AC. Vortruba, M. Bridges, JFP. Cebul, RD (2006). 'Overcoming bias in estimating the volume-outcome relationship.' *Health Services Research*, 41(1): 252–264.

Weiner, BJ. Shortell, SM. Alexander, J (1997). 'Promoting clinical involvement in hospital quality improvement efforts: the effects of top management, board, and physician leadership.' *Health Services Research*, 32(4): 491–510.

Zacharias, A. Schwann, TA. Riordan, CJ. Durham, SJ. Shah, A. Papadimos, TJ. Engoren, M. Habib, RH (2005). 'Is hospital procedure volume a reliable marker of quality for coronary artery bypass surgery? A comparison of risk and propensity-adjusted operative and midterm outcomes.' *Annals of Thoracic Surgery*, 79(6): 1961–1969.

Zyzanski, SJ. Flocke, SA. Dickinson, LM (2004). 'On the nature of analysis of clustered data.' *Annals of Family Medicine*, 2(3): 199–200.

3.4 Using composite indicators to measure performance in health care

MARIA GODDARD, ROWENA JACOBS

Introduction

Health-care performance is multi-dimensional and not easily captured by a single measure. Aspects of performance such as efficiency, quality, responsiveness, equity, outcomes and accessibility are all legitimate interests for the public and the policy-maker (Institute of Medicine 2001). It is not surprising therefore that there has been an explosion of interest in the generation, publication and interpretation of performance information in the health-care domain across the world, facilitated by the availability of information technology that allows for the capture of large amounts of complex data. This has occurred at all levels – whether individual practitioner, specific health services, health plans of provider organizations or entire health systems. However, the very abundance of such information can obscure users and policy-makers' ability to make overall judgments about relative performance. Complex information presented over many dimensions may be difficult to comprehend and a lack of transparency presents opportunities for poor performance to go undetected. Users faced with multiple and disparate performance information will need to weigh the evidence and make trade-offs between different performance dimensions, thus increasing their processing burden. Some users may base decisions on a single performance dimension simply because it is the most clear. However, this will not necessarily be the most important.

In response to such issues, the use of summary or composite measures has become widespread in health and social policy arenas (Freudenberg 2003; Nardo et al. 2005). Such measures seek to combine disparate indicators of performance into a single score or index which can be used to compare (and sometimes rank) the relative performance of individuals, organizations or systems. This approach is not peculiar to health care; there are examples of the use of composite indicators in many other sectors such as the environment, economy, technology, development, education and safety. It is also common practice to use composite measures to create league tables or rankings.

Composite indicators are in widespread use but their construction presents many methodological challenges. If not treated carefully and transparently these can leave them open to misinterpretation and potential manipulation. The accuracy, reliability and appropriateness of such indices need to be explored if major policy, financial and social decisions hinge on an organizations' performance as measured by composite indicators.

In this chapter we explore the advantages and disadvantages of constructing a composite indicator and describe the methodological choices made at each step in the construction. To illustrate these issues, we also describe some examples of current composite indicators in health care, highlighting good (and bad) practice in their development. We focus mainly on issues that are pertinent to the creation of composite measures rather than performance measurement in general, although of course there is much overlap.

Why use composite indicators to measure performance?

Composite indicators have a high profile in the media and play a potentially important role alongside the publication of individual performance indicators. However, they are not without drawbacks and any decision about the appropriateness of a composite measure will depend on a number of factors and the context in which they are to be used.

One of the main advantages of composite measures is that by focusing on a single measure they can give an overview of performance more readily than a plethora of diverse indicators. A single simple measure captures policy attention more easily and facilitates communication with the public about performance issues, thus enhancing public accountability. Composite measures also allow for the aggregation of a wide range of different types of performance data thereby ensuring that a rounded assessment of performance is presented rather than a focus on a single aspect. Comparison of single scores also means that it is easy to identify organizations that are performing poorly and should be priorities for improvement efforts.

On the other hand, composite indicators may lead to a number of dysfunctional consequences and there are several arguments against their use (Smith 2002). In particular, it is possible that a good composite score may mask serious shortcomings in some parts of a system. Transparency may be enhanced by summarizing performance but when performance is aggregated across a number of dimensions it may be difficult to determine the precise source of failings and therefore the remedial action required. In the health-care sector, data availability is often patchy across different domains and activities and therefore an indicator that is comprehensive in coverage is likely to rely on poor quality data along some dimensions. For example, outcome data are typically less readily available than process data and data on activity undertaken in the community are less accessible than those relating to secondary care. Conversely, unwanted behaviour can be induced by omitting measures for which data are unavailable as people focus only on what is measured.

The creation and publication of composite performance indicators can therefore generate both positive and negative outcomes, depending on the context in which they are used and the incentives they produce. The decision about whether composites are appropriate will always be a matter of judgment. However, where composites are used, the methodological choices made at each stage of construction will influence greatly their accuracy, reliability and appropriateness and have important implications for their impact. These include the choice of indicators; their transformation or standardization; the application of a system of weights; and the formation of the new composite. In the next section we provide some examples of the development and use of composite indicators in the health-care sector in order to illustrate issues arising from their construction and use.

Methodological issues and experience of using composite measures in health care

This section presents some of the methodological challenges that arise at each step of construction of a composite indicator. Where appropriate, these points are illustrated with discussions of composite measures of performance from health-care systems around the world.

Choosing units to assess and organizational objectives to encompass

These choices hinge on decisions about the boundaries of the units to be assessed and what aspects of performance these units will be held responsible for. They also depend on the target audience for the measures and the purpose of compiling the information. Measures of performance can be aggregated at a number of different levels – country, state, region, provider, health plan or physician. In addition, different elements of the health-care sector have overlapping boundaries – activities in one sector influence performance in another (e.g. primary care, secondary care, residential or long-term care and social services). Table 3.4.1 gives some examples of the coverage of composite indicator schemes.

Outside the health-care domain, many composite measures are reported at country level (e.g. environment, economic performance, quality of life). Within health, the WHO composite index of health system performance is probably the best known (WHO 2000). Despite much debate about the methodological detail, the publication of explicit rankings for 191 countries emphasized the potential power of using a single measure of performance to focus attention on important health-care issues. The Health Consumer Powerhouse has produced an annual health-care performance ranking for twenty-nine European countries (with recent addition of Canada) since 2005 (Health Consumer Powerhouse & Frontier Centre for Public Policy 2008).

The United States has produced composite measures of quality of care at state level for Medicare beneficiaries in fifty-two states, focusing on improvement as well as ratings. Jencks et al. (2000 & 2003) found that a state's average rank on the twenty-two indicators was highly stable over time with a correlation of 0.93 between the two periods. The better performing states appeared to be concentrated geographically in the northern and less populated regions (for both periods) but the geographical patterns of relative improvement by state were patchier.

Maclean's, a major mass-circulation magazine, publishes an annual health report that ranks Canadian regions according to their health-care performance. This is based on data published by the Canadian

Table 3.4.1 *Examples of domains included in composite indicators*

Index	Organizations ranked	Domains
Commonwealth Fund National Scorecard*	States (United States)	Access Quality Potentially avoidable use of hospitals Costs of care Healthy lives
ECHCI	EU countries (+ Canada in 2007)	Patient rights/information Waiting times Outcomes Generosity Pharmaceutical coverage
Maclean's magazine	Regions (Canada)	Outcomes Resources Community health Elderly services Prenatal care Efficiencies
World Health Report	Countries (worldwide)	Health outcomes Inequality in health Fairness in financing Responsiveness Inequality in responsiveness
Healthcare Commission annual rating (2007 version)	Hospitals (England) + primary care trusts	Quality of services Use of resources
Healthcare Commission star ratings (prior to 2005)	Hospitals (England)	Key target areas (e.g. waiting times, finance) Clinical focus Staff focus Patient focus

*Gives disaggregated results rather than a composite indicator but produces overall rankings

Institute for Health Information in a series of annual reports and a series of health indicators for the sixty-three largest regions, covering 90% of the population (Canadian Institute for Health Information 2001, 2001a & 2007). In the 2001 report, the composite performance scores ranged from 89.5 in North/West Vancouver, British Columbia to 73.4 in North Bay/Huntsville, Ontario.

Composite measures are created most commonly at provider level, usually a hospital. This focus is understandable because it is easier to see a direct line of accountability between the performance of that organization and the hospital management than (say) from the state, region or country downwards. The United States produces vast amounts of performance information; composite measures of performance have been constructed for hospitals and nursing homes for some time. For example, HealthGrades gives detailed performance information for consumers, providers and health plans (http://www. healthgrades.com). This organization gathers together a wide variety of information (e.g. Medicare inpatient data; range of specialized information provided by states) to provide detailed profile information on hospitals; star ratings (from one to five) for ten clinical areas; and (based on these individual star ratings) an overall ranking of the top fifty best hospitals. America's Best Hospitals guide (www.rti.org/page. cfm?objectid=EDFAA2A9-4725-488E-83AE91A9442C9727)   has operated for over fifteen years and is reported widely in the American press. This provider-level system ranks hospitals in sixteen specialties and by their overall performance. Hospitals that score at or near the top for a minimum of six specialties are classified as super elite.

In England, hospital trusts have been the focus of composite ratings for some time – the star ratings. A composite index score for each NHS organization places them in one of four categories: from three stars (highest levels of performance) to zero stars (poorest levels of performance). At the outset in 2001 only acute trusts were included (Department of Health 2001); specialist trusts, ambulance trusts and indicative ratings for mental health trusts were added later (Department of Health 2002). By 2003, all NHS providers were covered, including local purchasers of health care (primary care trusts). Further indicators have been published every year since but the nature of the performance assessment has altered over time and now there is less emphasis on summary measures (Healthcare Commission 2004, 2005 & 2007).

There are also composite measures for specialties such as paediatrics, cardiac surgery, long-term care and chronic conditions. At physician level, many different incentive schemes are based on linking income with performance but not all use a single composite score to measure performance. In New York, a demonstration project linked physician payment to performance on a composite compiled from process and outcome data for diabetes care (Beaulieu & Horrigan 2005).

As illustrated above, much of the measurement activity at national level has taken place in the acute hospital setting; even the star ratings for English primary care trusts were dominated by health-care activity in the secondary sector. There have been examples of composite indicators at primary-care level e.g. the Summary Quality Index (SQUID) in England (Nietert et al. 2007). These may be useful locally but tend not to have a national profile.

Choosing the indicators

This is probably one of the most important steps. Careful judgment is required as effort will be focused on the included indicators, potentially at the expense of achievement on those excluded.

Data availability

In practice, many composites are often opportunistic and incomplete (measuring aspects of performance captured in existing data) or are based on highly questionable sources of data. Either weakness can seriously damage the credibility of the composite (Smith 2002). The choice of indicators is most often constrained by data availability and thus may give an unbalanced picture of health services. The excluded indicators may be equally (or more) important but simply more difficult to measure.

The higher the level at which composites are created and the broader their scope the greater the issues of data availability and lack of comparability. The WHO composite index of health system performance was produced for 191 countries and sought to be comprehensive in coverage. It measured five domains: (i) overall health outcomes; (ii) inequality in health; (iii) fairness of financing; (iv) overall health system responsiveness; and (v) inequality in health system responsiveness. Much of the debate about the index has focused on appropriateness of the measures used to capture these domains and the source and robustness of the data (e.g. Almeida et al. 2001; Appleby & Street 2001; Navarro 2002; Nord 2002; Smith 2002; Williams 2001).

The Euro-Canada Health Consumer Index (ECHCI) aims to cover issues of relevance to the consumer and therefore focuses on five areas: (i) patient rights/information; (ii) waiting times; (iii) outcomes; (iv) generosity (activity rates); and (v) pharmaceuticals (e.g. access to new drugs, subsidies). A total of twenty-seven indicators were included in their most recent index but it was noted that the original, larger set had been pared down due to lack of data (Health Consumer Powerhouse & Frontier Centre for Public Policy 2008). It is clear that there will be a trade-off between an ambitious aim of deriving a composite measure, capturing complex and comprehensive health performance dimensions for a wide range of countries, and the practical issues of gathering good data on such dimensions.

The availability of data explains partly why most performance measures focus on hospital rather than community services. However, even within a sector there are many choices about the areas to be covered. For example, there has been criticism of the Canadian ratings of regions for excluding psychiatric care and the English star ratings for relying on process measures and focusing solely on indicators for which there are national targets. Also, many systems rely on indicators in only a few key disease areas. For example, the American state-level indicators for Medicare beneficiaries (Jencks et al. 2000 & 2003) cover six clinical areas: (i) acute myocardial infarction (six indicators); (ii) heart failure (two); (iii) stroke (three); (iv) pneumonia (seven); (v) breast cancer (one); and (vi) diabetes (three). The choice of indicators tends to over-represent inpatient and preventive services and under-represent ambulatory care and interventional procedures. However, an explicit rationale informed the selection of clinical areas according to the following criteria:

- disease is a major source of morbidity or mortality
- certain processes of care are known to improve outcomes
- measurement of these processes is feasible
- offers substantial scope for improvement in performance
- managerial intervention can potentially improve performance.

Lack of agreement about the data definitions and lack of consistency in interpreting the measures can also lead to partial representation of performance. The Canadian regional-level composites have been criticized on this basis but it has been noted that the number of indicators has expanded over time and new data have been incorporated as they become available (e.g. stroke survival in the latest round). In addition, this has prompted the quest for improvements in data quality. For example, only a handful of regions were able to provide waiting time information because of variations in definitions and collection methods. This will be addressed in future. The Canadian Institute for Health Information (http://secure.cihi.ca/cihiweb/dispPage.jsp?cw_page=home_e) notes that no comparable data were available for the public and providers five years ago so the rankings represent significant progress, despite the gaps in coverage. Improvements in data quality and availability may be a positive side-effect of attempts to create such indicators.

Data availability aside, the choice of indicators may reflect political priorities for performance. For example, the early stages of the English star ratings were dominated by waiting times and financial issues. Other indicators were included but given less weight in the final performance rating.

Type of indicators

There has been much debate about the pros and cons of different types of performance indicators in health care, particularly process and outcome measures (see Chapter 5.5). A focus on outcomes directs attention towards the patient (rather than the services provided by the organization). However, there can seldom be any confidence that outcome measures such as current health status are indicators of current health system performance. For example, it is clearly impractical to wait for some health outcomes (that may take years to emerge) before making a judgment on performance. Furthermore, the collection of outcome data may impose high costs on the health system. Finally, there are issues around attribution and the extent to which health status can be attributed solely to the health-care system (see Chapter 3.3). In such circumstances, it becomes necessary to rely on measures of health system process rather than health status outcome.

Process measures can be more meaningful for some users of performance ratings. For example, the SQUID composite measure of quality of care in primary care in England was created by combining thirty-six process and outcome measures (Nietert et al. 2007). More than one hundred ambulatory-care practices receive quarterly data on the patient level (proportion of recommended care received) and practice level SQUIDs (average proportion of recommended care received by the practice's patients). Measures of recommended care relate to indicators such as the proportion of the target population receiving specific interventions or tests (e.g. beta blockers, screening tests, counselling). The authors note that, unlike many composite measures, their SQUID score has a meaningful clinical interpretation which probably accounts for its acceptability to doctors.

Patients are becoming increasingly vocal in demanding that health care should be responsive to concerns over and above the health outcomes that result from treatments. This concern with the patient experience covers issues as diverse as promptness, autonomy, empowerment, privacy and choice (see Chapter 2.5). Such performance measures may be particularly appropriate when there are large variations in the responsiveness of organizations, as indicated by hospital waiting times in many publicly funded health systems. The WHO ratings of health-care systems included a measure of responsiveness to citizens as this was thought to be an important element in the health-care experience and one which might vary considerably between systems. The ECHCI is aimed at consumers and therefore many of the indicators relate to process issues of relevance to their audience, such as waiting times and the availability of a wide range of information via different media. The English performance ratings now include measures of patient satisfaction taken from annual surveys. In some circumstances (e.g. management of chronic diseases) process measures will be far more relevant to patients than outcome measures (Crombie & Davies 1998).

Collinearity between indicators
The final issue relating to the choice of indicator concerns the potential for performance indicators that measure similar aspects of performance to be highly correlated with each other. The concern is that the inclusion of variables which are highly collinear will effectively introduce some sort of double counting. It has therefore been argued that a chosen set of indicators should be reduced by selecting between indicators with high correlations. This may be desirable for reasons such as parsimony and transparency.

Multivariate statistical methods are available to investigate relationships between the indicators within a composite. Principal components analysis (PCA) and factor analysis (FA) may be used to extract statistical correlations between indicators to enable identification of a core group of indicators that statistically best represent the remaining excluded indicators (Joint Research Centre 2002). Factor analysis of individual measures used in two major performance schemes in the USA (HEDIS, CAHPS®) have frequently illustrated that it is feasible to achieve parsimony by aggregating indicators into one or a small number of composites. For example, for CAHPS, six out of thirty-three factors provided the best description of variation at patient level and three out of thirty-three explained much of the variation at hospital level (O'Malley et al. 2005). For HEDIS, a single composite explained 38% of the variation at hospital level and the use of three composites improved this to 60% (Lied et al. 2002). Similar analysis using a combination of all indicators in HEDIS and CAHPS illustrated that they could be separated into a four-factor solution that explained 64% of the variation in the measures (Zaslavsky et al. 2002). Other composite measures have been created from variables found to be generally uncorrelated with each other e.g. quality in cardiac surgery (O'Brien et al. 2007).

If statistical techniques are used to choose the variables for inclusion, it is likely that highly collinear variables will be excluded through model specification tests for multicollinearity. The choice of one variable over an alternative highly collinear variable may not alter rankings greatly but may affect the judgments on a small number of units, with extraordinary performance in either of those dimensions. It may therefore be subject to dispute and challenge.

Combining indicators to create a composite

The next stage is to aggregate the chosen indicators that are likely to be measured in different units and on different scales. Aggregation needs to be undertaken in a consistent manner in order to ensure that the composite measure produced is easily understood and has the intended incentive effects. The combination of the measurement scale used for individual indicators, and the weights applied to add them together, can affect the interpretation of changes in the composite indicator. The aim is to be transparent about how much improvement is required in one constituent indicator to compensate for deterioration in another.

Three key steps in aggregation are described below: (i) transformation of individual indicators; (ii) weighting; and (iii) application of decision rules.

Transformation of individual indicators

Transformation is less important if it is possible to specify a weight that indicates the relative value to the composite of an extra unit of attainment in that dimension at *all* levels of attainment. However, most indicators that make up a composite will be non-linear – an x-point change of the variable on one part of the scale will have a completely different effect on assessed performance than an x-point change on another. This requires them to be transformed in some way to enable aggregation into a composite. Other reasons for transformation include the need to allow for extreme values (outliers) which may otherwise skew the composite and the desire to add together indicators measured in different units.

A number of methods are available for transforming the underlying indicators including ranking, normalizing, re-scaling, generating various types of ratio variables, logarithmic transformation or transforming variables to a categorical scale. All of these can impact on the final outcome of the composite indicator. Table 3.4.2 shows some examples of the impact of choice of transformation method using hypothetical data for ten organizations. The methods have been surveyed elsewhere (Nardo et al. 2005) but not one model fits every set of circumstances – each is associated with pros and cons.

It is useful to explore how alternative measures for standardization impact on final performance rankings. For example, Lun et al. (2006) show that the use of Z scores (use the mean and standard deviation to adjust raw scores) rather than raw scores, dramatically changes the ranking of quality of life for 103 Italian provinces, with some moving 88 places in the ranking. This method gives greater weight to variables with extreme outliers. The use of Min-Max methods (use the differences between minimum and maximum scores) gives less weight to outliers but also changes rankings substantially. Similarly, Cherchye

Table 3.4.2 *Examples of impact of different transformation methods*

Unit	Raw data	Ranking	Standard-izing	Rescaling (best = 100, worst = 0)	Difference from mean (mean = 100)	Difference from leader (best = 100)	Threshold above and below mean (threshold = 20%)	Logarithmic	Categorical scale (percentiles = 0.75, 0.5 and 0.25)
Unit 1	2.85	1	2.01	100.00	174	100.00	1.37	0.45	3
Unit 2	2.08	2	1.09	71.01	94	71.93	0.65	0.31	3
Unit 3	1.58	3	0.54	53.99	47	55.44	0.22	0.20	3
Unit 4	1.35	4	0.28	45.65	24	47.37	0.02	0.13	2
Unit 5	1.03	5	-0.09	34.06	-8	36.14	-0.27	0.01	2
Unit 6	0.86	6	-0.29	27.90	-25	30.18	-0.43	-0.07	1
Unit 7	0.59	7	-0.60	18.12	-52	20.70	-0.67	-0.23	1
Unit 8	0.43	8	-0.79	12.32	-68	15.09	-0.81	-0.37	0
Unit 9	0.28	9	-0.96	6.88	-83	9.82	-0.95	-0.55	0
Unit 10	0.09	10	-1.18	0.00	-102	3.16	-1.12	-1.05	0

Unweighted average = 1.11
Standard deviation = 0.86

et al. (2007) illustrate the hypothetical impact of varying methods of normalization for country rankings and also question the wisdom of making statements about the resulting normalized scores e.g. that the global performance of organization/country X is 5% better than that of organization/country Y.

The choice of an appropriate method of transformation is therefore dependent on both the nature of the indicators and the composite's desired incentive effects on performance. For instance, it may be appropriate to allow extreme values on some indicators to influence overall performance on the composite when the intention is to reward exceptional behaviour on a few indicators, rather than average performance on all.

Weighting

In order to achieve a specific final score on the composite measure, the efforts required to improve performance on a sub-indicator will depend on the weight applied to it. The incentive effects of weighting are therefore potentially very powerful – the ranking of a particular organization can change dramatically if an indicator on which the organization excels or fails is given more weight. A weight indicates the relative opportunity cost of achieving each of the underlying indicators; it can be designed to equalize this across all indicators or to put more emphasis on some at the expense of others. This represents a trade-off in the efforts to achieve good performance on each indicator.

Differential weights are chosen for a variety of reasons although the usual interpretation is to reflect the importance of the underlying indicators (Cherchye et al. 2007). However, there should be consideration of the interaction between the way in which the indicators have been transformed (see above) and aggregated and the weights subsequently applied. In particular, in most methods of aggregation weights represent the trade-off between indicators. This suggests that it is acceptable for good performance in one domain to be offset by poor performance in another. However, if weights are meant to reflect relative importance then alternative methods of aggregation that do not allow for such compensatory behaviour must be used.

The impact of choices has been illustrated using health performance data from England where varying weights have been shown to have a

Table 3.4.3 *Examples of methods to determine weights*

Statistical approaches	Factor analysis
	Principal components analysis
	Data envelopment analysis
	Benefit of the doubt
Participatory approaches	Budget allocation
	Analytic hierarchy process
	Conjoint analysis
	Opinion polls and surveys

major effect on rankings (Jacobs et al. 2005). Also, it is observed that a region such as Edmonton can rate near the bottom of the rankings for low birth weight infants but still emerge at the top of the overall ranking within their group due to the combined impact of the complex set of weights used in the Canadian system (Page & Cramer 2001). Weights may also be chosen to reflect other characteristics of the indicators – for instance, those which have more reliable underlying data may be given greater weight in the final indicator. However, this may reinforce the dependence on easily measured and available data within performance results (Freudenberg 2003; Nardo et al. 2005).

Having decided on the purpose of the weighting system, the weights have to be derived. This can be achieved by using either a range of statistical techniques or participatory techniques that generally employ the judgment of individuals. Some of the relevant techniques for determining weights are listed in Table 3.4.3. The use of participatory methods involves fundamental consideration of the preferences used in the elicitation of those weights – whether those of policy-makers, providers, purchasers, patients or the public. The weights used will usually reflect a single set of preferences but the preferences of policy-makers, individual providers and the broader public are likely to vary.

Participatory techniques include direct interviews, surveys and public opinion polls. More advanced techniques enable the analyst to elicit trade-offs between several attributes or performance dimensions. These include the analytic hierarchy process (AHP) in which opinions are systematically extracted by a pair-wise comparison between different dimensions or attributes of performance (Saaty 1987). Conjoint analysis also has been used widely in the health-care context (Ryan &

Farrar 2000). This attempts to elicit values and trade-offs between the various attributes of a good service or, in this context, aspects of performance. Both approaches are able to deal with multiple attributes, particularly helpful in the context of health where there is likely to be interest in a wide range of dimensions of performance.

Three different approaches to eliciting preferences are illustrated by a British experiment organized by a television company; the WHO country performance rankings; and America's Best Hospitals in the United States. In 2000, a polling organization surveyed 2000 people across England, Scotland and Wales to obtain their preferences for selected aspects of health authority performance (Appleby & Mulligan 2000). Three methods were used to elicit preferences: (i) ranking from most to least desired indicator; (ii) budget-pie –respondents were asked to allocate a 'budget' of sixty chips between six performance indicators; and (iii) conjoint analysis. This offered the advantage of multi-attribute approaches as well as considering simpler trade-off methods. The authors spent considerable efforts to ensure that their weighting system reflected variations in views obtained from the different methods.

In contrast, the weighting system underlying much of the WHO rankings depended upon expert opinion. Dimensions of responsiveness were scored by around 2000 key informants from 35 countries who answered questions about their own countries and were then asked to score responsiveness as a whole. Another group of 1000 people ranked the 7 aspects of responsiveness in order of importance in a web-based exercise; weights were assigned based on the rankings. Mean scores on each aspect were multiplied by weights and summed to give an overall responsiveness score. The final dimension (equity in responsiveness) was calculated by asking informants to make judgments about the subgroups that they thought were treated with less responsiveness. Scores were assigned to subgroups based on the number of times that they were mentioned by country informants, multiplied by that group's share in the population. The products were summed and transformed to give an overall score. Finally, the individual scores on five dimensions of performance (including the responsiveness measure discussed above) were aggregated to create an overall attainment score. Individual measures were transformed to a 0–100 scale and summed using weights of either 0.25 or 0.125, based on the views of about 1000 people from 123 countries, half of whom were WHO staff. There has been widespread debate about the pros and cons of the approaches used (e.g. Almeida et al. 2001; Williams 2001).

America's Best Hospitals in the United States is another example of the use of expert opinion. This is based on survey responses and uses reputation as one of three dimensions of the composite indicator. A random sample of specialists (in each specialty) is asked to list the five best hospitals for 'difficult' cases in their specialty. This is undertaken without reference to geography or costs.

The use of statistical or empirical methods (rather than preferences) to create weights might be expected to raise fewer issues but the methodological challenges are still substantial (e.g. Lun et al. 2006). If it is possible to demonstrate that alternative approaches have little impact then this will help to build confidence in the results. For example, Zaslavasky et al. (2002) used three alternative statistical approaches to create weights for health performance and found similar final results (Mullen & Spurgeon 2000).

An entirely different approach uses data envelopment analysis (DEA) to create performance ratings without the need to incorporate fixed weighting systems. This is sometimes called the benefit of the doubt approach in the context of performance ratings. Essentially, this allows the use of flexible weights that vary across domains and between the organizations being assessed (Cherchye et al. 2007). For example, the weights assigned to different dimensions of performance for a country are derived from the country data. The core idea is that the country's good relative performance on a particular sub-indicator signals that the indicator has policy importance in that country and hence should be assigned a higher weight than in another country where relative performance on that dimension is weak. It is not possible to document all the pros and cons of such an approach (see Cherchye et al. for details) but one main drawback from a policy perspective is that the results may be difficult to reconcile with general views on the relative importance of different aspects of performance. For example, an organization may be excellent at a dimension of performance that is considered rather marginal in the overall healthcare context and it may seem inappropriate if their final composite score is influenced heavily by their performance along that dimension. This can be addressed to some extent through the use of restrictions – limiting the share of the total composite result that can be gained from specific sub-indicators. This can be achieved in several ways (depending on the strength of consensus about the importance of different indicators) and allows a great deal of flexibility in assigning weights using the revealed performance of organizations. This approach is probably of most value where the aim is to combine very disparate indicators at a high (e.g. country) level, where relative performance will be affected heavily by a wide range of factors.

In conclusion, there appears to be little consensus about the preferred technique for participatory methods (Dolan et al. 1996) and it is likely that the different methods will lead to the emergence of different preference sets. These examples illustrate the difficulties in eliciting preferences and devising weights and serve as reminders that a composite cannot be presented as 'objective' (Smith 2002). The choices about who and how to ask depend in part on the nature of the performance domains to be captured. Where responses require a great deal of technical or background knowledge it is legitimate to target experts, although the definition of expert may be controversial. For example, it could be argued that WHO staff may not necessarily have more knowledge than ordinary members of the public in some areas of questioning. In a complex area such as health care, multi-attribute approaches may be preferable to more simplistic methods. The former are more expensive to organize and are feasible only where a fairly limited set of domains is considered, otherwise the comparisons become too unwieldy. In all cases, comparisons between countries present particular challenges for ensuring consistency in elicitation methods. Statistical methods offer an alternative and may be especially valuable where high-level performance across countries is being considered. However, these can be difficult to explain and are less intuitive for the public and policy-makers than participatory approaches.

Application of decision rules

Rather than attaching explicit weights to transformed indicators, a set of decision rules can be applied to produce a composite indicator. Such rules reflect views on the importance of achieving certain standards. They set the boundaries within which performance scores will be allocated (e.g. defining what constitutes a good or poor score on an indicator); or they may disallow a good performance score if an organization fails to meet a particular target on a single indicator.

The rules are often applied sequentially and implicitly introduce a set of weights.

One example of this was the construction of the scorecard for acute hospitals in the star ratings system in England. This applied a complicated algorithm with a set of sequential decision rules to determine the ultimate star rating (composite indicator). The star ratings for trusts comprised four areas: (i) key government targets; (ii) clinical focus; (iii) patient focus; and (iv) capacity and capability. The key government targets were the most significant factors in determining overall performance ratings. Performance was assessed in terms of whether the target had been achieved; whether there was some degree of under-achievement; or whether the target was significantly underachieved (threshold type variables). The methodology broadly entailed transforming the underlying key targets and performance indicators into categorical variables of either three or five categories. The performance indicators in the patient, clinical, and capacity and capability focus areas were categorized into one of five performance bands (from five points for the best performance to one for the worst). The thresholds for deciding the cut-offs were not necessarily the same for each variable and individual band scores were combined to produce an overall score per area. All indicators were weighted equally within their scorecard area to ensure that each scorecard area carried the same weight, despite differing numbers of indicators. A complex six-step process imposed a sequential set of decisions on achievement on the various key variables to determine the final star rating. Evidence suggests that the application of such rules and subtle changes to their application can be hugely influential in the final outcome of the composite measure – small changes in decision rules can move hospitals from one end of the performance league table to the other (Jacobs et al. 2005). Reeves et al's (2007) comparison of five different methods of combining clinical quality indicators at primary-care provider level shows that the rules applied to the scoring of sub-indicators can change rankings dramatically. The pros and cons of using rules that set thresholds rather than dichotomous measures have also been analysed (Aron et al. 2007).

O'Brien et al. (2007) illustrate the impact of different approaches to aggregation on a composite score of provider ratings for quality in cardiac surgery. Their analysis investigated a wide set of options for combining eleven indicators of quality within and across four domains of care. They used data from over 133 000 procedures to test out methods such as scoring, scaling, opportunity-based approaches, latent variable models and all-or-nothing rules. In contrast to the analysis of the English data reported above, they concluded that 'inferences about a provider's quality were robust and largely insensitive to choice of methodology' (O'Brien et al. 2007, p. S21). However, they rejected some approaches (e.g. use of literature or expert views to assign importance weights to measures) and their range of measures was probably less diverse. O'Brien et al. focused on narrow definitions of quality for one specific type of care while the English system covered financial, clinical quality, staffing and other dimensions at the whole hospital level.

Sometimes the application of rules can produce a lack of transparency but there are often good reasons for such an approach. In particular, they can ensure that certain minimum requirements are met. For instance, O'Brien et al's (2007) analysis uses an all-or-nothing rule for some dimensions of quality – hospitals that do not *fully* meet the stated standard receive a zero score on that dimension with no credit for partial compliance (e.g. 100% of patients must receive the stated quality of care; 100% of patients must avoid complications). These approaches are common when it is felt appropriate to set a high benchmark on a particular domain of performance. Decision rules to attain minimum standards may be particularly pertinent for a hospital accreditation process. They are also useful stepping stones in performance reward systems where a baseline level of reward is contingent on attaining minimum standards in key areas and less stringent requirements are placed on other dimensions.

Interpretation and use of composite indicators

A composite indicator derived from a number of sub-indicators has the potential drawback that the indicators themselves will be subject to some degree of uncertainty. If they are combined into one composite without due regard for the underlying distribution of the variables their results may lack robustness. There are various methods for investigating the nature of the sub-indicators. Much research has been undertaken to look at the features of available sub-indicator data in terms of their appropriateness for incorporation into a composite performance measure – for example, looking at the extent of missing data, variability in performance, coverage of the relevant patient population, predictive properties of a process indicator etc. This has been undertaken in many different contexts e.g. paediatrics (Bethell et al. 2004) and nursing-home care (Berg et al. 2002). A more detailed approach attempts to separate out random fluctuations in the underlying variables from those attributable to actual differences in performance and to create confidence intervals around the resulting scores. Jacobs et al. (2005) explored this using English data and employing Monte Carlo simulation methods in order to demonstrate that there was a small group of providers who could – with confidence – be said to be performing better or worse than others but that such statements were less feasible for many in the middle ranks. Similarly, the authors of an analysis of Italian quality of life data were able to demonstrate some coarse groups of differentially performing provinces (Lun et al. 2006).

Another problem arises in interpretation – composite scores often feed into performance rankings and will produce conflicting results if slightly different composites are used. As illustrated earlier, small changes in methods can affect the resulting composites, even if similar data are used. Different data sources can cause even more confusion. This may be similar to the conflicting results that arise on individual indicators over a range of performance measures (when there are large variations in organizational rankings) but the conflicts are far more visible and stark and more likely to capture public interest. For example, several schemes in the United States receive a great deal of consumer attention but are constructed in slightly different ways. HealthGrade's composite scores for clinical areas are used to produce an overall ranking of the top fifty best hospitals. America's Best Hospitals ranks hospitals in sixteen specialties and by overall performance (US News & World Report 2007). Ratings are based on three areas: (i) reputation; (ii) mortality; and (iii) range of factors such as accreditation scores, inputs, availability of technology. The three elements are combined with equal weights and hospitals are ranked within each specialty. Hospitals that score at or near the top of the rank for a minimum of six specialties are classified as super elite. The Centers for Medicare and Medicaid Services (CMS) launched Hospital Compare in 2005 in order to provide patients with information on hospital quality, rather than targeting providers or regulators (www.cahps.ahrq.gov/content/products/HOSP/PROD_HOSP_Intro.asp). Data from 4000 hospitals are used to compile quality indicators.

Results from America's Best Hospitals and Hospital Compare have been compared in order to explore the consistency between rankings (Halasyamani & Davis 2007). Hospital Compare does not produce rankings using composite scores but its core performance measures were used to examine quality in three areas: acute myocardial infarction, congestive heart failure and community-acquired pneumonia. The scores were combined with equal weights to produce rankings of the hospitals. The properties of the indicators within each group were examined for statistical robustness and Hospital Compare scores were calculated for the hospitals included in America's Best Hospitals' rankings – for heart and heart surgery; respiratory disorders; and overall quality (roll of honour hospitals). The authors found that the separate measures for the three clinical areas had good internal consistency but there was little agreement between the Hospital Compare scores and America's Best Hospitals' ranks. Indeed, several of the 'best' hospitals scored below the national median in the disease area scores. There are reasonable explanations for some of the disparities – for instance, America's Best Hospitals relies heavily on mortality rates and on physicians' perceptions of reputation; Hospital Compare looks at delivery of disease-specific evidence-based practices. However, the analysis illustrates the difficulties of relying on a composite measure and ranking without adequate reflection on the nature of the underlying indicators.

Similarly, analysis of the HealthGrades rankings of hospitals has shown that these produce groups of hospitals that differ in the quality of care but do not differentiate well between any two hospitals' individual mortality rates. The authors claim that hospital performance is thus seriously misrepresented to the public (Krumholz et al. 2002). Similar results have been found by others (Werner & Bradlow 2006). Analysis of the rankings of cardiac hospitals produced by a national newspaper in the United States concluded that many of the newspaper's top-fifty hospitals were indeed performing significantly better than their peers but some were failing to provide evidence-based best practice. Also, some lesser-rated hospitals were in fact routinely providing cardiac care that accorded with national guidelines (Williams et al. 2006). It is debatable whether the public can be expected to appreciate the differences in scope and methodology and draw appropriate conclusions.

When incentives are attached to performance results, their accurate interpretation and robustness becomes even more vital. In the early days of the English star ratings much discontent was voiced at their use as a means of rewarding and penalizing managers – hospitals that obtained a three star rating for a consecutive number of years could apply for foundation status which confers significant financial and managerial decision-making freedoms and autonomy from central involvement (Cutler 2002; Kmietowicz 2003; Miller 2002; Snelling 2003). However, star ratings varied from year to year; in some extreme cases hospitals fell from three stars to zero stars within one year. These shifts seldom reflected dramatic changes in overall performance and usually were due to the application of varying decision rules that blocked a high overall score if hospitals fell below a minimum standard in one indicator. The Healthcare Commission subsequently broadened performance assessment in order to focus less on a composite score and more on a whole range of performance indicators (Healthcare Commission 2007).

The United States has been at the forefront of attaching financial incentives to performance ratings in health care. In July 2003, Premier (a nationwide organization of not-for-profit hospitals) and the CMS launched the Hospital Quality Incentive Demonstration Project (HQID) (Premier 2005; Centers for Medicare and Medicaid Services 2005) – the pay-for-performance scheme. CMS rewards participating hospitals that achieve superior performance by increasing their payment for Medicare patients. The project covers five clinical areas and hospital performance for each is aggregated into a composite score to establish baseline performance. Each composite consists of a process score (twenty-seven indicators) and outcome score component (seven indicators) weighted proportionally to the number of each type of indicator in the category. The composite *process* score in each category is created by summing the numerator and denominator values for each indicator and then dividing the totals. The composite *outcome* score in each category is created by generating a survival index of actual divided by expected survival rate. Each is then multiplied by the component weighting factor. The composite score is used to identify the hospitals eligible for incentive payments. Those in the top decile of quality for a given clinical area receive a 2% bonus of their Medicare payments for the given condition; hospitals in the second decile receive a 1% bonus. Composite quality scores are calculated annually. In year three, payments are adjusted for those hospitals that do not achieve performance improvements above baseline.

There has been much discussion about the impact of pay for performance. This is difficult to evaluate given the plethora of published quality ratings which may go some way towards encouraging performance improvement, even in the absence of financial incentives. A recent evaluation of composite measures compared public reporting of performance alone (through Hospital Compare ratings) and the pay-for-performance scheme and was able to make more relevant comparisons by careful matching of participating and excluded hospitals. This indicated that the incremental effect of financial incentives attached to the composite measures was between 2.6% and 4.1% (Lindenauer et al. 2007).

Conclusions

The use of composite measures of performance is common in many countries and sectors. Many of the technical and methodological issues associated with the construction of composites are similar to those faced in the general field of performance measurement and are not unique to the context of composite measures. However, in this chapter we have focused on some of the key issues that are particularly pertinent when attempting to combine indicators – mainly issues related to the choice of sub-indicators; the nature of their transformation; weighting schemes and decision rules; and the interpretation and use of composite scores and rankings. We have demonstrated that choices are made at each stage of their construction, often based on practical considerations such as data availability. These may appear largely technical or of minor significance but in fact can have a fundamental impact on the final performance results. This may call into question the utility of composite scores but it is hoped that the publication of composite measures can also lead to greater attention to issues of data quality and comparability and a search for a more satisfactory methodology.

Some recent moves have aimed to reduce reliance on composites alone. For example, in England the Healthcare Commission incorporated the overall ratings for providers (now designated as 'excellent', 'poor' etc) into a broader assessment process which contains a plethora of information (Healthcare Commission 2007). Dr Foster Intelligence (an independent organization set up to publish performance data) recently decided not to publish best-hospital rankings but to present a limited number of league tables based on single measures and selective reporting of other dimensions of performance (Dr Foster Intelligence 2007). In the United States, the Commonwealth Fund National Scorecard ranks states' overall performance across five dimensions but this is published alongside the detailed results and rankings disaggregated for all thirty-two indicators (Commonwealth Fund 2007).

An array of performance data can offer some advantages but we argue that composite scores play an important role in helping to focus attention on key aspects of performance in a way that the public can understand easily. They are therefore an important means of promoting accountability and providing the public with useful information about physicians, provider organizations and their overall health-care systems. Composite scores allow the best performers to be recognized easily and indicate those that need to improve. They can offer some flexibility at a local level if there is scope for managers to improve in their own priority performance domains and to make efforts where they will secure the most overall gain in performance.

Our main recommendation for policy-makers is to make methodological decisions explicit and at each stage to undertake detailed exploration of the nature of the underlying indicators and the final scores' sensitivity to the decisions to be made. Misleading results may result from underestimating the impact of what appear to be just technical decisions. The conceptual limits of composite indicators should be borne in mind and published with explanations of the choice of indicators, the transformation method and the weighting structure. Consideration should also be given to demonstrating the confidence intervals surrounding composite scores although it is a challenge to do this in a user-friendly way. Publication of the disaggregated data that underpin the composite or publication of additional supplementary data alongside the composite results may be a useful compromise as long as this does not obscure entirely the purpose of providing a concise summary of performance. Explanations of the limits of the composite may help interpretation and transparency by clarifying what policy objectives are being maximized. Composite measures are amenable to being linked with incentive mechanisms for good performance but powerful financial and other incentives should not be used unless there is confidence in the way in which the composites have been derived.

The creation of league tables and rankings is often one of the main purposes behind the construction of composite indicators as they facilitate easy comparisons. Such tables enjoy a high profile in the popular press and make very attractive headlines, especially when targeting the 'worst' performers. There is a danger that health-care organizations can be damaged by premature or inaccurate publication of such information without adequate accompanying health warnings. However, as long as there is open discussion of the processes by which they are derived and some careful interpretation then publication in this format may be an important first step in revealing important performance variations which might otherwise go undetected, unreported and unaddressed.

References

Almeida, C. Braveman, P. Gold, MR. Szwarcwald, CL. Ribeiro, JM. Miglionico, A. Millar, JS. Porto, S. Costa, NR. Rubio, VO. Segall, M. Starfield, B. Travessos, C. Uga, A. Valente, J. Viacava, F (2001). 'Methodological concerns and recommendations on policy consequences of *The world health report 2000.*' *Lancet*, 357(9269): 1692–1697.

Appleby, J. Mulligan, J (2000). *How well is the NHS performing? A composite performance indicator based on public consultation.* London: King's Fund.

Appleby, J. Street, A (2001). 'Health system goals: life, death and … football.' *Journal of Health Services Research*, 6(4): 220–225.

Aron, D. Rajan, M. Pogach, L (2007). 'Summary measures of quality of diabetes care: comparison of continuous weighted performance measurement and dichotomous thresholds.' *International Journal for Quality in Health Care*, 19(1): 29–36.

Beaulieu, N. Horrigan, D (2005). 'Putting smart money to work for quality improvement.' *Health Services Research*, 40(5 Pt. 1): 1318–1334.

Berg, K. Mor, V. Morris, J. Murphy, K. Moore, T. Harris, Y (2002). 'Identification and evaluation of existing nursing home quality indicators.' *Health Care Financing Review*, 23(4): 19–36.

Bethell, C. Peck Reuland, C. Halfon, N. Edward, L (2004). 'Measuring the quality of preventive and developmental services for young children.' *Paediatrics*, 113(Suppl. 6): 1973–1983.

Centers for Medicare and Medicaid Services (2005). *Medicare 'pay for performance (P4P)' initiatives.* Baltimore, MD: Centres for Medicare and Medicaid Services (http://www.cms.hhs.gov/apps/media/press/release.asp?counter=1343).

Cherchye, L. Moesen, W. Rogge, N. Van Puyenbroeck, T (2007). 'An introduction to 'benefit of the doubt' composite indicators.' *Social Indicators Research,* 82(1): 111–145.

CIHI (2001). *Health care in Canada 2001: a second annual report.* Ottawa: Canadian Institute for Health Information.

CIHI (2001a). *Health indicators 2001.* Ottawa: Canadian Institute for Health Information.

CIHI (2007). *Health indicators 2007.* Ottawa: Canadian Institute for Health Information.

Commonwealth Fund Commission on a High Performance Health System (2007). *Aiming higher: results from a state scorecard on health system performance.* New York: The Commonwealth Fund.

Crombie, I. Davies, HTO (1998). 'Beyond health outcomes: the advantages of measuring process.' *Journal of Evaluation in Clinical Practice,* 4(1): 31–38.

Cutler, T (2002). 'Star or black hole?' *Community Care,* 30 May: 40–41.

Department of Health (2001). *NHS performance ratings: acute trusts 2000/01.* London: Department of Health (http://www.dh.gov.uk/en/Publicationsandstatistics/Publications/PublicationsPolicyAndGuidance/DH_4003181).

Department of Health (2002). *NHS performance ratings and indicators: acute trusts, specialist trusts, ambulance trusts, mental health trusts 2001/02.* London: Department of Health (http://www.dh.gov.uk/en/Publicationsandstatistics/Publications/PublicationsPolicyAndGuidance/DH_4002706).

Dolan, P. Gudex, C. Kind, P. Williams, A (1996). 'Valuing health states: a comparison of methods.' *Journal of Health Economics,* 15(2): 209–231.

Dr Foster Intelligence (2007) [web site]. *How healthy is your hospital?* London: Dr Foster Intelligence (http://www.drfosterintelligence.co.uk/library/reports/hospitalGuide2007.pdf).

Freudenberg, M (2003). *Composite indicators of country performance: a critical assessment.* Paris: Organisation for Economic Co-operation and Development (STI Working paper DSTI/DOC 2003/16).

Halasyamani, L. Davis, M (2007). 'Conflicting measures of hospital quality: ratings from 'hospital compare' versus 'best hospitals'.' *Journal of Hospital Medicine,* 2(3): 128–134.

Healthcare Commission (2004). *2004 performance ratings.* London: Healthcare Commission (http://ratings2004.healthcarecommission.org.uk/).

Healthcare Commission (2005). *2005 performance ratings.* London: Healthcare Commission (http://ratings2005.healthcarecommission.org.uk/).

Healthcare Commission (2007). *Annual health check 2006/07. A national overview of the performance of NHS trusts in England.* London: Healthcare Commission (http://www.cqc.org.uk/_db/_documents/Annual_health_check_national_overview_2006–2007.pdf).

Health Consumer Powerhouse & Frontier Centre for Public Policy (2008). *Euro-Canada health consumer index 2008.* Brussels, Ottawa & Winnipeg (FC Policy Series No. 38).

Institute of Medicine (2001). *Crossing the quality chasm: a new health system for the 21st century.* Washington DC: Institute of Medicine of the National Academies, Committee on Quality of Health Care in America.

Jacobs, R. Goddard, M. Smith, PC (2005). 'How robust are hospital ranks based on composite performance measures?' *Medical Care,* 43(12): 1177–1184.

Jencks, S. Cuerdon, T. Burwen, D. Fleming, B. Houck, P. Kussmaul, A. Nilasena, D. Ordin, D. Arday, D (2000). 'Quality of medical care delivered to Medicare beneficiaries: a profile at state and national levels.' *Journal of the American Medical Association,* 284(13): 1670–1676.

Jencks, S. Huff, E. Cuerdon, T (2003). 'Change in the quality of care delivered to Medicare beneficiaries, 1998–1999 to 2000–2001.' *Journal of the American Medical Association,* 289(3): 305–312.

Joint Research Centre (2002). *State-of-the-art report on current methodologies and practices for composite indicator development.* Report prepared by the Applied Statistics Group. Brussels: European Commission, Institute for the Protection and Security of the Citizen (http://composite-indicators.jrc.ec.europa.eu/Document/state-of-the-art_EUR20408.pdf).

Kmietowicz, Z (2003). 'Star rating system fails to reduce variation.' *British Medical Journal,* 327(7408): 184.

Krumholz, H. Rathore, S. Chen, J. Wang, Y. Radford, M (2002). 'Evaluation of a consumer-orientated internet health care report card.' *Journal of the American Medical Association,* 287(10): 1277–1287.

Lied, T. Malsbary, R. Eisenberg, C. Ranck, J (2002). 'Combining HEDIS indicators: a new approach to measuring plan performance.' *Health Care Financing Review,* 23(4): 117–129.

Lindenauer, P. Remus, D. Roman, S. Rothberg, M. Benjamin, E. Ma, A. Bratzler, D (2007). 'Public reporting and pay for performance in hospital quality improvement.' *New England Journal of Medicine,* 356(5): 486–496.

Lun, G. Holzer, D. Tappeiner, G. Tappeiner, U (2006). 'The stability of rankings derived from composite indicators: analysis of the 'IL Sole 24 Ore' quality of life report.' *Social Indicators Research*, 77(2): 307–331.

Miller, N (2002). 'Missing the target.' *Community Care*, 21 November: 36–38.

Mullen, P. Spurgeon, P (2000). *Priority setting and the public*. Abingdon: Radcliffe Medical Press.

Nardo, M. Saisana, M. Saltelli, A. Tarantola, S. Hoffman, A. Giovanni, E (2005). *Handbook on constructing composite indicators: methodology and user guide*. Paris: Organisation for Economic Co-operation and Development (OECD Statistics Working Paper 2005/03).

Navarro, V (2002). '*The world health report 2000*: can health care systems be compared using a single measure of performance?' *American Journal of Public Health*, 92(1): 31–34.

Nietert, P. Wessell, A. Jenkins, R. Feifer, C. Nemeth, L. Ornstein, S (2007). 'Using a summary measure for multiple quality indicators in primary care: the Summary QUality InDex (SQUID).' *Implementation Science*, 2: 11.

Nord, E (2002). 'Measures of goal attainment and performance: a brief, critical consumer guide.' *Health Policy*, 59(3): 183–191.

O Brien, S. Shahian, D. Delong, E. Normand, SL. Edwards, F. Ferraris, V. Haan, C. Rich, J. Shewan, C. Dokholyan, R. Anderson, R. Peterson, E (2007). 'Quality measurement in adult cardiac surgery: Part 2 – statistical considerations in composite measure scoring and provider rating.' *Annals of Thoracic Surgery*, 83(Suppl. 4): 13–26.

O Malley, A. Zaslavsky, A. Hays, R. Heppner, K. Keller, S. Cleary, P (2005). 'Exploratory factor analyses of the CAHPS® hospital pilot survey responses across and within medical, surgical, and obstetric services. *Health Services Research*, 40(6 Pt 2): 2078–2095.

Page, S. Cramer, K (2001). 'Maclean's rankings of health care indices in Canadian communities, 2000: comparisons and statistical contrivance.' *Canadian Journal of Public Health* (*Revue Canadienne de Sante Publique*), 92(4): 295–298.

Premier (2005). CMS/ Premier Hospital Quality Incentive Demonstration (HQID). Washington, DC: Premier (http://www.premierinc.com/all/quality/hqi/index.jsp).

Reeves, D. Campbell, S. Adams, J. Shekelle, P. Kontopantelis, E. Roland, M (2007). 'Combining multiple indicators of clinical quality: an evaluation of different analytic approaches.' *Medical Care*, 45(6): 489–496.

Ryan, M. Farrer, S (2000). 'Using conjoint analysis to elicit preferences for health care.' *British Medical Journal*, 320(7248): 1530–1533.

Saaty, R (1987). 'The analytical hierarchy process: what it is and how it is used.' *Mathematical Modelling*, 9: 161–176.

Smith, PC (2002). Developing composite indicators for assessing health system efficiency. In: Smith, PC (ed.). *Measuring up: improving the performance of health systems in OECD countries*. Paris: Organisation for Economic Co-operation and Development.

Snelling, I (2003). 'Do star ratings really reflect hospital performance?' *Journal of Health Organization and Management*, 17(3): 210–223.

US News & World Report (2007). *America's Best Hospitals 2007 methodology*. Washington, DC. New York, NY: US News & World Health Report (http://www.usnews.com/usnews/health/best-hospitals/methodology_report.pdf).

Werner, R. Bradlow, E (2006). 'Relationship between Medicare's hospital compare performance measures and mortality rates.' *Journal of the American Medical Association*, 296(22): 2694–2702.

WHO (2000). *The world health report 2000. Health systems: improving performance*. Geneva: World Health Organization.

Williams, A (2001). 'Science or marketing at WHO? A commentary on world health 2000.' *Health Economics*, 10(2): 93–100.

Williams, S. Koss, R. Morton, D. Loeb, J (2006). 'Performance of top-ranked heart care hospitals on evidence-based process measures.' *Circulation*, 114(6): 558–564.

Zaslavsky, AM. Shaul, JA. Zaborski, LB. Cioffi, MJ. Cleary, PD (2002). 'Combining health plan performance indicators into simpler composite measures.' *Health Care Financing Review*, 23(4): 101–116.

PART IV

Performance measurement in specific domains

4.1 | *Performance measurement in primary care*

HELEN LESTER, MARTIN ROLAND

Introduction

This chapter explores the value and complexities of measuring performance in primary care. We begin with a definition of primary care and a description of its importance within the wider health-care system. We then explore the importance of measuring performance in this setting and provide an overview of some of the quality improvement strategies currently in use. The second part of the chapter describes a conceptual framework for quality measurement and reporting; the qualities of an ideal performance measure; and the relative value of process and outcome measures within primary care. The third part describes three very different primary-care focused systems in which performance measurement has been critical to improving health care: (i) Quality and Outcomes Framework in the United Kingdom; (ii) changes in the Veterans Health Administration in the United States; and (iii) European Practice Assessment. We conclude by highlighting challenges that policy-makers, researchers and clinicians face in future performance measurement in primary care.

Background to performance measurement in primary care

Defining primary care

WHO made the improvement of primary health care a core policy in the Alma-Ata declaration (WHO 1978) and the *Health for All by the Year 2000* strategy. The World Health Assembly renewed the commitment to global improvement in health (particularly for the most disadvantaged populations) in 1998 and this led to the *Health for All in the 21st Century* policy and programme.

The term 'primary care' has different meanings in different countries. The providers of primary care may be general practitioners, family physicians, specialists working in the community, nurses or nurse practitioners and (perhaps) physicians' assistants. These practitioners may work in solo practices or in large multi-professional groups and may or may not be integrated with social and community services. Some will have a gatekeeper function to secondary care. Methods of funding primary care also vary from payment by the patient to payment by the state, with a variety of combinations in between.

Primary care is better described in terms of its function rather than its location. The American Institute of Medicine (Donaldson et al. 1996) defined primary care as: 'the provision of integrated, accessible health care services by clinicians who are accountable for addressing a large majority of personal health care needs, developing a sustained partnership with patients and practising in the context of family and community'. This builds on Starfield's earlier definition of primary care as 'first-contact, continuous, comprehensive, and coordinated care provided to populations undifferentiated by gender, disease, or organ system' (Starfield 1994).

The critical elements of primary care are:

- first-contact accessible services where demands are clarified and information, reassurance or advice are given and diagnoses made;
- provision of comprehensive services to meet the needs of patients, with focus on generalism rather than specialism;
- provision of patient-centred rather than disease-centred care;
- provision of a longitudinal relationship between an individual patient and his/her health-care provider;
- coordination of care for individual patients;
- integration of biomedical, psychological and social dimensions of a patient's problem;
- focus on health promotion and disease prevention as well as management of established health problems.

In many countries, the primary-care provider also acts as an advocate for patients as they move through often complex health-care systems.

It has been demonstrated both between and within countries that those with a strong system of primary care have more efficient health systems and better health outcomes than those with a strong focus on hospital services (Macinko et al. 2007; Starfield 1998; Starfield et al. 2005). Countries with high primary care physician to population ratios (but not specialist to population ratios) have healthier populations and fewer social inequalities in the health of their populations. Primary care therefore has an equity-producing effect, at least for those measures of health that are most responsive to primary care (see Box 4.1.1).

Box 4.1.1 Benefits of primary care

Countries with strong primary care:

- have lower overall costs
- generally have healthier populations.

Within countries:

- areas with higher availability of primary-care physicians (but not specialists) have healthier populations;
- higher availability of primary-care physicians reduces the adverse effects of social inequality.

Source: from Starfield 1998

General practice or family medicine is a core discipline within primary care – in Europe, primary care is not easily conceptualized without general practice. However, primary care encompasses considerably more than general practice alone. In countries in which general practice is well-developed, the functions and characteristics of primary care largely overlap with those of general practice and general practice may have a preferred position in primary care. In other countries, specialists in internal medicine, paediatrics and gynaecology also provide primary medical care that is directly accessible.

Importance of measuring performance in primary care

In order to understand the importance of measuring performance in primary care it may be helpful to remember the ecology of medical care. White et al. (1961) published a framework for thinking about the organization of health care. Inspired in part by careful reporting on the part of British general practitioners (Horder & Horder 1954), this conceptualization suggested that in an average month and in a population of 1000 adults – 750 reported an illness, 250 consulted a physician, 9 were hospitalized, 5 were referred to another physician and just 1 was referred to a university medical centre. Analysis of 1995-1996 data on the use of health care in the United States (Green et al. 2001) had remarkably similar findings although undertaken thirty years later and in a different country. Among 1000 men, women and children they found that (on average each month) – 800 experienced symptoms, 327 considered seeking medical care, 217 visited a physician in the office (113 to a primary-care physician; 104 to other specialists), 65 visited a professional provider of complementary or alternative medical care, 21 visited a hospital-based outpatient clinic, 14 received professional health services at home, 13 received care in an emergency department, 8 were hospitalized and less than 1 (0.7) was admitted to an academic medical centre hospital (Green et al. 2001).

In essence, most people with symptoms manage them within the community; if they do seek help they use the equivalent of primary care, with very few people referred on for specialist care. Primary care is therefore the cornerstone of most health-care systems and measurement of its performance plays a critical part in ensuring that the whole system works effectively, efficiently and for the benefit of patients.

However, professional acceptance of the need to measure performance in primary care is relatively recent. Until the 1980s, there was a widespread notion in most European countries and in the United States that there was little variation in medical practice and that one doctor was much like another. The British government's attempts to introduce measures of performance in 1986 were described as 'political and provocative' (British Medical Association 1986). The international rise of evidence-based medicine (Sackett et al. 1996) and a growing realization of variations in practice meant that measurement of performance became a higher priority for both primary-care practitioners and policy-makers during the 1990s. Studies began to highlight inappropriate overuse, underuse and misuse of procedures in a variety of different fields (McGlynn et al. 1994). Much of the initial research focused on specialist practice but subsequent studies found considerable variation in the quality of primary care (Mangione-Smith et al. 2007; McGlynn et al. 2003; Seddon et al. 2001). This was accompanied by a wider general recognition that medical error can be an important cause of harm to patients (Kohn et al. 2000). In the United Kingdom, a series of well-publicized 'scandals' in primary and secondary care heightened concern that physicians should not be solely responsible for their own clinical governance and professional regulation (Smith 1998).

Over the last decade, many countries have therefore replaced implicit codes governing the health professional/patient relationship with explicit (often government controlled) rules and regulations for performance in primary care. Politicians' and payers' demands for efficiency increases also created pressure on managers to make decisions about which interventions and ways of working provided best value for money. Measuring performance provided one source of evidence for making such judgements.

Conceptual framework for assessing quality of care

It is helpful to have an overall understanding of the meaning of quality before deciding how to measure it. Campbell et al. (2000) describe a framework for assessing quality of care that distinguishes between care for individual patients and care for populations (see Box 4.1.2).

Quality of care for individual patients

For individual patients, the two central domains are access and effectiveness – can patients get to health care and is it any good when they arrive? Effectiveness covers both clinical and interpersonal care. It is not enough to provide good clinical care without good interpersonal care, and good interpersonal skills cannot substitute for poor clinical skills.

Clinical care may be subdivided into preventive care (staying healthy); care for acute illness (getting better); chronic disease management (living with illness or disability); and terminal care (coping with the end of life). The bracketed terms are those used by the Institute of Medicine in the United States. In addition, safety is sometimes included as a specific domain because of its high political profile and importance for patients. Interpersonal aspects of care are most frequently measured using patient questionnaires such as the General Practice Assessment Questionnaire (GPAQ) (www.gpaq.info) and the EUROPEP questionnaire for evaluating patient satisfaction and experience (Grol et al. 2000).

Good care cannot usually be delivered without good organization of care and attention to the environment in which that care is provided. Measuring organizational competence is therefore an important part of overall quality assessment.

Quality of care for populations

There are two additional domains of quality of care for populations of patients – equity and efficiency. Efficiency is an important marker of quality of care for populations as inefficient care (e.g. prescribing expensive but ineffective drugs) may have opportunity costs for the care that can be provided to other patients. Likewise, equity is a key element of quality especially where resources are distributed unevenly across population groups.

Box 4.1.2 Framework for assessing quality of care

Quality of care for individuals is determined by:

Access
Effectiveness of care
- clinical care
- interpersonal care (patient experience)
Organization of care/organizational development

Quality of care for populations is additionally determined by:

Equity
Efficiency

Source: from Campbell et al. 2000

Overview of quality improvement strategies in primary care

Quality improvement methods share three key elements:

1. *Specification of a desired performance* in the form of clinical guide-lines, care pathways, review criteria or clinical policies.
2. *Ways of changing clinical practice*. Numerous approaches have been used with varying degrees of success including lectures, small group education, one-to-one educational outreach visits, audit and feedback, reminder systems, computerized decision support, pub-lic release of information and financial incentives. Patient mediated interventions include guidelines for patients and training to increase patient assertiveness in consultation.

3. *Measurement.* Performance needs to be measured to determine whether and to what extent improvement has occurred so that further quality improvement strategies can be targeted appropriately (see Fig. 4.1.1).

Research shows that quality improvement strategies in primary care can make a difference but that no single method is always effective. Passive education tends to be least effective and multi-faceted interventions seem to have most effect, especially when sustained over time (Bero et al. 1998).

Baker et al. (2006) describe quality improvement systems that are being introduced into primary care in most European countries although the speed of introduction is dependent on the development of the profession of general practice in individual countries. Broadly, the European Union can be divided into first, second and third wave groups. The first wave includes Denmark, the Netherlands, Sweden and the United Kingdom. These have well-developed primary care systems with respected primary care practitioners and quality improve-

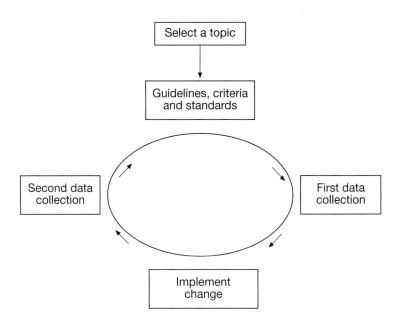

Fig. 4.1.1 Quality improvement cycle

ment systems that are now integral features of the health-care system. The second wave includes Austria, Belgium, France, Germany and Italy. These have made substantial progress since the early 1990s. The third wave is mainly composed of CEE countries. These have limited quality improvement initiatives, often hindered by the low status of general practitioners within the health-care system.

Developing performance measures for primary care

Underlying conceptual framework

The main purposes of a health-care system are to reduce the impact of the burden of illness, injury and disability and to improve the health and functioning of individuals in the population. Measuring the quality of care is one means of assessing how well this aim is being achieved. The Strategic Framework Board was established in the United States in 1999 to design a strategy for national quality measurement and reporting systems and to articulate the guiding principles and priorities for such a system. It produced a dynamic conceptual framework for a national quality measurement and reporting system (see Fig. 4.1.2).

This system aims to evaluate the degree to which the health system is providing safe, effective, timely and patient-centred care. It can also assess whether the delivery of high-quality care is efficient and equitable. It provides accessible information on quality to a variety of audiences including consumers, purchasers and providers to facilitate individual and collective decision-making. It also provides information that regulators, purchasers and providers can use to support continued improvement and achievement of goals (McGlynn 2003).

The Strategic Framework Board outlined a series of criteria and a process by which national goals for quality measurement and improvement could be selected. They suggested that goals should:

- be achievable within the health-care delivery system;
- represent areas in which patients experience a substantial burden of illness, injury or disability or problems with health and functioning;
- be based on evidence that progress on the goal is possible;
- be able to address the quality problems faced by diverse populations;

Fig. 4.1.2 Conceptual map of a quality measurement and reporting system
Source: McGlynn 2003

- be compelling to expert groups and relevant constituents (McGlynn et al. 2003a).

Performance measures can be developed once goals have been set and areas prioritized. Three preliminary issues need to be considered when developing measures.

1. Which aspects of care do you want to assess? Structure (e.g. staff, equipment, appointment systems); process (e.g. prescribing, investigations, interactions between professionals and patients); or outcomes (e.g. mortality, morbidity or patient satisfaction)? (Campbell et al. 2003).
2. Whose perspective is being prioritized? Different stakeholders will have different perspectives on the quality of care (Donabedian 1980). Patients may emphasize good communication skills whereas managers' views are more likely to be influenced by data on efficiency (Campbell et al. 2004).
3. What sort of supporting information or evidence is required? The type of indicator and the method of combining evidence and expert opinion when considering performance measurement are somewhat different in primary care than in other parts of the health system.

Many areas of health care have limited or methodologically weak evidence bases, especially within primary care (Naylor 1995). This requires performance measures to be developed using evidence along-side expert opinion. However, experts often disagree on the interpretation of evidence so rigorous methods are needed to combine the two. Consensus methods are structured facilitation techniques that explore general agreement amongst a group of experts in order to synthesize evidence with opinion. Group judgements are preferable to individual judgements as they are less prone to personal bias. Several consensus techniques exist including consensus development conferences; Delphi technique; nominal group technique; RAND appropriateness method; and iterated consensus rating procedures (Campbell et al. 2003; Murphy et al. 1998). The ideal qualities of a performance measure are shown in Box 4.1.3.

Box 4.1.3 Ideal qualities of a performance measure

An ideal performance measure has good:

- acceptability: acceptable to both those being assessed and those undertaking the assessment;
- feasibility: valid and reliable consistent data are available and collectable;
- reliability: minimal measurement error, reproducible findings when administered by different raters (inter-rater reliability);
- sensitivity to change: has capacity to detect changes in quality of care;
- predictive value: has capacity to predict quality of care outcomes.

Source: Campbell et al. 2002

Outcome measures are often seen as the gold standard but process measures are often more useful for performance in primary care. Hard outcomes such as mortality may relate to primary care but often occur long after the care has been given. They may be confounded by socio-demographic factors outside the control of primary care staff and also by the availability of secondary care services (Giuffrida et al. 1999). In theory, case-mix adjustment can be used to adjust outcomes for underlying differences in populations (Lilford et al. 2007). However, there is usually insufficient information in the medical record to allow this for primary care populations. Process measures based on scientific evidence which links them to effective outcomes (sometimes referred to as intermediate outcome measures) are generally recognized as the most useful indicators currently available in primary care. However, the development of methods of case-mix adjustment in primary care, e.g. the use of ambulatory care groups (Weiner et al. 1991), may provide new approaches to this problem.

The relative strengths and weaknesses of process and outcome measures are shown in Tables 4.1.1 and 4.1.2.

In the United Kingdom, coronary heart disease provides a practical example of the appropriate use of different types of performance measures. The Quality and Outcomes Framework has twelve primary care indicators focused on secondary prevention of coronary heart disease. These include producing a register of patients with the condition; a series of process measures aimed at ensuring that patents are given the most appropriate drug treatments; and two intermediate outcome measures that build on process measures of measuring blood pressure and cholesterol levels:

> *the percentage of patients with coronary heart disease whose last blood pressure reading was 150/90 or less.*

and:

> *the percentage of patients with coronary heart disease whose last measured total cholesterol was 5 mmol/l or less.*

In the longer term, there is strong evidence that control of blood pressure and high cholesterol are important in improving survival from coronary heart disease and therefore these intermediate outcomes may be related more closely to health outcomes than pure process measures.

However, for people with coronary heart disease within a secondary care setting, a cardiac surgeon's performance of coronary artery bypass graft **is** measured not only through their activity (process) figures but also through outcome measures. These include their overall mortality rates expressed as a percentage of all operations of that kind undertaken and compared to the national average. Whilst case-mix adjustment is often still necessary, the end result for the patient (death or improved quality of life) is more directly linked to the skill of the surgical team than the blood tests and prescribed medications that form the basis for performance measures in primary care. The use of an outcome measure such as mortality is more justifiable within a secondary care setting.

Table 4.1.1 *Relative advantages and disadvantages of process measures to measure quality*

Advantages	Disadvantages
Readily measured: utilization of health technologies is often measured relatively easily, without major bias or error.	**Salience**: processes of care may have little meaning to patients unless the link to outcomes can be explained.
Easily interpreted: utilization rates of different technologies can often be interpreted by reference to the evidence base without the need for case-mix adjustment or inter-unit comparisons.	**Specificity**: care processes are often quite specific to a single disease or single type of medical care therefore process measures across several clinical areas or aspects of service delivery may be required to represent quality for a particular group of patients.
Smaller sample size: can identify significant quality deficiencies with much smaller sample sizes than outcome indicators.	**Ossification**: focus on process may stifle innovation and the development of new modes of care.
Unobtrusive: care processes can frequently be assessed unobtrusively (e.g. data stored in administrative or medical records).	**Obsolescence**: usefulness may dissipate as technology and modes of care change.
Indicators for action: failures identified in the processes of care provide clear guidance on what must be remedied to improve health-care quality. Also, acted upon more quickly than outcome indicators which often become available only after a long time has elapsed.	**Adverse behaviour**: can be manipulated relatively easily and may give rise to gaming and other adverse behaviours.
Coverage: can capture aspects of care (e.g. speed of access; patient experience), other than health outcomes, that are often valued by patients.	

Source: Davies 2005

Table 4.1.2 *Relative advantages and disadvantages of outcome measures to measure quality*

Advantages	Disadvantages
Focus: directs attention towards the patient (rather than the service) and helps nurture a 'whole system' perspective.	**Measurement definition**: relatively easy to measure some outcome aspects validly and reliably (e.g. death) but others are notoriously difficult (e.g. wound infection).
Goals: represent the goals of care and the NHS more clearly.	**Attribution**: may be influenced by many factors outside the control of a health-care organization.
Meaningful: tend to be more meaningful to some of the potential users of clinical indicators (patients, purchasers).	**Sample size**: requires large sample sizes to detect a statistically significant effect even when there are manifest problems with the processes of care.
Innovation: focus on outcomes encourages providers to experiment with new modes of delivery to improve patient care and experience.	**Timing**: may take a long time to observe.
Far sighted: focus on outcomes encourages providers to adopt long-term strategies (e.g. health promotion) that may realize longer-term benefits.	**Interpretation**: observed outcomes may be difficult to interpret if the processes that produced them are complex or occurred distant to the observed outcome.
Manipulation: less open to manipulation than process indicators although providers can influence risk-adjusted outcome by exaggerating the severity of patients' conditions (upstaging).	**Ambiguity**: good outcomes can often be achieved despite poor processes of care (and vice versa).

Case studies of performance measurement in primary care

Three case studies are presented below, each chosen to illustrate a different way of developing and implementing quality improvement schemes that include measuring performance in primary care. Each describes the political and clinical context in which the measures were introduced; the measures themselves; the known intended and unintended consequences; and the critical factors that influenced implementation and changes to health and health care.

Case study 1: Quality and Outcomes Framework

The Quality and Outcomes Framework is a pay-for-performance scheme introduced in the United Kingdom in April 2004 as part of a new General Medical Services contract for general practitioners. Its introduction was facilitated by the alignment of a series of factors during the previous decade, including public disquiet over the quality of health-care services; the rise of evidence-based medicine; a change in the culture of the profession that enabled recognition of variations in the quality of primary care; and recognition of serious underfunding of health care in the United Kingdom in comparison to other countries (Roland 2004).

In these circumstances, professional representatives (General Practitioners Committee of the British Medical Association) were able and willing to negotiate with the government to provide elements of primary care through a system of performance related pay. The government was willing to invest up to 20% of the primary care budget, 90% of which was new money, in order to develop a series of incentivized evidence-based indicators across a range of clinical and organizational areas in primary care.

The Quality and Outcomes Framework consists of approximately 140 measures based on evidence or professional consensus. The majority (65%) of indicators are focused on clinical areas although the use of a balanced scorecard approach is reflected in a range of clinical, organizational and patient focused elements in the framework (see Box 4.1.4).

Points for individual indicators are awarded in relation to the level of achievement (e.g. percentage of people with diabetes with blood pressure below a defined target). A graduated scale of payments starts above a minimum threshold (25% initially but 40% since 2006) and ends at a maximum threshold (usually 90%). The framework is revised on a biennial basis – new clinical areas are added and issues that have become a standard part of primary care (usually within the organizational domain) are removed.

Box 4.1.4 Quality and Outcomes Framework: performance measure domains (2008)

Clinical: coronary heart disease, heart failure, stroke and transient ischaemic attacks, atrial fibrillation, hypertension, diabetes mellitus, chronic obstructive pulmonary disease, asthma, epilepsy, hypothyroidism, cancer, mental health, depression, dementia, learning disability, palliative care, chronic kidney disease, obesity, ethnicity coding.

Organizational: records and information, information for patients, education and training, practice management, medicines management.

Patient experience: length of consultations, patient surveys, patient experience of access to primary care.

Additional services: cervical screening, child health surveillance, maternity services, contraceptive services.

General practitioners can exclude patients from the quality calculation for a number of broadly defined reasons (exception reporting). This excludes them from both the numerator and the denominator of the quality calculation. Reasons for exception reporting include:

- patient is on maximum tolerated therapy
- patient refuses to participate
- patient is newly diagnosed or recently registered
- not clinically appropriate to include the patient.

Almost all practices in the United Kingdom now use an electronic medical record, a critical factor for successful implementation of the performance measurement system. Data on performance on each of the measures is collected at practice level through a national IT system. The Quality Management and Analysis System (QMAS) is used to calculate payments and as a public source of information on quality of care in individual practices. Practices can benchmark themselves against their performance in previous years and against other practices locally and nationally. Data are easily accessible on the Internet and patients can look up their own practice scores for each individual indicator (http://www.qof.ic.nhs.uk/index.asp).

The Quality and Outcomes Framework is a voluntary system but it has been taken up by over 99% of practices in the United Kingdom. During the first year, the levels of achievement exceeded those anticipated by the government – an average of 83.4% of the available incentive payments were claimed (Doran et al. 2006). Achievements were similarly high in the second and third years.

The indicators, particularly those in clinical areas, represent a mixture of process measures and intermediate outcome measures. Intermediate outcome indicators generally have more points attached to them as they are more difficult to achieve and represent a greater workload. The Quality and Outcomes Framework contains no pure outcome indicators since one of its central tenets is that the measure has to be within the control of primary care. This inevitably means that a majority of the clinical measures are process in nature (registers, improving systems). However, many of the clinical areas include a series of intermediate measures for which there is evidence that improvements in these parameters lead to better long-term outcomes, e.g. lowering blood pressure, lipid and glucose levels in conditions such as heart disease, stroke, hypertension, diabetes and kidney disease.

The process of developing new indicators involves multiple stakeholders. Every other year the general public, patients, national organizations, the Department of Health and health-care professionals submit ideas for inclusion. These are prioritized by representatives from the Department of Health and the medical profession. Evidence in each area is then reviewed by a panel of academic experts and summarized in a series of reports that are available for viewing by the general public once negotiations have been completed. Indicators in the reports are developed through a two-stage modified RAND process with primary care practitioners (Brook et al. 1986) and commented on by a national patient organization and by IT experts. The final set of evidence-based performance measures represents a negotiated compromise between the government (needing to ensure the best possible use of Treasury resources for public health benefit) and the British Medical Association (representing the medical profession). The negotiation is important for establishing a level of professional ownership.

Data on the impact of financial incentives in the Quality and Outcomes Framework are available from a study of forty-two representative practices in England – detailed data on quality of care were collected at a series of time points (1998, 2003, 2005, 2007), including some that predated the financial incentives. The results of the study show that the quality of care for the three major diseases studied (coronary heart disease, asthma, type 2 diabetes) was improving rapidly between 1998 and 2003 prior to the introduction of the incentives. Improvements continued after the introduction of financial incentives and the rate of improvement increased for asthma and diabetes. Care for coronary heart disease was increasing most rapidly before the financial incentives and continued to improve at the same rate. Overall, the results suggest that the introduction of pay for performance was associated with a modest acceleration in improvement in the quality of care (Campbell et al. 2007).

The findings of the study are consistent with previous work. This suggests that financial incentives can have a modest effect in changing professional behaviour (Epstein et al. 2004) and that patients receive higher-quality care in geographical areas where performance measures and monitoring have been established (Asch et al. 2004).

However, such schemes also have potential unintended consequences (McGlynn 2007). These include possible myopia (pursuit of short-term targets at the expense of legitimate long-term objectives) or misrepresentation (deliberate manipulation of data so that reported behaviour differs from actual behaviour) (Smith 1995). There is concern, as yet largely unfounded in the United Kingdom (Doran et al. 2006), that pay for performance may also increase racial and ethnic disparities (Casalino et al. 2007).

In the United Kingdom, family practitioners have expressed concerns that the financial incentives will produce adverse effects including reductions in continuity of care; fragmentation of care as a result of specialization within practices; and neglect of conditions for which financial incentives are not provided (Roland et al. 2006). More broadly, the introduction of the pay-for-performance programme has been associated with a general trend away from placing implicit trust in NHS health-care professionals and toward more active monitoring of their performance (Checkland et al. 2004). Despite these concerns, overall job satisfaction among family physicians was higher in 2004 than in 2001 (Whalley et al. 2006) and a recent report from the United States suggests that targeted quality improvement programmes have not resulted in any deterioration in quality of care in untargeted disease areas (Ganz et al. 2007). The results generally support the Institute of Medicine's view that pay-for-performance programmes can make a useful contribution to improving quality (Fisher & Davis 2006), particularly when part of a comprehensive quality improvement programme.

The size of the gains in quality in relation to the costs of pay for performance remains a political issue in the United Kingdom. The government now accepts that it paid more than expected for the improvements in performance (BBC 2007; National Audit Office 2008) – investing over £ 3 billion in primary care in the first three years of operation of the Quality and Outcomes Framework. General practitioners appear to have increased the proportion of practice income taken as profit since the new contract was introduced, suggesting that gains in quality could have been achieved at a lower cost. Payment is made at practice rather than individual physician level in order to reflect the significant degree of teamwork required to achieve a high level of performance and achievement. However, few non-physicians have received substantial pay rises as a result of the Quality and Outcomes Framework.

Case study 2: Veterans Health Administration

There has been health and social support for aged or injured soldiers in the United States since colonial times. However, a national programme for American veterans was consolidated with the establishment of the Veterans Administration (VA) in 1930. As resources were expanded following the Second World War the VA was elevated to Cabinet status and became the Department of Veterans Affairs in 1989. Its health-care system has grown from 54 hospitals in 1930 and now includes 155 medical centres with at least one in each state, Puerto Rico and the District of Columbia. VA operates more than 1400 sites of care, including 872 ambulatory care and community-based outpatient clinics, 135 nursing homes, 45 residential rehabilitation treatment programmes, 209 Veterans Centers and 108 comprehensive home-care programmes. Almost 5.5 million people were treated in VA health-care facilities in 2006 http://www1.va.gov/vetdata/docs/4X6_fall07_sharepoint.pdf).

Until the mid 1990s, the VA operated largely as a hospital system providing general medical and surgical services and long-term care. Medical centres and facilities were relatively independent of each other and even competitively duplicated services. In the late 1980s and early 1990s, the VA became increasingly criticized as an expensive and poor quality system with its failings publicized widely in the media, including popular movies. Members of Congress argued that the organization needed new management or even that funding should be discontinued. In 1996, the Veterans' Health Care Eligibility Reform Act enabled the system to be restructured from a hospital to a health-care system. Two documents – *Vision for Change* (Kizer 1995) and *Prescription for Change* (Kizer 1996) – outlined the challenges facing the VA and served as a strategic outline for organizational restructuring and a new strategy for systemizing quality and value.

There were three key reforms (Perlin et al. 2004).

1. Eligibility – broadly expanded the eligibility of veterans who could use the VA.

2. Operational – major structural change that established the Veterans Integrated Service Networks (VISNs) to move away from a hospital-centric service. Twenty-two regional networks assumed responsibility for the performance of all medical centres and clinics within their area. Resources were allocated according to the capitation formula and networks became responsible for coordinating care in order to reduce duplication and incentivize care coordination. At the same time, the VA began to expand the provision of primary care which was legalized and mandated by legislation in 1994. The VA also expanded and updated its IT system to allow better coordinated care, with the eventual introduction of a single electronic medical record across the whole system.

   Between 1995 and 1996 the VA closed 52% of its acute care hospital beds; ambulatory care visits increased by 43%; over 200 new outpatient clinics were funded by the redirected savings; and a pharmacy benefits programme and a national formulary were instituted. The VA introduced a new electronic medical record with tools for assessment and improvement such as reminders to carry out certain services and documentation of patient care that could be accessed first within the VISN and then nationwide. The VA implemented computerized order entry for medication, tests and consultation. The electronic medical record also enabled better integration of care and communication across providers, since all providers had access to it.

   Quality transformation – performance measurement of key indicators of chronic and preventative care and, more recently, acute hospital and palliative care are the cornerstones of this reform. To further motivate improvement, the VA has forged partnerships with health services researchers to measure quality and evaluate quality improvement interventions. The VA established nine quality enhancement research initiatives to help assess and improve quality in prevalent conditions like diabetes and heart failure and expanded the funding available for all VA health services researchers to focus on quality improvement. The VA also instituted annual patient surveys to assess access, satisfaction and health status.

3. Quality Transformation – quality measures are selected through an external peer review programme. Most of the measures come from major American quality monitoring organizations such as the NCQA but they also include measures of particular relevance to veterans. Data are collected quarterly by an external contractor who audits medical records from a sample in each facility. This is relatively expensive as the external contractor is paid several million dollars per year. Currently, there are approximately fifty quality measures within the system, collected with a level of clinical detail that makes them meaningful to clinicians (see Box 4.1.5).

To motivate improvement on the measures, VISN directors are accountable through a performance contract that either offers an incentive or withholds roughly 10% of salary. The VISN directors hold facilities and providers accountable through clear expectations of performance rather than direct individual monetary incentives. However, the VA administration is currently looking at ways to stimulate quality improvement through more direct use of pay for performance. The results at VISN and facility levels are publicized and recognized throughout the VA and stronger performances are recognized with awards. Much of the motivation therefore rests upon professional pride, on being recognized as a high-performing facility.

Within ten years, the VA moved from a reputation for providing poor quality care to being lauded for the provision of the best care within the United States (Longman 2005). Influenza vaccination rates rose from 28% in 1994 to 78% in 2000. Annual measurement of glycated haemoglobin in patients with diabetes rose from 51% to 94% and beta-blocker treatment following myocardial infarction rose from 70% to 95% in the same period (Jha et al. 2003). The absolute level of

Box 4.1.5 Veterans Administration performance measurement areas

Chronic and acute care	Preventive care
Diabetes e.g. low density lipoprotein cholesterol (LDLC) controlled (<130 mg/dl or 3.4 mmol/l)	Influenza vaccination
Acute myocardial infarction e.g. LDLC less than 130 mg/dl after heart attack and beta blocker on discharge after heart attack	Pneumococcal vaccination
Obstructive lung disease	Tobacco screening
Obesity	Mammography
Hypertension	Cervical cancer screening
Pain assessment	Colorectal cancer screening
Major depression	Hyperlipidaemia screening
Tobacco treatment	Alcohol screening
Community acquired pneumonia	Prostate screening
Heart failure	
Substance use disorders	

quality of care for veterans was also higher than for patients covered by Medicare. Kerr et al. (2004) showed that the quality of diabetes care in 2000-2001 was higher in the VA than in geographically matched commercial managed care plans for almost every aspect studied including timely eye screening, testing glucose and lipids concentrations and glucose and lipid control. Although overall care was higher for veterans than the community, the advantage was greatest for the measures that the administration was using to monitor quality (e.g. retinal screening for people with diabetes) and spilled over beyond the targeted measures to the conditions covered by the performance monitoring (e.g. diabetes). However, veterans had no advantage for conditions outside the performance monitoring system (Asch et al. 2004).

In summary, the change in quality of care in the VA over a relatively short time demonstrates the value of organizational change. This includes reorganization into networks; the shift to ambulatory settings; and the value of a high-quality information system. The VA's experience has shown that well-constructed and clinically detailed measures of performance play a valuable role in improving quality of care in the community even without large monetary incentives for individual doctors (Conrad et al. 2006). Extrinsic motivation of competition between regions and small financial incentives to regional directors helped to drive the change (as did an enabling environment) but the cornerstone for improving quality was the systematic use of data-driven measures to monitor performance.

Case study 3: European Practice Assessment

The European Practice Assessment Practice Management (EPA-PM) framework was developed between 2002 and 2004 as part of the TOPAS-EUROPE Association, in collaboration with the Bertelsmann Foundation (Engels et al. 2005). The framework was designed for use across a wide group of European countries. It aims to measure the quality of the management and organization of general practices in order to contribute to the assessment of, and improvements in, the quality of primary care and to enable comparisons to be made between primary-care practices, both within and between countries.

EPA-PM is based around a conceptual framework for practice management with five domains (see Box 4.1.6). The indicators relating to practice management were collated from published sets of indicators and literature; the conceptual framework was then used to organize the indicators into relevant dimensions. The indicators were rated in a systematic selection process by six national expert panels, taking account of both evidence and professional opinion – 62 out of 171 indicators met the criteria for validity across all countries (Engels et al. 2006). All the questionnaires and checklists in the EPA instrument are derived from these indicators. The instrument was piloted in 273 practices across 9 European countries in 2004 and resulted in the present version: EPA 2005.

EPA-PM has been used widely in Germany and Switzerland and integrated within existing accreditation systems in the Netherlands. It has also been used in Australia, Belgium, Canada, Denmark, Romania, Saudi Arabia and Slovenia. EPA-PM combines measurement and feedback tools to enable individual practices to monitor progress continuously against benchmarks. A trained facilitator visits each practice and conducts the EPA-PM process. This emphasizes an educational approach to encourage practice staff to conduct self-

Box 4.1.6 EPA-PM: performance domains

Domain	No. of indicators	Example of indicator
Infrastructure	27	Sufficient seating in the waiting room.
People/staff	7	Responsibilities within the team are clearly defined.
Information	16	Practice has computerized medical record system.
Finance	4	Practice produces annual financial report that includes all income and expenditure.
Quality and safety	8	All staff involved in quality improvements. Practice has sterilizer or autoclave.

assessments; to reflect on their own strengths and weaknesses; and to identify areas for quality improvement. There are also questionnaires for the practice manager, general practitioners and all other staff and a separate questionnaire (EUROPEP) for patients. Individual practice feedback is given on the same day. Each assessment is benchmarked so that practices can compare their performance with others and observe changes in their own practice over time. Benchmarks in Europe are available online (http://www.ru.nl/topas-europe/index.php?idcatside=13).

Unlike the Quality and Outcomes Framework and VA systems, EPA-PM is focused solely on organizational issues in primary care and is formative in nature, iteratively linking assessment with improvement. It is intended to promote an educative and reflective approach with team-based learning and practice-specific feedback. Like the Quality and Outcomes Framework it is voluntary but the levers for change are professional development rather than financial incentives. The enablers for change are largely systems based and motivations are intrinsic (professional) rather than extrinsic (financial rewards).

EPA-PM is still at a relatively early stage of development with few data on implementation and longer-term effect at practice level. Its ethos and the collaborative consensual nature of its piloting suggest that it may represent a future model of developing performance measures for and in primary care. Its ability to cross international borders echoes the wider political agenda of European unification and makes sense in a world of increasing economic migration of both patients and health professionals (Grol & Wensing 2007). However, it is also important to remember that comparisons across health systems can be misleading and that successful approaches will not necessarily work in the same way when transplanted to another system (Sheldon 2004).

The group that developed organizational indicators for use in general practice across Europe has used a similar approach to develop a set of indicators focusing on the prevention of cardiovascular disease – EPA-Cardio. An initial review of the literature was followed by selection of candidate indicators that were rated for validity by panels of informed general practitioners. Again, separate panels were convened in each of the nine participating countries. Overall, 44 out of 202 indicators (22%) were rated valid for inclusion on a 'European set'. These focused predominantly on secondary prevention and management of established cardiovascular disease and diabetes. There was less agreement on indicators of preventive care or for patients without established disease. Although 85% of 202 potential indicators assessed were rated valid by at least one panel, lack of consensus among panels meant that a smaller set was agreed by all panels. This was probably caused by a mixture of differences in health systems, cultures and attitudes to prevention and shows some of the problems in achieving agreement about the measurement of quality across different health-care systems (Campbell et al. 2008)

Conclusions

This chapter has outlined the central importance of performance measurement as a prerequisite for improving primary health care. Common themes have arisen across the different implementations described – the complexity of developing meaningful evidence-based measures that work in primary care; and the expense of setting up and maintaining a performance measurement system. We conclude with reflections on the issues raised by current schemes and some of the challenges that lie ahead for policy-makers, researchers and clinicians.

Where should performance measures be used?

The focus for performance measurement in primary care will vary by health economy but generic underpinning priorities would include health conditions with:

- high prevalence;
- significant morbidity or mortality;
- recognized gap between actual and potential performance;
- good evidence that introduction of a measure will lead to an improvement in care;
- political importance.

Is there an optimal way of improving performance?

There is no agreed optimal combination of methods to improve performance in health care and it is important to recognize that measurement is one of a series of levers that policy-makers and funders can use. Numerous approaches have been used, with varying degrees of success. These include educational programmes directed at the community and/or health workers; audit and feedback; reminder systems; computerized decision support; public release of information; and financial incentives.

Public reporting of performance data has been championed during the last decade as a mechanism for increasing accountability to payers and patients, though with limited evidence of its effectiveness (Fung et al. 2008). As yet, there is no evidence to suggest that patients change their medical provider if differences in quality are demonstrated (Galvin & McGlynn 2003). Rather, it seems that provider behaviour is stimulated by public release of information on quality of care (Marshall et al. 2000). One reason why the Quality and Outcomes Framework has stimulated general practitioner activity in the United Kingdom is that detailed results for every practice (down to individual indicators) are available on the Internet.

Financial incentives (pay for performance) are used increasingly commonly as a method of quality improvement. We reviewed some of the evidence behind this approach in the section on the Quality and Outcomes Framework. Pay for performance is far from a panacea and the results from most well-designed evaluations show only modest benefits. There is also a series of fundamental questions about which elements of primary care could or should be financially incentivized. Financial incentives are most likely to be effective in influencing professional behaviour when performance measures and rewards are aligned to the values of the staff being rewarded (Marshall & Smith 2003). Indeed, external incentives may crowd out motivation – the desire to do a task well for its own sake – if they clash with the professional's perceptions of his/her role or identity and of quality care (Gagné & Deci 2005). If measures and underlying data are not viewed as valid then physicians may see them as unfair or inappropriate (Bokhour et al. 2006).

Overall, Oxman et al's (2005) conclusion that there is 'no magic bullet' for quality improvement still stands. Single interventions are often disappointing and the best evidence for quality improvement comes from systems that have used multiple and sustained interventions designed to improve quality. However, it should not be inferred that nothing works. Examples such as the VA show that major system-wide change can be achieved with effective leadership which focuses on quality improvement as a key part of the delivery of health care.

Unintended consequences of performance measurement

It is important to monitor potential adverse effects of any quality improvement scheme that might selectively bring benefits to populations which are already advantaged. A clear example of a perverse and unintended consequence is the incentive designed to reduce waiting times to see general practitioners in the United Kingdom. Unexpectedly, this made it more difficult for patients to book appointments in advance (Salisbury et al. 2007).

There is also concern that financial incentives may lead to neglect of non-incentivized conditions (McGlynn 2007). This concern does not appear to have been realized in two recently published studies, from the United States (Ganz et al. 2007) and the United Kingdom (Steel et al. 2007), respectively. However, this type of study inevitably compares quality of care for those aspects that can be measured readily. Much of the criticism of the Quality and Outcomes Framework in the United Kingdom relates to the potential loss of the caring aspects of a general practitioner's work (Mangin & Toop 2007). There is a danger that measurement of isolated aspects of performance may fundamentally alter the concept of quality in primary care and begin to redefine what is important within it. There is a sense of urgency here since it may not be too long before the senior practitioners within primary care become those who have grown up in a climate that values what can be measured easily above less definable aspects of care (Lester & Roland 2007). We need to guard against this and remember that the science of performance measurement is just one element of the art of primary care.

One potential problem with quality improvement initiatives is that groups which are compliant or easy to treat may selectively benefit – because they present for treatment; their doctors selectively give them more attention; doctors or health plans selectively disenrol patients from disadvantaged groups for whom it may be more difficult to reach quality targets. This is an example of the inverse equity hypothesis (Victora et al. 2000) which suggests that public health interventions may produce an initial widening of inequalities. However, this effect was not seen when incentives were introduced for cervical cytology in the United Kingdom in 1990 as there was progressive narrowing of inequality in the delivery of health care (Baker & Middleton 2003; Middleton & Baker 2003). The introduction of the Quality and Outcomes Framework in the United Kingdom also appears to be associated with a reduction in inequality (Doran et al. 2008). Nevertheless, the issue remains important, especially in health-care systems in which doctors have a disincentive to enrol patients who may not reach quality targets.

Removing and refreshing measurement sets

Those thinking of adopting performance measures might do well to think through the rules for removing these measures beforehand. In the United States, 'the percentage of patients with acute myocardial infarction who receive a prescription for beta-blockers within seven days of hospital discharge' has been used to evaluate managed care plans since 1996. A decade ago, only two thirds of the patients who survived acute myocardial infarction received beta blockers; today, nearly all do. As the curve representing the tenth percentile crept above 90%, the NCQA found little variation among health plans and therefore retired the measure (Lee 2007). This methodology could be adopted and adapted to suit different measures and health expectations.

Future challenges

As population demography changes, patients are increasingly likely to present with more than one condition. Currently, 65% of Medicare beneficiaries have more than one condition and almost 20% have four or more (Berenson & Horvath 2003). Primary care will provide the majority of ongoing care for this growing population within most health systems. There is therefore a need to develop and validate sets of measures that make sense to primary care by taking account of the number and severity of conditions at an individual level. This may require piloting of new measures that are focused at patient level and can take into account the complexity of differing evidence bases for different conditions within the same patient. Indeed piloting of new performance measures is fast becoming the norm in both the United Kingdom and the United States and may provide an opportunity to experiment with new types of indicators, thresholds and the effects of differing financial incentives.

The consequences of co-morbidity will almost certainly include the potential for increasingly fragmented care, with the possibility of poor informational and interpersonal continuity. Coordination of care at the level of the individual patient pathway will present a series of challenges to clinicians and policy-makers and may well become a central focus of future performance measurement.

However, perhaps the greatest challenge facing primary performance measurement is to find the point of equipoise between trust and control (O'Neill 2003). In a system based on trust, it is a professional responsibility to measure performance and improve quality of care. Currently, many health-care systems appear to have a greater focus on control, accountability and public reporting – performance measurement is seen more as a societal or government responsibility. Is it possible that, in the longer term, this emphasis will erode an important part of the very medical professionalism that enabled quality improvement initiatives to flourish in the first place? Performance measurement, and the process of continuous quality improvement that it encourages, has enormous potential to improve the quality of primary care. The challenge is to develop more trust-promoting approaches that make sense to all actors and produce the greatest benefit for patients.

References

Asch, SM. McGlynn, EA. Hogan, MM. Hayward, RA. Shekelle, P. Rubenstein, L. Keesey, J. Adams, J. Kerr, EA (2004). 'Comparison of quality of care for patients in the Veterans Health Administration and patients in a national sample.' *Annals of Internal Medicine*, 141(12): 938–945.

Baker, D. Middleton, E (2003). 'Cervical screening and health inequality in England in the 1990s.' *Epidemiology of Community Health*, 57(6): 417–423.

Baker, R. Wensing, M. Gibis, V (2006). Improving the quality of performance. In: Saltman, R. Rico, A. Boerma, W (eds.). *Primary care in the driver's seat?* Maidenhead: Open University Press.

BBC (2007). *GP pay raise 'was mistake'.* BBC News Health. London: British Broadcasting Corporation (http://news.bbc.co.uk/player/nol/newsid_6280000/newsid_6280000/6280077.stm?bw=bb&mp=rm).

Berenson, RA. Horvath, J (2003). 'Confronting the barriers to chronic care management in Medicare.' *Health Affairs (Millwood)*, Suppl. web exclusives: W3-37-53.

Bero, L. Grilli, R. Grimshaw, JM. Harvey E. Oxman, AD. Thomson, MA (1998). 'Closing the gap between research and practice: an overview of systematic reviews of interventions to promote the implementation of research findings.' *British Medical Journal*, 317(7156): 465–468.

Bokhour, BG. Burgess, JF. Hook, J. White, B. Berlowitz, D. Guildin, MR. Meterko, M. Young, GJ (2006). 'Incentive implementation in physician practices: a qualitative study of practice executive perspectives on pay for performance.' *Medical Care Research and Review*, 63(Suppl. 1): 73–95.

British Medical Association (1986). *Report to Special Conference of Representatives of Local Medical Committees.* 13 November 1986. London: British Medical Association.

Brook, RH. Chassin, MR. Fink, A. Solomon, DH. Kosecoff, J. Park, RE (1986). 'A method for the detailed assessment of the appropriateness of medical technologies.' *International Journal of Technology Assessment in Health Care*, 2(1): 53–63.

Campbell, SM. Roland, MO. Buetow, SA (2000). 'Defining quality of care.' *Social Science and Medicine,* 51(11): 1611–1625.

Campbell, SM. Braspenning, J. Hutchinson, A. Marshall, MN (2002). 'Research methods used in developing and applying quality indicators in primary care. *Quality and Safety in Health Care*, 11(4): 358–364.

Campbell, SM. Braspenning, J. Hutchinson, A. Marshall, MN (2003). 'Research methods used in developing and applying quality indicators in primary care.' *British Medical Journal*, 326(7293): 816–819.

Campbell, S. Shield, T. Rogers, A. Gask, L (2004). 'How do stakeholder groups vary in a Delphi technique about primary mental health care and what factors influence their ratings?' *Quality and Safety in Healthcare*, 13(6): 428–434.

Campbell, S. Reeves, D. Kontopantelis, E. Middleton, E. Sibbald, B. Roland, M (2007). 'Quality of primary care in England with the introduction of pay for performance.' *New England Journal of Medicine*, 357(2): 181–190.

Campbell, S. Ludt, S. Van Lieshout, J. Boffin, N. Wensing, M. Petek, D. Grol, R. Roland, M (2008). 'Quality indicators for the prevention and management of cardiovascular disease in primary care in nine European countries.' *European Journal of Cardiovascular Disease Prevention and Rehabilitation*, 15(5): 509–515.

Casalino, LP. Elster, A. Eisenberg, A. Lewis, E. Montgomery, J. Ramos, D (2007). 'Will pay for performance and quality reporting affect health care disparities?' *Health Affairs (Millwood)*, 26(3): 405–414.

Checkland, K. Marshall, M. Harrison, S (2004). 'Re-thinking accountability: trust versus confidence in medical practice.' *Quality and Safety in Health Care*, 13(2): 130–135.

Conrad, DA. Saver, BG. Court, B. Heath, S (2006). 'Paying physicians for quality: evidence and themes from the field.' *Journal on Quality and Patient Safety*, 32(8): 443–451.

Davies, H (2005). *Measuring and reporting the quality of health care: issues and evidence from the international research literature*. Edinburgh: NHS Quality Improvement Scotland.

Donabedian, A (1980). *Explorations in quality assessment and monitoring. Vol. 1: The definition of quality and approaches to its assessment*. Ann Arbor, MI: Health Administration Press.

Donaldson, MS. Yordy, KD. Lohr, KN. Vanselow, NA (eds.) (1996). *Primary care: America's health in a new era*. Washington DC: National Academy Press.

Doran, T. Fullwood, C. Gravelle, H. Reeves, D. Kontopantelis, E. Hiroeh, U. Roland, M (2006). 'Pay-for-performance programs in family practices in the United Kingdom.' *New England Journal of Medicine*, 355(4): 375–384.

Doran, T. Fullwood, K. Kontopantelis, E. Reeves, D (2008). 'Effect of financial incentives on inequalities in the delivery of primary care in England: analysis of clinical activity indicators for the quality and outcomes framework.' *Lancet,* 372(9640): 728–736.

Engels, Y. Campbell, S. Dautzenberg, M. van den Hombergh, P. Brinkmann, H. Szécsényi, J. Falcoff, H. Seuntjens, L. Kuenzi, B. Grol, R. EPA Working Party (2005). 'Developing a framework of, and quality indicators for, general practice management in Europe.' *Family Practice,* 22(2): 215–222.

Engels,Y. Dautzenberg, M. Campbell, S. Broge, B. Boffin, N. Marshall, M. Elwyn, G. Vodopivec-Jamsek, V. Gerlach, FM. Samuelson, M. Grol, R (2006). 'Testing a European set of indicators for the evaluation of the management of primary care practices.' *Family Practice,* 23(1): 137–147.

Epstein, AM. Lee, TH. Hamel, MB (2004). 'Paying physicians for high-quality care.' *New England Journal of Medicine*, 350(4): 406–410.

Fisher, ES. Davis, K (2006). 'Audio interview: pay for performance – recommendations of the Institute of Medicine.' *New England Journal of Medicine,* 355(13): e14 (http://content.nejm.org/cgi/content/full/NEJMp068216/DC1).

Fung, C. Lim, Y-W. Mattke, S. Damberg, C. Shekelle, PG (2008). 'Systematic review: the evidence that publishing patient care performance data improves quality of care.' *Annals of Internal Medicine*, 148(2): 111–123.

Gagné, M. Deci, EL (2005). 'Self-determination theory and work motivation.' *Journal of Organizational Behavior,* 26(4): 331–362.

Galvin, RS. McGlynn, EA (2003). 'Using performance measurement to drive improvement. A road map for change.' *Medical Care*, 41(3): 48–60.

Ganz, DA. Wenger, NS. Roth, CP. Kamberg, CJ. Chang, JT. Maclean, Ch. Young, RT. Solomon, DH. Higashi, T. Min, L. Reuben, DB. Shekelle, PG (2007). 'The effect of a quality improvement initiative on the quality of other aspects of health care: the law of unintended consequences?' *Medical Care*, 45(1): 8–18.

Giuffrida, A. Gravelle, H. Roland, M (1999). 'Measuring quality of care with routine data: avoiding confusion between performance indicators and health outcomes.' *British Medical Journal*, 319(7202): 94–98.

Green, LA. Fryer, GE Jr. Yawn, BP. Lanier, D. Dovey, SM (2001). 'The ecology of medical care revisited.' *New England Journal of Medicine*, 344(26): 2021–2025.

Grol, R. Wensing, M (2007). 'Measuring performance quality in general practice: is international harmonization desirable?' *British Journal of General Practice,* 57(542): 691–692.

Grol, R. Wensing, M. Mainz, J. Jung, HP. Ferreira, P. Hearnshaw, H. Hjortdahl, P. Olesen, F. Reis, S. Ribacke, M. Szecsenyi, J (2000). 'Patients in Europe evaluate general practice care: an international comparison.' *British Journal of General Practice*, 50(460): 882–887.

Horder, J. Horder, E (1954). 'Illness in general practice.' *Practitioner*, 173(1034): 177–185.

Jha, AK. Perlin, JB. Kizer, KW. Dudley, RA (2003). 'Effect of the transformation of the Veterans Affairs Health Care System on the quality of care.' *New England Journal of Medicine*, 348(22): 2218–2227.

Kerr, EA. Gerzoff, RB. Krein, SL. Selby, JV. Piette, JD. Curb, JD. Herman, WH. Marrero, DG. Narayan, KM. Safford, MM. Thompson, T. Mangione, CM (2004). 'Diabetes care quality in the Veterans Affairs Health Care System and commercial managed care: the TRIAD study.' *Annals of Internal Medicine*, 141(4): 272–281.

Kizer, KW (1995). *Vision for change: a plan to restructure the Veterans Health Administration*. Washington, DC: Department of Veterans Affairs.

Kizer, KW (1996). *Prescription for change: the guiding principles and strategic objectives underlying the transformation of the Veterans Health Administration*. Washington, DC: Department of Veterans Affairs.

Kohn, LH. Corrigan, J. Donaldson, MS (eds.) (2000). *To err is human: building a safer health system*. Washington, DC: National Academies Press.

Lee, TH (2007). 'Eulogy for a quality measure.' *New England Journal of Medicine*, 357(12): 1175–1177.

Lester, HE. Roland, MO (2007). 'Measuring quality through performance. Future of quality measurement.' *British Medical Journal*, 335(7630): 1130–1131.

Lilford, RJ. Brown, CA. Nicholl, J (2007). 'Use of process measures to monitor the quality of clinical practice.' *British Medical Journal*, 335(7621): 648–650.

Longman, P (2005). 'The best care anywhere.' *Washington Monthly*, 37(1/2): 38–48.

Macinko, J. Starfield, B. Shi, L (2007). 'Quantifying the health benefits of primary care physician supply in the United States.' *International Journal of Health Services Research*, 37(1): 111–126.

Mangin, D. Toop, L (2007). 'The Quality and Outcomes Framework: what have you done to yourselves?' *British Journal of General Practice*, 57(539): 435–437.

Mangione-Smith, R. DeCristofaro, AH. Setodji, CM. Keesey, J. Klein, DJ. Adams, JL. Schuster, MA. McGlynn, EA (2007). 'The quality of ambulatory care delivered to children in the United States.' *New England Journal of Medicine*, 357(15): 1515–1523.

Marshall, M. Smith, P (2003). 'Rewarding results: using financial incentives to improve quality.' *Quality and Safety in Health Care*, 12(6): 397–398.

Marshall, MN. Shekelle, PG. Leatherman, S. Brook, RH (2000). 'The public release of performance data: what do we expect to gain? A review of the evidence.' *Journal of the American Medical Association*, 283(14): 1866–1874.

McGlynn, EA (2003). 'Introduction and overview of the conceptual framework for a national quality measurement and reporting system.' *Medical Care*, 41(Suppl. 1): 1–7.

McGlynn, EA (2007). 'Intended and unintended consequences. What should we really worry about?' *Medical Care*, 45(1): 3–5.

McGlynn, EA. Asch, M. Adams, A. Keesey, J. Kicks, J. DeCristofaro, A. Kerr, EA (2003). 'The quality of health care delivered to adults in the United States.' *New England Journal of Medicine*, 348(26): 2635–2645.

McGlynn, EA. Cassel, CK. Leatherman, ST. DeCristofaro, A. Smits, HL (2003a). 'Establishing national goals for quality improvement.' *Medical Care*, 41(Suppl. 1): 16–29.

McGlynn, EA. Naylor, CD. Anderson, GM. Leape, LL. Park, RE. Hilborne, LH. Bernstein, SJ. Goldman, BS. Armstrong, PW. Keesey, JW. Pinfold, SP. Damberg, C. Sherwood, MJ. Brook, RH (1994). 'Comparison of the appropriateness of coronary angiography and coronary artery bypass surgery between Canada and New York State.' *Journal of the American Medical Association*, 272(12): 934–940.

Murphy, MK. Black, NA. Lamping, DL. McKee, CM. Sanderson, CF. Askham, J. Martineau, T (1998). 'Consensus development methods and their use in clinical guideline development.' *Health Technology Assessment*, 2(3): 1–88.

National Audit Office (2008). *NHS pay modernisation: new contracts for general practice services in England*. London: National Audit Office.

Naylor, CD (1995). 'Grey zones of clinical practice: some limits to evidence-based medicine.' *Lancet*, 345(8953): 840–842.

O Neill, O (2003). 'Trust with accountability?' *Journal of Health Services Research and Policy*, 8(1): 3–4.

Oxman, AD. Thomson, MA. Davis, DA. Haynes, RB (1995). 'No magic bullets: a systematic review of 102 trials of interventions to improve professional practice.' *Canadian Medical Association Journal*, 153(10): 1423–1431.

Perlin, JP. Kolodner, RM. Roswell, RH (2004). 'The Veterans Health Administration: quality, value, accountability, and information as transforming strategies for patient-centered care.' *American Journal of Managed Care*, 10(11 Pt 2): 828–836.

Roland, M (2004). 'Linking physicians' pay to the quality of care – a major experiment in the United Kingdom.' *New England Journal of Medicine*, 351(14): 1448–1454.

Roland, MO. Campbell, SM. Bailey, N. Whalley, D. Sibbald, B (2006). 'Financial incentives to improve the quality of primary care in the UK: predicting the consequences of change.' *Primary Health Care Research and Development*, 7(1): 18–26.

Sackett, DL. Rosenberg, WMC. Gray, JAM (1996). 'Evidence-based medicine: what it is and what it isn't.' *British Medical Journal*, 312(7023): 71–72.

Salisbury, C. Goodall, S. Montgomery, AA. Pickin, DM. Edwards, S. Sampson, F. Simons, L. Lattimer, V (2007). 'Does advanced access improve access to primary health care? Questionnaire survey of patients. *British Journal of General Practice*, 57(541): 615–621.

Seddon, ME. Marshall, MN. Campbell, SM. Roland, MO (2001). 'A systematic review of the quality of clinical care provided in general practice in the UK, Australia and New Zealand.' *Quality in Health Care*, 10(3): 152–158.

Sheldon, T (2004). 'Learning from abroad or policy tourism?' *British Journal of General Practice*, 54(503): 410–411.

Smith, P (1995). 'On the unintended consequences of publishing performance data in the public sector.' *International Journal of Public Administration*, 18(2/3): 277–310.

Smith, R (1998). 'All changed, changed utterly.' *British Medical Journal*, 316(7149): 1917–1918.

Starfield, B (1994). 'Is primary care essential?' *Lancet*, 344(8930): 1129–1133.

Starfield, B (1998). '*Primary care: balancing health needs, services and technology.* Oxford: Oxford University Press.

Starfield, B. Shi, L. Macinko, J (2005). 'Contribution of primary care to health systems and health.' *Milbank Memorial Fund Quarterly*, 83(3): 457–502.

Steel, N. Maisey, S. Clark, A. Fleetcroft, R. Howe, A (2007). 'Quality of clinical primary care and targeted incentive payments: an observational study.' *British Journal of General Practice*, 57(539): 449–454.

Victora, CG. Vaughan, JP. Barros, F. Silva, AC. Tomasi, E (2000). 'Explaining trends in inequities: evidence from Brazilian child health studies.' *Lancet*, 356(9235): 1093–1098.

Weiner, JP. Starfield, BH. Steinwachs, DM. Mumford, LM (1991). 'Development and application of a population-oriented measure of ambulatory care case-mix.' *Medical Care*, 29(5): 452–472.

Whalley, D. Bojke, C. Gravelle, H. Sibbald, B (2006). 'GP job satisfaction in view of contract reform: a national survey.' *British Journal of General Practice*, 56(523): 87–92.

White, KL. Williams, TF. Greenberg, BG (1961). 'The ecology of medical care.' *New England Journal of Medicine*, 265: 885–892.

WHO (1978). *Primary health care.* Report of the International Conference on Primary Health Care, Alma-Ata, USSR, 6–12 September 1978. Geneva: World Health Organization.

4.2 | *Chronic care*

MARTIN MCKEE, ELLEN NOLTE

Introduction

This chapter examines the challenges inherent in assessing how health systems perform in response to chronic diseases. These are diseases that persist over an extended time and require a complex response involving coordinated inputs from a wide range of health professionals, access to essential medicines and (where appropriate) monitoring equipment. Ideally this is embedded within a system that promotes patient empowerment. There are many chronic diseases but in this chapter we draw extensively on experience with diabetes. The reasons for this are three-fold. First, diabetes was the first example of an acute disease that was transformed into a chronic disorder by the introduction of effective treatment. Second, it exemplifies the complex nature of chronic disease as its complications affect many different bodily systems and call upon the expertise of a wide range of specialists. Third, it provides a lens through which to view the performance of the overall health system.

Health system performance is the focus of the chapter and this volume. However, before looking specifically at performance it is necessary to understand the specificities of chronic diseases, many of which pose substantial challenges for performance measurement. It may also be helpful to reflect on the rapidly increasing contribution of chronic diseases to the overall burden of disease, a development that has important consequences for the assessment of health system performance more generally.

Growing importance of chronic disease

The discovery and subsequent purification of insulin in 1921 marked a fundamental transformation in the nature of health care. Until then, there was extremely limited scope for therapeutic intervention in the event of illness. Essentially, the physician could offer sympathy and symptomatic relief – perhaps using aspirin, first manufactured some twenty-five years previously – while the patient either recovered or died. The treatments available were largely useless and in some cases harmful. For the first time it was possible to treat patients who would otherwise die with effective, life-sustaining treatment.

For some years it seemed that the problem of diabetes had been solved. Certainly, people with insulin-dependent diabetes had to make significant changes to their lifestyles and adopt what are now seen as overly rigid diets. However, the complexity of diabetes was not yet apparent. By the 1950s the first generation of children whose lives had been saved by insulin were reaching middle age and manifesting a range of unexpected complications that affected vision, renal function and cardiovascular systems. Some complications (e.g. diabetic retinopathy) were quite new conditions; others (e.g. ischaemic heart disease) were also seen in the non-diabetic population but appeared earlier and more frequently in people with diabetes.

These developments posed major challenges. People with diabetes had typically developed long-term relationships with an individual physician or a small team of physicians specializing in diabetes. However, they now needed additional specialist care from ophthalmologists, renal physicians and vascular surgeons, among others. They also needed help from a range of paramedical staff such as dietitians and podiatrists. This was a new and very different model of care. Essentially, patients embarked on a journey to obtain appropriate specialized care at multiple destinations but often without either a map or a navigator. Inevitably, many perished along the way.

Diabetes is a simple biological problem (the inability to produce a particular hormone) that gives rise to a multi-system disease process. Yet, it is far from unique. A revolution in chemical engineering in the 1960s made available an increasing number of new classes of pharmaceuticals, many of which had the ability to transform the management of disease processes if they were taken indefinitely. Thiazide diuretics were joined by beta blockers and calcium antagonists in the management of hypertension. Inhaled beta sympathomimetics and steroids similarly transformed obstructive airways disease. Other classes of pharmaceuticals had a major impact on conditions such as arthritis, Parkinson's disease and epilepsy.

These new opportunities had profound consequences for the delivery of health care as a prescription was only the beginning of the process. These medicines required monitoring, first to ensure that parameters such as blood pressure or (for obstructive airways disease) respiratory function was being controlled adequately; second, to detect any side-effects at the earliest opportunity. The greatest changes were seen in the field of mental health, where the development of antidepressants and antipsychotics made it possible to close large psychiatric hospitals and replace them with community-based services.

Other changes have been less obvious but still profound. By the 1980s the advent of new chemotherapeutic agents had transformed many cancers from brief, fatal illnesses (like diabetes prior to 1922) into long-term chronic disorders which people died with, rather than from. More recently, the availability of life-sustaining treatment has similarly transformed the management of AIDS. In an unexpected parallel with diabetes it is only now that the long-term consequences are becoming clear. People on long-term treatment for AIDS are developing a range of complications, some of which relate to the underlying disease process (e.g. some malignancies) and others that are a consequence of the treatment (e.g. ischaemic heart disease linked to the atherogenic effects of antiretrovirals).

However, medical care is not the only factor driving increases in the numbers of people surviving with chronic diseases. The other is the ageing of populations. As the proportion of older people in the population grows so does the likelihood of developing a potentially disabling chronic condition because of accumulated exposure to chronic disease risk factors over a lifetime (Ben-Shlomo & Kuh 2002; Janssen & Kunst 2005). Data from Germany, the Netherlands and the United States suggest that about two thirds of those who have reached pensionable age have at least two chronic conditions (Deutsches Zentrum für Altersfragen 2005; van den Akker et al. 1998; Wolff et al. 2002).

To understand this phenomenon fully it is necessary to consider the ageing process. Populations are ageing rapidly in all industrialized countries but few commentators expect the maximum lifespan observed (currently 122 years) to increase significantly. They do expect that life expectancy at birth will continue to increase as it has in a linear fashion for over 150 years – those who would once have died young now survive for longer. At least in industrialized countries, much of this earlier gain was due to a marked decline in deaths in infancy and childhood. This now offers limited scope for further progress and future gains are expected to arise from the delay in deaths among adults.

Fries (1983) examined the process of ageing in depth and distinguished two processes, both involving the progressive loss of physiological function. The first set is essentially unmodifiable (although subsequent research has suggested that this may not be entirely true in all cases) and includes formation of cataracts and the loss of glomeruli in the kidneys that leads to a decline in renal function. Less importantly, this set also includes the greying of hair. The second set includes glucose intolerance, physical strength, cardiac reserve and cognitive function. These processes can be delayed by appropriate lifestyle changes and can also be compensated for by appropriate treatments. Fries proposed the compression of morbidity theory – while the maximum lifespan was unlikely to increase substantially, as populations adopted healthier lifestyles and as therapeutic advances continued, the period of illness (morbidity) that individuals would experience prior to their deaths would be compressed.

There is now considerable evidence that this has happened. Studies in several countries reveal that healthy life expectancy has increased at a faster rate than overall life expectancy. For example, a recent systematic review demonstrated how disability and limitations among older adults in the United States declined consistently during the 1990s (Freedman et al. 2002). However, accumulating evidence suggests that at least part of this improvement is a consequence of therapeutic advances, as complex combinations of treatment increasingly enable older people to function with multiple disorders. For example, Freedman et al. (2007) report that between 1997 and 2004 a rising prevalence of chronic conditions among older Americans (aged sixty-five and over) was accompanied by declines in the proportion reporting disability as a result of those conditions. This was supported by an analysis of the Swedish population which also reported an ageing population with a decline in disability over time but an increase in health problems among survivors (Parker & Thorslund 2007).

A typical 75-year-old may have disorders affecting multiple body systems (e.g. hypertension, arthritis, chronic airways disease, heart failure, Parkinson's disease). He/she may be undertaking treatment with perhaps ten different medications, all potentially interacting with each other and with a metabolism influenced by coexisting impairments in liver and kidney function. Such combinations of illnesses, treatments and physiological function are of such complexity that they are unlikely to become the subject of the randomized controlled trials that give rise to the evidence on which treatment decisions should be made. This situation poses severe problems for those seeking to assess the ability to respond to chronic disease and limits the scope of evaluations.

The ageing of populations is thus an important driver of increases in chronic disease but it is important to remember that these diseases are not limited to the older population. Especially in countries experiencing rising levels of obesity, increasing numbers of young and middle-aged people are developing some form of chronic health problem. It has been estimated that in 2002, 60% of all DALYs attributable to non-communicable diseases in Europe were lost before the age of sixty (WHO 2004). Recent evidence from the United States points to a rapid increase in the number of children and youths with chronic health conditions over the past four decades (Perrin et al. 2007), in particular as a response to growing levels of obesity. Rising rates of childhood chronic conditions imply subsequent higher rates of related conditions among adults (van der Lee et al. 2007).

This section, and the one preceding it, demonstrates clearly how the burden of disease is changing, with a transition from acute to chronic disease. The next section examines some of the implications for health systems.

Implications of the growth in chronic disease

The effects of the transition from acute to chronic disease are not trivial. In 2006, approximately 30% of the population in the European Union aged fifteen years and over reported a long-standing health problem, and one in four currently receives long-term medical treatment (TNS Opinion & Social 2007). Surveys undertaken in England and the United States suggest that one third and 45%, respectively, of the adult population has some form of chronic health problem (Hoffman et al. 1996; Wilson et al. 2005). People with chronic diseases are more likely to utilize health care, particularly when they have multiple problems. For example, in England people with chronic illness account for 80% of general practice consultations and about 15% of people who have three or more problems account for nearly 30% of inpatient days (Wilson et al. 2005). Estimates for the United States place the costs of chronic illness at around three quarters of the total national health expenditure (Hoffman et al. 1996). Some individual chronic diseases (e.g. diabetes) account for between 2% and 15% of national health expenditure in some European countries (Suhrcke et al. 2005).

This changing context has profound implications for policy-makers in the health sector. Health care is still largely built around an acute, episodic model of care that is ill-equipped to meet the requirements of those needing chronic care (Table 4.2.1). Experience in many countries shows that the responses required and their multiple interlinkages are very complex and it cannot be assumed that a model appropriate to these needs will simply emerge.

Table 4.2.1 *Features differentiating acute and chronic disease*

	Acute illness	**Chronic illness**
Onset	Abrupt	Generally gradual and often subtle
Duration	Limited	Lengthy and indefinite
Cause	Usually single	Usually uncertain
Diagnosis and prognosis	Usually accurate	Usually uncertain
Technological intervention	Usually effective	Often indecisive, adverse effects are common
Outcome	Cure possible	No cure
Uncertainty	Minimal	Pervasive
Knowledge	Professionals knowledgeable, patients inexperienced	Professionals and patients have complementary knowledge and experience

Source: Adapted from English Department of Health 2004

Health systems based on networks of semi-autonomous professionals and organizations struggle to ensure that the right combination of services is in the right place at the right time. In the past the standard response to complex illness was to restrict patients' movements by confining them to hospital beds to wait patiently for the appropriate services. This approach is still used in some countries but it is incompatible with a world in which patients with chronic diseases live and work in the community and go to the services they need rather than waiting for those services to come to them.

In these circumstances it is perhaps inevitable that those with chronic health problems often receive less than optimal quality of care. Chronic conditions frequently go untreated or are poorly controlled until more serious and acute complications arise. Where those conditions are recognized, there is often a large gap between evidence-based treatment guidelines and current practice. McGlynn et al. (2003) demonstrated that only about 45% of individuals with diabetes in the United States at the end of the 1990s had received the recommended package of care. The proportion was somewhat higher for patients with congestive heart failure (64%) but was still suboptimal. Similarly, a systematic review of the quality of clinical care in general practice in Australia, New Zealand and the United Kingdom found that only 49% of patients with diabetes had undergone routine foot examinations and only 47% of eligible patients had been prescribed beta blockers after a heart attack, even in the highest-achieving practices (Seddon et al. 2001).

Change will require the institution of new managerial and organizational skills, backed up by effective information systems, but this can happen only if the role of health systems is re-conceptualized. This is of particular importance for monitoring performance. Too often, the discourse surrounding health systems is based on a model of acute care that is relatively much less important than it was. This is apparent in the ways that many politicians judge the performance of health systems. Their focus on waiting lists and the numbers of procedures undertaken recalls the statement attributed to Einstein: "not everything that can be counted counts, and not everything that counts can be counted."

The challenges of assessing how well health systems respond to chronic illness are examined in the next section.

Assessing performance: different dimensions

Before looking at the specific issues that arise with chronic diseases, it is helpful to recall that performance assessment of health systems has multiple dimensions – the nature of the assessment undertaken will depend on the dimension in which the proposed question lies.

The first dimension is the level at which assessment takes place. For example, the different levels of decision-making within a health-care system can range from the primary process of patient care (micro level) to the organizational context (meso level) to the financing and policy or health system context (macro level) (Plochg & Klazinga 2002). This can be illustrated with reference to diabetes.

Beginning with the primary process of patient care, an assessment of performance may focus on doctor-patient interaction to communicate inevitably complex messages about the natural history of the disorder and to set out the options to manage the disease in ways that are appropriate for the patient's lifestyle and aspirations. Such an assessment might draw on, for example, techniques based on conversational analysis (Maynard & Heritage 2005).

At the meso level, assessment might focus on the extent to which different aspects of the disease process are managed by the appropriate member of the clinical team or organization. Ideally the clinical management of diabetes will be located on a related measure of the quality of primary care – the extent to which admissions (for complications and diabetic emergencies) to hospital are avoided. This measure of avoidable hospitalization has been shown to vary with access to effective care (Billings et al. 1996).

At the macro level, the rate of diabetes-related blindness or amputation among a population of people with diabetes may serve as an indicator of the performance of the whole health-care system. For example, the OECD Health Care Quality Indicators Project has identified amputation rates in people with diabetes as a potential key indicator for international comparisons of health-care quality across OECD countries (Armesto et al. 2007). These end results capture the performance of many different health professionals, including those who manage the underlying disease, those who identify complications at an early stage and those who treat them once they arise.

Finally, much of the growing epidemic of type II diabetes is fuelled by rising levels of obesity. This can be ameliorated by healthy public policies directed at the relative price, availability and marketing of energy-dense foods (reflecting, for example, restrictions on advertising or the use of 'fat taxes') and opportunities for energy expenditure through physical activity (reflecting, for example, construction of recreational facilities and cycle lanes). Thus, the mortality from type II diabetes might be considered a measure of the performance of government as a whole, with high rates signifying a failure to enact appropriate intersectoral health-promoting policies.

A second dimension differentiates the process and outcome of care. A typical process measure – used in many structured diabetes disease management programmes – is control of the metabolic disorder that characterizes diabetes. This is undertaken by monitoring HbA1c levels among patients to capture blood glucose levels over the preceding few weeks (Knight et al. 2005). For example, the United Kingdom's Quality and Outcomes Framework (Department of Health 2003) includes the frequency of undertaking regular HbA1c tests on patients with diabetes as a measure of quality of care. Many structured programmes use a related outcome measure – the proportion of patients with diabetes whose last HbA1c result was below a certain level.

Plochg and Klazinga (2002) argue for the necessity of considering each of the three levels of decision-making in the health-care system as each is characterized by distinct rationales addressing different dynamics. Thus, decision-making at the micro level (where patient care is delivered) is facing growing complexity due to the growth in available knowledge and technologies; an increase in the managerial complexity involved in the delivery of multidisciplinary health care; and, especially, patients' increasing engagement in decision-making.

The importance of involving patients fully in their own care was highlighted in the 1989 St. Vincent Declaration which set out a widely accepted set of goals and principles for the prevention, diagnosis and management of diabetes and its complications. This considers people with diabetes to be members of a therapeutic partnership in which they are linked with the various health professionals to whom they look for advice as they negotiate an appropriate therapeutic regime. Thus, performance measures must take account of the need to balance the evidence that imposing a strict and inflexible regime of diet and exercise will minimize the risk of complications against the knowledge that this comes at the cost of precluding the patient from leading a 'normal' life.

Different rationales prevail at the macro level, largely related to the question of how to allocate scarce resources in health care. For example, policy-makers faced with competing demands may have to decide whether the finite sums available are to be invested in the care of people with one or other chronic disease, or whether they will be used for the management of chronic disease or the reduction of waiting times for acute care. If the choices made at each level are not coordinated they can result in ambiguous goals, conflicting interests and excessive bureaucracy and ultimately limit the effectiveness of efforts to improve performance.

It is equally important to consider both process and outcome measures as they provide different, yet complementary, insights into the care process. Ultimately, the outcome of care is most important (e.g. in the amount of blindness, amputations and premature deaths avoided) but it is also important that those patients for whom these may be long-term outcomes receive care that is humane and reflects their expectations and lifestyles.

Finally, assessment of performance must take a broad perspective not least because the implementation of performance measures will change the behaviour of health-care providers, especially when supported by sanctions or incentives. This is an area that is fraught with the risk of unintended consequences as those whose performance is being assessed concentrate on what is being measured rather than what may be important.

The health system perspective

The preceding section showed how a comprehensive assessment of the ability to respond to chronic disorders necessarily requires evaluations of both process and outcomes, with inquiry at different levels. In this section the focus is on the level of the overall health-care system involved. Chronic disorders are complex and involve inputs from a wide range of health professionals equipped with appropriate knowledge and access to effective technology and pharmaceuticals. Hence, chronic disease is an ideal lens through which to assess the overall performance of the health-care system.

We propose a diagnostic hierarchy that involves a step-wise evaluation of health system performance. This approach begins by using existing data to identify potential problems. Normally this will not provide information on the precise reasons for any problem identified – this will require further steps using additional data. Once again we use the example of diabetes as an illustration.

Effective treatment reduces the risk of the disabling and potentially fatal complications of diabetes (Diabetes Control and Complications

Trial Research Group 1993; United Kingdom Prospective Diabetes Study Group (UKPDS) 1998; Writing team for the Diabetes Control and Complications Trial/Epidemiology of Diabetes Interventions and Complications Research Group 2002) and the risk of premature cardiovascular disease (Diabetes Control and Complications Trial Research Group 1995; Gaede et al. 2003). For this reason, several commentators have argued that any death from diabetes in a young person is a sentinel health event that should raise questions about the quality of health-care delivery at the level of the organization concerned (Connell & Louden 1983; McColl & Gulliford 1993; Nolte et al. 2002). However, such deaths occur in all health-care systems although the rates vary substantially between countries.

The Diabetes Epidemiology Research International (DERI) study monitored cohorts of young people with type I diabetes in the United States, Japan, Israel and Finland. It found large differences in ten-year survival with the worst outcomes in the United States and Japan, and the best in Israel (DERI Mortality Study Group 1995). A separate study conducted by the British Diabetic Association (Laing et al. 1999) found that survival in the United Kingdom was comparable to that in Israel; the death rate in Japan was between four and five times higher than those in the United Kingdom or Israel.

A subsequent study drew on data collected in a standardized form during the WHO DiaMond and EURODIAB studies (Nolte et al. 2006). This data on the incidence of type I diabetes among children aged 0–14 was combined with data on mortality at ages 0–39 (selected to capture ages where certification of deaths attributable to diabetes was likely to be relatively reliable) to generate a mortality-incidence ratio. This study covered twenty-nine countries and confirmed the existence of very great differences in outcomes. Again, the worst results were obtained for a number of eastern European countries and Japan. The best outcomes were seen in some European countries with national health services, including the United Kingdom, Sweden, Spain, Italy and Greece. Clearly, such studies are dependent on the quality of recording of mortality and thus can only be undertaken in high- and some middle-income countries (see Chapter 2.1 on population health). It is also necessary to use only data on deaths at young ages as, although diabetes is often a contributory factor in deaths at older ages, there is considerable variation in recording practices.

These studies demonstrate that there is a remarkable variation in diabetes outcomes across countries. This suggests that there are gross differences in health systems' ability to provide adequate care for people with chronic diseases but gives little indication of why such differences exist. The next step therefore involves the study of data that can shed light on the immediate causes of death that drive the differences in order to highlight possible underlying organizational and system failures.

In the DERI study, much of the observed excess mortality in the Japanese cohort was attributable to diabetic renal disease (Diabetes Epidemiology Research International Mortality Study Group 1991). This reflected the higher incidence of end-stage renal disease and less access to dialysis than in the United States (Matsushima et al. 1995). Another study demonstrated how lower survival among individuals with type I diabetes in Estonia and Latvia (in comparison to Finland) was driven by much higher rates of the acute complications of diabetes (Podar et al. 2000).

These findings suggest the need to examine the specificities of the health systems in question, so the next step is more detailed assessment of the actual processes of care. For example, Tabak et al. (2000) compared the management of diabetes in Hungary and the United States and found that American patients were less likely to receive education about their condition; to see an ophthalmologist or diabetologist; or to perform self-monitoring of blood glucose. Hungarian patients had a lower prevalence of retinopathy, registered blindness and albuminuria (an indicator of kidney damage) but were more likely to experience severe hypoglycaemia (suggesting over-restrictive treatment). Again, this highlights the need to look holistically at processes and outcomes at all levels of care.

A holistic approach was demonstrated in a series of studies in the former Soviet Union, following an observation that death rates from diabetes among young people had risen markedly since 1991 – as much as eight-fold in some countries such as Ukraine (Telishevska et al. 2001). An analytical framework was developed in which four sets of inputs were identified as being essential for the delivery of effective care at the whole-system level: (i) human resources, in the form of an appropriate combination of skilled professionals and informed patients; (ii) physical resources, in the form of pharmaceuticals (e.g.

insulin and oral hypoglycaemics) and equipment (e.g. glucometers and reagent strips); (iii) knowledge resources, in the form of evidence-based clinical guidelines; and (iv) social resources, in the form of social support for patients. For patients to survive, the right combination of resources must be brought together in the right place and at the right time.

This framework was operationalized to create an instrument that could be used to undertake a rapid appraisal of a health system and was applied in Kyrgyzstan (Hopkinson et al. 2004) and Georgia (Balabanova et al. 2009). The studies identified an array of individual weaknesses but the overriding problem concerned integration. For example, individual health professionals would be trained abroad in methods of foot care but would be unable to obtain the inexpensive equipment required to provide it on their return. Patients would have glucometers but not the reagent strips required to use them. Newly diagnosed patients would be discharged from hospital without a supply of insulin and would become ill while they waited for the distribution system to make it available in their local pharmacy. The studies clearly highlight the multiple challenges that these two systems face in providing comprehensive diabetes care. They demonstrate how a single intervention (e.g. training health professionals in foot care, providing adequate supplies of insulin) to address a key problem in low-income settings (Beran et al. 2005) may be necessary but by no means sufficient to improve diabetes care in these settings.

This chapter has focused on diabetes for several reasons, chiefly because it is the easiest to study among the common chronic disorders. Diabetes is a very common condition: worldwide prevalence is estimated to be 2.8% (2000) and expected to increase to 4.4% by 2030 (Wild et al. 2004). The onset of type I diabetes is relatively acute and the diagnosis is unambiguous. This contrasts with conditions such as hypertension or chronic airways disease in which the onset of disease is more insidious and where many of those affected will not be identifiable. The required treatment of diabetes is largely uncontroversial and the natural history of the condition is both well-understood and modifiable by effective care, as outlined earlier. However, the system response to diabetes involves the delivery of integrated individualized care and thus is essentially the same as that required for patients with any (or multiple) chronic disorders. As such, it is uniquely placed to act as a marker of health system performance in the field of chronic care. Essentially, a health-care system that is unable to deliver effective and timely care for patients with diabetes is unlikely to be able to do so for other chronic disorders (McKee & Nolte 2004).

Towards high-performing health systems

The preceding sections highlight the many challenges that exist in assessing the performance of health systems with regard to chronic disease. International comparisons of outcomes indicate clearly that health systems do matter and studies of the process of care identify the critical importance of coordinating the elements of care. Proposed models that seek to ensure the coordination of care have proven extremely difficult to evaluate – in part because they are often implemented in different ways in different settings (Wagner et al. 1999). The problems that need to be addressed may also differ between settings and make comparison problematic. Finally, those evaluations that have been undertaken have often been conducted in settings that cannot easily be generalized. Notwithstanding these problems, it is possible to propose some broad principles that are likely to underpin the delivery of optimal care for patients with chronic diseases (Singh 2005; Zwar et al. 2006).

The presence of appropriately skilled and motivated health professionals who have access to appropriate pharmaceuticals and technology and continuing professional development is a prerequisite for the delivery of optimal care. However, the challenge is how to organize them once they are in place.

Primary care plays a critical role. The complexity inherent in chronic disease means that patients will require assistance to navigate their path through the system in all but the simplest cases. This is best achieved by a partnership between the patient and his/her primary-care provider, with the latter able to take a holistic view of the patient's problems and propose solutions that are consistent with his/her lifestyle and expectations.

Multi-professional teams are important. The precise combination of skills required will vary with a patient's individual needs but will almost always include physicians, nurses and a range of other health professionals (e.g. dietitians, podiatrists, physiotherapists). There is now compelling evidence that physicians are not always the most appropriate providers of much of the routine care for chronic diseases

(Sibbald et al. 2004) and nurse-led clinics are becoming increasingly common in many countries (McKee et al. 2005). However, integrated care requires mechanisms that ensure strong linkages between all those involved in the delivery of care (Ouwens et al. 2005).

Patient self-management has been described as a 'cornerstone of treatment' (American Diabetes Association 2003) although the extent to which it is possible varies among different disease processes and in relation to the patient's functional ability, especially in terms of cognitive skills. Effective self-management gives patients greater motivation, skills and information. One study of diabetes identified this as the single most important factor in determining outcomes such as good metabolic control, reduced complication rates and hospitalization (Stam & Graham 1997). The means of supporting self-management are complex and can be resource intensive, requiring regular access to appropriate levels of care. Determination of the patient's needs, goals and treatment requires negotiation and not instruction (Fisher et al. 2005). It is much more than just patient education. Patient empowerment also requires strong health system governance structures that can secure patients' rights and protect vulnerable individuals.

Care should be responsive to the needs of patients and their carers, rather than trying to fit within rigid structures and models. It should be patient centred – 'respectful of and responsive to individual patient preferences, needs, and values and ensuring that patient values guide all clinical decisions' (National Diabetes Education Program 2005). The care of chronic disorders involves a partnership and therefore it should be delivered in ways that are acceptable to both patients and practitioners, ensuring that patients can participate fully in decision-making.

Care should also be evidence-based. The individual elements of the care process should be demonstrably effective on the basis of careful evaluations within representative samples of patients. This evidence should be available to practitioners in the form of guidelines and standards that should be sufficiently flexible to accommodate new technologies. However, this alone will not be sufficient to ensure high-quality care.

References

American Diabetes Association (2003). 'Standards of medical care for patients with diabetes mellitus.' *Diabetes Care*, 26(Suppl. 1): 33–50.

Armesto, S. Lapetra, M. Wei, L. Kelley, E (2007). *Health care quality indicators project*. 2006 data collection update report. Paris: OECD.

Balabanova, D. McKee, M. Koroleva, N. Chikovani, I. Goguadze, K. Kobaladze, T. Adeyi, O. Robles, S. (2009). 'Navigating the health system: diabetes care in Georgia.' *Health Policy Planning*, 24: 46–54.

Ben-Shlomo, Y. Kuh, D (2002). 'A life course approach to chronic disease epidemiology: conceptual models, empirical challenges, and interdisciplinary perspectives.' *International Journal of Epidemiology*, 31(2): 285–293.

Beran, D. Yudkin J. de Courten, M (2005). 'Access to care for patients with insulin-requiring diabetes in developing countries: case studies of Mozambique and Zambia.' *Diabetes Care*, 28(9): 2136–2140.

Billings, J. Anderson, GM. Newman, LS (1996). 'Recent findings on preventable hospitalizations.' *Health Affairs (Millwood)*, 15(3): 239–249.

Connell, FA. Louden, JM (1983). 'Diabetes mortality in persons under 45 years of age.' *American Journal of Public Health*, 73(10): 1174–1177.

Department of Health (2003). *Investing in general practice. The new general medical services contract*. (February 2003). London: Department of Health (http://www.dh.gov.uk/en/Publicationsandstatistics/Publications/PublicationsPolicyAndGuidance/DH_4071966).

Department of Health (2004). *Chronic disease management: a compendium for information*. London: Department of Health.

DERI Mortality Study Group (1995). 'International analysis of insulin-dependent diabetes mellitus mortality: a preventable mortality perspective.' *American Journal of Epidemiology*, 142(6): 612–618.

Deutsches Zentrum für Altersfragen (2005). *Gesundheit und Gesundheitsversorgung. Der Alterssurvey: Aktuelles auf einen Blick, ausgewählte Ergebnisse* [Health and health provision. The Alterssurvey: News and views, selected results]. Bonn: Bundesministeriums für Familie, Senioren, Frauen und Jugend.

Diabetes Control and Complications Trial Research Group (1993). 'The effect of intensive treatment of diabetes on the development and progression of long-term complications in insulin-dependent diabetes mellitus.' *New England Journal of Medicine*, 329(14): 977–986.

Diabetes Control and Complications Trial Research Group (1995). 'Effect of intensive diabetes management on macrovascular events and risk factors in the Diabetes Control and Complications Trial.' *American Journal of Cardiology*, 75(14): 894–903.

Diabetes Epidemiology Research International Mortality Study Group (1991). 'International evaluation of cause-specific mortality and IDDM.' *Diabetes Care*, 14(1): 55–60.

Fisher, EB. Brownson, CA. O'Toole, ML. Shetty, G. Anwuri, VV. Glasgow, RE (2005). 'Ecological approaches to self-management: the case of diabetes.' *American Journal of Public Health*, 95(9): 1523–1535.

Freedman, V. Martin, L. Schoeni, R (2002). 'Recent trends in disability and functioning among older adults in the United States.' *Journal of the American Medical Association*, 288(24): 3137–3146.

Freedman, V. Schoeni, R. Martin, L. Cornman, J (2007). 'Chronic conditions and the decline in late-life disability.' *Demography*, 44(3): 459–477.

Fries, JF (1983). 'The compression of morbidity.' *Milbank Memorial Fund Quarterly Health & Society*, 61(3): 397–419.

Gaede, P. Vedel, P. Larsen, N. Jansen, G. Parving, H. Pedersen, O (2003). 'Multifactorial intervention and cardiovascular disease in patients with type 2 diabetes.' *New England Journal of Medicine*, 348(5): 383–393.

Hoffman, C. Rice, D. Sung, H (1996). 'Persons with chronic conditions. Their prevalence and costs.' *Journal of the American Medical Association*, 276(18): 1473–1479.

Hopkinson, BD. Balabanova, D. McKee, M. Kutzin, J (2004). 'The human perspective on health care reform: coping with diabetes in Kyrgyzstan.' *International Journal of Health Planning & Management*, 19(1): 43–61.

Janssen, F. Kunst, A (2005). 'Cohort patterns in mortality trends among the elderly in seven European countries, 1950–99.' *International Journal of Epidemiology*, 34(5): 1149–1159.

Knight, K. Badamgarav, E. Henning, J. Hasselblad, V. Gano, A. Ofman, J. Weingarten, S (2005). 'A systematic review of diabetes disease management programs.' *American Journal of Managed Care*, 11(4): 242–250.

Laing, SP. Swerdlow, AJ. Slater, SD. Botha, JL. Burden, AC. Waugh, NR. Smith, AW. Hill, RD. Bingley, PJ. Patterson, CC. Qiao, Z. Keen, H (1999). 'The British Diabetic Association Cohort Study, I: all-cause mortality in patients with insulin-treated diabetes mellitus.' *Diabetic Medicine*, 16(6): 459–465.

Matsushima, M. Tajima, N. LaPorte, RE. Orchard, TJ. Tull, ES. Gower, IF. Kitagawa, T (1995). 'Markedly increased renal disease mortality and incidence of renal replacement therapy among IDDM patients in Japan in contrast to Allegheny County, Pennsylvania, USA.' *Diabetologia*, 38(2): 236–243.

Maynard, DW. Heritage, J (2005). 'Conversation analysis, doctor–patient interaction and medical communication.' *Medical Education*, 39(4): 428–435.

McColl, AJ. Gulliford, MC (1993). *Population health outcome indicators for the NHS. A feasibility study*. London: Faculty of Public Health Medicine and the Department of Public Health Medicine, United Medical and Dental Schools of Guy's and St. Thomas' Hospitals.

McGlynn, E. Asch, S. Adams, J. Keesey, J. Hicks, J. DeCristofaro, A. Kerr, E. (2003). 'The quality of health care delivered to adults in the United States.' *New England Journal of Medicine*, 348(26): 2635–2645.

McKee, M. Nolte, E (2004). 'Responding to the challenge of chronic diseases: ideas from Europe.' *Clinical Medicine*, 4(4): 336–342.

McKee, M. Dubois, C-A. Sibbald, B (2005). Changing professional boundaries. In: McKee, M. Dubois, CA. Nolte, E. *Human resources for health in Europe*. Buckingham: Open University Press: pp.63–78.

National Diabetes Education Program (2005). *Making systems changes for better diabetes care*. Bethesda, MD: National Diabetes Education Program (http://www.betterdiabetescare.nih.gov/WHATpatientcenteredcare.htm).

Nolte, E. Bain, C. McKee, M (2006). 'Diabetes as a tracer condition in international benchmarking of health systems.' *Diabetes Care*, 29(5): 1007–1011.

Nolte, E. Scholz, R. Shkolnikov, V. McKee, M (2002). 'The contribution of medical care to changing life expectancy in Germany and Poland.' *Social Science & Medicine*, 55(11): 1907–1923.

Ouwens, M. Wollersheim, H. Hermens, R. Hulscher, M. Grol, R (2005). 'Integrated care programmes for chronically ill patients: a review of systematic reviews.' *International Journal for Quality in Health Care*, 17(2): 141–146.

Parker, MG. Thorslund, M (2007). 'Health trends in the elderly population: getting better and getting worse.' *Gerontologist*, 47(2): 150–158.

Perrin, J. Bloom, S. Gortmaker, S (2007). 'The increase of childhood chronic conditions in the United States.' *Journal of the American Medical Association*, 297(24): 2755–2759.

Plochg, T. Klazinga, NS (2002). 'Community-based integrated care: myth or must?' *International Journal for Quality in Health Care*, 14(2): 91–101.

Podar, T. Solntsev, A. Reunanen, A. Urbonaite, B. Zalinkevicius, R. Karvonen, M. LaPorte, RE. Tuomilehto, J (2000). 'Mortality in patients with childhood-onset type 1 diabetes in Finland, Estonia, and Lithuania.' *Diabetes Care,* 23(3): 290–294.

Seddon, M. Marshall, M. Campbell, S. Roland, M (2001). 'Systematic review of studies of quality of clinical care in general practice in the UK, Australia, and New Zealand.' *Quality in Health Care,* 10(3): 152–158.

Sibbald, B. Shen, J. McBride, A (2004). 'Changing the skill-mix of the health care workforce.' *Journal of Health Services Research & Policy,* 9(Suppl. 1): 28–38.

Singh, D (2005). *Evidence about improving care for people with long-term conditions.* Birmingham: University of Birmingham, Surrey and Sussex PCT Alliance.

Stam, DM. Graham, JP (1997). 'Important aspects of self-management education in patients with diabetes.' *Pharmacy Practice Management Quarterly,* 17(2): 12–25.

Suhrcke, M. McKee, M. Sauto Arce, R. Tsolova, S. Mortensen, J (2005). *The contribution of health to the economy in the European Union.* Brussels: European Commission.

Tabak, AG. Tamas, G. Zgibor, J. Wilson, R. Becker, D. Kerenyi, Z. Orchard, TJ (2000). 'Targets and reality: a comparison of health care indicators in the US (Pittsburgh Epidemiology of Diabetes Complications Study) and Hungary (DiabCare Hungary).' *Diabetes Care,* 23(9): 1284–1289.

Telishevska, M. Chenet, L. McKee, M (2001). 'Towards an understanding of the high death rate among young people with diabetes in Ukraine.' *Diabetic Medicine,* 18(1): 3–9.

TNS Opinion & Social (2007). *Health in the European Union.* Special Eurobarometer 272e. Brussels: European Commission.

United Kingdom Prospective Diabetes Study Group (UKPDS) (1998). 'Intensive blood-glucose control with sulfonylureas or insulin compared with conventional treatment and risk of complications in patients with type 2 diabetes (UKPDS33).' *Lancet,* 352(9131): 837–853.

Van den Akker, M. Buntinx, F. Metsemakers, J. Roos, S. Knottnerus, J (1998). 'Multimorbidity in general practice: prevalence, incidence, and determinants of co-occurring chronic and recurrent diseases.' *Journal of Clinical Epidemiology,* 51: 367–375.

Van der Lee, J. Mokkink, L. Grootenhuis, M. Heymans, H. Offringa, M (2007). 'Definitions and measurement of chronic health conditions in childhood.' *Journal of the American Medical Association,* 297(24): 2741–2751.

Wagner, EH. Davis, C. Schaefer, J. von Korff, M. Austin, B (1999). 'A survey of leading chronic disease management programs: are they consistent with the literature?' *Managed Care Quarterly,* 7(3): 56–66.

WHO (2004). *Health statistics and health information systems. Revised Global Burden of Disease (GBD) 2002 estimates.* Geneva: World Health Organization (http://www.who.int/healthinfo/global_burden_disease/estimates_regional_2002_revised/en/).

Wild, S. Roglic, G. Green, A. Sicree, R. King, H (2004). 'Global prevalence of diabetes.' *Diabetes Care,* 27(5): 1047–1053.

Wilson, T. Buck, D. Ham, C (2005). 'Rising to the challenge: will the NHS support people with long-term conditions?' *British Medical Journal,* 330(7492): 657–661.

Wolff, J. Starfield, B. Anderson, GF (2002). 'Prevalence, expenditures, and complications of multiple chronic conditions in the elderly.' *Archives of Internal Medicine,* 162(20): 2269–2276.

Writing team for the Diabetes Control and Complications Trial/Epidemiology of Diabetes Interventions and Complications Research Group (2002). 'Effect of intensive therapy on the microvascular complications of type 1 diabetes mellitus.' *Journal of the American Medical Association,* 287(19): 2563–2569.

Zwar, N. Harris, M. Griffiths, R. Dennis, S. Roland, M. Powell Davies, G. Hasan, I (2006). *A systematic review of chronic disease management.* Canberra: Australian Primary Health Care Research Institute.

4.3 Performance measurement in mental health services

ROWENA JACOBS, DAVID MCDAID

Introduction

Mental health warrants a dedicated chapter within this book as it accounts for 14% of the global burden of disease. An estimated 450 million people worldwide are affected by mental health problems at any given time and one in five people will experience a psychiatric disorder (excluding dementia) within any given year (Horton 2007; WHO Regional Office for Europe 2003). Moreover, as we will indicate, assessment of the performance of mental health services presents challenges that may be unique within health care.

Within Europe, mental health problems account for approximately 20% of the total disability burden of ill health but often appear to be a lower policy priority than many other areas of health. This is despite the fact that nearly all countries readily admit that poor mental health has major impacts, not only on health but also on many other sectors of the economy (Taipale 2001).

The costs of poor mental health are conservatively estimated to account for 3%-4% of GDP in the European Union (EU) alone, yet none of these countries actually spends much more than 1% of GDP on mental health (Knapp et al. 2007). Differences in the boundaries between health and social care make cross-country comparisons difficult but health system funding for mental health in the EU ranges from almost 14% in England to much less than 4% in other countries including Bulgaria, the Czech Republic, Poland and Portugal.

One challenge for performance measurement is that many of the impacts of mental health go well beyond economic consequences – poor mental health has seriously marginalizing social consequences for individuals. These problems are compounded by deeply rooted stigma, fear, prejudice and discrimination; in some parts of Europe it remains effectively taboo to discuss the challenges that mental health raises for governments (Sayce & Curran 2007). Fundamental human

426

rights can also be affected as mental health is almost unique in its potential for compulsory detainment and treatment of individuals.

Another challenge arises because the organization and management of mental health services varies greatly within health-care systems across countries. A growing evidence base supports a community care centred approach, with substantial developments in pharmaceutical and psychosocial therapies and in services to help individuals reintegrate into the community. Many of these interventions appear to be cost effective in a variety of settings (Chisholm et al. 2004, Gutierrez-Recacha et al. 2006). This changing evidence base means that different countries are now at very different stages in rebalancing their mental health systems to make community based care the mainstay of the system. This principle was reaffirmed in the Mental Health Declaration for Europe and the Mental Health Action Plan for Europe endorsed by all fifty-two Members of the WHO European Region in 2005 (WHO Regional Office for Europe 2005).

Nearly all of western Europe has seen a shift in the balance of care with the closure of many psychiatric hospitals and the transfer of other beds to general hospitals. In much of northern Europe this has been accompanied by investment in social and community care based services. Mediterranean countries such as Italy, Portugal and Spain have made little investment in community based alternatives and much of the responsibility for support now rests with families. However, those services that are available often have very fragmented funding and delivery structures (McDaid et al. 2007), potentially leading to substantial variations in the type and quality of care provided (Hermann et al. 2006).

In contrast, very large and often isolated long-stay psychiatric hospitals and social care homes (*internats*) still dominate in much of central and eastern Europe. There are few incentives to change the balance of care, particularly where local communities rely on them for employment. The abuse of human rights within these institutions remains a key concern despite pressure from civil society organizations, the Council of Europe and judgements from the European Court of Human Rights (Parker 2007; Taipale 2001).

These challenges have caused the formal development of performance assessment procedures for mental health to lag behind that observed in many other sectors of the health system. Where aspects of performance have been assessed, measurement can be problematic.

Different countries have differences in social and cultural tolerance of what constitutes acceptable behaviour which in turn leads to differences in the size of the population deemed to have mental health problems. Assessment of the utilization of mental health services also needs to take account of the use of compulsory detention and treatment orders.

Some quality development initiatives sought better measurement of quality of life assessments by focusing initially on the cost effectiveness of some interventions, (Faria 1997), as well as monitoring the protection of human rights. However, the measurement of effectiveness can be complicated by difficulties with the reliability of psychiatric diagnoses and lack of consensus on the aetiology and treatment of many psychiatric illnesses (Evers et al. 1997). Moreover, in some limited circumstances, service users whose cognition is affected may find it difficult to express opinions and/or place a value on services received. Also, as with chronic conditions, the success of treatment may vary over time. In some circumstances it may be difficult to estimate the costs of treatment because of a lack of appropriate criteria for defining poor mental health. Crucially, as poor mental health can be stigmatizing, there is also a need to liaise with other sectors to measure key non-health outcomes such as changes in contact rates with the criminal justice system; levels of homelessness; and return to employment (Evers et al. 2007).

In this chapter we discuss some of the key developments in mental health performance measurement and provide international examples of how this has progressed. We reflect on the principal developments in the use of routine outcome and clinical process measurement. We also consider concerns about monitoring inequalities in mental health, looking at particular challenges for risk adjustment, attribution and causality. We end with a discussion of the key issues for mental health; the development of information technology and information management systems; and the policy implications of developments.

Performance measurement in mental health

As with other areas of health care, there are a number of potential dimensions for performance measures for mental health. Data on key outcomes and processes of care can facilitate improvement within provider organizations and provide insights into the quality and levels of performance that are feasible (Hermann et al. 2006). Many performance measures assess a range of aspects around the success of treatment, continuity, access, coordination and prevention; others may measure the treatment of specific disorders (Hermann et al. 2004b). In addition, there may be a set of useful performance measures specifically focused on carers.

Outcome measures in mental health can include health status (decrease in symptoms), social functioning, size of social network, quality of life, mortality, suicide, relapse and readmission. Non-health outcomes such as employment and housing status can be important. Process measures might include user satisfaction; rate of engagement and missed contacts; unplanned admissions or admissions under mental health legislation; length of stay; staff recruitment, retention and morale; as well as use of services and caseloads (Jenkins et al. 2000). More recently, some countries (e.g. Scotland) have begun to develop performance measures relating to mental health promotion and mental disorder prevention that incorporate measures of mental well-being or happiness (Health Scotland 2006; Tennant et al. 2007).

In principle, hundreds of performance indicators could be proposed for mental health system assessment but there may be huge variations in their evidence base, operational development, collection burden, availability, acceptability, reliability and validity. Stakeholders in the mental health-care system (e.g. payers, providers, regulators, clinicians, people with mental health problems and their families) often lack consensus on which aspects of performance should be used but several dimensions are considered to be of increasing importance. These include service access and integration and more user-focused standards of care such as responsiveness of service delivery, cultural appropriateness, consistency of services across a country and public protection (Clarkson & Challis 2002).

Recent work in Scotland investigated what would be the minimum requirements to help inform performance assessment. It was observed that, in the interim, systems do not have to be perfect. The "challenge is to develop good enough recording and reporting systems in the first instance that may only partially meet the needs of all the stakeholders, whilst developing a clear vision of the final shape of what is needed to support benchmarking and continuous improvement" (Donnelly 2008).

There have been a number of developments internationally – both to collect data on relevant performance indicators and to make use of these data within the context of performance measurement systems. Different dimensions of performance can be presented individually; form elements of a balanced scorecard comprising a range of measures across different domains; or be synthesized into a composite score or index of quality. For example, the reporting card systems being developed in Scotland use quality, efficiency, finance and future capability as the key dimensions (Donnelly 2008).

Reporting cards have long been used routinely in the United States (e.g. within VA-funded services) and have had a substantial impact on the types of care available and length of treatment (Rosenheck & Fontana 1999). Also, since 1986 the Colorado Division of Mental Health has implemented a performance contracting model to monitor a wide range of activity at both divisional and community mental health centre level. Indicators in the Colorado scheme are grouped around five dimensions considered important at the local level – financial viability, productiveness, responsiveness, comprehensiveness of services, outcomes. A standardized outcome measure is used to check compliance with standards.

In Australia, progress on the implementation of the National Mental Health Plan is assessed though examination of the delivery of services. For example, in the state of Victoria a number of different performance dimensions are monitored and a mental health dataset is collected. This covers information to support clinical standards at local level and planning and service standards at higher levels. Higher-level indicators include needs assessment, population indices, socio-economic status, homelessness and service utilization data, all of which are used for resource allocation purposes (Clarkson & Challis 2002). Supply-side indicators (e.g. number of beds and staff numbers per population) are used to monitor the shift towards more community-based care. Outcome indicators are also routinely collected.

Thus far, systems have tended to focus on administrative measures of quality because the data are more readily available and have lower collection costs (Druss et al. 1999). They also tend to be more developed for working age adult populations than for services for children and adolescents or older people. It can also be difficult to identify measurement approaches that specifically assess whether mental health systems meet the needs of minority populations. We now describe some of the principal developments in outcome and process measurement for mental health.

Outcome measures

Challenges in measuring health outcomes

Outcome measures can be used as a performance measure if they are summarized across the service users of a particular provider or across providers (Manderscheid 2006). A conventional definition of an outcome in mental health care is, 'the effect on a patient's health status attributable to an intervention by a health professional or health service' (Andrews & Peters 1994, p.4).

This definition raises a number of concerns as the link between health service interventions and outcomes is far from straightforward. Firstly, outcomes can also improve as a result of self-help, environmental changes or support from professionals outside the health sector. Moreover, maintaining (rather than improving) an individual's health status may be viewed as a positive outcome in some circumstances. Outcomes may also vary with different perspectives (e.g. of the clinician, person with mental health problems, their family or professional carer). Mental health interventions may also be delivered at different levels, for example using specific treatments, combinations of treatments or population-wide interventions. Outcomes may vary at these different levels and make outcome measurement in mental health extremely complex (Gilbody & Whitty 2002).

Routine outcome assessment requires either the clinician or the service user to monitor and rate changes in health status. Such outcome assessment reflects service-user reports of internal psychic phenomena which cannot be observed or verified externally. Classification systems such as the ICD diagnose illness according to the presence or absence of mental symptoms that are 'subjective' in their nature. This is not to say that there has not been significant work in producing standardized instruments to diagnose psychiatric disorders in a reliable manner and quantify the degree of severity of a disorder. The range of measures available tend to measure the frequency and intensity of specific psychiatric symptoms (psychopathological rating scales) or are instruments that judge a disorder's impact on the individual (measures of social functioning and global measures of outcome, or quality of life assessment). A wide number of these rating scales are used in psychiatric research or clinical trials but few are used routinely in clinical practice – too few to allow performance monitoring.

Clinicians complete most rating scales in psychiatry as the user voice has largely been ignored in the development of various instruments to rate health outcomes. Recently there has been more attention on the importance of the user voice and patient choice in decision-making (Ford 2006). Ideas of 'partnership' and 'shared decision-making' are becoming key in service delivery in some settings (Bower & Sibbald 1999). A multidimensional approach to rating which could incorporate user, clinician and family reports has been suggested (Dickey & Sederer 2001). However, clinicians and users have shown little agreement in ratings between different scales or even when using the same instrument (Garcia et al. 2002; Kramer et al. 2003). Nonetheless, clinician-, family- and user-rated instruments are now used routinely and successfully alongside each other in a number of settings. These are discussed in the next section.

International efforts towards routine health outcome assessment

Routine outcome measurement has been undertaken using a range of instruments and assessment scales internationally. Much of this work had been led by initiatives in Australia and the United States.

Australia

Australia has the most coherently developed approach to treatment-level routine outcome assessment. The first national mental health strategy included a systematic review of patient outcomes (Andrews & Peters 1994) which led to proposals for specific instruments for routine use. These instruments were independently field-tested for their utility; the resulting recommendations informed Australian practice in routine outcome assessment (Meehan et al. 2002).

The use of standard outcome measures for all mental health service users was mandated (Brooks 2000). All Australian states have signed agreements to submit routinely collected outcomes and casemix data to the Australian government on a regular basis (Callaly et al. 2006). This has involved a substantial commitment of resources by mental health providers and has produced a large national dataset.

Table 4.3.1 *Mandated outcome measures in Australia*

	Adult services	Child and adolescent services (CAMHS)	Older people's services
Clinician-rated	HoNOS Abbreviated Life Skills Profile (LSP)	Health of the Nation Outcome Scales for Children and Adolescents (HoNOSCA) Children's Global Assessment Scale (CGAS) Factors Influencing Health Status (FIHS)	Health of the Nation Outcome Scales for Elderly People (HoNOS 65+) Abbreviated Life Skills Profile (LSP) Resource Utilization Groups – Activities of Daily Living (RUG-ADL)
User-rated	BASIS-32 K-10+ MHI-38	Strengths and Difficulties Questionnaire (SDQ)	BASIS-32 K-10+ MHI-38

The measures mandated for use in Australia are listed in Table 4.3.1. Different combinations of indicators are used for those in receipt of adult, older people's or child and adolescent mental health services (CAMHS) (Callaly et al. 2006). All groups make use of the Health of the Nation Outcome Scales (HoNOS)[1] that include specialist variants for children and older people. Originally developed by the Royal College of Psychiatrists in England, the basic form of this instrument contains twelve items measuring behaviour, impairment, symptoms and social functioning on a five-point severity scale (Wing et al. 1996).

In addition to HoNOS, all adult and older people's mental health services are required to offer consumers one of three user-rated (self-report) instruments. Victoria, Tasmania and the Australian Capital Territory use the Behavior and Symptom Identification Scale (BASIS-32); New South Wales, South Australia, the Northern

---

[1] HoNOS is mandatory in Australia, England and New Zealand. There are also substantial programmes of use in Nova Scotia, Canada, the Netherlands, Norway and Italy.

Territory and Western Australia use the Kessler 10 plus (K-10+); and Queensland uses the Mental Health Inventory (MHI-38). All CAMHS are required to use the same self-report measure – the Strengths and Difficulties Questionnaire (Callaly et al. 2006).

There are mixed perceptions of the value of the outcome measurement system in Australia (Meehan et al. 2006). User-rated outcome measures are well-valued when they are seen to help service users to identify their own needs while allowing for better dialogue with clinicians and helping them to see the service-user point of view (Callaly et al. 2006). In practice, the greater the severity of illness the lower the likelihood that a service user will be offered the chance to complete the self-report measure. Those with more severe symptoms may also be more likely to decline to use the measure.

In contrast to user-rated outcome measures, the collection of clinical outcome data has received a much more lukewarm response. Initially, the majority of clinicians have perceived the Australian government's primary objective for introducing the measures to be financial management rather than to ensure the quality of services. Another limitation is that HoNOS cannot also be used to measure mental health outcomes in general practice. However, some acknowledge that national data collection could support the ability to compare services and treatment types and thus lead to more efficient and effective services (Callaly & Hallebone 2001, Callaly et al. 2003). This resistance to the use of outcome measures is not unique to Australia; the dominant driving force for the use of outcome measurement has been the need for aggregate data for management and accountability purposes rather than a desire to improve direct clinical utility.

England

In the early 1990s, the government's health strategy set the improvement of health and social functioning of people with severe mental health problems as its first mental health target and proposed that success against this target should be quantified (Department of Health 1992). The *Health of the Nation* led to the creation of the HoNOS instrument. A National Service Framework was also introduced in 1999. This put an emphasis on clinical governance and practice guidelines, service-user experience and the need to collect outcome data (Department of Health 1999). This framework and the increased focus on performance management were both intended to make managers more accountable through routine inspections; audit and publication of comparative data; and by encouraging engagement in activities that previously may not have been taken seriously (Rea & Rea 2002).

In 2002, 49% of all English mental health service providers were using HoNOS in at least one service delivery site; only 11% were routinely using the instrument in all service settings; and 34% were using the instrument routinely in more than half of their service settings. Collection of the Mental Health Minimum Dataset (MHMDS) for England, including HoNOS, became mandatory for all mental health provider organizations in the NHS in April 2003 (Appleby 2004).

The Mental Health Minimum Dataset is not specifically an indicator format but it can support the use of patient-centred indicators and is used by the Healthcare Commission (the regulator, now called the Care Quality Commission) at a more aggregate level for performance monitoring. A review by an outcomes advisory expert group concluded that local providers would need to develop expertise and systems to make effective use of the newly available outcomes data in order for the new system to inform local service delivery in England (Fonagy et al. 2004). However, work undertaken in Canada suggests that access to improved support materials and the use of initiatives to increase completion rates (including timely feedback to clinicians) can be useful at individual, team and service levels to significantly improve the uptake and ease of use of HoNOS (Kisely et al. 2008).

Netherlands
Overall assessment of health system performance in the Netherlands in 2006 includes a section devoted specifically to the mental health (including substance abuse) system, based on core indicators on mental health related outcomes. These include the uptake of prevention measures by target groups; changes in mental and social functioning (using the Global Assessment of Functioning – GAF); suicides and suicide attempts; discharge rates from the mental health system; and the percentage of the target population reached by professionals (Westert & Verkleij 2006). A mental health-care thermometer, a twenty-question instrument recording service-user satisfaction with involvement in treatment and care decisions has been introduced. In future this will allow service-user views of the system to be incorporated into the analysis.

United States of America

In the United States, the focus on outcome measurement as a measure of success has been driven largely by cost containment efforts. As in several European countries, difficulties in accurately quantifying the resources needed for DRGs for mental health and the increasing proportion of health expenditure devoted to mental health have led to a growing emphasis on outcome measures (Slade 2002). Purchaser-driven pressures have driven activity in routine outcome assessment here more than anywhere else. Outcomes measurement is increasingly being implemented in both public (e.g. VA) and private programmes.

Payers have variable mandates for outcomes measures and they are used more widely in specialist rather than generic managed-care organizations. Clinician ratings are used in some state hospitals (Ford 2006) and also within the VA mental health system where clinicians use the GAF tool to assess all mental health inpatients at discharge and all outpatients at least every ninety days of active treatment (Greenberg & Rosenheck 2005). The VA chose to use this tool because it had been used routinely for inpatient discharges since 1991 and therefore training needs were limited. Further implementation was incentivized by introducing a national performance measure on GAF recording compliance, with monitoring published monthly. Implementation was supported by national training initiatives.

User-rated instruments are used in the commercial public sector (for instance, in Medicaid carve-outs by some private psychiatric hospitals) and within some public mental health systems. Mental health service users have also been involved in the development of some outcome measurement systems, as illustrated in Ohio (Ohio Department of Mental Health 2007) (see Box 4.3.1).

Other outcome measures

Readmission rates

Measures other than specific outcome scales can be used to assess outcomes. These include rates of readmission to inpatient care services. The reductions in average length of stay observed in many high-income countries are more likely to be effective if appropriate levels of community based care and support are in place. Any increase in readmission rates might thus be seen as a potential indicator of poor

---

Box 4.3.1 Ohio Mental Health Consumer Outcomes System

A development task force commissioned by the Ohio Department of Mental Health focused on identifying what mattered to service users and their families. Pilot projects found that consumers liked being asked about their lives and seeing their outcomes instruments used in discussions with staff about their treatment plans.

The final approach, the Consumer Outcomes System, uses three instruments for adults and three for children and their families. The adult instruments include two service-user orientated outcome measurement instruments; those for children have one instrument targeted at young service users and a second targeted at parents/ guardians.

In 2003, the state introduced a rule requiring service providers to implement the Consumer Outcomes System. Implementation has been supported by training, technical support and subsidies. As of March 2005, reports were being generated by 277 provider agencies with records for 211 000 service users (Ford 2006).

---

quality initial treatment (including premature discharge) or it might reflect failure in the provision and quality of community based services (Lyons et al. 1997). However, several reviews have concluded that readmission rates are not a suitable indicator of quality of care in psychiatric hospitals, although appropriate discharge planning and follow-up visits may be associated with lower rates of readmission (Durbin et al. 2007; Lien 2002).

Readmission data require careful interpretation. Some studies suggest that a co-morbid substance-related disorder is the best predictor of readmission in a public hospital setting (Haywood et al. 1995, Lyons & McGovern 1989). Across countries there are often significant barriers in the cross-referral of patients with dual diagnoses to mental disorder and substance abuse treatment programmes. Readmission rates may also offer useful information for service providers on general admission policies and thresholds for admission. Subsequent analysis of the medical necessity of admissions might also be undertaken.

The availability of crude data on readmission rates in many countries can be misleading. There are a number of reasons why it may be problematic to determine accurately the rate of readmission. One key challenge in identifying whether treatment has been ineffective is that service users may be free to move between different public (and private) hospitals. This requires data to have unique patient identifiers that can be tracked not only over time but also to link each discharge with subsequent readmission in any facility for the same condition. Many national datasets are unable to meet these requirements. Moreover, individuals may also be re-institutionalized in facilities outside the health-care system, for example in social care facilities or within the prison system (Priebe et al. 2005). Such facilities are often not included in data collection systems. Another practical problem is that individuals who are readmitted may be treated primarily for a physical rather than a mental health problem. This reflects not only the high rate of physical co-morbidity in people with mental health problems but also the fact that tariffs set for health conditions may not cover the full costs of care (Halsteinli et al. 2006).

Suicide

Rates of suicide and deaths from unidentified causes are another commonly used measure for looking at the performance of both mental health treatment services and population-wide mental health strategies. For instance, suicide rates are used as a key indicator in assessing mental health performance against the National Service Framework for Mental Health in England (Department of Health 1999).

The majority of suicides are linked to mental health problems (Wilkinson 1982). Many people who ultimately complete suicide have come into contact with health (and other) care services. Appropriate suicide awareness training for front-line staff can be effective in reducing suicides by helping to identify individuals who may be particularly at risk (Mann et al. 2005). This suggests that some cases are potentially avoidable through appropriate early intervention from health and other services. Suicide rates may therefore be a good indicator of how well health and other local services in general are meeting the needs of people with mental health problems. High rates of suicide or undetermined death might suggest further investigation into areas such as access to treatment and the level of training for professionals at primary care level; integration of primary, secondary and social care services; clinical, organizational, staffing and resource management in psychiatric services; and follow-up procedures for service users (Renvoize & Clayden 1990).

Data on suicides are available in virtually all high-income countries but there are major challenges in using suicide rates as an indicator of a health system's effectiveness in dealing with mental health problems. Many factors well beyond the health system may influence rates of suicide, including changes in the economic climate, social isolation and rapid societal change as seen (for instance) in central and eastern Europe (Berk et al. 2006). This suggests the need for adequate risk adjustment for some of these factors.

At a statistical level some groups in the population have high suicide rates (e.g. older people, young men) but, even when including deaths from undetermined causes, the absolute number of deaths from suicide is often too low to assess change over time. This problem can be addressed to some extent by using data over a longer time period, for example over three years instead of one.

Another potential confounder in using suicides as a possible performance indicator for mental health is differences in the procedures for recording the cause of death in different countries. For instance, some require a coroner's investigation but may still have different legal definitions of suicide (Renvoize & Clayden 1990); others require police reports (e.g. at the site of a motor vehicle crash) before determining whether a suicide is recorded. Cultural and religious taboos may also discourage physicians and others from recording a death as suicide (Kelleher et al. 1998).

Physical health problems

One major gap in assessing changes in outcome for people receiving treatment for mental health problems are impacts on their physical health status. The evidence base consistently indicates that the mortality rates from many physical illnesses, most notably cardiovascular disease and diabetes, are significantly higher for people living with enduring mental illness than for those in the general population (Harris & Barraclough 1998; Fleischhacker et al. 2008). This is observed regardless of the type of mental health problem. People living with psychoses such as schizophrenia and those with more common problems (e.g. anxiety and depressive disorders) can be at greater risk of physical health problems (Osborn et al. 2007).

Moreover, the adverse effects of most antipsychotic medications for people with severe mental health problems include excessive weight gain (Allison et al. 1999; Newcomer 2005). People with depression and anxiety-related disorders are also at increased risk of weight gain – there is good evidence that long-term use of many older antidepressants (tricyclics) and of newer generation heavily prescribed selective serotonin reuptake inhibitors (SSRIs) can result in weight gain (Demyttenaere & Jaspers 2008; Gartlehner et al. 2008; Ness-Abramof & Apovian 2005).

There are strong links between poor mental and poor physical condition. To date, performance indicators have typically looked neither at changes in physical health status nor at whether individuals with mental health problems are treated for co-morbid physical health problems or receive advice and support to help minimize potential adverse health impacts of some treatments.

Is there any evidence that outcome measurement leads to service improvement?

There is consensus that outcomes should be routinely measured but is there any evidence that this is effective in improving services in any way? Overall evidence from various reviews seems scant (Gilbody et al. 2003) or mixed at best (Gilbody et al. 2001). The latter systematic review found only nine studies that looked at the addition of outcome measurement to routine clinical practice in both psychiatric and non-psychiatric settings. The results show that routine feedback of instruments had little impact on the recognition of mental disorders or longer term psychosocial functioning. Clinicians welcomed the information gained from the instruments but rarely incorporated these results into routine clinical decision-making. Given that routine outcome measurement can be costly the authors concluded that there was no robust evidence to suggest that it is of benefit in improving psychosocial outcomes in non-psychiatric settings (Gilbody & Whitty 2002).

Similarly, studies suggest that one-off outcome measurements do very little to shift clinical practice or change clinician behaviour (Ashaye et al. 2003). A more recent randomized controlled trial (Slade et al. 2006) on the effectiveness of standardized outcome measurement indicated that monthly outcome monitoring markedly reduced psychiatric admissions. However, it was not shown to be effective in improving primary outcomes of patient-rated unmet need and quality of life, nor did it improve other subjective secondary outcome measures. The study was longitudinal in nature and had more regular outcome measurement for patients (month on month assessment) and showed that this can prompt earlier intervention by clinicians to avert relapse which would otherwise lead to hospitalization, thus reducing admissions. The intervention therefore reduced psychiatric inpatient days and resulting service use costs and proved cost effective.

More evidence can be found in a six-country European study (Priebe et al. 2002) that examined how service-users' views could be fed into treatment decisions. The MECCA (Towards More Effective European Community Care for Patients with Severe Psychosis) trial tested the hypothesis that intervention would lead to better outcomes in terms of quality of life over a one-year period. A better outcome was assumed to be mediated through more appropriate joint decisions or a more positive therapeutic relationship. Results showed that while the intervention added time to clinical appointments it did lead to a significant improvement in quality of life.

The key message from these studies appears to be that one-off (or infrequent) outcome measurement seems to have equivocal results in terms of actually improving subjective outcomes. However, outcome measurement that is performed longitudinally and more regularly using a broad range of measures (ideally collected routinely in databases and backed up by regular monitoring) can significantly improve quality of life and/or reduce psychiatric admissions.

Process measures

A number of process measures related to mental health services can help to track performance variations within and between different providers. Typically process measures are used because they are more readily available in administrative datasets. Indicators of input (i.e. the level of resources invested in mental health) are a key component of many process measures.

Typical process measures include indicators such as length of stay and various measures of bed use or occupancy rates (Glover et al. 1990). These can include trends in very long stay service users (i.e. those living in institutions for more than one year). Other hospital-centric input measures can include the size of the hospital (number of inpatients) and staffing throughput measures, for example the number of service users per consultant, per nurse or per therapist (Geddis 1988). These crude ratios may provide useful information on staffing mixes, dependency levels and workload.

In Norway, for example, several process indicators for mental health are collected within the national system for measurement of quality within the health system – proportion of treatment undertaken compulsorily; waiting times for first outpatient consultation; duration of untreated psychosis; and the number of children and adolescents who have been diagnosed as having a mental health problem. In addition, in 2009 the government has commissioned the independent research organization SINTEF to publish information on service utilization, the number of therapists per service use and the skill mix/balance between psychologists and psychiatrists (Halsteinli 2008).

Community and ancillary service inputs that may be measured include quantification of the activities of community mental health teams supporting people to live in their homes; the provision of emergency out-of-hours services; and access to occupational rehabilitation services, sheltered housing and day care services (Jenkins & Glover 1997). Inputs from primary care services (e.g. general practitioners, nurses, health visitors, counsellors) also need to be counted on some notional basis, for example –the average number of patients presenting in primary care with a mental health problem. Other measurable indicators recently identified as important to quality assessment in Scotland include reducing and changing the pattern of antidepressant prescribing and then assessing whether or not any savings from these actions are reinvested in effective psychological therapies (Donnelly 2008). Box 4.3.2 provides an example of how traditional inpatient focused process indicators are being supplemented by additional community service indicators in Ireland (Health Research Board 2008).

Service-user experiences

In addition to data on inputs into the mental health system, data recording levels of service-user satisfaction are being used increasingly to help assess quality of care. The interest in assessing service-user satisfaction has been driven by a number of concerns. Service-user satisfaction with care has been found to be associated with better concordance

> ## Box 4.3.2 Collection of mental health system process indicators in Ireland
>
> In Ireland, the Health Research Board's Mental Health Research Unit collects a range of information. This includes the National Psychiatric Inpatient Reporting System that has recorded all admissions and discharges to inpatient psychiatric hospitals and units throughout the country – as well as related socio-demographic, diagnostic and service related information – over forty years.
>
> WISDOM is a new system being developed to gather information on the use of both community based and inpatient mental health services. Also, part of the Health Research Board's 2007–2011 research programme will work towards the further development of mental health specific performance indicators; an objective of the national mental health strategy – A Vision for Change.
>
> A proof of concept phase of WISDOM will be tested in the Donegal Local Health Area and comprehensively evaluated before the system is implemented more widely throughout the country. Evaluation of the proof of concept phase began in January 2008 with a review of evaluation literature, with a specific focus on the evaluation of information systems, user-focused evaluation and evaluation of training.

with treatment and outcomes. Also, there has been a shift towards greater consumer rights and a growth in mental health user movements (Callan & Littlewood 1998; Rose & Lucas 2007). Satisfaction measures may be useful to clinicians and managers because they can provide information on processes (e.g. satisfaction with treatment) as well as outcomes of care (e.g. a perspective on the success of treatment – see section on outcome measures).

Early studies seemed to report consistently high levels of user satisfaction with mental health services, often surpassing professionals' expectations (Kalman 1983). They also suggested that service users might have been reluctant to voice critical comments for fear of damaging the therapeutic relationship (Warner et al. 1994). Certainly there is a vocal community of individuals who regard themselves as 'survivors' of the psychiatric system (Rose & Lucas 2007).

The evidence on whether patient demographics are associated with satisfaction appears mixed (Lebow 1982) although some studies show some correlation with age, gender, legal status and ethnicity. Women, younger people, those involuntarily detained and ethnic minority service users historically may have had lower levels of satisfaction with the care that they received (Greenwood et al. 1999; Hansson 1989; Leavey et al. 1997; Perreault et al. 1996). Service users who were dissatisfied also tended to report more adverse experiences (Greenwood et al. 1999). Again, the reasons for different levels of patient satisfaction are complex – certain diagnostic categories (such as drug abuse or diagnoses of schizophrenia) tend to be associated with lower levels of satisfaction but other studies have found social problems to be more important than diagnosis in influencing satisfaction (Babiker & Thorne 1993).

As with other areas of the health system, there are a number of concerns when collecting what can be costly and time-consuming data on service-user satisfaction (Druss et al. 1999). For instance, there are risks that surveys suffer from both response and recall bias and it is not clear to what extent expressions are associated with prior expectations (Babiker & Thorne 1993; Callan & Littlewood 1998). Some questionnaires have also been too reductionist – it is not sufficient to know that service users are dissatisfied without knowing why. Many instruments have also been criticized for asking patients to rate only those aspects of care that the provider deems important rather than those which are important to service users (Rose et al. 2006). In addition, performance measures are usually conducted at provider level while data are collected at individual patient level and therefore require satisfaction scores to be aggregated to the provider level.

The detailed survey used in England and Wales is one example of an instrument that has been tailored to look at a range of issues. As Box 4.3.3 indicates, this gathers data on a number of different dimensions of service use that are of importance not just to service providers but also to service users.

Use of guidelines

It has been suggested that guidelines can help to improve quality of care by advocating evidence-based practice models with a view to improving patient outcomes and reducing variations in treatment

---

Box 4.3.3 Service-user satisfaction surveys in England and Wales

The Healthcare Commission has conducted a detailed survey of community mental health service users in England and Wales since 2004. This looks at the quality of care; communication with health professionals, crisis care and psychotherapy; and access to other support including help for family carers and social inclusion. The results of the survey are fed back to NHS providers with the aim of helping them to improve performance. In 2007, 75% of 15 900 service users in the survey reported care received to be good, very good or excellent; 81% indicated that their psychiatrist was 'definitely listening to them' (Healthcare Commission 2007). Reports are also prepared for the sixty-nine individual primary care providers, comparing service-user satisfaction against national benchmarks.

(Weinmann et al. 2007). The development and use of guidelines and national service plans for the promotion of mental health and for the treatment and rehabilitation of people with mental health problems are now considered of great importance in many countries. Well-developed guidelines and strategies are available (e.g. National Service Framework for Mental Health in England and Wales) but many guidelines and national service plans remain of low quality, leading some commentators to argue for the creation of institutions to support pan-national development of guidelines (Stiegler et al. 2005).

As with other areas of the health system, evidence also suggests that guideline implementation tends at best to have a modest impact on patient outcomes for a limited duration. Ongoing support or feedback has been identified as important in changing physician behaviour and improving patient outcomes on the back of guideline implementations (Bero et al. 1998; Grol 2001). Even if the performance of mental health professionals can be influenced, improving guideline adherence may not necessarily lead to better outcomes. Guidelines may be too artificial if the external validity of the trials on which they are based is limited by select patient groups (Weinmann et al. 2007). A corollary is that guideline adherence may be a poor performance measure for providers and a poor proxy measure for patient outcomes.

Table 4.3.2 *Twelve-month service use by severity of anxiety, mood and substance disorders in WMH Surveys (%)*

	Severe	Moderate	Mild	None
Belgium	60.9	36.5	13.9	6.8
France	48.0	29.4	21.1	7.0
Germany	40.0	23.9	20.3	5.9
Italy	51.0	25.9	17.3	2.2
Netherlands	50.4	31.3	16.1	7.7
Spain	58.7	37.4	17.3	3.9
USA	59.7	39.9	26.2	9.7

Source: Adapted from Wang et al. 2007

Inequalities in access and utilization

Inequalities in mental health care raise particular challenges, not only for the organization and management of services but also for how systems are able to monitor such inequalities in order to improve performance. The majority of those with mental disorders do not come into contact with mental health services (Thornicroft 2008). The challenge can be illustrated by looking at World Mental Health (WMH) Survey data on the use of services for anxiety, mood and substance abuse disorders. Conducted across seventeen countries, this survey reported that overall only around one third of those who could benefit from treatment actually made use of services (Wang et al. 2007).

Table 4.3.2 provides data on seven of the countries included in the WMH Surveys. Among individuals with the most severe of these mental disorders at least 39% (Belgium) and at most 60% (Germany) did not receive any treatment. Table 4.3.3 also indicates that no more than 42% of those who actually received services obtained what was deemed to be a minimally adequate level of treatment for their disorder. There were also substantial variations in the proportion of those with more severe disorders who received adequate treatment.

Again, there are complex reasons for low utilization of mental health services. The stigma surrounding poor mental health appears to be a major contributor to a lack of contact with services (Schomerus & Angermeyer 2008) and anticipated discrimination appears to deter

Table 4.3.3 *Minimally adequate treatment use for respondents using services in the WMH Surveys in previous twelve months (% of people by degree of severity)*

	Any severity	Severe	Moderate	Mild	None
Belgium	33.6	42.5	35.5	-	29.4
France	42.3	57.9	36.5	41.5	40.2
Germany	42.0	67.3	53.9	-	35.4
Italy	33.0	-	33.4	-	31.0
Netherlands	34.4	67.2	34.1	-	20.8
Spain	37.3	47.5	43.6	48.5	29.2
USA	18.1	41.8	24.8	4.9	-

Source: Adapted from Wang et al. 2007

people from coming into contact with services (Corrigan & Wassel 2008). Individuals may be fearful of being discriminated against if they are labelled as having a mental health problem. This under-utilization of services is reported even in those countries that require no out-of-pocket payments to access services. As members of the general population, these individuals are also exposed to common misconceptions surrounding mental disorders – for instance that they cannot be cured or that drug treatments do not work.

Contact rates also differ by mental health problem – highest for severe psychotic conditions (e.g. schizophrenia) but much lower for conditions perceived to be less serious (e.g. depression) (Wittchen & Jacobi 2005). Again this may be due to a lack of knowledge about mental health problems. People with psychosis may be more likely to come to the attention of services during the acute phases of their condition but there is some evidence to suggest that the general public do not believe that conditions such as depression always require intervention from mental health services. It is believed that these are caused by socio-environmental events or may reflect individual weakness – individuals just need to 'get a grip'(Thornicroft 2007). Troubling patterns of interaction with mental health services tend to include under-representation in outpatient care and over-representation in inpatient and emergency care. Failure to receive outpatient care may be associated with higher rates of hospitalization and longer lengths of stay.

Rates of contact with mental health services may also be lower in specific population groups than in the general population. The stigma of mental illness may be particularly acute in young people with mental health problems – one study reported that only 4% of these young people contacted their primary care practitioner about their problems (Potts et al. 2001). Performance measures need to be able to identify differences by population subgroups. One approach used in assessing Oregon's Medicaid State Plan compared population-based average health utilization data against normative benchmarks or performance guidelines for particular mental disorders and then examined outliers or unusual behaviour among provider organizations (McFarland et al. 1998). Guidelines were then risk adjusted to take account of co-morbidity in the target population and the outcome measured was the level of functioning. It was found to be a major challenge to incorporate outcomes data into administrative and claims databases which measured treatment processes.

Racial and ethnic disparities have also been demonstrated to lead to differences in the rates and patterns of treatment in mental health services. Many studies show that the probability of being diagnosed with schizophrenia is much higher among minority populations (Chow et al. 2003; Tapsell & Mellsop 2007). Afro-Caribbean people have been at higher risk of involuntary commitment and are likely to be referred by legal means, for example under the United Kingdom's Mental Health Act (Callan & Littlewood 1998; Fearon et al. 2006; Mohan et al. 2006), making the use of services more coercive.

There may also be a lack of cultural sensitivity in the provision of care, or taboos within the community. In some sections of the population there may be a tendency to attribute mental health problems to religious and other culturally sanctioned belief systems and lack of access to receptive culturally sensitive providers (Chow et al. 2003). People with mental health problems tend to be over-represented in poor neighbourhoods with high rates of unemployment, homelessness, crime and substance abuse and members of racial and ethnic minorities tend to be disproportionately represented in poor areas. The relationship between ethnicity, poverty and mental health service use is therefore complex.

These findings suggest the need to tailor services more carefully to meet the needs of minority groups; ensure fewer disparities in service access and use; and carefully monitor appropriate pathways in care. All of these concerns raise challenges for performance measurement within mental health systems. The issue is of particular interest in many western European countries experiencing recent new inward economic migration from countries in central and eastern Europe as these new migrants can be highly vulnerable to mental health problems. In addition, refugees present very different challenges to mental health systems as individuals may experience severe post-traumatic stress disorders. Yet, not one of eighteen OECD countries recently surveyed had the most basic of data on service follow-up for ethnic minority groups (Garcia-Armesto et al. 2008).

Reviews of services in Europe suggest that few mental health services are yet equipped to meet these needs (Watters 2007; Watters & Ingleby 2004). In New Zealand, culturally specific measures of mental health status (Hua Oranga) are being used to help develop appropriate outcome measures and performance indicators integral to the National Mental Health Information Strategy. This experience may be of use to those seeking to develop equally culturally appropriate indicators in other countries (Ministry of Health 2006).

Productivity measurement

The literature on price indices for mental health care in the United States is particularly relevant for measurement of the productivity of mental health services. Rising expenditure on mental health has generated considerable interest in constructing price indices, in particular for major depression, schizophrenia and bipolar disorder. The literature indicates that it is important to focus on the direct medical costs of treating an episode of illness rather than changes in the prices of the inputs used in treatment. For all three disorders, studies suggest that the price of treating an episode or individual have declined in recent years. This is contrary to many of the officially reported figures, for example those from the Bureau of Labour Statistics.

This literature improves on previous methods by attempting to define the units of output of medical care that reflect the changing bundles of inputs required to treat these problems. Output is also defined in a way that incorporates measures of the quality of treatment. Outputs had been considered solely in terms of services used in the treatment of disease, for example physician visits, hospital stays, prescriptions. The newer approach views these as inputs into the treatment of mental health problems. Output is viewed as a course of treatment over a specified period, combining a number of treatment inputs which produce health benefits. The studies focus on the episodes of poor mental health. This involves pooling a number of treatments into bundles that are ex ante expected to lead to similar outcomes. This conception of output allows for a change in the composition of inputs or substitution among inputs as a result of technological change.

Many of the studies show that changes in the composition of treatment enable treatment episode costs to fall, even when input costs are rising. Berndt (2004) argues that this can be explained by the fact that official (Bureau of Labour Statistics) statistics do not make allowances for changes in the mix of treatment over time. Studies have also reported a considerable shift over time in the composition of treatment for depression (Berndt et al. 1998; Berndt et al. 2001; Berndt et al. 2002; Frank et al. 1998; Frank et al. 1998a), schizophrenia (Frank et al. 2004; Frank et al. 2006) and bipolar disorder (Ling et al. 2004).

For example, the studies found a shift in the mix of treatment for depression over recent years. The combination of psychotherapy and tricyclic antidepressants (TCAs) is being replaced by the use of newer selective SSRIs, sometimes in combination with psychotherapy. The move away from more costly psychotherapy-intensive treatment to less costly psychopharmacological treatments has had a significant impact on the average cost of treating an episode of acute phase major depression. Since expenditures on depression were thought to have increased over the study period, the source of this increase was likely to be an increase in volume rather than price as the cost of treating an episode of depression fell. Quality also improved because episodes that met guideline standards increased over the period (Berndt 2004).

Similarly, for schizophrenia, one study constructed treatment bundles which consisted of both single treatments (e.g. any antipsychotic medication) and more than one form of treatment such as medication and psychotherapy (Frank et al. 2004). Output was defined as the course of treatment over an entire year, given that schizophrenia is a severe and persistent mental disorder. The study found significant compositional changes in treatment with various forms of psychosocial therapy and older pharmaceutical treatments being replaced by newer atypical antipsychotics, in line with guidance. It was concluded that, as the cost of treating an individual per annum had declined, the observed increase in overall expenditure indicated that there had been an increase in the number of individuals being treated. Compositional changes in the types of treatment for bipolar disorder have been more gradual than those for either depression or schizophrenia. Four treatment bundles were defined: no treatment; psychotherapy only; mood stabilizers only; and psychotherapy and mood stabilizers combined (Berndt 2004; Ling et al. 2004).

Taking the evidence from the above studies, one recent study examined the level and composition of all mental health spending in the United States (Berndt et al. 2006). Quality-adjusted price indices for several major mental disorders (anxiety; schizophrenia; bipolar disorder; major depressive disorders; and all others) were applied to national mental health expenditure account estimates to examine changes in real output for the whole mental health sector. The study used estimates on depression, schizophrenia and bipolar disorder from previous research and aggregated results across all categories of mental health problem to arrive at overall price indices. These price indices reveal large gains in real output (70%–75%) relative to those used by the Bureau of Labour Statistics (16%–17%).

An alternative to calculating price and output indices for productivity calculations is to use a non-parametric approach such as data envelopment analysis (DEA) to calculate a productivity index. DEA was used to calculate a Malmquist productivity index for Norwegian psychiatric outpatient clinics to examine whether any change is related to personnel mix, budget growth or financial incentives (Evers et al. 2007). Bootstrapping methods were used to construct confidence intervals for the technical productivity index and its decomposition. A second stage regression was run on the productivity index to examine variables that may potentially be statistically associated with productivity growth. Overall the study reported substantial technical productivity growth. Personnel growth had a negative impact on productivity growth but a growth in personnel with university education increased productivity. Other than taking staff education as a proxy for staff quality on the input side, this study did not take account of any other changes in the quality of the output or interventions over time. The researchers call for more research to explore this. Further data on productivity in the Norwegian mental health system will be published in 2009 (Halsteinli 2008).

Risk adjustment

Comparisons of performance across different providers and over time rely on the assumption that organizations have similar basic characteristics and structures. This is seldom the case in mental health as services can be highly diverse. Moreover, there is a strong association between poor mental health and socio-economic deprivation. This greatly increases the need to make more equitable comparisons between mental health providers serving different populations. Risk adjustment in performance measures can be used to take account of differences in factors that are beyond facilities' control (Schacht & Hines 2003). One objection to statistical methods of risk adjustment is that the confounding cannot be completely removed as groups may differ on a number of characteristics other than the risk-adjustment variable used (Dow et al. 2001). Risk adjustment is only ever a partial fix but it allows more equitable and valid comparisons.

Statistical adjustment is not expected to make groups more comparable on all confounding variables but rather to make them more equal than they would have been with no adjustment (Hendryx & Teague 2001). The goal is to reduce the risk of drawing incorrect conclusions about the performance of some providers. Variables used to take account of group differences in the mental health context include age, gender, legal status and admission-referral source. It is often particularly challenging to control for casemix in mental health – DRGs (and their equivalents in other countries) are typically used for casemix and are based on diagnosis but they have been shown to be problematic and poor predictors of service use (Halsteinli et al. 2006; McCrone 1995).

There has been a lot of work on the risk adjustment of outcomes for specific interventions in mental health and some on risk adjustment for the development of payment systems (Ettner et al. 1998). However, there has been very little work on the risk adjustment of indicators for the purpose of comparing the performance of multiple providers (Dow et al. 2001).

Hendryx et al. (1999) developed models for risk adjusting outcome data to compare provider performance. Demographic and diagnostic data were used to risk adjust client functional status, quality of life and satisfaction ratings. Risk adjustment resulted in somewhat different rankings of provider performance although there was no statistical comparison of rankings with and without adjustment. Dow et al. (2001) risk adjusted two outcome measures (global rating of functioning; consumer satisfaction measure) using data on 7000 individuals over a three-year period from 24 state-funded providers in Florida. There was significant variation between providers on the two outcome measures but the risk adjustment had a fairly small impact on their overall rank ordering. However, it had a major effect for a few specific providers, particularly those with small caseloads.

Data comparability across providers and data quality largely determines whether these types of risk-adjustment models can be implemented in practice. The Behavioral Healthcare Performance Measurement System (BHPMS) for state psychiatric inpatient facilities in the United States is one example of the use of risk adjustment to facilitate benchmarking (see Box 4.3.4).

There is very little use of such risk adjustment mechanisms outside the United States and a number of challenging questions must be answered in order to facilitate their development and greater use. For example, does the collection of service-user self-report and clinician-rated variables make a difference to models built exclusively on the demographic and clinical indicators available in administrative databases? Investment in resources to collect additional data may not be merited if models from administrative databases perform as well (Hendryx & Teague 2001). Inappropriate or ineffective risk adjustment raises the possibility that providers will treat performance comparisons with scepticism, mistrust or even active opposition, thereby jeopardizing any performance measurement system. On the other hand, valid risk-adjustment models may encourage providers to use comparative findings as an opportunity for improvement.

Expanding the dimensions of performance assessment

Potentially important indicators of performance may lie outside the health system yet are influenced by inputs from it. A major report on social inclusion and mental health in England highlighted the importance of reintegration into employment. It reported that health service professionals were reluctant to encourage individuals to seek employment for fear that they might be unsuccessful and would have diffi-

> ## Box 4.3.4 Making use of risk adjustment in performance measurement
>
> The United States National Association of State Mental Health Program Directors Research Institute developed the BHPMS for state psychiatric inpatient facilities. The programme covers around 240 psychiatric facilities in 50 states and is approved by the Joint Commission.[2]
>
> A standardized set of data definitions and reporting requirements allows the development of benchmarks. A risk-adjustment method using logistic regression is applied using individual and organizational characteristics that show significant relationships. Monthly performance data allow the models to be updated if necessary (Schacht & Hines 2003). A time-series graphical display with confidence intervals is developed for each indicator for each organization and sent to providers in a confidential report.
>
> Risk-adjustment models have now been developed for readmission, seclusion and restraint. The characteristics used in the models include age, gender, race, marital status, diagnoses, living arrangements, legal status and referral source on admission. Institutional characteristics include unit mission (expected length of hospitalization) and specialty, bed capacity, security level and locked status.
>
> Each organization's rate of performance is now compared to a predicted risk-adjusted rate for the specific population that it serves. This represents an improvement on the previous system in which each service was simply compared against the average.

culty in regaining social welfare benefits (Social Exclusion Unit 2004). Yet employment has been shown to be a protective factor for mental health. One randomized controlled trial in six European countries has shown that supported employment schemes (in which health professionals work alongside specialist employment staff) are highly effective in helping people with severe mental health problems to return to work (Burns et al. 2007).

The promotion of reintegration into the workplace is a specific goal of mental health policy in England. However, it is challenging to mea-

---

[2] Previously known as Joint Commission on Accreditation of Healthcare Organizations and Affiliates.

sure the performance of the mental health system by taking account of inputs from outside the health service – namely the workplace. There are inputs within the workplace where employers may contribute to the promotion, prevention or treatment of mental health problems (Jenkins & Glover 1997). It is extremely challenging for the public mental health system to gauge accurately the contributions made by managers, human resources teams and occupational health teams in private companies. Indeed, few countries are able to measure these inputs accurately amongst public sector employers.

Mental health services can have inputs in partnership with other sectors including housing and education. For example, potential mental health inputs in a school setting might include a notional share of the contribution made by teachers or educational psychologists (Jenkins & Glover 1997). This could be calculated by looking at the epidemiology of mental health problems in schools or the extent of specific help given to pupils in schools.

Performance data and IT

Information systems and the development of databases and informatics in mental health remain one of the biggest challenges for performance measurement. Information systems and databases provide vital information for performance assessment and performance management for: assessing needs; resource management and planning; joint working between health and social care professionals; ensuring the effective delivery of appropriate care; measuring the effectiveness of different treatments and different settings; clinical audit and research; more refined contracting; and assessing costs (Jenkins & Glover 1997).

The measurement of performance in mental health is often opportunistic and piecemeal, reflecting the availability of data rather than performance dimensions that should be measured and monitored. The shift from hospital-based to community care; hospital closures; and the reconfiguration of services have largely not been accompanied by investment in computing systems. This makes it difficult to evaluate policies and develop services on a sound basis for decision-making (Glover 1995).

The geographical dispersal of many services to smaller community sites requires the development of wider computer networks. Furthermore, the nature of care is changing significantly – moving towards an integrated care pathway that is multidisciplinary in nature. Typically, integrated care cannot be identified readily as datasets still tend to be episodic and based on hospital care alone. Many information systems were not appropriately networked and datasets that have been available have tended to produce data that are inappropriate or unhelpful (Glover 1995).

Data analysis for performance management purposes still tends to be focused at the macro level; it is less common for individual teams or clinicians to use electronic data collection systems to guide decision-making at the micro level (Clarkson & Challis 2002). Moreover, policy-makers, providers and purchasers require different types of information to make decisions about the numbers of service users to treat; range of clinical problems; outcomes of care; and value of the services provided. Rea and Rea (2002) suggest that there should be a distinction between performance management and the management of performance and their very different informational requirements. Performance management requires information after the event and is used to make comparisons and devise league tables between different organizations for central government purposes. The management of performance requires users and practitioners to be involved in the development of systems and routines.

Routine collection of data requires careful and explicit definition of which data items are to be collected and the points in the care pathway at which data returns are to be made. Historically, hospital admission and discharge have been the main triggers for data returns but these systems of data collection are no longer suitable. Clinical staff tend to be more accurate at data recording than administrative staff but will have significant involvement in the data gathering process only if it has some clinical value. Computerized information systems should be designed to ensure that they meet the information requirements of clinical professionals and can safely replace a paper-based system (Jenkins & Glover 1997). An audit of information systems and their local use can help to identify gaps in systems that may be addressed as part of a performance measurement system (Donnelly 2008).

Collection of the Mental Health Minimum Dataset for England has been mandatory within the NHS since April 2003. Information on mental health service use stored within an electronic record has been recognized to be critical to the usefulness of this. When electronic records are fully implemented it will be possible to monitor outpatient attendances which may extend over many years as well as hospital, community and day care attendances which may commonly overlap. For each institution it should be possible to track the characteristics of the patient; health organizations involved; nature of the problems, including their range and severity; amounts of different interventions delivered to the patient; the way these interventions are combined as packages and scheduled over time; and changes in the patient's condition over time. Cost data are not included.

Outside the United Kingdom, there is still very limited use of unique identifiers for individual service users to enable system performance to be tracked. A recent survey reported that individual service-user records could be linked to different output measures in only six out of seventeen countries (Garcia-Armesto et al. 2008). Denmark is one such country, collecting highly detailed administrative data on health service use by people with mental health problems. Such information is absent in Australia where it has proved difficult to develop computer systems that reliably collect useful data and provide feedback and reports that are of sufficient quality to help clinicians and managers to guide service development (Callaly et al. 2005). Nonetheless, there has been a tremendous effort to develop an electronic medical record and to reduce duplication of data collection by different health agencies involved with the same patient (i.e. to integrate electronic health records between service providers) (Callaly et al. 2005).

In contrast, the routine datasets that provide activity data for Medicaid billing in the United States are extremely well-kept, up to date and almost entirely accurate (Huxley & Evans 2002). When a capitation scheme was introduced in Colorado State it was feared that data quality would decline because of the lack of direct financial incentive, however the State countered this by offering mental health providers a cash incentive for the best outcomes (Huxley & Evans 2002).

Conclusions

Poor mental health is one of the principal causes of disability and morbidity worldwide. It has a major impact on economies and public health but typically has not received the requisite level of policy priority in comparison to other areas for health action. Of course, additional resources cannot be invested in mental health (or any other aspect of health) without ensuring that the proposed interventions are of high quality; meet the needs of service users; are distributed fairly; lead to improvements in health and other outcomes; and are likely to be cost effective.

Monitoring the many dimensions of performance of the mental health system can help to facilitate better use of the resources allocated to mental health. However, these performance measurement systems face what may be unique challenges – defining the social and cultural boundaries of what constitutes poor mental health; difficulties in making diagnoses; and ensuring that there is a clear understanding of the different elements of service provision. For instance, outpatient care is very different to community care yet is sometimes used as an indicator of the implementation of the latter.

Issues of human rights and dignity are of paramount importance given that the mental health system uses involuntary detention and treatment in some circumstances. It is increasingly recognized that mental health system impacts on health outcomes cannot be assessed by looking at changes in mental and physical health status alone. Other key outcomes include individuals' ability to live independently and, particularly, to return to employment. Additional measurement difficulties are created by poor quality data and by shifting boundaries between health, social care and other sectors, e.g. where vocational rehabilitation services may be provided.

To a large extent, progress in performance assessment to date has depended on political agendas and the differing national priorities accorded to mental health. The majority of developments have been initiated in the United States but there are different examples of how this is being driven forward across the globe. Often initiatives are undertaken at regional level. For example, the Australian government developed national standards reflecting a number of important dimensions of performance for the national mental health strategy initiated in 1992. These nationally agreed indicators have since been monitored in different ways across the different states and territories (Andrews & Peters 1994; Rosen et al. 1989).

Significant developments in performance assessment initiatives are in place or due to be implemented in some parts of Europe, notably in England, Iceland, Ireland, the Netherlands, Norway and Scotland. However, these are exceptions rather than the rule. Wahlbeck's (2006) recent survey of twenty-five European Union countries noted that data on suicide rates and the number of psychiatric beds were readily available but other data were scarce. The report concluded that 'clearly, there is a need for Member States to develop their mental health monitoring systems'. A survey of eighteen OECD countries suggests that much information that would be useful to performance assessment is already available (e.g. in Denmark or Sweden) but is not used as part of a performance assessment process (Garcia-Armesto et al. 2008).

Drives towards performance monitoring have often been initiated through a desire to inform programmes and systems or to reduce expenditure rather than to inform treatment decisions for individual service users. This means that some systems may have been designed to use data that meet the needs of policy-makers or system managers rather than clinical staff. Of course, it is essential to provide information to inform policy-making. However, there may be an adverse impact on implementation if clinicians perceive the process of performance measurement as a threat or a paper-filling exercise, with no clinical value. This challenge was acknowledged in the development of a new benchmarking system for mental health in Scotland. This stressed the need to set up an expert implementation group charged with working with local health bodies and other stakeholders to develop and agree on the dimensions of the system to be measured in order to help facilitate uptake. The recommendations also emphasize the need for stakeholders to work together to align costs with service definitions and functions (Donnelly 2008).

We have highlighted the challenge posed by the need not only to develop effective information and data systems that make use of administrative data but also (ideally) to use integrated data systems with information on measurable and appropriate indicators across the different dimensions of performance. Initiatives to develop and make use of such indicators can be identified. Both the OECD and the European Union have recognized the importance of mental health performance indicators and are developing plans to monitor aspects of mental health in member countries, although these policy drives are still in their infancy. The OECD HCQI project identified a number of measures for international benchmarking of the quality of mental health care (Hermann et al. 2004a; Hermann et al. 2006). Actual benchmarking has been delayed because of the difficulties in ensuring common definitions of services across countries (Garcia-Armesto et al. 2008).

The MINDFUL (Mental Health Information and Determinants for the European Level) project also put forward a plan for a comprehensive mental health information system to cover not only mental health problems but also positive mental health, mental health promotion and the prevention of mental disorders (Lavikainen et al. 2006). Supported by the European Commission, this project has been revising mental health indicators that appear in the European Community Health Indicators list in order to support the development of the proposed European Health Survey System.

At a European level, WHO has relied on self report by countries to publish some basic data on the structure of mental health systems within the region. However, some of the major variations in the availability and balance of services in this report can be attributed to difficulties in obtaining comprehensive data and in how different countries (despite the provision of guidance) defined different services and types of mental health and related professionals (Petrea & Muijen 2008).

At a global level, WHO has developed the Assessment Instrument for Mental Health Systems (WHO-AIMS) to collect essential information on the mental health system of a country or region. Both a brief and a long-form instrument are provided to collect a broad range of data in a common format across countries, primarily low- and middle-income. A number of European countries are participating including Portugal, Greece and Ukraine (WHO 2005a). WHO has also published two editions of an atlas on adult mental health. This contains brief basic information on the structure of mental health systems on a country by country basis, including the development of new policies, funding for mental health and the level of resources available (WHO 2005a). This information has many limitations and gaps but has increased awareness of disparities in coverage for mental health across Europe and elsewhere. Atlases on child mental health and people with learning difficulties are also available.

Policy-makers face another key challenge – it is not sufficient to improve access to information on the services provided within the health-care system alone. The greater focus on the promotion of mental well-being in health policy-making across Europe and beyond also implies the need to develop initiatives that promote and maintain this. Developments in indicators for well-being are still in their infancy. We have already noted that the boundaries between health and social care vary considerably across countries (McDaid et al. 2007).

Clearly, performance frameworks that can integrate data from health and social care and provide a coherent set of performance measures have considerable advantages (Clarkson & Challis 2002). However, key services and supports may also be provided entirely outside of this system. For instance, interventions may be delivered by education services within a school setting and employment services may focus on helping and supporting individuals with mental health problems to be fully integrated into the workplace. Such developments will become critical as policy-makers increasingly embrace the language of service-user empowerment and choice. They are also necessary for adequate assessment of new mechanisms for funding mental health services. This includes the direct allocation of budgets to service users which in theory allows them to purchase services that best meet their needs – within health, social care or other sectors.

Finally, from a policy-making perspective, institutional arrangements need to be in place to promote participation in any system of performance assessment. Our analysis indicates that improvements in system performance can be encouraged by mechanisms such as collaboration with multiple stakeholders in system design; financial incentives; routine data collection; and feedback to providers. Some emerging evidence suggests that performance assessment may also help to improve individual health outcomes but much more evaluation and analysis is required. There should be careful consideration of how information arising from performance assessment systems can best be used to help facilitate change in both policy and practice.

References

Allison, DB. Mentore, JL. Heo, M. Chandler, LP. Cappelleri, JC. Infante, MC. Weiden, PJ (1999). 'Antipsychotic-induced weight gain: a comprehensive research synthesis.' *American Journal of Psychiatry,* 156(11): 1686–96.

Andrews, G. Peters, L (1994). Measurement of consumer outcome in mental health. In: CRUFAD (ed.). *A report to the National Mental Health Information Strategy Committee.* Sydney: CRUFAD.

Appleby, L (2004). *The national service framework for mental health – five years on.* London: Department of Health.

Ashaye, O. Livingston, G. Orrell, M (2003). 'Does standardized needs assessment improve the outcome of psychiatric day hospital care for older people? A randomized controlled trial.' *Aging & Mental Health,* 7(3): 195–199.

Babiker, IE. Thorne, P (1993). 'Do psychiatric patients know what is good for them?' *Journal of the Royal Society of Medicine,* 86(1): 28–30.

Berk, M. Dodd, S. Henry, M (2006). 'The effect of macroeconomic variables on suicide.' *Psychological Medicine,* 36(2): 181–189.

Berndt, ER (2004). 'Changes in the costs of treating mental health disorders: an overview of recent research findings.' *Pharmacoeconomics,* 22(2 Suppl. 2): 37–50.

Berndt, ER. Bir, A. Busch, SH. Frank, RG. Normand, SL (2002). 'The medical treatment of depression, 1991–1996: productive inefficiency, expected outcome variations, and price indexes.' *Journal of Health Economics,* 21(3): 373–396.

Berndt, ER. Busch, SH. Frank, RG (1998). *Price indexes for acute phase treatment of depression.* Cambridge, MA: National Bureau of Economic Research (NBER Working Paper no. 6799).

Berndt, ER. Busch, SH. Frank, RG (2001). Treatment price indexes for acute phase major depression. In: Cutler, DM. Berndt, ER (eds.). *Medical care output and productivity.* Chicago: University of Chicago Press.

Berndt, ER. Busch, AB. Frank, RG. Normand, SL (2006). 'Real output in mental health care during the 1990s.' *Forum for Health Economics & Policy,* 9(1): 1–17.

Bero, LA. Grilli, R. Grimshaw, JM. Harvey, E. Oxman, AD. Thomson, MA (1998). 'Closing the gap between research and practice: an overview of systematic reviews of interventions to promote the implementation of research findings. The Cochrane Effective Practice and Organization of Care Review Group.' *British Medical Journal,* 317(7156): 465–468.

Bower, P. Sibbald, B (1999). 'On-site mental health workers in primary care: effects on professional practice.' *Cochrane Database of Systematic Reviews,* Issue 4.

Brooks, R (2000). 'The reliability and validity of the Health of the Nation Outcome Scales: validation in relation to patient derived measures.' *Australian and New Zealand Journal of Psychiatry,* 34(3): 504–511.

Burns, T. Catty, J. Becker, T. Drake, RE. Fioritti, A. Knapp, M. Lauber, C. Rossler, W. Tomov, T. van Busschbach, J. White, S. Wiersma, D (2007). 'The effectiveness of supported employment for people with severe mental illness: a randomised controlled trial.' *Lancet,* 370(9593): 1146–1152.

Callaly, T. Hallebone, EL (2001). 'Introducing the routine use of outcomes measurement to mental health services.' *Australian Health Review,* 24(1): 43–50.

Callaly, T. Arya, D. Minas, H (2005). 'Quality, risk management and governance in mental health: an overview.' *Australasian Psychiatry,* 13(1): 16–20.

Callaly, T. Coombs, T. Berk, M (2003). 'Routine outcome measurement by mental health-care providers.' *Lancet,* 361(9363): 1137–1138.

Callaly, T. Hyland, M. Coombs, T. Trauer, T (2006). 'Routine outcome measurement in public mental health: results of a clinician survey.' *Australian Health Review,* 30(2): 164–173.

Callan, A. Littlewood, R (1998). 'Patient satisfaction: ethnic origin or explanatory model?' *International Journal of Social Psychiatry,* 44(1): 1–11.

Chisholm, D. Sanderson, K. Ayuso-Mateos, JL. Saxena, S (2004). 'Reducing the global burden of depression: population-level analysis of intervention cost-effectiveness in 14 world regions.' *British Journal of Psychiatry,* 184: 393–403.

Chow, JC. Jaffee, K. Snowden, L (2003). 'Racial/ethnic disparities in the use of mental health services in poverty areas.' *American Journal of Public Health,* 93(5): 792–797.

Clarkson, P. Challis, D (2002). 'Developing performance indicators for mental health care.' *Journal of Mental Health,* 11(3): 281–294.

Corrigan, PW. Wassel, A (2008). 'Understanding and influencing the stigma of mental illness.' *Journal of Psychosocial Nursing and Mental Health Services,* 46(1): 42–48.

Demyttenaere, K. Jaspers, L (2008). 'Review: Bupropion and SSRI-induced side effects.' *Journal of Psychopharmacology,* 22(7): 792–804.

Department of Health (1992). *The health of the nation: a strategy for England.* London: HMSO.

Department of Health (1999). *National service framework for mental health: modern standards and service models.* London: Department of Health.

Dickey, B. Sederer, LI (2001). *Improving mental health care: commitment to quality.* Washington, DC: American Psychiatric Publishing, Inc.

Donnelly, RR (2008). *Mental Health Project final report: National Benchmarking Project. Report 2.* Edinburgh: The Scottish Government.

Dow, MG. Boaz, TL. Thornton, D (2001). 'Risk adjustment of Florida mental health outcomes data: concepts, methods, and results.' *Journal of Behavioral Health Services & Research,* 28(3): 258–272.

Druss, BG. Rosenheck, RA Stolar, M (1999). 'Patient satisfaction and administrative measures as indicators of the quality of mental health care.' *Psychiatric Services,* 50(8): 1053–1058.

Durbin, J. Lin, E. Layne, C. Teed, M (2007). 'Is readmission a valid indicator of the quality of inpatient psychiatric care?' *Journal of Behavioral Health Services and Research*, 34(2): 137–150.

Ettner, SL. Frank, RG. McGuire, TG. Newhouse, JP. Notman, EH (1998). 'Risk adjustment of mental health and substance abuse payments.' *Inquiry*, 35(2): 223–239.

Evers, S. Salvador-Carulla, L. Halsteinli, V. McDaid, D. The MHEEN Group (2007) 'Implementing mental health economic evaluation evidence: building a bridge between theory and practice.' *Journal of Mental Health*, 16(2): 223–241.

Evers, SM. Van Wijk, AS. Ament, AJ (1997). 'Economic evaluation of mental health care interventions. A review.' *Health Economics*, 6(2): 161–177.

Faria, JG (1997). 'Quality development in mental health care in Europe. Recent contributions by WHO.' *Epidemiologia e Psichiatria Sociale*, 6(Suppl. 1): 211–215.

Fearon, P. Kirkbride, JB. Morgan, C. Dazzan, P. Morgan, K. Lloyd, T. Hutchinson, G. Tarrant, J. Fung, WL. Holloway, J. Mallett, R. Harrison, G. Leff, J. Jones, PB. Murray, RM (2006). 'Incidence of schizophrenia and other psychoses in ethnic minority groups: results from the MRC AESOP Study.' *Psychological Medicine*, 36(11): 1541–1550.

Fleischhacker, WW. Cetkovich-Bakmas, M. De Hert, M. Hennekens, CH. Lambert, M. Leucht, S. Maj, M. McIntyre, RS. Naber, D. Newcomer, JW. Olfson, M. Osby, U. Sartorius, N. Lieberman, JA (2008). 'Comorbid somatic illnesses in patients with severe mental disorders: clinical, policy, and research challenges.' *Journal of Clinical Psychiatry*, 69(4): 514–519.

Fonagy, P. Matthews, R. Pilling, S (2004). *The Mental Health Outcomes Measurement Initiative: report from the Chair of the Outcomes Reference Group*. London: National Collaborating Centre for Mental Health.

Ford, D (2006). 'Counting hoops: measuring the quality of mental health services in the US.' *The Mental Health Review*, 11:15–20 (http://www.commonwealthfund.org/Content/Fellowships/Harkness-Fellowships/2004-2005-Fellows/Dominic-Ford--U-K.aspx).

Frank, RG. Berndt, ER. Busch, AB. Lehman, AF (2004). 'Quality-constant "prices" for the ongoing treatment of schizophrenia: an exploratory study.' *Quarterly Review of Economics and Finance*, 44(3): 390–409.

Frank, RG. Berndt, ER. Busch, SH (1998). *Price indexes for the treatment of depression*. Cambridge, MA: National Bureau of Economic Research (NBER Working Paper no. W6417).

Frank, RG. Busch, SH. Berndt, ER (1998a). 'Measuring prices and quantities of treatment for depression.' *American Economic Review,* 88(2): 106–111.

Frank, RG. McGuire, TG. Normand, SL (2006). *Cost-offsets of new medications for treatment of schizophrenia.* Cambridge, MA: National Bureau of Economic Research (NBER Working Paper no. W12643).

Garcia-Armesto, S. Medeiros, H. Wei, L (2008). *Information availability for measuring and comparing quality of mental health care across OECD countries.* Paris: OECD.

Garcia, R. Joseph, T. Turk, J. Basu, R (2002). 'A comparison of parent and therapist ratings of outcome in a child mental health clinic.' *Child and Adolescent Mental Health,* 7(4): 168–172.

Gartlehner, G. Thieda, P. Hansen, RA. Gaynes, BN. Deveaugh-Geiss, A. Krebs, EE. Lohr, KN (2008). 'Comparative risk for harms of second-generation antidepressants : a systematic review and meta-analysis.' *Drug Safety,* 31(10): 851–865.

Geddis, PW (1988). 'Health service performance indicators.' *Ulster Medical Journal,* 57(2): 121–128.

Gilbody, S. Whitty, P (2002). 'Improving the delivery and organisation of mental health services: beyond the conventional randomised controlled trial.' *British Journal of Psychiatry,* 180: 13–18.

Gilbody, S. Whitty, P. Grimshaw, J. Thomas, R (2003). 'Educational and organizational interventions to improve the management of depression in primary care: a systematic review.' *Journal of the American Medical Association,* 289(23): 3145–3151.

Gilbody, SM. House, AO. Sheldon, TA (2001). 'Routinely administered questionnaires for depression and anxiety: systematic review.' *British Medical Journal,* 322(7283): 406–409.

Glover, G (1995). 'Mental health informatics and the rhythm of community care.' *British Medical Journal,* 311(7012): 1038–1039.

Glover, G. Farmer, R. Preston, D (1990). 'Indicators of mental hospital bed use.' *Health Trends,* 22(3): 111–115.

Greenberg, GA. Rosenheck, R (2005). 'Using the GAF as a national mental health outcome measure in the Department of Veterans Affairs.' *Psychiatric Services,* 56(4): 420–426.

Greenwood, N. Key, A. Burns, T. Bristow, M. Sedgwick, P (1999). 'Satisfaction with in-patient psychiatric services. Relationship to patient and treatment factors.' *British Journal of Psychiatry,* 174: 159–163.

Grol, R (2001). 'Successes and failures in the implementation of evidence-based guidelines for clinical practice.' *Medical Care,* 39(8 Suppl. 2): II46–54.

Gutierrez-Recacha, P. Chisholm, D. Haro, JM. Salvador-Carulla, L. Ayuso-Mateos, JL (2006). 'Cost-effectiveness of different clinical interventions for reducing the burden of schizophrenia in Spain.' *Acta Psychiatrica Scandanavica. Supplementum,* 432: 29–38.

Halsteinli, V (2008). Personal communication. November 2008.

Halsteinli, V. Ose, SO. Torvik, H. Hagen, TP (2006). 'Allocation of labour to somatic and psychiatric specialist care – the effects of earmarked grants.' *Health Policy,* 78(2–3): 115–127.

Hansson, L (1989). 'Patient satisfaction with in-hospital psychiatric care: a study of a 1-year population of patients hospitalized in a sectorized care organization.' *European Archives of Psychiatry & Neurological Sciences,* 239(2): 93–100.

Harris, EC. Barraclough, B (1998). 'Excess mortality of mental disorder.' *British Journal of Psychiatry,* 173: 11–53.

Haywood, TW. Kravitz, HM. Grossman, LS. Cavanaugh, JL. Davis, JM. Lewis, DA (1995). 'Predicting the "revolving door" phenomenon among patients with schizophrenic, schizoaffective, and affective disorders.' *American Journal of Psychiatry,* 152(6): 856–861.

Health Research Board (2008). *WISDOM.* Dublin (http://www.hrb.ie/health-information-in-house-research/mental-health/information-systems/wisdom/).

Health Scotland (2006). *Establishing national mental health and well-being indicators for Scotland.* Edinburgh.

Healthcare Commission (2007). *Survey of users of mental health services 2007.* London.

Hendryx, MS. Dyck, DG. Srebnik, D (1999). 'Risk-adjusted outcome models for public mental health outpatient programs.' *Health Services Research,* 34(1 Pt 1): 171–195.

Hendryx, MS. Teague, GB (2001). 'Comparing alternative risk-adjustment models.' *Journal of Behavioral Health Services & Research,* 28(3): 247–257.

Hermann, R. Mattke, S. & Members of the OECD Mental Health Care Panel (2004). *Selecting indicators for the quality of mental health care at the health systems level in OECD countries.* Paris: Directorate for Employment, Labour and Social Affairs (OECD Health Technical Papers no. 17).

Hermann, RC. Mattke, S. Somekh, D. Silfverhielm, H. Goldner, E. Glover, G. Pirkis, J. Mainz, J. Chan, JA (2006). 'Quality indicators for international benchmarking of mental health care.' *International Journal for Quality in Health Care,* 18(Suppl. 1): 31–38.

Hermann, RC. Palmer, H. Leff, S. Shwartz, M. Provost, S. Chan, J. Chiu, WT. Lagodmos, G (2004b). 'Achieving consensus across diverse stakeholders on quality measures for mental healthcare.' *Medical Care*, 42(12): 1246–1253.

Horton, R (2007). 'Launching a new movement for mental health.' *Lancet*, 370(9590): 806.

Huxley, P. Evans, S (2002). 'Quality of life routine outcomes measurement: lessons from experience in the USA and the UK.' *Epidemiologia e Psichiatria Sociale*, 11(3): 192–197.

Jenkins, R. Glover, G (1997). 'The importance of service level measures for mental health policy.' *Epidemiologia e Psichiatria Sociale*, 6(Suppl. 1): 229–237.

Jenkins, R. Strathdee, G. Carr, S. Rawaf, S (2000). Equity in mental health. In: Rawaf, S. Orton, P (eds.). *Current issues in health care – health improvement programmes*. London: Royal Society of Medicine.

Kalman, TP (1983). 'An overview of patient satisfaction with psychiatric treatment.' *Hospital & Community Psychiatry*, 34(1): 48–54.

Kelleher, MJ. Chambers, D. Corcoran, P. Williamson, E. Keeley, HS (1998). 'Religious sanctions and rates of suicide worldwide.' *Crisis*, 19(2): 78–86.

Kisely, S. Campbell, LA. Crossman, D. Campbell, J (2008). 'Routine measurement of mental health service outcomes: Health of the Nation Outcome Scales in Nova Scotia.' *Psychiatric Bulletin*, 32: 248–250.

Knapp, M. McDaid, D. Amaddeo, F. Constantopoulos, A. Oliveira, M. Salvador-Carulla, L. Zechmeister, I. Mheen Group (2007). 'Financing mental health care in Europe.' *Journal of Mental Health*, 16(2): 167–180.

Kramer, TL. Owen, RR. Wilson, C. Thrush, CR (2003). 'Relationship between self-report and clinician-rated impairment in depressed outpatients.' *Community Mental Health Journal*, 39(4): 299–307.

Lavikainen, J. Fryers, T. Lehtinen, V (eds.) (2006). *Improving mental health information in Europe*. Helsinki: STAKES.

Leavey, G. King, M. Cole, E. Hoar, A. Johnson-Sabine, E (1997). 'First-onset psychotic illness: patients' and relatives' satisfaction with services.' *British Journal of Psychiatry*, 170: 53–57.

Lebow, J (1982). 'Consumer satisfaction with mental health treatment.' *Psychological Bulletin*, 91(2): 244–259.

Lien, L (2002). 'Are readmission rates influenced by how psychiatric services are organized?' *Nordic Journal of Psychiatry*, 56(1): 23–28.

Ling, DYC. Busch, AB. Frank, RG (2004). *Treatment price indexes for bipolar disorder*. Harvard: Harvard Medical School.

Lyons, JS. McGovern, MP (1989). 'Use of mental health services by dually diagnosed patients.' *Hospital & Community Psychiatry*, 40(10): 1067–1069.

Lyons, JS. O'Mahoney, MT. Miller, SI. Neme, J. Kabat, J. Miller, F (1997). 'Predicting readmission to the psychiatric hospital in a managed care environment: implications for quality indicators.' *American Journal of Psychiatry*, 154(3): 337–340.

Manderscheid, RW (2006). 'Some thoughts on the relationships between evidence based practices, practice based evidence, outcomes, and performance measures.' *Administration and Policy in Mental Health*, 33(6): 646–647.

Mann, JJ. Apter, A. Bertolote, J. Beautrais, A. Currier, D. Haas, A. Hegerl, U. Lonnqvist, J. Malone, K. Marusic, A. Mehlum, L. Patton, G. Phillips, M. Rutz, W. Rihmer, Z. Schmidtke, A. Shaffer, D. Silverman, M. Takahashi, Y. Varnik, A. Wasserman, D. Yip, P. Hendin, H (2005). 'Suicide prevention strategies: a systematic review.' *Journal of the American Medical Association*, 294(16): 2064–2074.

McCrone, P (1995). 'Predicting mental health service use: diagnosis based systems and alternatives.' *Journal of Mental Health*, 4(1): 31–40.

McDaid, D. Oliveira, M. Jurczak, K. Knapp, M. & the Mheen Group (2007). 'Moving beyond the mental health care system: an exploration of the interfaces between health and non-health sectors.' *Journal of Mental Health*, 16(2): 181–194.

McFarland, BH. George, RA. Goldman, W. Pollack, DA. McCulloch, J. Penner, S. Angell, RH (1998). 'Population-based guidelines for performance measurement: a preliminary report.' *Harvard Review of Psychiatry*, 6(1): 23–37.

Meehan, T. Bergen, H. Stedman, T (2002). 'Monitoring consumer satisfaction with inpatient service delivery: the Inpatient Evaluation of Service Questionnaire.' *Australian & New Zealand Journal of Psychiatry*, 36(6): 807–11.

Meehan, T. McCombes, S. Hatzipetrou, L. Catchpoole, R (2006). 'Introduction of routine outcome measures: staff reactions and issues for consideration.' *Journal of Psychiatric & Mental Health Nursing*, 13(5): 581–587.

Ministry of Health (2006). *National Mental Health Information Strategy: implementation plan 2006*. Wellington: New Zealand Ministry of Health.

Mohan, R. McCrone, P. Szmukler, G. Micali, N. Afuwape, S. Thornicroft, G (2006). 'Ethnic differences in mental health service use among patients with psychotic disorders.' *Social Psychiatry and Psychiatric Epidemiology*, 41(10): 771–776.

Ness-Abramof, R. Apovian, CM (2005). 'Drug-induced weight gain.' *Drugs of Today*, 41(8): 547–555.

Newcomer, JW (2005). 'Second-generation (atypical) antipsychotics and metabolic effects: a comprehensive literature review.' *CNS Drugs*, 19(Suppl. 1): 1–93.

Ohio Department of Mental Health (2007). Ohio Mental Health Consumer Outcomes Initiative (http://www.mh.state.oh.us/oper/outcomes/outcomes.index.html).

Osborn, DP. Levy, G. Nazareth, I. Petersen, I. Islam, A. King, MB (2007). 'Relative risk of cardiovascular and cancer mortality in people with severe mental illness from the United Kingdom's General Practice Research Database.' *Archives of General Psychiatry,* 64(2): 242–249.

Parker, C (2007). Developing mental health policy: a human rights perspective. In: Knapp, M. McDaid, D. Mossialos, E. Thornicroft, G (eds.). *Mental health policy and practice across Europe.* Buckingham: Open University Press.

Perreault, M. Rogers, WL. Leichner, P. Sabourin, S (1996). 'Patients' requests and satisfaction with services in an outpatient psychiatric setting.' *Psychiatric Services,* 47(3): 287–292.

Petrea, I. Muijen, M (2008). *Policies and practices for mental health in Europe – meeting the challenges.* Copenhagen: WHO.

Potts, Y. Gillies, M. Wood, S (2001). 'Lack of mental well-being in 15-year-olds: an undisclosed iceberg?' *Family Practice,* 18(1): 95–100.

Priebe, S. Badesconyi, A. Fioritti, A. Hansson, L. Kilian, R. Torres-Gonzales, F. Turner, T. Wiersma, D (2005). 'Reinstitutionalisation in mental health care: comparison of data on service provision from six European countries.' *British Medial Journal,* 330(7483): 123–126.

Priebe, S. McCabe, R. Bullenkamp, J. Hansson, L. Rossler, W. Torres-Gonzales, F. Wiersma, D (2002). 'The impact of routine outcome measurement on treatment processes in community mental health care: approach and methods of the MECCA study.' *Epidemiologia e Psichiatria Sociale,* 11(3): 198–205.

Rea, CA. Rea, DM (2002). 'Managing performance and performance management: information strategy and service user involvement.' *Journal of Management in Medicine,* 16(1): 78–93.

Renvoize, E. Clayden, D (1990). 'Can the suicide rate be used as a performance indicator in mental illness?' *Health Trends,* 22(1): 16–20.

Rose, D. Lucas, J (2007). The user and survivor movement in Europe. In: Knapp, M. McDaid, D. Mossialos, E. Thornicroft, G (eds.). *Mental health policy and practice across Europe.* Buckingham: Open University Press.

Rose, D. Thornicroft, G. Slade, M (2006). 'Who decides what evidence is? Developing a multiple perspectives paradigm in mental health.' *Acta Psychiatrica Scandinavica,* 113(Suppl. 429): 109–114.

Rosen, A. Miller, V. Parker, G (1989). 'Standards of care for area mental health services.' *Australian and New Zealand Journal of Psychiatry,* 23(3): 379–395.

Rosenheck, R. Fontana, A (1999). 'Changing patterns of care for war-related post-traumatic stress disorder at Department of Veterans Affairs medical centers: the use of performance data to guide program development.' *Military Medicine,* 164(11): 795–802.

Sayce, L. Curran, C (2007). Tackling social exclusion across Europe. In: Knapp, M. McDaid, D. Mossialos, E. Thornicroft, G (eds.). *Mental health policy and practice across Europe.* Buckingham: Open University Press.

Schacht, LM. Hines, H (2003). 'Recent applications of risk adjustment for performance measures used by state inpatient psychiatric facilities.' *Harvard Review of Psychiatry,* 11(4): 220–224.

Schomerus, G. Angermeyer, MC (2008). 'Stigma and its impact on help-seeking for mental disorders: what do we know?' *Epidemiologia e Psichiatria Sociale,* 17(1): 31–37.

Slade, M (2002). 'What outcomes to measure in routine mental health services, and how to assess them: a systematic review.' *Australian & New Zealand Journal of Psychiatry,* 36(6): 743–753.

Slade, M. McCrone, P. Kuipers, E. Leese, M. Cahill, S. Parabiaghi, A. Priebe, S. Thornicroft, G (2006). 'Use of standardised outcome measures in adult mental health services: randomised controlled trial.' *British Journal of Psychiatry,* 189: 330–336.

Social Exclusion Unit (2004). *Mental health and social exclusion.* London: Office of the Deputy Prime Minister.

Stiegler, M. Rummel, C. Wahlbeck, K. Kissling, W. Leucht, S (2005). 'European psychiatric treatment guidelines: is the glass half full or half empty?' *European Psychiatry,* 20(8): 554–558.

Taipale, V (2001). 'Mental health and quality of mental health care.' *Medicine & Law,* 20(4): 531–542.

Tapsell, R. Mellsop, G (2007). 'The contributions of culture and ethnicity to New Zealand mental health research findings.' *International Journal of Social Psychiatry,* 53(4): 317–324.

Tennant, R. Joseph, S. Stewart-Brown, S (2007). 'The Affectometer 2: a measure of positive mental health in UK populations.' *Quality of Life Research,* 16(4): 687–695.

Thornicroft, G (2007). 'Most people with mental illness are not treated.' *Lancet,* 370(9590): 807–808.

Thornicroft, G (2008). 'Stigma and discrimination limit access to mental health care.' *Epidemiologia e Psichiatria Sociale,* 17(1): 14–19.

Wahlbeck, K (2006). Mental health in EU health monitoring systems. In: Lavikainen, J. Fryers, T. Lehtinen, V (eds.). *Improving mental health information in Europe.* Helsinki: STAKES.

Wang, PS. Aguilar-Gaxiola, S. Alonso, J. Angermeyer, MC. Borges, G. Bromet, EJ. Bruffaerts, R. De Girolamo, G. De Graaf, R. Gureje, O. Haro, JM. Karam, EG. Kessler, RC. Kovess, V. Lane, MC. Lee, S. Levinson, D. Ono, Y. Petukhova, M. Posada-Villa, J. Seedat, S. Wells, JE (2007). 'Use of mental health services for anxiety, mood, and substance disorders in 17 countries in the WHO world mental health surveys.' *Lancet*, 370(9590): 841–850.

Warner, JP. Singhal, S. Dutta, A (1994). 'How well do we assess patients' satisfaction?' *Medical Audit News*, 4(6): 157–158.

Watters, C (2007). The mental health care of asylum seekers and refugees. In: Knapp, M. McDaid, D. Mossialos, E. Thornicroft, G (eds.). *Mental health policy and practice across Europe*. Buckingham: Open University Press.

Watters, C. Ingleby, D (2004). 'Locations of care: meeting the mental health and social care needs of refugees in Europe.' *International Journal of Law and Psychiatry*, 27(6): 549–570.

Weinmann, S. Koesters, M. Becker, T (2007). 'Effects of implementation of psychiatric guidelines on provider performance and patient outcome: systematic review.' *Acta Psychiatrica Scandinavica*, 115(6): 420–433.

Westert, GP. Verkleij, H (eds.) (2006). *Dutch health care performance report*. Bilthoven: National Institute for Public Health and the Environment.

WHO Regional Office for Europe (2003). *Mental health in the WHO European region*. Copenhagen & Vienna (Fact sheet EURO 03/03) WHO Regional Office for Europe.

WHO Regional Office for Europe (2005). *Mental health action plan for Europe. Facing the challenges, building solutions*. Copenhagen: WHO Regional Office for Europe.

WHO (2005). *Mental health atlas 2005*. Geneva: World Health Organization.

WHO (2005a). *The World Health Organization assessment instrument for mental health systems (WHO-AIMS)*. Geneva: World Health Organization.

Wilkinson, DG (1982). 'The suicide rate in schizophrenia.' *British Journal of Psychiatry*, 140(2): 138–141.

Wing, JK. Curtis, RH. Beevor, AS (1996). *HoNOS: Health of the Nation Outcome Scales: report on research and development July 1993-December 1995*. London: Royal College of Psychiatrists.

Wittchen, HU. Jacobi, F (2005). 'Size and burden of mental disorders in Europe – a critical review and appraisal of 27 studies.' *European Neuropsychopharmacology*, 15(4): 357–376.

4.4 Long-term care quality monitoring using the interRAI common clinical assessment language

VINCENT MOR, HARRIET FINNE-SOVERI,

JOHN P. HIRDES, RUEDI GILGEN,

JEAN-NOËL DUPASQUIER

Introduction

Residential care has been the mainstay of long-term care delivery systems in industrialized countries for decades. However, changes in acute care financing; individuals' preferences for remaining in the community; and the ageing of the elderly population mean that individuals with increasing frailty and impairments occupy these long-term care facilities. Most long-term care systems have evolved idiosyncratically as countries have faced different demographic imperatives and responded to different regulatory and medical-care systems. The need to characterize the needs of the population of long-term care users and the types and quality of services they receive has come to the forefront as the acuity of long-term care facilities has increased and as countries attempt to rebalance these budgets in order to provide more community support.

This chapter describes the development of a comprehensive clinical and functional assessment instrument – the nursing home Resident Assessment Instrument (RAI), more commonly known as the Minimum Data Set (MDS). This was designed in the United States on the basis that the proper provision of the complex care needed by frail older persons is predicated upon a comprehensive clinical assessment and it is the absence of such that underlies deficient quality of care. Originally intended as a clinical care planning tool, this minimum set of clinical and demographic data on all nursing home residents has been adapted as a vehicle for determining payment levels and to monitor the quality of care.

Several European countries have adopted the RAI within their long-term care systems. Similar applications are in place, either by governmental mandate or on a voluntary basis, in Canada and several European countries such as Switzerland and Finland. Various provinces in other countries are currently considering adopting this approach. The long-term care sector shares many of the conceptual and technical difficulties that health policy-makers face when attempting to compare quality performance in hospitals or medical groups. However, long-term care facilities are also individuals' homes and therefore the adequacy of the living experience must be addressed by understanding quality of life, not just quality of care, issues.

In this chapter we document how the RAI-MDS has been transformed into an assessment based data system that serves multiple research and applied policy functions, ranging from casemix reimbursement to outcomes measurement and quality performance monitoring. Since all industrialized countries are facing rising ageing populations and are therefore grappling with how to develop and/or modify their long-term care systems, there is substantial international interest in the development of the RAI for clinical assessment, educational purposes and for policy applications. The second half of this chapter focuses on the use of RAI data for benchmarking nursing home quality via public reporting and quality improvement efforts in the United States, Canada, Finland and Switzerland.

Origin of the RAI in the United States

Complaints about the quality of nursing home care began soon after Medicare began reimbursing for post-hospital nursing home care and Medicaid began paying for long-term nursing home care in 1966. Scandals about the quality of care in nursing homes have occurred periodically and prompted the formation of a new investigatory commission, the promulgation of new regulations, or both (Davis 1991). In 1984, the Institute of Medicine initiated a study of the quality of care in nursing homes, led by Sidney Katz.

Recommendations from the committee's report *Improving the Quality of Care in Nursing Homes* (Institute of Medicine 1986) were translated almost entirely into the 1987 Nursing Home Reform Act of the Omnibus Budget Reconciliation Act. One of the key recommendations was to mandate a comprehensive assessment that would provide a uniform basis for establishing a nursing home resident's care plan. This was based on the observation that the lack of training and education among direct line nursing home staff meant that they were unable to identify patient needs. It was thought that a systematic assessment would structure the clinical information necessary for care planning and form the basis for a common lexicon for describing patients and their needs. Like the ICD, the MDS for nursing home resident assessment was designed to become a common language of functional impairment and disability for long-term care (Mor 2004).

The MDS was designed by a consortium of academic medical centres under contract from the Health Care Financing Administration (now the Centers for Medicare and Medicaid Services – CMS). Hundreds of experts representing the academic disciplines and professional organizations serving geriatrics, psychiatry, nursing, physical and occupational therapies, nutrition, social work and resident rights advocates participated in the design and testing of the instrument between 1989 and 1991. The goal was to create an instrument that captures the basic information needed to determine whether patients have various common geriatric problems and to develop a care plan that considers individuals' co-morbidities as well as their strengths and residual capacities. The domains of problems to be included in the assessment were specified in the 1987 Nursing Home Reform Act (Hawes et al. 1997; Hawes et al. 1997).

Version 1.0 of the RAI-MDS was implemented in all nursing homes in the United States in 1991. As a 'condition of participation' in the Medicare or Medicaid programmes, nursing homes had to complete the assessments for all residents regardless of their payer source. Thus, the population of all nursing home residents was represented in the data in all certified facilities. Assessments were required upon admission; re-admission; when the resident experienced a significant change in condition; and quarterly following the initial admission assessment. In 1999 an updated version (RAI 2.0) of the instrument was implemented along with a mandate that all facilities must computerize all assessments and submit them to CMS (Morris et al. 1997) With the adoption of a subset of RAI items as a measure of casemix acuity for casemix reimbursement, Medicare post-acute hospital nursing home admissions had to be assessed more frequently in the weeks following admission in order to determine the level of reimbursement based upon residents' assessed acuity.

Various studies have evaluated the impact of the Nursing Home Reform Act. One focused on understanding the impact of introducing the RAI-MDS in nursing homes in the United States, based upon a longitudinal study of 250 randomly selected facilities in 10 states with all data collected by independent research nurses. The investigators found that processes of care in several areas (restraint use and pressure ulcer prevention services) improved between the period prior to and after the implementation of the RAI (Hawes et al. 1997). Using MDS-based measures of cognitive function and ADL and mobility as outcome measurement scales, residents were found to be less likely to decline functionally and less likely to be hospitalized than they were before the Omnibus Budget Reform Act (Fries et al. 1997; Phillips et al. 1997; Mor et al. 1997) This study revealed that, when used by trained research staff, RAI-MDS has the capacity to identify specific care process problems and to measure changes in functional status.

Reliability and validity of the MDS

The MDS was tested repeatedly for inter-rater reliability among trained nurse assessors in large and small, for-profit and voluntary nursing homes throughout the country. These tests revealed high average levels of reliability as measured by kappa. The MDS was implemented nationally in late 1990; a modified version was designed and retested in 1995 and found to have improved reliability (Hawes et al. 1995; Mor et al. 2003; Morris et al. 1990)

Subsequent epidemiological and health services research studies using data from several states that used computerized versions of MDS found considerable evidence for construct validity. For example, Gambassi et al. (Gambassi et al. 1998) linked MDS assessment records with the Medicare hospital discharge claim that immediately preceded the MDS nursing home assessment. They found that the positive predictive value of an MDS-based diagnosis of a chronic condition affecting function or treatment exceeded 0.7 when compared to the hospital claim discharge diagnosis. In addition, in comparisons between drugs taken by residents and their MDS-based diagnoses they observed high levels of correspondence between the diagnosis and the appropriate class of drug for its treatment. Subsequent analyses of patients with diagnoses ranging from Parkinson's disease to congestive heart failure revealed similar positive associations (Bernabei et al. 1998; Bernabei et al. 1999; Gambassi et al. 1998) Finally, a series of analyses examining the relationship between the presence of selected diagnoses and functional and cognitive status found that each of these measures strongly predicted mortality in the expected direction (Gambassi et al. 1999; Gambassi, Lapane et al. 1999).

The discriminant validity of the MDS was also established by a series of smaller studies that compared summary indices derived from selected MDS data elements. Morris and colleagues created the Cognitive Performance Scale (CPS) by crosswalking variables in the MDS with the mini-mental state examination administered by research staff (Hartmaier, Sloane et al. 1995; Morris, Fries et al. 1994). They (and others) found the CPS to be strongly correlated to clinical and research tools assessing cognition and to a diagnosis of Alzheimer's disease and subsequent mortality (Gambassi et al. 1999; Gruber-Baldini et al. 2000). Various forms of ADL indices have been constructed using MDS variables characterizing patients' mobility; self-care performance; and the amount of assistance required to perform those tasks. Morris reported that both hierarchical and additive versions of the ADL scale were found to be strongly related to staff time – residents with more ADL impairment receiving more assistance (Morris et al. 1999) Other multi-item summary indices based upon the MDS assessment have been developed for domains such as pain; distressed mood and behavioural disturbances; and social engagement (Mor et al. 1995; Frederiksen, Tariot et al. 1996; Fries et al. 2001). Each of these manifested discriminant validity, clearly differentiating patients with different diagnoses, levels of functioning and nursing care needs.

Policy applications of the RAI

The RAI was designed as an assessment tool to facilitate care planning for nursing home residents but it was not long before the assessment data were being applied to very different functions ranging from reimbursement to quality monitoring. The precedent for this multifaceted use of clinical assessment data was established in the original studies that tested their utility and validity for research purposes since part of the evaluation required the creation of summary indices of residents' outcomes. Indeed, as described below, much of the work on applying the assessment data for reimbursement purposes was performed contemporaneously.

Casemix reimbursement

Casemix reimbursement came to long-term care in the 1980s in states such as New York, which was intent upon controlling its nursing home costs in the Medicaid programme. This was initially based on the Resource Utilization Group (RUG) system, a mandated, uniform data collection tool that classified patients largely by functional status (Fries and Cooney 1985). During the 1990s, many other states began adopting a prospective reimbursement system based on casemix (Feng, Grabowski et al. 2006). This trend was greatly accelerated by the universal availability of the MDS and by revision of the RUG system to incorporate new data elements that captured the characteristics of the more clinically complex patients entering nursing homes in increasing numbers. RUG was revised under the federally funded Nursing Home Case-Mix and Quality Demonstration project to include the far richer and clinically more complex data elements contained in the MDS. Thus, RUG-III was created for application to the Medicaid and Medicare patients in facilities from six states that participated in the demonstration project (Fries et al. 1994) Although not without controversy, the Medicare programme adopted the RUG classification system and applied it to a per diem payment for Medicare-reimbursed skilled nursing facility stays (Davis et al. 1998; Matherlee 1999).

It is interesting that virtually all evaluations of the impact of introducing casemix reimbursement at both federal and state level have relied upon the MDS data. Numerous researchers have merged nursing home level data on staffing levels with resident level data from the MDS. The resulting hierarchical and longitudinal data have been used to test the effect of introducing casemix reimbursement on staffing levels and skill mix; and the average acuity of residents and the outcomes they experience, for both Medicare and Medicaid beneficiaries (Feng et al. 2006; Konetzka et al. 2006; Konetzka et al. 2004; Wodchis et al. 2004).

Creating quality indicators to monitor provider performance

Researchers have frequently proposed and used measures of nursing home quality but generally only for a small number or select groups of facilities. Until recently, most such measures were based upon aggregate data reported by the home as part of the federal requirement for survey and certification (Zinn 1994). Many early studies of the determinants of quality of care in nursing homes produced contradictory findings because they used facility-level data that could not be risk-adjusted for differences in casemix (Davis 1991).

The availability of clinically relevant, universal, uniform and computerized data on all nursing home residents raised the possibility of using this information to improve care quality. Several approaches were suggested. The MDS data were thought to have utility in directly guiding efforts to improve the quality of care in a single nursing home (Popejoy et al. 2000; Zimmerman 2003). Several states instituted the use of MDS-based indicators of nursing home quality as part of the Case Mix Reimbursement and Quality Demonstration (Reilly et al. 2007). As with most efforts designed to improve health-care quality, this offered multifaceted incentives and targets. First, government regulators anticipated that the creation of indicators of nursing homes' quality performance would guide and systematize existing regulatory oversight processes that had been characterized as idiosyncratic. Secondly, more enlightened facility administrators felt that such information could facilitate their own existing quality improvement activities. Finally, advocates for nursing home residents thought that making this information available would create greater transparency to guide consumers' choice of a long-term care facility.

Initially, few nursing facilities across the country had the sophistication to use the MDS for institutional planning, staff loading or outcome monitoring but now many are actively using the MDS for one or more of these functions. Some states, particularly those that began statewide computerization of their MDS data before the CMS mandate in June 1998, began rudimentary efforts to report aggregated quality indicators from a variety of different MDS domains (Castle & Lowe 2005) These efforts were designed to make facilities aware of the potential uses of the MDS and to allow comparisons between their quality of care and the state-wide averages.

As part of the Nursing Home Case-Mix and Quality Demonstration, Wisconsin's Center for Health Systems Research and Analysis (CHSRA) was charged with developing an array of readily useable facility and resident quality indicators based upon computerized data from the resident assessment instrument (Zimmerman 2003; Reilly et al. 2007). Numerous versions of these proposed indicators were reviewed by various clinical and industry panels for appropriateness, meaningfulness and their potential for attributing problems to the care provided in the facility. Indicators included the prevalence of pressure ulcers; prevalence of use of anti-psychotics; and the incidence of late loss ADL. The CHSRA team created algorithms to identify individual residents and aggregate them to the level of the facility and then designed reports to help facilities and state inspectors to use this information to isolate problem areas.

Various other efforts were undertaken to develop and test quality indicators focused on quality of life issues such as mood or well-being. As it was easier to gain expert consensus on the meaning of clinically pertinent quality indicators, far fewer broader quality of life measures have been developed and promulgated (Castle et al. 2007; Mukamel et al. 2007). Furthermore, psychosocial measures included in the RAI-MDS have been shown to have poorer inter-rater reliability and suffer from ascertainment bias – under-identification of pain, mood and behaviour problems, for example (Bates-Jensen et al. 2004; Simmons et al. 2004; Roy & Mor 2005; Wu et al. 2005). Additionally, the MDS contains information on distressed mood and even involvement in social activities but does not capture patients' preferences or satisfaction. However, a separate 'industry' has arisen to produce resident satisfaction surveys in the United States over the last decade and these are increasingly available in facilities across the country (Lowe et al. 2003; Castle 2006; Straker et al. 2007).

In the late 1990s, CMS expanded their commitment to use quality indicators in their efforts to improve nursing home quality (Clauser & Fries 1992; Harris & Clauser 2002). The first objective was to improve and expand upon extant clinically relevant quality indicators based upon the universally available MDS information (Berg, Mor et al. 2002). The second objective was to develop measures that were fully responsive to the quality of life concerns of long-term care facility residents, such as food quality and preferences, autonomy and perception of treatment with respect (Kane 2003). These updated measures of quality performance were intended to meet the information needs of four distinct audiences: providers, regulators, purchasers and consumers. The first two groups had had some experience of interpreting and working with the MDS-based quality indicators developed under the Nursing Home Case-Mix and Quality Demonstration. However, the involvement of purchasers and consumers meant introducing some level of public reporting of the information. Public reporting has presented challenges to both the National Committee for Quality Assurance (in the managed care plan realm) and to the Joint Commission, which has been struggling with hospitals on this issue. Data can be misinterpreted or tell only part of a story and providers and insurers are uncomfortable that data are made available to a public who may not understand the meaning of the performance measures. This reluctance has frequently resulted in disagreements about the precise definitions and construction of the performance measures, particularly whether and how to risk adjust the data (Sangl et al. 2005; Zinn et al. 2005; Castle et al. 2007; Gerteis et al. 2007; Phillips et al. 2007).

CMS quality measures cover both long- and short-stay nursing home residents, with a numerator and denominator defined for each measure. Cross-sectional measures such as the proportion of residents with physical restraints are repeated quarterly as are longitudinal measures such the proportion of long-stay residents with declining physical functioning. However, longitudinal measures require the residents to have two measures and ignore censoring due to death or discharge. Rules on reporting are based on the number of patients for whom a measure can be calculated. However, the result can be quite volatile even when there are at least twenty or thirty patients (Mor 2005; Sangl, Saliba et al. 2005). For example, it is not uncommon for the measure of the proportion of patients declining through late onset ADL impairments to be well over 30% in one quarter and well under 20% in another, shifting the providers' quality ranking from near the top to near the bottom (Mor 2004). Statistically, less than 25% of the variation in a quality measure reflecting one quarter's performance can be explained by that of the next quarter. Even more importantly, the correlation between clinical quality measures (e.g. rate of functional decline, pressure ulcer prevalence) is less than .05, meaning that providers doing well in one area may not be doing well in another (Mor et al. 2003; Baier et al. 2005; Mor 2005). Consumers, families and advocates who use this information to choose a provider do so because they believe that the past will be a good predictor of the future. When quality measures are volatile they will not be good predictors of future performance – nor will they guarantee that good performance in one area means good performance in another.

Comparisons of data quality problems in relation to the prevalence or incidence of selected quality indicators revealed that almost half of the observed inter-state differences are due to systematic coding differences in the assessment items that make up the quality measures (Wu et al. 2005a). This is consistent with several small studies that compared nursing home providers' performance in areas such as pain management or incontinence care. The authors found substantial inter-facility and inter-state differences in the prevalence of clinical conditions that seemed unrelated to differences in the patients studied (Schnelle et al. 2003; Simmons et al. 2004).

In spite of concerns about the validity of data and consumers' use of publicly reported quality information, in 2002 the CMS began posting aggregated quality measures on their Nursing Home Compare web site (see below). This had previously contained information about staffing levels and the results of annual inspections of facilities (Castle & Lowe 2005; Castle et al. 2007; Mukamel et al. 2007). The resulting publicly reported data are now promulgated widely throughout the Internet. Many companies repackage the information in a more user-friendly format to help consumers and their families to choose a facility and many states have gone beyond CMS by adding selected information about facilities (Castle et al. 2005). At present CMS is initiating a demonstration project that pays nursing homes extra. These bonuses are based on performance on the publicly reported quality measures for reductions in acute hospitalizations and associated costs which are presumed to accompany improvements in quality (Rahman 2006).

Use of RAI for quality monitoring and benchmarking: international examples

Nursing Home Compare in the United States

CMS initiated a six-state pilot project in April 2002 in which facility-specific, MDS-based quality measures were promulgated for every Medicare/Medicaid certified nursing facility in each state. Applied to both long and short-stay post-acute patients, the quality measures included items such as pressure ulcer prevalence, restraint use, mobility improvement, pain and ADL decline. Advertisements presenting the rankings of area nursing homes were taken out in every major newspaper in every community in these six states.

Most nursing homes in the state were ranked and data on all measures for all facilities were included on the Nursing Home Compare web site (http://www.medicare.gov/NHCompare/home.asp). These data are readily accessible to consumers and advocates who may be seeking a facility. Having indicated a chosen geographical location, any number of facilities can be selected by various characteristics such as size, ownership or specialized services. This generates printable reports that compare the selected facilities in terms of staffing levels, inspection results and quality measures. Fig. 4.4.I provides an example of a comparison of one of the RAI-MDS based quality measures in several facilities in the state of Rhode Island. The comparative report includes information on the national and state average of the measure in order to provide context for the performance of each facility.

As noted above, consumers and their advocates are not the only users of these data. State inspectors of nursing home quality use the information on quality measure performance to guide their inspections, focusing on those aspects of the care process in which the facility appears to perform most poorly. Additionally, the Quality Improvement Organizations (QIOs), contracted by CMS to help facilities to institute quality improvement programmes, generally focus on improving those aspects identified as problematic in the publicly reported quality measurements. Finally, both CMS and some states are experimenting with pay-for-performance programmes that pay bonuses to high-performing facilities, based on the quality measures and selected structural factors such as staffing levels (Rahman 2006; Arling et al. 2007).

To date the impact of public reporting of nursing homes' perform ance is poorly understood. A recent survey of administrators suggests that most providers are keenly aware of how they compare to their local competition or peers; those who see their performance as sub-par report having instituted quality improvement programmes (Mukamel et al. 2007). Another recent study revealed that fewer than half of all consumers correctly interpreted the meaning of the bar graphs on Nursing Home Compare (see Fig. 4.4.I), suggesting that the quality

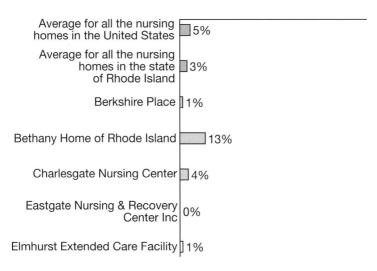

Fig. 4.4.1 Percentage of long-stay residents who were physically restrained

Source: http://www.medicare.gov/NHCompare/Include/DataSection/Questions/ProximitySearch.asp

information has relatively low utility to the end user (Gerteis et al. 2007). Similar results have been observed from efforts to inform consumers about the quality of insurers, hospitals and even physicians (McGee et al. 1999; Sofaer & Firminger 2005).

Benchmarking initiatives involving interRAI data in Canada

Multiple organizations undertake efforts to improve the quality of health care in Canada. The Canadian Institute for Health Information (CIHI) is an independent agency that houses and reports on data related to health expenditures, health services, health human resources and population health. It provides national reports on a range of health indicators for a variety of sectors including acute care, continuing care, home care, rehabilitation and mental health. The Canadian Council on Health Services Accreditation (CCHSA) works at the organizational level to evaluate and identify opportunities to improve quality in health care. Its accreditation standards require performance indicators to be used within internal quality improvement efforts but the organization does not produce provincial or national comparative reports based on those indicators. Following a national commission on the future of health care, the Health Council of Canada was founded to promote public accountability and transparency. Its reports have focused on progress related to federal and provincial governments' commitments in the 2004 ten-year plan for health system renewal. Since the establishment of this national agency, a number of provincial governments have created parallel agencies to perform similar functions at their level.

There is widespread implementation of interRAI instruments in Canada. For example, the nursing home Resident Assessment Instrument 2.0 (RAI 2.0) was first mandated as the standard assessment instrument for all patients in Ontario's Complex Continuing Care (CCC) hospitals/units in 1996. Seven other provinces/territories have since undertaken to implement the instrument and CIHI established the Continuing Care Reporting System (CCRS) to serve as the national data warehouse for RAI 2.0 data. As noted in the summary, versions of the RAI assessment instrument appropriate for home care and other populations with disabilities are also being implemented in multiple Canadian provinces.

The Ontario Hospital Report initiative was the first large scale effort to report on the quality of care using interRAI data in Canada. Data from CCC hospitals/units were used as part of a scorecard that aims to report on clinical utilization and outcomes; patient and family satisfaction; financial performance; and system integration and change. Of particular interest here, quality indicators developed by Morris and colleagues are used to benchmark hospital performance in thirteen areas including depression, communication decline, falls, pain, pressure ulcers and physical restraint use (http://www.cms.hhs. gov/NursingHomeQualityInits/Downloads/NHQISnapshot.pdf). The reports include provincial level distributions, regional rates and hospital-specific performance on individual quality indicators. The financial quadrant of the report uses resource utilization groups to provide a casemix adjustment for benchmarking the direct costs of care per weighted day (Fries et al. 1994). The system integration and change quadrant examines trends toward improved care through evidence based practice; use of information technology; integration of care; and use of the RAI 2.0 to inform clinical practice. All reports from this initiative are publicly available through the research collaborative (www. hospitalreport.ca). Fig. 4.4.2 provides an example of a report compar-

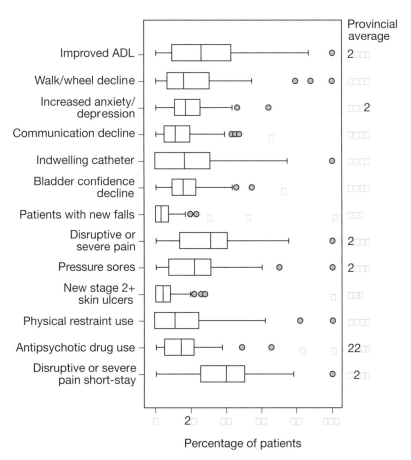

Fig. 4.4.2 Distribution of provincial indicator results

Source: Continuing Care Reporting Systems 2005–2006, CIHI.

ing CCC providers on a number of different quality measures. Box plots for each measure indicate the median facility score and the distribution of providers that are outside the range of most providers on each measure. Fig. 4.4.3 compares a number of providers on a given quality measure (new pressure ulcers) and indicate the provincial average of all other CCCs in much the same way as the CMS Nursing Home Compare report.

There was some initial concern about how public reporting would impact on hospital performance but such transparency is now accepted as common practice in Ontario hospitals. Long-term care facilities

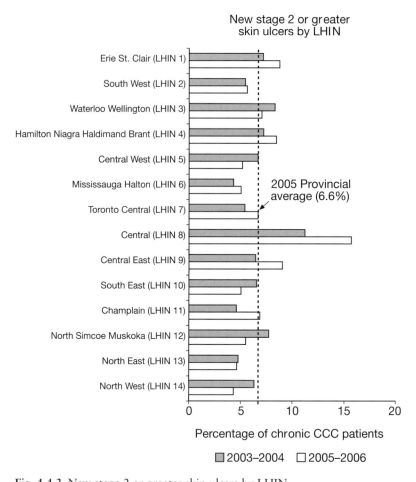

Fig. 4.4.3 New stage 2 or greater skin ulcers by LHIN

Source: Continuing Care Reporting Systems 2003–2004 and 2005–2006, CIHI.

have not yet fully implemented the RAI 2.0 and so it has not been possible to produce equivalent reports for that sector. Recent high-profile media coverage of several instances of poor care in nursing homes has increased demands for improved quality in that sector. Indeed, there is now general agreement on the need for increased accountability and transparency in all continuing care settings. However, the issue of risk adjustment has been a source of some concern, given the great heterogeneity of CCCs and nursing homes. For example, Ontario's CCC hospitals/units serve a considerably more clinically complex, post acute population than is typical of nursing home residents in that (or other) province(s). Early quality indicators based on the RAI 2.0 included some resident level risk adjusters but these are acknowledged to be inadequate to control for the substantial facility-level differences in the populations served. A CIHI-funded research initiative is exploring the use of direct adjustment methods to control more adequately for these differences without over-adjusting the indicator. A report on this new approach is expected by mid 2008.

Comparing performance of nursing facilities in Finland

In Finland, long-term care for older individuals has traditionally been divided into two categories: (i) hospital based long-term care delivered in health centres; and (ii) residential homes (nursing homes). The population aged 65 or over will increase by nearly 75% between now and 2030. However, particularly the proportion of the oldest old; the number of long-term beds; and the proportion of the elderly population living in them have been decreasing during the past ten years.[1]

The National Institute for Health and Welfare (STAKES) is a research and analysis unit that functions immediately under the Ministry of Social Affairs and Health. Its responsibilities include enhancement of best practices in the care of older persons in addition to collecting data and maintaining national registers on this field. However, it has no controlling or regulatory power. The counties are responsible for overseeing and supervising nursing homes but regular visits for these purposes are practically nonexistent. Also, data about conditions and the nature of the population served were sporadic and lacking information about performance until the RAI-benchmarking project was launched.

RAI benchmarking project in long-term care

STAKES and collaborating organizations in the RAI benchmarking project launched RAI activities as a pilot study in 2000. Project aims included implementing the RAI assessment system in Finnish long-term care facilities; educating facility staff and management in RAI assessment technology; developing performance measures to monitor efficiency and quality of care; creating software for facility manage-

---

[1] STAKES: http://www.stakes.fi/EN/Aiheet/olderpeople/statistics.htm?KwPath=S tatistics&TextSize=medium accessed Dec. 26, 2007.

ment to monitor web-based reports; and creating a forum for ongoing educational and best practice dissemination. Participation has been voluntary but facilities that committed to participation were required to assess every resident.

The performance measures adopted were based upon the models available in 2001. The nursing home casemix index had been validated in Finland in 1995, as had several RAI-MDS based summary outcome scales (Bjorkgren et al. 1999; Morris et al. 1999). (Burrows et al. 2000; Fries et al. 2001) The only nursing home quality indicators internationally tested at that time were those created by the University of Wisconsin-Madison and therefore that form was adopted (Zimmerman 2003). There were twenty-six indicators with set thresholds – twenty-two prevalence based; four incidence based. Five of the indicators were also risk adjusted (stratified by risk status).

The RAI benchmarking project established continuous feedback between the facilities and STAKES. A copy of the RAI assessment data is sent to STAKES biannually for benchmarking and research purposes. Within a month STAKES produces web-based, password-protected benchmarking results together with individual reports for each of the wards in the facility. STAKES organizes biannual two-day seminars in order to educate facility managers and clinical leaders and to facilitate sharing of best practices among providers. Over the eight years of the project, the number of voluntarily participating facilities increased from 41 in health centres and 43 in residential homes (overall 84) to 110 in health centres and 261 in residential homes (overall 371). The number of semi-annual RAI-assessments conducted increased from 2300 to 9000 and the number of nurses participating in semi-annual training seminars increased from 100 to 1000.

In order to highlight the comparisons possible with the benchmarking data, we have drawn upon examples that include only those communities in which every long-term care facility uses RAI. The performance measures embedded in the RAI assessments can first inform management of changes in the mix of residents' acuity levels. Fig. 4.4.4 reveals differences in means of the casemix and proportions (%) of light-care residents in four small or medium size towns. Light-care residents are independent in the personal activities of daily living and have minimal cognitive impairment. Presumably, health-care resources should be allocated accordingly.

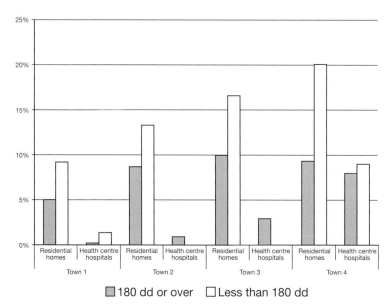

Fig. 4.4.4 Light-care residents (%) by type of long-term care facility in four medium or small sized towns, 2006

Source: Noro 2005

Town 4 has a smaller difference between casemix in the two different types of care (health centre hospitals, residential homes) than other towns. In addition, Town 4's intake of light-care residents is considerably higher than in the peer towns. These data indicate potential inefficiency in the case management processes designed to sustain older persons in their own homes in Town 4, where the eligibility criteria for long-term care settings are worth revisiting. Conversely, Town 1 has the lowest overall prevalence of light-care residents but there is also a small proportion of newly admitted light-care residents in health-care centres.

In order to benchmark quality of care, the facilities are first encouraged to ensure that peer groups are selected correctly, e.g. they have reasonably similar acuity levels in terms of cognitive and physical functioning. Fig. 4.4.5 shows a comparison of casemix index, staffing ratios and the prevalence of grade 2-4 pressure ulcers in four residential homes belonging to same organization. This shows some vari-

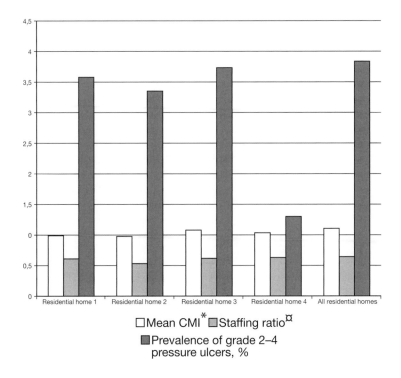

$\square$Mean CMI*$\blacksquare$Staffing ratio$^{\alpha}$
$\blacksquare$Prevalence of grade 2–4
pressure ulcers, %

Fig. 4.4.5 Mean case-mix index, staffing ratio, and prevalence of grade 2–4 pressure ulcers (%) in four residential homes compared to their peers in 2006

* CMI: casemix index, range 0.42–2.52
¤ Staffing ratio: number of licensed and practical nurses in the ward per number of residents
Overall number of assessed residents in the residential home numbers 1–4 is 885
Source: Noro 2005

ability in the prevalence of grade 2-4 pressure ulcers but comparable casemix and staffing ratios across the four facilities.

Benchmarking in intra-facility management

Intra-facility comparisons between wards follow the same guidelines as inter-facility comparisons. However, individual wards may have special profiles based upon management decisions such as concentrating ambulating persons with dementia and behavioural problems in some wards and relatively independent residents with mental illness in others. In these cases the wards are encouraged to compare themselves with ward-specific peer groups calculated by STAKES. This grouping of wards according to the severity of the casemix index and percentage of residents with dementia produces fourteen categories of ward, regardless of the type of facility. Every ward receives the suggested peer grouping values independently. Identification of the appropriate peers helps to create networks between similar units, to set reasonable goals for the units and to enable systematic work to reach them. Facilities are encouraged to identify target areas for which particular improvement can be expected and to set specific goals for each of the performance measures. One successful effort substantially reduced the use of psychotropic drugs but it is a challenge to hit a moving target when all residential homes improve their performance (Noro 2005).

In summary, RAI benchmarking was implemented successfully in Finland in 2000. Apart from measures for psychotropic medications, nursing rehabilitation and new pressure ulcers, the overall level of performance measures has remained relatively stable. However, looking only at those facilities involved in the project since 2001, eight of the twenty-six quality indicators have remained stable; four show deteriorated quality of care and fourteen have improved. This suggests that monitoring performance measures on a regular basis is a valuable tool for nursing managers in long-term care facilities. The observed changes in care patterns have occurred as a consequence of strong management actions within the facilities. These actions have not resulted from external pressures such as sanctions or changes in legislation or requirements. It is also evident that the changes have occurred only where both leaders and staff have used the measures for multiple purposes.

Nursing home performance measurement in Swiss cantons: Q-Sys approach

Since the late 1990s seven cantons in the German-speaking part of Switzerland have adopted the RAI. This serves as the basis for health sector reimbursements to facilities and for measuring nursing home quality as part of a broader voluntary adoption of the RAI in all facilities in participating cantons. By 2006 over 300 facilities in 7 cantons serving over 20 000 residents were participating in the RAI residents' assessment, facility payment and quality improvement system operated by a company called Q-Sys AG, led by geriatricians and software engineers (http://www.rai.ch/). Instituted primarily as a care planning tool with substantial educational content for skilled and unskilled staff in Swiss nursing homes, the RAI-MDS has been used for both financing and quality monitoring and improvement efforts. The long-term care funding agencies in each canton have accepted the RAI based RUG-III casemix reimbursement financing model, a system that has been validated in many other countries (Ikegami et al. 1994; Hirdes et al. 1996; Ljunggren and Brandt 1996; Jorgensen et al. 1997; Carpenter et al. 2003).

Much of the movement towards the adoption of the RAI in selected Swiss cantons is attributable to the Health Insurance Law revised in 1994. This altered the basis for payment of nursing homes to produce a more uniform system of coverage for long-term care in all Swiss Cantons. The regulations required a geriatric assessment using a standardized instrument for all residents of nursing homes who wished to be reimbursed under the new long-term care financing law. Furthermore, nursing home providers were obliged to undertake some form of quality assurance and improvement programme in order to continue receiving reimbursements. A health information services company devoted to processing RAI data and producing the reports and data that nursing home providers need to generate quality reports was founded in 1999. Q-Sys AG receives RAI assessment data from all participating nursing facilities in the seven Swiss cantons which have adopted this approach to reimbursement and quality monitoring. The report produced for each provider summarizes their performance on twenty-four different quality indicators first developed by Zimmerman and his colleagues (Zimmerman 2003).

Many different presentations of performance are generated in the form of reports to each provider and to the consortium of providers in each canton. Fig. 4.4.6 provides an example of the variable performance among providers in eight different areas, displaying intra- and inter-cantonal differences in the distribution of the proportion of residents receiving psychotropic medications in the absence of a psychiatric diagnosis. These data cover 2006 but similar reports are generated semi-annually. Other reports made available to all providers within a canton and to specific providers demonstrate changes in the prevalence of the quality indicators in participating nursing homes over a four- or five-year period. Most recently, Q-Sys investigators

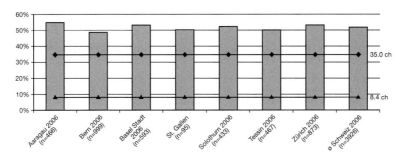

Fig. 4.4.6 Inter- and intra-canton comparisons of psychotropic drug use

Source: Q-Sys AG web site (http://www.rai.ch/)

and other European colleagues collaborated to produce some cross-national comparisons of these longitudinal data. These are intended to engage providers and cantons in a wider understanding of quality improvement by providing an opportunity to view their activities in a broader international context.

Summary and implications

The availability of uniform clinical data on nursing home residents' characteristics makes it viable to create quality performance measures for multiple purposes. Like uniform discharge abstracts for hospitals in the United States, the availability of the RAI-MDS on all facilities in selected geographical regions makes it possible to compare providers' performance on important parameters relevant to quality of care. There are still numerous conceptual and technical problems associated with interpreting differences among providers on the quality performance measures. However, the examples from the United States, Canada, Finland and Switzerland clearly reveal that the impetus for quality improvement is greatly stimulated by comparative data.

Provider quality performance measures can be used as a management tool to identify areas for quality improvement. This is reinforced when providers come together as a consortium to share best practices in quality improvement strategies and track performance changes, as in Finland. Performance measures can also be used to assist governmental or non-governmental inspectors charged with ensuring that providers meet minimum standards in order to retain certification for reimbursement, as in the United States. Public reporting of performance measures can help consumers and their advocates to select high-quality facilities that provide the types of services they require. Finally, governmental or insurance entities charged with reimbursing long-term care providers can use performance measures as a basis for bonuses for high quality or to adjust payment levels in accordance with the quality of care provided (Rahman 2006; Grabowski 2007; Kane et al. 2007).

Policy challenges

Numerous policy challenges arise when common assessment systems are introduced to evaluate residential care facilities' quality in a country. First and foremost, should these systems be mandatory or voluntary? A related policy challenge is whether it is viable to use data intended for clinical use for policy applications such as casemix reimbursement and public reporting of quality performance. Finally, if the data are to be used to drive quality improvement through public reporting of results that influences consumers' choices, there needs to be an understanding of the policy implications if consumers are not able to interpret or use publicly reported quality data to make such choices.

The RAI was introduced in the United States as part of a legislative mandate designed to improve the quality of long-term care facilities, about which there was substantial consensus. Some Canadian provinces followed this example; others began with voluntary, more limited implementation only to determine that the logic of universal comparative data is so strong that mandatory implementation was required. Comparisons of the manner in which nursing home assessment systems have been implemented in North America and Europe show some interesting differences. The approach to mandating implementation in the United States and Canada is associated with public reporting uses of the information; the quasi-voluntary approach used in Finland and selected Swiss cantons is associated with a much greater focus on facility quality improvement and managerial education. It is true that quality improvement is a major focus of the performance benchmarking process introduced by both CMS and CIHI. In the United States, CMS has made a major investment in quality improvement efforts under the direction of specialized organizations in each state that work with providers to devise strategies to institute quality improvement projects.[2] In Canada, the HRCC collaborative also undertakes continuing quality improvement projects that seek to identify strategies for performance improvement and to promulgate these as best practices among other chronic care hospitals in the consortium.[3] It is anticipated that a similar approach will be undertaken once all the nursing homes in the Ontario province have implemented performance measurement processes using the RAI-MDS.

Whether for casemix reimbursement or quality monitoring, these secondary uses of the RAI data raise questions about the validity and clinical utility of the basic resident assessment information. There was precedent in the case of hospitals' use of ICD diagnosis and procedure coding to document case mix acuity and associated payments before and after the introduction of DRGs (Hsia et al. 1988) As with RAI assessment data, hospitals had reasonably high error rates in their ICD coding, but tended to 'up-code'. To date, research in nursing homes in the United States suggests that error rates tend to be random but that systematic bias can creep readily into the process. Also, as when hospitals were paid on the basis of DRGs, clinical coding decisions became too important to leave to clinicians. Virtually all nursing home organizations now employ nurse assessors to coordinate MDS assessments, many of whom belong to rapidly growing national membership organizations that offer professional identity and education.[4] Even without responding to the incentive to up-code the MDS items, the original notion that all residents' needs would be assessed by an interdisciplinary team of professionals has fallen by the wayside as reimbursement is predicated upon the assessment information. It is not known whether this is changing the manner in which the data are used.

Research suggests that consumers find public reports of provider quality complicated and difficult to use. Also, significant unresolved technical problems may undermine the validity of direct comparisons between different providers in any one area. This raises questions about the strong push for public reporting of variations in provider quality in the United States and Canada. Certainly, the ideological rationale that underpins transparency and quality provides a strong impetus for public reporting. Nonetheless, there is increasing evidence

[2] http://www.cms.hhs.gov/QualityImprovementOrgs/01_Overview. asp#TopOfPage
[3] http://www.hospitalreport.ca/projects/QI_projects/IC5.html
[4] http://www.aanac.org/pages/membership_opp.asp.

that providers are stimulated to engage in serious quality improvement efforts precisely because their performance is open to all, including their local competition. This suggests that, despite the associated technical or conceptual problems, performance measurement that spurs providers into greater efforts to identify and improve quality problems may still have a very positive influence on long-term care in the United States and in developed economies where long-term care needs are growing rapidly. It is not clear whether providers' emphasis on quality improvement or even the validity of the underlying data might change under a regime of pay for performance (Rahman 2006).

Research needs

In all the countries that use the RAI data to develop benchmarks to which individual providers can aspire (or attempt to supercede), there is an underlying assumption that providers know how to re-organize their care processes to improve quality. It is true that the first step in quality improvement is accepting that improvements are necessary but it is far more difficult to understand which processes need to be changed and how. The provision of care in long-term care residential settings is a complex set of activities that combines medical treatments and social ministrations to enhance individuals' well-being; ensuring a safe and secure environment while allowing maximal independence in what is now the residents' home. Meeting all these needs requires innovative staff training, supervision and flexibility not normally associated with institutional care systems. The United States is introducing changes in both the physical and organizational environment in to change the culture of long-term care institutions (Rahman & Schnelle 2008). Enthusiasm for these changes appears to have outstripped the evidence for their effectiveness but it is evident that there is interest in changing institutional care to meet residents' needs more appropriately.

Research on the applicability of RAI data across providers is needed in order to better understand the implications of benchmarking for long-term care. In most countries there is considerable overlap between the needs of older people who live at home and those who enter institutions. Is it possible to develop comparable measures that are relevant to the outcomes experienced by frail older people whether they are at home or in an institution?

As noted, interRAI has developed quality indicators for home care that are in use in selected American states, Canadian provinces, Swiss cantons and Italian regions.[5] These take an approach similar to that used in the nursing home context. Initial efforts have been directed at monitoring performance measures designed to understand the sources of variation across providers in an area and to work with them to increase understanding of how to use the information for management and (ultimately) quality improvement purposes (Hawes et al. 2007). In the United States, a different assessment instrument has been mandated for all Medicare beneficiaries served by certified home health agencies. These data are used for both casemix-based reimbursement and public reporting of provider performance on a set of quality measures (Ahrens 2005). As with the MDS-RAI for nursing homes, individual agencies and consortia use these data for quality improvement (Stadt & Molare 2005; Scharpf et al. 2006).

A related research challenge with considerable policy importance is the development of measures that assess connections to the acute care setting. In the United States, almost 20% (with considerable inter-state variation) of Medicare beneficiaries entering nursing homes or even receiving home care are re-hospitalized within thirty days (Intrator et al. 2007). This may be a particular problem in that country since large differences were found in earlier comparisons of the hospitalization rates of nursing home residents in the United States and the Netherlands (Frijters et al. 1997). Nonetheless, performance measurement systems may provide incentives for facilities to discharge deteriorating residents to hospital in order to avoid reporting them. Future research will have to examine precisely how quality measures classify residents who are discharged to hospital and therefore may not contribute to the facility quality measure. It is not clear whether this is an issue in other countries but clearly the same incentives may be operating.

Conclusions

The emergence of a standardized assessment system and clinical language that is useful for educating and orienting long-term care providers has been the stimulus for standardized quality benchmarking systems in the United States and several other developed countries with rapidly ageing populations. Institutional care is always likely to be an option

---

[5] http://interrai.org/applications/hcqi_table_final.pdf.

for those needing long-term care in developed countries and therefore it is important to have a means of measuring and comparing quality of care. Computerized health records facilitate performance measurement but it is possible to use a uniform assessment to characterize the needs of the population of nursing home residents without considerable investment in high tech equipment. A common assessment language helps to structure the information for subsequent reporting using simple manual summaries. Less well-developed countries – with rapidly growing ageing populations and an increasingly mobile society e.g. China – could institute an assessment system. There is considerable expertise that can be tapped to design web-based data collection and management tools appropriate to particular populations.

References

Ahrens, J (2005). 'The impact of Medicare home health policy changes on Medicare beneficiaries: part II.' *Policy Brief (Center for Home Care Policy and Research)*, (19): 1–6.

Arling, G. Lewis, T. Kane, RL. Mueller, C. Flood, S (2007). 'Improving quality assessment through multilevel modeling: the case of nursing home compare.' *Health Services Research*, 42(3 Pt 1): 1177–1199.

Baier, RR. Gifford, DR. Mor, V (2005). 'Reporting nursing home quality in Rhode Island.' *Medicine and Health, Rhode Island*, 88(6): 186–1877, 191.

Bates-Jensen, BM. Alessi, CA. Cadogan, M. Levy-Storms, L. Jorge, J. Yoshii, J. Al-Samarrai, NR. Schnelle, JF (2004). 'The Minimum Data Set bed-fast quality indicator: differences among nursing homes.' *Nursing Research*, 53(4): 260–272.

Berg, K. Mor, V. Morris, J. Murphy, KM. Moore, T. Harris, Y (2002). 'Identification and evaluation of existing nursing homes quality indicators.' *Health Care Financing Review*, 23(4): 19–36.

Bernabei, R. Gambassi, G. Lapane, K. Landi, F. Gatsonis, C. Dunlop, R. Lipsitz, L. Steel, K. Mor, V (1998). 'Management of pain in elderly patients with cancer. SAGE Study Group. Systematic Assessment of Geriatric Drug Use via Epidemiology.' *Journal of the American Medical Association*, 279(23): 1877–1882.

Bernabei, R. Gambassi, G. Lapane, K. Sgadari, A. Landi, F. Gatsonis, C. Lipsitz, L. Mor, V (1999). 'Characteristics of the SAGE database: a new resource for research on outcomes in long-term care. SAGE (Systematic Assessment of Geriatric drug use via Epidemiology) Study

Group.' *Journals of Gerontology Series A: Biological Sciences and Medinal Sciences,* 54(1): M25–33.

Bjorkgren, MA. Häkkinen, U. Finne-Soveri, UH. Fries, BE (1999). 'Validity and reliability of Resource Utilization Groups (RUG-III) in Finnish long-term care facilities.' *Scandinavian Journal of Public Health,* 27(3): 228–234.

Burrows, AB. Morris, JN. Simon, S. Hirdes, J. Phillips, C (2000). 'Development of a minimum data set-based depression rating scale for use in nursing homes.' *Age and Ageing,* 29(2): 165–172.

Carpenter, I. Perry, M. Challis, D. Hope, K (2003). 'Identification of registered nursing care of residents in English nursing homes using the Minimum Data Set Resident Assessment Instrument (MDS/RAI) and Resource Utilisation Groups version III (RUG-III).' *Age and Ageing,* 32(3): 279–285.

Castle, NG (2006). 'Family members as proxies for satisfaction with nursing home care.' *Joint Commission Journal on Quality and Patient Safety,* 32(8): 452–458.

Castle, NG. Lowe TJ (2005). 'Report cards and nursing homes.' *Gerontologist,* 45(1): 48–67.

Castle, NG. Degenholtz, H. Engberg, J (2005). 'State variability in indicators of quality of care in nursing facilities.' *Journals of Gerontology Series A: Biological Sciences and Medical Sciences* 60(9): 1173–1179.

Castle, NG. Engberg, J. Liu, D (2007). 'Have Nursing Home Compare quality measure scores changed over time in response to competition?' *Quality and Safety in Health Care,* 16(3): 185–191.

Clauser, SB. Fries BE (1992). 'Nursing home resident assessment and case-mix classification: cross-national perspectives.' *Health Care Financing Review,* 13(4): 135–155.

Davis, MA (1991). 'On nursing home quality: a review and analysis. *Medical Care Review,* 48(2): 129–166.

Davis, MA. Freeman, JW. Kirby, EC (1998). 'Nursing home performance under case-mix reimbursement: responding to heavy-care incentives and market changes.' *Health Services Research,* 33(4 Pt 1): 815–834.

Feng, Z. Grabowski, DC. Intrator, O. Mor, V (2006). 'The effect of state medicaid case-mix payment on nursing home resident acuity.' *Health Services Research,* 41(4 Pt 1): 1317–1336.

Frederiksen, K. Tariot, P. De Jonghe, E (1996). 'Minimum Data Set Plus (MDS+) scores compared with scores from five rating scales.' *Journal of the American Geriatrics Society,* 44(3): 305–309.

Fries, BE. Cooney, LM Jr. (1985). 'Resource utilization groups. A patient classification system for long-term care.' *Medical Care,* 23(2): 110–122.

Fries, BE. Hawes, C. Morris, JN. Phillips, CD. Mor, V. Park, PS (1997). 'Effect of the National Resident Assessment Instrument on selected health conditions and problems.' *Journal of the American Geriatrics Society,* 45(8): 994–1001.

Fries, BE. Schneider, DP. Foley, WJ. Gavazzi, M. Burke, R. Cornelius, E. (1994). 'Refining a case-mix measure for nursing homes: Resource Utilization Groups (RUG-III).' *Medical Care,* 32(7): 668–685.

Fries, BE. Simon, SE. Morris, JN. Flodstrom, C. Bookstein, FL (2001). 'Pain in US nursing homes: validating a pain scale for the minimum data set.' *Gerontologist,* 41(2): 173–179.

Frijters, DH. Mor, V. DuPaquier JN. Berg, K. Carpenter, GI. Ribbe, MW(1997). 'Transitions across various continuing care settings.' *Age and Ageing,* 26(Suppl. 2): 73–76.

Gambassi, G. Landi, F. Lapane, KL. Sgadari, A. Mor, V. Bernabei, R(1999). 'Predictors of mortality in patients with Alzheimer's disease living in nursing homes.' *Journal of Neurolology, Neurosurgurgery, and Psychiatry,* 67(1): 59–65.

Gambassi, G. Landi, F. Peng, L. Brostrup-Jensen, C. Calore, K. Hiris, J. Lipsitz, L. Mor, V. Bernabei, R (1998). 'Validity of diagnostic and drug data in standardized nursing home resident assessments: potential for geriatric pharmacoepidemiology. SAGE Study Group. Systematic Assessment of Geriatric drug use via Epidemiology.' *Medical Care,* 36(2): 167–179.

Gambassi, G. Lapane, K. Sgadari, A. Landi, F. Carbonin, P. Hume, A. Lipsitz, L. Mor, V. Bernabei, R (1998a). 'Prevalence, clinical correlates, and treatment of hypertension in elderly nursing home residents. SAGE (Systematic Assessment of Geriatric Drug Use via Epidemiology) Study Group.' *Archives of Internal Medicine,* 158(21): 2377–2385.

Gambassi, G. Lapane, KL. Landi, F. Sgadari, A. Mor, V. Bernabei, R. (1999a). 'Gender differences in the relation between co-morbidity and mortality of patients with Alzheimer's disease. Systematic Assessment of Geriatric drug use via Epidemiology (SAGE) Study Group.' *Neurology,* 53(3): 508–516.

Gerteis, M. Gerteis, JS. Newman, D. Koepke, C. (2007). 'Testing consumers' comprehension of quality measures using alternative reporting formats.' *Health Care Financing Review,* 28(3): 31–45.

Grabowski, DC (2007). 'Medicare and Medicaid: conflicting incentives for long-term care. *Milbank Memorial Fund Quarterly,* 85(4): 579–610.

Gruber-Baldini, AL. Zimmerman, SI. Mortimore, E. Magaziner, J (2000). 'The validity of the minimum data set in measuring the cognitive impairment of persons admitted to nursing homes.' *Journal of the American Geriatrics Society,* 48(12): 1601–1606.

Harris, Y. Clauser SB (2002). 'Achieving improvement through nursing home quality measurement.' *Health Care Financing Review,* 23(4): 5–18.

Hartmaier, SL. Sloane, PD. Guess, HA. Koch, GG. Mitchell, CM. Phillips, CD (1995). 'Validation of the Minimum Data Set Cognitive Performance Scale: agreement with the Mini-Mental State Examination.' *Journals of Gerontology Series A: Biological Sciences and Medical Sciences,* 50(2): M128–133.

Hawes, C. Fries, BE. James, ML. Guihan, M (2007). 'Prospects and pitfalls: use of the RAI-HC assessment by the Department of Veterans Affairs for home care clients.' *Gerontologist,* 47(3): 378–387.

Hawes, C. Mor, V. Phillips, CD. Fries, BE. Morris, JN. Steele-Friedlob, E. Greene, AM. Nennstiel, M (1997). 'The OBRA-87 nursing home regulations and implementation of the Resident Assessment Instrument: effects on process quality.' *Journal of the American Geriatrics Society,* 45(8): 977–985.

Hawes, C. Morris, JN. Phillips, CD. Fries, BE. Murphy, K. Mor, V (1997a). 'Development of the nursing home Resident Assessment Instrument in the USA.' *Age and Ageing,* 26(Suppl. 2): 19–25.

Hawes, C. Morris, JN. Phillips, CD. Mor, V. Fries, BE. Nonemaker, S (1995). 'Reliability estimates for the Minimum Data Set for nursing home resident assessment and care screening (MDS).' *Gerontologist,* 35(2): 172–178.

Hirdes, JP. Botz, CA. Kozak, J. Lepp, V (1996). 'Identifying an appropriate case mix measure for chronic care: evidence from an Ontario pilot study.' *Healthcare Management Forum,* 9(1): 40–46.

Hsia, DC. Krushat, WM. Fagan AB. Tebbutt, JA. Kusserow, RP (1988). 'Accuracy of diagnostic coding for Medicare patients under the prospective-payment system.' *New England Journal of Medicine,* 318(6): 352–355.

Ikegami, N. Fries, BE. Takagi, Y. Ikeda, S. Ibe, T (1994). 'Applying RUG-III in Japanese long-term care facilities.' *Gerontologist,* 34(5): 628–639.

Institute of Medicine (1986). *Improving the quality of care in nursing homes.* Washington DC: National Academies Press.

Intrator, O. Grabowski, DC. Zinn, J. Schleinitz, M. Feng, Z. Miller, S. Mor, V (2007). 'Hospitalization of nursing home residents: the effects of states' Medicaid payment and bed-hold policies.' *Health Services Research,* 42(4): 1651–1671.

Jorgensen, LM. el Kholy, K. Damkjaer, K. Deis, A. Schroll, M (1997). ''RAI' – an international system for assessment of nursing home residents [in Danish].' *Ugeskrift for Laeger,* 159(43): 6371–6376.

Kane, RA (2003). 'Definition, measurement, and correlates of quality of life in nursing homes: toward a reasonable practice, research, and policy agenda.' *Gerontologist,* 43(Spec. No. 2): 28–36.

Kane, RL. Arling, G. Mueller, C. Held, R. Cooke, V (2007). 'A quality-based payment strategy for nursing home care in Minnesota.' *Gerontologist,* 47(1): 108–115.

Konetzka, RT. Norton, EC. Sloane, PD. Kilpatrick, KE. Stearns, SC (2006). 'Medicare prospective payment and quality of care for long-stay nursing facility residents.' *Medical Care,* 44(3): 270–276.

Konetzka, RT. Yi, D. Norton, EC. Kilpatrick, KE (2004). 'Effects of Medicare payment changes on nursing home staffing and deficiencies.' *Health Services Research,* 39(3): 463–488.

Ljunggren, G. Brandt L (1996). 'Predicting nursing home length of stay and outcome with a resource-based classification system.' *International Journal of Technology Assessment in Health Care,* 12(1): 72–79.

Lowe, TJ. Lucas, JA. Castle, NG. Robinson, JP. Crystal, S (2003). 'Consumer satisfaction in long-term care: state initiatives in nursing homes and assisted living facilities.' *Gerontologist,* 43(6): 883–896.

Matherlee, K (1999). 'Implementing the BBA: the challenge of moving Medicare post-acute services to PPS.' *Issue Brief National Health Policy Forum,* (743): 1–8.

McGee, J. Kanouse, DE. Sofaer, S. Hargraves, JL. Hoy, E. Kleimann, S (1999). 'Making survey results easy to report to consumers: how reporting needs guided survey design in CAHPS. Consumer Assessment of Health Plans Study.' *Medical Care,* 37(Suppl. 3): MS32–40.

Mor, V (2004). 'A comprehensive clinical assessment tool to inform policy and practice: applications of the minimum data set.' *Medical Care,* 42(Suppl. 4): III50–59.

Mor, V (2005). 'Improving the quality of long-term care with better information.' *Milbank Memorial Fund Quarterly,* 83(3): 333–364.

Mor, V. Angelelli, J. Jones, R. Roy, J. Moore, T. Morris, J (2003). 'Inter-rater reliability of nursing home quality indicators in the US' *BMC Health Services Research,* 3(1): 20.

Mor, V. Berg, K. Angelelli, J. Gifford, D. Morris, J. Moore, T (2003a). 'The quality of quality measurement in US nursing homes.' *Gerontologist,* 43(Spec. No. 2): 37–46.

Mor, V. Branco, K. Fleishman, J. Hawes, C. Phillips, C. Morris, J. Fries, B (1995). 'The structure of social engagement among nursing home residents.' *Journals of Gerontology Series B, Psychological Sciences and Social Sciences,* 50(1): 1–8.

Mor, V. Intrator, O. Fries, BE. Phillips, C. Teno, J. Hiris, J. Hawes, C. Morris, J (1997). 'Changes in hospitalization associated with introducing the

Resident Assessment Instrument.' *Journal of the American Geriatrics Society,* 45(8): 1002–1010.

Morris, JN. Fries, BE. Mehr, DR. Hawes, C. Phillips, C. Mor, V. Lipsitz, LA (1994). 'MDS Cognitive Performance Scale.' *Journal of Gerontology,* 49(4): 174–182.

Morris, JN. Fries, BE. Morris, SA (1999). 'Scaling ADLs within the MDS.' *Journals of Gerontology Series A, Biological Sciences and Medical Sciences,* 54(11): 546–553.

Morris, JN. Hawes, C. Fries, BE. Phillips, CD. Mor, V. Katz, S. Murphy, K. Drugovich, ML. Friedlob, AS (1990). 'Designing the national resident assessment instrument for nursing homes.' *Gerontologist,* 30(3): 293–307.

Morris, JN. Nonemaker, S. Murphy, K. Hawes, C. Fries, BE. Mor, V. Phillips, C (1997). 'A commitment to change: revision of HCFA's RAI.' *Journal of the American Geriatrics Society,* 45(8): 1011–1016.

Mukamel, DB. Spector, WD. Zinn, JS. Huang, L. Weimer, DL. Dozier, A (2007). 'Nursing homes' response to the nursing home compare report card.' *Journals of Gerontology Series B, Psychological Science and Social Science,* 62(4): 218–225.

Noro, A (2005). Vertailukehittämishanke [Benchmarking Project]. In: Noro, A. Finne-Soveri, H. Björkgren, M. Vähäkangas, P (eds.). *Ikääntyneiden laitoshoidon laatu ja tuottavuus – RAI-järjestelmä vertailukehittämisessä [Quality and efficiency of the institutional long-term care for older persons - RAI-systems in benchmarking].* Saarijärvi: STAKES.

Phillips, C. Hawes, C. Lieberman, T. Koren, MJ (2007). 'Where should Momma go? Current nursing home performance measurement strategies and a less ambitious approach.' *BMC Health Services Research,* 7(1): 93.

Phillips, CD. Morris, JN. Hawes, C. Fries, BE. Mor, V. Nennstiel, M. Iannacchione, V (1997). 'Association of the Resident Assessment Instrument (RAI) with changes in function, cognition, and psychosocial status.' *Journal of the American Geriatrics Society,* 45(8): 986–993.

Popejoy, LL. Rantz, MJ. Conn, V. Wipke-Tevis, D. Grando, VT. Porter, R (2000). 'Improving quality of care in nursing facilities. Gerontological clinical nurse specialist as research nurse consultant.' *Journal of Gerontological Nursing,* 26(4): 6–13.

Rahman, A (2006). 'The Pay for Performance demonstration program.' *Journal of the American Medical Directors Association,* 7(2): 133.

Rahman, AN. Schnelle JF (2008). 'The nursing home culture-change movement: recent past, present, and future directions for research.' *Gerontologist,* 48(2): 142–8.

Reilly, KE. Mueller, C. Zimmerman, DR (2007). 'The Centers for Medicare and Medicaid Services' Nursing Home Case-Mix and Quality Demonstration: a descriptive overview.' *Journal of Aging and Social Policy,* 19(1): 61–76.

Roy, J. Mor V (2005). 'The effect of provider-level ascertainment bias on profiling nursing homes.' *Statistics in Medicine,* 24(23): 3609–3629.

Sangl, J. Saliba, D. Gifford, DR. Hittle, DF (2005). 'Challenges in measuring nursing home and home health quality: lessons from the First National Healthcare Quality Report.' *Medical Care,* 43(Suppl. 3): I24–32.

Scharpf, TP. Colabianchi, N. Madigan, EA. Neuhauser, D. Peng, T. Feldman, PH. Bridges, JF (2006). 'Functional status decline as a measure of adverse events in home health care: an observational study.' *BMC Health Services Research,* 6: 162.

Schnelle, JF. Cadogan, MP. Yoshii, J. Al-Samarrai, NR. Osterweil, D. Bates-Jensen, BM. Simmons, SF (2003). 'The minimum data set urinary incontinence quality indicators: do they reflect differences in care processes related to incontinence?' *Medical Care,* 41(8): 909–922.

Simmons, SF. Cadogan, MP. Cabrera, GR. Al-Samarrai, NR. Jorge, JS. Levy-Storms, L. Osterweil, D. Schnelle, JF (2004). 'The minimum data set depression quality indicator: does it reflect differences in care processes?' *Gerontologist,* 44(4): 554–564.

Sofaer, S. Firminger K (2005). 'Patient perceptions of the quality of health services.' *Annual Review of Public Health,* 26: 513–559.

Stadt, J. Molare E (2005). 'Best practices: that improved patient outcomes and agency operational performance.' *Home Healthcare Nurse,* 23(9): 587–593.

Straker, JK. Ejaz, FK. McCarthy, C. Jones, JA (2007). 'Developing and testing a satisfaction survey for nursing home residents: the Ohio Experience.' *Journal of Aging and Social Policy,* 19(2): 83–105.

Wodchis, WP. Fries, BE. Hirth, RA (2004). 'The effect of Medicare's prospective payment system on discharge outcomes of skilled nursing facility residents. *Inquiry,* 41(4): 418–434.

Wu, N. Miller, SC. Lapane, K. Roy, J. Mor, V (2005). 'Impact of cognitive function on assessments of nursing home residents' pain.' *Medical Care,* 43(9): 934–939.

Wu, N. Miller, SC. Lapane, K. Roy, J. Mor, V (2005a). 'The quality of the quality indicator of pain derived from the minimum data set.' *Health Services Research,* 40(4): 1197–1216.

Zimmerman, DR (2003). 'Improving nursing home quality of care through outcomes data: the MDS quality indicators.' *International Journal of Geriatric Psychiatry,* 18(3): 250–257.

Zinn, J. Spector, W. Hsieh, L. Mukamel, DB (2005). 'Do trends in the reporting of quality measures on the nursing home compare web site differ by nursing home characteristics?' *Gerontologist,* 45(6): 720–730.

Zinn, JS (1994). 'Market competition and the quality of nursing home care.' *Journal of Health Politics, Policy and Law,* 19(3): 555–582.

PART V

Health policy and performance measurement

5.1 Targets and performance measurement

PETER C. SMITH, REINHARD BUSSE

Introduction

Targets are a tool designed to improve health and health system performance. They can facilitate the achievement of health policy by expressing a clear commitment to achieve specified results in a defined time period and facilitating the monitoring of progress towards the achievement of broader goals and objectives. They may be quantitative (e.g. $x\%$ increase in the immunization rate) or qualitative (e.g. introduction of national screening programme); based on health outcomes (e.g. reduction in mortality) or processes (e.g. reduction of waiting time). The introduction of the concept of targets into the health sector is often traced to the 1981 publication of WHO's *Health for All* strategy which presented targets as a tool with which to improve health policy (WHO Regional Office for Europe 2005).

Earlier chapters of this book discuss the manifest need for tools designed to improve performance and accountability. Thus it is not surprising that targets' role in health policy has grown and an increasing number of countries and/or regions now use them as tools to improve performance. Various mapping exercises have documented growing and sustained interest in health targets among governments and international organizations (Busse & Wismar 2002; Ritsatakis et al. 2000; van de Water & van Herten 1998). The 2005 update of the WHO European *Health for All* policies reported that forty-one of the (then) fifty-two Member States of the Region had either adopted or drafted policies which included health targets (WHO Regional Office for Europe 2005). Most recently, Wismar et al. (2008) offered many national and sub-national examples from Europe, primarily in population health. The Millennium Development Goals introduced important health targets at the international level.

A large body of literature has developed to provide increasing insights into the various dimensions of target setting and monitoring.

For example, there has been much discussion about the relative merits of goals that are process or outcome oriented. As explained below, we would argue that in reality this is a false dichotomy. Other debates have focused on the extent to which targets should set a general direction of travel or be detailed road maps, indicating every point along the way. This has been addressed by separating aspirational, managerial and technical targets that are ranked in terms of the extent to which they prescribe what should be achieved and how (van Herten & Gunning-Schepers 2000). Similarly, much has been written about the optimal characteristics of targets. At the risk of simplification, this literature has been reduced to a mnemonic, indicating that targets should be SMART – specific, measurable, achievable, realistic and timed.

Rather than providing a systematic review of the issues surrounding the use of targets in the health sector, this chapter seeks to illustrate the general issues and to explore how targets contribute to improving health system performance. We use the specific example of the extensive English experience (possibly one of the most ambitious of such innovations to date) but also take account of experience in other European countries. The chapter begins with a brief history of targets in England. We then describe in some detail experience with the Public Service Agreement (PSA) targets introduced in 1998, under which targets assumed a much more central role. The chapter assesses the strengths and weaknesses of the PSA targets regime and concludes with the general lessons that can be learned from the English and European experiences.

Targets in the English health system

England has an extended history of targets in health and health care (Hunter 2002) but the first concerted attempt to introduce targets into English public health was the *Health of the Nation* strategy, launched in 1992 (Department of Health 1992). Owing a heavy debt to the WHO *Health for All* initiative, this was intended to encourage health authorities to focus on securing good health for their population. *Health of the Nation* can be seen as an attempt to set the public health agenda for local health authorities in the reformed NHS. Initially, five key areas were selected for action:

1. coronary heart disease and stroke
2. cancers

3. mental illness
4. HIV/AIDS and sexual health
5. accidents.

A small number of national targets were specified for each key area. For example, the targets for the first key area were:

- to reduce death rates for both coronary heart disease and stroke in people under 65 by at least 40% by the year 2000;
- to reduce the death rate for coronary heart disease in people aged 65-74 by at least 30% by the year 2000;
- to reduce the death rate for stroke in people aged 65-74 by at least 40% by the year 2000.

A careful independent evaluation of *Health of the Nation* in 1998 concluded that its: 'impact on policy documents peaked as early as 1993; and, by 1997, its impact on local policymaking was negligible' (Department of Health 1998). It found that health authorities felt that they had more pressing concerns than public health and therefore concentrated on operational issues, such as reducing waiting times and securing budgetary control. The evaluation concluded that the high-level national targets did not resonate with local decision-makers: 'National targets were a useful rallying point, but the encouragement to develop local targets would have been welcomed within the national framework as a reflection of local needs.' There was also seen to be a lack of incentives and institutional capacity for local managers.

Hunter (2002) summarizes the weaknesses of the *Health of the Nation* strategy under six broad headings.

1. Appeared to be a lack of leadership in the national government.
2. Policy failed to address the underlying social and structural determinants of health.
3. Targets were not always credible and were not formulated at a local level.
4. Poor communication of the strategy beyond the health system.
5. Strategy was not sustained.
6. Partnership between agencies was not encouraged.

The overarching theme was that the *Health of the Nation* strategy, and the associated targets, did not permeate the health system strongly enough to make a material difference.

The Labour government came to power in 1997 with a commitment to evidence-based policy; systematic priority setting; and explicit performance targets throughout the public services. A series of biennial spending reviews was implemented in 1998, setting three-year budgets in advance for each government department. Following the conclusion of the budgetary agreements, a set of PSAs with each department was announced. These were intended to signal priorities across the entire range of government activity and took the form of a series of specific objectives, expressed as a target in measurable form, that were expected to be achieved within a designated time frame. In common with other ministries, the Department of Health was set a series of PSA targets – for health and health care.

One distinctive feature of PSAs was the intention to focus on the outcomes of the public services rather than the operational activities of public service delivery. The PSA process signalled the government's determination to make the management of public services more transparent and to give departments clear statements of priorities. In the first round, the detail, specificity and measurability of the PSA targets were highly variable. However, over subsequent series of spending reviews the targets have become fewer and focused increasingly on outcomes.

An example: 2004 PSAs for the Department of Health

We illustrate the issues by describing the 2004 PSA targets which were based on four broad objectives.

1. Improve the health of the population. By 2010 increase life expectancy at birth in England to 78.6 years for men and to 82.5 years for women.
2. Improve health outcomes for people with long-term conditions.
3. Improve access to services, in particular waiting times.
4. Improve the patient and user experience.

The detailed targets associated with the objectives are given in Box 5.1.1; the four standards that must be maintained are shown at the bottom. These reflect targets secured through previous PSAs that must continue to be achieved. A set of even more detailed technical notes accompanies the targets, giving the context, data sources and measurement instruments. Box 5.1.2 gives an example, showing the technical note for the obesity target.

Box 5.1.1 Department of Health PSA Targets, 2004

Objective I: Improve the health of the population. By 2010 increase life expectancy at birth in England to 78.6 years for men and to 82.5 years for women.

1. Substantially reduce mortality rates by 2010:

   • from heart disease and stroke and related diseases by at least 40% in people under 75, with at least a 40% reduction in the inequalities gap between the fifth of areas with the worst health and deprivation indicators and the population as a whole;
   • from cancer by at least 20% in people under 75,with a reduction in the inequalities gap of at least 6% between the fifth of areas with the worst health and deprivation indicators and the population as a whole; and
   • from suicide and undetermined injury by at least 20%.

2. Reduce health inequalities by 10% by 2010 as measured by infant mortality and life expectancy at birth.
3. Tackle the underlying determinants of ill health and health inequalities by:

   • reducing adult smoking rates to 21% or less by 2010, with a reduction in prevalence among routine and manual groups to 26% or less;
   • halting the year-on-year rise in obesity among children under 11 by 2010 in the context of a broader strategy to tackle obesity in the population as a whole; and
   • reducing the under-18 conception rate by 50% by 2010 as part of a broader strategy to improve sexual health.

Objective II: Improve health outcomes for people with long-term conditions.

4. To improve health outcomes for people with long-term conditions by offering a personalized care plan for vulnerable people most at risk; and to reduce emergency bed days by 5% by 2008, through improved care in primary care and community settings for people with long-term conditions.

Box 5.1.1 cont'd

Objective III: Improve access to services.

5. To ensure that by 2008 no-one waits more than 18 weeks from GP referral to hospital treatment.
6. Increase the participation of problem drug users in drug treatment programmes by 100% by 2008 and increase year on year the proportion of users successfully sustaining or completing treatment programmes.

Objective IV: Improve the patient and user experience.

7. Secure sustained national improvements in NHS patient experience by 2008, as measured by independently validated surveys, ensuring that individuals are fully involved in decisions about their healthcare, including choice of provider.
8. Improve the quality of life and independence of vulnerable older people by supporting them to live in their own homes where possible by:

   • increasing the proportion of older people being supported to live in their own home by 1% annually in 2007 and 2008; and
   • increasing, by 2008, the proportion of those supported intensively to live at home to 34% of the total of those being supported at home or in residential care.

Standards

• A four hour maximum wait in Accident and Emergency from arrival to admission, transfer or discharge.
• Guaranteed access to a primary care professional within 24 hours and to a primary care doctor within 48 hours.
• Every hospital appointment booked for the convenience of the patient, making it easier for patients and their GPs to choose the hospital and consultant that best meets their needs.
• Improve life outcomes of adults and children with mental health problems, by ensuring that all patients who need them have access to crisis services and a comprehensive Child and Adolescent Mental Health Service.

Source: HM Treasury 2004

**Box 5.1.2 Example of a PSA Technical Note – 2002
Joint Obesity Target for Department of Health (DH) and
Department for Education and Skills (DfES)**

PSA Target: Halting the year-on-year rise in obesity among children under eleven by 2010, in the context of a broader strategy to tackle obesity in the population as a whole.

Scope: children aged between two and ten years (inclusive) in England.

Obesity: prevalence of obesity as defined by the National BMI percentile classification (from the 1990 reference population from TJ Cole et al.) and measured through the Health Survey for England. Children above the 95th percentile of the 1990 reference curve are defined as obese.

Halt the year-on-year increase: obesity in two- to ten-year-olds rose, on average, by 0.8% per year between 1995 and 2002. Halting the increase would mean no significant change in prevalence between the two three-year periods 2005/06/07 and 2008/09/10.

Data source: Health Survey for England. We are also exploring with colleagues in DH and DfES the cost and feasibility of options for other sources of data in order to obtain more local level information.

Baseline year: due to the small sample size, the baseline will be the weighted average for the three-year period 2002/03/04.

Target year: by 31 December 2010, in practice this will mean 2010–2011 financial year.

Reporting: annually (aggregate trend data will be available every three years). The lag between the end of the collecting period and data being published is around twelve to fifteen months.

OGD contributions to PSA: delivery of this joint PSA target will be supported by a range of programmes including:

a) joint DfES and DCMS[1] PE, School Sport and Club Links project which seeks to increase the percentage of school children who

[1] Department for Culture, Media and Sport

Box 5.1.2 cont'd

  spend a minimum of two hours each week on high quality PE
  and school sport within and beyond the curriculum;
b) joint DfES and DH National Healthy Schools Programme which
  seeks to promote a whole school approach to healthy living;
c) joint DfES and DH 'Food in Schools' programme which seeks to
  promote a whole school approach to a range of food issues.

Throughout the PSA regime, one of the Department of Health's central tasks has been to devise operational instruments that transmit the national PSA targets to the local level. To this end, the most important initiative was the development of a system of performance ratings for individual NHS organizations. Beginning in 2001, every organization (including local health authorities and NHS providers of care) was ranked annually on a four-point scale (zero to three stars) according to a series of about forty performance indicators. The indicators were intended directly to reflect the objectives of the NHS, as embodied in the national PSA targets (Department of Health 2001).

For each NHS organization, the star rating was produced by combining the indicators according to a complex algorithm. The most important determinant of an organization's rating was its performance against a set of about ten 'key indicators', which were then dominated by measures of various aspects of patient waiting times. This was augmented by a composite measure of performance based on the thirty or so subsidiary indicators, combined in the form of a balanced scorecard view of the organization. Clinical quality comprised only a small element of the calculation. In 2004 the health-care regulator took over responsibility for preparing the star ratings.

The most striking innovation associated with performance ratings was the introduction of very strong managerial incentives dependent on the level of attainment. Some commentators characterize this as a regime of terror (Bevan & Hood 2006b). The jobs of senior executives of poorly performing organizations came under severe threat and the performance indicators (especially the key targets) became a prime focus of managerial attention. Rewards for performing well included some element of increased organizational autonomy. For example, the best performers in the acute hospital sector became eligible to apply for Foundation status which carries considerably greater autonomy from direct NHS control.

NHS managers have shown a mixed response to performance ratings. Many have criticized the system because of some of the apparently arbitrary ways in which the ratings are calculated and their sensitivity to small data fluctuations (Barker et al. 2004). However, some acknowledge that the system gives managers better focus and a real lever with which to affect organizational behaviour and clinical practice. Healthcare professionals have shown less ambiguous reactions and there is a widespread view that the ratings distort clinical priorities and undermine professional autonomy (Mannion et al. 2005). This is hardly surprising, as one of the aims of the national and local targets was precisely to challenge traditional clinical behaviour and to direct more attention to issues that had not always been a high priority e.g. waiting times.

There is no doubt that performance ratings have delivered major improvements in the aspects of NHS care targeted (Bevan & Hood 2006b). They have also secured marked progress towards some of the PSA targets. For example, very long waits for non-urgent inpatient treatment were a prime focus of the PSA regime and have been rapidly eliminated. Moreover, targeted aspects of English health care have improved markedly in comparison to Wales and Scotland, even though they have higher funding levels. These countries have not been subject to the PSA regime and have not implemented performance ratings (Hauck & Street 2007; Propper et al. 2008).

Less satisfactorily, the high level PSAs shown in Box 5.1.1 included important public health targets under objective 1, such as improved reduced mortality rates from heart disease and cancer; reductions of health inequalities; and reduced rates of smoking, childhood obesity and teenage pregnancy. Converting these high-level public health objectives into meaningful local targets through the medium of the performance ratings system proved far less straightforward than in the waiting time domain. Public health has not received anything like the sustained managerial attention enjoyed by the health service delivery targets (Marks & Hunter 2005). This raises concerns that local managers concentrated on targeted and readily managed aspects of health care (most notably objective 3 – waiting times) at the expense of less controllable and less immediate concerns, such as public health (objective 1).

Whilst retaining the principle of rating performance on a simple composite measure, it is noteworthy that in 2006 the Healthcare

Commission implemented a major change to the assessment regime that pays more attention to a broader spectrum of performance, most notably clinical quality (Healthcare Commission 2005). This places greater emphasis on self reporting and reports clinical performance and financial performance separately.

Discussion

PSAs and, in particular, the associated targets have become a central element of political discourse in England. Without question they have succeeded in shaping the priorities and delivery of public services in general, and health services in particular, although it remains a matter of fierce debate whether that influence is for the good. On the one side are those who claim that their focus on outcomes and setting of firm measurable targets have helped to modernize those services. On the other are those who claim that their simplistic view of priorities has undermined the traditional public service ethos and rendered those services dysfunctional.

In the health domain PSA targets have certainly delivered noteworthy successes, such as the reduction in NHS waiting times. However, alongside the manifest intended improvements in many of the measured PSA targets there are widespread reports of adverse side effects in other, often unmeasured, aspects of public services (Bevan & Hood 2006a). Many of these reports are anecdotal and may be apocryphal, but some have been credibly documented by the House of Commons Public Administration Select Committee (2003) and Bevan and Hood (2006b). These include neglect of unmeasured aspects of performance (e.g. sacrificing clinical priorities in the pursuit of reduced waiting times); distorted behaviour (e.g. refusing to admit patients to accident departments until a four-hour waiting time target was achievable); and fraud (manipulation of waiting lists).

Unintended and adverse responses such as these were readily predictable from the Soviet literature (Nove 1980). They offer a powerful caution against relying solely on a targets regime to secure improvement and indicate the need for countervailing instruments (Smith 1995). These might include: strong national data audit and surveillance capacity; system of professional inspection that monitors and reports on unintended consequences; careful scrutiny of performance beyond targets by organizational boards of governors; some sort of democratic 'voice' in the control of local public service organizations; and empowerment of service users through improved information and systems of redress.

The Social Market Foundation (2005) summarized the criticisms of the targets regime under five headings:

1. there are too many targets
2. they are too rigid and undermine the morale of staff
3. they have perverse and unintended consequences
4. not always clear who is responsible for meeting the target
5. data are often not credible.

Over its ten-year lifetime, the PSA infrastructure has been adapted as difficulties have arisen and remedial measures put in place. Drawing on the experience of other countries (where available) this section discusses some of the most important questions that have arisen in the development of the English system under eight headings: (i) Who should choose the targets? (ii) What targets should be chosen? (iii) When should outcomes be used as a basis for targets? (iv) How should targets be measured and set? (v) How should cross-departmental targets be handled? (vi) How should attainment be scrutinized? (vii) How should departmental objectives be transmitted to local organizations?

Who should choose the targets?

In principle, it seems perfectly reasonable (and indeed honourable) for a legitimately elected government to set out its objectives and targets in an explicit fashion. Targets serve many purposes, one of which is to enhance political accountability. Indeed, lack of an adequate accountability framework may lead to failure to achieve the objectives of target setting (see Box 5.1.3). The PSAs enable parliament and the electorate to hold the government to account for both its choice of priorities and its performance against the targets. Indeed, it is a sign of the success of the process that much of the public debate surrounding targets referred less to the principle of setting targets and more to the details of what they should be.

However, disagreement remains about the processes by which priorities are chosen and targets are set. For example, many argue that the government's excessive emphasis on waiting times in NHS targets has posed a threat to clinical quality by ignoring the prime objective of

---

Box 5.1.3 Lack of accountability in Hungarian target setting

In Hungary, the lack of an accountability framework was identified as one of the reasons why target setting failed to achieve its objectives. Political will served as the sole determinant of whether or not a health policy would be target-based. Ten years after the development of the first target-based health policies, there is still no legal pressure to develop the policies further (Vokó & Ádány 2008). The following have been recognized as contributory factors in the failure to establish an accountability framework.

1. An overall feeling of lack of ownership resulted from the realization that the Hungarian health monitoring system was capable of providing information only at the national level and thus could not take account of huge social and geographical inequalities.
2. Policy-makers and those involved from outside the health sector were rarely involved in the development of the targets. An inter-ministerial committee was set up to coordinate the targets and to try to bridge the gap between the various sectors but its work was hindered by the very limited financial resources allocated to targets in Hungary.
3. Slow acceptance of the new public health approach in Hungary reflected a lack of awareness among health professionals. Health is not a priority issue for other sectors and so they were reluctant to incorporate health considerations into their own policies.

As a result, Hungarian targets lack regulation, ownership, consensus and financing and have failed to induce behaviour change.

Source: Vokó & Ádány 2008

---

health care – to improve health. Such outcomes have led some to argue that the professionals who deliver the public services should have a greater say in the nature of the targets. There is an element of good sense in this principle, especially in health services where outcomes rely very heavily on the engagement and commitment of front-line professionals. Yet it is also the case that the priorities and working practices of those professionals may impede progress towards better performance. To some extent, the PSA process seeks to challenge traditional ways of delivering services and therefore at times will come into conflict with the professions.

Some argue that parliament should have a greater say in target setting. Parliament already plays a crucial role by scrutinizing the choice of priorities and the attainment of targets and it is difficult to see how the legislature's involvement in choosing targets would enhance the PSA process. No government will pursue objectives with total commitment when it does not fully control their nature. Of course, this also applies to the devolved organizations charged with delivering services and gives rise to some of the problems of morale and alienation discussed below.

It is frequently suggested that service users should have more say in setting PSA targets and of course there is much to commend wide consultation with user groups when identifying priorities for improvement. However, the setting of objectives involves considerations beyond immediate users of a particular service, such as the taxpayer perspective; the interests of future users; and the interests of users of other services. The user perspective is important but cannot be the sole influence on priority setting, which in any case involves judgements about the relative importance of different user groups.

Consensus and ownership have nevertheless usually been seen as vital to elicit acceptance of country-based targets. In Catalonia, health councils were created at central and provincial levels to encourage citizens' groups to take an active part in target setting. In Flanders, Belgium, local health networks (LHN) were established to encourage the exchange of information between local organizations and create possibilities for collaboration by offering a focal point for preventive actions. The organizations were encouraged to undertake collaborations with local government and other sectors to achieve the health targets (Van den Broucke 2008). France saw the establishment of national and regional health conferences which allowed stakeholders the opportunity to debate existing health problems and foster partnerships. It is clear that targets without consensus and ownership will have difficulty achieving success.

In isolation, neither consensus and ownership nor legislation can guarantee results. Implementation of an accountability framework demands vertical and horizontal coordination, which can be difficult. In Flanders, the five health targets were repeatedly reaffirmed between 1998 and 2003 when a decree was passed to outline the procedures for formulating new targets and updating existing ones. This decree helped to streamline the process of target setting and provided a legal basis for synchronizing the activities of the different players involved. Ten years after the first targets were introduced in Flanders, it is clear that health targets have become a well-established mechanism to support prevention policies. They may not have produced the anticipated results in terms of health gain or changes in health-related behaviour but they have spurred changes in the policy environment that may assist in achieving targets in the future.

Hence, any prudent government seeking to implement a PSA type process would be well-advised to consult many relevant stakeholders to reach consensus on the choice of objectives and the nature of the targets. However, uncritical accommodation of every interest group would render the target process meaningless, for example by leading to an unwieldy proliferation of priorities. One of a government's prime roles is to balance conflicting claims on public resources and targets should be an explicit and succinct statement of the government's decisions.

What targets should be chosen?

Multiple objectives are a characteristic of health services. Indeed, it can be argued that the existence of multiple objectives is one of the defining characteristics of public services such as health care and one of the reasons why they cannot (at least in their entirety) be delivered by competitive markets.

However, one intention of any targets regime is to focus on a limited number of objectives. The initial 1998 suite of English PSAs failed to recognize that this requires tough political choices and therefore failed to have a detectable impact in many domains. This mistake was not confined to England but visible in many other target programmes developed around that time such as the 1998 programmes in Italy (100 targets) and in Andalucia (84 targets) (Busse & Wismar 2002). Subsequent English spending reviews addressed this issue by focusing on a greatly reduced number of targets. Nevertheless, it is important to note that some of the numerical reduction was deceptive – the 2004 example given above indicates how some targets became multidimensional, for example seeking to address both overall health improvement and reductions in inequalities in health. Also as noted above a number of previous targets were converted into standards, indicating a level of attainment secured in previous periods. To many, these retained the appearance of targets albeit in a different guise.

Having identified a priority, it is noteworthy that the English government sought to include an associated objective into the targets regime, even when attainment is hard to measure (e.g. patient experience target in Box 5.1.1.) Without question quantification is a good principle to pursue as it generally allows the government to set concrete targets for departments. However, it runs the risk of distracting managerial attention from important qualitative aspects of performance and suggests that reports of progress towards quantified targets should be accompanied by a narrative that describes success and failure in more qualitative terms.

The move towards specifying standards indicates that targets should focus on domains where manifest change is required, as the Social Market Foundation suggests. If a domain is not included in the targets regime, this does not necessarily indicate that it is unimportant. Rather, it may suggest that it is not a priority for urgent change and should instead be considered a standard. The key focus of targets should be where change is required and maintenance of standards in other domains should be secured through other instruments, such as routine regulation, inspection or market mechanisms.

When should outcomes be used as a basis for targets?

From the outset, the architects of the English targets system recognized that the outcomes of public services usually matter to most service users and the broader public. In principle, the outcomes focus should enable health service organizations to look beyond traditional ways of delivering their services and traditional organizational boundaries.

However, the focus on outcomes can give rise to difficulties. For example, some outcomes (e.g. many aspects of health system responsiveness) are intrinsically difficult to measure. Even if they can be measured, some outcomes (e.g. reduced mortality from smoking) can take years to materialize – beyond the lifetime of most governments. Furthermore, some outcomes (e.g. most conventional mortality rates) are particularly vulnerable to influences beyond the control of the health ministry. Each of these difficulties offers the ministry an excuse for apparent failure and can undermine the targets process.

On the other hand, it is clear that the use of process measures can distort behaviour and lead to unintended outcomes. For example, the attempt to guarantee access to a primary care professional within twenty-four hours led to widespread reports of primary care practices refusing to allow patients to arrange appointments more than twenty-four hours in advance, even when that was their preference. Patients could secure access to appointments only by telephoning on the day they required a consultation, often leading to uncertainty and inconvenient timing of appointments. The real objective (securing quicker and more convenient access to a doctor) was subverted by the use of an incomplete and poorly articulated target. Thus, if the chosen output target is pursued without regard to the eventual outcomes, additional assurance will be needed to ensure that the desired outcomes have indeed been secured. In this example, if the real objective was to increase patient satisfaction, it would have been preferable to use a direct measure of patient satisfaction (rather than a highly imperfect proxy measure) as the basis for the target.

In short, outcome measures address what matters to the service user and the citizen and are less vulnerable to distortion. It therefore seems incontestable that outcomes should inform all targets. However, there will be occasions when a carefully chosen output or process measure – which evidence shows to be clearly linked to the eventual outcome – may form a more effective basis for a target.

How should targets be measured and set?

A central feature of the English targets debate has been how (once objectives have been identified) the associated targets should be set, in terms of the required measurement instrument and level of attainment. The use of SMART targets was advocated in the United Kingdom (HM Treasury et al. 2001) as in other countries and the Treasury has sought to pursue these principles when setting PSA targets.

The Royal Statistical Society (Bird et al. 2005) put forward a more comprehensive set of desirable general principles for setting targets.

- Indicators should be directly relevant to the primary objective, or be an obviously adequate proxy measure.
- Definitions need to be precise but practicable.

- Survey-based indicators, such as those of user satisfaction, should use a shared methodology and common questions between institutions.
- Indicators and definitions should be consistent over time.
- Indicators and definitions should obviate, rather than create, perverse behaviours.
- Indicators should be straightforward to interpret, avoiding ambiguity about whether the performance being monitored has improved or deteriorated.
- Indicators that are not collected for the whole population should have sufficient coverage to ensure against misleading results, that is: potential bias compared to measuring the target population should be small.
- Technical properties of the indicator should be adequate.
- Indicators should have the statistical potential to exhibit or identify change within the intended timescale.
- Indicators should be produced with appropriate frequency, disaggregation and adjustment for context.
- Indicators should conform to international standards if these exist.
- Indicators should not impose an undue burden – in terms of cost, personnel or intrusion – on those providing the information.
- Measurement costs should be commensurate with the likely information gain.

The National Audit Office (2005 and 2006) scrutinized the data systems used to monitor and report progress against all 2002 PSA targets and found varying levels of success – only 30% were deemed strictly fit for purpose. The Statistics Commission (2006) scrutinized all 2004 targets in detail to assess whether the statistical evidence to support PSA targets was adequate for the purpose of achieving government policy objectives. It noted numerous problems with poor specification; undue complexity; and availability, transparency, independence and timeliness of the data.

A number of approaches exist to overcome some of these weaknesses. For example, the Royal Statistical Society advocates a multistage measurement 'protocol' for each target that would explicitly explain all stages of the measurement process, from choice of indicator to publication of results (Bird 2005). It also recommends publication of levels of uncertainty alongside all attainment measures. In the same vein, the Statistics Commission (2006) advocates publication of interim attainment measures for longer-term targets.

The specification of explicit levels of attainment is a particular feature of targets regimes. However, this important element of the process is usually applied with inconsistent rigour. Some targets might be little more than unattainable aspirations whilst others can be secured with little effort on the part of ministries. Furthermore, there are conflicting pressures within any targets regime. To be effective managerial instruments, targets should be stretching but attainable, suggesting (say) a one in three risk of failure. However, few governments would want to be confronted with such a high proportion of failures. From an accountability perspective, they would wish to feel that there was a good chance of attaining all targets.

This was seen in the Netherlands during the early 1990s when the Secretary of State for Health avoided using quantitative health targets because of the political accountability that they would create (van Herten & Gunning-Schepers 2000). Similarly, Russia has experienced politically driven target setting in which the targets set were neither especially relevant nor necessary. Health was seldom a priority on the policy agenda in the USSR or subsequently in the Russian Federation and generally those targets that were set were broadly defined, infrastructure-oriented and almost never outcome-oriented. In many cases, achievement of the targets required no change in policy (Danishevski 2008). It is difficult to see how this tension can be resolved satisfac-torily as it requires a political process mature enough to recognize that some failure is inevitable and not necessarily adverse if progress is also being secured.

A note of caution is helpful in this context. A target that is not achieved is easily dismissed as 'too ambitious' (as in the Netherlands); a target that is achieved is sometimes dismissed as 'would have been reached anyway' (e.g. coronary heart disease death rate target in England). These deserve closer examination. The first statement requires a thorough knowledge of the potential effect sizes (efficacy) of various intervention strategies (and possible combinations of interventions); the second assumes that longitudinal trends remain constant over time. This is not the case since external factors also exercise large influences.

Life expectancy in Central and Eastern Europe provides a good example of this point. If, in 1990, Russia had passed a target to keep life expectancy constant until 2000, it would have been accused of setting a target that would be reached anyway. In reality, if this target had resulted in halving the actual decline it would have been a success even though most evaluation strategies would label it a failure. The same holds true in reverse. If a target that 'experts' have judged to be neither overambitious nor trivial has been reached successfully, it is rather difficult to attribute this to the strategy itself. This argues for an independent assessment of the attribution of success or failure. However, it is usually not possible to differentiate with any confidence how the different elements have contributed to the measured outcome and we shall probably never be able to control for all factors contributing to good or ill health (Busse 1999).

How should cross-departmental targets be handled?

The many determinants of health involve actions by organizations in many different sectors and effective coordination among responsible actors has emerged as a key issue in securing system improvements. In particular, a focus on health outcomes sometimes gives rise to strategies that are not obviously attached to a particular ministry, leading to the need to specify joint targets that transcend departmental boundaries. These are particularly important in the public health domain and have produced difficulties in the English PSA process. A joint report by the National Audit Office and the Audit Commission (2006) examines complex cross-departmental targets, including efforts to halt the rise in child obesity. They find no ready solutions, but advocate much stronger collaboration between national and local government and stronger engagement with non-governmental organizations.

In short, cross-sectoral targets give rise to problems of coordination, persuasion and engagement that must be addressed if they are to be successful. Effective coordination depends on the structures already in place, particularly the system of governance and the forums within which key actors can meet. This may be easier where responsibility for health lies within local or regional government, as in Scandinavia, but it is possible to convene relevant actors from many different sectors in other ways.

The Social Market Foundation (2005) recognizes that some targets cannot be broken down into individual components and therefore require joint effort by two or more ministries. However, it recommends that there should always be a 'lead' ministry that takes responsibility for meeting the target. It is noteworthy that the 2007 Comprehensive

Spending Review placed special emphasis on cross-departmental collaboration, with a view to seeking innovative solutions for the challenges posed by joint targets.

Other countries have faced a different challenge with intersectoral targets. Having stressed the need to involve the many sectors whose actions contribute to health, often they have not included the healthcare sector itself. This has made health targets an issue for actors only at the sideline, thereby often diluting their potential impact (Busse & Wismar 2002).

How should attainment be scrutinized?

A persistent theme in any discussion of targets is how to scrutinize, understand and report on progress. Given that this mechanism has played such a central part in the recent development of English public services, there has been surprisingly little attention to public reporting and scrutiny of attainment against targets.

One exception was the House of Commons Public Administration Select Committee (2003) report which sought to identify attainment of 249 measurable targets from 1998. These results were not readily available but research revealed that 67.1% had been met; 7.6% partially met; 10.0% not met; and 14.9% had inadequate data on achievement. In their original form, performance reports were found in a variety of formats and with varying levels of clarity in the annual reports of individual ministries. The Treasury web site merely offered links to these reports. The Committee recommended that progress towards targets and eventual attainment should be reported consistently and regularly on a single, authoritative web site.

Within many parliamentary systems, the parliament appoints scrutiny committees for most ministries. These would be the natural focus for holding a government to account through routine reporting of progress towards targets. However, systematic parliamentary scrutiny has not yet become routine in England and the Health Select Committee has referred to PSA targets only periodically. Thus, scrutiny has been piecemeal – e.g. in the form of occasional reports from pressure groups, the media and regulators.

Within any targets regime it is particularly important to ensure independent audit of the reliability of the data used to assess attainment. Within government, few have an interest in challenging information that reports apparent performance improvements and attainment of targets. In England this has led to considerable popular scepticism about the veracity of information that the government provides on its own performance. The National Audit Office examines the processes for data collection but is not in a position to assure the accuracy of all data. It is noteworthy that the British Government has made the Office for National Statistics more independent of government by creating the UK Statistics Authority, accountable directly to parliament. An important objective of this initiative is to dispel the perception that reports of government performance may be unreliable.

Within government there has been far greater attention to scrutiny of progress towards English targets. Service delivery agreements with departments were the initial instruments for assuring the implementation of PSA targets. When these proved unwieldy and ineffective they were replaced by the Prime Minister's Delivery Unit, a very important element of the more mature PSA system. This indicates a perception within government that continuous monitoring; strong and timely intervention powers; and continued political attention at the highest level have made essential contributions to the longevity and sustained high profile of the system.

How should departmental objectives be transmitted to local organizations?

Attainment of national ministerial targets usually relies on securing satisfactory improvement in local organizations charged with the delivery of health services. Therefore, much depends on how ministerial targets are transmitted to local services. For example, it would be clearly inappropriate to set the same mortality targets for every locality, regardless of existing levels of attainment and the difficulty of local circumstances. Such approaches lead to manifest problems. Organizations that are already performing well have no incentive to improve; those with disadvantaged populations may stand no chance of success and become alienated. Indeed, if such regimes are sustained, existing problems may be exacerbated as it becomes difficult to recruit key managers and professionals in disadvantaged areas. As a result, many ministries have introduced more subtle target regimes for local organizations and sought to encourage all organizations to improve in the chosen measures, whatever their baseline.

The tension between national objectives and local discretion has become an important unresolved issue within the English regime. In particular, the 'must do' nature of local health targets has put especially severe pressure on some local organizations, precluding any serious consideration of separate local priorities. The prevailing lack of flexibility was highlighted in a report by the Audit Commission (2003) that criticized the neglect of local government discretion in earlier PSA targets. The Treasury responded by setting up a review of devolved decision-making to examine how national priorities and local flexibility can be accommodated within the targets system. It is moving towards the publication of local performance data as an alternative to national targets (HM Treasury 2004b). The aim is to allow local people (rather than national government) to hold local services to account for their chosen priorities and performance. However, whilst a policy of devolution clearly has relevance to health systems delivered through local governments, it is not clear how local accountability can be secured in health systems that do not have a local democratic decision-making mechanism.

This problem is not confined to England. All countries need to develop a sense of ownership and accountability amongst those required to implement health targets. Unfortunately, this is often not the case. As a previous review has noted, target programmes are disseminated in a top-down manner with little effort to ensure the involvement of key actors at the grass-roots level (Wismar & Busse 2002).

Conclusions

The use of targets is becoming widespread in health systems and therefore is clearly perceived to be an important mechanism for securing health system improvement and accountability. In particular, the English health system's experience with targets has developed very rapidly over a period of fifteen years. The first tentative steps in the domain of public health were largely ineffective and initial ambitions were modest when attention switched to health service delivery. However, the introduction of a targets 'culture' throughout English public services rapidly increased the prominence and impact of targets in the NHS, most notably in the form of performance ratings of NHS organizations.

The government had a number of objectives when it introduced the PSA system in 1998 (House of Commons Public Administration Select Committee 2003):

- to offer a clear statement of what it is trying to achieve
- to give a clear sense of direction and ambition
- to introduce a focus on delivering results
- to form a basis for deciding what is and what is not working
- to improve accountability.

It is difficult to argue with the claim that, at least in parts of the health domain, the PSA system has been successful in these respects. Smith (2008) suggests a number of reasons for the increasing influence of targets. First, their range and specificity has increased markedly – moving from long-term general objectives towards very precise short-term targets. Second, the specification has moved progressively from the national to the organizational level. This local interpretation of national targets is likely to have much more resonance with local decision-makers. Third, some attempts have been made to engage professionals with the design and implementation of the targets regime. This runs the risk of capture by professional interests but also increases the chance that professionals will take notice of the targets. Fourth, organizations have been given increased capacity to respond to challenging targets, in the form of extra finance, information and managerial expertise. Finally, very concrete incentives have been attached to the targets.

It is noteworthy that the English target initiatives have in effect combined a multiplicity of targets into a single indicator of performance at the local level (the performance ratings). As discussed in Chapter 3.4, if the method of aggregating individual indicators is in line with national objectives then these composite measures of success can play a particularly important role in capturing the attention of local decision-makers and allowing local organizations to choose the areas of endeavour that they wish to concentrate on. The alternative – requiring improvement in every domain – diminishes such local autonomy and may be less effective.

The use of targets remains a work in progress that has introduced numerous challenges and anomalies, as documented in this chapter. As experience unfolds, it is becoming clear that a targets regime must be augmented by a number of other mechanisms. In a series of departmental Capability Reviews by the Cabinet Office (2006) in the United Kingdom it was noted that '... whilst progress against PSAs and other top targets is necessary and welcome, it is not sufficient for delivering high-quality performance across the whole system.'

Some of the more important institutional requirements for the implementation of regimes such as the English PSA system are listed below.

- Sustained political commitment to the targets system, at the very highest level.
- A nimble central government organization (Prime Minister's Delivery Unit) responsible for timely monitoring, reporting and (where necessary) intervention.
- Continued monitoring and regulation in domains not directly covered by targets.
- High-quality performance management skills within the ministry.
- Carefully crafted mechanisms for transmitting national targets to the local level.
- Strong collaborative arrangements, where necessary, for domains that cross traditional ministerial boundaries.
- Careful integration of central and local priorities.
- Engagement as appropriate with relevant stakeholders, including user groups, professional organizations and the voluntary sector.

A number of commentators have offered suggestions on the architecture of the targets regime. For example, the Social Market Foundation (2005) raises several issues.

- Targets should be set only when change is required or for aspects of public services which are exceptionally important.
- There should be a fairly small number of targets in place at any one time.
- Whilst an outcome orientation is desirable, process and input targets may sometimes be appropriate, especially if the organization in question has limited influence over the outcome.
- Targets add most value where other mechanisms such as user choice and the threat of exit, or the contestability of providers, are not in place.
- Proportionate sanctions and incentives are important. An organization that misses a stretching target by a narrow margin should not be sanctioned for failure, but rather rewarded for its progress.

- Targets should be fully integrated into ministerial performance management, audit and inspection regimes.
- Joint targets that need to be delivered by more than one department should always have a lead ministry that takes responsibility for meeting the target.
- Greater use could be made of targets relating to public satisfaction.

In addition, the Royal Statistical Society and the Statistics Commission have given detailed guidance on technical aspects of performance measurement (Bird et al. 2005; Statistics Commission 2006). The work of the National Audit Office emphasizes the need to improve data quality and there is clear evidence that genuinely independent scrutiny and audit of the data has become a central requirement of any targets regime.

Notwithstanding a cautiously positive commentary on recent English experience with targets in health, Smith (2008) has noted some serious risks drawn from the English experience, including those listed here.

- Targets are selective and untargeted aspects of the health system may suffer from neglect.
- Unless incentives are designed carefully, managers and practitioners are likely to concentrate on short-term targets directly within their control at the expense of targets addressing longer-term or less controllable objectives.
- The targets system is very complex, requiring capacity to implement and giving rise to the scope for capture by professional interests.
- Excessively aggressive targets may undermine the reliability of the data on which they depend.
- Excessively aggressive targets may induce gaming or other undesirable labour market responses, as clinicians seek to create favourable environments for achieving those targets.
- The targets regime may replace altruistic professional motivation with a narrow mercenary viewpoint.

A full evaluation of the costs and benefits of any English targets system is likely to be intrinsically difficult and is still awaited. However, most of the risks can be mitigated to some extent by careful monitoring and the introduction of countervailing instruments where necessary. Targets have secured a real change in the behaviour of the English health system, probably to a much greater extent than any previous policy instruments. The challenge for any health system that relies on targets is to monitor carefully; to nurture the benefits of targets; and to neutralize their harmful side-effects.

References

Audit Commission (2003). *Targets in the public sector.* London: The Stationery Office (http://www.audit-commission.gov.uk/reports/ NATIONAL-REPORT.asp?CategoryID=&ProdID=B02E376A-01D5-485b-A866-3C7117DC435A).

Barker, R. Pearce, M. Irving, M (2004). 'Star wars, NHS style.' *British Medical Journal*, 329(7457):107–109.

Bevan, G. Hood, C (2006). 'What's measured is what matters: targets and gaming in the English public health care system.' *Public Administration*, 84(3): 517–538.

Bevan, G. Hood, C (2006a). 'Have targets improved performance in the English NHS?' *British Medical Journal*, 332(7538): 419–422.

Bird, SM. Cox, D. Farewell, VT. Goldstein, H. Holt, T. Smith, P (2005). 'Performance indicators: good, bad and ugly,' *Journal of the Royal Statistical Society, Series A*, 168(1): 1–25 (http://www.rss.org.uk/PDF/ PerformanceMonitoring.pdf).

Busse, R (1999). 'Evaluation and outcomes of health targets.' *Eurohealth*, 5(3):12–13.

Busse, R. Wismar, M (2002). 'Health target programmes and health care services - any link? A conceptual and comparative study (part 1).' *Health Policy*, 59(3): 209–221.

Cabinet Office (2006). *Capability reviews: the findings of the first four reviews.* London: Cabinet Office (http://www.civilservice.gov.uk/ reform/capability_reviews/reports.asp).

Danishevski, K (2008). The Russian Federation: difficult history of target setting. In: Wismar, M. McKee, M. Ernst, K. Srivastava, D. Busse, R (eds.). *Health targets in Europe: learning from experience.* Copenhagen: WHO Regional Office for Europe on behalf of the European Observatory on Health Systems and Policies.

Department of Health (1992). *The Health of the Nation.* London: HMSO.

Department of Health (1998). *Health of the Nation: a policy assessed.* London.

Department of Health (2001). *NHS performance ratings Acute Trusts 2000/01.* (http://www.doh.gov.uk/performanceratings/).

Hauck, K. Street, A (2007). 'Do targets matter? A comparison of English and Welsh national health priorities. *Health Economics*, 16(3): 275–290.

Healthcare Commission (2005). *Assessment for improvement. The annual health check. Measuring what matters.* London: The Healthcare Commission (http://annualhealthcheckratings.healthcarecommission.org.uk/annualhealthcheckratings.cfm).

HM Treasury (2004). *Stability, security and opportunity for all: investing for Britain's long-term future. New public spending plans 2005-2008.* London: The Stationery Office (http://www.hm-treasury.gov.uk/spending_review/spend_sr04/spend_sr04_index.cfm).

HM Treasury (2004a). *Devolving decision making: 1- delivering better public services: refining targets and performance management.* London: The Stationery Office (http://www.hm-treasury.gov.uk/media//53886/devolving_decision1_409.pdf).

HM Treasury, Cabinet Office, National Audit Office, Audit Commission, Office for National Statistics (2001). *Choosing the right fabric: a framework for performance information.* London: HM Treasury (http://www.hm-treasury.gov.uk/media/EDE/5E/229.pdf).

House of Commons Public Administration Select Committee (2003). *On target? Government by measurement. Fifth Report of Session 2002–03.* London: House of Commons (http://www.publications.parliament.uk/pa/cm200203/cmselect/cmpubadm/62/6202.htm).

Hunter, D (2002). England. In: Marinker, M (ed.). *Health targets in Europe.* London: BMJ Books.

Mannion, R. Davies, H. Marshall, M (2005). 'Impact of star performance ratings in English acute hospital trusts.' *Journal of Health Services Research and Policy*, 10(1): 18–24.

Marks, L. Hunter, D (2005). 'Moving upstream or muddying the waters? Incentives for managing for health.' *Public Health*, 119(11): 974–980.

National Audit Office (2005). *Public service agreements: managing data quality – compendium report.* London: The Stationery Office (http://www.nao.org.uk/pn/04-05/0405476.htm).

National Audit Office and Audit Commission (2006). *Delivering efficiently: strengthening the links in public service delivery chains.* London: The Stationery Office (http://www.nao.org.uk/pn/05-06/0506940.htm).

Nove, A (1980). *The Soviet economic system, second edition.* London: Allen and Unwin.

Propper, C. Sutton, M. Whitnall, C. Windmeijer, F (2008). 'Did "targets and terror" reduce waiting times in England for hospital care?' *B.E. Journal of Economic Analysis & Policy*, 8(2): 1863.

Ritsatakis, A. Barnes, R. Dekker, E. Harrington, P. Kokko, S. Makara, P (2000). *Exploring health policy development in Europe.* Copenhagen: WHO Regional Office for Europe.

Smith, P (1995). 'On the unintended consequences of publishing performance data in the public sector.' *International Journal of Public Administration*, 18(2/3): 277–310.

Smith, PC (2008). England: intended and unintended effects. In: Wismar, M. McKee, M. Ernst, K. Srivastava, D. Busse, R (eds.). *Health targets in Europe: learning from experience*. Copenhagen: WHO Regional Office for Europe on behalf of the European Observatory on Health Systems and Policies.

Social Market Foundation (2005). *To the point: a blueprint for good targets. Report of the Commission on Targets in the Public Services*. London: Social Market Foundation.

Statistics Commission (2006). *PSA targets: the devil in the detail*. London: Statistics Commission (http://www.statscom.org.uk/media_pdfs/reports/Final%20PSA%20Targets%20Report.pdf).

Van den Broucke, S (2008). Flanders: health targets as a catalyst for action. In: Wismar, M. McKee, M. Ernst, K. Srivastava, D. Busse, R (eds.). *Health targets in Europe: learning from experience*. Copenhagen: WHO Regional Office for Europe on behalf of the European Observatory on Health Systems and Policies.

Van de Water, HPA. van Herten, LM (1998). *Health policies on target? Review of health target and priority setting in 18 European countries*. Leiden: TNO.

van Herten, LM. Gunning-Schepers, LJ (2000). 'Targets as a tool in health policy. Part I: lessons learned.' *Health Policy*, 53(1): 1–11.

Vokó, Z. Ádány, R (2008). Hungary: targets driving improved health intelligence. In: Wismar, M. McKee, M. Ernst, K. Srivastava, D. Busse, R (eds.). *Health targets in Europe: learning from experience*. Copenhagen: WHO Regional Office for Europe on behalf of the European Observatory on Health Systems and Policies.

WHO Regional Office for Europe (2005). *The Health for All policy framework for the WHO European Region: 2005 update*. Regional Committee for Europe. Fifty-fifth session. Copenhagen: WHO Regional Office for Europe (http://www.euro.who.int/Document/RC55/edoc08.pdf).

Wismar, M. Busse, R (2002). 'Outcome-related health targets – political strategies for better health outcomes. A conceptual and comparative study (part 2).' *Health Policy*, 59(3): 223–241.

Wismar, M. McKee, M. Ernst, K. Srivastava, D. Busse, R (eds.) (2008). *Health targets in Europe: learning from experience*. Copenhagen: WHO Regional Office for Europe on behalf of the European Observatory on Health Systems and Policies.

5.2 | *Public performance reporting on quality information*

PAUL G. SHEKELLE

Introduction

The public reporting of information about the quality of health care delivered by identified providers has become increasingly popular in developed countries. In part this is due to a general trend towards increasing the transparency of the performance of a variety of services (e.g. test scores in schools). Within health care this is also promoted as a mechanism to help improve the quality of care. Berwick et al's (2003) framework for quality improvement shows that public reporting can improve quality via two pathways. In the first (selection pathway), consumers (patients) select providers of better quality. In the second (change pathway), performance data help providers to identify areas of underperformance and public release of the information acts as a stimulus for improvement (Fig. 5.2.1).

Colleagues and I recently completed a systematic review of the published evidence regarding the public release of performance data to improve quality, identifying forty-five articles (Fung et al. 2008). This

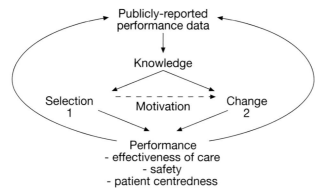

Fig. 5.2.1 Two pathways for improving performance through release of publicly-reported performance data

Source: Berwick et al. 2003

updated the earlier review on the same topic (Marshall et al. 2000). In this chapter I discuss the evidence from these reviews in the context of key questions and conclusions for the WHO conference.

Public reporting: effect on selection pathway

There is evidence that public reporting has little effect on the selection pathway. In our review, we identified twenty-one studies that assessed the effect of public reporting on the selection of health plans, hospitals or providers. Studies were mostly observational in design, being time series analyses of market share during the period of the introduction of public reporting. Experimental studies of consumers' response to hypothetical quality ratings revealed some willingness to trade access restrictions for higher quality (Harris 2002; Spranca et al. 2000). However, two randomized trials of Medicare beneficiaries' use of data from the Consumer Assessment of Healthcare Providers and Systems (CAHPS) in the United States showed that this public reporting had no overall effect on the selection of health plans (Farley et al. 2002 & 2002a). We know of one other randomized trial of the effect of the release of actual quality information on health plan selection – this has not yet been published.

For hospitals, nine studies of four different American public reporting systems showed no or (at most) modest short-term effects on market share (Baker et al. 2003; Chassin 2002; Hannan et al. 1994a; Hibbard et al. 2005; Jha & Epstein 2006; Mennemeyer et al. 1997; Mukamel & Mushlin 1998; Vladeck et al. 1988). For example, two analyses of one of the earliest public reporting systems – the Health Care Financing Administration (now CMS) release of hospital mortality rates – reported statistically significant but small changes in utilization (Mennemeyer et al. 1997) or no statistically significant changes in bed occupancy rates (Vladeck et al. 1988).

Among studies that assessed the effect on market share of the New York State CSRS, three out of four concluded that effects (if any) were minimal (Chassin 2002; Hannan et al. 1994a; Jha & Epstein, 2006; Mukamel & Mushlin 1998). We found seven studies regarding individual providers. Public reporting of performance data was associated with ceasing practice for low volume cardiac surgeons in the New York State CSRS, but other effects were small or inconsistent (Hannan et al. 1994a & 1995; Jha & Epstein 2006; Mukamel & Mishlin 1998; Mukamel et al. 2000, 2002 & 2004–2005).

Public reporting: effect on quality improvement activities (change pathway)

By hospitals

There is good evidence that public reporting stimulates quality improvement activities by hospitals (change pathway). We identified eleven studies, almost all of which found that the public release of performance data stimulated activities at the hospital level. For example, a controlled trial by Hibbard and colleagues showed that the quantity of quality improvement activities was greater in hospitals subject to public reporting than in those receiving confidential reporting of the same quality information (Hibbard et al. 2003 & 2005). Similarly, Tu and Cameron (2003) found that more than half of the hospitals responded to a Canadian hospital-specific report on acute myocardial infarction by implementing quality improvement activities. Chassin (2002) conducted a series of interviews and case studies that documented the steps taken to try to improve cardiac surgery programmes within New York hospitals. Other studies reported similar findings – hospitals acted in response to public reporting of performance data (Bentley & Nash 1998; Dziuban et al. 1994; Longo et al. 1997; Mannion et al. 2005; Rosenthal et al. 1998). For example, Rosenthal et al. (1998) assessed hospitals participating in the Cleveland Health Quality Choice programme. Examining one academic and three community hospitals, they found increases in quality improvement activities such as interdisciplinary process improvement teams; review of processes of care; and development of practice guidelines. Only two studies reported that public reporting had little effect on hospital activity, both concerned the same system – the California Hospital Outcomes Project (Luce et al. 1996; Rainwater et al. 1998).

By health plans or individual providers

We identified no studies that assessed the effect of the public reporting of performance information on quality improvement activities by health plans of individual providers. However, the changes observed in hospitals are expected to carry over to health plans and individual providers and there are nonsystematic data about the changes instituted by health plans in order to improve performance on public quality measures. For example, a recent commentary on performance measurement reported that an American insurance company and health plan (Aetna) developed a plan to respond to the HEDIS requirement to use the administration of beta blockers following myocardial infarction as a performance measure. The use of beta blockers was integrated within the 'scripts' used by their case managers following Aetna members who had suffered a myocardial infarction. The company also started to send information about beta blockers to patients and their physicians (Lee 2007).

It is likely that the lack of published studies documenting the effect of public reporting on quality improvement activities by health plans or individual providers is due not to any lack of effect but rather because this is happening outside the usual sphere in which academic physicians work, research and publish.

Public reporting: effect on clinical outcomes

There is scant direct evidence that public reporting improves clinical outcomes. Without doubt, the greatest number of published studies about the effects of the public release of performance data concern mortality associated with cardiac surgery, specifically the New York State CSRS. Eight studies assessed the effect of public reporting on hospital clinical outcomes focused on the CSRS (Dranove et al. 2003; Dziuban et al. 1994; Ghali et al. 1997; Hannan et al. 1994 & 1994a; Moscucci et al. 2005; Omoigui et al. 1996; Peterson et al. 1998). All are in agreement that there has been a marked decline in mortality during the time that the CSRS has been in place. The issue is whether this decline is greater than in other areas of the United States that have no public reporting (i.e. is a secular trend unassociated with the CSRS) or whether the decline is due to New York cardiac surgeons' avoidance of high-risk patients and/or outmigration of such cases to other states. Suffice to say that this issue has generated many passionately held views. Peterson et al. (1998) have produced the methodologically strongest study. They demonstrate that reductions in mortality associated with cardiac surgery in New York State are greater than the national trend in the United States. They found no evidence of decreased access to cardiac surgery among elderly patients with acute myocardial infarction or among higher-risk elderly subsets.

Outside of cardiac surgery, few studies provide direct evidence for clinical benefits and their results are mixed (Baker et al. 2002 & 2003; Clough et al. 2002; Hibbard et al. 2005; Longo et al. 1997; Rosenthal et al. 1997). However, indirect evidence suggests that there have been clinical benefits. For example, Lee (2007) reported that the NCQA in the United States had retired the measure used to assess the use of beta blockers in patients hospitalized with acute myocardial infarction. This was because the average performance by managed care organizations participating in the HEDIS has risen from about 60% to more than 90% over the past ten years, with little variation among plans. Since this quality measure was not implemented in a controlled fashion, caution is required when drawing causal inferences about its use in public reporting systems and this dramatic improvement over time. Lee points out that no single organization (or policy) can claim credit for this success but case studies support the premise that public reporting, and the health plans' response to it, was a contributory factor. This contribution to the increased use of beta blockers after myocardial infarction must translate into lives saved. Thus, there is indirect evidence that the use of public reporting stimulates process improvements on the part of providers and that those process improvements translate into meaningful health gains for patients.

Public reporting: potential for unintended consequences

Numerous articles have discussed the potential for adverse unintended consequences resulting from the public reporting of performance data. However, the research data on this topic are relatively scant and consist mostly of surveys of how public reporting may have changed providers' practice. For example, three articles reported that cardiac surgeons in the United States thought that public reporting had made them more reluctant to operate on high-risk patients (Burack et al. 1999; Narins et al. 2005; Schneider & Epstein 1996). Similarly, Mannion et al. (2005) found that senior managers and clinicians believed that the English star performance ratings had led to a distortion of clinical priorities, erosion of public trust and reduced staff morale. However, Bridgewater et al's (2007) study in England found no evidence that public reporting had resulted in a decrease in the number of high-risk cardiac surgery cases. In fact, the proportion of high-risk cases increased from 14.1% to 16.8% over an eight-year period in which public reporting of cardiac surgery outcomes occurred.

We have already reviewed the American data about whether or not the improvement in mortality following cardiac surgery is due to real change or to avoidance of operations for high-risk patients (Dranove et al. 2003; Moscucci et al. 2005; Omoigui et al. 1996; Peterson et al. 1998). Baker et al. (2002) reported that any benefits in in-hospital mortality rates were offset by increases in mortality post discharge in Cleveland hospitals participating in the Cleveland Health Quality Choice programme. There have been no studies of the vital issue of whether providers' attention to areas subject to public reporting comes at the expense of attention to other areas of care that may be equally or more important.

Evidence about public reporting

Public reporting has been operating in the United States for almost twenty years; perhaps unsurprisingly the source of virtually all the published data about evaluations of public reporting. However, these data concern only a small handful of the numerous public reporting systems in use.

The lack of data from other countries gives some reason to pause. If policy-makers judge that a cultural component is contributing to the effect of public reporting, then (without their own data) they must guess how the demonstrated effects in the United States might translate to their country. One conclusion seems likely to remain unchanged as the evidence suggests that public reporting of performance data has little effect on consumers' choice of providers – even in a country known for consumerism and choice in health care. It is unlikely that this result would be any different in countries with less consumerist cultures. Conversely, in countries with a greater culture of professional responsibility than the United States the public release of performance data could exert an even greater effect on providers.

Even within the United States, only a handful of public reporting systems have been subject to evaluations. Most studies consider the New York State CSRS; CAHPS; QualityCounts; California Hospital Outcomes Project; Cleveland Health Quality Choice; Pennsylvania Health Care Cost Containment Council; and HEDIS. The effects of other major reporting systems have not received peer-reviewed evaluations.

Conclusions and the challenges ahead

Our review of the literature suggests that implementation of the public reporting of quality information will stimulate providers to start or enhance activities in order to improve their performance on publicly reported measures. In Chapter 5.5, Epstein suggests a variety of criteria to consider when choosing a performance measure – strong scientific underpinning, risk adjustment for outcome measures, allow exclusions, etc. An additional criterion is required for policy-makers considering the implementation of public reporting – choose measures that assess the most important aspects of health care. This is because a measure's inclusion in a public reporting system drives the health-care system to do it and can have good effects: for example, the lives saved by near universal use of beta blockers following acute myocardial infarction or the lowering of mortality associated with cardiac surgery.

But there is also potential for negative effects. No health effect will be gained from a measure that is not linked tightly to outcomes and the resources spent might be better used on, or at the expense of, some other aspect of care. Too often the items that have been reported are those that are most expediently measured, chosen from existing data-sets that will require no new data collection. Policy-makers should focus on what is important for their health-care system and aim towards a measurement system that reflects that, rather than letting the availability of existing data drive the decision about which measures will be reported.

Countries with, or considering, public reporting systems[1]

United States

The United States has numerous public reporting systems and it is not possible to list them all in this chapter. Some of the more prominent systems are described below.

HEDIS

One of the oldest and most mature public reporting systems, HEDIS is run by the NCQA (www.ncqa.org), a private not-for-profit corporation. It reports publicly on health plans that voluntarily agree the

1 Additional material from Jako Burghers

number of changes in measures from year to year. Thirty-five measures of 'the effectiveness of health care' were included in 2007.

New York State CSRS/PCI Reporting System
Oldest, best-known and most studied system for reporting short-term outcomes of cardiac interventions (www.nyhealth.gov/statistics/).

Pennsylvania Health Care Cost Containment Council – cardiac care
Another cardiac surgery system that is mature and has been the subject of research reports (www.phc4.org/reports/cabg/).

California Outcomes Reports
With a population of similar size to that of England, California is the largest American state to report some health outcomes – all at the hospital level. Outcomes are reported for cardiac surgery, community acquired pneumonia and myocardial infarction (www.oshpd.state.ca.us/HID/DataFlow/HospQuality.html).

HealthGrades
For-profit company that sells reports about doctors, hospitals and nursing homes (www.healthgrades.com/).

QualityNet
Established by the CMS, QualityNet (www.qualitynet.org/) provides the health-care quality improvement news; resources; and data reporting tools and applications used by health-care providers and others. Publicly reported quality information is made available through a companion site – Hospital Compare (see below).

Hospital Compare
Established by the CMS and members of the Hospital Quality Alliance, Hospital Compare (www.hospitalcompare.hhs.gov/) is a public-private collaboration to promote reporting on hospital quality. It displays rates for process of care measures as well as thirty-day risk adjusted mortality rates. Process measures include the antibiotic, vaccine and oxygenation status of patients with pneumonia and the provision of ACE inhibitors, aspirin and beta blockers to patients admitted for myocardial infarction; smoking cessation counselling to certain patients; and prophylactic antibiotics prior to surgery.

England

Dr Foster

Dr Foster (www.drfoster.co.uk/) is a partnership between the Health and Social Care Information Centre and Dr Foster, a private company. Its reports about Trusts in England include information about the number of operations; lengths of stay; readmission rates; nurses per 100 beds, etc., as well as hospital standardized mortality ratios.

Heart Surgery in the United Kingdom

Developed by the Care Quality Commission in collaboration with the Society for Cardiothoracic Surgery in Great Britain and Ireland and patients who have had experience of heart surgery, this web site (www. heartsurgery.cqc.org.uk/) presents risk-adjusted outcomes for cardiac surgery at thirty-nine hospitals. The EuroSCORE logistic model is used to calculate expected survival rates.

Denmark

National Indicator Project

Established in 1999, the National Indicator Project (www.nip.dk) is the result of concerted action between a number of Danish institutions, including the Ministry of Health. It measures the quality of care provided by hospitals in order to create public awareness about the extent to which health services meet quality standards. Sets of performance indicators are used to collect information on eight common conditions (stroke, hip fracture, schizophrenia, acute surgery, heart failure, lung cancer, diabetes, chronic obstructive pulmonary disease). Participation is mandatory for all hospitals. Data are published nationally, allowing benchmarking of hospitals.

Unit of Patient Evaluation

This organization has conducted a biennial survey of patients' experiences of hospital care since 2000. The data are aggregated on a national level that enables information to be used for improving hospital quality but not for hospital selection.

Other relevant organizations and web sites
Several Danish websites provide information on public and private hospitals, e.g. waiting times, treatment options, number of surgical interventions, follow-up care.

Relevant organizations and web sites include:

- Danish HealthCare Quality Programme (http://www.ikas.dk/English.aspx)
- Sundhed.dk (http://www.sundhed.dk/wps/portal/_s.155/18 6)
- Sundhedskvalitet (Health Quality) (http://www.sundhedskvalitet.dk).

Germany

Several organizations report on the quality of healthcare.

Bundesgeschäftsstelle Qualitätssicherung (BQS)
Independent organization established by the government, responsible for clinical performance assessment which is mandatory for all hospitals in Germany (used 212 indicators in 2004; 169 in 2005). Results are integrated in quality reports that include recommendations for improvement. Data on individual hospitals are not published, so consumers cannot use them for selection purposes (www.bqs-online.com).

Bertelsmann Stiftung
Conducts an annual health survey (Gesundheitsmonitor) of the experiences and needs of professionals and consumers. Since 2008, quality information has been provided through a web site (weisse-liste.de) developed and maintained by the Bertelmanns Stiftung (www.bertelsmann-stiftung.de).

Institut für Qualität und Wirtschaftlichkeit im Gesundheitswesen (IQWiG)
Independent scientific institute (http://www.iqwig.de) established in the course of the health care reform in 2004. Evaluates the quality and efficiency of health care and also publishes health information for patients and the general public. Primary goal is to contribute to

improvements in health care in Germany. German/English web site was launched in July 2005 as part of IQWiG's legislative remit to inform the public (http://www.Gesundheitsinformation.de). Web site includes information for consumers and patients, based on the Institute's own scientific publications and topics of its choice, but does not contain quality information on individual hospitals.

Other relevant organizations and web sites
Patienten-information (www.patienten-information.de).

Netherlands

There is increasing attention on the transparency of health-care quality in the Netherlands. Several organizations (governmental, professional and insurance companies) have developed performance indicators in many disease areas. Initially health-care practitioners and hospitals were targeted in order to encourage quality improvement and to enable benchmarking.

In 2006, a reform of the Dutch health-care system offered consumers more opportunities for choice. Health-care insurers invested heavily in promoting their plans and, as a result, 20%-30% of consumers changed their insurance plan. However, this proportion is now decreasing (no more than 5% change was expected in 2008). In 2005, the Ministry of Health, Welfare and Sport launched a web site (www.kiesbeter.nl) to provide consumers with health information and comparative information on hospital care and health insurers in order to enable better choices. The web site includes quality information and performance assessment of individual hospitals.

Private initiatives include the top 100 hospitals list produced by the daily newspaper, *Algemeen Dagblad*; the Best Hospitals list published by Elsevier; and web sites that offer comparisons of hospitals and other health-care services (e.g. www.mediquest.nl; www.independer.nl).

As in Denmark and Germany, there are no systematic data available on the effect of public reporting on the selection of health-care services, quality improvement and patient outcomes. Nevertheless, politicians and policy-makers in particular have a strong belief that quality information will result in improvements in the quality of health care and more informed decision-making among consumers.

Other relevant organizations and web sites
National Institute for Public Health and the Environment (http://www. rivm.nl).
DGN Publishers BV (private) (www.zorgkiezer.nl).

Norway

National quality indicators for the specialized health-care services were introduced in Norway in 2003. In 2006, data for twenty-one indicators were registered (11 for somatic care; 10 for psychiatric care) including patient experience surveys. The reporting of data is compulsory and they are published online (www.frittsykehusvalg.no) together with information about waiting times for different treatments and initiatives. Data are presented at an organizational (hospital) level and on the national average. Developments over time are also shown.

References

Baker, DW. Einstadter, D. Thomas, CL. Husak, SS. Gordon, NH. Cebul, RD (2002). 'Mortality trends during a program that publicly reported hospital performance.' *Medical Care*, 40(10): 879–890.

Baker, DW. Einstadter, D. Thomas, C. Husak, S. Gordon, NH. Cebul, RD (2003). 'The effect of publicly reporting hospital performance on market share and risk-adjusted mortality at high-mortality hospitals.' *Medical Care*, 41(6):729–740.

Bentley, JM. Nash, DB (1998). 'How Pennsylvania hospitals have responded to publicly released reports on coronary artery bypass graft surgery.' *Joint Commission Journal on Quality Improvement*, 24(1): 40–49.

Berwick, DM. James, B. Coye, MJ (2003). 'Connections between quality measurement and improvement.' *Medical Care*, 41(Suppl. 1): I30–38.

Bridgewater, B. Grayson. AD. Brooks, N. Grotte, G. Fabri, BM. Au, J. Hooper, T. Jones, M. Keogh B. North West Quality Improvement Programme in Cardiac Interventions (2007). 'Has the publication of cardiac surgery outcome data been associated with changes in practice in northwest England: an analysis of 25,730 patients undergoing CABG surgery under 30 surgeons over eight years.' *Heart*, 93(6): 744–748.

Burack, JH. Impellizzeri. P. Homel, P. Cunningham, JN Jr. (1999). 'Public reporting of surgical mortality: a survey of New York State cardiothoracic surgeons.' *Annals of Thoracic Surgery*, 68(4): 1195–1200; discussion: 1201–1202.

Chassin, MR (2002). 'Achieving and sustaining improved quality: lessons from New York State and cardiac surgery.' *Health Affairs (Millwood)*, 21(4): 40–51.

Clough, JD. Engler, D. Snow. R. Canuto, PE (2002). 'Lack of relationship between the Cleveland Health Quality Choice project and decreased inpatient mortality in Cleveland.' *American Journal of Medical Quality*, 17(2): 47–55.

Dranove, DEA. Kessler, D. McClellan, M. Satterthwaite, M (2003). 'Is more information better? The effects of "report cards" on health care providers.' *Journal of Political Economy*, 111(3): 555–588.

Dziuban, SW Jr. McIlduff, JB. Miller, SJ. Dal Col, RH (1994). 'How a New York cardiac surgery program uses outcomes data.' *Annals of Thoracic Surgery*, 58(6): 1871–1876.

Farley, DO. Elliott, MN. Short, PF. Damiano, P. Kanouse, DE, Hays, RD (2002). 'Effect of CAHPS performance information on health plan choices by Iowa Medicaid beneficiaries.' *Medical Care Research and Revue*, 59(3): 319–336.

Farley, DO. Short, PF. Elliott, MN. Kanouse, DE. Brown, JA. Hays, RD (2002a). 'Effects of CAHPS health plan performance information on plan choices by New Jersey Medicaid beneficiaries.' *Health Services Research*, 37(4): 985–1007.

Fung, CH. Lim, Y. Mattke, S. Damberg, C. Shekelle, PG (2008). 'Systematic review: the evidence that releasing performance data to the public improves quality of care.' *Annals of Internal Medicine*, 148(2): 111–123.

Ghali, WA. Ash, AS. Hall, RE. Moskowitz, MA (1997). 'Statewide quality improvement initiatives and mortality after cardiac surgery.' *Journal of the American Medical Association*, 277(5): 379–382.

Hannan, EL. Kilburn, H Jr. Racz, M. Shields, E. Chassin, MR (1994). 'Improving the outcomes of coronary artery bypass surgery in New York State.' *Journal of the American Medical Association*, 271(10): 761–766.

Hannan, EL. Kumar, D. Racz, M. Siu, AL. Chassin, MR (1994a). 'New York State's Cardiac Surgery Reporting System: four years later.' *Annals of Thoracic Surgery*, 58(6): 1852–1857.

Hannan, EL. Siu, AL. Kumar, D. Kilburn, H Jnr. Chassin, MR (1995). 'The decline in coronary artery bypass graft surgery mortality in New York State. The role of surgeon volume.' *Journal of the American Medical Association*, 273(3): 209–213.

Harris, KM (2002). 'Can high quality overcome consumer resistance to restricted provider access? Evidence from a health plan choice experiment.' *Health Services Research*, 37(3):551–571.

Hibbard, JH. Stockard, J. Tusler, M (2003). 'Does publicizing hospital performance stimulate quality improvement efforts?' *Health Affairs (Millwood)*, 22(2): 84–94.

Hibbard, JH. Stockard, J. Tusler, M (2005). 'Hospital performance reports: impact on quality, market share, and reputation.' *Health Affairs (Millwood)*, 24(4): 1150–1160.

Jha, AK. Epstein, AM (2006). 'The predictive accuracy of the New York State coronary artery bypass surgery report-card system.' *Health Affairs (Millwood)*, 25(3): 844–855.

Lee, TH (2007). 'Eulogy for a quality measure.' *New England Journal of Medicine*, 357(12): 1175–1177.

Longo, DR. Land, G. Schramm, W. Fraas, J. Hoskins, B. Howell, V (1997). 'Consumer reports in health care. Do they make a difference in patient care?' *Journal of the American Medical Association*, 278(19): 1579–1584.

Luce, JM. Thiel, GD. Holland, MR. Swig, L. Currin, SA. Luft, HS (1996). 'Use of risk-adjusted outcome data for quality improvement by public hospitals.' *Western Journal of Medicine*, 164(5): 410–414.

Mannion, R. Davies, H. Marshall, M (2005). 'Impact of star performance ratings in English acute hospital trusts.' *Journal of Health Services Research and Policy*, 10(1): 18–24.

Marshall, MN. Shekelle, PG. Leatherman, S. Brook, RH (2000). 'The public release of performance data: what do we expect to gain? A review of the evidence.' *Journal of the American Medical Association*, 283(14): 1866–1874.

Mennemeyer, ST. Morrisey, MA. Howard, LZ (1997). 'Death and reputation: how consumers acted upon HCFA mortality information.' *Inquiry*, 34(2):117–128.

Moscucci, M. Eagle, KA. Share, D. Smith, D. De Franco, AC. O'Donnell, M. Kline-Rogers, E. Jani, SM. Brown, DL (2005). 'Public reporting and case selection for percutaneous coronary interventions: an analysis from two large multicenter percutaneous coronary intervention databases.' *Journal of the American College of Cardiology*, 45(11): 1759–1765.

Mukamel, DB. Mushlin, AI (1998). 'Quality of care information makes a difference: an analysis of market share and price changes after publication of the New York State Cardiac Surgery Mortality Reports.' *Medical Care*, 36(7): 945–954.

Mukamel, DB. Mushlin, AI. Weimer, D. Zwanziger, J. Parker, T. Indridason, I (2000). 'Do quality report cards play a role in HMOs' contracting practices? Evidence from New York State.' *Health Services Research*, 35(1 Pt 2): 319–332.

Mukamel, DB. Weimer, DL. Zwanziger, J. Gorthy, SF. Mushlin, AI (2004–2005). 'Quality report cards, selection of cardiac surgeons, and racial disparities: a study of the publication of the New York State Cardiac Surgery Reports.' *Inquiry*, 41(4): 435–446.

Mukamel, DB. Weimer, DL. Zwanziger, J. Mushlin, AI (2002). 'Quality of cardiac surgeons and managed care contracting practices.' *Health Services Research*, 37(5): 1129–1144.

Narins, CR. Dozier, AM. Ling, FS. Zareba, W (2005). 'The influence of public reporting of outcome data on medical decision making by physicians.' *Archives of Internal Medicine*, 165(1): 83–87.

Omoigui, NA. Miller, DP. Brown, KJ. Annan, K. Cosgrove, D 3rd. Lytle, B. Loop, F. Topol, EJ (1996). 'Outmigration for coronary bypass surgery in an era of public dissemination of clinical outcomes.' *Circulation*, 93(1): 27–33.

Peterson, ED. DeLong, ER. Jollis, JG. Muhlbaier, LH. Mark, DB (1998). 'The effects of New York's bypass surgery provider profiling on access to care and patient outcomes in the elderly.' *Journal of the American College of Cardiology*, 32(4): 993–999.

Rainwater, JA. Romano, PS. Antonius, DM (1998). 'The California Hospital Outcomes Project: how useful is California's report card for quality improvement?' *Joint Commission Journal on Quality Improvement*, 24(1): 31–39.

Rosenthal, GE. Hammar, PJ. Way, LE. Shipley, SA. Doner, D. Wojtala, B. Miller, J. Harper, DL (1998). 'Using hospital performance data in quality improvement: the Cleveland Health Quality Choice experience.' *Joint Commission Journal on Quality Improvement*, 24(7): 347–360.

Rosenthal, GE. Quinn, L. Harper, DL (1997). 'Declines in hospital mortality associated with a regional initiative to measure hospital performance.' *American Journal of Medical Quality*, 12(2): 103–112.

Schneider, EC. Epstein, AM (1996). 'Influence of cardiac-surgery performance reports on referral practices and access to care. A survey of cardiovascular specialists.' *New England Journal of Medicine*, 335(4): 251–256.

Spranca, M. Kanouse, DE. Elliott, M. Short, PF. Farley, DO. Hays, RD (2000). 'Do consumer reports of health plan quality affect health plan selection?' *Health Services Research*, 35(5 Pt 1): 933–947.

Tu, JV. Cameron, C (2003). 'Impact of an acute myocardial infarction report card in Ontario, Canada.' *International Journal for Quality in Health Care*, 15(2): 131–137.

Vladeck, BC. Goodwin, EJ. Myers, LP. Sinisi, M (1988). 'Consumers and hospital use: the HCFA "death list".' *Health Affairs (Millwood)*, 7(1):122–125.

5.3 Developing information technology capacity for performance measurement

THOMAS D. SEQUIST, DAVID W. BATES

Introduction

Health information technology (IT) plays a substantial role in perform-ance measurement in many locations, particularly as such measure-ment programmes seek to involve a broad-based collection of health systems, payers, hospitals and individual clinicians. This role should soon become even greater as information technologies (e.g. electronic health records, data warehouses, electronic claims) can provide ready access to the clinical information required to assess quality of care across a broad spectrum of conditions and among large populations.

Electronic information systems have distinct advantages over paper review and administrative data, including the standardization of data collection; provision of expanded clinical detail; and the ability to update information in real time. However, these benefits are accompan-ied by significant upfront and ongoing challenges such as developing the infrastructure for installing and maintaining such systems; stan-dardizing data collection; and ensuring comparability across systems. Despite this, clinical information systems should soon become the key platform for performance measurement in developed countries and will also play a substantial role in future programmes for improving health-care quality.

This chapter explores several key issues regarding the use of IT for performance measurement, including the required infrastructure for, and penetration of, such technology; its potential capabilities; and spe-cific issues that arise when IT is used to measure quality of care.

Infrastructure of health information network

Health IT requires a robust infrastructure if it is to be used for perform-ance measurement. This infrastructure can be viewed at the local, regional or national level; all with distinct yet complementary goals. Local implementation of health information networks facilitates quality measurement and reporting for a given health plan, hospital or clinic and allows the development of local initiatives to improve care and to assess their effectiveness. However, such local efforts present challenges to attempts to assess performance across settings. Comparisons can be difficult as independent health information systems may not share the same standards for data representation and are likely to have even more variable data collection methods. However, the implementation of national standards for data representation and measurement and regional and national health information networks can standardize measure reporting at the regional and local levels and allow broader assessments of clinical performance.

Infrastructure requirements at the level of local hospitals and clinics depend to some extent on the type of health information to be used for performance assessment, ranging from the use of administrative claims data to a fully functional electronic health record. The former are dependent on electronic claims submissions, requiring the establishment of computerized databases that function in the background with no real-time interaction with the live clinical environment. These data warehouses can be maintained by technical support staff and updated at intervals that fit performance measurement and quality improvement. Claims data have been convenient sources for some time but it is likely that they will be superseded by clinical data from electronic health records.

The implementation of a fully functional electronic health record entails a much larger commitment than a claims database, to both support and maintain (Poon et al. 2004). The infrastructure needs to encompass live clinical environments including patient scheduling; laboratory, radiology and pharmacy systems; and clinical notes. Background data systems are also vital as consistent and reliable data entry provides the basis for valid performance measurement. This will include certain key elements: (i) ensuring the availability of networked personal computer access in all clinical workspaces; (ii) maintaining high speed interactivity among these computers; (iii) allowing structured data entry of those fields that inform performance measurement activities; and (iv) eliminating the need and potential for data entry workarounds that will not be captured (e.g. hand-written or verbal orders). Relevant data collected in the live clinical environments can be backed up routinely to create general data warehouses and data marts focused on particular diseases, such as a diabetes registry. Data warehouses are essential for queries across large numbers of patients, as required for quality assessment. The architecture of clinical databases is not suited to such queries which can bring operational databases to a grinding halt.

The extension of performance measurement from the local level to the regional or national level requires consideration of the involved parties; determination of a focus on hospital versus office-based care; and data storage and exchange. Ideally this will ensure comprehensive performance measurement by involving clinical providers, payers, clinical laboratories and pharmacies (Kaushal et al. 2005). A comprehensive selection of clinical providers (including hospitals, physician office practices, skilled nursing facilities, home health agencies) allows the collection of data on the full spectrum of clinical care, including patient demographics; diagnoses and procedures; medication utilization; and laboratory testing and results across hospital and office-based settings (Kaushal et al. 2005).

Performance measurement can take place in either the hospital or the office setting. However, quality assessment sometimes requires knowledge of care across both settings and the importance of transitions has been increasingly recognized. The targeted areas of performance assessment will guide the decision to focus on a particular setting for the purposes of establishing an adequate infrastructure. Some measures of care are largely hospital-based, e.g. the Hospital Quality Alliance measures on timing of antibiotic administration for treatment of pneumonia and use of aspirin for treatment of acute myocardial infarction (Jha et al. 2005). Some are focused largely on office-based care, including mammography for breast cancer screening (Trivedi et al. 2005). Others require knowledge of care in both the hospital and the office setting – for example, asthma management focuses on both medication use and the frequency of hospital visits. Once a set of measures has been identified the spectrum of required providers can be narrowed or expanded to ensure adequate data capture. The key issue for health IT is what variables need to be collected, ideally as a part of routine care. It can be especially onerous to collect some exclusion criteria and contraindications and those who develop the measures should consider whether or not they are all worthwhile.

A variety of models can be employed for data storage and exchange at the regional and national level. These might differ according to the heterogeneity of systems used to collect data; site of electronic data storage; and the strength of networking among sites. One model uses a single information system – participating organizations use one network to feed information into a central server that acts as a hub for storage and analysis. This model facilitates ready access to a completely standardized set of clinical data that allows immediate performance assessment at the national level. This creates substantial potential for uniform performance measurement but requires a system that is built from the ground up – installing the unique hardware and software at all participating clinical provider sites, for pharmacy and laboratory systems and for payer groups. In addition, the storage of data from local clinical sites on a single national server creates substantial concern about data security and the privacy of health information and necessitates the implementation of policies and procedures to safeguard such information. These policies include regulations regarding who may access the clinical data and for what specific purpose; and also to determine whether patient permission to store data outside of the local clinical site needs to be obtained prospectively. Such homogeneity is difficult to achieve and is the rare exception.

The national health information infrastructure in the United Kingdom is similar to the model described above although it does include multiple different electronic health records (Chantler et al. 2006). In 2002, the NHS began large investments in a national health information system that would facilitate widespread measurement and improvement of health-care delivery. Within the resulting national broadband network, the Spine stores demographic information on every citizen in England (including name, date of birth, address, registered primary care physician, unique patient identifier). Connected to over 98% of general practices in England, this provides a near complete listing of all patients in the country. Five regional service providers were created to direct the implementation of electronic patient records at all clinics in the country and several vendors operate electronic health records within each service area. Detailed clinical data are abstracted automatically from these records to create patient summaries of important diagnoses and procedures, laboratory results and prescriptions. Patient summary records are stored on the Spine to allow regional and national assessments of health-care delivery. This model highlights the vast potential of a planned implementation of a national health information infrastructure. However, there are concerns about the ongoing expense of maintaining the infrastructure; shortcomings in the system's technical capacity to manage the vast amount of clinical data being generated; and the transferability of the system to new regions including Scotland and Wales.

An alternative approach would allow local organizations to implement their own technologies (around a set of data representation and exchangeability standards) and to create health information exchanges that would transfer, rather than store, clinical information. A model close to this is being developed in the United States. Under the leadership of the Office of the National Coordinator for Health Information Technology (ONCHIT), regional centres or health information exchanges will facilitate the merging of data from disparate sites to allow the combination of data within larger geographical units. This model has the advantage of allowing local health organizations to use existing systems and avoids the permanent storage of data outside the local clinical organization. However, there are also significant disadvantages – for example, difficulties with the standardization of data formats may impede data merging. In addition, data ownership ultimately resides at the local level which will need to be approached for each new performance assessment or national estimates of quality of care. One key issue is how many electronic records to include in each region – the interoperability in the United Kingdom system is due in part to the limited number of vendors in each region. This process is being implemented to a variable extent in the United States, e.g. the Massachusetts eHealth Collaborative [www.maehc.org].

The systems in the United Kingdom and the United States are examples of two conceptual models for implementing a national health IT infrastructure (Fig. 5.3.1). Other examples demonstrate variations of these concepts. Finland is a leader in the use of electronic health records: over 90% of practices use electronic records to document care and there is a strong push towards national use of e-prescription. Rather than creating a national spine for information transfer and storage, Finland has adopted a national IT roadmap to transmit health information between entities over secure commercially owned virtual private networks restricted to health-care purposes. The roadmap actively promotes the use of standardized formats to allow data

---

Finland
- Strong penetration of electronic health records.
- No national architecture dedicated to health-care information exchange.
- Data exchange accomplished via secure connections on commercially owned broadband network.
- Emphasis on adherence to data standards to ensure exchangeability.

Germany
- Focus on patient electronic health cards.
- Identify patients across providers and regions.
- Carry pertinent health information at discretion of patient.

United Kingdom
- Nationally owned and implemented infrastructure.
- Information Spine stores health information on all patients.
- Costly to implement but allows relatively complete capture of population health delivery.

United States
- Local development and implementation of health information technology tools, including electronic health records.
- Creation of regional health information exchanges.
- Reliance on adherence to data standards to ensure exchangeability.

Fig. 5.3.1 Conceptual models of IT infrastructure plans

Many countries have developed roadmaps for implementing a health IT infrastructure within improvement performance measurement and quality of care. These models often vary according to the underlying structure of the health-care delivery system within a country, including issues of finance and ownership.

exchange between systems. Countries such as Austria and Germany have focused efforts on electronic patient cards that protect health information but also identify patients across multiple components of the health-care system. This requires substantial initial investment in technical architecture to ensure that the card is compatible across the system. However, it also offers the promise of a true patient health record containing portable health information that can be used to improve the quality, safety and efficiency of health care.

Penetration of health IT

Widespread use of IT for performance measurement is dependent on the penetration of such technology among key stakeholder organizations including clinical providers; payers; and laboratory and pharmacy systems. The accuracy of performance reporting that relies solely on electronic data depends on all potential sources of data utilizing an electronic platform to store and transfer information. The use of paper systems by any one of these stakeholders could result in gaps in information and inaccurate estimates of health-care delivery. For example, an analysis of acute myocardial infarction care may miss vital information if pharmacy records are not available in an electronic form, e.g. use of beta blocker therapy following hospital discharge.

In addition, high rates of penetration are necessary to assure that performance estimates derived from electronic data provide an accurate reflection of population health and are not biased by reliance on data obtained from a unique subset of clinics that chose to implement IT. Early adopters may be more interested in quality measurement and improvement and thus provide performance assessments that are not representative of the entire population.

Specific information technologies show varying levels of adoption. One report estimates that the penetration of electronic claims submission is already relatively high in the United States and will approach 100% within the next two years (Kaushal et al. 2005). It is more challenging to estimate the use of electronic health records in the United States due to the lack of a uniform definition of what constitutes an electronic health record. This can range from a system that shows only laboratory results to a fully functional system that includes clinical decision support tools, computerized order entry and electronic note authoring (Friedman 2006). However, it is clear that most other industrialized nations have progressed further (Ash & Bates 2005).

The definition of an electronic health record can vary according to its need and purpose. There are two distinct types of electronic patient records in the United Kingdom: (i) those that describe care provided by a single institution; and (ii) those that describe a system that allows the exchange of electronic clinical data across settings to provide a complete, longitudinal representation of health-care delivery (Friedman 2006). However, there is no current requirement for specific functionalities beyond these general descriptions.

Several efforts to standardize the definition are underway in the United States. Based on much more specific requirements, these processes all endorse the need for electronic health records to support a reporting function. The Institute of Medicine has defined eight core functions of an electronic health record: (i) health information and data; (ii) results management; (iii) order management; (iv) decision support; (v) electronic communication and connectivity; (vi) patient support; (vii) administrative processes and reporting; and (vii) reporting and population health (Board on Health Care Services & Institute of Medicine 2003). In 2005, the federal government formed the Certification Commission for Healthcare Information Technology (www.cchit.org) to establish a certification process for IT based on minimum standards for functionality, security and interoperability. These standards will be used to certify not only electronic health records but also health networks that allow the exchange of data among hospitals and clinics. The CCHIT certified more than seventy-five outpatient records in its first year and is currently certifying inpatient records. There has been attention to ensuring that some quality measures can be addressed and a current process is attempting to define what atomic data elements will be needed but most functions are currently certified as either present or absent.

Despite the limitations inherent in defining electronic health records, some estimates of penetration increase understanding of the current status of IT and its potential for performance measurement (Fig. 5.3.2). The United Kingdom has made the most progress in creating a national health information architecture and implementing an electronic health record system. Recent estimates suggest that over 90% of general practices in England use electronic patient records (Chantler et al. 2006; Schoen et al. 2006), facilitating a rather complete picture of office-based care. There are similar adoption rates in most Scandinavian countries, Australia and New Zealand. North America lags behind – electronic health records are used by only 28% of physicians in the United States and 23% in Canada (Jha et al. 2006; Schoen et al. 2006). Adoption rates vary with the size of practices – larger practices have implemented electronic health records approximately two to three times more than smaller practices and solo physician practices (Jha et al. 2006). Furthermore, many systems tend to be focused on the collection of data in the ambulatory setting; fewer are designed to capture both hospital and office-based care (Chantler et al. 2006; Schoen et al. 2006).

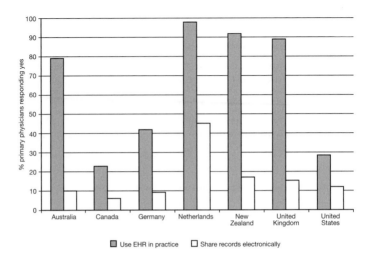

Fig. 5.3.2 International penetration of electronic health records and data exchangeability: responses from primary care physicians across seven countries, 2006

Source: Schoen et al. 2006

There are limited data regarding the use of such programmes for health information exchange at the broader regional and national levels. The United Kingdom has the most fully functioning system, storing patient level data in central repositories that allow performance reporting on a national level (Campbell et al. 2007). In the United States, the ONCHIT Nationwide Health Information Network has instituted a pilot programme in nine regional networks to investigate the feasibility of using regional health information exchanges.

Many factors affect the adoption rates for IT, particularly electronic health records, but the perception of clinical providers is paramount. It is clear that enlisting the support of management and clinicians is an essential component of successful implementation (Poon et al. 2004; Scott et al. 2005). Some high profile examples of failed implementation have resulted from clinicians' dissatisfaction with the system (Connolly 2005). Diffusion of innovations research suggests that the 'late majority' of technology adopters represent a constituency that provides the 'critical mass' necessary to ensure continued widespread use (Rogers 2003). In order to develop this critical mass, health system leaders need to develop implementation plans that minimize upfront challenges to clinicians' workflow and efficiency and make the benefits of adoption more transparent to the general workforce.

It is equally important to understand patients' views on the adoption and use of IT. Some data suggest that patients feel that electronic health records may reduce the amount of time that their physician spends talking with them during an office visit, but very few feel that the quality of the overall interaction is diminished (Rouf et al. 2007). Innovative use of technology such as cell phones, Internet patient portals and portable electronic health records has vast potential to improve health care and patient experiences of care and to increase patients' engagement in their own health-care delivery (Smith & Barefield 2007). However, while many patients are in favour of advancing the use of IT, many also express legitimate concerns regarding the security and privacy of their health information (Chhanabhai & Holt 2007).

Capabilities of electronic health records

Having installed the IT infrastructure, it is necessary to consider electronic health records' suitability for valid assessments of performance. Performance assessment can be categorized according to the six domains identified by the Institute of Medicine to assess whether care is equal, effective, safe, efficient, patient-centred and timely (Institute of Medicine 2001). Data from electronic health records are likely to be most valuable for assessing the effectiveness, safety, efficiency and equality of health-care delivery, in both office and hospital settings.

Health-care effectiveness

Electronic health records offer clear benefits over the use of paper record reviews and administrative claims data when assessing health-care effectiveness. Paper record reviews require more personnel to identify charts for abstraction; training of chart abstracters to ensure uniformity; and manual recording of data needed for performance measurement. Given the complexity of this process, including time and personnel commitment, most performance measurement that relies on manual chart review is completed on only a limited sample of the total population.

Administrative claims data offer the substantial advantage of being available in electronic form in the vast majority of settings, thereby allowing automated identification of data for the entire population with limited expenditure. However, they offer a limited spectrum of data for useful performance measurement. Administrative claims data are intended primarily as a source for financial accounting and therefore often lack the clinical detail needed to assess important health outcomes (e.g. blood pressure control) or counselling efforts (e.g. tobacco counselling). In addition, in a multi-payer system such as that in the United States, administrative data need to be pooled across multiple payers to provide a complete performance assessment for one provider, e.g. a hospital or clinic. Electronic health record systems incur substantial capital costs (Chantler et al. 2006; Kaushal et al. 2005a) but once in place may allow performance measurement with substantially fewer resources than paper chart reviews and offer increased clinical detail that is not available in administrative claims data.

Electronic health records require several key data elements to enable reliable assessment of health-care effectiveness across a spectrum of conditions. These include patient demographics, diagnosis and procedure codes, laboratory and radiology results, pharmacy data and allergy information. All of these elements contribute to the standard assessment of quality metrics for health-care effectiveness, which includes identification of the eligible denominator and numerator populations. The creation of the eligible denominator population is reliant on all patients being assigned a unique patient identifier within the electronic health record. This is particularly important for performance measurement across multiple clinical sites in which duplicate identification of patients could threaten the validity of the analysis. In addition, metrics are often assessed by provider and this requires patients to be assigned to a specific provider, such as the primary care provider or specialist for a given condition. When unique patients have been identified and linked (if necessary) to specific providers, further eligibility criteria for the denominator population can be applied from electronic health record data. These structured fields typically include patient demographics (e.g. age and sex) and diagnostic codes (e.g. congestive heart failure or diabetes). Finally, exclusion criteria must be applied, often by using medication allergy information or other relevant data. Identification of the appropriate numerator population from electronic health record data most often relies on laboratory and radiology results, as well as pharmacy data.

There is a growing number of examples of the use of electronic health record data to assess quality based on the principles described above (Baker et al. 2007; Benin et al. 2005; O'Toole et al. 2005; Persell et al. 2006; Tang et al. 2007). Identification of eligible denominator populations for some screening measures is straightforward and unlikely to be biased, regardless of data source. For example, quality measures constructed from electronic health record data that are strictly age-based (e.g. breast or colorectal cancer screening rates) are unlikely to include or exclude patients inappropriately. However, those measures that are based on the presence of a specific disease require increased attention to ensure that the appropriate denominator population is identified accurately.

Benin et al. (2005) assessed acute pharyngitis care by comparing electronic health record data with administrative claims data, using manual chart review as the gold standard. For identification of cases of pharyngitis they found that the electronic health record had a higher sensitivity than claims data (96% versus 62%), but a lower specificity (34% versus 55%). However, this may not provide an accurate reflection of the potential for accuracy of electronic health record data as this study identified cases through free text searches rather than coded data.

The ability to identify accurately the eligible denominator populations for chronic disease care has also been examined. In one study of Medicare patients, coded electronic health record data had substantially higher sensitivity than claims data for identification of diabetic patients (97% versus 75%), with a near perfect specificity (99.6%) (Tang et al. 2007). This high level of data accuracy was achieved primarily by using coded information in the electronic problem list; the presence of a diabetes medication on the electronic medication list; and laboratory results consistent with the presence of uncontrolled diabetes.

Electronic health record data also offer the opportunity to further refine the identification of patients with diabetes. For example, standard definitions of quality measurement for diabetes care require the presence of at least two visits for diabetes during the measurement period. This is intended to improve the specificity of the denominator population despite the fact that only 75% of patients with diabetes meet this requirement (Tang et al. 2007). Electronic health record data can be less reliant on the number of office visits and track more patients with diabetes through electronic problem and medication lists, as well as the availability of historical laboratory data. However, diabetes is much easier to detect than many other chronic conditions (coronary artery disease, congestive heart failure, chronic obstructive pulmonary disease) since some drugs are used almost exclusively to treat diabetes and there are good laboratory markers.

There have also been assessments of the accuracy of electronic health record data for identifying appropriate numerator populations. For management of pharyngitis, electronic health record data had slightly lower rates of identified testing for Group A streptococcus than administrative data (71% versus 76%) (Benin et al. 2005). The most detailed assessment of the accuracy of numerator data comes from two studies of cardiovascular disease care in the office setting. Electronic health record data were used to evaluate standard performance measures for patients with coronary artery disease, such as measurement of cholesterol, measurement of blood pressure and use of appropriate medications (antiplatelet drugs, lipid lowering drugs, beta blockers, angiotensin converting enzyme [ACE] inhibitors). Rates of appropriate care were consistently lower when using coded electronic health record data rather than manual chart review, with absolute differences between the two methods ranging from as low as 1.8% (cholesterol control) to as high as 14.3 % (antiplatelet drug use). The high discrepancy rate for antiplatelet drug use in this study is likely due to the availability of aspirin as an over-the-counter treatment. This provides less incentive for clinicians to document prescriptions in coded format in the electronic medication list.

Similar findings are available for the assessment of quality of care for congestive heart failure in which quality metrics included assessment of left ventricular ejection fraction; use of beta blockers and ACE inhibitors; and prescription of warfarin for patients in atrial fibrillation. Again, coded electronic health record data showed lower rates of appropriate care than manual chart review data, ranging from a low of 1.9% for use of beta blocker therapy to a high of 23.2% for use of warfarin therapy (Baker et al. 2007). In contrast to the previous study, the high discrepancy rate for use of warfarin therapy among patients with atrial fibrillation was attributable to the lack of identification of valid exclusion criteria in the electronic health record, such as a history of bleeding or mental disorder that precluded anticoagulation.

Possibly the largest scale demonstration of performance measurement based on electronic health record data originates from the United Kingdom, where the national information architecture has allowed measurement of health-care delivery across a spectrum of conditions (Campbell et al. 2007). Focused on health-care effectiveness, these measurements form the basis for a nationwide pay-for-performance programme targeting general practitioners. A remarkably high rate of quality performance has been achieved across a very large number of parameters. However, a very large amount (around 30%) of payment was based on quality. One issue emerged from providers being allowed to remove patients from the numerator and denominator for any measure – exception reporting. A few practices used this option for a very large number of their patients and the next iteration of this programme will include auditing around this issue for practices that use this option frequently.

The findings above highlight several key components in the use of electronic health records to measure the effectiveness of health-care delivery. The first is that the data contained within electronic health records can be used in a feasible manner to conduct performance assessment across a wide range of conditions. The second is that the identification of denominator and numerator populations presents challenges within the context of electronic health record data. Some assessment of validation of individual performance measures is advisable before implementing their routine use and those developing the measures should particularly consider the relative importance of specific exceptions. Finally, it is important to note that the above findings provide only an early window into the potential opportunities and pitfalls of using electronic health record data. This will require more information on the extension of these findings to other practice settings that use a range of electronic health record systems.

Patient safety

The standardized assessment of patient safety is a crucial imperative given the large body of evidence documenting the unintended consequences of medical care (Institute of Medicine 1999). Adverse events are historically substantially underreported in hospital settings (Bates et al. 2003) as systematic identification and reporting systems have been difficult to implement. Clearly many injuries occur in other settings but data about these adverse events are even more limited and it has been suggested that the magnitude of harm outside the hospital may be as great as inside. Electronic health records have the potential to improve dramatically the measurement of patient safety across many areas.

The AHRQ has developed a set of hospital-based patient safety indicators (PSIs) that allow hospitals to assess patient safety and evaluate interventions to improve safety (Agency for Healthcare Research and Quality 2006). These rely on diagnostic codes to identify potential threats to patient safety such as the occurrence of incident decubitus ulcers or foreign bodies left during procedures. This information can be abstracted readily from inpatient electronic medical record systems but these codes for adverse events are not well-represented in the overall coding schemes and are not used consistently by clinicians. These sensitivity and specificity problems limit their potential to detect patient safety issues (Bates et al. 2003).

Additional strategies to detect threats to patient safety may be employed using electronic health records in hospital settings. Once electronic data are widely available, algorithms can be developed and validated to detect adverse medical events. For example, searches for key words in electronic discharge summaries can identify a spectrum of adverse events including falls, decubitus ulcers, postoperative complications, adverse drug events and unexpected death (Murff et al. 2003). Other elements of inpatient electronic health records can also be utilized. Pharmacy records can be searched for the use of medications (e.g. diphenhydramine, naloxone) commonly associated with adverse events (Classen et al. 1991). Laboratory records can be searched for out-of-range values associated with adverse events such as abnormal coagulation studies (Classen et al. 1991). Radiology reports can be searched to identify evaluations following patient falls, such as X-rays and head computed tomograms (Hripcsak et al. 1995). More advanced solutions have also been developed – natural language processing is used to discern patterns within unstructured data such as radiology reports – and their use is likely to increase as the software continues to advance (Bates et al. 2003). Alternatively, as more structured reporting of results is implemented (e.g. pathology and radiology reporting) the use of structured electronic health record data will become increasingly relevant to the detection of adverse events. The general approach uses IT to detect signals that an adverse event might be present and follows this with further chart review. This needs refinement but is likely to represent the approach of the future.

There is no widely accepted set of patient safety indicators in the office setting but electronic health records have been used to detect adverse events. In particular, one study identified a substantial number of adverse drug events by using an ambulatory electronic health record and a variety of searching techniques including text search, allergy records and administrative billing codes (Honigman et al. 2001). This study highlighted the fact that the predominance of adverse events was detected using free text searches rather than structured data fields. However, increased attention to structured data entry and improvements in natural language processing will likely result in improved identification of adverse events in the office setting.

Electronic health records also have the potential to increase dramatically the measurement of another key aspect of patient safety. Follow-up of abnormal test results is a problem in many settings but may be a particular problem in the office setting where care is coordinated across many providers and health centres. Findings such as abnormal mammograms (McCarthy et al. 1996) and abnormal faecal occult blood tests (Etzioni et al. 2006) often lack adequate follow-up, diminishing the effectiveness of population based screening programmes. Through innovative use of laboratory and radiology data, electronic health records can be used to identify abnormal test results and measure the adequacy of follow-ups according to rigorously defined guidelines (Poon et al. 2004a).

Similarly, transitions in care from the hospital to the office setting are often cited as sources of considerable concern for patient safety (Roy et al. 2005). In this setting, data from electronic health records can be employed to identify abnormal test results and measure whether appropriate follow-up has occurred. One challenge to this use of electronic data is the availability of structured information to identify such abnormal results. Blood test results may have clear thresholds but other findings may be subtler and require clearly structured definitions.

Categorization schemes have been implemented in the clinical setting for topics such as mammogram interpretations, pap smear findings and colorectal polyp characteristics. However, automated identification is difficult as they are often entered into free text reports. Increased use of advanced coding systems such as the Systemized Nomenclature of Medicine (SNOMED) algorithm will provide the structured fields that will help to solve this issue (College of American Pathologists 1984).

Health-care efficiency

Currently, there is no widely accepted set of metrics for health-care efficiency although electronic health records present an opportunity to increase measurement in this area. According to the Institute of Medicine (2001), inefficiency in health-care systems is a product of quality waste and administrative costs. Quality waste includes redundant test ordering (often due to a lack of access to prior clinical information) as well as inappropriate test use (e.g. routine use of imaging for lower back pain). Prior analyses have indicated that repeat laboratory testing in the absence of a clinical indication accounts for up to 30% of all utilization and is a particular problem in the hospital setting (van Walraven & Raymond 2003). Electronic health records hold particular promise for the measurement of such quality waste within health-care systems – they provide ready access to data on laboratory test utilization and can be used to measure rates of redundant test ordering in a reliable manner (Bates et al. 1998 & 1999).

There is increasing attention on the development of more robust measurement of health-care efficiency in both hospital and office settings. The episode treatment group is one potential option, focusing on the longitudinal management of specific conditions in both settings (Forthman et al. 2000). This technique requires access to a combination of hospital-, ambulatory- and pharmacy-based information to represent accurately the management of a specific condition, such as chronic sinusitis. Episode treatment groups can be used to identify variation in the use of procedures and medications as well as repeat office visits. Electronic health records with complete integration between hospital and office settings provide ready access to the required data and thus offer the potential to use such methodologies to assist in the measurement of efficiency.

Health-care equality

Inappropriate differences in the quality of health care are widespread throughout many health-care systems in the world and disadvantaged populations often receive poorer quality care (Institute of Medicine 2002). These differences are based on patient socio-demographic features including sex, race, income and educational attainment. Reliable and routine measurement of such differences in care represents an important first step in the development of programmes to ensure the delivery of equal treatment to all patients. This requires the use of health information systems that can not only produce reliable data on standard measures of clinical performance but also combine these with patient level socio-demographic features. Patient gender is routinely available in administrative claims data, allowing an analysis of gender differences in health care (Ayanian & Epstein et al. 1991). However, data on patient race, income and educational attainment are far less complete (Nerenz & Currier 2004). Analyses of racial disparities in health care are often limited to black-white differences in care due to a lack of data on other racial and ethnic groups (Sequist & Schneider 2006). Similarly, patient-level income and educational attainment are often estimated at larger geographical levels, despite the known limitations of these estimates (Krieger et al. 2003).

Electronic health records can provide a reliable means of measuring health disparities according to a wide range of patient socio-demographic features (Sequist et al. 2006). Patient information (including patient race and educational attainment) can be collected as part of routine care and combined with clinical data to construct stratified measures of health-care quality.

Key issues concerning use of electronic data

Electronic health record data have the potential to improve dramatically performance measurement as outlined above. However, this potential will not be realized without careful consideration of the key issues of data quality and patient privacy.

Data quality

Electronic health records offer access to increased clinical detail for use in performance measurement. However, it is important to understand the accuracy of these data before using them for high stakes reporting, such as pay for performance or public reporting efforts. Some work has highlighted potential limitations in the use of electronic medical record data for performance measurement (Baker et al. 2007; Persell et al. 2006). These limitations relate largely to two main issues. The first is that populations can be highly mobile, shifting care between physician practices within and across geographical regions. This creates challenges for complete capture of clinical care for the purposes of performance measurement, particularly when measurements rely on care delivered over a continuum. For example, accurate assessment of colorectal cancer screening rates requires knowledge of the performance of colonoscopy within the previous ten years. This presents a significant challenge when patients are quite likely to have relocated or changed health-care providers during this extended timeframe. A critical solution to this issue is to facilitate electronic data exchange among health-care systems or to institute shared data warehouses that allow complete capture of clinical care processes.

The second issue is that data are entered into electronic health records for the primary purpose of routine clinical care rather than performance measurement. This may lead to deficiencies in documentation or lack of use of the structured data fields required for reporting in lieu of more convenient free text documentation of care. Similarly, exclusions that apply to specific performance measures may not be coded routinely in electronic health records, either through technical limitations or because clinicians are not aware of the need to enter such structured documentation. If it is clear that specific exclusions are important it is possible to create coded fields and stress the importance of documentation to clinicians. A recent study analysed the use of electronic health record data to assess quality of care for coronary artery disease in the office setting. This revealed that 15% to 81% of cases deemed to have failed to achieve the quality metric were found on manual chart review to have met either the quality metric or valid exclusion criteria (Persell et al. 2006). The study identified three important causal factors for both numerator and denominator inconsistencies. First, clinicians often used the diagnosis of coronary artery disease inappropriately, frequently when they were ordering tests to exclude this condition (though current reimbursement models sometimes reward this approach). Second, data were often entered in non-structured data fields – such as noting aspirin use in free text rather than the formal electronic medication list. Third, valid exclusions were not captured in structured data fields, including concepts such as patient preference and adverse medication effects.

Data collected via electronic health records are primarily for the purpose of clinical care and will certainly lack data required for broad-based performance assessment. This is a significant problem but one that can be expected to improve with time, especially if clinicians are made more aware. Missing data are less likely to be a significant concern for laboratory- or radiology-based measures that already form part of routine clinical care. The completeness of the data may be of particular relevance when assessing performance measures focused on patient education or counselling, or those in which patient refusal may play a large role. Busy clinicians typically document this type of information in unstructured notes rather than in the coded fields that allow automated performance assessments. The use of coded fields can be increased through the effective design of electronic health records that encourage their use in the context of streamlined clinical workflows and through training and performance feedback on their use (Porcheret et al. 2004). It is crucial to demonstrate a clinical 'return on investment', such as basing clinical decision support tools (electronic reminders) or performance feedback reports on data entered in these coded fields (Friedman 2006). Finally, it is important to discourage the entry of free text diagnoses by ensuring that coded fields cover the full spectrum of clinical care through the use of advanced coding systems such as the SNOMED algorithm (College of American Pathologists 1984).

When encouraging the use of coded fields, it is important to consider the special case of behaviour counselling, such as smoking status. These fields should include a 'not assessed' option set as the default response in all records to avoid the pitfall of erroneously assigning a smoking status to a patient in whom such behaviour has not actually been assessed. This will allow differentiation between those patients whose smoking status has been assessed and those with missing data.

Potential solutions can be implemented to improve data quality from electronic health records and other information systems but still it is critical to ensure the reliability of the data via routine audit or other quality assurance means. This is particularly important if data are to be used for high stakes purposes such as public reporting or pay for performance. There are relatively straightforward options for ensuring data reliability, such as crosschecking data from multiple sources. For example, discrepancies arising from comparisons of administrative claims data and the electronic health record can be examined further by a more labour intensive manual chart review of a small subset of patients. More complex options would include random chart audits conducted by trained staff. Clearly, these are more labour intensive but may be necessary initially as performance measurement programmes that are reliant on information from new electronic systems become more widespread.

Patient privacy

As electronic health record data become increasingly available and are able to provide a greater level of clinical detail on large populations of patients, it will become more important to protect the privacy of such information when assessing performance. At the local level, safeguards need to be established to ensure that passwords and network security limit access to patient information to approved personnel only and that audit trails verify individual access. Where health information is exchanged across health systems with the ultimate goal of aggregation at the regional or national level there will need to be consideration of what type of patient information can be transmitted securely and how to transmit it. This will require a careful balance between the protection of privacy and the collection and transmission of data with enough detail to allow clinically meaningful performance assessment. The level of security of electronic transmissions should be commensurate with the level of detail contained in the data, employing encryption techniques when necessary.

The United Kingdom has been at the forefront of issues related to the privacy of patient health information and data sharing outside of the local sites for performance measurement purposes (Chantler et al. 2006). As outlined earlier, the Spine stores basic demographic information on all citizens in England. These data can be augmented in a personal summary record that contains more detailed information regarding clinical diagnoses and treatments, including prescriptions, procedures and hospital discharge summaries. The demographic information stored on the Spine is compulsory for all patients but they can dictate to what extent, if at all, more detailed information is available in the personal summary record. Access to patient medical records is monitored in order to ensure data security – smart cards identify health professionals as they access information and maintained audit trails detail access to each record. However, these safeguards are not perfect. A junior official recently extracted banking data on 25 million people in the United Kingdom. The data were saved on two disks (with little protection), mailed and subsequently lost. Such incidents have generated understandable concern.

The United States has enacted the Health Insurance Portability and Accountability Act (HIPAA) which in part regulates the use of private health information. This has implications for the use of data to measure the delivery of health care (Kamoie & Hodge 2004). ONCHIT is actively considering the options for data security and patient privacy – security is one of the core components of successful certification of electronic heath record systems through this office (http://healthit. hhs.gov/portal/server.pt). The criteria required for certification under this system are similar to those in the United Kingdom, including the requirement of secure monitored access to electronic health record information as well as maintenance of a complete audit trail of access to these records.

Key policy issues

A number of lessons emerge for policy-makers in developed nations. One clear immediate priority is to create international agreement on key quality metrics. The European Union has begun this but has not yet reached broad agreement for most metrics. This creates significant challenges and resultant unnecessary incremental work when performing international comparisons.

It is clear that financial incentives are powerful motivators for the adoption of electronic health records in the outpatient sector. Some countries (e.g. United Kingdom) have achieved near universal adoption of electronic health records in general practice by paying for these systems; other countries (e.g. Australia) have used incentives-based approaches to achieve high levels of implementation. The United Kingdom has also been extremely successful with performance measurement by offering large financial incentives based on providers' performance on quality metrics extracted from the electronic record. The requirement that providers bill electronically can also provide an important incentive. Such incentive programmes have enabled a large proportion of Europe to achieve high levels of adoption of electronic health records in the outpatient setting. The current challenge is to improve the records so as to deliver better decision support; allow providers to work efficiently; and ensure that the records can be used readily to measure performance and improve care.

Less evidence is available about how best to achieve high levels of adoption and how to use records to measure performance in the inpatient setting. In most nations, levels of implementation in inpatient facilities lag behind what is available in the outpatient sector. This requires better incentives to encourage institutions to adopt this technology and additional approaches for routine measurement of the quality of inpatient care in order to align incentives with high quality. A clear note of caution is required as financial incentives can be a double-edged sword and may promote undesirable behaviour. Incentive programmes should be viewed from a variety of perspectives and include consideration of the possibility of gaming. The effect on the quality of care should be monitored as closely in areas that are not reliant on incentives as in those that are.

Low-income countries have far less experience of how best to proceed although some transitional countries such as Brazil have achieved notable success, particularly around the larger population centres. Furthermore, it appears likely that health IT will be useful even in very low-resource environments such as Kenya (Siika et al. 2005). More research is urgently needed on how best to increase adoption of electronic health records in the inpatient setting; to address the benefits of clinical data exchange; and to identify which solutions will be most beneficial in transitional and developing nations in particular. Further evaluation of decision support and the relative costs and benefits of implementation is needed in all settings. Furthermore, research is needed to identify quality metrics which can be implemented directly through electronic records.

The future

Looking ahead, we believe that electronic health records and patient computing will remain the key technologies for measuring and improving quality. Patient computing is likely to mature within the next ten to twenty years and patients will likely begin to manage much more of their care with the assistance of health IT (Delbanco & Sands 2004).

The influence of electronic health records in the inpatient and outpatient setting will also continue to expand – with a focus on computerized provider order entry, clinical data exchange and clinical decision support.

The use of electronic health records in the ambulatory setting is essential for capturing the health of populations and moving to the next level of performance measurement. The latter should be possible in developed nations within the next five to ten years. Most actions in the inpatient setting occur as the result of an order and electronic health records should prompt providers on appropriate actions, simultaneously improving quality and facilitating performance measurement.

Today, it is technically feasible to implement widespread clinical data exchange. It should be possible to obtain a much more comprehensive picture of quality within the next ten years, once the political and social obstacles to data exchange have been overcome. Pilot programmes are required in order to determine how best to implement data exchange in a manner that does not encroach on patient privacy. Clinical decision support is one of the keys to truly dramatic improvement. Decision support is often single-synapse but could be much more sophisticated. A number of challenges for reaching the next level have been put forward recently, including: prioritizing recommendations for presentation to providers; using free text information to create recommendations; and combining decision support recommendations for patients with multiple co-morbid conditions (Sittig et al. 2008).

Conclusions

Health information technologies, particularly electronic health records, have enormous potential to increase performance measurement in a variety of areas as outlined. The ability to achieve ready access to detailed clinical information on a spectrum of conditions with minimal resource utilization is an appealing alternative to the current system of labour-intensive manual chart reviews and increasingly unsuitable administrative claims data. Used effectively, electronic health record systems can provide real-time, clinically relevant measures of health-care delivery. This potential is yet to be realized in most health-care settings as additional work is required to overcome the substantial challenges that still exist.

Challenge 1: *increase penetration of electronic health records*

As discussed earlier, widespread use of electronic health records is essential to ensure the validity of performance measurement comparisons across health-care settings. Some countries have very high adoption rates but others are lagging behind, particularly among small and solo physician practices. In addition, implementations in hospitals generally lag behind office practices. Policy solutions are needed to increase the adoption of electronic health records in these settings. The need for central leadership to support adoption has been highlighted repeatedly (Poon et al. 2004). In addition, successful implementation depends on minimizing the impact on clinician workflow and efficiency, with clear demonstrations of potential care improvements. Financial barriers must be overcome (Bates 2005) and better alignment of financial incentives is needed, e.g. increased reimbursements based on the presence of electronic health records or use of key functionalities such as computerized order entry.

Challenge 2: *ensure data exchangeability*

Successful performance measurement and the delivery of good clinical care depend on the ability to merge data from multiple systems (including pharmacy, radiology, laboratory) into a single electronic health record (McDonald 1997). If these data exist in isolation, rather than as part of a uniform clinical record, this not only increases the complexity of performance measurement but also discourages further adoption of electronic health records.

Similarly, successful coordination to produce a single electronic health record will require further efforts to ensure that this health information can be exchanged as part of a compatible regional and national health information system. This will allow performance measurement at levels that extend from the local clinical site to international comparisons. The United Kingdom has implemented what is arguably the most successful model to date, although many difficulties remain; the United States is in the process of testing a model of regional health information exchanges (Adler-Milstein et al. 2008).

Challenge 3: increase reliability of electronic health record data

Preliminary studies indicate that electronic health record data can be used for performance measurement, but the accuracy of these data varies according to the metric. Sources of inaccuracy are related to the variable entry of data into structured fields and to the lack of complete data capture across health-care settings. Efforts to improve the use of structured fields within electronic health records should focus on increasing their visibility as part of the standard clinical workflow and on providing direct benefits of the collection of such information, such as using these data to drive electronic clinical decision support tools. Improved capture of data across health-care settings will involve ensuring that all possible key stakeholders have deployed electronic data systems. This will include hospital- and office-based providers as well as pharmacy and laboratory systems. Electronic gaps in any of these systems will challenge the validity of performance assessment based on electronic health record data.

When these challenges have been addressed, health IT can realize its true potential to advance the field of performance measurement. This will facilitate widespread assessments of health-care delivery and ultimately improve the health status of the population.

References

Adler-Milstein, J. McAfee, AP. Bates, DW. Jha, AK (2008). 'The state of regional health information organizations: current activities and financing.' *Health Affairs (Millwood)*, 27(1): 60–69.

AHRQ (2006). *Patient safety indicators overview*. Rockville, MD: Agency for Healthcare Research and Quality (http://www.qualityindicators.ahrq.gov/psi_overview.htm).

Ash, JS. Bates, DW (2005). 'Factors and forces affecting EHR system adoption: report of a 2004 ACMI discussion.' *Journal of the American Medical Informatics Association*, 12(1): 8–12.

Ayanian, JZ. Epstein, AM (1991). 'Differences in the use of procedures between women and men hospitalized for coronary heart disease.' *New England Journal of Medicine*, 325(4): 221–225.

Baker, DW. Persell, SD. Thompson, JA. Soman, NS. Burgner, KM. Liss, D. Kmetik, KS (2007). 'Automated review of electronic health records to assess quality of care for outpatients with heart failure.' *Annals of Internal Medicine*, 146(4): 270–277.

Bates, DW (2005). 'Physicians and ambulatory electronic health records.' *Health Affairs (Millwood)*, 24(5): 1180–1189.

Bates, DW. Boyle, DL. Rittenberg, E. Kuperman, GJ. Ma'Luf, N. Menkin, V. Winkelman, JW. Tanasijevic, MJ (1998). 'What proportion of common diagnostic tests appear redundant?' *American Journal of Medicine*, 104(4): 361–368.

Bates, DW. Evans, RS. Murff, H. Stetson, PD. Pizziferri, L. Hripcsak, G (2003). 'Detecting adverse events using information technology.' *Journal of the American Medical Informatics Association*, 10(2): 115–128.

Bates, DW. Kuperman, GJ. Rittenberg, E. Teich, JM. Fiskio, J. Ma'Luf, N. Onderdonk, A. Wybenga, D. Winkelman, J. Brennan, TA. Komaroff, AL. Tanasijevic, M (1999). 'A randomized trial of a computer-based intervention to reduce utilization of redundant laboratory tests.' *American Journal of Medicine*, 106(2): 144–150.

Benin, AL. Vitkauskas, G. Thornquist, E. Shapiro, ED. Concato, J. Aslan, M. Krumholz, HM (2005). 'Validity of using an electronic medical record for assessing quality of care in an outpatient setting.' *Medical Care*, 43(7): 691–698.

Board on Health Care Services and Institute of Medicine (2003). *Key capabilities of an electronic health record system: letter report*. Washington, DC: National Academies Press.

Campbell, S. Reeves, D. Kontopantelis, E. Middleton, E. Sibbald, B. Roland, M (2007). 'Quality of primary care in England with the introduction of pay for performance.' *New England Journal of Medicine*, 357(2): 181–190.

Chantler, C. Clarke, T. Granger, R (2006). 'Information technology in the English National Health Service.' *Journal of the American Medical Association*, 296(18): 2255–2258.

Chhanabhai, P. Holt, A (2007). 'Consumers are ready to accept the transition to online and electronic records if they can be assured of the security measures.' *Medscape General Medicine*, 9(1): 8.

Classen, DC. Pestotnik, SL. Evans, RS. Burke, JP (1991). 'Computerized surveillance of adverse drug events in hospital patients.' *Journal of the American Medical Association*, 266(20): 2847–2851.

College of American Pathologists (1984). *Systemized nomenclature of medicine, second edition*. Skokie. IL: Vol. 1 & 2.

Connolly, C (2005). 'Cedars-Sinai doctors cling to pen and paper.' *Washington Post*, 21 March 2005: p.A01.

Delbanco, T. Sands, DZ (2004). 'Electrons in flight – e-mail between doctors and patients.' *New England Journal of Medicine*, 350(17):1705–1707.

Etzioni, DA. Yano, EM. Rubenstein, LV. et al (2006). 'Measuring the quality of colorectal cancer screening: the importance of follow-up.' *Diseases of the Colon and Rectum,* 49(7): 1002–1010.

Forthman, MT. Dove, HG. Wooster, LD (2000). 'Episode Treatment Groups (ETGs): a patient classification system for measuring outcomes performance by episode of illness.' *Topics in Health Information Management,* 21(2): 51–61.

Friedman, DJ (2006). 'Assessing the potential of national strategies for electronic health records for population health monitoring and research.' *Vital and Health Statistics Series 2,* (143): 1–83.

Honigman, B. Lee, J. Rothschild, J. Light, P. Pulling, RM. Yu, T. Bates, DW (2001). 'Using computerized data to identify adverse drug events in outpatients.' *Journal of the American Medical Information Association,* 8(3): 254–266.

Hripcsak, G. Friedman, C. Alderson, PO. DuMouchel, W. Johnson, SB. Clayton, PD (1995). 'Unlocking clinical data from narrative reports: a study of natural language processing.' *Annals of Internal Medicine,* 122(9): 681–688.

Institute of Medicine (1999). *To err is human: building a safer health system.* Washington, DC: National Academies Press.

Institute of Medicine (2001). *Crossing the quality chasm. A new health system for the 21st century.* Washington, DC: National Academies Press.

Institute of Medicine (2002). *Unequal treatment. Confronting racial and ethnic disparities in health care.* Washington, DC: National Academies Press.

Jha, AK. Ferris, TG. Donelan, K. DesRoches, C. Shields, A. Rosenbaum, S. Blumenthal, D (2006). 'How common are electronic health records in the United States? A summary of the evidence.' *Health Affairs (Millwood),* 25(6): w496–507.

Jha, AK. Li, Z. Orav, EJ. Epstein, AM (2005). 'Care in U.S. hospitals – the Hospital Quality Alliance program.' *New England Journal of Medicine,* 353(3): 265–274.

Kamoie, B. Hodge, JG Jr (2004). 'HIPAA's implications for public health policy and practice: guidance from the CDC.' *Public Health Reports,* 119(2): 216–219.

Kaushal, R. Bates, DW. Poon, EG. Jha, AK. Blumenthal, D (2005). 'Functional gaps in attaining a national health information network.' *Health Affairs (Millwood),* 24(5): 1281–1289.

Kaushal, R. Blumenthal, D. Poon, EG. Jha, AK. Franz, C. Middleton, B. Glaser, J. Kuperman, G. Christino, M. Fernandopulle, R. Newhouse, JP. Bates, DW (2005a). 'The costs of a national health information network.' *Annals of Internal Medicine,* 143(3): 165–173.

Krieger, N. Chen, JT. Waterman, PD. Rehkopf, DH. Subramanian, SV (2003). 'Race/ethnicity, gender, and monitoring socioeconomic gradients in health: a comparison of area-based socioeconomic measures – the public health disparities geocoding project.' *American Journal of Public Health,* 93(10): 1655–1671.

McCarthy, BD. Yood, MU. Boohaker, EA. Ward, RE. Rebner, M. Johnson, CC (1996). 'Inadequate follow-up of abnormal mammograms.' *American Journal of Preventive Medicine,* 12(4): 282–288.

McDonald, CJ (1997). 'The barriers to electronic medical record systems and how to overcome them.' *Journal of the American Medical Informatics Association,* 4(3): 213–221.

Murff, HJ. Forster, AJ. Peterson, JF. Fiskio, JM. Heiman, HL. Bates, DW (2003). 'Electronically screening discharge summaries for adverse medical events.' *Journal of the American Medical Informatics Association,* 10(4): 339–350.

Nerenz, DR. Currier, C (2004). Collection of data on race/ethnicity by health plans, hospitals and medical groups. In: Ver Ploeg, M. Perrin, E (eds.). *Eliminating health disparities: measurement and data needs.* Washington, DC: National Academies Press.

O'Toole, MF. Kmetik, KS. Bossley, H. Cahill, JM. Kotsos, TP. Schwamberger, PA. Bufalino, VJ (2005). 'Electronic health record systems: the vehicle for implementing performance measures.' *American Heart Hospital Journal,* 3(2): 88–93.

Persell, SD. Wright, JM. Thompson, JA. Kmetik, KS. Baker, DW (2006). 'Assessing the validity of national quality measures for coronary artery disease using an electronic health record.' *Archives of Internal Medicine,* 166(20): 2272–2277.

Poon, EG. Blumenthal, D. Jaggi, T. Honour, MM. Bates, DW. Kaushal, R (2004). 'Overcoming barriers to adopting and implementing computerized physician order entry systems in U.S. hospitals.' *Health Affairs (Millwood),* 23(4): 184–190.

Poon, EG. Gandhi, TK. Sequist, TD. Murff, HJ. Karson, AS. Bates, DW (2004a). '"I wish I had seen this test result earlier!" Dissatisfaction with test result management systems in primary care.' *Archives of Internal Medicine,* 164(20): 2223–2228.

Porcheret, M. Hughes, R. Evans, D. Jordan, K. Whitehurst, T. Ogden, H. Croft, P. (2004). 'Data quality of general practice electronic health records: the impact of a program of assessments, feedback, and training.' *Journal of the American Medical Informatics Association,* 11(1): 78–86.

Rogers, EM (2003). *Diffusion of innovations, fifth edition.* New York: Free Press.

Rouf, E. Whittle, J. Lu, N. Schwartz, MD (2007). 'Computers in the exam room: differences in physician-patient interaction may be due to physician experience.' *Journal of General Internal Medicine,* 22(1): 43–48.

Roy, CL. Poon, EG. Karson, AS. Ladak-Merchant, Z. Johnson, RE. Maviglia, SM. Gandhi, TK (2005). 'Patient safety concerns arising from test results that return after hospital discharge.' *Annals of Internal Medicine,* 143(2): 121–128.

Schoen, C. Osborn, R. Huynh, PT. Doty, M. Peugh, J. Zapert, K (2006). 'On the front lines of care: primary care doctors' office systems, experiences, and views in seven countries.' *Health Affairs (Millwood),* 25(6): 555–571.

Scott, JT. Rundall, TG. Vogt, TM. Hsu, J (2005). 'Kaiser Permanente's experience of implementing an electronic medical record: a qualitative study.' *British Medical Journal,* 331(7528): 1313–1316.

Sequist, TD. Schneider, EC (2006). 'Addressing racial and ethnic disparities in health care: using federal data to support local programs to eliminate disparities.' *Health Services Research,* 41(4 Pt 1): 1451–1468.

Sequist, TD. Adams, A. Zhang, F. Ross-Degnan, D. Ayanian, JZ (2006). 'Effect of quality improvement on racial disparities in diabetes care.' *Archives of Internal Medicine,* 166(6): 675–681.

Siika, AM. Rotich, JK. Simiyu, CJ. Kigotho, EM. Smith, FE. Sidle, JE. Wool-Kaloustian, K. Kimaiyo, SN. Nyandiko, WM. Hannan, TJ. Tierney, WM (2005). 'An electronic medical record system for ambulatory care of HIV-infected patients in Kenya.' *International Journal of Medical Informatics,* 74(5): 345–355.

Sittig, DF. Wright, A. Osheroff, JA. Middleton, B. Teich, JM. Ash, JS. Campbell, E. Bates, DW (2008). 'Grand challenges in clinical decision support.' *Journal of Biomedical Informatics,* 41(2): 387–392.

Smith, SP. Barefield, AC (2007). 'Patients meet technology: the newest in patient-centered care initiatives.' *The Health Care Manager (Frederick),* 26(4): 354–362.

Tang, PC. Ralston, M. Arrigotti, MF. Qureshi, L. Graham, J (2007). 'Comparison of methodologies for calculating quality measures based on administrative data versus clinical data from an electronic health record system: implications for performance measures.' *Journal of the American Medical Informatics Association,* 14(1): 10–15.

Trivedi, AN. Zaslavsky, AM. Schneider, EC. Ayanian, JZ (2005). 'Trends in the quality of care and racial disparities in Medicare managed care.' *New England Journal of Medicine,* 353(7): 692–700.

van Walraven, C. Raymond, M (2003). 'Population-based study of repeat laboratory testing.' *Clinical Chemistry,* 49(12): 1997–2005.

5.4 Incentives for health-care performance improvement

DOUGLAS A. CONRAD

Introduction

In March 2007, there were approximately 148 pay-for-performance programmes in the United States (The Leapfrog Group and Med-Vantage ® 2007). This marked increase (from thirty-nine in 2003) reflects the growing concern to seek increased value from the expenditures of health plans and organized health-care purchasers (predominantly government, private employers, unions, consumer groups, multiple-employer trusts). The General Medical Services Contract introduced in 2004 radically transformed the NHS in England, introducing 146 quality indicators to measure primary care team performance and encompassing 10 chronic conditions, care organization and patient experience. This new set of quality performance incentives offered general practice partnerships the potential to increase their annual income by as much as 25% (Roland 2004). Similarly, policymakers in continental Europe are moving toward strategic purchasing which optimizes population health through service mix, contract design, payment systems and choice of health care (Figueras et al. 2005).

When designing appropriate performance incentives, decision-makers must incorporate the varying socio-demographic, political, economic, cultural and organizational conditions that prevail in local, regional and national environments. The incentive options available in different polities and markets largely mirror the nature of funding and health-care delivery in those areas. Particulars of policy and practice are not only influenced substantially by specific circumstances but also (at any point in time) are somewhat 'path-dependent'– shaped by history (Figueras et al. 2005). Initial conditions are important.

This book examines multiple dimensions of health system performance: population health; financial protection; individual health outcomes; clinical quality and appropriateness; responsiveness; equity;

582

and health system productivity. Incentives are one type of policy instrument for improving performance and inevitably confront trade-offs among these objectives. For example, improvements in clinical quality and appropriateness and individual health outcomes might be accompanied by increased cost. Similarly, improvements in the efficiency of financial protection (e.g. risk-rating health insurance premiums) may compromise financial protection for high-risk population groups and raise questions of equity.

The theoretical framework predicts how distinct incentives will impact on health system performance. The empirical evidence review emphasizes the effects on cost and quality because incentives are generally targeted most directly to those two dimensions of performance.

Definitions and distinctions

Incentives can be conceptualized as reinforcers, stimuli or catalysts of behaviour. This chapter differentiates between incentives and other mechanisms designed to influence behaviour – measurement, information, reporting, rules, constraints and organizational structures. These interact with incentives but are not incentives per se. For example, performance measurement logically must precede application of a performance incentive but should not be confused with the incentive itself. Similarly, external (public) and internal performnce reports (e.g. peer comparisons within medical groups) may induce physicians to change behaviour in response to potential doctor-switching among patients in local markets or internal competition. Behaviour change can be motivated by the possible gain or loss in self-perceived or external reputation resulting from performance reports but the actual behavioural stimulus is the indirect dollar gain (or loss) from patient-switching or the internal psychological gain (or loss) associated with a change in reputation.

Theoretical framework

Incentives vary along several margins:

- nature of incentive (reward versus penalty)
- target entity (group or individual; provider or consumer)
- type (financial or non-financial, general versus selective)

- extrinsic versus intrinsic
- behaviour subject to incentive
- magnitude
- certainty of application (ex ante versus ex post)
- frequency and duration (short- versus long-term)
- base of comparison (relative versus absolute performance).

Nature of incentives: rewards versus penalties

In classic expected utility theory (Arrow 1963; von Neumann & Morgenstern 1944) risk-averse individuals will purchase insurance at above actuarially fair prices (i.e. when the premium reflects expected losses due to the risky event) – the excess premium reflecting risk aversion. An expected penalty will trigger a larger behavioural response (loss avoidance) than a reward of equal magnitude (gain-seeking).

Kahneman and Tversky (1979) found that the certainty effect (relative over-weighting of certain prospects compared to uncertain ones) drives decision-makers to weigh losses more heavily than similar size gains. Tversky and Kahneman (1986) noted that decision-makers tend to ignore common outcomes across prospects and focus on incremental gains or losses relative to their reference point. Incentive theory provides two important lessons: (i) penalties may be more powerful stimuli than rewards; (ii) the same decision-maker will gamble or seek insurance according to his/her initial point of reference and assessment of the probabilities and magnitudes of gain or loss.

Target entity

Other things being equal, a group-level incentive payment is a less powerful motivator of individual-level behaviour change than an individual-level incentive of identical expected amount for each individual. Individual agents tend to coast on the expected efforts of others unless there is an active monitoring or disciplinary mechanism. Accordingly, if the principal (e.g. medical group practice owner) wishes individual agents (e.g. physician employees or other owners) to perform well, individual incentives such as high-powered compensation tied to individual performance are critical to success (cf. Conrad et al. 2002; Gaynor & Gertler 1995). Gaynor and Gertler's work on physician productivity shows that physicians in larger groups are more responsive to high-powered (individual production-based) compensation, as might be expected if smaller groups are inherently more able to use informal monitoring and peer pressure to enforce productivity norms.

In contrast, group or team incentives are expected to induce better performance for tasks that require cooperation and coordination among individuals. Group incentives also dominate individual incentives when the desired behaviour involves organization-level structural change, e.g. adoption of IT, chronic disease registries or electronic health records. The basic principle is to incentivize at the level of the entity responsible for a given action and which stands to capture most directly the benefits and costs.

Types of incentive

There are two general types of incentives: financial and non-financial. In turn, these can be either general or selective. For example, 'pure' forms of health plan payment to medical practices (Gosden et al. 2000) – capitation, per episode of care/case, fee for service – are general, indirect financial incentives as they do not target a particular behaviour (cost per unit of service, service volume or clinical quality). Under pure capitation, physicians bear the full cost of services for each enrollee but receive no incremental dollars per service. Capitation thus encourages the lowest level of service volume per enrollee of all plan payment types. On the same reasoning, payment per case (e.g. hospital DRG rates) and per episode (package pricing for pre- and post-surgical care) induce somewhat higher levels of service; fee for service induces the highest (Conrad & Christianson 2004).

Individual physician compensation has subtler impacts within provider organizations. For example, the salaried non-owner physician will not directly realize the marginal revenues or marginal costs of his/her treatment decisions. With fee for service, non-owner physicians will directly capture those individual marginal revenues and their pro rata or individual share of marginal costs; owner-physicians will perceive the same marginal revenue incentive and even stronger marginal cost incentive. A fixed salary might create even stronger volume incentives if the salaried physician attaches a sufficiently high decision weight to marginal health benefits delivered to patients versus marginal profit per unit under fee for service. This matches Kralewski et al's (2000) findings in medical group practices.

The ownership status of the individual physician also affects economic incentives. The owner is a *residual claimant* of practice net income, i.e. captures a share of after-tax, after-cost practice returns (Fama & Jensen 1998). Thus, independent of the general compensation method (salary, fee for service or some hybrid), owners will perceive a high-powered individual incentive to manage revenues and costs. Moreover, ownership confers a non-financial, *reputational* incentive to take actions that will enhance the brand name of the practice, such as the optimization of quality, access, cost and equity.

As discussed in Chapter 5.2, public performance reporting also acts as an indirect economic incentive. The improved reputation that results from credible public performance reporting is a capital asset. Reputation has psychological value to the individual as well as economic value to the individual provider or organization. A better reputation stimulates patient demand and thus confers a competitive advantage, allowing higher prices and higher net income.

Selective incentives (e.g. incremental payments for immunization or screening tests) might be expected to induce a stronger response in the targeted behaviour than a general incentive of equivalent size. For example, capitation payment encourages general efforts in health maintenance and promotion but direct fee-for-service increments for particular preventive and health promotion activities are more likely to lead to increases in those activities.

In economic theory, non-financial incentives are less efficient reinforcers than financial incentives. Whereas the dollar value of a financial reward is identical across persons and organizations, the utility of non-financial incentives such as recognition, administrative simplification and IT grants varies by individual and by organizational context. For example, direct transfer of dollars (cash subsidy) leads to greater improvement in the welfare of the recipient than an in-kind subsidy that costs the grantor the same. The recipient receives more advantage from allocating the dollar between different goods and services according to his/her personal preferences than from a dollar's worth of one particular commodity. Analogously, a producer would rather receive a dollar in subsidy to allocate between different inputs of capital and labour than a subsidy for a dollar's worth of labour. Selective contingent incentives alter the relative price of different activities while general non-contingent incentives provide general rewards or penalties that influence behaviour only indirectly.

Extrinsic and intrinsic incentives

Traditional microeconomic theory does not imply any direct effect of external incentives (such as financial rewards or penalties) on the internal motivation of the individual. The neoclassical model takes consumers' tastes and preferences as given and demonstrates that (irrespective of those subjective values and holding consumer wealth constant) lowering the relative price of any given activity or service will induce the consumer to use more of it. In this model, tastes and personal values such as intrinsic motivation are independent of market conditions and relative prices, for example. Financial rewards and penalties alter the relative prices of behaviour but will not directly affect intrinsic incentives for the same behaviours. Thus, financial incentives for quality improvement would not directly reduce (or accentuate) physicians' inherent interest in optimizing the health benefits for patients.

There are at least two reasons to be cautious about such a conclusion. First, relative price changes (incremental rewards or penalties) have income effects on behaviour by increasing or decreasing provider income. In the balance between net income and the intrinsic payoffs of patient health benefit, as net income rises financial rewards will strengthen the intrinsic motivation of providers who favour patient benefit whereas penalties will weaken it. There is no way to know a priori whether financial rewards reinforce or weaken the provider's intrinsic valuation of patient benefit (Congelton 1991; Frey 1997).

Second, cognitive psychology provides strong evidence that extrinsic incentives (financial and non-financial) crowd out intrinsic motivation (Kohn 1999). Deci et al's (1999) meta-analysis of 128 studies found that all forms of reward – whether contingent on engagement in the activity, completion or level of performance – significantly reduced free-choice intrinsic motivation. Positive feedback (without additional reward) led to increased levels of the activity (free-choice behaviour) as well as self-reported interest in the activity. Deci and Ryan (1985) concluded:

> ... by far the most detrimental type of performance-contingent rewards – indeed, the most detrimental type of rewards – is one that is commonly used in applied settings, namely, one in which rewards are administered as a direct function of people's performance. If people do superlatively, they get large rewards,

but if they do not display optimal performance, they get smaller rewards.

These experimental findings do not imply that financial (and non-financial) incentives will fail to direct behaviour towards the target in the short-term. However, they do raise caution regarding potential long-term negative effects on intrinsic motivation, especially if rewards are accompanied by increased monitoring, assessment and peer competition (Deci & Ryan 1985). The cognitive psychology and industrial psychology literature demonstrates the importance of supporting what Amabile and Kramer (2007) call 'inner work life' – enabling people to progress in their work and treating them decently. Deci and Ryan (1985) argue that intrinsic motivation is grounded in psychological needs for autonomy and competence. Incentive structures that conform to these values would be less likely to undermine intrinsic motivation and are particularly salient for self-regulating professions such as medicine.

Behaviour targeted by the incentive

Narrowly circumscribed incentives oriented on a few discrete tasks or performance measures risk encouraging providers to sub-optimize by multi-tasking or treating to the test (Holmstrom & Milgrom 1991). Such incentives also encourage cream-skimming, i.e. selecting patients for whom it is inherently easier to achieve good performance. Eggleston (2005) demonstrates that mixed payment systems of partial capitation and fee for service will improve performance when incentive contracts fail to specify the full range of provider behaviours necessary to achieve optimal patient outcomes by: (i) muting the adverse effects of incomplete pay-for-performance incentives; and (ii) balancing the cost control incentives of capitation with the quality-promoting potential of fee-for-service payment.

Providers may have differing valuations of patient health benefit relative to net income. Jack (2005) has shown that the best balance between greater provider participation and lower cost to the payer is likely to be achieved by offering provider groups an array of payment contracts with varying degrees of supply side cost-sharing (capitation = 100% provider cost-share; fee-for-service reimbursement approximates 0% cost-share). Providers with higher marginal valuation for patient benefit will select a higher proportion of fee-for-service payment; those who place greater weight on net income will favour capitation. For example, between 1991 and 1999 general practices in the United Kingdom had the option to become fundholders, receiving a budget to pay for non-emergency, hospital-based specialty care. This voluntary contracting regime captures two points along Jack's schema as fundholding general practices accept partial capitation and non-fundholding practices continue with no direct referral incentives (effectively a type of fee for service). Having adjusted for physician self-selection, Dusheiko et al. (2006) found that fundholding was related to lower hospital admission rates, as expected.

Mixed payment models are designed to address two interrelated performance goals – maximum patient health benefit at least cost. To the extent that policy-makers wish to achieve goals of population access to health benefits and equity, tools other than provider incentives are likely to be more effective and efficient.

Finally, the performance measures that underlie incentives inevitably blend structure, process and outcomes of care (Conrad & Christianson 2004; Kuhn 2003; Young & Conrad 2007). Chalkley and Khalil (2005) show that outcomes-based incentives may be superior when patients are not knowledgeable about their own medical conditions and costs of care but do respond to perceived differences in treatment. Similarly, they demonstrate that outcomes-based payment may be superior for not-for-profit providers who are more intrinsically motivated by patient health benefit.

Policy- and decision-makers deciding on the mix of structure, process and outcome to incentivize must balance the cost and gains of achieving various policy goals. The approach is two-fold (Prendergast 1999):

1. Craft incentives that induce providers not only to treat patients cost-effectively but also, in turn, to reveal their superior information about costs and benefits of different preventive, diagnostic and treatment regimens (incentive compatibility).
2. Pay amounts sufficient at the margin to make providers at least as well off under the incentive regime as they were before (participation constraint).

These two conditions can be satisfied best by predominantly incentivizing behaviour (structure and processes of care) under the proximate control of providers and also including outcomes in the incentive formulae. On this logic, payment formulae weight the structures and processes chosen as behavioural targets positively (according to the present value of their expected benefits net of costs) and negatively (according to the errors in estimating those net benefits). Other things being equal, process and structure measures strongly related to patient health outcomes (i.e. with large and statistically significant estimated dose-response coefficients) would receive more weight, as would outcome measures that a provider can control more directly and cost-effectively. Conversely, for a given dose-response, measures with less estimating precision would be weighted less in the incentive. In practice, this decision rule places substantial demands on the clinical and economic evidence base but the public, providers and policy-makers should demand nothing less.

Magnitude of incentive

The size of an incentive is optimized by balancing two factors. First, the incentive payment must cover a provider's marginal costs for adjusting behaviour in the targeted direction (Avery & Schultz 2007). This will motivate provider response. There is a subsidiary benefit from tailoring the size of the incentive payment to the marginal cost of performance improvement. When incremental returns (revenues minus costs) are equalized approximately across different dimensions of performance (cost control, clinical effectiveness [quality], patient satisfaction) this attenuates providers' tendency to treat to the test or optimize only certain behaviours. Second, payment should not be higher than is necessary to induce provider participation in the incentive programme. This will contain programme costs by minimizing the 'rents' (payments above marginal cost) captured by providers. Of course, this optimal trade-off is easier to state than to achieve.

Certainty of incentive application

The power of incentives is closely tied to their certainty; the signal-to-noise ratio of incentives is diminished by uncertainty regarding their size, behaviours rewarded, achievability and duration. It is especially important to be clear about the expected duration of incentives and the achievability of underlying performance targets. Incentives that are expected to be short-term and/or implausible will not stimulate behaviour change, even if they are large and broad-gauged.

Frequency and duration

In principle, more frequent incentive payments will be stronger reinforcers. This reflects the heightened salience that accompanies increased frequency. Also, greater frequency connects reward or penalty more proximately to behaviour and raises the present value of the incentive revenue. The useful life of the provider's investment in quality and efficiency improvement lengthens as the expected duration of the incentive increases, thereby enhancing the expected return on those investments. Moreover, as Kohn (1999) has argued, long-term incentives pose a lesser risk to long-term intrinsic motivation.

Base of comparison: relative versus absolute performance measures

Relative performance measures directly reveal comparative information on providers and, if disclosed publicly, potentially heighten competition. Transparent identification of performance differences also accentuates reputational incentives. Comparative performance incentives adjust implicitly for exogenous shocks common to providers in the same area (e.g. changes in input prices, shifts in area socio-demographics).

The aggregate budget for relative performance incentive payments is fixed by policy and therefore is actuarially predictable (Rosenthal & Dudley 2007). Once the eligible pool of providers is fixed and the structure of rewards and/or penalties is determined then the corresponding incentive budget is known with certainty for a given period. For example, consider an eligible panel of 1000 primary care providers participating in an incentive budget which pays $ 2000 to each provider in the top-performing decile and $ 1000 per provider in the second (80th-89th percentile). In this case the incentive budget equals $ 20 000 (2000 X 10) + $ 10 000 (1000 X 10), or $ 30 000. However, this budgetary certainty is accompanied by uncertainty regarding peer performance which is beyond the individual provider's control. Major gains in quality or cost control may still fall short of the incentive threshold if others achieve even better performance.

Whether payments are increased continuously along a gradient of performance improvement or based on exceeding a specific threshold, absolute performance-based incentives offer providers greater control in attaining the reward. Between the two absolute incentive structures, continuously increasing incentive payments create stronger motivation by avoiding the all-or-nothing property of specific thresholds. Continuously increasing incentive payments account for increasing marginal costs for achieving higher levels of performance (Avery & Schultz 2007; Conrad et al. 2006), strengthening their incentive properties in comparison to relative performance schema. The superior incentive power of absolute performance-based rewards and penalties must be weighed against the greater actuarial uncertainty for incentive payers who must predict the distribution of provider performance and consequent level of payout.

Empirical evidence on performance incentives

This chapter examines performance incentives at two levels. The first is between a health plan (e.g. private insurer in the United States; sickness or statutory health funds in Germany or the Netherlands; general practice partnerships in the United Kingdom) and a provider organization (e.g. medical group practice or independent practice association in the United States; primary care team or general practice fundholder in the United Kingdom). The second is between a provider organization and an individual provider in all health systems. Incentives for the former are determined by health plan payment to providers (general incentives of fee for service, case rates, capitation or a hybrid, coupled with selective incentives for quality or efficiency). For the latter, within the provider organizations, individual physician compensation methods and ownership forms determine the incentive structure.

Health plan to provider organization incentives

The core of this chapter is devoted to selective incentives for quality performance but also presents evidence of how capitation, per case and fee-for-service payments affect physician behaviour. These general incentives establish the overall payment framework within which specific incentives are applied. To date, no published research has compared the effects of selective quality incentives within capitation, per case and fee-for-service payment regimes. Early pay-for-performance incentives have been applied principally in health maintenance organizations (HMOs). They mitigate the problem of attribution by assigning each enrollee to a particular practice organization or individual provider. This subsection concentrates on the main effects on physician behaviour of general health plan payment methods because the pay-for-performance evidence base does not allow the analyst to isolate interaction effects between general payment methods and selective incentives.

The evidence base in this domain is summarized in two major review papers (Chaix-Couturier et al. 2000; Gosden et al. 2000) and Miller and Luft's (1997 & 2002) reviews in the United States. Chaix-Couturier et al. report that fundholding in the United Kingdom has had no impact on specialist referral or hospital admission rates among general practitioners (Coulter & Bradlow 1993) but has produced consistent reductions in drugs per prescription (Bradlow & Coulter 1993; Himmel et al. 1997; Maxwell et al. 1993; Whynes et al. 1995; Wilson et al. 1996). The shift from fee for service to fundholding led to fewer referrals for elective surgery and to private clinics. Relative to fee for service, capitation payment reduced the number of hospital days by up to 80%.

Chaix-Couturier et al. (2000) synthesized the results of several randomized trials of general financial incentives. Among second and third year paediatric residents Hickson et al. (1987) tested the effect of \$ 2 per patient visit (fee for service) against a \$ 20 per month salary – payment levels calibrated to yield equal expected income per group, based on historical use rates. The fee-for-service group had significantly more visits per patient; saw their own patients more often (increased continuity); and their patients had fewer emergency room visits. Davidson et al. (1992) assessed the effects of fee-for-service versus capitation (prepaid) payment among physicians participating in the Children's Medicaid programme. Each physician was assigned responsibility for a panel of children. The prepaid physicians' patients had fewer primary care visits; fewer visits to non-primary care office-based specialists; and fewer emergency visits. Assessing the effects of payment method on the care of elderly persons receiving Medicaid, Lurie et al. (1994) found significantly fewer physician visits and inpatient stays and marginally better self-reported general health (p<.06) and well-being (p <.07) in the capitation group.

Gosden et al. (2000) summarized two other studies of general incentives not captured in the Chaix-Couturier et al. (2000) review. Krasnik et al. (1990) conducted a controlled before and after study of general practitioners in Copenhagen whose remuneration was changed from capitation to mixed fee for service and capitation. Compared to control practices continuing on mixed fee for service/capitation payment, those shifting from capitation to mixed fee for service/capitation demonstrated a significant rise in face-to-face consultations per 1000 patients in the initial six months, followed by a decline in the second six months to rates insignificantly different from baseline. Referrals to specialists and hospital admissions declined more for the intervention group – significantly so by the second six-month period. Compared to the controls, telephone consultations increased significantly more for the intervention group in both post-periods, as did the rate of diagnostic and curative services. Hutchison et al. (1996) found no significant change in hospital-utilization rates among patients of primary care physicians changing from fee for service to capitation (with an additional incentive payment for low hospital-utilization rates) compared to physicians continuing on a fee-for-service basis.

Physician organization-based (group-level) selective incentive studies

This section summarizes the findings of the three most recent structured reviews of the literature on the effects of quality incentives on physician behaviour (Frolich et al 2007; Petersen et al. 2006; Rosenthal & Frank 2006). These are augmented by studies published since the period spanned by those reviews and by earlier literature reviews covering a broader scope of performance measures.

Petersen et al's (2006) review is the most comprehensive, highlighting the effects of selective payment incentives on clinical quality and, secondarily, on access. Overall, they report that explicit quality incentives produced statistically significant quality improvement in two of nine studies at the provider organization level (Christensen et al. 2000; Kouides et al. 1998) and a partial effect in five other studies, i.e. some but not all provider behaviours showed significant improvement (Casalino et al. 2003; Clark et al. 1995; McMenamin et al. 2003; Rosenthal et al. 2005; Roski et al. 2003). Kouides et al. (1998) reported the positive effects on immunization rates of a stepped bonus per influenza immunization; Christensen et al. (2000) showed an increase in cognitive services interventions by pharmacists in response to enhanced fee for service. Two studies found that group bonuses had no statistically significant effect on cancer screening for women aged fifty or more (Hillman et al. 1998); or on paediatric immunization and well-child visit rates (Hillman et al. 1999).

A recent study of the pay-for-performance incentives applied by Partners Community HealthCare in Massachusetts (Levin-Scherz et al. 2006) demonstrated partial effects. Potential for bonus distribution and return of withholds was associated with increased development of medical management programmes and improved diabetes care processes but no significant impact on paediatric asthma measures.

The financial incentive demonstration of largest scope and incentive size is represented by the General Medical Services contract enacted in the United Kingdom in 2004 (Doran et al. 2006). The results of this new Quality and Outcomes Framework are discussed in more detail in Chapter 4.1 (Lester and Roland 2009). On balance, performance incentives were related to a modest increase in the improvement rate of quality of care (Campbell et al. 2007).

Hospital-based selective incentive studies

Four recent studies of hospital quality incentives complement the physician organization-level studies summarized above. Lindenauer et al. (2007) assessed differential changes in adherence to process quality measures for 10 conditions and 4 composite quality scores in 207 hospitals participating voluntarily in public quality reporting plus pay-for-performance financial incentives and in 406 hospitals participating only in the public reporting initiative. Participating hospitals were part of the CMS/Premier Hospital Quality Incentive Demonstration (HQID). Under this national demonstration programme Medicare hospital inpatient case rates would be increased by 1% for hospitals performing at the 80th-89th percentile and 2% for those at or above the 90th percentile. In comparison with the control group, pay-for-performance hospitals improved significantly more on process measures for acute myocardial infarction; heart failure; pneumonia; and a composite of all ten measures. Baseline performance was inversely associated with improvement – in pay-for-performance hospitals, the composite of all ten measures improved by 16.1% in those with the lowest quintile of baseline performance and 1.9% for those in the highest quintile (P<0.001). After adjustments for differences in baseline performance and other hospital characteristics, pay for performance was associated with improvements ranging from 2.6% to 4.1% over the two-year period.

Glickman et al. (2007) examined a subpopulation of acute myocardial infarction patients (those with non-ST-segment elevation) in hospitals participating in CRUSADE, a voluntary quality improvement initiative of the American College of Cardiology and the American Heart Association. They compared processes of care and outcomes for the 54 CRUSADE hospitals participating in the CMS/Premier HQID with those of the 446 non-participating CRUSADE hospitals (the controls). The authors found no significant differences in overall improvement between the incentive and control hospitals. However, incentive hospitals did achieve (small but statistically significant) greater improvement than controls in two domains of adherence – aspirin at discharge and smoking cessation counselling. In parallel, the researchers assessed eight guideline-based measures not scored in the incentive programme and found no significant difference in improvement between the incentive and control group. The latter evidence is inconsistent with a hypothesis of treating to the test.

Grossbart's (2006) comparative study of participating pay-for-performance and public reporting only hospitals, affiliated with the Catholic Healthcare Partners health system, identified somewhat weaker effects of the HQID programme. Overall quality scores improved 2.6% more in pay-for-performance incentive hospitals than in other participant (control) hospitals. However, differences were seen solely among congestive heart failure patients, with no significant differences for those with acute myocardial infarction or pneumonia.

A fourth study of hospital quality incentives estimated the cost effectiveness of a voluntary incentive programme adopted by Blue Cross Blue Shield of Michigan (Nahra et al. 2006). In years one to three this programme added up to 1.2% to the participating hospital's DRG (case) rate for the organization's degree of adherence to predetermined heart care guidelines (for acute myocardial infarction and congestive heart failure patients). In year 4 it added up to 2%, contingent on the hospital exceeding the median performance of participant hospitals. This incentive blends elements of relative and absolute performance criteria. There was no comparison group of hospitals but the authors estimated the cost effectiveness of the incentive programme by summing a programme's administrative costs and incentive payments and comparing these to the estimated QALYs gained by the changes in adherence to heart care guidelines. Nahra and colleagues (2006) concluded that improved guideline adherence saved between $ 12 967 and $30 081 in costs per QALY.

Individual physician-based selective incentive studies

Appraising the external incentives applied to the individual physician, Petersen et al. (2006) indicate that five out of six reviewed studies found significant positive or partial effects (Beaulieu & Horrigan 2005; Fairbrother et al. 1999 & 2001; Pourat et al. 2005; Safran et al. 2000). The initial study by Fairbrother et al. (1999) applied a bonus for improvement from baseline plus enhanced fee for service per immunization delivered. The authors concluded that the stepped bonus improved children's up-to-date immunization status but the enhanced fee-for-service incentive showed no significant effect. In a subsequent study, with an increased bonus for up-to-date immunizations, Fairbrother et al. (2001) reported significant positive effects for both the bonus and the enhanced fee for service.

Safran et al. (2000) conducted a cross-sectional survey of physicians in eight network/independent practice association HMOs. They found that physician financial incentives based on patient satisfaction were associated with higher patient ratings on two of the dimensions of care assessed (access to and comprehensiveness of care) but not to other rated dimensions (continuity, integration, clinical interaction, interpersonal treatment, trust). Pourat et al. (2005) conducted a cross-sectional survey of primary care physicians contracting with Medicaid HMOs in eight Californian counties with the highest rates of Chlamydia trachomatis infection and HMO enrolment. Sexually active females were screened for Chlamydia more often by physicians receiving a salary in conjunction with a quality of care incentive than those paid in other ways (capitation plus financial performance, salary plus productivity, salary and financial performance).

Beaulieu and Horrigan (2005) evaluated the impact of an annual bonus for attaining composite scores exceeding a predetermined target (or for achieving 50% improvement) of process and outcomes of medical care for diabetes patients. Physicians participating in the incentive programme also were provided with a diabetes registry and met in groups to discuss progress in achieving goals for improvement. Physician performance in the incentive group improved significantly over baseline for five of six process measures and two of three outcome measures.

The study did not formally test the difference-in-differences between the incentive and control groups, but the authors note, 'Improved performance in the study group is an order of magnitude greater than the improved performance in the control group' (Beaulieu & Horrigan 2005, p.1327). For example, changes in the percentage of patients with HbA1c levels ≤ 9.5 between the base year of 2001 and the end of the intervention period of 2002 were 13.9% and 1.8% for the intervention and control groups, respectively. Both absolute and percentage improvements in care process were inversely related to baseline performance. The researchers cautioned that the results could not distinguish explicitly between the effect of the financial incentive and the provision of a diabetes registry and group meetings for tracking progress.

In the sole peer-reviewed study of a relative performance incentive for primary care physicians, Young et al. (2007) evaluated the effect of a 5% withhold. A potential return of between 50% and 150% of the withheld contribution was dependent on the provider's ranking on measures of adherence to four process quality measures of caring for patients with diabetes. Except for a single first-year increase in eye examinations there were no significant differences in pre-intervention and post-intervention trends.

Unintended consequences of performance incentives

One salutary feature of the research on provider performance incentives in health care has been the attention paid to potential unintended consequences. This includes providers' sub-optimizing behaviour such as cream-skimming; stinting on care; or directing exclusive attention to measured performance, to the detriment of important but unmeasured dimensions of care (treating to the test).

Petersen et al. (2006) point to four studies indicating the unintended effects of incentives. Shen (2003) uncovered evidence suggestive of cream-skimming in a Medicaid programme for treating substance abuse. The analysis compared the probability of substance abuse programme clients being classified as 'most severe' by providers participating in performance-based contracting and providers who were not (the controls). They identified a drop of 7% among clients of participating providers and a rise of 2% among the control group. Three other studies (Fairbrother et al. 1999 & 2001; Roski et al. 2003) found that improved documentation in response to the financial incentive, rather than an increase in preventive services per se, was the source of the positive study findings.

Rosenthal and Frank (2006) cite other examples of unintended consequences. The state of Ohio created financial incentives for increased outreach to persons with severe mental illness – basing the extra payment on the number of such people identified by the provider. The researchers (Frank & Gaynor 1994) concluded that there were increases in the census of such persons identified per provider but found no significant increase in actual treatment for these individuals. A variety of other gaming responses have been documented:

- seemingly intentional miscoding of diagnoses, for provider and/or patient economic benefit (Wynia et al. 2000);
- upcoding of discharge diagnoses in order to enhance hospital reimbursement in response to the incentives of the Medicare hospital inpatient prospective payment system (Carter et al. 1990);
- favourable selection of patients and avoidance of high-cost patients under New York State Cardiac Surgery Reporting System, even with risk-adjustment to control for poorer outcomes of high-risk patients (Burack et al. 1999; Moscucci et al. 2005).

Evidence summary

This section has presented extant empirical research on performance incentives, including general payment incentives and selective incentives in the form of pay-for-performance. The paper's theoretical framework will be used briefly to summarize this evidence.

Nature of the incentive (reward versus penalty)

Empirical studies shed little light on whether penalties or rewards evoke a stronger behavioural response. However, available research does confirm that both negative sanctions and positive rewards induce provider responses in the expected direction. Interestingly, Strunk and

Hurley (2004) report that health plans tend to favour positive incentives (carrots) in lieu of penalties (sticks) in their pay-for-performance programmes.

Target entity (group or individual)

The evidence on which level of incentive exerts more powerful effects on performance is ambiguous. In summarizing the existing peer-reviewed literature, Petersen et al. (2006) observe that seven of nine studies of provider group-level incentives showed positive or partial effects on quality; five of six studies of individual-level studies found positive effects on quality. Frolich et al. (2007) indicated that positive effects were demonstrated in one of three group-level randomized trials and five of seven individual-level studies. Private HMOs appear to be mixing their strategies for levels of incentive (Rosenthal & Dudley 2007). Rosenthal et al. (2006) found that 14% of physician pay-for-performance programmes in commercial HMOs solely incentivize individual physician performance; 61% solely incentivize group-level performance; and the remaining 25% blend the two approaches. Where system failure (rather than individual clinician's deficiencies) is the major source of quality problems, group incentives would be expected to dominate those for individuals, as these figures reflect.

Type of incentive

Extant studies demonstrate that behaviour is influenced by general payment system-level incentives (fee for service, per case, capitation), selective pay for performance and indirect incentives of public reporting. Reviews by Miller and Luft (1997 & 2002) confirm that HMOs' system-level capitation incentives produce somewhat lesser use of hospitals and other expensive resources than do indemnity payments based on fee for service. HMO and non-HMO settings deliver roughly comparable quality of care levels but HMO enrollees report inferior experience on many measures of access to care and lower levels of satisfaction with certain domains, including physician-patient interaction (Miller & Luft 2002). The results for capitation payment in Europe and fundholding in the United Kingdom are consistent with studies in the United States (cf. Gosden et al. 2000; Mossialos et al. 2005).

Extrinsic incentives: effects on intrinsic motivation

No peer-reviewed research of pay-for-performance programmes in health care has estimated the direct impact of selective financial incentives on provider altruism in serving patient needs. Certain forms of sub-optimizing behaviour in response to pay for performance are consistent with diminution in intrinsic motivation: 'treating to the test' (Frank & Gaynor 1994) or avoiding high-cost, low-margin patients (Burack et al. 1999; Moscucci et al. 2005; Shen 2003). At best, these illustrations provide weak evidence of extrinsic rewards crowding out internal aspirations for patient benefit – as Rosenthal and Frank (2006) argue, there are no data to suggest that the pre-incentive overall level of treatment benefits minus costs was superior to the post-incentive level. Glickman et al. (2007) also offer an important counter-example to the posited trade-off of intrinsic for extrinsic reward – non-measured domains of clinical quality did not decline even as certain rewarded types of performance improved.

Nature of behaviour subject to incentive

The first generation of pay-for-performance programmes for physicians emphasized process measures (Petersen et al. 2006) but that is changing. By 2006 over 94% of twenty-four early adopters of pay for performance were using outcomes measures, compared to 59% in 2003 (Rosenthal et al. 2007). No peer-reviewed papers made direct comparisons of outcome- and process-based incentives' effects on actual provider behaviour. However, changes in incentive structure (towards more emphasis on outcomes) constitute survivorship evidence in support of blending outcomes and process incentives.

Only one study (Young et al. 2007) has explicitly evaluated the impact of a relative performance incentive for individual physicians but the authors report no significant effect. Existing pay-for-performance programmes for individual physicians and medical groups favour absolute performance thresholds – 70% of the programmes surveyed by Rosenthal and Dudley (2007). The same survey found that 25% favour pay for improvement, so the predominant pattern in physician pay for performance is one of absolute performance criteria rather than rankings.

Prior studies of physician performance incentives (and the programmes themselves) have targeted preventive services and chronic care. The former reflect the predominance of HMOs in the first generation of programmes; the latter capture the major quality improvement and cost challenges in primary care practice. These clinical domains may offer the most easily achievable quality and efficiency gains but current trends manifest a broadening of the scope of incentives to encompass cost-efficiency, IT and patient experience (Rosenthal & Dudley 2007), as well as specialty practice (Rosenthal et al. 2006).

Incentive size
As Frolich et al. (2007) affirm, previous studies have not identified the dose-response relationship between incentives and the medical care processes or outcomes. The diverse nature of the incentives evaluated and the limited range of variation in the magnitude of any one type (e.g. hospital or medical group, process or outcome, chronic or acute condition) precludes the estimation of robust, precise incentive effects. Petersen et al. (2006) postulate that no or small effects of incentives in several studies (Hillman et al. 1998 & 1999; Kouides et al. 1998) are at least partially attributable to the smallness of the incremental payments.

By combining data on the size of pay-for-performance incentive payments with evidence that previously evaluated programmes have led to modest but typically statistically significant performance improvement it is possible to establish a range for the minimum incentive required to achieve gains. For example, Baker and Carter's (2005) survey of national pay-for-performance programmes indicates that the maximum physician performance bonus was 9%. Rosenthal et al's (2007) look-back interviews of early pay-for-performance adopters reveal that the average physician performance bonus in their sample was 2.3% of total payment. This 2%-9% range in incentive size probably represents an array of tipping points for the first stage of modest change in provider behaviour.

Certainty, frequency and duration of incentive
State-of-the-art empirical work on health-care performance incentives cannot yield direct estimates of the impact of uncertainty in weakening provider response to incentives. Also, available evidence does not allow assessment of the incremental effects on performance of

increased frequency or duration of incentive payment. However, some clues emerge from a small sample of diverse studies. Petersen et al. (2006) indicate that end-of-year payments may contribute to lack of awareness and salience of the bonus, as exhibited in the Hillman et al. (1999) analysis of a paediatric immunization and well-child visit incentive programme. Similarly, lack of frequent performance feedback seemed to inhibit performance improvement in the smoking cessation incentive programme evaluated by Roski et al. (2003).

With no studies of incentive duration, it is possible only to speculate on the size of the boost in quality and efficiency that might be achieved by establishing incentives that would be predictable and endure over a timeframe sufficiently long to prompt providers to make sustained investments in improved clinical infrastructure and care processes.

Implications for research and policy in performance incentive design

This chapter has identified several remaining challenges for empirical research. The research community should develop study designs to differentiate more clearly the performance effects of: (i) distinct types of incentives (financial and non-financial); (ii) group- versus individual-level incentive mechanisms; (iii) external rewards and intrinsic motivation; (iv) process versus outcome measures; (v) varying sizes of incentive payment; and (vi) differences in the certainty, frequency and duration of incentives.

It is imperative to perform side-by-side comparisons of incentives, differing along one dimension at a time. A mix of purposive and randomized controlled trials will be necessary to isolate each key dimension. Also, when experimenting with new incentive arrangements, it is critical that policy-makers collaborate with researchers to design proper pilot demonstrations and monitoring and evaluation mechanisms. This specificity will deliver more targeted information for policy-makers, executives and practitioners as they refine future performance incentives.

The empirical evidence reported in this chapter leads to certain general observations for policy-makers and the design of incentive mechanisms. First, pressures for cost containment in all types of health systems necessitate a type of dynamic budget neutrality in any new quality or cost incentives. Over the long run, resources available for new incentives are likely to be limited to the rate of growth in the population and input prices for medical care. Accordingly, it will not be possible to sustain incremental rewards for high-performing providers without dampening growth in payments to those attaining lower levels of quality and efficiency. Such reductions are less likely to be perceived as explicit penalties but will send a signal that there is a price premium for quality and efficiency. This reasoning also implies that marginal increases in the rewards for absolute performance are more likely to catalyse quality and cost improvement than relative performance-based incentives.

Second, a mix of group- and individual-level incentive structures will produce the best results, especially if both types are vetted carefully with the professionals and organizations concerned. Quality and efficiency problems are traceable to individual as well as systemic and organizational failures and both levels of structure and behaviour must be confronted. Considerations of sample size and attribution must be addressed in fashioning the optimal mix of organization- and individual-level incentives.

This writer considers that two substantial policy benefits can be achieved by tipping the balance in favour of group-level incentives. Firstly, organizational decision-makers are given maximal discretion to distribute incentives to individual providers in a manner that reflects group norms and practice priorities. This reinforces the salience and professional credibility of any incentive payment (or withhold). Secondly, by directing funds to the group the incentive payers facilitate improvements in the quality and efficiency infrastructure that are necessary conditions for performance improvement.

A third policy recommendation is to follow the natural evolution of incentive implementation. Specifically, process measures for performance incentives should be recalibrated periodically to ensure achievability and consistency with the state of the art. These should be combined with outcome measures that encourage providers to attain results.

Risk-adjustment of patient populations will be increasingly important to the technical and political sustainability of outcomes-based incentive payments. General incentives (as in capitation, per case and fee-for-service payment systems) also interact with selective pay-for-performance and performance reporting incentives. In particular, risk-adjusted and outcomes-adjusted capitation payment could significantly reinforce provider response to public reporting and pay-for-performance initiatives.

Different dimensions of performance necessitate distinct incentive structures. Preventive services may be incentivized best by mixing increased fee-for-service payments to individual clinicians with multi-year risk- and outcome-adjusted capitation contracts with the organization. Chronic care management is probably facilitated most effectively by quality-adjusted, salaried compensation to individual physicians, blended with team incentives and organizational capitation.

A substantial body of evidence reveals that significant quality and efficiency improvement is more likely to occur in organized practice settings (McGlynn 2007; Mehrotra et al. 2006; Rittenhouse et al. 2004). Consequently, incentive design should experiment with explicit subsidies for IT and implicit inducements for modest increases in practice scale. For example, implicit incentives for larger-scale practices could take the form of per-provider infrastructure grants that do not compensate small practices for their lack of scale economies in adopting and using advanced technology or in re-configuring practice infrastructure to improve quality or efficiency. Pay-for-performance and performance reporting initiatives targeted at the organization can create a much more robust infrastructure and context for performance improvement than individual physician incentives alone.

References

Amabile, TM. Kramer, SJ (2007). 'Inner work life: understanding the subtext of business performance.' *Harvard Business Review*, (1 May): pp.72–83.

Arrow, KJ (1963). 'Uncertainty and the welfare economics of medical care.' *American Economic Review*, 53(5): 941–973.

Avery, G. Schultz, J (2007). 'Regulation, financial incentives, and the production of quality.' *American Journal of Medical Quality*, 22(4): 265–273.

Baker, G. Carter, B (2005). *Provider pay-for-performance incentive programs: 2004 national study results*. San Francisco, CA: Med-Vantage, Inc.

Beaulieu, ND. Horrigan, DR (2005). 'Putting smart money to work for quality improvement.' *Health Services Research*, 40(5 Part 1): 1318–1334.

Bradlow, J. Coulter, A (1993). 'Effect of fundholding and indicative prescribing schemes on general practitioners' prescribing costs.' *British Medical Journal*, 307(6913): 1186–1189.

Burack, JH. Impellizzeri, P. Homel, P. Cunningham, JN Jr (1999). 'Public reporting of surgical mortality: a survey of New York cardiothoracic surgeons.' *Annals of Thoracic Surgery*, 68(4): 1195–1202.

Campbell, S. Reeves, D. Kontopantelis, E. Middleton, E. Sibbald, B. Roland, M (2007). 'Quality of primary care in England with the introduction of pay for performance.' *New England Journal of Medicine*, 357(2): 181–190.

Carter, GM. Newhouse, JP. Relles, DA (1990). 'How much change in the case-mix index is DRG creep?' *Journal of Health Economics*, 9(4): 411–428.

Casalino, L. Gillies, RR. Shortell, SM. Schmittdiel, JA. Bodenheimer, T. Robinson, JC. Rundall, T. Oswald, N. Schauffler, H. Wang, MC (2003). 'External incentives, information technology, and organized processes to improve health care quality for patients with chronic diseases.' *Journal of the American Medical Association*, 289(4): 434–441.

Chaix-Couturier, C. Durand-Zaleski, I. Jolly, D. Durieux, P (2000). 'Effects of financial incentives on medical practice: results from a systematic review of the literature and methodological issues.' *International Journal for Quality in Health Care*, 12(2): 133–142.

Chalkley, M. Khalil, F (2005). 'Third party purchasing of health services: patient choice and agency.' *Journal of Health Economics*, 24(6): 1132–1153.

Christensen, DB. Neil, N. Fassett, WE. Smith, DH. Holmes, G. Stergachis, A (2000). 'Frequency and characteristics of cognitive services provided in response to a financial incentive.' *Journal of the American Pharmacy Association*, 40(5): 609–617.

Clark, RE. Drake, RE. McHugo, GJ. Ackerson, TH (1995). 'Incentives for community treatment: mental illness management services.' *Medical Care*, 33(7): 729–738.

Congleton, RD (1991). 'The economic role of a work ethic.' *Journal of Economic Behavior and Organization*, 15(3): 365–385.

Conrad, DA. Christianson, JB (2004). 'Penetrating the "black box": financial incentives for enhancing the quality of physician services.' *Medical Care Research and Review*, 61(Special Suppl. 3): 37S–68S.

Conrad, DA. Sales, A. Liang, SY. Chaudhuri, A. Maynard, C. Pieper, L. Weinstein, L. Gans, D. Piland, N (2002). 'The impact of financial incentives on physician productivity in medical groups.' *Health Services Research*, 37(4): 885–906.

Conrad, DA. Saver, BG. Court, B. Health, S (2006). 'Paying physicians for quality: evidence and themes from the field.' *Joint Commission Journal on Quality and Patient Safety*, 32(8): 443–451.

Coulter, A. Bradlow, J (1993). 'Effect of NHS reforms on general practitioners' referral patterns.' *British Medical Journal*, 306(6875): 433–437.

Davidson, SM. Manheim, LM. Werner, SM. Hohlen, MM. Yudowsky, BK. Fleming, GV (1992). 'Prepayment with office-based physicians in publicly funded programs: results from the children's Medicaid program.' *Pediatrics*, 89(4 Pt 2): 761–767.

Deci, EL. Ryan, RM (1985). *Intrinsic motivation and self-determination in human behavior*. New York: Plenum.

Deci, EL. Koestner, R. Ryan, RM (1999). 'A meta-analytic review of experiments examining the effects of extrinsic rewards on intrinsic motivation.' *Psychological Bulletin*, 125(6): 627–668.

Doran, T. Fullwood, C. Gravelle, H. Reeves, D. Kontopantelis, E. Hiroeh, U. Roland, M (2006). 'Pay-for-performance programs in family practices in the United Kingdom.' *New England Journal of Medicine*, 355(4): 375–384.

Dusheiko, M. Gravelle, H. Jacobs, R. Smith, P (2006). 'The effect of financial incentives on gatekeeping doctors: evidence from a natural experiment.' *Journal of Health Economics*, 25(3): 449–478.

Eggleston, K (2005). 'Multitasking and mixed systems for provider payment.' *Journal of Health Economics*, 24(1): 211–223.

Fairbrother, G. Hanson, KL. Friedman, S. Kory, PD. Butts, GC (1999). 'The impact of physician bonuses, enhanced fees, and feedback on childhood immunization coverage rates.' *American Journal of Public Health*, 89(2): 171–175.

Fairbrother, G. Siegel, MJ. Friedman, S. Kory, PD. Butts, GC (2001). 'Impact of financial incentives on documented immunization rates in the inner city: results of a randomized controlled trial.' *Ambulatory Pediatrics*, 1(4): 206–212.

Fama, E. Jensen, M (1998). Agency problems and residual claims. In: Jensen, MC. *Foundations of Organizational Strategy*. Cambridge, MA: Harvard University Press: pp.153–174.

Figueras, J. Robinson, R. Jakubowski, E (2005). Purchasing to improve health system performance: drawing the lessons. In: Figueras, J (ed.). *Purchasing to improve health systems performance*. Maidenhead: Open University Press: pp.44–80.

Frank, RG. Gaynor, M (1994). 'Organizational failure and transfers in the public sector: evidence from an experiment in the financing of mental health care.' *Journal of Human Resources*, 29(1): 108–125.

Frey, BS (1997). 'On the relationship between intrinsic and extrinsic work motivation.' *International Journal of Industrial Organization,* 15(4): 427–439.

Frolich, A. Talavera, JA. Broadhead, P. Dudley, RA (2007). 'A behavioral model of clinician responses to incentives to improve quality.' *Health Policy,* 80(1): 179–193.

Gaynor, M. Gertler, P (1995). 'Moral hazard and risk-spreading in partnerships.' *RAND Journal of Economics,* 26(4): 591–613.

Glickman, SW. Ou, FS. DeLong, ER. Roe, MT. Lytle, BL. Mulgund, J. Rumsfeld, JS. Gibler, WB. Ohman, EM. Schulman, KA. Peterson, ED (2007). 'Pay for performance, quality of care, and outcomes in acute myocardial infarction.' *Journal of the American Medical Association,* 297(21): 2373–2380.

Gosden, T. Forland, F. Kristiansen, IS. Sutton, M. Leese, B. Giuffrida, A. Sergison, M. Pederson, L (2000). 'Capitation, salary, fee-for-service and mixed systems of payment: effects on the behavior of primary care physicians (review).' *Cochrane Database of Systematic Reviews (online),* (3): CD002215.

Grossbart, SR (2006). 'What's the return? Assessing the effect of "pay-for-performance" initiatives on the quality of care delivery.' *Medical Care Research and Review,* 63(Special Suppl. 1): 29S–48S.

Hickson, GB. Altemeier, WA. Perrin, JM (1987). 'Physician reimbursement by salary or fee-for-service: effect on physician practice behavior in a randomized prospective study.' *Pediatrics,* 80(3): 344–350.

Hillman, AL. Ripley, K. Goldfarb, N. Nuamah, I. Lusk, E (1998). 'Physician financial incentives and feedback: failure to increase cancer screening in Medicaid managed care.' *American Journal of Public Health,* 88(11): 1699–1701.

Hillman, AL. Ripley, K. Goldfarb, N. Nuamah, I. Weiner, J. Lusk, E (1999). 'The use of physician financial incentives and feedback to improve pediatric preventive care in Medicaid managed care.' *Pediatrics,* 104(4): 931–935.

Himmel, W. Kron, M. Thies-Zajonc, S. Kochen, M (1997). 'Changes in drug prescribing under the Public Health Reform Law - a survey of general practitioners' attitudes in East and West Germany.' *International Journal of Clinical Pharmacology and Therapeutics,* 35(4): 164–169.

Holmstrom, B. Milgrom, P (1991). 'Multitask principal-agent analyses: incentive contracts, asset ownership, and job design.' *Journal of Law, Economics, and Organization,* 7(Special Issue): 24–52.

Hutchison, B. Birch, S. Hurley, J. Lomas, J. Stratford-Devai, F (1996). 'Do physician payment mechanisms affect hospital utilisation?

A study of health services organizations in Ontario.' *Canadian Medical Association Journal*, 154(5): 653–661.

Jack, W (2005). 'Purchasing health care services from providers with unknown altruism.' *Journal of Health Economics*, 24(1): 73–93.

Kahneman, D. Tversky, A (1979). 'Prospect theory: an analysis of decision under risk.' *Econometrica*, 47(2): 263–291.

Kohn, A (1999). *Punished by rewards: the trouble with gold stars, incentive plans, A's, praise, and other bribes*. Boston: Houghton Mifflin Company.

Kouides, RW. Bennett, NM. Lewis, B. Cappuccio, JD. Barker, WH. LaForce, FM (1998). 'Performance-based physician reimbursement and influenza immunization rates in the elderly: the primary-care physicians of Monroe County.' *American Journal of Preventive Medicine*, 14(2): 89–95.

Kralewski, JE. Rich, EC. Feldman, R. Dowd, BE. Bernhardt, T. Johnson, C. Gold, W (2000). 'The effects of medical group practice and payment methods on costs of care.' *Health Services Research*, 35(3): 591–613.

Krasnik, A. Grenewegen, PP. Pedersen, PA. von Scholten, P. Mooney, G. Gottschau, A. Flierman, HA. Damsgaard, MT (1990). 'Changing remuneration systems: effects on activity in general practice.' *British Medical Journal*, 300(6741): 1698–1701.

Kuhn, M (2003). *Quality in primary care: economic approaches to analysing quality-related physician behavior*. London: Office of Health Economics.

Landon, BE. Normand, SL. Blumenthal, D. Daley, J (2003). 'Physician clinical performance assessment: prospects and barriers.' *Journal of the American Medical Association*, 290(9): 1183–2289.

Lester, H. Roland, M (2009). Performance measurement in primary care. In: Smith, PC. Mossialos, E. Papanicolas, I. Leatherman, S (eds.). *Performance management for health system improvement: experiences, challenges and prospects*. Cambridge: Cambridge University Press.

Levin-Scherz, J. DeVita, N. Timbie, J (2006). 'Impact of pay-for-performance contracts and network registry on diabetes and asthma HEDIS® measures in an integrated delivery network.' *Medical Care Research and Review*, 63(Special Suppl. 1): 14S–28S.

Lindenauer, PK. Remus, D. Roman, S. Rothberg, MB. Benjamin, EM. Ma, A. Bratzler, DW (2007). 'Public reporting and pay for performance in hospital quality improvement.' *New England Journal of Medicine*, 356(5): 486–496.

Lurie, N. Christianson, J. Finch, M. Moscovice, I (1994). 'The effects of capitation on health and functional status of Medicaid elderly: a randomized trial.' *Annals of Internal Medicine*, 120(6): 506–511.

Maxwell, H. Heaney, D. Howie, JGR. Noble, S (1993). 'General practice fundholding: observations on prescribing patterns and costs using the daily dose method.' *British Medical Journal*, 307(6913): 1190–1194.

McGlynn, EA (2007). 'Intended and unintended consequences: what should we really worry about?' *Medical Care*, 45(1): 3–5.

McMenamin, SB. Schauffler, HH. Shortell, SM. Rundall, TG. Gillies, RR (2003). 'Support for smoking cessation interventions in physician organizations: results from a national study.' *Medical Care*, 41(12): 1396–1406.

Mehrotra, A. Epstein, AM. Rosenthal, MB (2006). 'Do integrated medical groups provider higher quality medical care than individual practice associations?' *Annals of Internal Medicine*, 145(11): 826–833.

Miller, RH. Luft, HS (1997). 'Does managed care lead to better or worse quality of care?' *Health Affairs*, 16(5): 7–25.

Miller, RH. Luft, HS (2002). 'HMO plan performance update: an analysis of the literature, 1997–2001.' *Health Affairs*, 21(4): 63–86.

Moscucci, M. Eagle, KA. Share, D. Smith, D. De Franco, AC. O'Donnell, M. Kline-Rogers, E. Jani, SM. Brown, DL (2005). 'Public reporting and case selection for percutaneous coronary interventions: an analysis from two large multicenter percutaneous coronary intervention databases.' *Journal of American College of Cardiology*, 45(11): 1759–1765.

Mossialos, E. Walley, T. Rudisill, C (2005). 'Provider incentives and prescribing behavior in Europe.' *Expert Reviews of Pharmacoeconomics Outcomes Research*, 5(1): 1–13.

Nahra, TA. Reiter, KL. Hirth, RA. Shermer, JE. Wheeler, JRC (2006). 'Cost-effectiveness of hospital pay-for-performance incentives.' *Medical Care Research and Review*, 63(Special Suppl. 1): 49S–72S.

Petersen, LA. Woodard, LD. Urech, T. Daw, C. Sookanan, S (2006). 'Does pay-for-performance improve the quality of health care?' *Annals of Internal Medicine*, 145(4): 265–272.

Pourat, N. Rice, T. Tai-Seale, M. Bolan, G. Nihalani, J (2005). 'Association between physician compensation methods and delivery of guideline-concordant STD care: is there a link?' *The American Journal of Managed Care*, 11(7): 426–432.

Prendergast, CR (1999). 'The provision of incentives in firms.' *Journal of Economic Literature*, 37(1): 7–63.

Rittenhouse, DR. Grumbach, K. O'Neil, EH. Dower, C. Bindman, A (2004). 'Physician organization and care management in California: from cottage to Kaiser.' *Health Affairs*, 23(6): 51–62.

Roland, M (2004). 'Linking physician pay to quality of care – a major experiment in the United Kingdom.' *New England Journal of Medicine*; 351(14): 1448–1454.

Rosenthal, MB. Dudley, RA (2007). 'Pay-for-performance: will the latest payment trend improve care?' *Journal of the American Medical Association*, 297(7): 740–744.

Rosenthal, MB. Frank, RG (2006). 'What is the empirical basis for paying for quality in health care?' *Medical Care Research and Review*, 63(2): 135–157.

Rosenthal, MB. Frank, RG. Li, Z. Epstein, AM (2005). 'Early experience with pay-for-performance: from concept to practice.' *Journal of the American Medical Association*, 294(14): 1788–1793.

Rosenthal, MB. Landon, BE. Howitt, K. Song, HR. Epstein, AM (2007). 'Climbing up the pay-for-performance learning curve: where are the early adopters now?' *Health Affairs*, 26(6): 1674–1682.

Rosenthal, MB. Landon, BE. Normand, SL. Frank, RG. Epstein, AM (2006). 'Pay for performance in commercial HMOs.' *New England Journal of Medicine*, 355(18): 1895–1902.

Roski, J. Jeddeloh, R. An, L. Lando, H. Hannan, P. Hall, C. Zhu, SH (2003). 'The impact of financial incentives and a patient registry on preventive care quality: increasing provider adherence to evidence-based smoking cessation practice guidelines.' *Preventive Medicine*, 36(3): 291–299.

Safran, DG. Rogers, WH. Tarlov, AR. Inui, T. Taira, DA. Montgomery, JE. Ware, JE. Slavin, CP (2000). 'Organizational and financial characteristics of health plans: are they related to primary care performance?' *Archives of Internal Medicine*, 160(1): 69–76.

Shen, Y (2003). 'Selection incentives in a performance-based contracting system.' *Health Services Research*; 38(2): 535–552.

Strunk, BC. Hurley, RE (2004). *Paying for quality: health plans try carrots instead of sticks*. Center for Studying Health System Change (Issue Brief No. 82: pp.1–7).

Tversky, A. Kahneman, D (1986). 'Rational choice and the framing of decisions.' *Journal of Business*, 59(4): 251– 278.

von Neumann, J. Morgenstern, O (1944). *Theory of games and economic behavior*. Princeton, NJ: Princeton University Press.

Whynes, DK. Baines, DL. Tolley, KH (1995). 'GP fundholding and the costs of prescribing.' *Journal of Public Health Medicine*, 17(3): 323–329.

Wilson, RPH. Hatcher, J. Barton, S. Walley, T (1996). 'Influences of practice characteristics on prescribing in fundholding and non-fundholding general practices: an observational study.' *British Medical Journal*, 313(7057): 595–599.

Wynia, MK. Cummins, DS. VanGeest, JB. Wilson, IB (2000). 'Physician manipulation of reimbursement rules for patients: between a rock and a hard place.' *Journal of the American Medical Association*, 283(14): 1858–1865.

Young, GJ. Conrad, DA (2007). 'Practical issues in the design and implementation of pay-for-quality programs.' *Journal of Healthcare Management,* 52(1): 10–18.

Young, GJ. Meterko, M. Beckman, H. Baker, E. White, B. Sautter, KM. Greene, R. Curtin, K. Bokhour, BG. Berlowitz, D. Burgess, JF Jnr. (2007). 'Effects of paying physicians based on their relative performance for quality.' *Journal of General Internal Medicine,* 22(6): 872–876.

5.5 | *Performance measurement and professional improvement*

ARNOLD M. EPSTEIN

Introduction

As many of the preceding chapters have established, measurement is clearly the first step in improving quality of care. If performance cannot be measured, you cannot genuinely determine how well you are doing or whether different approaches to health-care delivery are associated with higher or lower quality. However, measurement is only part of the answer. Most health care is provided by individual clinicians practising in a variety of sites and there will be no predictable and systematic progress in improving quality unless these professionals become engaged in collecting and using performance data to effect change. This chapter focuses specifically on these issues, particularly the relationship between various aspects of performance measurement and professional improvement.

Quality assurance, quality improvement and performance measurement

Historically, quality management was the province of individual doctors, their professional organizations and the state; the latter exercising control largely through licensure (Epstein 1996). Institutional quality assurance developed in the latter half of the twentieth century as a result of the increasing scientific basis of clinical care; complexity of technology; congregation of different sorts of providers (e.g. physicians, nurses, nutritionists, pharmacists) in hospitals and group practice settings; and the advent of accreditation.

Initial quality assurance efforts in hospitals focused largely on structure and process indicators. Analyses of insurance claims data employed to identify providers who overused services for different clinical conditions or in particular clinical circumstances were also deemed quality assurance efforts in some instances. Particularly at the outset, quality assurance often focused on identifying performers providing low-quality care, the so-called bad apples. Traditional quality assurance probably did not lead to large improvements in the quality of care and was not popular with providers. Undoubtedly at least some of this attitude arose because physicians saw the effort to identify sub-par performers as an attack on their professionalism and autonomy.

Quality improvement arose in part as a counterpoint to traditional quality assurance and has become increasingly important in the last two decades. It builds on managerial and statistical approaches first applied on a wide scale in Japan after the Second World War and rests on seven central ideas (Epstein 1996).

1. Failure to provide optimal care often reflects remediable systemic problems rather than misconduct by individual providers who generally work hard to provide high-quality care.
2. It is essential to encourage teamwork and cooperation because groups of providers dispense complex care in hospitals and medical groups.
3. Quality of care is an organization's product and commitment to quality must be evident throughout the organizational structure and in all personnel.
4. Continuing measurement, characterization of variation and identification of innovative approaches can improve quality of care across the entire performance spectrum.
5. It is crucial to involve patients and workers across the delivery system and to empower them to identify more effective approaches to delivering care.
6. Feedback from health-care 'customers' is an essential part of assessing quality of care and the impact of improvement interventions.
7. Improvement can be performed most effectively in cycles that include the design of new approaches, implementation and continued monitoring of system performance.

Within quality improvement, performance measurement is used to monitor performance; feed data to providers for benchmarking (normative and comparative); and identify high performers or best practices that characterize particularly effective approaches to care. Performance measurement is central to both quality assurance and quality improvement. However, while quality improvement involves a component of monitoring for poor quality, it places less emphasis on it, unlike quality assurance.

Engaging professionals in quality of care improvement efforts: what does and does not work

Numerous approaches have been used to encourage physicians to change their practice patterns to improve quality of care. Eisenberg and Williams (1981) and Eisenberg (1986) published early reviews of these approaches but these have now been superseded by hundreds of studies and scores of reviews. Some of the most important approaches based on, or incorporating, performance measurement for professional improvement are described below.

Education

Education is possibly the most basic approach to behavioural change. While it need not be combined with performance measurement, evidence of low performance has often been the trigger for educational efforts. Moreover, as described below, failure to catalyse important changes in behaviour through education alone has led to the use of additional strategies that sometimes incorporate performance measurement.

A large range of educational interventions have been extensively studied and reviewed. These include passive traditional educational strategies, usually consisting of didactic educational meetings (e.g. conferences, seminars, lectures) or dissemination of printed educational materials (e.g. publications, audiovisual material). Several factors likely affect the impact of educational interventions on physician behaviour, including the source of the information; presentation format; mode of delivery; frequency and timing of intervention; and specific content (Framer et al. 2003).

A number of studies and reviews suggest that generally the passive dissemination of information (through lecture-based presentations or printed educational materials) has, at most, a small effect on physician practice and patient outcomes (Bero et al. 1998; Grimshaw et al. 2001; Oxman et al. 1995). For example, Browner et al. (1994) examined the impact of a continuing medical education (CME) programme focused on the recommendations of the National Cholesterol

Education Program (NCEP) in the United States. They found that a three-hour seminar had no impact on screening for high serum cholesterol or compliance with guidelines. Even when the educational intervention was intensified by follow-up meetings and printed materials, it failed to elicit change in physician practice. In a major review, Grimshaw et al. (2001) summarized the outcomes of forty-one prior reviews of a wide range of interventions and concluded that passive educational approaches are largely ineffective and unlikely to change physicians' practices significantly.

The development and promulgation of clinical practice guidelines by prestigious professional organizations or other sources may be regarded as a variant of the traditional educational approaches described above, albeit with an intervention that is often regional or national. As with other educational strategies, the passive dissemination of clinical guidelines has often been found to have little impact. For example, Lomas et al. (1989) examined how guidelines recommending reduced use of Caesarian section affected use rates in Canada. A third of the hospitals and obstetricians reported changing their practice as a consequence of these guidelines and obstetricians reported reduced rates in women with histories of a previous Caesarean section. However, data on actual practice showed only a slight decrease. Lomas (1991) also reviewed prior studies of passive dissemination of guidelines and found little evidence that this approach induced change in provider behaviour. Grimshaw et al's (2004) more recent review has similar findings.

Passive strategies alone thus appear to have little impact on physician behaviour but educational strategies that employ interactive methods to engage medical providers can be more effective. Admittedly, the implementation of active approaches may require more resources since they are inevitably more expensive and difficult logistically then simply mailing written materials or publicizing educational information. Thomson O'Brien et al. (2001) demonstrated that interactive workshops that utilize small group discussions and practice sessions can result in moderately large changes in clinical practice. Other studies of active educational approaches such as outreach visits or educational sessions by charismatic opinion leaders have also often shown positive outcomes, although effectiveness varies (Grimshaw et al. 2001; Oxman et al. 1995).

Moreover, multifaceted interventions that use several strategies are generally more effective than single interventions (Grimshaw & Russell 1993; Grimshaw et al. 2001). For example, Headrick et al. (1992) compared three approaches for improving physician compliance with clinical guidelines for the NCEP. Physicians were grouped in three categories (i) standard lecture; (ii) standard lecture + reminder of NCEP guidelines; (iii) standard lecture + patient-specific feedback. This study found that the didactic lectures alone did not improve compliance with NCEP guidelines but the latter two groups experienced some improvement. Box 5.5.1 provides additional examples from the literature of studies incorporating active approaches to education in five countries.

Box 5.5.1 Studies of education coupled with outreach

- In Australia, Cockburn et al. (1992) compared three approaches for marketing a smoking cessation intervention kit to 264 general practitioners: (i) personal delivery and presentation by an educational facilitator; (ii) delivery to receptionist by a volunteer courier; (iii) postal delivery. Doctors receiving the first approach were significantly more likely to see the kit; rate the method of delivery as motivating; use one of the intervention components from the kit; report that they found the kit less complicated; and report greater knowledge of how to use the kit.
- In England, Berings et al. (1994) studied 128 primary practitioners and compared the impact of providing: (i) written information about the indications and limitations of benzodiazepines; (ii) both written and oral information from specially trained general practitioners; (iii) no information at all. The number of benzodiazepines prescribed per 100 patient contacts decreased by 24% among physicians who received both oral and written information; 14% among those provided with only written information; and 3% in the control group.
- In Canada, Lomas et al. (1991) evaluated the education of local opinion leaders as well as audit and feedback as methods of encouraging compliance with a guideline for the management of women who had had a previous Caesarean section. The overall Caesarean section rate dropped only in the opinion leader education group.

Box 5.5.1 cont'd

- In Sweden, Diwan et al. (1995) observed a similar effect for pre-scribing lipid-lowering drugs in primary care. Health centres that offered four group educational sessions, conducted by a phar-macist, on guidelines for managing hyperlipidaemia showed an increase in the number of prescriptions of lipid-lowering drugs per month compared to the control group.
- In the United States, Stross and colleagues showed the effective-ness of medical education programmes at the community hospital level by training and deploying local opinion leaders whom their peers identified as influential and respected clinicians. One pro-gramme resulted in a series of significant positive changes in the management of chronic obstructive pulmonary disease (Stross et al. 1983). Another demonstrated substantial improvement in the utilization of diagnostic procedures and management of patients with rheumatoid arthritis (Stross & Bole 1980). More recently, Raisch et al. (1990) showed that one-to-one educational meet-ings between prescribers and pharmacists improved the prescrib-ing of anti-ulcer agents for outpatients in a health maintenance organization.

The success of active educational strategies, often using outreach or opinion leaders, has not gone unnoticed in the commercial world. The pervasiveness and perceived impact of these approaches is demon-strated by pharmaceutical companies' common use of representatives who visit physicians in their offices and clinical specialists who are hired to present educational sessions for primary care practitioners on newly developed medications.

Audit, profiling and feedback

The variable and sometimes limited effectiveness of education has been partly responsible for widespread efforts to audit physicians, profile their practice and provide feedback on their performance in relation to their peers. The rationale for this approach is the assumption that phy-sicians will be more willing to change their practice if they learn that their behaviour is far below the norm or some recognized high-quality benchmark. Sometimes the profiling data are used to characterize performance on indicators of clinical quality (e.g. use of beta blockers for the treatment of acute myocardial infarction) but frequently they are also used to measure 'efficiency', or what is often literally risk-adjusted utilization. These measures might include rates of specialty referral for primary care practitioners; use of radiographic testing; or comparative prescription rates for generic and branded medications.

In the United States, numerous national efforts are underway to capture clinical performance data and provide feedback to hospitals and physicians on comparisons between their performance over time and national benchmarks. For example, the Society of Thoracic Surgeons (STS) has been collecting data since 1989 for the STS National Database. Currently this has over 900 active surgeon participants; in some instances the surgeon's hospital serves as a co-participant. Extensive data are collected for each individual patient undergoing adult cardiac surgery, congenital heart surgery or general thoracic surgery, including pre-operative risk factors; history of previous interventions; specifics on the operative procedure; and post-operative complications. Every six months participants receive a case-mix adjusted outcomes report comparing their practice to regional and national benchmarks. The outcomes report provides longitudinal data on outcomes such as mortality and length of stay by procedure and complexity level. Fig. 5.5.1 provides an example of the national data on length of stay provided by the STS.

In addition to these national profiling efforts, many health plans in the United States collect and distribute data on participating individual doctors and medical groups in an attempt to reduce variation and utilization. For example, in a recent national survey of quality management by more than 240 health plans, Landon et al. (2008) examined the collection of data for 7 quality indicators included as part of the HEDIS battery (e.g. screening for breast cancer, control of high blood pressure). Depending on the quality indicator, they found that 50% to 81% of health plans collected quality performance data on individual doctors or medical groups and 38% to 69% of health plans reported these data back to the providers responsible.

The compelling rationale for audit and feedback and its broad use in patient care organizations might imply that it is a highly effective strategy for changing physicians' behaviour. However, early studies in the 1990s indicated that audit and feedback was neither a consistent

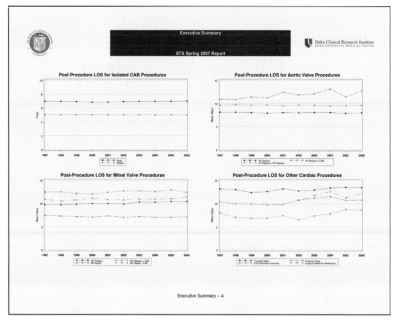

Fig. 5.5.1 Sample of length-of-stay report from STS database

Source: STS database (http://www.sts.org/documents/pdf/
ndb/1stHarvestExecutiveSummary_-_2009.pdf)

nor a particularly effective intervention (Axt-Adam et al. 1993; Balas
et al. 1996). Reviews of the literature by the Cochrane Collaboration
initially affirmed that the effects of audit and feedback varied and
it was unfeasible to determine which, if any, features contributed to
effectiveness (Jamtvedt et al. 2006). More recently, Jamtvedt et al.
(2006) undertook a literature review in which they examined 118 randomly controlled studies to determine the impact of audit and feedback, either alone or in concert with various other interventions such
as education, involvement of opinion leaders or outreach visits. This
review also concluded that audit and feedback on performance generally has a small to moderate impact. Greater changes occur when there
is low baseline adherence to recommended practice and when feedback, with or without educational meetings, is given more intensely
(e.g. more frequently). Boxes 5.5.2 and 5.5.3 provide examples
from five countries of prior studies of audit and feedback that have
addressed different clinical areas or that have been combined with differing interventions.

Box 5.5.2 Studies of audit and feedback by area of health care

Pathology and radiology

In the Netherlands, Buntinx et al. (1993) compared three feedback methods to improve the quality of cervical smears among 179 doctors. Cytologists judged the smears on a three-point scale. Feedback of increasing intensity was provided to: (i) low-intensity group – received written feedback on the technical quality of their sample; (ii) medium-intensity group – received same written feedback plus monthly summaries of their quality performance relative to their peers; and (iii) high-intensity group – received both forms of written feedback plus specific advice concerning their deficiencies. A positive but not statistically significant correlation was observed between improvement in the quality of cervical smears and the increasing intensity of the feedback.

Operative procedures

In the United States, Ferguson et al. (2003) examined the effect of a multi-faceted set of low-intensity interventions to increase the use of beta blocker therapy and internal mammary artery grafting in patients undergoing CABG surgery. Three types of interventions were used: (i) call-to-action by a physician leader; (ii) educational products; and (iii) nationally benchmarked, longitudinal, site-specific feedback. The intervention groups showed modest increases in the use of both process measures, with a significant impact at lower-volume CABG sites.

Prescribing

In Australia, O'Connell et al. (1999) examined the impact of unsolicited written and graphical feedback on the prescribing patterns of over 2000 general practitioners practising in non-urban settings. The test group received mailed, unsolicited, graphical displays of their prescribing rates for two years relative to those of their peers, in addition to educational letters on prescription issues. The authors found no significant change in the prescription patterns of the participants overall or within the subgroups of high and low prescribers.

Box 5.5.3 Studies of different audit and feedback approaches

Audit & feedback with guidelines

In Denmark, Søndergaard et al. (2003) studied the impact of feedback on general practitioners' prescriptions for antibiotics for respiratory tract infections. The control group received clinical guidelines only; the intervention group received guidelines coupled with data on prescription rates versus county averages for various classes of antibiotics. The addition of feedback on prescription patterns failed to change general practitioners' behaviour significantly.

Audit & feedback with education

In Canada, Pimlott et al. (2003) studied how feedback in combination with educational materials affected the rate of physician prescriptions for benzodiazepines in elderly patients. The intervention group received evidence-based educational bulletins and profiling for benzodiazepine prescriptions written for elderly patients. The control group received similar educational materials and profiling for antihypertensive drug prescribing for elderly patients. The authors found that the feedback intervention produced no significant change for either total benzodiazepine prescription rates or for rates of benzodiazepine prescriptions in combination with other psychoactive medications.

Audit & feedback using a multi-faceted approach

In the Netherlands, Verstappen et al. (2003) examined how a multi-faceted approach to audit and feedback impacted on the test ordering performance of primary care physicians. Two test groups focused on different clinical problems (Group A: cardiovascular and abdominal complaints. Group B: chronic pulmonary disease and asthma; general complaints; and degenerative joint complaints). Both groups received mailed feedback benchmarking their test ordering practices against their colleagues. This feedback was followed up with dissemination of national evidence-based guidelines and with regular small group meetings on quality improvement. The study found an improvement in physicians' test ordering

> **Box 5.5.3 cont'd**
>
> practices in both study groups and Group A showed a significant reduction in the number of inappropriate tests ordered.
>
> In the United States, Soumerai et al. (1998) examined how clinician education by local opinion leaders and performance feedback impacted on improving the quality of treatment of acute myocardial infarction. The intervention group received feedback on adherence to treatment guidelines and took part in small and large group educational discussions on treatment guidelines with a local opinion leader. The control group received only mailed feedback on adherence to treatment guidelines. The use of local opinion leaders accelerated the adoption of some beneficial therapies (e.g. aspirin, beta blockers) but had no significant impact on the use of effective but riskier treatments (e.g. thrombolytics for elderly patients).

Accreditation and recertification

Increasingly, quality performance measurement is incorporated into individual and institutional providers' requirements for accreditation and recertification. For the latter, mandated performance measurement is often used as a method for focusing survey processes on substandard or deficient performance areas.

In the United States, the two major accreditors of provider institutions (NCQA and Joint Commission) require the submission of performance data for health plans and for hospitals. NCQA requires health plans to submit both HEDIS and CAHPS. The HEDIS battery includes seventy-one indicators covering eight domains and is described in more detail below. The national oversight committee from NCQA reviews on- and off-site survey team evaluations and performance scores on HEDIS and CAHPS and assigns accreditation ratings in the form of a star system. At present the HEDIS-CAHPS results account for approximately 35% of the overall accreditation points.

Since 2004, the Joint Commission has required hospitals to submit data on three (increased to four in 2008) standardized core measure sets. Each set is a group of indicators covering one of five clinical conditions: (i) acute myocardial infarction; (ii) congestive heart failure; (iii) pneumonia; (iv) surgical infection prevention; and (v) pregnancy and related conditions. The Joint Commission provides a summary of the reported data using statistical process control techniques for organizational and surveyor use; populates a management tool that compares organizational performance against self-selected cohorts for organizational use; and publishes the data on the Internet (www.qualitycheck.org). The Joint Commission uses performance measurement data to help identify clinical service groups and prioritize focus areas for the on-site survey process. Performance on HEDIS-CAHPS and the core measures reflects overall health plan and hospital performance.

While effective institutional quality management is central to high performance, it would be very difficult for health plans and hospitals to improve without the cooperation of individual providers. Certification of individual health-care providers is gaining attention in multiple countries. One early innovator is The American Board of Medical Specialties (ABMS). In 2002, the ABMS approved a new framework for the maintenance of certification comprising four components: (i) evaluation of clinical performance; (ii) maintenance of an unrestricted licence; (iii) evidence of lifelong learning; and (iv) passing an examination of medical knowledge. The twenty-four specialty boards overseen by the ABMS are required to have recertification programmes that conform to this framework by 2010.

The American Board of Internal Medicine (ABIM) implemented its new programme in 2006. All physicians seeking their ten-year recertification must complete a four-step practice improvement module (PIM): (i) collection of practice data from some combination of medical record audit, patient surveys and a survey about clinical management in their practice; (ii) generation of quality performance measures for review by the physician; (iii) selection of a performance measure to improve, implementation of a strategy to accomplish improvement, and conduct of a rapid cycle test of change involving a small sample of patients over a relatively short period (e.g. several weeks); and (iv) physician's reflections on the impact of the improvement plan and indication of further changes that are intended. The PIMs focus on common issues and concerns such as diabetes, hypertension and preventive cardiology. To date more than 11 000 physicians have completed one of the PIMs and some preliminary data are available about the acceptability of the recertification programme and the quality indicators used in the diabetes PIM (Holmboe et al. 2006; Lipner et al. 2007). However, there is still a lack of information about the approach's success in teaching quality improvement techniques or actually leading to improved care.

Publicly released performance data

The performance measurement efforts described above (perhaps excluding accreditation) are employed largely for internal purposes – to guide quality assurance and quality improvement within healthcare organizations. However, concerted efforts to develop and disseminate publicly information on quality indicators over the last fifteen years have also engendered public, standardized reports on quality of care, commonly known as quality report cards. In the United States, these sorts of data are available much more commonly for hospitals or health plans than for medical groups. Public performance reporting is discussed at length by Shekelle (Chapter 5.2) but this chapter provides brief descriptions of the key reports, targeting United States' hospitals and health plans specifically.

The Hospital Quality Alliance (HQA) is arguably the most extensive current effort to measure hospital quality of care. Developed by a consortium including the CMS, the Joint Commission and the American Hospital Association, since 2003 the HQA has provided regular public reporting for an increasing number (now over twenty) of process indicators of clinical quality for acute myocardial infarction, pneumonia, congestive heart failure and surgical care. Hospitals report these measures on a voluntary basis but the CMS has provided financial incentives for reporting a subset of the measures since 2004. As a result almost all hospitals with sufficient numbers of patients provide the data. The HQA data set has expanded to include risk-adjusted mortality after acute myocardial infarction, congestive heart failure and pneumonia and the Hospital Consumer Assessment of Healthcare Providers and Systems (HCAHPS).

The gold standard for performance measurement of hospitals and individual physicians is perhaps the regular release of statistics on risk-adjusted mortality due to coronary artery bypass graft (CABG) surgery for hospitals and individual surgeons in New York State and Pennsylvania. These data have been made public in periodic reports since the early 1990s. Several other states (e.g. California, Massachusetts, New Jersey) have developed similar systems, although the data from California and New Jersey are at the hospital level only. The CABG reports are notable because researchers have relatively long experience with them and they incorporate extensive efforts to risk adjust the mortality data.

Overseen by NCQA, HEDIS has been the most commonly used report card for health plans for more than fifteen years. The HEDIS battery includes not only information on quality of care but also access to care, enrollees' satisfaction with care and utilization of services. In 2008 HEDIS included indicators covering twenty-three clinical conditions addressing overuse, misuse and underuse of care. HEDIS data released in 2007 included performance results from more than 500 health plans and 80 million HMO, point of service (POS) and preferred provider organization (PPO) enrollees.

Providers' response to report cards

Quality report cards are designed with audiences other than providers in mind – patients who might use them to select providers; large-scale purchasers of health care for contracting or commissioning; and regulators of care who might use them to assure accountability. Each of these audiences may use the data somewhat differently but it is hoped that all of these efforts will result in improved quality performance among health-care professionals.

Evidence suggests that hospitals and health systems (and presumably the doctors and medical groups that populate them) often respond to publicly released data with efforts to improve on measured aspects of care. For example, studies have documented substantial improvement in risk-adjusted mortality after CABG surgery in New York and several other states have initiated public reporting of these data (Hannan et al 1994; National Committee for Quality Assurance 2004). Similarly, NCQA's public release of serial HEDIS data on health plans has been associated with fairly broad improvement in the publicly released indicators. However, success has been variable and some areas (e.g. mental health) have proved intransigent.

Furthermore, even when public performance reports catalyse quality improvement by providers, some critics have raised concerns about unintended responses. For example, Green and Wintfeld (1995) reported data from New York State showing that surgeons began to report higher rates of co-morbidities for their patients after the CABG mortality reporting system was introduced, perhaps leading to a factitious reduction in risk-adjusted mortality over time.

A survey of Pennsylvania cardiologists showed that most respondents thought that the risk adjustment was inadequate and that surgeons and hospitals might manipulate the data to their benefit (Schneider & Epstein 1996). Only 13% of those cardiologists surveyed considered that the reporting system had a moderate or substantial influence on their referral recommendations.

Others have worried that a focus on publicly reported quality indicators will cause physicians to ignore the performance and improvement of other important but unreported aspects of care. Two recent studies have tried to address this concern (Glickman et al. 2007; Landon et al. 2007). They found no evidence of such negative spillovers but the possibility of this kind of skewed emphasis remains.

Finally, there has been substantial concern about potential inequity of care; specifically that physicians or hospitals might limit access to care for patients with greater severity of illness or higher levels of co-morbidity which cannot be addressed fully by the risk adjustment. Studies in the United States have linked better performance on health plan quality indicators with white race and higher socio-economic status (Zaslavsky & Epstein 2005; Zaslavsky et al. 2000) giving rise to concern that patients from racial minorities and lower socio-economic groups also may be at risk of exclusion.

Thus far these concerns about access have been difficult to study or document effectively. When surveyed, 59% of the cardiologists in Pennsylvania reported more difficulty finding a surgeon for severely ill patients needing CABG surgery after adoption of the public reporting system on risk-adjusted CABG mortality; 63% of those surveyed said that they were less willing to operate on such patients (Schneider & Epstein 1996). Omoigui et al. (1996) reported that the number of patients transferred to Cleveland Clinic from New York State increased by more than 30% after the initiation of CABG mortality reporting in New York and that these patients tended to be higher risk than patients transferred from other states. Peterson et al. (1998) found no evidence of restrictions in access to care in New York State when they studied national Medicare data. In fact, the severity of illness of CABG patients in the state increased after the adoption of CABG reporting; and New York State residents who sought CABG surgery in other states had lower co-morbidity than those who received their CABG surgery within the state.

Pay for performance

Public reporting has successfully spawned quality improvement but there are many concerns that the rate of improvement in care is still too low. This has produced increasing interest in tying performance measurements to financial incentives. Financial incentives have been used in medicine for many years. For example, as far back as 1990, general practitioners in England began receiving incremental payments for performing immunizations and Papanicolaou smears (Roland 2004). In the United States, health plans have often provided physicians with small incentives based on patients' satisfaction with care or the use of screening measures such as mammography (Epstein et al. 2004). Incentives have grown and are now being applied to a broader set of quality indicators (including structural measures such as the adoption of IT).

Possibly the best known pay-for-performance programme is that adopted for NHS primary care doctors in 2004. This system provides payment for quality indicators related to clinical care for 10 chronic diseases (including diabetes and asthma); organization of care; and patient experience. The average family practitioner had earned between £ 70 000 and £ 75 000 but average gross income rose by £ 23 000 after the pay-for-performance programme was implemented (Doran et al. 2006).

Pay-for-performance systems have been widely adopted in the private sector in the United States. By 2006, more than half of the health plans covering 80% of plan enrollees had adopted pay for performance for physicians or medical groups; a smaller but substantial number adopted them for hospitals (Rosenthal et al. 2006). In some instances, financial payments have been used to provide incentives indirectly. For example, some employers have incorporated financial incentives in the form of tiering arrangements – patients pay more for providers with lower quality performance or efficiency. Even the federal government has served notice of its interest in a pay-for-performance approach. In the Deficit Reduction Act of 2005, Congress mandated the Secretary of Health and Human Services to develop plans for incorporating performance incentives into the Medicare programme for hospitals by 2009.

Despite the considerable interest in pay for performance, the data on its effectiveness are inconclusive. Petersen et al. (2006) found mixed results in seventeen studies published between 1980 and 2005, with few strongly positive findings. Four of the studies reviewed showed unintended effects of pay-for-performance programmes (including adverse selection and improved documentation) rather than improved quality of care. Only one study examined cost effectiveness. No studies examined whether improvements in quality persisted over a long period or changes in quality of care as measured by overuse. Similarly, Campbell et al. (2007) found that the quality of care had been improving for diabetes, asthma and congestive heart failure before pay for performance was implemented. The new NHS programme modestly accelerated improvement for diabetes and asthma but not congestive heart failure. Conversely, the same study demonstrated that there was no difference in the rate of improvement between specific clinical indicators associated with financial incentives and unassociated indicators. However, the authors caution that the NHS study was not designed specifically to analyse the difference between indicators with and without incentive attachments and therefore this finding per se cannot be interpreted as proof of the pay-for-performance programme's ineffectiveness.

Two recent studies of a voluntary demonstration programme by CMS in the United States were equally inconclusive. Starting in the last quarter of 2003, hospitals that chose to participate in the Medicare demonstration were eligible for an increase of 2% in their Medicare payments if they reached the top performance decile for one of five clinical conditions: congestive heart failure, acute myocardial infarction, pneumonia, total hip replacement and total knee replacement. Hospitals reaching the second performance decile were eligible for an additional 1% payment; hospitals that failed to exceed the performance levels of the bottom 40% by the third year were penalized. Lindenauer et al. (2007) examined care for acute myocardial infarction, congestive heart failure and pneumonia within this programme. They compared this to care provided by a comparison group of matched hospitals with similar characteristics but no monetary incentive to improve and found improvements averaging 4.1% to 5.2% over two years for those receiving the financial incentive. Glickman et al. (2007) examined acute myocardial infarction using a different comparison group and found no statistical impact from the financial incentives.

In short, review of the literature to date shows clearly the lack of conclusive data on the effectiveness of pay for performance. It seems likely that multiple factors impact on the success of efforts to spur improvement with financial incentives. These include the nature of the clinical conditions targeted; the size and shape of the incentive programme; and the time lag between initiation of the programme and the measurement of care. All that can be said with confidence is that performance incentives certainly have the potential to work but also the potential to fail.

Quality measurement to encourage professional participation

If performance measurement is to prompt professional improvement, the specific types of indicators used are likely to be as important as the approach through which they are employed. In particular, it seems that physicians are most likely to find indicators acceptable and useful if they serve the functions listed below.

- *Reflect meaningful aspects of clinical practice with strong scientific underpinning.* The most credible indicators are those that reflect important aspects of what physicians perceive that they do; are statistically reliable; and have strong scientific evidence of validity.
- *Assure close risk adjustment of outcome indicators and specify process indicators.* Professionals are intimate with the clinical and social characteristics of patients that lead them to choose different diagnostic and therapeutic approaches. The plaintive refrain, 'my patients are sicker,' accompanies almost every effort in practice profiling. Physicians recognize that outcomes are critically important but the ability to specify process measures more closely to fit a narrow clinical spectrum often makes these more acceptable.
- *Allow exclusions.* Every physician is aware of patients whose medical or social condition made them inappropriate for a particular service, even when they seemed to fit the official clinical profile. The classic complaints concern colorectal screening for patients with dementia, although the problems extend far beyond this. The NHS has addressed this problem by adopting a broad system of exclusions from performance measurement – physicians can exclude patients with atypical clinical situations and for whom performance scoring would be misleading. Proponents of this approach argue that it

has enabled the NHS in England to garner physician support and thereby increase the validity of the performance measurements.

- *Facilitate interpretability.* Process measures are most effective when they indicate clearly what physicians need to do to improve performance. Professionals are likely to mistrust process measures where it is not clear whether higher or lower means better quality of care. Measures such as the proportion of generic medications fall into this category – greater use of generics is often preferable but 100% use is clearly too high. Measures such as these can be confusing and less effective in spurring improvement.
- *Represent services under a provider's control.* Clinicians are most comfortable with quality indicators for which measured performance does not depend greatly on institutional systems or other factors such as patients' compliance. For example, surgeons have complained that risk-adjusted surgical mortality may reflect a hospital's quality of care more than their own individual performance. This may be true, at least for certain procedures. Birkmeyer et al. (2003) have shown that surgical outcomes for some highly technical surgical procedures (e.g. endarterectomy) likely reflect primarily the surgeon's technical skill whereas outcomes for complicated procedures (e.g. pneumonectomy) carried out by operative teams are related more closely to hospital quality.
- *Assure high accuracy.* Health-care providers will strongly favour measures that accurately measure performance. Close specification that yields high reliability; sufficient sample size; and resistance to gaming will all serve to achieve this goal.
- *Minimize cost and burden.* The cost and administrative burden of data collection often falls on the providers who are the subject of performance measurement. Indicators that rely on existing electronic administrative data systems can minimize this burden and thus reduce potential objections.

Policy questions and future challenges for performance measurement and professionals

Performance measurement may be well-advanced but numerous questions and challenges persist.

Should we continue reporting on institutions such as health plans and hospitals or move to performance reports on medical groups and individual doctors?

This question is enormously controversial. In the United States, publicly available performance reports have commonly focused on larger aggregations of providers in hospitals or health plans. This focus reflects easy data availability; the need for adequate sample size; political sensitivity; and concerns about confidentiality. However, there is tremendous impetus to focus on smaller aggregations or even individual clinicians. In England, data are commonly tied to the practice site which generally reflects care by a small number of clinicians. Most patients believe that their individual health-care provider is the person most responsible for their care and data on that provider's practice are the most relevant.

Although systems of care are important determinants of quality and safety, leaders of hospitals and health plans and large practices recognize that they are unlikely to improve quality without the cooperation and changes in the behaviour of individual doctors. Thus far performance measurement seems to reflect acceptable middle ground, with most reports at the individual level remaining confidential. At this point there is no clear consensus about the desirability or practicality of providing a more personal focus.

How can physicians be encouraged to utilize performance measurement and engage more actively in quality improvement?

Part of the answer to this question lies in fostering the use of those quality indicators that are most likely to be acceptable to professionals and employing the strategies that are most likely to engage them. These measures and strategies are discussed at some length above. It would also be helpful to acquaint physicians with performance measurement early in their careers – as a tool to further lifelong professional quality improvement rather than an instrument for inspection and punishment. Better training might also help to foster different attitudes among doctors, encouraging them to recognize their own foibles; the importance of system design in delivering high-quality care; and the primacy of the needs and health outcomes of their patients. Regulators, accreditors and large-scale purchasers are showing substantial interest in using performance measurement to guide professional improvement. Physicians (and their patients) will benefit if they can be induced to take leadership roles in designing systems to measure and improve the quality of care.

How to create quality indicators to assess specialty care and measure efficiency?

Partly because of the need for sufficient sample size, most quality indicators reflect aspects of care that are very common and under the purview of primary care practitioners. Yet the majority of care, especially expenditure for care, concerns services provided by specialists. For example, in the United States less than 25% of expenditures for office based visits are due to visits to primary care doctors in general practice, family practice or internal medicine (Kurtz 2008). Similarly, most of the process quality indicators employed reflect underuse rather than overuse and exacerbate the growing health-care costs in this country. This trend can be mitigated by introducing more measures of overuse.

Finally, in the last fifteen years the armoury of quality measures has expanded from indicators of appropriate screening and preventive care to a much more comprehensive array of indicators focused on managing chronic disease. These new tools should be used to focus attention on measures that can gauge the performance of specialists and the efficiency of care delivery more specifically.

How to create consortia to better map performance and provide consistent signals?

This is already a particular challenge in countries like the United States, in which physicians contract with multiple payers, and may emerge with increasing use of private insurance in other countries. Several problems may co-exist – significant differences in payers' patient populations can cause scores for the same entity to vary in unexpected ways; no single payer is likely to have enough patients to measure an individual physician's performance reliably without pooling data from other payers; and different specifications for performance indicators for the same clinical task multiply the administrative burden for those providing the data and may lead to confusing information or false conclusions about performance. These problems have long been recognized but the creation of national (and possibly even international) standards for measures is an ad hoc process that remains a challenge.

When financial incentives are tied to publicly reported data, what are the most appropriate targets (attainment or improvement) and what are the levers that will prompt change most effectively (the magnitude of the incentive or professional ethos)?

Despite considerable experience with pay for performance, many questions remain. Existing pay-for-performance systems show large variations in how they structure incentives, including the magnitude of money at stake and whether targets are tied to attaining certain performance goals or to actual improvement. Rewards for attaining certain performance goals may offer little incentive to improve when providers are already performing well, and may not incentivize very poor performers as they are unlikely to meet goals based on the achievements of the very top performers. Rewards based on relative improvement can be useful – making it possible to reward improvements in very poor performers but disadvantaging those already performing well. These two approaches can be combined in various ways but the resulting complexity and multiplicity of rewards often dilutes the incentive.

There is a need for better understanding of how the magnitude of reward impacts any resulting behavioural change. This is a complicated issue since financial incentives tied to performance provide not only a monetary inducement to improve care but also a signal that draws greater attention to poor performance and the need to improve care. Recent studies have highlighted certain situations in which the signalling function of financial incentives may be particularly important. For example, Rosenthal et al. (2005) and Lindenauer et al. (2007) showed the greatest improvement among providers whose baseline level of performance was so low that they were unlikely to reach the payment target. In these situations the authors concluded that the financial incentives may well have heightened attention to clinical performance and (because of professional ethos) elicited a response from even very poor performers, particularly in settings where initially low levels of performance facilitated quality gains. Understanding these issues continues to be critically important in programme design and for setting incentives of appropriate magnitude.

Conclusions

In concluding, it seems appropriate to emphasize that performance measurement has become part of everyday life for many practising physicians and already is indispensable in monitoring the quality of care and constructing effective quality improvement efforts. The reality is that none of the methodologies used to date – whether involving confidential profiling; public reporting with aggressive use of incentives; or any other variation – has proven clearly and consistently superior for promoting high quality of care.

Performance measurement is already ubiquitous but many questions and nuances require further exploration in order to increase its usefulness and relevance. Increasing use of IT in health care is likely to make efforts to measure performance even more widespread. The ultimate utility of these efforts will depend on answering the questions and addressing the challenges identified in this chapter.

References

Axt-Adam, P. van der Wouden, JC. van der Does, E (1993). 'Influencing behavior of physicians ordering laboratory tests: a literature study.' *Medical Care*, 31(9): 784–794.

Balas, EA. Boren, SA. Brown, GD. Ewigman, BG. Mitchell, JA. Perkoff, GT (1996). 'Effect of physician profiling on utilization: meta-analysis of randomized clinical trials.' *Journal of General Internal Medicine*, 11:584–590.

Berings, D. Blondeel, L. Habraken, H (1994). 'The effect of industry-independent information on the prescribing of benzodiazepines in general practice.' *European Journal of Clinical Pharmacology*, 46(6): 501–505.

Bero, L. Grilli, R. Grimshaw, JM. Harvey, E. Oxman, AD. Thomson, MA (1998). 'Closing the gap between research and practice: an overview of systematic reviews of interventions to promote the implementation of research findings.' *Journal of the American Medical Association*, 317(7156): 465–468.

Birkmeyer, JD. Stukel, TA. Siewers, AE. Goodney, PP. Wennberg, DE. Lucas, FL (2003). 'Surgeon volume and operative mortality in the United States.' *New England Journal of Medicine*, 349(22): 2117–2127.

Browner, WS. Baron, RB. Solkowitz, S. Adler, LJ. Gullion, DS (1994). 'Physician management of hypercholesterolemia. A randomized trial of continuing medical education.' *Western Journal of Medicine*, 161(6): 572–578.

Buntinx, F. Knottnerus, JA. Crebolder, HF. Seegers, T. Essed, GC. Schouten, H (1993). 'Does feedback improve the quality of cervical smears? A randomized controlled trial.' *British Journal of General Practice*, 43(370): 194–198.

Campbell, S. Reeves, D. Kontopantelis, E. Middleton, E. Sibbald, B. Roland, M (2007). 'Quality of primary care in England with the introduction of pay for performance.' *New England Journal of Medicine*, 357(2): 181–190.

Cockburn, J. Ruth, D. Silagy, C. Dobbin, M. Reid, Y. Scollo, M. Naccarella, L (1992). 'Randomised trial of three approaches for marketing smoking cessation programmes to Australian general practitioners.' *British Medical Journal*, 304(6828): 691–694.

Diwan, VK. Wahlström, R. Tomson, G. Beermann, B. Sterky, G. Eriksson, B (1995). 'Effects of "group detailing" on the prescribing of lipid-lowering drugs: a randomized controlled trial in Swedish primary care.' *Journal of Clinical Epidemiology*, 48(5): 705–711.

Doran, T. Fullwood, E. Gravelle, H. Reeves, D. Kontopantelis, E. Hiroeh, U. Roland, M (2006). 'Pay for performance programs in family practices in the United Kingdom.' *New England Journal of Medicine*, 355(4): 375–384.

Eisenberg, JM (1986). *Doctors' decisions and the cost of medical care: the reason for doctors' practice patterns and ways to change them.* Ann Arbor: Health Administration Press.

Eisenberg, JM. Williams, SV (1981). 'Cost containment and changing physicians' practice behavior. Can the fox learn to guard the chicken coop?' *Journal of the American Medical Association*, 246(19): 2195–2201.

Epstein, AM (1996). 'The role of quality measurement in a competitive marketplace.' *Baxter Health Policy Review*, 2: 207–234.

Epstein, AM. Lee, TH. Hamel, MB (2004). 'Paying physicians for high-quality care.' *New England Journal of Medicine*, 350(4): 406–410.

Ferguson, TB Jr. Peterson, ED. Coombs, LP. Eiken, MI. Carey, ML. Grover, FL. DeLong, ER (2003). 'Use of continuous quality improvement to increase use of process measures in patients undergoing coronary artery bypass graft surgery: a randomized controlled trial.' *Journal of the American Medical Association*, 290(1): 49–56.

Framer, AP. Légaré, F. McAuley, LM. Thomas, R. Harvey, EL. McGowan, J. Grimshaw, JM. Wolf, FM (2003). 'Printed educational material: effects on professional practice and health care outcomes (protocol).' *Cochrane Database of Systematic Reviews*, (3): CD004398.

Glickman, SW. Ou, FS. DeLong, ER. Roe, MT. Lytle, BL. Mulgund, J. Rumsfeld, JS. Gibler, WB. Ohman, EM. Schulman, KA. Peterson, ED (2007). 'Pay for performance, quality of care, and outcomes in acute myocardial infarction.' *Journal of the American Medical Association*, 297(21): 2373–2380.

Green, J. Wintfeld, N (1995). 'Report cards on cardiac surgeons. Assessing New York State's approach.' *New England Journal of Medicine*, 332(18): 1229–1232.

Grimshaw, JM. Russell, IT (1993). 'Effect of clinical guidelines on medical practice: a systematic review of rigorous evaluations.' *Lancet*, 342(8883): 1317–1322.

Grimshaw, JM. Shirran, L. Thomas, R. Mowatt, G. Fraser, C. Bero, L. Grilli, R. Harvey, E. Oxman, A. O'Brien, MA (2001). 'Changing provider behavior: an overview of systematic reviews of interventions.' *Medical Care*, 39(8 Suppl. 2): 2–45.

Grimshaw, JM. Thomas, RE. MacLennan, G. Fraser, C. Ramsay, CR. Vale, L. Whitty, P. Eccles, MP. Matowe, L. Shirran, L. Wensing, M. Dijkstra, R. Donaldson, C (2004). 'Effectiveness and efficiency of guideline dissemination and implementation strategies.' *Health Technology Assessment*, 8(6): iii–iv, 1–72.

Hannan, EL. Kilburn, H Jr. Racz, M. Shields, E. Chassin, MR (1994). 'Improving the outcomes of coronary artery bypass surgery in New York State.' *Journal of the American Medical Association*, 271(10): 761–766.

Headrick, LA. Speroff, T. Pelecanos, HI. Cebul, RD (1992). 'Efforts to improve compliance with the National Cholesterol Education Program guidelines. Results of a randomized controlled trial.' *Archives of Internal Medicine*, 152(12): 2490–2496.

Holmboe, ES. Meehan, TP. Lynn, L. Doyle, P. Sherwin, T. Duffy, FD (2006). 'Promoting physicians' self-assessment and quality improvement: the ABIM diabetes practice improvement module.' *Journal of Continuing Education in the Health Professions*, 26(2): 109–119.

Jamtvedt, G. Young, JM. Kristoffersen, DT. O'Brien, MA. Oxman, AD (2006). 'Audit and feedback: effects on professional practice and health care outcomes.' *Cochrane Database of Systematic Reviews*, (2): CD000259.

Kurz, R (2008). '7 interesting statistics and facts about office-based physician visits.' *Becker's ASC Review* (http://www.beckersasc.com/news-analysis-asc/business-financial-benchmarking/7-interesting-statistics-and-facts-about-office-based-physician-visits-by-specialty.html).

Landon, BE. Hicks, LS. O Malley, AJ. Lieu, TA. Keegan, T. McNeil, BJ. Guadagnoli, E (2007). 'Improving the management of chronic disease at community health centers.' *New England Journal of Medicine*, 356(9): 921–934.

Landon, BL. Rosenthal, MB. Norman, SL. Frank, RG. Epstein, AM (2008). 'Quality monitoring and management in commercial health plans.' *American Journal of Managed Health Care*, 14(6): 377–386.

Lindenauer, PK. Remus, D. Roman, S. Rothberg, MB. Benjamin, EM. Ma, A. Bratzler, DW (2007). 'Public reporting and pay for performance in hospital quality improvement.' *New England Journal of Medicine*, 356(5): 486–496.

Lipner, RS. Weng, W. Arnold, GK. Duffy, FD. Lynn, LA. Holmboe, ES (2007). 'A three-part model for measuring diabetes care in physician practice.' *Academic Medicine*, 82(Suppl. 10): 48–52.

Lomas, J (1991). 'Words without action? The production, dissemination, and impact of consensus recommendations.' *Annual Review of Public Health*, 12: 41–65.

Lomas, J. Anderson, GM. Domnick-Pierre, K. Vayda, E. Enkin, MW. Hannah, WJ (1989). 'Do practice guidelines guide practice? The effect of a consensus statement on the practice of physicians.' *New England Journal of Medicine*, 321(19): 1306–1311.

Lomas, J. Enkim, M. Anderson, GM. Hannah, WJ. Vayda, E. Singer, J (1991). 'Opinion leaders vs audit and feedback to implement practice guidelines. Delivery after previous cesarean section.' *Journal of the American Medical Association*, 265(17): 2202–2207.

National Committee for Quality Assurance (2004). 2004 state of health care quality report. Washington, DC: National Committee for Quality Assurance.

O'Connell, DL. Henry, D. Tomlins, R (1999). 'Randomised control trial of effect of feedback on general practitioners' prescribing in Australia.' *British Medical Journal*, 318(7): 507–511.

Omoigui, NA. Miller, DP. Brown, KJ. Annan, K. Cosgrove, D 3rd. Lytle, B. Loop, F. Topol, EJ (1996). 'Outmigration for coronary bypass surgery in an era of public dissemination of clinical outcomes.' *Circulation*, 93(1): 27–33.

Oxman, AD. Thomson, MA. Davis, DA. Haynes, RB (1995). 'No magic bullets: a systematic review of 102 trials of interventions to improve professional practice.' *Canadian Medical Association Journal*, 153(10): 1423–1431.

Peterson, ED. DeLong, ER. Jollis, JG. Muhlbaier, LH. Mark DB (1998). 'The effects of New York's bypass surgery provider profiling on access to care and patient outcomes in the elderly.' *Journal of the American College of Cardiology*, 32(4): 993–999.

Petersen, LA. Woodard, LD. Urech, T. Daw, C. Sookanan, S (2006). 'Does pay-for-performance improve the quality of health care?' *Annals of Internal Medicine*, 145(4): 265–272.

Pimlott, NJ. Hux, JE. Wilson, LM. Kahan, M. Li, C. Rosser, WW (2003). 'Educating physicians to reduce benzodiazepine use by elderly patients: a randomized controlled trial.' *Canadian Medical Association Journal*, 168(7): 835–839.

Raisch, DW. Bootman, JL. Larson, LN. McGhan, WF (1990). 'Improving antiulcer agent prescribing in a health maintenance organization.' *American Journal of Hospital Pharmacy*, 47(8): 1766–1773.

Roland, M (2004). 'Linking physicians' pay to the quality of care – a major experiment in the United Kingdom.' *New England Journal of Medicine*, 351(14): 1448–1454.

Rosenthal, MB. Frank, RG. Li, Z. Epstein, AM (2005). 'Early experience with pay-for-performance: from concept to practice.' *Journal of the American Medical Association*, 294(14): 1788–1793.

Rosenthal, MB. Landon, BE. Normand, SL. Frank, RG. Epstein, AM (2006). 'Pay-for-performance in commercial HMOs.' *New England Journal of Medicine*, 355(18): 1895–1902.

Schneider, EC. Epstein, AM (1996). 'Influence of cardiac-surgery performance reports on referral practices and access to care. A survey of cardiovascular specialists.' *New England Journal of Medicine*, 335(4): 251–256.

Søndergaard, J. Andersen, M. Støvring, H. Kragstrup, J (2003). 'Mailed prescriber feedback in addition to a clinical guideline has no impact: a randomized, controlled trial.' *Scandinavian Journal of Primary Health Care*, 21(1): 47–51.

Soumerai, SB. McLaughlin, TJ. Gurwitz, JH. Guadagnoli, E. Hauptman, PJ. Borbas, C. Morris, N. McLaughlin, B. Gao, X. Willison, DJ. Asinger, R. Gobel, F (1998). 'Effect of local medical opinion leaders on quality of care for acute myocardial infarction: a randomized controlled trial.' *Journal of the American Medical Association*, 279(17): 1358–1363.

Stross, JK. Bole, GG (1980). 'Evaluation of a continuing education program in rheumatoid arthritis.' *Arthritis and Rheumatism*, 23(7): 846–849.

Stross, JK. Hiss, RG. Watts, CM. Davis, WK. Macdonald, R (1983). 'Continuing education in pulmonary disease for primary-care physicians.' *American Review of Respiratory Disease*, 127(6): 739–746.

Thomson O Brien, MA. Freemantle, N. Oxman, AD. Wolf, F. Davis, DA. Herrin, J (2001). 'Continuing education meetings and workshops: effects on professional practice and health care outcomes.' *Cochrane Database of Systematic Reviews*, 1: CD003030.

Verstappen, WH. van der Weijden, T. Sijbrandij, J. Smeele, I. Hermsen, J. Grimshaw, J. Grol, RP (2003). 'Effect of a practice-based strategy on test ordering performance of primary care physicians: a randomized trial.' *Journal of the American Medical Association*, 289(18): 2407–2412.

Zaslavsky, AM. Epstein, AM (2005). 'How patients' sociodemographic characteristics affect comparisons of competing health plans in California on HEDIS quality measures.' *International Journal for Quality in Health Care*, 17(1): 67–74.

Zaslavsky, AM. Hochheimer, JN. Schneider, EC. Cleary, PD. Seidman, JJ. McGlynn, EA. Thompson, JW. Sennett, C. Epstein, AM (2000). 'Impact of sociodemographic case mix on the HEDIS measures of health plan quality.' *Medical Care*; 38(10): 981–992.

International health system comparisons: from measurement challenge to management tool

JEREMY VEILLARD, SANDRA GARCIA-ARMESTO, SOWMYA KADANDALE, NIEK KLAZINGA

Introduction

International comparisons of health system performance provided by multilateral organizations such as WHO and the OECD generate much interest. The provision of comparative data presents vast methodological challenges but offers considerable potential for cross-country learning. Policy-makers are looking for examples, benchmarks and solutions to address the pressures imposed by the epidemiological, economic, societal and technological demands on all European health-care systems.

The use of international performance indicators to assess national economies and public domains such as education, transport and environment has paved the way for their acceptance in the health-care field. Dating back to the 1930s (e.g. Mountin & Perrott 1947), studies on health insurance programmes in western Europe show that international comparisons of health systems were used as a means to guide policy processes (Nolte et al. 2006). Several decades ago, such international assessments focused mainly on structural characteristics (e.g. numbers of physicians, nurses, hospitals) and a few specific outcome parameters (e.g. perinatal mortality, under-five mortality, maternal death, incidence and prevalence of infectious diseases, average life expectancy at birth). In the European region these parameters were complemented by the work on avoidable deaths (Rutstein et al.1976) and release of the first atlas of avoidable deaths in the European Union (Holland 1988 & 1990), thus introducing attempts to assess the contribution of health care to the overall health of populations. Coupled with data on health expenditures (OECD 2001; World Bank 1993), these produced the first picture on the performance of national health systems in relation to the resources used.

The publication of WHO's *The world health report 2000* and the OECD's *Health at a Glance 2001* received (and continues to receive) much attention. *The world health report 2000* was based on a generic conceptual performance framework and ranked Member States in a league table. Despite many criticisms (see Box 5.6.1), the report placed international health system performance on the political agenda; raised awareness about performance issues; and resulted in many initiatives to improve the perceived health situation in different countries. The latest version of *Health at a Glance* (OECD 2007) contains a comprehensive array of performance indicators without attempting to group the findings in league tables. This has elicited a more nuanced reaction from participating countries. The OECD experience underscores the fact that comparative data help primarily by raising questions about the performance of health-care systems rather than explaining why one country performs better than another.

Box 5.6.1 Debates around *The world health report 2000*

The world health report 2000 was subject to a great deal of controversy. The following points summarize the key controversies pertaining to its political, technical and methodological aspects (McKee 2001):

- Underlying political philosophy – in political and ideological debates the report was accused of being too medical-model based and criticized for its failure to consider the importance of primary health-care systems.
- Face validity – experts questioned the actual rankings of certain countries. For example, the United States ranks higher than Denmark in the responsiveness measure despite the latter having a system of universal health-care coverage.
- Coherence of performance measures – the report was criticized for focusing mainly on health-care systems (instead of considering broader social and educational factors) and not accounting for the lag between health interventions and their measurable impact.
- Data availability – the use of estimates rather than actual data was one of the greatest areas of contention.

Box 5.6.1 cont'd

- Health levels and distribution – critics questioned the use of specific measures such as disability-adjusted life expectancy and equality measures.
- Responsiveness levels and distribution – the use of limited key informants for assessing the responsiveness of health systems and failure to consider the political contexts that could impact this measure was another major area of contention.
- Fairness of financing – critics disputed the definitions and methods used to assess the fairness of financing measures.
- Estimating performance – several debates questioned the 'achievement of performance in health system' concept used in the report.
- Composite index – the use of a composite index (especially the weighting methods used in the report) to measure health systems was heavily questioned.
- Use of evidence – many criticized the report for using a narrow evidence base.

Despite these debates, *The world health report 2000* fostered the importance of health systems. Its publication emphasized the need for health stewardship within national governments and played a significant role in raising the profile of accountability for health on political agendas. Following the release of the report, numerous countries (e.g. Kyrgyzstan) asked WHO for technical support to revise their national health system policies and strategies. Furthermore, it created an impetus for further cross-national discussions around the importance of developing comparable data standards that can be utilized for strengthening health system performance in countries.

This chapter discusses some of the main issues involved in international health system comparisons. The first two sections examine the rationale (why) and the scope (what) of cross-national health system performance assessments, emphasizing the various functions of comparisons (accountability, strategy development, learning) and the scope of such efforts (whole systems, specific services, specific diseases, subnational approaches). Using the OECD's HCQI project as an example, the third section deals with outstanding methodological issues and challenges (how) such as population variations, data standardization problems, differences in coding practices and definitional issues that arise during international comparisons. The final section addresses the question of how countries can move from measurement to management by illustrating new initiatives that ensure that cross-system data comparisons become an integral part of health system performance management and decision-making processes.

Increased interest in international health system comparisons

Several reasons underlie the increased interest in international health system comparisons. Firstly, policy-makers in resource-scarce environments are increasingly held accountable by the public and the media. International data therefore play a key role in the *accountability* agenda which enables countries to demonstrate that their performance on specific items is equivalent to (or better than) that reported in other countries. Various surveys indicate that accountability can be a generic function of governments towards their citizens but user's negative experiences of health systems can also increase the pressure for governments to seek out best practices and policy lessons from other settings (Schoen et al. 2005). Additionally, the issue of patient responsiveness has recently gained momentum at the European level and could impact on future policy agendas in several countries. Furthermore, patient mobility adds an additional layer of public pressure on governments as borders become more porous in the European region (Legido-Quigley et al. 2008; Rosenmöller et al. 2006).

Secondly, performance information from international comparisons, along with trend data and careful policy analysis, can form the input for national *strategy development* (Hsiao 1992). Following the application of balanced scorecards and strategy maps in the private finance industry (Kaplan & Norton 1992 & 2000), a growing number of countries are in the process of developing frameworks to assess their health systems through national performance reports and strategy development. Examples of such reports are found in the United States (Agency for Healthcare Research and Quality 2008 & 2008a); Ontario, Canada (Veillard et al. 2009); and the Netherlands (Westert & Verkleij 2006). Similarly, the use of balanced scorecards has impacted the establishment of information systems and the management and delivery of health-care services at national and sub-system levels (Goodspeed 2006; Zelman et al. 2003). International bench-marking data can thus help in formulating the national policy pro-gramme. However, it is necessary to use a cautious approach when using comparative data for strategy development purposes since hid-den political agendas and selective perception can distort the perform-ance evidence (Klein 1997).

Thirdly, other systems gain opportunities to learn from and emulate the efforts of effective restructuring successes based on performance data from health systems such as the Veterans Health Administration in the United States (Kerr & Fleming 2007). Thus mutual *learning* constitutes the third function of international health system com-parisons. As data become more robust it becomes feasible to analyse the factors contributing to better performance – this constitutes an important part of the still limited evidence-based knowledge on health system engineering. The value of sharing similar challenges and expe-riences is greatly enhanced when governments identify peer groups for comparison. For example, the Nordic Council of Ministers is involved in efforts to compare the quality of care among their countries – Denmark, Finland, Iceland, Norway and Sweden. The results of the study are intended for use in monitoring and evaluating health serv-ices while providing a forum for sharing learning experiences amongst participating countries (Wait & Nolte 2005).

In summary, accountability and strategy development are currently the major functions driving governments to engage in international health system comparisons. However, mutual learning is gaining fur-ther interest with the increasing scientific robustness of knowledge cre-ated through health systems research.

Scope of international health system comparisons

The scope of international health system comparisons varies by coun-try, type of established health information system and availability of resources. The first stage in setting up an international comparison comprises the development or identification of a conceptual frame-work against which the utility and validity of a set of indicators can be assessed. International organizations have presented conceptual frame-works that aim to describe the underlying constructs and domains and their mutual relations. For example, WHO and the OECD developed such frameworks for health system performance assessment to form the basis for *The world health report 2000* and a frame for the HCQI project, respectively (Kelley & Hurst 2006) (see Box 5.6.2).

Box 5.6.2 Standardization of performance concepts in international health system comparisons – WHO and OECD conceptual frameworks

WHO *health system performance measurement*: WHO chose multidimensional tiers to conceptualize performance, reflecting those considered to be the main goals of a health system – improvement of population health, responsiveness to population expectations and fairness in financial contribution across the population. The main features of this framework are summarized below. Additionally, four main functions were identified (stewardship, financing, service provision, resource generation) in order to provide a relevant policy context for the performance of a health system.

WHO health system performance framework

Components for assessment goals	Average level	Distribution
Health improvement	✓	✓
Responsiveness to expectations	✓	✓
Fairness in financial contribution	–	✓

Source: Murray & Frenk 2000

Boundaries of health systems in the WHO conceptual framework

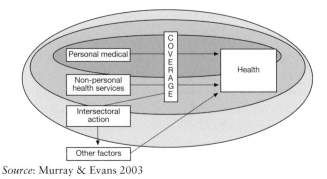

Source: Murray & Evans 2003

Box 5.6.2 cont'd

OECD HCQI conceptual framework: The OECD also adopted a multidimensional approach. The framework below presents a visual summary of the dimensions of health-care performance including: quality, access, cost, efficiency and equity. It also presents a picture of factors related to, but distinct from, health system performance, such as: health system design, policy and context; non-health care determinants of health; and overall levels of health. Finally, it highlights the particular dimensions of quality of care that are the focus of the HCQI project: effectiveness, safety and responsiveness or patient experience.

Conceptual framework for HCQI project

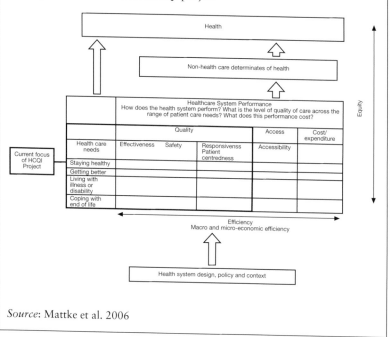

Source: Mattke et al. 2006

The design of a proper set of indicators within such frameworks necessitates the initial, unavoidable task of answering fundamental questions relating to the definition of health system performance, selection of measures and interaction among the individual indicators.

The set cannot be a random list of measures or a simple repository of information and is normally conceived as a system articulating information with a certain purpose – in the case of WHO and OECD, to inform the comparative performance of health systems. There is consensus that indicators selected to compare performance should: (i) be scientifically solid; (ii) be politically relevant; (iii) be available across a sufficient number of countries; and (iv) allow for sustainable and feasible data collection across time (Hurtado et al. 2001; Kelley & Hurst 2006).

The frameworks developed by international organizations encompass structures used in several existing national performance reports and, as Arah et al. (2003) noted, contain many similar dimensions and perspectives. For a classification of the ongoing health system comparisons one can also look at whole system, multilateral, bilateral, disease, sector- or domain-specific approaches. Table 5.6.1 provides a broad categorization of different types of international comparisons of health systems. Some are undertaken on a regular, systematic basis (e.g. OECD HCQI project); others were one-time comparisons (e.g. between United Kingdom's NHS and California's Kaiser Permanente). Although the list is by no means comprehensive, many of these endeavours seek to overcome epidemiological, economic or geopolitical considerations by identifying specific components of the health system and measuring performance on those factors.

As noted earlier, initiatives such as those undertaken by the WHO and OECD assess a broader set of health measures than those studied in traditional comparisons of health systems (e.g. health expenditures among countries; indicators such as life expectancy). Taken a step further, countries and international agencies are increasingly implementing sub-level comparisons, especially at the European Union level. For example, Ben RHM and ISARE are two European Commission funded projects that identified European regions with some common features in their political, socio-demographic and epidemiological development and initiated benchmarking efforts to determine the structural, functional and quality differences of health services within the selected countries. Experiences from these projects show that smaller countries often prefer comparative efforts in which they are evaluated against regions, rather than the entire national health system, of bigger countries (Fédération Nationale des Observatoires Régionaux de la Santé 2007). Furthermore, sub-level comparisons enabled network-

Table 5.6.1 *General classification of health system comparisons*

Type of initiative	Systems/factors involved	Selected examples
Entire health system	Broad comparisons of overall health systems	• *The world health report 2000*[1] • Commonwealth Fund studies comparing high-performing health systems in the United States, United Kingdom, Canada, Germany, Australia and New Zealand[2]
Multi-lateral	Comparisons between national or sub-national health systems	• Commonwealth Fund study on health system comparisons of six countries that measure various dimensions of health-care systems including quality, access, equity, efficiency and healthy lives[3] • European Commission-funded project: Indicateurs de Santé des Régions Europeénnes (ISARE) covers 283 health regions in 24 European countries[4]
Bilateral	Comparisons between national health systems; national health systems and provincial regional health systems; or national health systems and health-care organizations	• Comparison of health system in Canadian province of Ontario and health system in the Netherlands[5] • Comparison of the United Kingdom's NHS and California's Kaiser Permanente in the United States[6]
Disease-specific	Comparisons of specific health conditions across countries/regions	• Joint WHO/European Commission project: Benchmarking Regional Health Management (Ben RHM) covering 19 regions in 15 European countries and tracking 3 conditions – diabetes, breast cancer and measles[7] • Nordic Council of Ministers' comparisons of specific disease conditions in Denmark, Finland, Iceland, Norway and Sweden[8]

Table 5.6.1 *cont'd*

Sector-specific	Comparisons of segments of the health-care system e.g. primary care	• Comparison of primary care systems for 18 OECD countries from 1970-1998[9]
Domain-based	Comparisons among components of the health-care system e.g. waiting times, patient experiences	• OECD HCQI project involving 30 countries[10] • Commonwealth Fund study on patient experiences in 7 countries[11]

Sources: [1]WHO 2000; [2,3]Davis et al. 2007; [4] Fédération Nationale des Observatoires Régionaux de la Santé 2007; [5]Tawfik-Shukor et al. 2007; [6]Feachem et al. 2002; [7]Brand et al. 2007; [8]Wait & Nolte 2005; [9]Macinko et al. 2003; [10]Kelley & Hurst 2006; [11]Schoen et al. 2007.

ing opportunities among health experts and fostered mutual learning experiences (Schröder-Bäck 2007).

A major reform of the health system provides a unique opportunity for countries to undertake comparative studies, allowing related policy and performance changes to be monitored. In 2006, following such a restructuring, the Netherlands initiated a comparative study of their health sector and that of Ontario, Canada, which had undergone reforms during a similar time period. Both Ontario and the Netherlands invested in the development of reliable health system performance assessment frameworks. The study mapped various dimensions of these and compared each of the systems. Conceptual and contextual problems prevent the two systems from being completely comparable but they still provide a starting point for such benchmarking efforts and highlight the range of issues involved in international comparisons (Tawfik-Shukor et al. 2007).

Some researchers have attempted to overcome the larger methodological barriers of cross-country assessments by examining specific components of health systems. For example, a controversial study by Feachem et al. (2002) compared performance factors such as access and responsiveness in the British NHS to the California branch of Kaiser Permanente in the United States. The authors concluded that Kaiser Permanente performed better and had a better integrated and managed system than the NHS, despite similar costs. The study was heavily criticized for flaws in both its methodology and its assumptions (Himmelstein & Woolhandler 2002) and illustrates that, while individual components of health systems can be compared, it is imperative that such exercises are approached with caution.

This discussion of the various comparative projects is far from complete but illustrates the type of work currently being implemented. In addition, it should be mentioned that major developments are underway to increase the potential of international comparisons in health care at the level of both international research and cross-system databases. At the research level, studies in areas such as cancer care, cardiovascular diseases and diabetes have largely increased the availability of international comparative data. Research projects funded by the European Commission (e.g. Ben RHM, ISARE) are good examples of this type of work currently being implemented. The field of health systems analysis has also expanded and various targeted research groups have been established over the past decade.

Apart from these research processes, expert working groups in international organizations are leading efforts to increase data comparability among countries. Along with WHO's work on the classification of diseases (ICD-9, ICD-10, ICD-11) (WHO 2007) and the OECD's focus on comparing national health accounts and health financing data (OECD System of Health Accounts), there is active collaboration among WHO, OECD and the European Union (Eurostat 2008) to improve the comparability of national data systems.

By contrast, several transition countries in the European region are still establishing their health information systems and therefore comparative studies occur on a limited basis. However, as a first step, a number of countries are involved in the Health Metrics Network (http://www.who.int/healthmetrics) which is hosted by WHO and enables them to overcome problems of data availability and improve the quality and reliability of their information systems. Although some transition countries lack optimal quality control measures, many are increasing investments in efforts to align their health systems with international standards. For example, WHO recently led initiatives by which Armenia and Kyrgyzstan developed performance assessment frameworks to aid them in strengthening their health sectors. In the long run such endeavours will lead to benchmarking among comparable countries in the WHO European Region and highlight areas for improvement in health system performance.

As seen in this section, international health system performance comparisons have a broad scope. Such assessments depend largely on project aims, policy opportunities and the availability of resources and data. Each type of comparison – from multilateral to domain specific – serves an important function in drawing attention to a particular health system and possible ways to strengthen its performance.

Methodological issues in conducting international health system comparisons: lessons from the OECD experience

Initiatives to build relevant and meaningful indicators across different countries face numerous challenges. This section provides an overview of the operational and methodological issues involved in such efforts. The matters explored follow the experience within the OECD HCQI project but can be generalized to comparative efforts in similar international health systems.

The OECD HCQI project started in 2002 with the objective of developing a set of health-care quality indicators that can be reported reliably and regularly across thirty OECD countries. The purpose was to help raise questions for further investigation into differences in the quality of care across countries. The number of countries involved in the HCQI project has recently expanded to include all European Union Member States, including non-OECD nations, following an agreement between the European Commission's Directorate-General for Health and Consumers and the OECD.

The HCQI project has undergone several phases. The initial list of indicators consisted of eighty-six potential measures in five priority areas of care (patient safety; mental health care; health promotion, prevention and primary care; cardiac care; and diabetes care). However, data availability proved to be a major hurdle.[1] There has been a two-pronged strategy to overcome this barrier: (i) initiate regular data collection of widely available indicators; and (ii) simultaneously work with countries to improve information systems and enhance the comparability of indicators. At the current state of development, the regularly updated set covers health areas outlined in Table 5.6.2 (Garcia-Armesto et al. 2007). In addition, fourteen measures for patient safety and two for mental health care have reached the

---

[1] For a complete description of the short-list building process, refer to entire issue of Mattke et al. 2006.

Table 5.6.2 HCQI project indicators

Care for acute conditions	
Outcome	**Process**
In-hospital acute myocardial infarction case-fatality rates	Waiting times for surgery after hip fracture, age 65+
In-hospital ischaemic/haemorrhagic stroke case-fatality rates	

Cancer care	
Outcome	**Process**
Survival rate for colorectal cancer	Mammography screening
Survival rate for breast cancer	Cervical cancer screening
Survival rate for cervical cancer	

Care for chronic conditions	
Outcome	**Process**
Hospital admission rate for asthma (age 18+)	Annual retina examination for diabetics
Asthma mortality rates (age 5-39)	

Prevention of communicable diseases	
Outcome	**Process**
Incidence of measles	Vaccination against measles
Incidence of pertussis	Vaccination against pertussis (+ diphtheria + tetanus)
Incidence of Hepatitis B	Vaccination against Hepatitis B
	Vaccination against influenza (age 65+)

Other
Smoking rates

last phase of piloting and it is envisioned that they will be included in the regular set for 2009 data collection. The indicator set includes both process and outcome measures since they provide different but complementary insights – information derived from process indicators is easier to translate into specific improvements; outcome indicators may be subject to multifactor causal attribution but are indispensable in aligning performance assessment with health system objectives. The key is to establish a balance between these two types of measures.

Within the HCQI project, indicators are considered ready for international comparisons once the agreed threshold of ten countries can provide data from well-identified and stable databases according to agreed definitions (age group, codes, methods of identification). Indicators are added and deleted in order to ensure that the set remains responsive to changes in data availability or measurement quality. The tension between maintaining a stable set over time and the imperative to convey a concise message to policy-makers should be balanced while making decisions about adding and deleting indicators. Furthermore, there is a trade-off between implementing rigorous methodological approaches and including all countries in the calculations. A balance point is achieved when the methodology is strict enough to provide policy insights but flexible enough to allow participation by the maximum number of countries.

Another compromise is to achieve homogeneous information systems without overburdening the countries that are required to comply with such constraints, especially those bearing the cost of adding new data items to their collection structures. The improvement of national health information systems can be considered a positive side effect of involvement in international performance assessment initiatives but any changes must take account of existing structures.

The OECD HCQI project provides rich empirical experience of dealing with complex methodological barriers. Several key issues that need to be considered when establishing and monitoring cross-country performance indicators are listed below.

1. Specifying indicators using internationally standardized definitions.
2. Controlling for differences in population structures across countries.
3. Adjusting for differences in information systems' ability to track individual patients.
4. Controlling variability of data sources.

5. Identifying nationally representative data.
6. Determining retrospective completeness of the time series.

These are described in the following sub-sections together with suggestions to overcome them.

Specifying indicators using internationally standardized definitions

Standardization constitutes the best way to ensure data comparability across countries since it is applied across all stages of data production, storage and report.

WHO leads the main initiative in this field through the WHO Family of International Classifications (WHO-FIC) programme, comprising three types of systems:

1. International Classification of Diseases (ICD)
2. International Classification of Health Interventions (ICHI)
3. International Classification of Functioning, Disability and Health (ICF)

The ICD is used to classify diseases and other health problems and has become the international standard diagnostic classification for epidemiological and health management purposes, ICD-10 is the latest version (an updated ICD-11 is currently under development). However, countries can find it difficult to update to new versions of ICD as its impact in shaping national information systems involves issues such as staff training, adapting to new definitions and changes to funding schemes. For example, ICD-10 contains 12 640 codes while ICD-9 had only 6969. As a consequence, the use of different versions of ICD across countries is a real issue when attempting to identify indicators for international comparison.

In the absence of an internationally accepted system for reconciling ICD-9 and ICD-10, the HCQI project has opted to develop ad hoc validated crosswalks for the indicators relying on them. The first initiative comprises fourteen patient safety indicators that are currently being tested for adoption in 2009. The International Methodology Consortium for Coded Health Information (IMECCHI) is an expert network that has worked with the HCQI project to develop and validate a manual for the calculation of these measures. Consideration of both ICD versions and the national adaptations of ICD-10 provides a solid basis for 'translation' and enhancing comparability across countries (Drösler 2008).

There are other outstanding issues concerning the calculation of indicators based on standardized codified databases. For instance, actions to address variation in documentation and coding practices across countries will entail some cultural changes that take time. However, participation in international initiatives has the beneficial effect of drawing attention to practices that might be regarded as adequate at the national level, but become less acceptable when compared to those in similar countries.

The current lack of an international classification system for procedures is another relevant aspect, especially for the specification of process indicators. The ICHI covers a wide range of measures for curative and preventive purposes but is still in its beta trial version and entering extensive field trials before being submitted for endorsement by the governing bodies of WHO (WHO 2007). Despite encouraging progress, it may be several years before ICHI is ready for adoption and therefore the HCQI project currently utilizes ICD-9-CM and ICD-10 to specify procedures.

Endorsed in 2001, the ICF seems promising. However, it is not yet used widely across countries and its specific applicability in defining outcome indicators needs to be explored further.

Controlling for differences in population structures across countries

A number of indicators can be affected by a country's demographic structure. For example, survival or mortality rates are influenced by the age and gender structure of the population. This demographic composition has an impact on the epidemiology of diseases and becomes a confounding factor that assessments need to adjust for. Age and sex standardization facilitates comparisons across countries by controlling for these differences in national populations.

When selecting a reference population it is important to decide whether to use the general population or one that is disease-specific (i.e. has the distribution of patients with the respective disease). As the incidence and prevalence of most diseases increases with age, disease-specific populations tend to weigh older population segments more heavily. A disease-specific reference population is therefore theoretically superior but is frequently not feasible as it requires the construction of a population for each disease. Many research projects overcome this problem by using general population weights. Another technique reduces distortion by removing the segment of the population that is less affected by the disease, truncating the sample to include only those above a certain age, e.g. forty (Lousbergh et al. 2002).

The HCQI project initially considered the 1980 OECD population structure for age-standardization calculations. This decision is now being revised because: (i) the structure of this population is becoming outdated with the demographic ageing trends in OECD societies; and (ii) the OECD has expanded from twenty-four to thirty countries and therefore the 1980 reference has limited validity. The transition to a 2005 OECD reference population is under assessment. The adoption of a truncated population is also being analysed, especially as countries such as Japan face a higher prevalence of myocardial infarction in the elderly group rather than the typical middle-age range.

There is a trade-off in updating the structure of the reference population and maintaining valid comparable data over time. Other international comparative projects face similar challenges caused by ageing populations and incorporating new member countries, e.g. European Union's development of the European Community Health Indicators Monitoring project (2008) or the European Health Interview Survey (2008). Steps should be taken to ensure that the data remain valid and comparable over time.

Adjusting for differences in information systems' ability to track individual patients

Indicators often take the form of rates in which the denominator is a specific group of patients – this cluster of indicators includes hospital fatality rates among patients with certain diagnoses or rates of specific procedures among chronically ill patients. Two interrelated issues affect the feasibility of these indicators: (i) the need to distinguish between different patients and repeated events affecting the same patient; and (ii) the necessity of detecting a patient's contact at any level of care and across different institutions. However, national information systems do not have a uniform ability to identify patients and often the only data available are activity records which count each episode of care separately, even if the same patient was involved.

There is a clear need to harmonize calculations across countries to ensure data comparability; Mattke et al. (2006) illustrate the effect of different bases of calculation on thirty-day hospital fatality rates for myocardial infarction and stroke. Currently, the most generally feasible approach is events-based calculations in which it can reasonably be argued that the validity of a specific indicator is not affected. However, a unique patient identifier is the most efficient tool for performing patient-based calculations and the OECD recently began encouraging member countries to establish these across their key health information systems.

Controlling variability of data sources

National information systems comprise a variety of data sources with substantial differences in their structure; the nature of data recorded; and the purpose for which they were conceived. Data systems have been shaped to serve monitoring functions within each country. Often, the purpose of such monitoring is neither performance comparison nor quality measurement but rather to support administrative activities such as budget distribution or system management (see Box 5.6.3 for a summary of the main data sources and their general strengths and weaknesses). This means that a fair assessment of the available sources across countries and their suitability (on an indicator by indicator basis) will be required when building indicators for international comparison. For instance, process indicators such as vaccination or screening rates can be built from data from varying sources across countries but the nature of the available data will vary with the structure of health service provisions in each system.

In some countries, prevention activities are organized in large-scale national programmes with routine databases that can be used for analysis. However, data in other countries are managed by each municipality and therefore registries are fragmented and not always accessible at the national level. In addition, registries for prevention activities often do not cover settings outside the health-care system (e.g. work or school) and private organizations that provide this type of care can vary by country, complicating the retrieval of documented

---

Box 5.6.3 Sources of information available to assess quality of care across countries

Source	Weaknesses	Strengths
1. **Administrative data** *Admission/ discharge records* *Minimum set of data* *Insurance-reimbursement* *DRGs accounting* *Prescription*	Limited/no information on processes of care and physiological measures of severity Limited/no information on timing (co-morbidities vs. onset or adverse events) Heterogeneous severity within some ICD codes Accuracy depends on documentation and coding Data are used for other purposes, subject to gaming Variation in how administrative data are collected and used, in particular DRG-based payment versus global budgeting versus service-based payment Time lag may limit usefulness Poor development outside the hospital setting	Data availability improving Coding systems (international classifications of diseases) and practices are improving Large data sets optimize precision Comprehensiveness (all hospitals, all payers) avoids sampling/selection bias Data are used for other purposes and therefore subject to auditing and monitoring
2. **National surveys** *Health status* *Health services use* *Pharmaceutical consumption*	Self-reported (recall bias, lack of accuracy due to lay approach of those interviewed) Inability to identify and follow up subjects	Population based rather than patient based information, including individuals that health information systems cannot account for Can provide a basis for access and needs assessments

Box 5.6.3 cont'd

3. National registries *Cancer* *Chronic diseases* *Adverse events* *Certain procedures* *Mortality*	When not mandatory, some eventual selection bias may deem them not representative Resource intensive to register the detailed specific features (e.g. adding cancer staging data to the diagnosis in cancer registries) Not always linkable to other sources of information	Precise specific information
4. Medical records	Data retrieval is work intensive and therefore expensive, even with electronic records Difficult to sustain over time	Complete clinical information and good chronology
5. Patients surveys *Satisfaction* *Experience* *Access*	Low degree of standardization in patient survey tools, often even within countries Cultural influences on concepts such as satisfaction, expectations and experience hinder comparability across countries	Most reliable method of assessing system responsiveness and obtaining information about how patients perceive and experience the care provided Leads to improvements in designing trans-cultural assessment tools

activity. In other cases, programmes are non-existent and services are provided on a demand basis. In all these situations, population surveys might be the most valid source of information.

The key question is whether data from so many different data sources (registries and population surveys) are comparable. As part of a methodological refinement, the HCQI project assessed the data comparability of surveys and programme registries for cancer screening indicators. Median rates of mammography and cervical cancer screening for each available year were calculated separately for programme and survey data. Based on surveys compared to registries, the variation over time is remarkable and suggests that both sources of data should be utilized with caution. Furthermore, international health system comparisons should use the source factor to adjust differences in the indicators.

Identifying nationally representative data

Cross-national assessments should reflect country-wide data. This is especially true when using process indicators (e.g. measuring care for chronic diseases) where data are often derived from pilots or ad hoc registries and raises serious concerns about the representativeness of data. Unique patient identifiers could make patients much more traceable within routinely collected information and thereby increase the reliability of data collected.

To ensure data comparability across countries, the HCQI project recently adopted a system of classification of the quality of data. This comprises three levels:

- A – corresponds to national administrative registries, with demonstrated non-selection bias;
- B – accounts for non-national administrative registries with demonstrated non-selection bias;
- C – applies to ad hoc registries (e.g. research and pilots) and any other source not classified elsewhere.

Such a system has the advantage of enabling data collection at different levels of quality and using all available data sources, while preserving the rigour of the analysis. For instance, only data within categories A and B can be utilized but C type data can be collected and efforts made to raise them to the two higher categories.

Determining retrospective completeness of the time series

Almost all international comparative efforts face problems in obtaining uninterrupted, reliable data over a given time period. This limits the validity of trend analysis and affects the ability to interpret related indicators together. The time lag between policy implementation (e.g. breast cancer screening for a target population) and expected outcomes (improvement in breast cancer survival rates) can hardly be accounted for in the absence of time series. Prospective time series rely on regularly updated, sustainable data sources; retrospective completeness could be hindered by problems with (for example) the availability of data that need to be considered during international comparisons.

Comparative projects of health systems similar to those developed and implemented by the OECD have great potential in driving health policy. There can be numerous methodological barriers but the process of identifying and overcoming these pitfalls can lead to valid, reliable conclusions that enable effective health decision-making for overall system improvement.

Turning international health system comparisons into health system performance management

International comparisons of health systems can offer governments a valuable tool to revise their policies, review accountability agreements and reassess resource allocation procedures. However, to strengthen health systems it is necessary to use these comparisons for performance management purposes and, as a first step, to integrate performance data needs into the policy-making process. An example from the Ontario Ministry of Health and Long-Term Care illustrates the systematic use of performance information and its flow through the decision-making cycle (Fig. 5.6.1). The diagram shows that comparative data can be used at different stages of the health ministry's business cycle which, as a continuous improvement process, facilitates the use of strategic performance information for performance improvement purposes.

Similar examples can be found in the United States Veterans Health Administration where performance indicators were used to monitor the effects of health system reforms while driving accountability agreements at sub-system and individual levels (Kerr & Fleming

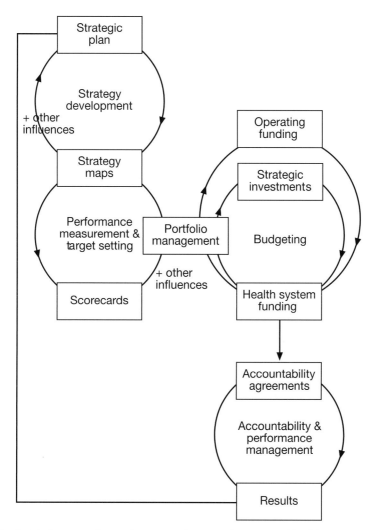

Fig. 5.6.1 Conceptualizing the range of potential impacts of health system performance comparisons on the policy–making process

Source: Veillard et al. 2009

2007). Other successful case studies range from health-care organiza-tions (Kaplan & Norton 2005) to private industry (Kaplan & Norton 2000). In order to guide health policy-makers in the delivery of better results, it is critical to turn strategy-based performance information into performance management systems.

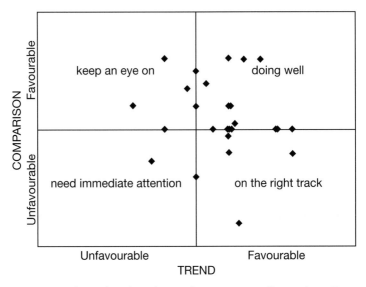

Fig. 5.6.2 Translating benchmarking information to policy-makers. Example from the Ministry of Health and Long-Term Care, Ontario, Canada

Source: Health Results Team for Information Management 2006

Translating performance information for policy-makers

Another crucial aspect of performance management is translating performance information to make it simple and clear to policy-makers (Lavis 2006). For instance, the Ontario Ministry of Health and Long-Term Care represented health system performance measures from two different perspectives: variation in performance over time and against selected benchmarks (or comparators), respectively. These approaches are interesting examples of how to present performance information to health policy-makers in relevant ways. For instance, Fig. 5.6.2 indicates to Ontarian decision-makers whether performance is improving; if it is favourable compared to pre-defined benchmarks (standards, international comparators, provincial comparators); and the policy actions required for different levels of performance. This approach suffered from standardization difficulties but with comparable performance data can be a promising practice for governments wishing to benchmark their health system performance in a concrete fashion.

Funnel plots are another tool for benchmarking performance management and are used increasingly by countries such as the United

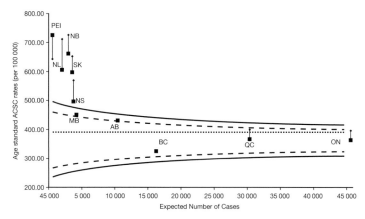

Fig. 5.6.3 Funnel plots for ambulatory care sensitive conditions for different Canadian provinces, 2006 data

Source: Health Results Team for Information Management 2006

Kingdom and Canada (Spiegelhalter 2005). Fig. 5.6.3 shows a set of funnel plots that represent the performance indicator (in this case, rate of ambulatory care conditions) with deviations from the average. A trend component is incorporated by using an arrow to indicate whether performance has improved or declined; the length of the arrow shows the relative magnitude of change over time. The calculation of funnel plots is associated with some statistical problems but they can provide policy-makers with a visual representation of their country's relative performance against comparators that is easy to interpret and helps to identify areas for improvement (Spiegelhalter 2005).

Benchmarking health system performance

Despite the methodological difficulties of comparative efforts, the diversity of benchmarking initiatives shows that national and regional health authorities are gaining increasingly from comparing their performance and learning policy lessons from better performers. The selection of benchmarks is becoming more pragmatic and increasingly is driven by the specific strategies of health systems and by their performance expectations. Performance measurement thus becomes the basis for policy discussions concerning how to improve health system performance and specifically about sharing how others have achieved higher performance in a particular context. For instance, a number of

---

Box 5.6.4 Benchmarking for better health system performance: example of the Commonwealth Fund in the United States

The Commonwealth Fund, a private organization in the United States, established the Commission on a High Performance Health System in 2005. This group of experts was assembled to analyse best practices from several health systems. Their benchmarking shows that Denmark performs better than any other country in Europe on measures of patient satisfaction and primary care; Germany is a leader in national hospital quality benchmarking; and the Netherlands and the United Kingdom lead on transparency in reporting quality data (Davis 2007).

Within the United States, the Commission also benchmarked states against each other across five key dimensions of health system performance – access, quality, avoidable hospital use and costs, equity, healthy lives (The Commonwealth Fund Commission on a High Performance Health System 2006). Cumulative and dimension-specific ranks were published along with an analysis of the policy implications. The results are publicly available and are intended to assist states to identify opportunities better to meet the population's health needs and learn from high-performing states (Cantor et al. 2007).

European countries have invested in efforts to benchmark their performance against countries such as Australia, Canada, New Zealand and the United States through the work of the Commonwealth Fund (Box 5.6.4).

In this perspective, a well-designed benchmarking system has the potential to guide policy development and can be used both prospectively and retrospectively (Nolte et al. 2006). It can support better understanding of past performance and the rationale behind certain performance patterns (retrospective use) and also help to revise strategies for improving future performance (prospective use).

Such strategy-based performance benchmarking systems have certain characteristics.

• Strategic focus: link between health system strategies and international benchmarking efforts ensures that policy lessons will be designed for those who can act upon the findings (the policy-makers).

- Adaptability and flexibility: benchmarking efforts can undertake both large (full health system comparisons) and narrower scope studies, using tools that can be administered in a time frame that matches the policy-makers' agendas (e.g. using patient survey comparisons such as that of the Commonwealth Fund).
- Data standardization: efforts are made to standardize data and facilitate credible comparisons.
- Policy focus rather than research focus: benchmarking systems are driven not by experts or researchers but by policy-makers supported by experts and researchers.
- Efforts to translate performance information and policy lessons for decision-makers: new tools (e.g. funnel plots) are used increasingly to represent performance information in rigorous yet explicit ways, conveying data in a meaningful manner while reducing the need to rank health systems in league tables.
- Sensitivity to political and contextual issues: interpretation of indicator data should not lose sight of the policy context within which they are measured; of the players involved in formulating and implementing policy; of the time lag needed to assess the impact of different policies; and of aspects of health care that remain unmeasured by available data.

Conclusions

This chapter reviews the reasons for increased governmental interest in international health system performance comparisons – they offer greater accountability and transparency and support strategy review and development. However, mutual learning is a third function that is becoming more important with the increasing scientific robustness of knowledge created through health systems research. Projects such as the OECD HCQI project or the Commonwealth Fund's cross-national benchmarking initiatives in the United States are two good examples of comparative efforts in this direction. The scope of experiences is growing and covers comparisons at different levels of the health system and from different perspectives. The methodological difficulties of such exercises can be classified and addressed over time but require investment from countries. Governments can achieve superior health system performance through the powerful policy instruments offered by linking performance measurement to performance management;

translating performance information in ways that are meaningful for policy-makers; and investing in benchmarking and mutual learning.

Finally, important requirements for fostering the value of international comparisons and their practical use for performance improvement are listed below.

- Recognize the value of information and make substantial investments in improving minimum data quality for developing and transition countries (e.g. through the Health Metrics Network) and data quality for developed countries (through projects such as the OECD HCQI).
- Build upon knowledge of how to resolve methodological issues in health system performance comparisons in order to strengthen such comparisons.
- Encourage international organizations to provide active support for data standardization efforts within their member states.
- Achieve a balance between process and outcome indicators in comparisons of health system performance in order to provide different but complementary insights into health-care processes.
- Avoid inconsistencies, strategic misalignment and (ultimately) health system sub-performance by selecting indicators that cascade across different (macro, meso, micro) levels of the health system through performance measurement and accountability mechanisms.
- Set up benchmark networks structured against common strategic objectives and performance patterns to build stronger analytical capacities within and between countries.
- Evaluate indicator data across countries with an adequate understanding of the regulatory and evaluative policies that underpin them.
- Develop and use graphic tools to convey performance information to policy-makers in a meaningful way.
- Undertake further research in health system performance management and share the results effectively among countries.

References

Agency for Healthcare Research and Quality (AHRQ) (2008a). *National healthcare disparities report 2007*. Rockville: US Department of Health and Human Services.

Agency for Healthcare Research and Quality (AHRQ) (2008b). *National healthcare quality report 2007*. Rockville: U.S. Department of Health and Human Services.

Arah, OA. Klazinga, NS. Delnoij, DM. ten Asbroek, AH. Custers, T (2003). 'Conceptual frameworks for health systems performance: a quest for effectiveness, quality, and improvement.' *International Journal for Quality in Health Care*, 15(5): 377–398.

Brand, H. et al. (2007). *Benchmarking Regional Health Management II (Ben RHM II) final report*. Bielefeld: Institute of Public Health of Nordrhein-Westfalen.

Cantor, JC. Schoen, C. Belloff, D. How, SKH. McCarthy, D. (2007). *Aiming higher: results from a state scorecard on health system performance*. New York: The Commonwealth Fund Commission on a High Performance Health System (http://www.commonwealthfund.org/publications/publications_show.htm?doc_id=494551).

Davis, K. (2007). *Learning from high performance health systems around the globe*. New York: The Commonwealth Fund. (http://www.commonwealthfund.org/publications/publications_show.htm?doc_id=441618).

Davis, K. Schoen, C. Schoenbaum, SC. Doty, MM. Holmgren, AL. Kriss, JL. Shea, KK (2007). *Mirror, mirror on the wall: an international update on the comparative performance of American health care*. New York: The Commonwealth Fund.

Drösler, S (2008). *Facilitating cross-national comparisons of indicators for patient safety at the national health-system level in the OECD countries*. Paris: Organisation for Economic Co-operation and Development (OECD Health Technical Papers no.19).

European Community Health Indicators Monitoring (ECHIM) (2008). *European Community Health Indicators Monitoring project*. Brussels: European Commission (http://www.echim.org/index.html).

European Health Interview Survey (EHIS) (2008). *European Health Interview Survey*. Brussels: European Commission (http://ec.europa.eu/health/ph_information/dissemination/reporting/ehss_01_en.htm).

Eurostat (2008). *Eurostat database*. Brussels: European Commission (http://epp.eurostat.ec.europa.eu/portal/page?_pageid=1090,30070682,1090_33076576&_dad=portal&_schema=PORTAL).

Feachem, R. Sekhri, NK. White, KI (2002). 'Getting more for their dollar: a comparison of the NHS with California's Kaiser Permanente.' *British Medical Journal*, 324(7330): 135–143.

FNORS (2007). *Project ISARE 3: Health indicators in the European regions*. Paris: Fédération Nationale des Observatoires Régionaux de la Santé.

Garcia-Armesto, S. Lapetra, MLG. Wei. L. Kelley, E. & Members of HCQI Expert Group (2007). *Health care quality indicators project 2006. Data collection update report*. Paris: Organisation for Economic Co-operation and Development (OECD Health Working Papers no. 29).

Goodspeed, SW (2006). 'Metrics help rural hospitals achieve world-class performance.' *Journal for Healthcare Quality*, 28(5): 28–32.

Health Results Team for Information Management (2006). *Strategy mapping*. Toronto: Ontario Ministry of Health and Long-Term Care (unpublished).

Himmelstein, DU. Woolhandler, S (2002). 'Getting more for their dollar: Kaiser v the NHS. Price adjustments falsify comparison.' *British Medical Journal*, 324(7349): 1332–1339.

Holland, WW (ed.) (1988). *The European community atlas of avoidable death*. Oxford: Oxford University Press.

Holland, WW (1990). 'Avoidable death as a measure of quality.' *Quality Assurance in Health Care*, 2(3-4): 227–233.

Hsiao, WC (1992). 'Comparing health care systems: what nations can learn from one another.' *Journal of Health Politics, Policy and Law*, 17(4): 613–636.

Hurtado, MP. Swift, EK. Corrigan, JM (eds.) (2001). *Envisioning the National Health Care Quality report*. Washington: National Academies Press.

Kaplan, R. Norton, D (1992). 'The balanced scorecard: measures that drive performance.' *Harvard Business Review*, 70(1): 71–79.

Kaplan, R. Norton, D (2000). 'Having trouble with your strategy? Then map it.' *Harvard Business Review*, 78(5): 167–176.

Kaplan, R. Norton, D (2005). 'Office of strategy management.' *Harvard Business Review*, 83(10): 72–80.

Kelley, E. Hurst, J (2006). *Health care quality indicators project conceptual framework paper*. Paris: Organisation for Economic Co-operation and Development (Health Working Papers no. 23).

Kerr, E. Fleming, B (2007). 'Making performance indicators work: experiences of US Veterans Health Administration.' *British Medical Journal*, 335(7627): 971–973.

Klein, R (1997). 'Learning from others: shall the last be the first?' *Journal of Health Politics, Policy and Law*, 22(5): 1267–1278.

Lavis, J (2006). 'Research, public policymaking, and knowledge-translation processes: Canadian efforts to build bridges.' *Journal of Continuing Education in the Health Professions*, 26(1): 37–45.

Legido-Quigley, H. McKee, M. Walshe, K. Suñol, R. Nolte, E. Klazinga, N (2008). 'How can quality of health care be safeguarded across the European Union?' *British Medical Journal*, 336(7650): 920–923.

Lousbergh, D. Buntinx, F. Geys, H. Du Bois, M. Dhollander, D. Molenberghs, G (2002). 'Prostate-specific antigen screening coverage and prostate cancer incidence rates in the Belgian province of Limburg in 1996–1998.' *European Journal of Cancer Prevention*, 11(6): 547–549.

Macinko, J. Starfield, B. Shi, L (2003). 'The contribution of primary care systems to health outcomes within Organisation for Economic Co-operation and Development (OECD) countries, 1970–1998.' *Health Services Research*, 38(3): 831–865.

Mattke, S. Epstein, AM. Leatherman, S (eds.) (2006). *International Journal for Quality in Health Care*, 18 (Suppl. 1): 1–56.

Mattke, S. Kelley, E. Scherer, P. Hurst, J. Lapetra, MLG. & HCQI Expert Group Members (2006). *Health care quality indicators project. Initial indicators report*. Paris: Organisation for Economic Co-operation and Development (OECD Health Working Papers No. 22).

McKee, M (2001). *The world health report 2000: advancing the debate*. Prepared for the European Regional Consultation on *The world health report 2000*, Copenhagen, Denmark, 3–4 September 2001. Copenhagen: WHO Regional Office for Europe (http://www.euro.who.int/document/obs/HSPAMcKeebackgrounddocument.pdf.).

Mountin, JW. Perrott, GS (1947). 'Health insurance programs and plans of western Europe: summary of observations.' *Public Health Report*, 62: 369–399.

Murry, CJL. Frenk, J (2000). *A framework for assessing the performance of health systems*. Geneva: World Health Organization.

Murray, CJL. Evans, D (eds.) (2003). *Health systems performance assessment. Debates, methods and empiricism*. Geneva: World Health Organization.

Nolte, E. Wait, S. McKee, M (2006). *Investing in health: benchmarking health systems*. London: The Nuffield Trust.

OECD (2001). *Health at a glance 2001*. Paris: Organisation for Economic Co-operation and Development.

OECD (2007). *Health at a glance 2007*. Paris: Organisation for Economic Co-operation and Development.

Rosenmöller, M. McKee, M. Baeten, R, Glinos, IA (2006). Patient mobility: the context and issues. In: Rosenmöller, M. McKee, M. Baeten, R (eds.) *Patient mobility in the European Union. Learning from experience*. Copenhagen: WHO Regional Office for Europe.

Rutstein, DD. Berenberg, W. Chalmers, TC. Child, CG. Fishman, AP. Perrin, EB (1976). 'Measuring the quality of medical care. A clinical method.' *New England Journal of Medicine*, 294(11): 582–588.

Schoen, C. Osborn, R. Doty, M. Bishop, M. Peugh, J. Murukutla, N (2007). 'Toward higher-performance health systems: adults' health care experiences in seven countries, 2007.' *Health Affairs*, 26(6): 717–734.

Schoen, C. Osborn, R. Huynh, PT. Doty, M. Zapert, K. Peugh, J. Davis, K (2005). 'Taking the pulse of health care systems: experiences of patients with health problems in six countries.' *Health Affairs (Millwood)*, 16(Suppl. web exclusives): 509–525.

Schröder-Bäck, P. (2007). *Results from the Benchmarking Regional Health Management II (BEN II) study* [PowerPoint presentation]. Bielefeld: Institute of Public Health of Nordrhein-Westfalen.

Spiegelhalter, DJ. (2005). 'Funnel plots for comparing institutional performance.' *Statistics in Medicine*, 24(8): 1185–1202.

Tawfik-Shukor, A. Klazinga, NS. Arah, OA (2007). 'Comparing health system performance assessment and management approaches in the Netherlands and Ontario, Canada.' *BMC Health Services Research*, 7: 25.

The Commonwealth Fund Commission on a High Performance Health System (2006). *Why not the best? Results from a national scorecard on U.S. health system performance* [online]. New York, The Commonwealth Fund (http://www.commonwealthfund.org/publications/publications_show.htm?doc_id=401577).

Veillard, J. Huymh, T. Kadandale, S. Ardal, S. Klazinga, N. Brown, A (2009). 'Making health system performance measurement useful to policy makers: aligning strategies, measurement and local health system accountability in Ontario.' *Healthcare Policy,* forthcoming.

Wait, S. Nolte, E (2005). 'Benchmarking health systems: trends, conceptual issues and future perspectives.' *Benchmarking: An International Journal*, 12(5): 436–448.

Westert, GP. Verkleij, H (eds.) (2006). *Dutch health care performance report 2006*. Bilthoven: National Institute for Public Health and the Environment.

WHO (2000). *The world health report 2000 – Health systems: improving performance*. Geneva: World Health Organization.

WHO (2007). *International classification of health interventions*. Geneva (http://www.who.int/classifications/ichi/en/).

WHO (2008). *European Health for All database* (HFA-DB) [online database]. Copenhagen: WHO Regional Office for Europe (http://www.euro.who.int/hfadb).

World Bank (1993). *World development report 1993: investing in health*. New York: Oxford University Press.

Zelman, WN. Pink, GH. Matthias, CB (2003). 'Use of the balanced scorecard in health care.' *Journal of Health Care Finance*, 29(4): 1–16.

PART VI

Conclusions

6.1 Conclusions

PETER C. SMITH, ELIAS MOSSIALOS,
IRENE PAPANICOLAS, SHEILA LEATHERMAN

In the opening chapter we argue that the goals of any performance measurement instrument are twofold: to promote accountability and to improve the performance of the health system. The modern health system is immensely complex, comprising of diverse agents such as insurers, provider organizations, health-care professionals and central and local governments. Measurement of the actions and outcomes of these agents is a necessary condition if the health system is to be held properly to account by citizens and patients. That accountability may be considered a good thing in its own right as it enhances transparency and promotes informed debate about the health system. Furthermore, by providing reassurance that finances are being used effectively, performance measurement can increase government and citizens' willingness to invest additional resources in the health system. In this book the prime focus is how performance measurement and the increased accountability it offers directly promotes the achievement of health system objectives – higher quality and more cost-effective health care and improved population health.

Measurement alone is not sufficient to achieve these objectives. In this book we cite numerous instances of technically satisfactory performance measurement initiatives that have failed to make material impacts on health systems (or indeed have had perversely adverse impacts). For example, there are examples of public performance reporting schemes being ignored; professional improvement efforts becoming moribund; and the use of centrally mandated targets inducing perverse results. To have maximum effect, performance measurement needs to be aligned with other aspects of system design such as financing, market structure, governance arrangements and regulation. Moreover, great attention needs to be paid to the political context within which any performance measurement scheme is implemented. Without careful attention to these broader health system considerations the best performance measurement system will be ineffective.

The effectiveness of any performance measurement initiative should be evaluated not only in relation to (often important) statistical properties such as accuracy and validity but also more broadly – by the extent to which it promotes or compromises broader health system objectives. This book has sought to reflect this broader view of performance measurement. Part 2 describes some recent major technical advances in seeking to measure aspects of health system performance. Part 3 examines some of the analytical techniques currently used to gain a greater understanding of the information contained in performance measures, whilst Part 4 examines advances in some particularly challenging areas of the health system. Part 5 seeks to complete the accountability cycle by examining some of the policy initiatives that have been introduced to promote more effective use of performance measures.

In this chapter we draw out the most important lessons for policy-makers. We begin by emphasizing the need for a conceptual framework to inform the development of performance measurement. Such a framework must be in place in order to undertake a systematic choice of performance indicators, as discussed in the next section. We then examine statistical issues that must be addressed satisfactorily if performance measurement is to be effective and the necessity for indicators to be embedded within an appropriate set of incentives. We go on to discuss the intrinsically political nature of performance measurement, as noted by many authors. In the penultimate section we examine government's role in promoting, facilitating and implementing performance measurement. The concluding section summarizes what we consider to be the main priorities for any health system seeking to improve the measurement of performance.

Conceptual framework

We believe that a fundamental requirement for any performance measurement system is the development of a robust conceptual framework within which specific performance measures can be developed, tested and implemented routinely. The framework should ensure that all major domains of health system performance are covered. The chapters in Part 2 offer an oversight of the main categories of measures that are likely to be useful in most systems. They are summarized below.

Align with health system objectives

It is important that the conceptual framework for performance measurement is aligned with other aspects of health system design. Important considerations might be the payment system; market structure; accountability and governance arrangements; IT infrastructure; and regulation. For example, if a DRG payment system is used it may be sensible to ensure that certain performance measures are consistent with DRG codes. This will enable provider performance to be linked directly with expenditure and will facilitate judgments about efficiency.

Integrate with IT and routine data collection

The link between the performance measurement framework and health system IT arrangements is critical. Rapid changes in technology and analytical methodology, coupled with changing public and professional attitudes, have made the use of large-scale information systems for performance assessment and improvement increasingly feasible (Power 1999). So far, there has been patchy and largely idiosyncratic experience of realizing the potential of new data sources to improve system performance; with little consensus across countries and disparate health systems in technical development. Yet technology has transformed the capacity to store a greater volume of information at a great level of detail; distribute this widely, rapidly and flexibly; and update it quickly. The development of the electronic health record, containing all information on a patient's health history, offers vast potential for capturing performance in many areas.

Sequist and Bates (Chapter 5.3) show that many challenges need to be addressed if such potential is to be transformed into reality. First, the sheer amount of data and the speed at which they can be processed makes it increasingly important and challenging to audit their accuracy. If increasing reliance is to be placed on performance data then the possibility of error carries severe implications. Second, the constant development of technology calls for continual infrastructure investment and maintenance. There will be a need to ensure that the increasing numbers of information systems are mutually compatible if their full value is to be exploited. Policy-makers should work to ensure smooth implementation of IT systems that do not disrupt workflow or hinder efficiency in the short term. Third, there is a crucial coordination role in ensuring that information collected is comparable across institutions and settings. Finally, the storage and use of so much information raises ethical concerns about individual privacy. In short, IT strategy and the performance measurement framework should be considered as an integrated system, developed jointly rather than in isolation.

Include high-priority hard-to-measure areas

Part 4 of the book highlights progress in certain hard-to-measure parts of the health system: primary care, chronic care, mental illness and long-term care. We believe these to be especially important priorities – they represent major expenditure commitments in most health systems, although clinical practice (and therefore the outcomes of services) is especially variable. Furthermore, without adequate performance measurement it becomes very difficult to identify what works in these challenging domains. Paradoxically, it is this shortage of evidence that makes these domains such high priorities for future initiatives.

More generally, the conceptual framework is intended to help identify priorities for new developments and to ensure that collection and analysis efforts are neither misdirected nor duplicated. In short, the eventual requirement is to develop an optimal portfolio of performance measurement instruments that fits a health system's existing organizational structure and accountability arrangements and the available levels of resources and analytical capacity. This may seem a demanding requirement. However, the alternative to maintaining the necessary holistic view will be continued fragmentation and underperformance in some parts of the health system

Design for international comparability

One final consideration in the development of a conceptual framework is the increasing need to harmonize national data with international practice and standardize the definitions of indicators that are compared internationally. The OECD HCQI project is assembling a suite of performance indicators that are common to a large number of national performance measurement schemes (Box 6.1.1), leading

> ## Box 6.1.1 OECD HCQI project
>
> ### Background
>
> Begun in 2001, the OECD HCQI project aims to assess international health-care quality by developing a set of indicators based on comparable data that can be used to investigate quality differences in health care amongst countries.
>
> ### Indicators
>
> Indicators are being collected in five areas:
>
> 1. patient safety
> 2. quality of mental health care
> 3. quality of health promotion, prevention and primary care
> 4. quality of diabetes care
> 5. quality of cardiac care.
>
> The collection of indicators is a two-fold process. Firstly, data are gathered from a limited set of new indicators prepared by teams of internationally renowned experts in each of the five fields. Secondly, country experts in all five areas conduct focus work that will provide the basis for improving quality data systems across member countries.
>
> *Source*: OECD web site (https://www.oecd.org/health/hcqi)

to increased potential for international comparison. Such comparison makes an especially strong contribution to national accountability and is one of the most important stimuli for policy reform.

Choosing performance measures

The selection of performance measures is not only critical for sound assessment but also plays a larger role in defining what is considered important at every level of a health system. In Part 2 we have summarized health system objectives under a limited number of headings such as the health conferred on citizens by the health system; responsiveness to citizen preferences; financial protection offered by the health system; and health system productivity. Furthermore, as well as a concern with the overall attainment in each of these domains, we highlight the importance of distributional (or equity) issues expressed in terms of inequity in health outcomes, in responsiveness and in payment. Table 6.1.1 summarizes these largely universal dimensions of health performance measurement considered in this book and some example indicators in each.

The chapters show that there is variable progress in the development of performance measures and data collection techniques in the different dimensions of health performance. Some areas (e.g. population health) have well-established indicators such as infant mortality and life expectancy (sometimes adjusted for disability). Yet even here there is scope for important further work. With population health measures there is a particular difficulty in estimating the health system's specific contribution to health. Chapter 2.1 highlights the devel-

Table 6.1.1 *Dimensions of health performance measures*

Measurement area	Description of measure	Examples of indicators
Population health	Measures of aggregated data on the health of the population.	Life expectancy Years of life lost Avoidable mortality DALYs
Individual health outcomes	Measures of individual's health status; can be relative to the whole population or amongst groups. Some indicators also apply utility rankings to different health states.	Generic measures: • SF-36 • EQ-5D Disease specific measures: • Arthritis Impact Measurement Scales • PDQ-39
Clinical quality and appropriateness of care	Measures of the services and care patients receive to achieve desired outcomes. Used to determine if best practice takes place and that these actions are carried out in a technologically sound manner	Outcome measures: • health status • specific post-operative readmission and mortality rates Process measures: • frequency of blood pressure measurement

Table 6.1.1 *cont'd*

Responsiveness of health system	Measures of the way individuals are treated and environment in which they are treated during health system interactions. Responsiveness is concerned with issues of patient dignity, autonomy, confidentiality, communication, prompt attention, social support and quality of basic amenities.	Patient experience measures Patient satisfaction measures
Equity	Measures of extent to which there is equity in health, access to health care, responsiveness and financing.	Utilization measures Rates of access Use-needs ratios Spending thresholds Disaggregated health outcome measures
Productivity	Measures of productivity of the health-care system, health-care organizations and individual practitioners.	Labour productivity Cost-effectiveness measures (i.e. for interventions) Technical efficiency (measures of output/input) Allocative efficiency (i.e. measured by willingness to pay)

opment of more recent instruments such as the concept of *avoidable* mortality (Holland 1988; Nolte & McKee 2004).

In the health-care domain Chapter 2.2 notes increasing interest in measures of improvements in patient health status, often in the form of PROMs, derived from simple surveys of subjective health status administered directly to patients. There is now a plethora of measurement instruments ranging from detailed condition-specific questionnaires to broad-brush generic measures of patient outcome. For performance measurement purposes one central policy challenge is to identify the most appropriate choice of instrument. For example, in England the government recently mandated the use of the EQ-5D generic PROM instrument for all NHS patients undergoing four common procedures: hip replacement, knee replacement, hernia repair and varicose vein surgery. This experiment will assess the feasibility and costs of such routine use and test whether the resistance to PROMs among some health professionals is sustained. Also, PROMs have clear relevance to acute care but their application to domains such as chronic disease and mental illness remains less well-developed.

Chapter 2.3 concerns the ambiguous concept of clinical quality. Most performance measurement schemes consider the outcomes of health care to be a principal focus but their use can be problematic, for example if the outcomes cannot realistically be assessed in a timely or feasible fashion. This is particularly important for chronic diseases. Measures of process then become important signals of future success (Donabedian 1966). Process measures are based on actions or structures known to be associated with health system outcomes in either the health or the responsiveness domains. An example might be appropriate prescribing, known from research evidence to contribute eventually to good outcomes. The concept of effective coverage is an important population health process measure (Shengelia et al. 2003) that seeks to move beyond crude measures of activity in order to adjust for ineffective or inappropriate care. Box 6.1.2 summarizes the basic advantages and disadvantages of outcome and process indicators and the areas of performance measurement for which they are most useful.

Financial protection from catastrophic expenditure associated with ill-health is a fundamental health system concern and has been the driving force behind the systems of universal health insurance enjoyed in most high-income countries. However, the issue remains acute in many lower-income countries that show massive variations in the extent to which households (especially the poor) are protected from catastrophic expenditure. Chapter 2.4 notes that one major challenge is to move beyond the immediate expenditure on health care in order to trace longer-term implications for households' wealth and savings.

Chapter 2.5 shows that work in the responsiveness domain is at an early stage. Patient satisfaction, timely care and respect are important

Box 6.1.2 Usefulness of structural outcome and process indicators

Type of indicator	Advantages	Disadvantages	Areas best used
Outcome indicators	▪ Stakeholders often find outcome measures more meaningful ▪ Direct attention to, and focus on, health goals of the patient ▪ Encourage long-term health promotion strategies ▪ Not easily manipulated	▪ May be ambiguous and difficult to interpret as they are the result of many factors that are difficult to disentangle ▪ Take time to collect ▪ Require large sample sizes to detect statistically significant effects ▪ Can be difficult to measure (i.e. wound infection)	▪ To measure quality of homogeneous procedures ▪ To measure quality of homogeneous diagnoses with strong links between interventions and outcomes ▪ To measure quality of interventions in heterogeneous populations with a common condition
Process indicators	▪ Easily measured without major bias or error ▪ More sensitive to quality of care ▪ Easier to interpret ▪ Require smaller sample size to detect statistically significant effects ▪ Can often be observed unobtrusively ▪ Provide clear pathways for action ▪ Capture aspects of care that are valued by patients, aside from outcomes	▪ Often too specific, focusing on a particular intervention or condition ▪ May quickly become dated as models of care and technology develop ▪ May have little value for patients unless they understand how they relate to outcomes ▪ May be manipulated easily	▪ To measure quality of care, especially for treatments in which technical skill is relatively unimportant ▪ To measure quality of care of homogeneous conditions in different settings

Source: Adapted from Davies 2005; Mant 2001

issues and many countries are experimenting with patient administered questionnaires but there are very few generally accepted measures of performance that can be compared readily across systems.
Measurement of even apparently straightforward concepts such as
waiting time has been surprisingly problematic (Sicilliani & Hurst
2005). Development of generally accepted summary measures of
responsiveness is therefore a priority for future research.

Equity is a central concern of many health systems and increased use
of sample household health surveys in many countries is increasing the
potential to develop meaningful performance measures. Chapter 2.6
shows that considerable progress has been made in developing summary measures of equity that permit comparison across health systems
and over time. Whenever relying on self-reported health or health-care
utilization, a fundamental methodological concern is whether variations are in some sense due to reporting bias. The increased use of
electronic health records and objective measures such as biomarkers
may help to address this.

Productivity measurement offers an intellectual framework for
drawing together the various measures of performance discussed
above and relating levels of achievement to the resources consumed.
As discussed in Chapter 2.7, this is an immensely challenging undertaking in practice. For example, comparisons between hospitals must
allow for patients' different types of case-mix. The challenges become
even more daunting in comparisons of health systems. However, there
is progress in the methodology for addressing issues of comparability
– the notion of adopting disease-based approaches to measure productivity appears especially promising.

Statistical issues

The attribution problem is fundamental when seeking to interpret performance data. This refers to the process of determining what has
caused the observed performance and to which practitioners, organizations or agencies any variations in performance should be attributed.
It is critical that the causality behind observed measures is attributed to
the correct sources in order to inform policy, improve service delivery
and ensure accountability. The sensitive nature of correct attribution
becomes even more important with increased use of publicly reporting performance data and performance-based payments. Chapter 3.1

stresses that researchers and policy-makers should be careful to control properly for measurement and attribution error when using statistical methods to evaluate causal relationships and inform policy. The key considerations are summarized in Box 6.1.3.

Risk adjustment is the usual approach for addressing the attribution problem. It seeks to adjust performance data to account for variations in patient or population characteristics and can be used for detailed comparison of health-care providers or broad comparisons of population health. Since the early efforts with DRGs in the United States the methods of risk adjustment have been steadily refined over a forty-year period, particularly for adjusting for outcomes for specific diseases or health-care treatments. It is noteworthy that risk adjustment (for co-morbidity, age and other patient risk factors) was central to the New York scheme for public reporting of providers' mortality rates for coronary artery bypass graft surgery.

Chapter 3.2 describes the major progress made within risk adjustment in health care but also highlights many remaining challenges. The key lessons learnt to date are summarized below.

- Optimal risk-adjustment models result from a multidisciplinary effort in which clinicians interact with statisticians as well as experts in information systems and data production.
- Different practice patterns, patient characteristics and data specifications may limit the transferability of models across different countries. Clinicians and methodologists should examine clinical validity and statistical performance before applying a model developed in another setting.
- Decision-makers should be wary of using statistical summary measures (e.g. R-squared values) to draw conclusions about performance on risk-adjustment models as these values may not capture the model's predictive ability for different patient subgroups.
- Where it is believed that patient characteristics may also influence differences in the treatment patients receive it may be more appropriate to apply risk stratification instead of (or alongside) risk adjustment.

A central concern in health care remains the quality (especially completeness) of the data on which risk adjustment is undertaken, especially the presence of co-morbidities or other complications. Recording of these data is ultimately dependent on the practitioners whose per-

Box 6.1.3 Key considerations when addressing causality and attribution bias

Users of performance measures should consider the following recommendations when addressing causality and attribution bias.

- Assess existing reports of research investigating a possible causal and attributable link between the agents being assessed and the quality outcome proposed, with particular attention to:
  - the study methodology;
  - its controls for confounding variables; and
  - generalizability of the study sample.

- Undertake prospective analyses to identify critical pathways involved in the achievement of desired and undesired processes and outcomes of care. These analyses should try to identify:
  - possible confounders; and
  - extent to which agents under assessment are/can be clustered into homogeneous groupings.

- In new performance measurement initiatives, carefully consider sources of random and systematic error in measurement and sampling when developing the design. Institutionalize data collection procedures that maximize the reliability and accuracy of data (both primary and secondary) used for quality assessment.

- Employ risk adjustment techniques when evaluating the relationship between agents under assessment and the quality indicators. Use hierarchical models to account for the clustering of data within different levels of the health system under analysis. Consider using statistical methods such as propensity scores or instrumental variables.

- Causality and attribution bias cannot be eliminated completely, even when utilizing best practice. Monitor carefully any unintended impacts from biases in assessment of performance, especially when reimbursement or other incentives are linked to the measures.

Source: Adapted from Terris & Aron 2009

formance is being assessed, with an ever-present threat to the integrity of the data if the incentives associated with performance comparison are too stark. Furthermore, most risk adjustment efforts are still work in progress. Consequently, there is often a need for careful qualitative clinical commentary on any risk-adjusted data as technical limitations are common. However, as risk adjustment is almost always essential for performance measurement to secure credibility with practitioners it is important to sustain efforts to improve current methodologies.

In the public health domain, it is key that risk adjustment establishes what the agency under scrutiny is accountable for. For example, in the short run a health system has to deal with inherited epidemiological patterns and risky behaviours. This implies a major need for risk adjustment when comparing different health systems. In the longer run, the health system might be expected to be accountable for improving epidemiological patterns and health-related behaviour. This changes the nature of risk adjustment as the health system can now be considered accountable for at least some of the underlying causes of measured outcomes.

Proper statistical treatment of performance indicators is essential if appropriate policy inferences are to be drawn, given the large degree of random variation present in most performance indicators. The Royal Statistical Society has produced a protocol that seeks to summarize best practice for the selection, collection, analysis and presentation of performance data (Bird et al. 2005). One of the most important issues is the need to present measures of uncertainty (e.g. confidence intervals) alongside any performance measure. For example, it is noteworthy that confidence intervals were a central feature of the New York cardiac surgery public reporting initiative. The intention is to signal when a variation in performance is a matter for concern and the potential urgency of the need for intervention. Chapter 3.3 gives a particular example of how this approach can be applied – statistical control charts track a provider's performance over time and identify in a timely fashion any systematic deviation from expected levels of attainment. The authors discuss the criteria for selecting statistical methods including utility, verity, simplicity and responsiveness. These can be applied to most statistical methods of analysis applied to performance measurement although any choice involves some trade-offs. However, improved treatment of uncertainty is essential if performance measures are to retain credibility with patients, professionals and regulators.

Chapter 1.1 highlights the many different uses and users of performance measurement in the health system – it will often be the case that different levels of aggregation of performance measures will be needed for different uses. Chapter 3.4 discusses the role of composite measures of performance of whole systems and organizations. The chapter highlights the considerable controversy that exists as the science of composite measurement is still embryonic. However, while composite measures are of questionable direct use to patients or professionals they serve as a crucial element in promoting accountability to legislatures, governments and citizens in general. It is therefore important that (to the extent that data permit) they are credible; are constructed using transparent methods; and that users of composite indicators, including the media, are made aware of their limitations.

The choice of weights (or importance) attached to the component measures is fundamental to composite indicators. All the evidence suggests that individual citizens attach widely varying importance to aspects of performance. This indicates that the choice of weights is first and foremost a political undertaking, requiring the decision-maker to have political legitimacy. Analysis can therefore inform but should not determine the choice of weights. The body of economic methodology for inferring weights includes methods for calculating willingness to pay valuations or to elicit patients' preferences from rankings of alternative scenarios or direct choice experiments. However, these have not been applied widely to the construction of composite indicators of health system performance (Smith 2002). Box 6.1.4 summarizes the advantages and disadvantages of using composite indicators for health performance assessment.

Incentives and performance information

Accountability is not just about the production of performance measures, it also requires mechanisms with which to hold agents to account. In other words, the agent needs an incentive to take notice of the performance measures. For example, it is noteworthy that important comparative data on hospital performance in Scotland (including risk adjusted mortality rates in various specialties) were routinely fed back to hospital boards, albeit without any deliberate publicity. However, they appear to have had little impact on boards or clinicians and many senior managers and physicians claimed to have no knowl-

---

Box 6.1.4 Advantages and disadvantages of composite indicators

Advantages

- Offer a broad assessment of system performance.
- Place system performance at centre of the policy arena.
- Enable judgment and cross-country comparison of health system efficiency.
- Offer policy-makers at all levels the opportunity to set priorities and seek out performance improvement in these areas.
- Clearly indicate which systems represent the best overall performance and improvement efforts.
- Can stimulate better data collection and analytical efforts across health systems and nations.

Disadvantages

- Composite indicators may disguise failings in specific parts of the health-care system.
- Composite indicators make it difficult to determine where poor performance is occurring and consequently may make policy and planning more difficult and less effective.
- Indicators often have high positive correlation which can lead to double counting.
- In seeking to cover many areas, composite indicators may use feeble data that may also question the methodological soundness of the entire indicator.
- Aggregation of the data may conceal contentious individual measures within the composites.
- Composite indicators may ignore dimensions of performance that are difficult to measure, leading to adverse behavioural effects.
- Methodology on applying weights to composite indicators is not adequately developed and may reflect only certain preferences.

Source: Adapted from Smith 2002

---

edge of the data (Mannion & Goddard 2001). In contrast, the star ratings report cards prepared for English hospitals had a profound impact on behaviour because the data were publicly reported and had some very real incentives and sanctions attached to them, for the organizations and for the senior managers.

Incentives can arise as an incidental by-product of other system reforms. For example, almost all finance mechanisms introduce accidental incentives that may be benign or indeed reinforce a desire to secure improved performance. Accidental incentives can also lead to adverse consequences. Performance data can often fulfil an important role in correcting adverse incentives – for example, careful monitoring of performance can abate the common incentive to skimp on quality of care that results from hospital case payment (DRGs). However, performance measurement itself can give rise to unintended outcomes especially when explicit incentives are attached. Part 5 of the book explores the role of performance incentives under a number of headings: performance targets; public performance reporting; direct financial incentives; and professional improvement.

Health system targets are a specific type of performance measurement and incentive scheme. They comprise a quantitative expression of an objective to be met in the future. Brought to health policy from the business world, the main idea is that more organized and efficient efforts will be made to meet goals that are defined explicitly as targets. Targets are expected to be SMART – specific, measurable, accurate, realistic and time bound (van Herten & Gunning-Schepers 2000). The governments of many countries (including United States, United Kingdom, European Member States, Australia, New Zealand) have experimented with targets in health care.

Health system targets have traditionally been used extensively in public health but Chapter 5.1 indicates that reports of measurable success are rare. The English experience with the 1992 *Health of the Nation* strategy is typical. Based on WHO's *Health for All* initiative this set a series of ambitious public health targets. However, a careful independent evaluation in 1998 concluded that: '[its] impact on policy documents peaked as early as 1993; and, by 1997, its impact on local policymaking was negligible' (Department of Health 1998). Hunter (2002) summarizes its failings under six broad headings:

1. Appeared to be a lack of leadership in the national government.
2. Policy failed to address the underlying social and structural determinants of health.
3. Targets were not always credible and were not formulated at a local level.
4. Poor communication of the strategy beyond the health system.
5. Strategy was not sustained.
6. Partnership between agencies was not encouraged.

In the past decade, targets have featured especially strongly in English health-care policy. Starting in 1998 the Treasury issued strategic targets (PSAs) to all government departments including the health ministry (Smith 2007). PSAs were focused primarily on outcomes such as the improvement of mortality rates; reductions in smoking and obesity; and reductions in waiting times. The health ministry used star rating report cards as a key instrument to achieve these objectives. In contrast to most national target systems this proved notably effective in securing some of the targeted objectives in health care (Bevan & Hood 2006). This success can be attributed to the following characteristics.

- Targets were precise, short-term objectives rather than long-term and general.
- Targets were based on the local level rather than the national level.
- Professionals were engaged in the design and implementation of some of the targets. This ran the risk of leading to capture by professional interests but also served to increase awareness of objectives.
- Organizations were given increased finance, information and managerial capacity to respond to challenging targets.
- Concrete incentives were attached to the targets.

However, this success in health care was not replicated in the public health domain. This was almost certainly because managers felt that health-care targets were much more amenable to health system intervention.

Targets provide a straightforward way of highlighting key objectives and can be very successful if designed and implemented correctly. However, some of the notable risks associated with their use are summarized in Box 6.1.5. The conclusions from this experience indicate that performance targets offer some scope for focusing system attention on specific areas of endeavour but are unlikely to secure performance improvement unless they are implemented carefully alongside other improvement initiatives such as more general inspection and regulation.

Public performance reporting is established within health care and is congruent with an increasing broader trend for transparency in society. Even if it had no discernable impact on health system performance, it would be necessitated by growing public demand for important outcome information to be made available to patients and the pub-

---

Box 6.1.5 Risks associated with increased reliance on targets

- Untargeted aspects of the health system may be neglected.
- Managers and practitioners may concentrate on short-term targets directly in their control at the expense of targets that address long-term or less controllable objectives.
- Excessively aggressive targets may undermine the reliability of the data on which they are based.
- Excessively aggressive targets may induce gaming or other undesirable behavioural responses.
- Targets may encourage a narrow, mercenary attitude rather than altruistic professional motivation.
- Targets require continual monitoring and updating to verify that they remain relevant and are not undermined by professional interests.

Source: Smith 2008

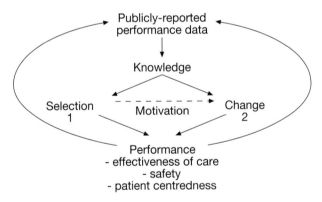

Fig. 6.1.1 Pathways for improving performance through publicly reported data
Source: Berwick et al. 2003

lic, both to enhance public accountability and to inform health-care consumers. Moreover, public reporting can improve quality through two pathways (Fig. 6.1.1): (i) selection pathway by which consumers become better informed and select providers of higher quality; and

(ii) change pathway by which information helps providers to identify areas of underperformance and thus acts as a stimulus to improve.

Chapter 5.2 examines the growing experience of placing information in the public domain and reports considerable evidence that publication of provider performance measures leads to performance improvement (Hibbard et al. 2005). Although the immediate purpose has often been to facilitate and inform patient choice, there is little evidence that patients make direct use of report cards. However, report cards do appear to promote performance improvements in providers by means of their impact on reputation – the change pathway. For example, long-standing use of coronary artery bypass graft report cards in two American states (New York and Pennsylvania) has unequivocally been associated with improvements in risk-adjusted mortality. Nevertheless, there is continuing debate about whether these results necessarily imply that they have been beneficial and a number of adverse outcomes associated with the schemes have also been reported (Dranove et al. 2003; Schneider & Epstein 1996).

- Coronary artery bypass graft report cards led to increased selection by New York and Pennsylvania providers who were more inclined to avoid sicker patients (who might benefit from treatment) and to treat increased numbers of healthier patients (for whom the benefits of treatment are more contested).
- Initiative has increased Medicare expenditures with only a small improvement in population health.
- Practitioners were concerned about the absence of quality indicators other than mortality; inadequate risk adjustment; and unreliability of data provided by physicians and hospitals.

This experience underlines the importance of carefully monitoring and evaluating the outcomes of incentive schemes, such as public reporting. It suggests several points that should be taken into account when implementing public disclosure of data.

- Give careful consideration to the purpose of the disclosure and the type of information that different stakeholders of the health system will want and are able to use.
- Give careful consideration to the impact on quality of care that may result from public disclosure of information. Where appropriate, public disclosure of information should be integrated with other quality improvement strategies (Marshall et al. 2000).

- Enhance the credibility and usefulness of public performance reports by creating them in collaboration with physicians and other legitimate interest groups (Marshall et al. 2000; Schneider & Epstein 1996).
- When reporting data, implement careful risk adjustment in order to assure legitimacy of the scheme with providers and offer accurate comparisons between outcomes and providers (Iezzoni 2009; Marshall et al. 2000). Detailed information on the risk adjustment strategies used should be made available for public scrutiny alongside the reported information.

There is no doubt that clinicians and other actors in the health system generally do respond to financial incentives (Dudley 2005). When performance measurement is incorporated into financial incentive regimes it offers a potentially promising avenue for future policy and a number of experiments that attach financial rewards to reported performance are now under way. Historically, the use of indirect financial incentives in health care has been offered through systems of accreditation that offer rewards in the form of access to markets or extra payments for meeting structural requirements. Germany has an accreditation system of this sort at the regional level in which specific quality indicators are used for accreditation (www.G-BA.de).

Yet accreditation is a very blunt incentive instrument and Chapter 5.4 summarizes the evidence that policy is shifting towards very much more direct and focused incentives, for individuals and for organizations. The author indicates that most experiments so far have been small scale and it is difficult to draw strong conclusions as the results are difficult to assess with any confidence. Notwithstanding, there is evident need for increased experimentation and research.

Chapter 5.4 also highlights the many issues that need to be considered when designing performance incentive schemes, summarized in Box 6.1.6 below. This complexity is one reason why it is difficult to make a definitive evaluation of financial incentives. Furthermore, translation of results from one institutional setting to another must be treated with caution because other health system instruments (e.g. financing mechanism) may interact with the incentives to produce unexpected results. In short, any scheme requires constant monitoring to ensure that there are no unintended responses to incentives (e.g. cream-skimming, gaming); that the incentive scheme does not jeopardize the reliability of the performance data on which it relies; and that it does not compromise unrewarded aspects of performance.

Box 6.1.6 Design issues for pay-for-performance schemes

The behaviour induced by a financial incentive varies according to its design along each of the following dimensions (discussed in more detail in Chapter 5.4).

Organizational vs. individual

Financial incentives can be awarded at either group or individual level. A group-level payment may be less likely to motivate individual behaviour and may encourage free-riding but may be better at inducing cooperation and coordination. The incentive should be offered at the level at which it most directly motivates the party responsible for the action being incentivized.

Absolute vs. relative

Incentives based on relative performance measures may increase competition amongst providers, especially if this information is made publicly available. Absolute incentive payments offer the payee more certainty about the attainment of payment and may increase motivation.

Short term vs. long term

Long-term payments can lead to greater investment in structural change and processes of care and provide a longer time frame in which to observe results. Short-term payments may have the benefit of appearing more salient and corresponding more closely to the action being incentivized. They may also impose greater administrative costs and encourage more myopic behaviour.

Reward vs. penalty

Incentives structured as rewards or penalties (e.g. withholding payment) may affect providers' attitudes towards performance and therefore have differential incentive effects.

Size and power of payment

It is important to ensure that an incentive payment is large enough to cover the marginal costs involved in adjusting behaviour to achieve the targeted results. However, payment levels should not be higher than the level required to encourage participation in the incentive scheme. Furthermore, the link between performance and reward (power of the incentive) needs to be calibrated carefully.

Box 6.1.6 cont'd

Choice of performance measures

The best performance measures on which to attach financial incentives are those which lie within the control of the physician. Usually these are structural or process of care indicators. Outcome indicators are more likely to be influenced by external factors and are therefore less favourable.

Source: Conrad 2009

Another important use of performance measurement is to provide clinical practitioners with feedback on their performance relative to their peers, with the intention of stimulating performance improvement. Databases serving this purpose exist in many countries. For example, providers in Sweden contribute to quality registers by voluntarily collecting individual-based data on patient characteristics, diagnosis, treatments, experiences and outcome that are shared with other members of the register. The quality registers have an explicit aim to facilitate the improvement of quality in clinical work through continuous learning and development (Rehnqvist 2002). Indeed there is a strong argument that performance measurement should become an inherent element in a professional's lifelong learning. This suggests the need for a prominent role for performance measurement principles in early clinical training.

There is much debate on whether information for professional improvement should be anonymized or made available to the public. Evidence suggests that such performance measurement schemes need to be designed and owned by the professionals who use them in order to be effective (Rowan & Black 2000). It is argued that the most constructive systems are those that encourage positive and cooperative behaviour amongst practitioners and avoid public threats to their professional or commercial standing. The latter may encourage defensive behaviour that could lead to gaming or cream-skimming. Indicators used for professional improvement should therefore:

- reflect meaningful aspects of clinical practice with strong scientific underpinning;
- assure close risk adjustment of indicators;

- allow exclusions of certain patients, e.g. those who refuse to comply with treatment;
- facilitate interpretability;
- represent services under a provider's control;
- assure high accuracy;
- minimize cost and burden.

Furthermore, it is important to measure not only the outcomes of care but also the extent of inappropriate care (overuse or underuse of treatments).

The requirements of a successful professional improvement performance measurement system may therefore come into conflict with the requirements of information systems designed to promote accountability and patient choice. This is not to say that the tension between these different needs and demands cannot be resolved. Experience from Sweden and elsewhere (e.g. Netherlands, Denmark) suggests that public and professional needs can be reconciled. For example, quality registers such as the Danish National Indicator Project (www.nip.dk) publish outcomes on individual practitioners. In any case, it is likely that patient advocacy groups will increasingly demand that more performance data should be made available. The challenge for the professions is to ensure that this trend is harnessed for good rather than leading to defensive professional behaviour. One solution lies in careful development of acceptable statistical risk adjustment schemes and careful presentation of statistical data so that the public and media are better equipped to understand and interpret the information made available to them.

Politics of performance measurement

It is inevitable that performance information of any power creates winners and losers. A recurring theme throughout the book is therefore the immensely political nature of any attempt to measure performance within the health system. Inspired by pioneers such as Florence Nightingale and Ernest Codman, the very earliest efforts to measure performance were ultimately frustrated by the opposition of elements within the medical profession and a lack of resolve amongst politicians (Spiegelhalter 1999). One hundred and fifty years later, the earliest opposition to Nightingale's proposals to measure surgical outcomes still sounds remarkably familiar to contemporary readers.

The political nature of performance measurement is an inevitable consequence of its power to challenge vested interests within the health system. There is an enormous range of interest groups, often encompassing (amongst others):

- taxpayers
- voters
- patient groups
- clinical professionals
- insurers and other purchaser organizations
- provider organizations
- pharmaceutical companies
- governments
- geographical interests
- age groups
- social groups (income, ethnicity).

Performance information often serves the interests of some of these groups but will also challenge others. The natural response of those under challenge will be to contest the veracity, completeness and relevance of the information provided. High-quality statistical analysis of data, such as risk adjustment, is therefore imperative to assure the credibility of the performance measurement.

Chapter 1.1 argues that performance information plays a prime role in enabling principals to hold agents to account more effectively within the health system. Transparency, in the form of performance information, is a fundamental requirement for enhancing the accountability of governments, provider organizations, professionals and insurers to patients and the broader citizenry. Furthermore, as summarized in Chapter 5.2 on public reporting, many authors have argued that enhanced accountability leads to improved performance in a virtuous improvement circle.

If performance indicators are to promote accountability they must address the specific questions of each discrete audience and be presented with appropriate clarity that resonates with the various constituencies. These may include patients, the broader public, professionals, the media and researchers. A key requirement in the accountability cycle is to identify the targets and shape the analysis and presentation of the measures to suit their needs.

In most health systems the many actors formally charged with governance of institutions and professions form an especially important constituency. These might include the boards of governors of provider organizations; professional conduct committees; a wide range of regulators; and elected representatives in local and central government. Performance information plays a particularly important role in enabling these constituencies to discharge their roles effectively. Comparative performance information should be an important resource and all those charged with governance should be given the capacity to demand and understand such data.

One specific issue highlighted by Busse and Smith is performance measurement's potential to undermine the traditional approach of clinical professionalism that encourages clinicians to do the best for their patients, regardless of pecuniary or other incentives. Pursued to excess, reliance on a limited range of specific indicators may distort professional behaviour by encouraging treating to the test – concentrating on measured aspects of care at the expense of the unmeasured.

This argument has some force when applied to a system with very partial or distorted performance information but in our view does not compromise the argument for performance measurement. Rather it suggests the need for redoubled efforts to broaden the scope of measurement; to shift from measuring processes to measuring health outcomes wherever possible; to improve the quality of statistical analysis; to ensure that incentives are not distortionary; and to ensure that performance data are used constructively to help professionals to improve the care they offer.

The political element of performance measurement will always exist and therefore one of the fundamental roles of governments will be to nurture informed political debate. This includes ensuring that legitimate interests are empowered to make their case using the best available performance information and that the information is fit for purpose. In particular, it is important to ensure that key constituencies such as the public, patients and professionals are fully engaged in the development, analysis and interpretation of performance measures.

Stewardship perspective on performance measurement

Governments play a major stewardship role in harnessing the full potential of performance measurement to improve the health system. *The world health report 2000* defined stewardship as: '…defining the vision and direction of health policy, exerting influence through regulation and advocacy, and collecting and using information' (WHO 2000). This summary seeks to outline how performance measurement can help governments to fulfil each of these tasks. We argue that performance measurement offers major opportunities to secure performance improvement and that no health system can be steered adequately without good performance information and intelligence. The overarching role of performance measurement is to enhance the decisions made by actors throughout the health system.

Performance information can help a government directly in the formulation and evaluation of policy and in undertaking regulation. However, government's broader stewardship role is to assure that the necessary flows of information are available, functioning properly and aligned with the design of the health system. Performance measurement is a public good that will not occur naturally and therefore government has the fundamental role of ensuring that maximum benefit is secured from performance measurement, whether through law, regulation, coordination or persuasion. Implementation requires sustained political and professional leadership at the highest level and assurance that the necessary analytical capacity is available throughout the health system.

Some of the stewardship responsibilities of government are summarized in Box 6.1.7. While these functions and tasks must be in place, government itself is not necessarily required to perform them.

Box 6.1.7 Stewardship responsibilities associated with performance measurement

Development of a clear conceptual framework and a clear vision of the purpose of the performance measurement system:

- align with accountability relationships
- align with other health system mechanisms (e.g. finance, market structure, IT)

Design of data collection mechanisms:

- detailed specification of individual indicators
- alignment with international best practice

Box 6.1.7 cont'd

Information governance:

- data audit and quality control
- assuring public trust in information
- assuring well-informed public debate

Development of analytical devices and capacity to help understand the data:

- commissioning appropriate research on (e.g.) risk adjustment, uncertainty, data feedback mechanisms
- ensuring analysis is undertaken efficiently and effectively
- ensuring local decision-makers understand the analysis

Development of appropriate data aggregation and presentational methods:

- ensuring information has appropriate impact on all parties
- mandating public release of summary comparative information
- ensuring comparability and consistency

Design of incentives to act on performance measures:

- monitoring impact of performance information on behaviour
- acting to enhance beneficial outcomes and negate any adverse consequences

Proper evaluation of performance measurement instruments:

- ensuring money is spent cost effectively on information resources

Managing the political process

- developing and monitoring policy options
- ensuring that specific interest groups do not capture the performance information system
- encouraging healthy political debate

Future priorities

Given increasing demand and the wide set of actors and responsibilities it is important that policy-makers consider what makes performance indicators effective in improving system performance and accountability. Although there is no conclusive answer to this question, experience suggests that any policy development should take account of the following recommendations.

1. Develop a clear conceptual framework and a clear vision of the purpose of the performance measurement system in alignment with the accountability relationships inherent in the health system.
2. Ensure that definitions of performance indicators are clear and consistent and fit the chosen conceptual framework.
3. Indicators should:

   - aim to measure what matters, specifically to: promote health, improve patient care and ensure prudent utilization of health system resources;
   - be statistically sound and presented in ways that are straightforward to interpret in order to reduce the likelihood of manipulation or misinterpretation;
   - fully acknowledge any data limitations, including levels of uncertainty and lack of timeliness.

4. Pay more attention to improving the comprehensibility and utility of performance data, particularly how to improve its interpretation by patients, providers and practitioners.
5. Enhance managers' and clinicians' capacity to understand and use information. Use of performance data should become an intrinsic part of clinical education and lifelong professional development.
6. Incentives to act upon performance measures should be designed carefully. Monitor closely how performance information impacts on behaviour and take action to enhance beneficial outcomes and negate adverse consequences.
7. Policy-makers should pay particular attention to the broader health system, ensuring that performance measurement is aligned with the design of mechanisms such as finance and market structures and recognizing the organizational context within which performance data are collected and disseminated.
8. Performance measurement systems should be monitored frequently and evaluated to identify opportunities for updating and improvement and any unintended side effects.

9. Ensure effective management of the political process of performance measurement. Amongst other things, encourage healthy political debate and ensure that specific interest groups do not capture the performance information system.

While arguing very strongly for increased use of performance measurement throughout the health system we recognize that this is a costly undertaking that diverts valuable resources from health services. It is imperative that all performance measurement initiatives are undertaken effectively and justified with the same cost-effective criteria that should be applied to more conventional health technologies. Many performance measurement initiatives will involve relatively low-cost capture of data that are already required to assure the delivery of high-quality services. However, their utility should be evaluated rigorously when they do involve significant additional costs.

The effectiveness of any performance measurement instrument ultimately should be evaluated not in relation to statistical properties (e.g. accuracy and validity) but more broadly – by the extent to which it promotes or compromises health system objectives. Effective performance measurement alone is not enough to ensure performance improvement – the functions of analysis and interpretation of performance data are also crucial. Furthermore, performance measurement is only one (albeit very important) instrument for securing system improvement. For maximum effect it needs to be aligned with other levers for system reform such as financing, market structure, accountability arrangements and regulation. Without careful attention to these broader health system considerations the performance measurement system will be ineffective.

Health systems are in the early days of performance measurement and there is still huge potential to improve the effectiveness of measurement systems. However, performance measurement offers scope for major health system improvements. Advances in technology are likely to increase this potential still further and increasing public demands for accountability and information will reinforce current trends. There is therefore a policy-making imperative to consider carefully the role of performance measurement within the health system; implement initiatives of proven effectiveness; undertake careful trials of less established mechanisms; and monitor and update performance measurement systems as new knowledge and capacity emerge.

References

Berwick, DM. James, B. Coye, MJ (2003). 'Connections between quality measurement and improvement.' *Medical Care*, 41(1): I30–I38.

Bevan, G. Hood, C (2006). 'Have targets improved performance in the English NHS?' *British Medical Journal*, 332(7538): 419.

Bird, S. Cox, D. Farewell, VT. Golstein, H. Holt, T. Smith, PC (2005). 'Performance indicators: good, bad, and ugly.' *Journal of the Royal Statistical Society*, 168(1): 1–27.

Conrad, D (2009). Incentives for health-care performance improvement. In: Smith, PC. Mossialos, E. Papanicolas, I. Leatherman, S (eds.). *Performance measurement for health system improvement: experiences, challenges and prospects*. Cambridge: Cambridge University Press.

Davies, H (2005). *Measuring and reporting the quality of health care: issues and evidence from the international research literature*. NHS Quality Improvement Scotland.

Department of Health (1998). *Health of the Nation: a policy assessed*. London.

Donabedian, A (1966). 'Evaluating the quality of medical care.' *Milbank Memorial Fund Quarterly*, 44(3): 166–206.

Dranove, D. Kessler, M. McClellan, M. Satterthwaite, M (2003). 'Is more information better? The effects of 'report cards' on health care providers.' *Journal of Political Economy*, 111(3): 555–588.

Dudley, RA (2005). 'Pay-for-performance research: how to learn what clinicians and policy makers need to know.' *Journal of the American Medical Association*, 283(14): 134–148.

Hibbard, JH. Stockard, J. Tusler, M (2005). 'Hospital performance reports: impact on quality, market share, and reputation.' *Health Affairs*, 24(4): 1150–1160.

Holland, WW (1988). *European Community atlas of 'avoidable death'*. Oxford: Oxford Medical Publications (Commission of the European Communities Health Services Research Series No. 3).

Hunter, DJ (2002). England. In: Marinker, M. McKee, M (eds.). *Health targets in Europe: polity, progress and promise*. London: BMJ Books.

Iezzoni, L (2009). Risk adjustment for performance measurement. In: Smith, PC. Mossialos, E. Papanicolas, I. Leatherman, S (eds.). *Performance measurement for health system improvement: experiences, challenges and prospects*. Cambridge: Cambridge University Press.

Mannion, R. Goddard, M (2001). 'Impact of published clinical outcomes data: case study in NHS hospital trusts.' *British Medical Journal*, 232(7307): 260–263.

Mant, J (2001). 'Process versus outcome indicators in the assessment of quality of health care.' *International Journal for Quality in Health Care*, 13(6): 475–480.

Marshall, MN. Shekelle, PG. Leatherman, S. Brook, RH (2000). 'Public disclosure of performance data: learning from the US experience.' *Quality in Health Care*, 8(1): 53–57.

Nolte, E. McKee, M (2004). *Does health care save lives? Avoidable mortality revisited*. London: The Nuffield Trust.

Power, M (1999). *The audit society: rituals of verification*. Oxford: Oxford University Press.

Rehnqvist, N (2002). Improving accountability in a decentralized system: a Swedish perspective. In: Smith, PC (ed.). *Measuring up: improving the performance of health systems in OECD countries*. Paris: Organisation for Economic Co-operation and Development.

Rowan, K. Black, N. (2000). 'A bottom-up approach to performance indicators through clinician networks.' *Health Care UK*, Spring: 42–46.

Schneider, EC. Epstein, AM (1996). 'Influence of cardiac-surgery performance reports on referral practices and access to care.' *New England Journal of Medicine*, 335(4): 251–256.

Sequist, T. Bates, D (2009). Developing information technology capacity for performance measurement. In: Smith, PC. Mossialos, E. Papanicolas, I. Leatherman, S (eds.). *Performance measurement for health system improvement: experiences, challenges and prospects*. Cambridge: Cambridge University Press.

Shengelia, B. Murray, CJL. Adams, OB (2003). Beyond access and utilization: defining and measuring health system coverage. In: Murray, CJL. Evans, DB. *Health systems performance assessment: debates, methods and empiricism*. Geneva: World Health Organization.

Sicilliani, L. Hurst, J (2005). 'Tackling excessive waiting times for elective surgery: a comparative analysis of policies in 12 OECD countries.' *Health Policy*, 72(2): 201–215.

Smith, PC (2002). Developing composite indicators for assessing health system efficiency. In: Smith, PC (ed.). *Measuring up: improving the performance of health systems in OECD countries*. Paris: Organisation for Economic Co-operation and Development.

Smith, PC (2007). Performance budgeting in England: experience with Public Service Agreements. In: Robinson, M (ed.). *Performance budgeting: linking funding and results*. Washington DC: International Monetary Fund.

Smith, PC (2008). England: intended and unintended effects. In: Wismar, M. McKee, M. Ernst, K. Srivastava, D. Busse, R (eds.). *Health targets in Europe: learning from experience*. Copenhagen: WHO Regional Office for Europe on behalf of the European Observatory on Health Systems and Policies.

Spiegelhalter, DJ (1999). 'Surgical audit: statistical lessons from Nightingale and Codman.' *Journal of the Royal Statistical Society*, 162(1): 45–58.

Terris, DD. Aron, DC (2009). Attribution and causality in health-care performance measurement. In: Smith, PC. Mossialos, E. Papanicolas, I. Leatherman, S (eds.). *Performance measurement for health system improvement: experiences, challenges and prospects*. Cambridge: Cambridge University Press.

van Herten, L. Gunning-Schepers, LJ (2000). 'Targets as a tool in health policy. Part I: lessons learned.' *Health Policy*, 53(1): 1–11.

WHO (2000). *The world health report 2000*. Geneva: World Health Organization.

Index